ALGEBRAIC AND AUTOMATA-THEORETIC PROPERTIES OF FORMAL LANGUAGES

Fundamental Studies in Computer Science

VOLUME 2

NORTH-HOLLAND PUBLISHING COMPANY — AMSTERDAM · OXFORD
AMERICAN ELSEVIER PUBLISHING COMPANY, INC. — NEW YORK

Algebraic and Automata-Theoretic Properties of Formal Languages

SEYMOUR GINSBURG

Professor of Computer Science
University of Southern California
Los Angeles, California

1975

NORTH-HOLLAND PUBLISHING COMPANY — AMSTERDAM · OXFORD
AMERICAN ELSEVIER PUBLISHING COMPANY, INC. — NEW YORK

Library of Congress Catalog Card Number: 73-86082

North-Holland ISBN Series: 0 7204 2500 X

North-Holland ISBN Volume: 0 7204 2506 9

American Elsevier ISBN: 0 444 10586 7

Published by:

NORTH-HOLLAND PUBLISHING COMPANY — AMSTERDAM

NORTH-HOLLAND PUBLISHING COMPANY, LTD. — OXFORD

Sole distributors for the U.S.A. and Canada:

AMERICAN ELSEVIER PUBLISHING COMPANY, INC.

52 VANDERBILT AVENUE

NEW YORK, N.Y. 10017

PRINTED IN HUNGARY

To my family

PREFACE

During the years 1955–1966 a large number of families of formal languages, arising from either computer science or linguistics, were investigated for their mathematical properties. With few exceptions, these families were found to have a common core of closure operations, e.g., closure under inverse homomorphism, closure under intersection with regular sets, and my personal favorite, closure under ϵ-free generalized sequential machines. In August of 1966, Sheila Greibach and I decided to see if certain of these closure operations could be used to derive others. We eventually selected six "elementary" ones (many different sets would have served equally well) which allowed us to prove closure under ϵ-free generalized sequential machines and other complicated operations. We called any family of languages satisfying these six operations an AFL (for *a*bstract *f*amily of *l*anguages).

In the same spirit, we next inquired if we could find a model for families of one-way nondeterministic acceptors which incorporated the essential features of most extant types such devices. Excluding some minor technical conditions added later, this goal was soon reached. We called any family in this model an AFA (for *a*bstract *f*amily of *a*cceptors). And then, to our great surprise, we found that AFL could be used to characterize the families of languages accepted by AFA, and conversely. Now AFL theory was no longer just an academic sport but a potentially important tool—one that might permit a unified approach to formal languages and automata theory as well as suggest the formulation of new questions about familiar friends.

Since that fruitful month in 1966, a flock of papers on AFL and other structures defined by closure operations have been written. In 1968, Greibach noticed [Gr3] that many results held, not only for AFL, but for more general structures called semi-AFL. And in the process of writing this book I observed that much could also be said for still a more general structure called a trio. (A structure called AFDL, which characterizes the families of languages accepted by families of one-way deterministic devices, was introduced by my student W. J. Chandler in his Ph. D. thesis [Ch]. And a structure called

AF2DL, which characterizes the families of languages accepted by families of two-way deterministic devices, was given by Aho and Ullman [AU].)

Has the developed theory been successful in

(1) permitting a unified treatment of formal languages and automata theory? and

(2) suggesting new ideas or relationships about established concepts?

My replies to both questions are a resounding yes. One justification for an affirmative answer to (1) is that any family of languages either satisfying the axioms for a (semi-)AFL or defined by a new type of AFA is now known to be automatically closed under a variety of operations, thereby obviating the need to re-prove these closure operations over and over again. Another reason is that certain general conditions on an AFA now allow us to infer that the resulting family of languages is closed under reversal, a fact that, in earlier times, was proved for many individual families of devices. One justification for a positive response to (2) is the introduction of the "algebraic" notion of a principal (semi-)AFL and the knowledge it has shed on a flock of well-known families of languages. An example of the influence of the concept of a principal (semi-)AFL is the formulation and subsequent proof of the existence of a "Chomsky–Schutzenberger representation theorem" for several families of languages, such as the one-way stack languages. Another reason for yes on (2) is the many deep properties of languages brought to light by investigation on substitution of (semi-)AFL. A beautiful illustration of this is the result that each substitution-closed full principal AFL, excluding the family of regular sets, properly contains a (unique) largest full AFL. Thus there exists a largest full AFL properly contained in the family of context-free languages (or in the family of recursively enumerable sets).

The purpose of this text is to present the basic important features of trios, semi-AFL, and AFL, *especially* the last. These include

(a) concepts employed frequently throughout the development of the subject, such as a-transducers,

(b) theorems on broad topics, such as principal (semi-)AFL and substitution, which give a sense of achievement or deep understanding to the field,

(c) results, such as a sufficiency condition on an AFA to guarantee closure under reversal of the associated (semi-)AFL, which are pertinent to many families of languages or families of acceptors, and

(d) results, such as the characterization of multitape AFA languages by the wedge operator, which demonstrate the use of algebraic methods to device-oriented problems.

In addition, some material is included which, for one reason or another, offers promise of potential value. Foremost here would be the topic of (semi-)AFL generated by families of bounded languages.

The text itself developed from lecture notes used at the University of Southern California, and is suitable for a one-semester course by eliminating results and sections labelled with (+). The level is geared to graduate students in computer science, computer engineering, and mathematics who have had at least one previous course in automata and formal languages. (A knowledge of Chapters 1–3 of [Sm], or Chapters 1–7 of [Kn], or 1–9 of [HUl], or Chapters 1–4 of [Gi] with some supplementary material on context-sensitive and recursively enumerable languages, would suffice.)

The subject matter is divided into two preliminary chapters and five main ones. In particular, the initial two chapters are review, the first on general mathematical and language notions, and the second on the Chomsky hierarchy of languages and automata. The study of formal structures properly begins with Chapter 3. There the three language structures "trio", "semi-AFL" and "AFL" are introduced, as well as the basic transformation device "a-transducer". The language structures are characterized in terms of a-transducers, and their closure under various operations considered. Chapter 4 concerns AFA, both single tape and multitape. The fundamental theorems of (full) AFL and semi-AFL are established, namely, characterizations of families of languages accepted by AFA by means of (full) AFL and semi-AFL. Two other noteworthy results which appear are the equality of $\mathscr{L}(\mathscr{D}_1 \wedge \mathscr{D}_2)$ and $\hat{\mathscr{H}}(\mathscr{L}(\mathscr{D}_1) \wedge \mathscr{L}(\mathscr{D}_2))$ for arbitrary AFA $\mathscr{D}_1$ and $\mathscr{D}_2$, and the fact that the smallest full AFL containing $\{L_1 \cap L_2/L_1 \text{ in } \mathscr{L}_1, L_2 \text{ in } \mathscr{L}_2\}$, $\mathscr{L}_1$ and $\mathscr{L}_2$ both AFL with $\{a^nb^n/n \geqq 1\}$ in them, contains every recursively enumerable set. Chapter 5 concerns [full] principal (semi-)AFL. These (semi-)AFL are characterized in terms of finitely encoded AFA, and various generators for well-known AFL determined. The essential preservation of [full] principal (semi-)AFL by the binary operator $\wedge$ is also presented. Chapter 6 deals with the substitution operator. The preservation of [full] principal trios, semi-AFL, and AFL under substitution is established and a characterization of Sub($\mathscr{L}_1$, $\mathscr{L}_2$), $\mathscr{L}_1$ and $\mathscr{L}_2$ AFL, in terms of nested multitape AFA proved. Substitution closure is extensively discussed. Here, for example, appears the result mentioned earlier, that each substitution-closed full principal AFL, excluding the family of regular sets, properly contains a unique largest full AFL. Chapter 7 discusses generation by families of bounded languages. For example, it is shown that there is no family $\mathscr{L}_1$ of bounded languages and substitution-closed nonregular AFL $\mathscr{L}_2$ so that $\mathscr{L}_2 \subseteq \hat{\mathscr{F}}(\mathscr{L}_1)$. Necessary conditions are obtained on certain kinds of bounded languages U and V in order for V to be in the smallest [full] (semi-)AFL [fully] generated by U. As a consequence, various [full] principal (semi-)AFL, [fully] generated by bounded languages, are shown to be different. By way of illustration, these methods enable one to show the rather startling fact that $\hat{\mathscr{F}}(\{a^{n^2}b^{n^2}/n \geqq 0\})$ and $\hat{\mathscr{F}}(a^{n^2}b^{(n+1)^2}/n \geqq 0\})$ are different.

Historical references are summarized at the end of each chapter. In general, documentation is made only for (i) main results and (ii) central concepts whose importance first arose in (semi-)AFL theory. Thus the operations substitution and $+$, well-known from context-free language theory, are not referenced. Many of the lesser results usually occur implicitly, and are practically impossible to trace to initial sources. Almost all leading ideas were originally conceived for AFL, but were later found to generalize to semi-AFL and/or trios. Since the extensions to semi-AFL and trios, when true, are usually quite straightforward, citations made are to first appearances, even though just one structure is considered.

An extensive bibliography, which also includes papers not referenced in the corpus of the book, is listed after Chapter 7. A goodly supply of exercises is provided to test the reader's understanding, as well as to cover material not mentioned in the text. While many of them are either straightforward or require just a little ingenuity, a few, marked by the asterisk*, are quite difficult. A number of open problems and questions are presented, both to indicate gaps in our knowledge and to suggest possible new developments. It is my fond hope that solutions to many of these problems and questions will be achieved by readers. For in a sense, two of the aims of any advanced book in a scientific field should be to put known material into proper perspective and to prepare the way for exploring the unknown.

In conclusion, I wish to acknowledge my indebtedness to many people for their assistance in various aspects of the work. I have benefited from conversations with the following professional colleagues: Armen Gabrielian, Jonathan Goldstine, Sheila A. Greibach, Gene F. Rose, and Edwin H. Spanier. Many of the exercises arose in discussions with those five individuals. Last, but certainly not least, I have profited from the suggestions of a score of students, especially Rodney Hoffman, Richard McHard, Jeffrey Outwater, and Branislav Rovan, on such diverse pedagogical matters as motivation, organization, proofs, and symbolism. To all of the above I render my thanks.

CONTENTS

CHAPTER 1

MATHEMATICAL AND FORMAL LANGUAGE PRELIMINARIES

Some concepts of either a mathematical or formal language nature are briefly reviewed here. The reader is advised to omit this chapter, and refer to it only as needed.

1.1 Mathematical Preliminaries

The set of those elements having a property P is written as $\{x/x$ has property $P\}$.

The set with no elements in it, called the *empty* set, is denoted by $\emptyset$.

For sets A and B, A is a *subset* of B (alternatively, B *contains* A), written $A \subseteq B$ or $B \supseteq A$, if each element of A is an element of B. A is a *proper* subset of B (alternatively, B *properly contains* A), written $A \subsetneq B$, if $A \subseteq B$ but there is an element of B not in A.

Sets A and B are *equal*, written $A = B$, if $A \subseteq B$ and $B \subseteq A$.

Given a set $\{x_\alpha/\alpha \text{ in } \mathscr{I}\}$, $\mathscr{I}$ is called an *index* set.

The *set union* or *union* of a family $\{A_\alpha/\alpha\}$ of sets, written $\bigcup_\alpha A_\alpha$, is the set of elements in at least one of the A_α. The set union of no sets is defined to be the empty set.

The *set intersection* or *intersection* of a family $\{A_\alpha/\alpha\}$ of sets, written $\bigcap_\alpha A_\alpha$, is the set of elements in all of the A_α.

If there is a finite (infinite) number $A_1, \ldots, A_n$ $(A_1, \ldots, A_n, \ldots)$ of sets involved, then the set union is written as $A_1 \cup A_2 \cup \ldots \cup A_n$ or $\bigcup_{1 \leqq i \leqq n} A_i$ or $\bigcup_{i=1}^{n} A_i \left(\bigcup_{i \geqq 1} A_i \text{ or } \bigcup_{i=1}^{\infty} A_i\right)$, and the set intersection as $A_1 \cap \ldots \cap A_n$ or $\bigcap_{1 \leqq i \leqq n} A_i$ or $\bigcap_{i=1}^{n} A_i \left(\bigcap_{i \geqq 1} A_i \text{ or } \bigcap_{i=1}^{\infty} A_i\right)$.

Sets A and B are *disjoint* if $A \cap B = \emptyset$.

For sets A and B, $A - B$, called *set difference*, is the set of those elements in A which are not in B.

If $A \subseteq B$, then the *complement of A with respect to B* is the set $B-A$. Usually B is understood. The act of taking complements is called *complementation.*

For each set A, the set of all subsets of A is denoted by 2^A, i.e., $2^A = \{B/B \subseteq A\}$.

A set A is said to be the *smallest* set having properties $P_1, \ldots, P_k$ if A has properties $P_1, \ldots, P_k$ and $A \subseteq B$ for each set B having properties $P_1, \ldots, P_k$.

The number of elements in a finite set A is denoted by $\#(A)$.

A set consisting of a single element x is sometimes written as x instead of $\{x\}$.

The *cartesian product* of a finite sequence of sets $A_1, \ldots, A_n$, denoted by $A_1 \times \ldots \times A_n$, is the set of all n-tuples $(a_1, \ldots, a_n)$, where each a_i is in A_i.

For n-tuples $(a_1, \ldots, a_n)$ and $(b_1, \ldots, b_n)$, let $(a_1, \ldots, a_n) = (b_1, \ldots, b_n)$ if $a_i = b_i$ for each i.

A *relation* ϱ on a set A is a subset ϱ of $A \times A$. We write $x\varrho y$ or "$x\varrho y$ holds" to indicate that (x, y) is in the relation ϱ. We write $x\varrho y$ to indicate that $x\varrho y$ does not hold.

A relation ϱ on A is *symmetric* if $x\varrho y$ implies $y\varrho x$.

A relation ϱ on A is *transitive* if $x\varrho y$ and $y\varrho z$ imply $x\varrho z$.

For each relation ϱ on A let ϱ^0 be the relation $\{(a, a)/a \text{ in } A\}$ on A. For each $k \geqq 1$ let ϱ^k be the relation $\{(a_0, a_k)/a_i \varrho a_{i+1},\ 0 \leqq i < k, \text{ for some } a_1, \ldots, a_{k-1}\}$ on A. Let $a_0 \varrho a_1 \ldots \varrho a_k$ denote the fact that $a_i \varrho a_{i+1}$ for each i, $0 \leqq i < k$. Let $\varrho^+ = \bigcup_{k \geqq 1} \varrho^k$ and $\varrho^* = \bigcup_{k \geqq 0} \varrho^k$. The relation ϱ^+ is called the *transitive closure* of ϱ, and ϱ^* is the *reflexive transitive closure* of ϱ.

The two most frequently employed relation symbols are $\Rightarrow$ and $\vdash$. These symbols are customarily defined with respect to some given structure X ($\Rightarrow$ with "grammars" and $\vdash$ with "acceptors"). When the related structure is to be emphasized, then $\underset{X}{\Longrightarrow}$ or $\underset{X}{\vdash}$ is written. For example, if $\Rightarrow$ is used in conjunction with a grammar G, then $\Rightarrow$ and $\underset{G}{\Longrightarrow}$ are interchangeable symbols.

The symbols $\overset{k}{\Longrightarrow}$, $\overset{k}{\vdash}$, $\overset{+}{\Longrightarrow}$, $\overset{+}{\vdash}$, $\overset{*}{\Longrightarrow}$, and $\overset{*}{\vdash}$ are used instead of $\Rightarrow^k$, $\vdash^k$, $\Rightarrow^+$, $\vdash^+$, $\Rightarrow^*$, and $\vdash^*$, respectively.

A *partial order* on a set A is a relation $\leqq$ on A such that (i) $x \leqq x$ for all x in A, (ii) if $x \leqq y$ and $y \leqq z$, then $x \leqq z$, and (iii) if $x \leqq y$ and $y \leqq x$, then $x = y$, i.e., x is y.

A pair $(A, \leqq)$ is called a *partially ordered* set.

Let $(A, \leqq)$ be a partially ordered set. x_0 in A is *minimal* if $x \leqq x_0$ implies $x = x_0$. x_0 in A is *maximal* if $x_0 \leqq x$ implies $x = x_0$. x_0 in A is *largest* if

$x \leqq x_0$ for all x in A. Elements x and y are *incomparable* if $x \leqq y$ and $y \leqq x$ are both false.

A *simply ordered set*, or *chain*, is a partially ordered set $(A, \leqq)$ such that for all x and y in A either $x \leqq y$ or $y \leqq x$.

Unless otherwise specified, when referring to a family $\mathscr{L}$ of sets as a partially ordered set, the partial order is set containment, i.e., $A \leqq B$ if and only if $A \subseteq B$. Thus the terms "$\mathscr{L}$ has a maximal element", "$\mathscr{L}$ has incomparable elements", etc. may be used.

A *function* (or *mapping*, *operation*, or *operator*) is a triple (A, B, f) where A and B are nonempty sets and to each element x in A there corresponds an element, denoted by $f(x)$, in B. (A, B, f) is also called a *function* f, *from* A *into* B.

A function f is *one to one* if $f(x_1) \neq f(x_2)$ whenever $x_1 \neq x_2$.

The *inverse* of a function (A, B, f) is the function $(B, 2^A, f^{-1})$ defined by $f^{-1}(y) = \{x \text{ in } A/f(x) = y\}$ for each y in B.

Let (A, B, f) and (C, B, f') be functions, with $C \subseteq A$ and $f'(x) = f(x)$ for each x in C. Then f' is said to be the *restriction* of f to C, and f is said to be an *extension* of f'.

Let f be a function from A into B and g a function of C into D, with $B \subseteq C$. Then gf is the function from A into D defined by $gf(x) = g[f(x)]$ for each x in A.

Whenever gf is written, with (A, B, f) and (C, D, g) functions, it is to be assumed that $B \subseteq C$.

Let f be a function from A into B. If $E \subseteq A$, then $f(E) = \{f(x)/x \text{ in } E\}$. If $f(A) = B$, then f is said to be *onto* B.

It is easily seen that for each function (A, B, f) and all sets $C \subseteq A$ and $D \subseteq B$, $f(C) \cap D = f[C \cap f^{-1}(D)]$.

A *permutation* of a finite set A is a one-to-one function (A, A, f).

A set A is *countable* if there exists a one-to-one function f from A into the set of positive integers. A is *countably infinite* if it is countable and infinite.

An infinite sequence $\{x_n\}$ of elements is said to be *ultimately periodic* if there exist integers n_0 and n_1 such that $x_{n+n_1} = x_n$ for every integer $n \geqq n_0$. A set A of nonnegative integers is said to be *ultimately periodic* if either A is finite or $y_1, y_2 - y_1, \ldots, y_{n+1} - y_n, \ldots$ is an ultimately periodic sequence, where $y_1, y_2, \ldots$, are the elements of A ordered by increasing magnitude.

Let N denote the nonnegative integers.

A function f from N into N is said to be *nondecreasing* if $f(n+1) \geqq f(n)$ for all n in N. f is said to be *strictly increasing* (on the set $\{x/x \geqq x_0\} \subseteq N$) if $f(n+1) > f(n)$ for all n (in $\{x/x \geqq x_0\}$).

For each positive integer n let $N^n = N \times \ldots \times N$ (n times) For all elements $x = (x_1, \ldots, x_n)$ and $y = (y_1, \ldots, y_n)$ of N^n and c in N, let $x+y = (x_1+y_1, \ldots, x_n+y_n)$ and $cx = (cx_1, \ldots, cx_n)$.

$L \subseteq N^n$ is said to be a *linear* set if there exists a finite subset $\{p_1, \ldots, p_r, c\}$ of N^n such that $L = \left\{c + \sum_{i=1}^{r} k_i p_i / \text{each } k_i \text{ in } N\right\}$. A subset of N^n is said to be *semilinear* if it is a finite union of linear sets.

If $k_1, \ldots, k_r$ are nonnegative integers, then $\max\{k_i / 1 \leqq i \leqq r\}$ is the largest number among the k_i.

The *degree of the polynomial* $f(x) = a_n x^n + \ldots + a_1 x + a_0$ is the largest integer j such that $a_j \neq 0$.

For integers k, m, and n, write $m \equiv n \pmod{k}$ if there exists an integer i such that $m - n = ik$.

1.2 Language Preliminaries

An *alphabet* is a set of abstract symbols. Unless otherwise indicated, Σ subscripted is always to be a finite alphabet.

Each element in an alphabet is called a *symbol*.

A *word* (of *length* $k \geqq 0$) over an alphabet Δ is a finite sequence $x_1, \ldots, x_k$ of elements in Δ. A word $x_1, \ldots, x^k$ is usually written without commas, i.e., as $x_1 \ldots x_k$.

The word of length zero, called the *empty* word, is denoted by ϵ.

The length of a word w is denoted by $|w|$.

$x_1 \ldots x_k$ is a Δ-word if $k \geqq 1$ and each x_i is in Δ.

Δ-words $x_1 \ldots x_r$ and $y_1 \ldots y_s$ are *equal*, written $x_1 \ldots x_r = y_1 \ldots y_s$, if $r = s$ and $x_i = y_i$ for each i.

If $x = x_1 \ldots x_r$ and $y = y_1 \ldots y_s$ are words, then $x \cdot y$, called the *concatenation* or *product* of x and y, is the word $x_1 \ldots x_r y_1 \ldots y_s$. We usually write xy instead of $x \cdot y$.

The set of all words, including ϵ, over an alphabet Δ is denoted by Δ^*.

Let x and y be words in Δ^*. x is a *subword* of y if $y = uxv$ for some u and v in Δ^*. x is an *initial* subword of y if $y = xv$ for some v in Δ^*. x is a *terminal* (or *final*) subword of y if $y = ux$ for some u in Δ^*. x is a *proper* subword of y if x is a subword of y, but $x \neq y$.

For each word w and each symbol a, let $\#_a(w)$ denote the number of occurrences of a in w.

Let $\Sigma_1 = \{a_1, \ldots, a_n\}$. Let $\psi_{\langle a_1, \ldots, a_n\rangle}$, or ψ when $\langle a_1, \ldots, a_n\rangle$ is understood, be the mapping from Σ_1^* into N^n defined by $\psi(w) = (\#_{a_1}(w), \ldots, \#_{a_n}(w))$ for each w in Σ_1^*. Such a function is called a *Parikh* mapping.

For each finite alphabet Σ_1, each subset $L \subseteq \Sigma_1^*$ is called a *language*.

We shall expand upon the notion of a language in Chapter 3.

A language which does not contain ϵ is called an ϵ-*free* language.

For languages X and Y, the *concatenation* (or *product*) of X and Y, written $X \cdot Y$ or XY, is the language $\{xy/x \text{ in } X, y \text{ in } Y\}$.

For each language L let $L^0 = \{\epsilon\}$. For each $n \geqq 1$ let $L^n = L^{n-1}L$. Let $L^* = \bigcup_{i=0}^{\infty} L^i$ and $L^+ = \bigcup_{i=1}^{\infty} L^i$. The operations $*$ and $+$ etc. are also called *Kleene*$*$ and *Kleene*$+$.

Thus, for a word w, $w^0 = \epsilon$, $w^n = w^{n-1}w$ for each $n \geqq 1$, $w^* = \{w^n/n \geqq 0\}$, and $w^+ = \{w^n/n \geqq 1\}$.

Note that $\Sigma_1^+ = \Sigma_1^* - \{\epsilon\} = \Sigma_1\Sigma_1^*$.

Let $\underline{P}_1, \ldots, \underline{P}_m$ be distinct symbols not in Σ_1, and $U_1, \ldots, U_m$ subsets of Σ_1^*. A *general Post production* (over Σ_1, with $\underline{P}_i$ over U_i, $1 \leqq i \leqq m$) is an ordered pair $(\alpha(\underline{P}_1, \ldots, \underline{P}_m), \beta(\underline{P}_1, \ldots, \underline{P}_m))$, written $\alpha(\underline{P}_1, \ldots, \underline{P}_m) \to \beta(\underline{P}_1, \ldots, \underline{P}_m)$, where $\alpha(\underline{P}_1, \ldots, \underline{P}_m)$ and $\beta(\underline{P}_1, \ldots, \underline{P}_m)$ are words in $(\Sigma_1 \cup \{\underline{P}_i/1 \leqq i \leqq m\})^*$. Given a set Π of general Post productions (over Σ_1, with $\underline{P}_i$ over U_i, $1 \leqq i \leqq m$), let $\Rightarrow$ be the relation on Σ_1^* defined as follows: Write $w \Rightarrow y$ if there exists $\alpha(\underline{P}_1, \ldots, \underline{P}_m) \to \beta(\underline{P}_1, \ldots, \underline{P}_m)$ in Π and $u_1, \ldots, u_m$, each u_i in U_i, so that $w = \alpha(u_1, \ldots, u_m)$ and $y = \beta(u_1, \ldots, u_m)$.

Let $\epsilon^R = \epsilon$ and for each Σ_1-word $x_1 \ldots x_k$ let $(x_1 \ldots x_k)^R = x_k \ldots x_1$. For each language L let $L^R = \{w^R/w \text{ in } L\}$. For each set $\mathcal{L}$ of languages let $\mathcal{L}^R = \{L^R/L \text{ in } \mathcal{L}\}$. The operation R is called (*word*) *reversal*.

For all words x and y, $(xy)^R = y^R x^R$. For all languages L_1 and L_2, $(L_1L_2)^R = L_2^R L_1^R$.

Let h be a function from Σ_1^* into Σ_2^* such that $h(xy) = h(x)\,h(y)$ for all x and y in Σ_1^*. Then h is called a *homomorphism* (on Σ_1^*).

For each homomorphism h, $h(\epsilon) = \epsilon$.

A homomorphism on Σ_1^* is uniquely defined by its values for all a in Σ_1. Moreover, let $h(a)$ be an arbitrary word for each a in Σ_1. Then h can be extended over Σ_1^* to be a homomorphism, and this homomorphism is unique.

Let h be a homomorphism on Σ_1^*. If $h(x) \neq \epsilon$ for each $x \neq \epsilon$ in Σ_1^*, then h is said to be ϵ-*free*. If $|h(x)| \leqq |x|$ for each x in Σ_1^*, then h is said to be *decreasing*. If $|h(x)| = |x|$ for each x in Σ_1^*, then h is said to be *length preserving*.

A homomorphism h on Σ_1^* is ϵ-free if and only if $h(a) \neq \epsilon$ for each a in Σ_1.

h is decreasing if and only if $|h(a)| \leqq 1$ for each a in Σ_1. h is length preserving if and only if $|h(a)| = 1$ for each a in Σ_1.

For each element a in Σ_1 let Σ_a be a finite alphabet and $\tau(a)$ a subset of Σ_a^*. Let $\tau(\epsilon) = \{\epsilon\}$ and $\tau(x_1 \ldots x_r) = \tau(x_1) \ldots \tau(x_r)$ for each Σ_1-word $x_1 \ldots x_r$. Then the function τ from Σ_1^* into $2^{(\bigcup_a \Sigma_a)^*}$ is called a *substitution* (on Σ_1^*). The substitution τ on Σ_1^* is extended to $2^{\Sigma_1^*}$ by letting $\tau(L) = \bigcup_{w \text{ in } L} \tau(w)$ for each $L \subseteq \Sigma_1^*$.

A substitution τ on Σ_1^* is said to be ϵ-*free* if $\tau(a)$ is ϵ-free for each a in Σ_1.

For each substitution τ on Σ_1^* and each x and y in Σ_1^*, $\tau(xy) = \tau(x)\,\tau(y)$.

Suppose τ is a substitution on Σ_1^* such that for each a in Σ_1, $\tau(a)$ contains exactly one word. Then τ may be regarded as a homomorphism which maps Σ_1^* into $\left(\bigcup_a \Sigma_a\right)^*$.

Let $\mathcal{L}$ be a set of languages and F a set of functions. If each f in F is a mapping from a subfamily of $\mathcal{L} \times \ldots \times \mathcal{L}$ (n_f times) into $\mathcal{L}$, then $\mathcal{L}$ is said to be *closed under* the functions in F.

Thus $\mathcal{L}$ is closed under $+$ if L^+ is in $\mathcal{L}$ for each L in $\mathcal{L}$. $\mathcal{L}$ is closed under union (intersection) if $L_1 \cup L_2$ ($L_1 \cap L_2$) is in $\mathcal{L}$ for all[1] L_1, L_2 in $\mathcal{L}$. $\mathcal{L}$ is closed under homomorphism if $h(L)$ is in $\mathcal{L}$ for each Σ_1, each homomorphism h on Σ_1^*, and each $L \subseteq \Sigma_1^*$ in $\mathcal{L}$.

For the purposes of the concept "$\mathcal{L}$ is closed under substitution", only substitutions τ on Σ_1^* are considered in which $\tau(a)$ is in $\mathcal{L}$ for each a in Σ_1. In other words, a family $\mathcal{L}$ of languages is closed under (ϵ-free) substitution if $\tau(L)$ is in $\mathcal{L}$ for each Σ_1, each $L \subseteq \Sigma_1^*$ in $\mathcal{L}$, and each (ϵ-free) substitution τ on Σ_1^* such that $\tau(a)$ is in $\mathcal{L}$ for each a in Σ_1.

[1] Clearly closure under union (intersection) implies closure under the union (intersection) of each finite number of languages.

CHAPTER 2

THE CHOMSKY HIERARCHY

In this chapter we recall some elementary facts about the Chomsky hierarchy, i.e., about the four families of languages: regular sets, context-free languages, context-sensitive languages, and recursively enumerable sets; and their defining acceptors. The presentation is of a review nature and is intended solely to provide background for the study of formal languages later in the text. Very little discussion is given and all proofs are omitted. A more detailed exposition, including proofs, is in [Gi; HU1; Kn; Sm]. As in Chapter 1, the reader is advised to omit this material until such time as needed.

2.1 Turing Acceptors and Recursively Enumerable Sets

In this section we recall Turing acceptors and recursively enumerable sets, and some related concepts.

The version of a Turing acceptor we consider (i) has an input tape, read from left to right, (ii) receives inputs one at a time, on demand, (iii) has one work tape, and (iv) on the work tape performs the operation of either write, overprint, move left, move right, or stay stationary. Acceptance of a word is by reading the entire word and ending in an accepting state. Formal details are now given.

A *nondeterministic Turing acceptor* is a 7-tuple $A = (K_1, \Sigma_1, \Gamma_1, \beta, \delta, p_0, F)$, where

(i) K_1, Σ_1, and Γ_1 are finite nonempty sets (of *states*, *inputs*, and *working symbols*, respectively);

(ii) β (the *blank* symbol) is an element in Γ_1;

(iii) δ (the *transition* function) is a mapping from $K_1 \times (\Sigma_1 \cup \{\epsilon\}) \times \Gamma_1$ into $2^{K_1 \times (\Gamma_1 - \{\beta\}) \times \{-1, 0, 1\}}$;

(iv) p_0 is in K_1 (the *start* state); and

(v) $F \subseteq K_1$ (the set of *accepting* states).

Let $\uparrow$ be a new symbol (*left pointer*) and let $\vdash$ be the relation on $K_1 \times \Sigma_1^* \times$

$\Gamma_1^* \uparrow \Gamma_1^*$ defined as follows: Let x and y be in $(\Gamma_1-\{\beta\})^*$, Y in $\Gamma_1-\{\beta\}$, Z in Γ_1, a in $\Sigma_1 \cup \{\epsilon\}$, and p in K_1. If $(p', Z', -1)$ is in $\delta(p, a, Z)$, write $(p, aw, xYZ \uparrow y) \vdash (p', w, xY \uparrow Z'y)$ and $(p, aw, Z \uparrow y) \vdash (p', w, \beta \uparrow Z'y)$. If $(p', Z', 0)$ is in $\delta(p, a, Z)$, write $(p, aw, xZ \uparrow y) \vdash (p', w, xZ' \uparrow y)$. If $(p', Z', 1)$ is in $\delta(p, a, Z)$, write $(p, aw, xZ \uparrow Yy) \vdash (p', w, xZ'Y \uparrow y)$ and $(p, aw, xZ \uparrow) \vdash (p', w', xZ'\beta \uparrow)$.

For each nondeterministic Turing acceptor $A = (K_1, \Sigma_1, \Gamma_1, \beta, \delta, p_0, F)$ let

$$T(A) = \{w \text{ in } \Sigma_1^*/(p_0, w, \beta \uparrow) \overset{*}{\vdash} (p, \epsilon, y_1 \uparrow y_2) \quad \text{for some } p \text{ in } F \text{ and } y_1, y_2 \text{ in } \Gamma_1^*\}.$$

Each word in $T(A)$ is said to be *accepted* by A.

A *deterministic Turing acceptor* is an 8-tuple $A = (K_1, \Sigma_1, \$, \Gamma_1, \beta, \delta, p_0, F)$, where

(i) $(K_1, \Sigma_1 \cup \{\$\}, \Gamma_1, \beta, \delta, p_0, F)$ is a nondeterministic Turing acceptor;
(ii) $\$$ is a symbol not in Σ_1; and
(iii) $\#(\delta(p, a, Z) \cup \delta(p, \epsilon, Z)) \leqq 1$ for each p in K_1, a in Σ_1, and Z in Γ_1.

Let $A = (K_1, \Sigma_1, \$, \Gamma_1, \beta, \delta, p_0, F)$ be a deterministic Turing acceptor. The relation $\vdash$ is defined on $(K_1 \times (\Sigma_1 \cup \{\$\})^* \times \Gamma_1^* \uparrow \Gamma_1^*$ as in the nondeterministic Turing acceptor $(K_1, \Sigma_1 \cup \{\$\}, \Gamma_1, \beta, \delta, p_0, F)$. The set $T(A)$ is defined as $\{w \text{ in } \Sigma_1^*/(p_0, w\$, \beta \uparrow) \overset{*}{\vdash} (p, \epsilon, y_1 \uparrow y_2)$ for some p in F and y_1, y_2 in $\Gamma_1^*\}$.

The role of the endmarker $\$$ is to permit the deterministic Turing acceptor to know when it is at the end of its input tape. Condition (iii) guarantees that each configuration of a deterministic Turing acceptor has at most one next configuration.

We now consider the languages defined by Turing acceptors.

Let $\mathscr{L}_{RE} = \{T(A)/A$ a nondeterministic Turing acceptor$\}$. Each language in $\mathscr{L}_{RE}$ is called a *recursively enumerable* (r.e.) set.

If $L \subseteq \Sigma_1^*$ is in $\mathscr{L}_{RE}$ and $\Sigma_1^* - L$ is in $\mathscr{L}_{RE}$, then L is called a *recursive* set. Let $\mathscr{L}_{rec}$ be the family of all recursive sets.

The family of recursive sets is properly contained in the family of recursively enumerable sets, i. e., $\mathscr{L}_{rec} \subsetneq \mathscr{L}_{RE}$.

We next consider r. e. sets in connection with certain sets of "rules".

A *rewriting system* (or *phrase structure grammar*) is a 4-tuple $G = (V, \Sigma_1, P, \sigma)$, where

(i) V is a finite set of abstract symbols (the *total vocabulary*);
(ii) $\Sigma_1 \subseteq V$ (the set of *terminals*);
(iii) P is a finite subset of $(V-\Sigma_1)^+ \times V^*$, i. e., P is a finite set of ordered pairs (u, v), u in $(V-\Sigma_1)^+$ and v in V^*; and

(iv) σ is a distinguished element of $V-\Sigma_1$ (the *start* variable).

Elements (u, v) in P are called *productions* and are usually written $u \to v$.

Let $G = (V, \Sigma_1, P, \sigma)$ be a rewriting system. For each y and z in V^* write $y \Rightarrow z$ if there exist u_1, u_2, u, and v such that $y = u_1uu_2$, $z = u_1vu_2$, and $u \to v$ is in P.

A sequence $y_0, \ldots, y_k$ such that $k \geqq 1$, $y = y_0$, $z = y_k$ and $y_0 \Rightarrow y_1 \Rightarrow \ldots \Rightarrow y_k$ is called a *derivation* or *generation* of z from y.

A set $L \subseteq \Sigma_1^*$ is called a *phrase structure language* if $L = L(G)$ for some phrase structure grammar $G = (V, \Sigma_1, P, \sigma)$, where $L(G) = \{w \text{ in } \Sigma_1^* / \sigma \overset{*}{\Longrightarrow} w\}$.

For each set $U \subseteq \Sigma_1^*$, the following statements are equivalent:

(a) $U = T(A)$ for some nondeterministic Turing acceptor A.

(b) $U = T(A)$ for some deterministic Turing acceptor A.

(c) $U = L(G)$ for some rewriting system G.

The family $\mathscr{L}_{\text{RE}}$ is closed under union, concatenation, $+$, $*$, intersection with regular sets, homomorphism, inverse homomorphism, reversal, and substitution.

The family $\mathscr{L}_{\text{rec}}$ is closed under union, concatenation, $+$, $*$, intersection with regular sets, ϵ-free homomorphism, inverse homomorphism, ϵ-free substitution, reversal, and complementation. $\mathscr{L}_{\text{rec}}$ is not closed under arbitrary homomorphism or arbitrary substitution. Indeed, the homomorphism (substitution) closure of $\mathscr{L}_{\text{rec}}$ is $\mathscr{L}_{\text{RE}}$.

2.2 Finite-State Acceptors and Regular Sets

We now review some elementary ideas associated with finite-state acceptors and regular sets.

A *nondeterministic finite-state acceptor* (abbreviated *nondeterministic fsa*) is a 5-tuple $A = (K_1, \Sigma_1, \delta, p_0, F)$, where

(i) K_1 and Σ_1 are finite sets (of *states* and *inputs*, respectively);

(ii) δ is a function from $K_1 \times \Sigma_1$ into 2^{K_1};

(iii) p_0 is in K_1 (the *start* state); and

(iv) $F \subseteq K_1$ (the set of *accepting* states).

If, in addition, $\#(\delta(p, a)) = 1$ for each p in K_1 and a in Σ_1, then A is said to be a (*deterministic*) *finite-state acceptor* (abbreviated *fsa*).

Let $\vdash$ be the relation on $K_1 \times \Sigma_1^*$ defined as follows: For p and q in K_1, a in Σ_1, and x in Σ_1^*, write $(p, ax) \vdash (q, x)$ if q is in $\delta(p, a)$. If A is deterministic, then for each p in K_1 and w in Σ_1^* let $\delta(p, w) = q$, where $(p, w) \overset{*}{\vdash} (q, \epsilon)$.

For each nondeterministic fsa $A = (K_1, \Sigma_1, \delta, p_0, F)$ let $T(A) = \{w$ in

$\Sigma_1^*/(p_0, w) \stackrel{*}{\vdash} (p, \epsilon)$ for some p in $F\}$. Each word in $T(A)$ is said to be *accepted* by A.

Let $\mathcal{R} = \{T(A)/A$ an fsa$\}$ and $\mathcal{R}_0 = \{L$ in $\mathcal{R}/L$ is ϵ-free$\}$. Each set in $\mathcal{R}$ is called a *regular* set.

For each nondeterministic fsa A, $T(A)$ is regular.

Regular sets may be characterized algebraically as follows:

KLEENE THEOREM: *$\mathcal{R}(\mathcal{R}_0)$ is the smallest family containing the (ϵ-free) finite sets of words and closed under union, concatenation, and*[1] $*$ $(+)$.

The Kleene theorem may be rephrased as "$\mathcal{R}(\mathcal{R}_0)$ is the smallest family containing $\{a\}$, for each symbol a, and closed under union, concatenation, and $*$ $(+)$".

$\mathcal{R}(\mathcal{R}_0)$ is closed under intersection, (ϵ-free) homomorphism, inverse homomorphism, substitution, reversal, and set difference.

Let a be a symbol. A set $L = \{a^j/j$ in $E\}$ is regular if and only if E is an ultimately periodic set of integers.

Let $G = (V, \Sigma_1, P, \sigma)$ be a phrase structure grammar. A production is called *right linear* (*left linear*) if it is of the form $\xi \to u$ or $\xi \to uv$ ($\xi \to vu$), where u is in Σ_1^* and ξ, v are in $V - \Sigma_1$. The phrase structure grammar is said to be *right linear* (*left linear*) if each production in it is right linear (left linear).

A set L is regular if and only if $L = L(G)$ for some right-linear (left-linear) phrase structure grammar G.

For each regular set R there exists a positive integer p with the following property: Each word w in R, $|w| > p$, is of the form $w_1w_2w_3$, where $w_2 \neq \epsilon$ and $w_1w_2^kw_3$ is in L for every $k \geqq 1$.

2.3 Context-Free Languages and Pushdown Acceptors

We now review certain features of context-free language theory.

A *context-free* grammar is a phrase structure grammar $G = (V, \Sigma_1, P, \sigma)$ in which each production in P is of the form $\xi \to v$, where ξ is in $V - \Sigma_1$ and v is in V^*. Let $\mathcal{L}_{CF} = \{L(G)/G$ a context-free grammar$\}$. Each L in $\mathcal{L}_{CF}$ is called a *context-free language*.

[1] This smallest family is to be interpreted as containing $\emptyset$ since the union of no sets is $\emptyset$.

$\mathcal{L}_{CF}$ is closed under union, concatenation, $*$, $+$, reversal, homomorphism, inverse homomorphism, intersection with regular sets, and substitution.

$\mathcal{R} \subsetneq \mathcal{L}_{CF}$.

Each context-free language $L \subseteq a^*$, a in Σ_1, is regular.

BAR-HILLEL, PERLES, AND SHAMIR LEMMA: *For each context-free language L there exists an integer n with the following property: Each word z in L,* $|z| > n$, *is of the form uvwxy, where* $|vwx| \leqq n$, $vx \neq \epsilon$, *and* $uv^m wx^m y$ *is in L for all* $m \geqq 1$.

Let $\Sigma_1 = \{a_1, \ldots, a_n\}$ and $\Sigma_1' = \Sigma_1 \cup \{a_1^E, \ldots, a_n^E\}$, Σ_1' being a set of $2n$ elements. Let G be the context-free grammar $(\{\sigma\} \cup \Sigma_1', \Sigma_1', P, \sigma)$, where $P = \{\sigma \rightarrow \epsilon, \sigma \rightarrow \sigma a_i \sigma a_i^E \sigma / 1 \leqq i \leqq n\}$. Then $L(G)$ is called the *Dyck set on* Σ_1.

CHOMSKY–SCHUTZENBERGER THEOREM: *For each alphabet* Σ_1 *there exists an alphabet* Σ_1', *a Dyck set* $D \subseteq \Sigma_1'^*$, *and a homomorphism h from* $\Sigma_1'^*$ *onto* Σ_1^* *with the property that for each context-free language* $L \subseteq \Sigma_1^*$ *a regular set R can be found such that* $h(D \cap R) = L$.

Given a context-free grammar $G = (V, \Sigma_1, P, \sigma)$, $\xi = w_0 \Rightarrow \ldots \Rightarrow w_r$ is a *leftmost derivation* if for each i, $w_i = u_i v_i y_i$ and $w_{i+1} = u_i z_i y_i$, with $v_i \rightarrow z_i$ in P and u_i in Σ_1^*.

A *pushdown acceptor* (abbreviated *pda*) is a 7-tuple $A = (K_1, \Sigma_1, \Gamma_1, \delta, Z_0, p_0, F)$, where

(i) K_1, Σ_1, and Γ_1 are nonempty finite sets (of *states*, *inputs*, and *pushdown symbols*, respectively);

(ii) δ is a mapping from $K_1 \times (\Sigma_1 \cup \{\epsilon\}) \times \Gamma_1$ into the finite subsets of $K_1 \times \Gamma_1^*$;

(iii) Z_0 is an element of Γ_1 (the *start* pushdown symbol);

(iv) q_0 is in K_1 (the *start* state); and

(v) $F \subseteq K_1$ (the set of *accepting* states).

Given a pda $A = (K_1, \Sigma_1, \Gamma_1, \delta, Z_0, p_0, F)$ let $\vdash$ be the relation on $K_1 \times \Sigma_1^* \times \Gamma_1^*$ defined as follows: For Z in Γ_1 and x in $\Sigma_1 \cup \{\epsilon\}$ write $(p, xw, \alpha Z) \vdash (q, w, \alpha\gamma)$ if $\delta(p, x, Z)$ contains (q, γ).

For each pda $A = (K_1, \Sigma_1, \Gamma_1, \delta, Z_0, p_0, F)$ let $T(A) = \{w$ in $\Sigma_1^* / (p_0, w, Z_0) \overset{*}{\vdash} (p, \epsilon, \alpha)$ for some p in F and α in $\Gamma_1^*\}$. Each word in $T(A)$ is said to be *accepted* by A.

A language L is context free if and only if $L = T(A)$ for some pda A.

For each pda $A = (K_1, \Sigma_1, \Gamma_1, \delta, Z_0, p_0, F)$ let $Null(A) = \{w/(q_0, w, Z_0) \overset{*}{\vdash} (q, \epsilon, \epsilon)$ for some $q\}$.

A language L is context free if and only if $L = \text{Null}(A)$ for some pda A.

For each context-free language L there exists a pda A with no ϵ-moves, i. e., $\delta(p, \epsilon, Z) = \emptyset$ for each p and Z, such that $L = T(A)$.

A pda $A = (K_1, \Sigma_1, \Gamma_1, \delta, Z_0, p_0, F)$ is said to be *deterministic* if $\#(\delta(p, a, Z) \cup \delta(p, \epsilon, Z)) \leqq 1$ for each p in K_1, a in Σ_1, and Z in Γ_1. A set L is said to be a *deterministic pda language* if $L = T(A)$ for some deterministic pda A.

The family of deterministic pda languages is neither closed under union nor under ϵ-free homomorphism.

A context-free grammar $G = (V, \Sigma_1, P, \sigma)$ is said to be *linear* if each production is of the form $\xi \rightarrow u$ or $\xi \rightarrow uvv$, u and v in Σ_1^*, v in $V - \Sigma_1$. A set L is said to be a *linear context-free* language if $L = L(G)$ for some linear context-free grammar G.

Let $\mathscr{L}_{\text{lin}}$ be the family of all linear context-free languages.

$\mathscr{L}_{\text{lin}}$ is closed under union, homomorphism, inverse homomorphism, intersection with regular sets, and reversal.

2.4 Context-Sensitive Languages and Linear-Bounded Acceptors

We conclude our review of the Chomsky hierarchy with a discussion of context-sensitive languages and linear bounded acceptors.

A *context-sensitive grammar* is a phrase structure grammar $G = (V, \Sigma_1, P, \sigma)$ in which each production is of the form $u \rightarrow v$, with $|u| \leqq |v|$. If $L = L(G)$ for some context-sensitive grammar G, then L is said to be a *context-sensitive language*.

Let $\mathscr{L}_{\text{CS}} = \{L/L$ context sensitive$\}$ and $\mathscr{L}_{\text{ECS}} = \{L, L \cup \{\epsilon\}/L$ in $\mathscr{L}_{\text{CS}}\}$. (A language in $\mathscr{L}_{\text{ECS}}$ is an *extended* context-sensitive language.)

$$\mathscr{L}_{\text{CF}} \subsetneqq \mathscr{L}_{\text{ECS}} \quad \text{and} \quad \mathscr{L}_{\text{ECS}} \subsetneqq \mathscr{L}_{\text{rec}}.$$

$\mathscr{L}_{\text{CS}}$ ($\mathscr{L}_{\text{ECS}}$) is closed under union, intersection, concatenation, $+$, intersection with regular sets, ϵ-free homomorphism, inverse homomorphism, reversal, and (ϵ-free) substitution.

$\mathscr{L}_{\text{CS}}$ ($\mathscr{L}_{\text{ECS}}$) is *not* closed under arbitrary homomorphism. Indeed, the homomorphism closure of $\mathscr{L}_{\text{CS}}$ ($\mathscr{L}_{\text{ECS}}$) is $\mathscr{L}_{\text{RE}}$.

A *linear bounded acceptor*, abbreviated *lba*, is a 6-tuple $A = (K_1, \Sigma_1, W, \delta, p_0, F)$, where

(i) K_1 and W are finite nonempty sets (of *states* and *working symbols* respectively);

(ii) $\Sigma_1 \subseteq W$;

(iii) δ is a mapping from $K_1 \times W$ into $2^{K_1 \times W \times \{-1, 0, 1\}}$;

(iv) p_0 is in K_1 (the *start* state); and

(v) $F \subseteq K_1$ (the set of *accepting* states).

If $\#(\delta(p, a)) \leqq 1$ for each p in K_1 and a in Σ_1, then A is said to be a *deterministic lba*.

The lba is a 2-way read-write device as follows:

Let $\upharpoonright$ be a new symbol (*right pointer*) and let $\vdash$ be the relation on $K_1 \times W^* \upharpoonright W^*$ defined as follows: Let x and y be in W^*, a and b in W, and p in K_1. If $(p', a', 1)$ is in $\delta(p, a)$ write $(p, x \upharpoonright ay) \vdash (p', xa' \upharpoonright y)$. If $(p', a', 0)$ is in $\delta(p, a)$ write $(p, x \upharpoonright ay) \vdash (p', x \upharpoonright a'y)$. If $(p', a', -1)$ is in $\delta(p, a)$ write $(p, xb \upharpoonright ay) \vdash (p', x \upharpoonright ba'y)$.

For each lba $A = (K_1, \Sigma_1, W, \delta, p_0, F)$ let

$$T(A) = \{w \text{ in } \Sigma_1^+/(p_0, \upharpoonright w) \overset{*}{\vdash} (p', w' \upharpoonright) \text{ for some } p' \text{ in } F \text{ and } w' \text{ in } \Sigma_1^*\}.$$

$T(A)$ is called an *lba language*.

It is an open question whether the family of lba languages coincides with the family of deterministic lba languages.

A language is context sensitive if and only if it is an lba language.

The deterministic lba languages are closed under union, concatenation, $+$, ϵ-free homomorphism, intersection, intersection with regular sets, substitution, inverse homomorphism, reversal, and set difference.

Each ϵ-free context-free language is a deterministic lba language.

2.5 Two Variations

Besides $\mathcal{R}$, $\mathcal{L}_{CF}$, $\mathcal{L}_{CS}$, and $\mathcal{L}_{RE}$, many other families of languages have been studied (often in conjunction with associated families of acceptors). As an indication of the variety possible, so that a need to systematize the treatment of families of languages will be better appreciated, the two which have received the most attention are now briefly, informally, mentioned. A more theoretical and extensive treatment of these two families, as well as numerous others, will appear in later chapters, especially in the examples and exercises.

The first family is $\mathcal{L}_S$, the "(one-way) stack-acceptor languages". A stack acceptor is essentially a pda which can enter and read, but not alter, the contents of the auxiliary storage. (Thus stack acceptors can store "symbol tables" on the storage and then access them without erasing any storage.) Acceptance is by accepting state (or equivalently, by simultaneous accepting state and empty storage.) Formal details are given in Example. 4.1.4.

The stack languages have a number of closure properties similar to those in the Chomsky hierarchy. For example, they are closed under union, concatenation, inverse homomorphism, and reversal.

The stack languages fit between the context-free and the extended context-sensitive languages, i.e., $\mathcal{L}_{\text{CF}} \subsetneq \mathcal{L}_{\text{S}} \subsetneq \mathcal{L}_{\text{ECS}}$. In particular, $\{a^n b^n c^n / n \geqq 1\}$ is in $\mathcal{L}_{\text{S}} - \mathcal{L}_{\text{CF}}$ and, [Og, b], $\{a^{n^2} b^{n^2} c^{n^2} / n \geqq 1\}$ is in $\mathcal{L}_{\text{CS}} - \mathcal{L}_{\text{S}}$.

The second family is $\mathcal{L}_{\text{C}}$, the "counter" languages. A counter is a push-down acceptor in which the auxiliary storage alphabet contains just one element. In effect, the auxiliary storage at each moment is a number, namely the length of the storage. (As a result, counters, in essence, can only compare "weighted" lengths of parts of a word.) Formal details are given in Example 4.1.3.

The closure properties of the counter languages are also similar to those in the Chomsky hierarchy. For example, they are closed under union, concatenation, intersection with regular sets, and inverse homomorphism.

The counter languages lie between the regular sets and the context-free languages, i. e., $\mathcal{R} \subsetneq \mathcal{L}_{\text{C}} \subsetneq \mathcal{L}_{\text{CF}}$. In particular, $\{a^n b^n / n \geqq 1\}$ is in $\mathcal{L}_{\text{C}} - \mathcal{R}$ and the Dyck set on $\{a, b\}$ is in $\mathcal{L}_{\text{CF}} - \mathcal{L}_{\text{C}}$.

CHAPTER 3

TRIOS, SEMI-AFL, AND AFL

During the years 1955–1966 numerous families of formal languages from computer science, automata theory, and mathematical linguistics were investigated for their mathematical properties. In time, it was noticed that many of these families, as for example those in Chapter 2, had common properties. This suggested the presence of underlying general structures, of which the families already considered were but specific examples. If these underlying structures could be abstracted, then a general theory of families of languages, giving greater insight and ultimately leading to codification and classification, might be attainable.

A search for these more general structures was begun in 1966 with the introduction of the notion of an AFL (acronym for *a*bstract *f*amily of *l*anguages). Since then, other mathematical models have also been studied, but AFL have remained pre-eminent and have received the most attention. The aim of this text is to describe the main results of the developed theory, especially as they relate to AFL. In the present chapter, we first define an AFL and the accessory concepts of trio and semi-AFL. We then discuss connections between these concepts and a-transducers. For example, we characterize the smallest AFL containing a given family of languages in terms of a-transducers and substitution. In the remaining chapters, we treat other aspects of AFL theory.

3.1 Families of Languages

In the present section we first consider the notion of a "family of languages". Then we introduce three progressively more restricted models of families of languages, the last being that of an AFL.

Before considering "families of languages", let us deal with the notion of a "language". Intuitively, one thinks of a language as a set of rules (grammar) which then selects the gramatically correct words (or sentences) of the language. This view is too narrow for our purposes since many of the languages we shall treat do not have an apparent generating set of rules.[1] Instead, we shall regard a language as any set of words. Additionally, we shall demand that all the words be over a finite alphabet. More exactly, we have

Def: A *language* is a set L for which there exists a finite set Σ_1 of abstract symbols such that[2] $L \subseteq \Sigma_1^*$. For each language L, let Σ_L be the smallest set Σ_1 such that $L \subseteq \Sigma_1^*$.

Obviously Σ_L exists, consisting of those symbols which occur in at least one word of L. In particular, $\Sigma_{\{\epsilon\}} = \emptyset$.

EXAMPLE 3.1.1: Let $\Sigma = \{a_i \mid i \geqq 1\}$. Then $\{a_1^n a_2^n \mid n \geqq 1\}$ is a language, but $\{a_i^i a_{i+1}^i \mid i \geqq 1\}$ is not.

In general, we are not interested in single languages but in collections of languages. As already mentioned, we are especially concerned with families of languages, such as the regular sets, the context-free languages, and the context-sensitive languages, which have arisen in computer science, automata theory, and mathematical linguistics. An examination of such families indicates that while each language is over a finite alphabet, an infinite alphabet is required to meaningfully discuss all the languages in a family. Thus we shall deal with families of languages over an infinite alphabet as now formalized.

Def: A *family of languages* is an ordered pair $(\Sigma, \mathscr{L})$, or $\mathscr{L}$ when Σ is understood, where

(1) Σ is an infinite set of symbols,
(2) $\mathscr{L}$ is a set of sets of words over Σ,
(3) For each L in $\mathscr{L}$ there is a finite set $\Sigma_1 \subseteq \Sigma$ such that $L \subseteq \Sigma_1^*$, and
(4) $L \neq \emptyset$ for some L in $\mathscr{L}$.

Condition 4 eliminates the family $\{\emptyset\}$ and the empty family.

Henceforth, Σ will always denote a given infinite set of symbols and Σ subscripted a finite subset of Σ. All symbols given or constructed, and then used in a language, will be assumed to be in Σ. Also, L and $\mathscr{L}$, with or without a subscript, will always denote a language and a family of languages, respectively, over Σ.

[1] The last phrase must be taken philosophically since we do not make precise what we mean by a "rule".

[2] This coincides with the concept of language given in Section 1.2. It is repeated here, with additional background, in order to provide the proper mood with which to deal with structures of families of languages.

The notion of a family of languages is too general a concept for the families of languages we are trying to model. We need further restrictions. The properties to be added are certain closure operations. The main concept to be studied, an AFL, has six axiomatic closure operations. We shall find it convenient to first introduce the auxiliary notions of "trio" and "semi-AFL".

Def: A (*full*) *trio* is a family of languages closed under the operations of ϵ-free homomorphism (arbitrary homomorphism), inverse homomorphism, and intersection with regular sets.

EXAMPLE 3.1.2: $\mathcal{L}_{\text{lin}}$, $\mathcal{R}$, $\mathcal{L}_{\text{CF}}$, and $\mathcal{L}_{\text{RE}}$ are full trios.

EXAMPLE 3.1.3: $\mathcal{L}_{\text{CS}}$, $\mathcal{L}_{\text{ECS}}$, $\mathcal{L}_{\text{rec}}$, and $\mathcal{R}_0$ are trios which are not full.

EXAMPLE 3.1.4: The family $\mathcal{L}$ of deterministic context-free languages is not a trio since $\mathcal{L}$ is not closed under ϵ-free homomorphism.

Note (Exercise 3.1.2) that $L - R$ is in $\mathcal{L}$ for each trio $\mathcal{L}$, each language L in $\mathcal{L}$, and each R in $\mathcal{R}$.

We shall see in Section 3.2 that (full) trios have a characterization in terms of certain general finite-state devices.

Observe that a trio $\mathcal{L}$ contains $\{\epsilon\}$ if and only if $\mathcal{L}$ contains some language with ϵ in it.

As indicated above, $\mathcal{R}_0(\mathcal{R})$ is a (full) trio. We now show that each (full) trio contains $\mathcal{R}_0(\mathcal{R})$, so that $\mathcal{R}_0(\mathcal{R})$ is the smallest (full) trio.

LEMMA 3.1.1: *Let $\mathcal{L}$ be a trio with a language containing ϵ. Then $\mathcal{R} \subseteq \mathcal{L}$.*

Proof: Let L in $\mathcal{L}$ contain ϵ. Then $L \cap \{\epsilon\} = \{\epsilon\}$ is in $\mathcal{L}$. Let R be in $\mathcal{R}$. Let h be the homomorphism on Σ_R^* defined by $h(a) = \epsilon$ for each a in Σ_R. Then $h^{-1}(\{\epsilon\}) \cap R = \Sigma_R^* \cap R = R$ is in $\mathcal{L}$. Hence $\mathcal{R} \subseteq \mathcal{L}$.

THEOREM 3.1.1: *For each* (*full*) *trio* $\mathcal{L}$, $\mathcal{R}_0 \subseteq \mathcal{L}$ ($\mathcal{R} \subseteq \mathcal{L}$).

Proof: Let L be a nonempty language in $\mathcal{L}$ and w some element in L. Let R be in $\mathcal{R}_0$. For each a in Σ_R, let $\bar{a}$ be a new symbol and $\Sigma_2 = \{\bar{a}/a \text{ in } \Sigma_R\}$. Let h_1 be the homomorphism on $(\Sigma_R \cup \Sigma_2)^*$ defined by $h_1(a) = \epsilon$ and $h_1(\bar{a}) = w$ for each a in Σ_R. Let h_2 be the ϵ-free homomorphism on $(\Sigma_R \cup \Sigma_2)^*$ defined by $h_2(a) = h_2(\bar{a}) = a$ for each a in Σ_R. Then $h_1^{-1}(L) \cap \Sigma_R^* \Sigma_2 \Sigma_R^* = \Sigma_R^* \Sigma_2 \Sigma_R^*$, so that $\Sigma_R^* \Sigma_2 \Sigma_R^*$ is in $\mathcal{L}$ since $\mathcal{L}$ is closed under inverse homomorphism and intersection with regular sets. Since h_2 is an

ϵ-free homomorphism, $\Sigma_R^+ = h_2(\Sigma_R^*\Sigma_2\Sigma_R^*)$ is in $\mathcal{L}$. Then $R = \Sigma_R^+ \cap R$ is in $\mathcal{L}$, so that $\mathcal{R}_0 \subseteq \mathcal{L}$.

Suppose $\mathcal{L}$ is a full trio. Let h_3 be the homomorphism on Σ_L^* defined by $h_3(a) = \epsilon$ for all a in Σ_L. Then $h_3(L) = \{\epsilon\}$, so that $\{\epsilon\}$ is in $\mathcal{L}$. By Lemma 3.1.1, $\mathcal{R} \subseteq \mathcal{L}$.

In passing, we note two properties of trios.

PROPOSITION 3.1.1: (a) *Each (full) trio is closed under union with ϵ-free (arbitrary) regular sets.*

(b) *If $\mathcal{L}$ is a trio, then LR and RL are in $\mathcal{L}$ for each L in $\mathcal{L}$ and R in $\mathcal{R}$.*

Proof: (a) Let $\mathcal{L}$ be a trio and L in $\mathcal{L}$. Suppose R is an ϵ-free regular set. It suffices to assume that $\Sigma_L \cap \Sigma_R = \emptyset$. [Otherwise, for each a in Σ_R let a' be a new symbol. Let h be the ϵ-free homomorphism mapping each a in Σ_R onto a'. Let h' be the ϵ-free homomorphism which is the identity for a in Σ_L and which maps a' onto a for each a'. Then $h(R)$ is regular, $\Sigma_L \cap \Sigma_{h(R)} = \emptyset$, $h'(L \cup h(R)) = L \cup R$, and $L \cup R$ is in $\mathcal{L}$ if $L \cup h(R)$ is in $\mathcal{L}$.] If $L = \emptyset$ then $L \cup R$ is in $\mathcal{L}$ by Theorem 3.1.1. Thus suppose $L \neq \emptyset$. Let w be a word in L. For each a in Σ_R let $\bar{a}$ be a new symbol and $\Sigma_1 = \{\bar{a} / a$ in $\Sigma_R\}$. Let h_1 be the homomorphism on $(\Sigma_L \cup \Sigma_R \cup \Sigma_1)^*$ defined by $h_1(a) = a$ for a in Σ_L, $h_1(\bar{a}) = w$ for $\bar{a}$ in Σ_1, and $h_1(a) = \epsilon$ for a in Σ_R. Then $h_1^{-1}(L) \cap (\Sigma_L^* \cup \Sigma_1 R) = L \cup \Sigma_1 R$ since Σ_L, Σ_1, and Σ_R are pairwise disjoint. Clearly $L \cup \Sigma_1 R$ is in $\mathcal{L}$. Let h_2 be the homomorphism on $(\Sigma_L \cup \Sigma_R \cup \Sigma_1)^*$ defined by $h_2(a) = a$ for a in $\Sigma_L \cup \Sigma_R$ and $h_2(\bar{a}) = \bar{a}a$ for $\bar{a}$ in Σ_1. Let h_3 be the ϵ-free homomorphism on $(\Sigma_L \cup \Sigma_R \cup \Sigma_1)^*$ defined by $h_3(a) = a$ for a in $\Sigma_L \cup \Sigma_R$ and $h_3(\bar{a}) = a$ for $\bar{a}$ in Σ_1. Then $h_3(h_2^{-1}(L \cup \Sigma_1 R)) = L \cup R$, since R is ϵ-free, and is in $\mathcal{L}$.

Suppose $\mathcal{L}$ is a full trio. In view of the previous paragraph it suffices to show that $L \cup \{\epsilon\}$ is in $\mathcal{L}$ for each L in $\mathcal{L}$. Let b be a new symbol. Then $L \cup \{b\}$ is in $\mathcal{L}$ since $\{b\}$ is an ϵ-free regular set. Let h_4 be the homomorphism on $(\Sigma_L \cup \{b\})^*$ defined by $h_4(a) = a$ for a in Σ_L and $h_4(b) = \epsilon$. Then $h_4(L \cup \{b\}) = L \cup \{\epsilon\}$ is in $\mathcal{L}$ since $\mathcal{L}$ is full.

(b) Let $\mathcal{L}$ be a trio, L in $\mathcal{L}$, and R in $\mathcal{R}$. As in (a), we may assume that $\Sigma_L \cap \Sigma_R = \emptyset$. Let h be the homomorphism on $(\Sigma_L \cup \Sigma_R)^*$ defined by $h(a) = a$ for a in Σ_L and $h(a) = \epsilon$ for a in Σ_R. Then $h^{-1}(L) \cap \Sigma_L^* R = LR$, $h^{-1}(L) \cap R\Sigma_L^* = RL$, and both languages are in $\mathcal{L}$.

The notion of a (full) trio has been abstracted because a number of elementary results of interest involve, in either the hypothesis or the conclusion, a family of languages closed under inverse homomorphism, ϵ-free homomorphism (arbitrary homomorphism), and intersection with regular sets. In general though, (full) trios are rather weak structures and not too much will be said about them. It turns out that by adding the property of closure under union to (full) trios, significantly stronger structures are obtained. This leads to the following concept.

Def: A *(full) semi-AFL* is a (full) trio closed under union, i.e., a family of languages closed under ϵ-free homomorphism (arbitrary homomorphism), inverse homomorphism, intersection with regular sets, and union.[1]

Each of the families in Example 3.1.2 is a full semi-AFL. Each of the families in Example 3.1.3 is a semi-AFL which is not full.

Semi-AFL are interesting structures and much will be said about them. Nevertheless, they are not the main objects of our study. The families of languages of paramount importance to us are AFL. These families are obtained by adding to a semi-AFL the remaining closure operations in the Kleene theorem for $\mathcal{R}_0$.

Def: A *(full) AFL* is a (full) semi-AFL closed under concatenation and $+$. Expressed otherwise, a (full) AFL is a family of languages closed under union, concatenation, $+$, intersection with regular sets, ϵ-free homomorphism (arbitrary homomorphism), and inverse homomorphism.

EXAMPLE 3.1.5: $\mathcal{R}$, $\mathcal{L}_{CF}$, and $\mathcal{L}_{RE}$ are full AFL.

EXAMPLE 3.1.6: $\mathcal{R}_0$, $\mathcal{L}_{CS}$, $\mathcal{L}_{ECS}$, and $\mathcal{L}_{rec}$ are AFL which are not full.

EXAMPLE 3.1.7: $\mathcal{L}_{lin}$ is a full semi-AFL which is not an AFL. (See Exercise 3.1.8.)

We wish to stress the following. The principal concern in this text is with the study of AFL, not trios or semi-AFL. When convenient though, we state results for trios and semi-AFL. While there are numerous connections between AFL and semi-AFL, nevertheless AFL and semi-AFL have separate theories.[2]

It is readily seen (Exercise 3.1.3) that the arbitrary union of (full) trios is a (full) trio. This is not true for either semi-AFL or AFL. In fact, for (full)

[1] Recall that closure under union means closure under the union of each two languages.

[2] An analogous situation in classical mathematics is the separate theories of groups and semi-groups.

semi-AFL, resp. AFL, $\mathcal{L}_1$ and $\mathcal{L}_2$, $\mathcal{L}_1 \cup \mathcal{L}_2$ is a (full) semi-AFL, resp. AFL, if and only if either $\mathcal{L}_1 \subseteq \mathcal{L}_2$ or $\mathcal{L}_2 \subseteq \mathcal{L}_1$. (See Exercise 3.1.4.)

Note that $\mathcal{L}$ is a (full) trio, semi-AFL, AFL, resp. if and only if $\mathcal{L}^R$ is a (full) trio, semi-AFL, AFL, resp. (See Exercise 3.1.6.)

The definition of an AFL involves closure under six operations. It turns out that these operations are not independent of each other.[1] In particular, we now show that concatenation is dependent on the remaining operations.

THEOREM 3.1.2: *Each (full) semi-AFL closed under* $+$ *is a (full) AFL.*

Proof: Let $\mathcal{L}$ be a semi-AFL closed under $+$. Let L_1 and L_2 be in $\mathcal{L}$, and $\Sigma_1 = \Sigma_{L_1} \cup \Sigma_{L_2}$. For each a in Σ_1, let a' and a'' be new symbols. Let $\Sigma_2 = \{a'/a \text{ in } \Sigma_1\}$, $\Sigma_3 = \{a''/a \text{ in } \Sigma_1\}$, and $\Sigma_4 = \Sigma_1 \cup \Sigma_2 \cup \Sigma_3$. Let h be the ϵ-free homomorphism from Σ_4^* into Σ_1^* defined by $h(a) = h(a') = h(a'')$ $= a$ for each a in Σ_1. Let

$$L_1' = h^{-1}(L_1) \cap \Sigma_2\Sigma_1^*,$$

$$L_2' = h^{-1}(L_2) \cap \Sigma_3\Sigma_1^*,$$

and $L_3 = (L_1' \cup L_2')^+ \cap \Sigma_2\Sigma_1^*\Sigma_3\Sigma_1^*$

$$= \{a'w_1b''w_2 \,/\, aw_1 \text{ in } L_1,\ bw_2 \text{ in } L_2,\ a \text{ and } b \text{ in } \Sigma_1\}.$$

Clearly L_1' and L_2' are in $\mathcal{L}$, so that L_3 is in $\mathcal{L}$. Then

(i) $L_1L_2 = h(L_3)$ if ϵ is not in $L_1 \cup L_2$.

(ii) $L_1L_2 = h(L_3) \cup L_1$ if ϵ is in $L_2 - L_1$.

(iii) $L_1L_2 = h(L_3) \cup L_2$ if ϵ is in $L_1 - L_2$.

(iv) $L_1L_2 = h(L_3) \cup L_1 \cup L_2$ if ϵ is in $L_1 \cap L_2$.

In all cases, L_1L_2 is in $\mathcal{L}$, so that $\mathcal{L}$ is closed under concatenation. Hence $\mathcal{L}$ is an AFL.

We shall return to the study of the dependency of the AFL operations in Section 3.7.

In general, the empty word plays a nuisance role in language structure theory. Many proofs require a division into two cases, namely when $\{\epsilon\}$ is in the structure and when it is not. Proposition 3.1.2 below exhibits a simple relation between structures with and without $\{\epsilon\}$.

[1] It is not unusual to define a mathematical structure in terms of dependent axioms. For example, the customary axioms [MB] for a group are known to be dependent.

PROPOSITION 3.1.2: *For each trio, semi-AFL, AFL* $\mathcal{L}$, *resp. let* $\mathcal{L}_1 = \{L$ *in* $\mathcal{L}/L$ *is* ϵ*-free*$\}$ *and* $\mathcal{L}_2 = \{L, L \cup \{\epsilon\}/L$ *in* $\mathcal{L}\}$. *Then*

(a) $\mathcal{L}_1$ *and* $\mathcal{L}_2$ *are trios, semi AFL, AFL, resp.*,

(b) $\mathcal{L}_1 = \{L-\{\epsilon\}/L$ *in* $\mathcal{L}\}$, *and*

(c) *in case* $\mathcal{L}$ *is a semi-AFL,* $\mathcal{L}$ *is either* $\mathcal{L}_2$ *or* $\mathcal{L}_1$, *according as* $\mathcal{L}$ *does or does not have a language with* ϵ *in it.*

Proof: Clearly we need only prove (a) and (b).

Turning to (a), consider $\mathcal{L}_1$. By Theorem 3.1.1, $\mathcal{R}_0 \subseteq \mathcal{L}$. Therefore $\mathcal{R}_0 \subseteq \mathcal{L}_1$ and $\mathcal{L}_1$ contains a nonempty language. Since intersection with regular sets, ϵ-free homomorphism, and inverse homomorphism do not introduce ϵ, $\mathcal{L}_1$ is closed under these operations, i. e., $\mathcal{L}_1$ is a trio. Suppose $\mathcal{L}$ is a semi-AFL. Let L_1 and L_2 be in $\mathcal{L}_1 \subseteq \mathcal{L}$. Then $L_1 \cup L_2$ is ϵ-free and in $\mathcal{L}$, thus in $\mathcal{L}_1$. Hence $\mathcal{L}_1$ is a semi-AFL. Suppose $\mathcal{L}$ is an AFL. Since $+$ does not introduce ϵ, $\mathcal{L}_1$ is closed under this operation. Hence $\mathcal{L}_1$ is an AFL by Theorem 3.1.2.

Consider $\mathcal{L}_2$. Since $\mathcal{L} \subseteq \mathcal{L}_2$, $\mathcal{L}_2$ contains a nonempty language. Now let L_1 and L_2 be in $\mathcal{L}_2$. Clearly, $L_1' = L_1-\{\epsilon\}$ and $L_2' = L_2-\{\epsilon\}$ are in $\mathcal{L}$. Then $L_1 \cup L_2 = L_1' \cup L_2'$ if $L_1 \cup L_2$ is ϵ-free, and $L_1 \cup L_2 = L_1' \cup L_2' \cup \{\epsilon\}$ if ϵ is in $L_1 \cup L_2$. If $\mathcal{L}$ is a semi-AFL, then $L_1' \cup L_2'$, thus $L_1 \cup L_2$, is in $\mathcal{L}_2$. Let R be a regular set. Two cases arise.

(α) Suppose L_1 is ϵ-free. Then L_1 is in $\mathcal{L}$. Hence $h_1(L_1)$, $h_2^{-1}(L_1)$, and $L_1 \cap R$ are in $\mathcal{L} \subseteq \mathcal{L}_2$ for every ϵ-free homomorphism h_1 and every homomorphism h_2. If $\mathcal{L}$ is an AFL then L_1^+ is in $\mathcal{L} \subseteq \mathcal{L}_2$.

(β) Suppose L_1 contains ϵ. For every ϵ-free homomorphism h_1 and every homomorphism h_2, $h_1(L_1) = h_1(L_1') \cup \{\epsilon\}$ and $h_2^{-1}(L_1) = h_2^{-1}(L_1') \cup h_2^{-1}(\{\epsilon\})$. Obviously $h_1(L_1)$ is in $\mathcal{L}_2$. Since $\{\epsilon\}$ is a regular set, $h_2^{-1}(\{\epsilon\})$ is a regular set containing ϵ. Thus $h_2^{-1}(\{\epsilon\}) = R_0 \cup \{\epsilon\}$, where R_0 is in $\mathcal{R}_0$. By Proposition 3.1.1, $h_2^{-1}(L_1') \cup R_0$ is in $\mathcal{L}$. Thus $h_2^{-1}(L_1) = h_2^{-1}(L_1') \cup R_0 \cup \{\epsilon\}$ is in $\mathcal{L}_2$. Also, $L_1 \cap R = (L_1' \cap R) \cup (\{\epsilon\} \cap R)$ is in $\mathcal{L}_2$. Since $L_1^+ = L_1'^+ \cup \{\epsilon\}$, L_1^+ is in $\mathcal{L}_2$ if $\mathcal{L}$ is an AFL.

In either case, $\mathcal{L}_2$ is a trio, semi-AFL, AFL according as $\mathcal{L}$ is a trio, semi-AFL, AFL (by Theorem 3.1.2) resp.

Consider (b). For each L in $\mathcal{L}$, $L-\{\epsilon\}$ is in $\mathcal{L}$. Thus $\{L-\{\epsilon\}/L$ in $\mathcal{L}\} \subseteq \mathcal{L}_1$. On the other hand, suppose that L is in $\mathcal{L}_1 \subseteq \mathcal{L}$. Then $L = L-\{\epsilon\}$ is in $\{L'-\{\epsilon\}/L'$ in $\mathcal{L}\}$, so that $\mathcal{L}_1 \subseteq \{L'-\{\epsilon\}/L'$ in $\mathcal{L}\}$, whence equality.

Note that (c) of Proposition 3.1.2 need not hold if $\mathcal{L}$ is a trio. For let $\mathcal{L} = \mathcal{R} \cup \mathcal{L}_{CS}$. Then $\mathcal{L}_1 = \mathcal{L}_{CS}$ and $\mathcal{L}_2 = \mathcal{L}_{ECS}$. Clearly $\mathcal{L} \neq \mathcal{L}_1$ and $\mathcal{L} \neq \mathcal{L}_2$.

Open Question: Does there exist an AFL $\mathcal{L}_1$, properly containing $\mathcal{R}$, with the following property: If $\mathcal{L}$ is an AFL such that $\mathcal{R} \subseteq \mathcal{L} \subseteq \mathcal{L}_1$, then either $\mathcal{L} = \mathcal{R}$ or $\mathcal{L} = \mathcal{L}_1$? Phrased otherwise, among all AFL properly containing $\mathcal{R}$, is there a minimal one? [It is shown in [GGo2] that there is no smallest AFL properly containing $\mathcal{R}$.]

EXERCISE 3.1.1: (a) Prove that $\mathcal{L}_{CS} \cup \mathcal{R}$ is a trio but not a semi-AFL.
(b) Generalize (a) to the following: Let $\mathcal{L}_1$ and $\mathcal{L}_2$ be two incomparable trios. Prove that $\mathcal{L}_1 \cup \mathcal{L}_2$ is a trio but not a semi-AFL.

EXERCISE 3.1.2: Let $\mathcal{L}$ be a trio. Prove that $L-R$ is in $\mathcal{L}$ for all L in $\mathcal{L}$ and R in $\mathcal{R}$.

EXERCISE 3.1.3: Prove that the arbitrary union of (full) trios is a (full) trio.

EXERCISE 3.1.4: Prove that for (full) semi-AFL, resp. AFL, $\mathcal{L}_1$ and $\mathcal{L}_2$, $\mathcal{L}_1 \cup \mathcal{L}_2$ is a (full) semi-AFL, resp. AFL, if and only if either $\mathcal{L}_1 \subseteq \mathcal{L}_2$ or $\mathcal{L}_2 \subseteq \mathcal{L}_1$.

EXERCISE 3.1.5: Prove that $\bigcap_{\alpha \text{ in } A} \mathcal{L}_\alpha$ is a (full) trio, semi-AFL, AFL, resp. for each nonempty collection $\{\mathcal{L}_\alpha/\alpha \text{ in } A\}$ of (full) trios, semi-AFL, AFL, resp.

EXERCISE 3.1.6: Prove that $\mathcal{L}$ is a (full) trio, semi-AFL, AFL, resp. if and only if $\mathcal{L}^R$ is a (full) trio, semi-AFL, AFL, resp.

EXERCISE 3.1.7: Prove that each (full) trio, semi-AFL, AFL, resp. contains a largest reversal-closed (full) trio, semi-AFL, AFL, resp. [GHa2].

EXERCISE 3.1.8: Prove that $\mathcal{L}_{\text{lin}}$ is not closed under concatenation. [Hint: Let $L_1 = \{a^n b^n/n \geqq 1\}$ and $L_2 = \{c^n d^n/n \geqq 1\}$. Then show that L_1 and L_2 are in $\mathcal{L}_{\text{lin}}$, but $L_1 L_2$ is not in $\mathcal{L}_{\text{lin}}$.]

EXERCISE 3.1.9: Prove that the set of all languages (over Σ) is a full AFL.

EXERCISE 3.1.10: For each context-free grammar $G = (V, \Sigma_1, P, \sigma)$ and each $n \geqq 1$, let $L_n(G)$ be the set of all words w in Σ_1^* with the following property: There exists a leftmost derivation $\sigma = w_0 \underset{L}{\Rightarrow} \ldots \underset{L}{\Rightarrow} w_r = w$ such that $|h(w_i)| \leqq n$ for all w_i, where h is the homomorphism on V^* defined by $h(a) = \epsilon$ for each a in Σ_1 and $h(\xi) = \xi$ for each ξ in $V - \Sigma_1$. Given $n \geqq 1$, a language L is called *n-left derivation bounded* if $L = L_n(G)$ for some G. Let $\mathcal{L}_{\text{LDB}(n)}$ be the family of all n-left derivation bounded languages. Prove the following:

(a) $\mathcal{L}_{\text{LDB}(n)}$ is a full semi-AFL for all $n \geqq 1$ [Wa].
(b) For no n is $\mathcal{L}_{\text{LDB}(n)}$ an AFL.

(c) $\mathscr{L}_{\text{LDB}} = \bigcup_{n \geqq 1} \mathscr{L}_{\text{LDB}(n)}$ is a full AFL [Wa]. (Each language in $\mathscr{L}_{\text{LDB}}$ is called *left derivation bounded.*)

(d) $\mathscr{L}_{\text{LDB}} \subseteq \mathscr{L}_{\text{CF}}$.

(e) $\mathscr{L}_{\text{LDB}(n)} \subsetneqq \mathscr{L}_{\text{LDB}(n+1)}$ for each $n \geqq 1$.

EXERCISE 3.1.11: Give an example of an AFL $\mathscr{L}$ containing $\{\epsilon\}$ for which the family $\{\Sigma_1^* - L/L \text{ in } \mathscr{L}, \Sigma_1 \subseteq \Sigma\}$ is not an AFL.

EXERCISE 3.1.12: A 6-tuple $G = (K_1, V, \Sigma_1, P, p_0, \sigma)$ is said to be a *state grammar* if (i) K_1 is a finite nonempty set (of *states*), (ii) V is a finite set of symbols, (iii) $\Sigma_1 \subseteq V$, (iv) σ is in $V - \Sigma_1$, (v) p_0 is in K_1, and (vi) P is a finite subset of $K_1 \times (V - \Sigma_1) \times K_1 \times V^+$. Each element (p, ξ, q, u) of P is said to be a *state-production, applicable* (*under* p) *at* ξ. Each element of $V - \Sigma_1$ is called a *variable*. Write $(p, x) \Rightarrow (q, y)$ if there exist u_1, u_2, ξ, and v such that $x = u_1 \xi u_2$, $y = u_1 v u_2$, (p, ξ, q, v) is in P, and there is no state-production applicable at a variable in u_1. For $n \geqq 1$, write $(p, x) \underset{(n)}{\Longrightarrow} (q, y)$ if, in addition, $u_1 \xi$ has at most n occurrences of variables. Let $L(G) = \{w \text{ in } \Sigma_1^+ / (p_0, \sigma) \overset{*}{\Longrightarrow} (p, w)$ for some p in $K_1\}$ and $L(G; n) = \{w \text{ in } \Sigma_1^+ / (p_0, \sigma) \underset{(n)}{\overset{*}{\Longrightarrow}} (p, w)$ for some p in $K_1\}$. Let $\mathscr{L}_n$ be the family of all $L(G)$ such that $L(G) = L(G; n)$. Prove the following [Ka]:

(a) $\mathscr{L}_1$ is the AFL of ϵ-free context-free languages.

(b) $\{L(G)/\text{all } G\} = \mathscr{L}_{\text{CS}}$.

(c) For each n, $\mathscr{L}_n$ is closed under (i) union, (ii) concatenation, (iii) $+$, (iv) intersection with regular sets, and (v) ϵ-free homomorphism. [Closure under inverse homomorphism occurs in Exercise 3.7.7.]

EXERCISE 3.1.13: A 4-tuple $G = (\Sigma_1, \delta, w_0, F)$ is called a *PE0L system* if δ is a function from Σ_1 into the finite nonempty subsets of Σ_1^+, w_0 is in Σ_1^+, and $F \subseteq \Sigma_1$. Let $\Rightarrow$ be the relation on Σ_1^+ defined by $u \Rightarrow v$ if there exist $k \geqq 1$, $u_1, \ldots, u_k$ in Σ_1, and $v_1, \ldots, v_k$ in Σ_1^+ such that $u = u_1 \ldots u_k$, $v = v_1 \ldots v_k$, and v_i is in $\delta(u_i)$ for each i. Let $L(G) = \{w \text{ in } F^* / w_0 \overset{*}{\Longrightarrow} w\}$ and $\mathscr{L} = \{L(G)/G \text{ a PE0L system}\}$. Prove the following [He]:

(a) $\mathscr{L}$ is closed under union, concatenation, $+$, intersection with regular sets, and ϵ-free homomorphism.

(b) Let h be the homomorphism on $\{a, b\}^*$ defined by $h(a) = a$ and $h(b) = \epsilon$. Let $L_1 = \{a^{2^i}/i \geqq 0\}$ and $L_2 = h^{-1}(L_1)$. Then L_1 is in $\mathscr{L}$, but L_2 is not in $\mathscr{L}$.

3.2 a-Transducers

We now study a special type of finite-state transformation device, the a-transducer, which plays an important role in the theory of families of languages. The main result of the section characterizes the images, under a-transducers, of a family $\mathscr{L}$ of languages in terms of the smallest full trio containing $\mathscr{L}$. This characterization theorem is then used to infer a number of closure properties of AFL.

Intuitively, an a-transducer is a finite-state device with accepting states which, in a nondeterministic manner, moves under input words to give output words. The output is recorded only if the device lands at an accepting state after reading the entire input. Formally, we have:

Def: A *sequential transducer with accepting states*, abbreviated *a-transducer*, is a 6-tuple $M = (K_1, \Sigma_1, \Sigma_2, H, p_0, F)$, where
(i) K_1, Σ_1, and Σ_2 are finite sets (of *states*, *inputs*, and *outputs*, resp.).
(ii) H is a finite subset of $K_1 \times \Sigma_1^* \times \Sigma_2^* \times K_1$ (the *moves*).
(iii) p_0 is in K_1 (the *start* state).
(iv) $F \subseteq K_1$ (the set of *accepting* states).
If $H \subseteq K_1 \times \Sigma_1^* \times \Sigma_2^+ \times K_1$, then M is called *ϵ-free*.

The moves cause M to function in the following manner.

Notation: Let $\vdash$ be the relation on $K_1 \times \Sigma_1^* \times \Sigma_2^*$ defined by letting $(p, xw, z_1) \vdash (q, w, z_2)$ for each w in Σ_1^* if (p, x, y, q) is in H and $z_2 = z_1 y$.

The triple (p, w, z) represents the fact that M is in state p, with w the input still to be read, and z the accumulated output. $(p, w, z) \overset{*}{\vdash} (p', w', z')$ means that M can go from (p, w, z) to (p', w', z') by a sequence of zero or more elementary moves.

The purpose of an a-transducer is to act as a transformation device. The manner in which this is accomplished is now given.

Def: Let $M = (K_1, \Sigma_1, \Sigma_2, H, p_0, F)$ be an a-transducer. For each word w in Σ_1^*, let $M(w) = \{z/(p_0, w, \epsilon) \overset{*}{\vdash} (p, \epsilon, z) \text{ for some } p \text{ in } F\}$. For every set $W \subseteq \Sigma_1^*$, let $M(W) = \bigcup_{w \text{ in } W} M(w)$. The mapping M from $2^{\Sigma_1^*}$ into $2^{\Sigma_2^*}$ so defined is called an *a-transducer mapping* or *a-transduction*.

Note that for an ϵ-free a-transducer $M = (K_1, \Sigma_1, \Sigma_2, H, p_0, F)$, $M(w)$ is ϵ-free for $w \neq \epsilon$, and $M(\epsilon)$ contains ϵ if and only if p_0 is in F.

EXAMPLE 3.2.1: Let $M = (K_1, \Sigma_1, \Sigma_2, H, p_0, F)$, where $K_1 = \{p_0, p_1, p_2, p_3\}$, $\Sigma_1 = \{a, b\}$, $\Sigma_2 = \{c, d\}$, $F = \{p_2, p_3\}$, and $H = \{(p_0, \epsilon, c, p_0), (p_0, ab, d, p_1), (p_1, b, cd, p_0), (p_1, b, d^2, p_2), (p_2, a, dc, p_3), (p_2, b, \epsilon, p_3), (p_3, a, c, p_1)\}$. Then

$$M(ab) = \{z/(p_0, ab, \epsilon) \overset{*}{\vdash} (p, \epsilon, z), p \text{ in } F\} = \emptyset$$

and
$$\begin{aligned} M(ab^3) &= \{z/(p_0, ab^3, \epsilon) \overset{*}{\vdash} (p, \epsilon, z), p \text{ in } F\} \\ &= \{z/(p_0, ab^3, \epsilon) \overset{*}{\vdash} (p_0, ab^3, c^i) \overset{*}{\vdash} (p, \epsilon, z), p \text{ in } F, i \geqq 0\} \\ &= \{z/(p_0, ab^3, \epsilon) \overset{*}{\vdash} (p_1, b^2, c^i d) \overset{*}{\vdash} (p, \epsilon, z), p \text{ in } F, i \geqq 0\} \\ &= c^* d^3. \end{aligned}$$

REMARK: As defined above, an a-tranducer has just one input tape. The device can be generalized to one having n input tapes as follows: An *n-tape a-transducer* is a 6-tuple $M = (K_1, (\Sigma_1, \ldots, \Sigma_n), \Sigma_{n+1}, H, p_0, F)$, where

(i) $n \geqq 1$.

(ii) K_1, p_0, and F are as in an a-transducer.

(iii) $\Sigma_1, \ldots, \Sigma_{n+1}$ are finite sets (with Σ_i, $1 \leqq i \leqq n$, the *inputs on the ith input tape* and with Σ_{n+1} the *outputs*).

(iv) H is a finite subset of $K_1 \times (\Sigma_1^* \times \ldots \times \Sigma_n^*) \times \Sigma_{n+1}^* \times K_1$ (the *moves*). If $H \subseteq K_1 \times (\Sigma_1^* \times \ldots \times \Sigma_n^*) \times \Sigma_{n+1}^+ \times K_1$, then M is called *ϵ-free*. For words $w = (w_1, \ldots, w_n)$ and $y = (y_1, \ldots, y_n)$ in $\Sigma_1^* \times \ldots \times \Sigma_n^*$, let $wy = (w_1 y_1, \ldots, w_n y_n)$. Define $\vdash$ as in an a-transducer. For each w in $\Sigma_1^* \times \ldots \times \Sigma_n^*$ and $W \subseteq \Sigma_1^* \times \ldots \times \Sigma_n^*$ define $M(w)$ and $M(W)$ as in an a-transducer. Our interest in n-tape a-transducers, $n > 1$, will be confined to occasional exercises.

We now turn to the main result of the section.

Notation: For each family $\mathcal{L}$ of languages let

$$\mathcal{M}(\mathcal{L}) = \{M(L)/L \text{ in } \mathcal{L}, M \text{ an } \epsilon\text{-free a-transducer}\} \text{ and}$$

$$\hat{\mathcal{M}}(\mathcal{L}) = \{M(L)/L \text{ in } \mathcal{L}, M \text{ an a-transducer}\}.$$

Note that in defining $\mathcal{M}(\mathcal{L})$ and $\hat{\mathcal{M}}(\mathcal{L})$, we require $\mathcal{L}$ to be a *family* of languages instead of a *set* of languages. This is done so that Theorem 3.2.1 below, the main result of the section, will have an attractive form. In particular, Theorem 3.2.1 provides two characterizations of $\mathcal{M}(\mathcal{L})(\hat{\mathcal{M}}(\mathcal{L}))$: (1) $\mathcal{M}(\mathcal{L})(\hat{\mathcal{M}}(\mathcal{L}))$ is the family of all languages of the form $h_2(h_1^{-1}(L) \cap R)$, where L is in $\mathcal{L}$, R is in $\mathcal{R}$, h_1 is a homomorphism, and h_2 is an ϵ-free (arbitrary) homomorphism; and (2) $\mathcal{M}(\mathcal{L})(\hat{\mathcal{M}}(\mathcal{L}))$ is the smallest (full) trio containing $\mathscr{L}$. We shall establish this theorem with the assistance of a sequence of lemmas.

LEMMA 3.2.1: *For each subset T of $\Sigma_1 \times \Sigma_1$,*

$$R = \{a_1 \ldots a_k / k \geqq 2, (a_i, a_{i+1}) \text{ in } T \text{ for } 1 \leqq i < k\} \cup \Sigma_1$$

is a regular set.

Proof: Let $E = \{\epsilon\} \cup \bigcup_{(a,b) \text{ in } (\Sigma_1 \times \Sigma_1) - T} \Sigma_1^* ab \Sigma_1^*$. Since E is a finite union of regular sets, E is regular. From the definition, $R = \Sigma_1^* - E$. Hence R is regular.

Using the preceding lemma we get:

LEMMA 3.2.2: *Let M be an (ϵ-free) a-transducer. Then there exist a regular set R and two homomorphisms h_1 and h_2 (with h_2 ϵ-free) such that $M(L) = h_2[h_1^{-1}(L) \cap R]$ for all languages L.*

Proof: Let $M = (K_1, \Sigma_1, \Sigma_2, H, p_0, F_1)$ be an a-transducer. For each (p, w, y, p') in H, let $\overline{(p, w, y, p')}$ be a new symbol. Let Σ_3 be the set of all such symbols $\overline{(p, w, y, p')}$. Let h_1 be the homomorphism from Σ_3^* into Σ_1^* defined by $h_1(\overline{(p, w, y, p')}) = w$ for all $\overline{(p, w, y, p')}$. Let h_2 be the homomorphism from Σ_3^* into Σ_2^* defined by $h_2(\overline{(p, w, y, p')}) = y$ for all $\overline{(p, w, y, p')}$. Let $i_0 = 0$. Let

$$R_1 = \Sigma_3 \cup \{\overline{(p_{k_0}, w_{k_1}, y_{k_1}, p_{k_1})} \ldots \overline{(p_{k_{n-1}}, w_{k_n}, y_{k_n}, p_{k_n})} / n \geqq 2, \text{ each } \overline{(p_{k_j}, w_{k_{j+1}}, y_{k_{j+1}}, p_{k_{j+1}})} \text{ in } \Sigma_3\}$$

and $$R_2 = \{\overline{(p_{i_0}, w_{i_1}, y_{i_1}, p_{i_1})} \ldots \overline{(p_{i_{n-1}}, w_{i_n}, y_{i_n}, p_{i_n})} / n \geqq 1, \text{ each } \overline{(p_{i_j}, w_{i_{j+1}}, y_{i_{j+1}}, p_{i_{j+1}})} \text{ in } \Sigma_3, p_{i_n} \text{ in } F_1\}.$$

By Lemma 3.2.1, R_1 is regular. Since

$$R_2 = R_1 \cap \{\overline{(p_0, w, y, p)} / \overline{(p_0, w, y, p)} \text{ in } \Sigma_3\} \Sigma_3^* \cap \Sigma_3^* \{\overline{(p, w, y, p')} / p' \text{ in } F_1\},$$

R_2 is regular. Let $R_3 = R_2 \cup \{\epsilon / p_0 \text{ in } F_1\}$. Clearly $M(L) = h_2(h_1^{-1}(L) \cap R_3)$ for each language L. Also, h_2 is ϵ-free if and only if M is ϵ-free.

Lemma 3.2.2 gives containment one-way in the first part of the characterization result. We now turn to the reverse containment. We shall need two lemmas to achieve this. The first is of a technical nature. The second asserts that the composition of (ϵ-free) a-transducers is an (ϵ-free) a-transducer.

Def: An a-transducer $M = (K_1, \Sigma_1, \Sigma_2, H, p_0, F)$ is said to be *1-output* if $H \subseteq K_1 \times \Sigma_1^* \times \Sigma_2 \times K_1$, and *1-bounded* if $H \subseteq K_1 \times (\Sigma_1 \cup \{\epsilon\}) \times (\Sigma_2 \cup \{\epsilon\}) \times K_1$.

Thus an a-transducer is 1-output if the output from each single move is an element of Σ_2. Hence, a 1-output a-transducer is ϵ-free. An a-transducer is 1-bounded if the length of the input and the length of the output in each move is at most one.

LEMMA 3.2.3: *For each a-transducer M_1, there exists a 1-bounded a-transducer M_2 such that $M_2(L) = M_1(L)$ for each language L. For each ϵ-free a-transducer M_1 there exists a 1-output a-transducer M_2 such that $M_2(L) = M_1(L)$ for each language L.*

Proof: Let $M_1 = (K_1, \Sigma_1, \Sigma_2, H_1, p_0, F_1)$, with $H_1 = \{(p_i, u_i, v_i, q_i)/1 \leqq i \leqq n\}$.

Suppose M_1 is ϵ-free. For each i let $v_i = b_{i1} \ldots b_{ir(i)}$, $r(i) \geqq 1$, each b_{ij} in Σ_2. Let $p_{i1}, \ldots, p_{i(r(i)-1)}$ be new symbols. Let $K_2 = K_1 \cup \{p_{ij}/\text{all } i, j\}$. Let H_2 consist of the following 4-tuples (for each i):

(1) (p_i, u_i, v_i, q_i) if $r(i) = 1$.

(2) $(p_i, u_i, b_{i1}, p_{i1})$, $(p_{ij}, \epsilon, b_{i(j+1)}, p_{i(j+1)})$ for $1 \leqq j < r(i)-1$, and $(p_{i(r(i)-1)}, \epsilon, b_{ir(i)}, q_i)$, if $r(i) > 1$.

Clearly $M_2 = (K_2, \Sigma_1, \Sigma_2, H_2, p_0, F_1)$ is 1-output, and $M_2(L) = M_1(L)$ for every language L.

Now suppose M_1 is an arbitrary a-transducer. The idea here is to split up both the input and the output. In particular, for each i let $u_i = a_{i1} \ldots a_{ir(i)}$ and $v_i = b_{i1} \ldots b_{ir(i)}$, each a_i in $\Sigma_1 \cup \{\epsilon\}$, each b_i in $\Sigma_2 \cup \{\epsilon\}$, and each $r(i) \geqq 2$. Again let $p_{i1}, \ldots, p_{i(r(i)-1)}$ be new symbols and $K_2 = K_1 \cup (p_{ij}/\text{all } i, j\}$. Let

$$H_2 = \{(p_i, a_{i1}, b_{i1}, p_{i1}), (p_{ij}, a_{i(j+1)}, b_{i(j+1)}, p_{i(j+1)}), (p_{i(r(i)-1)}, a_{ir(i)}, b_{ir(i)}, q_i)/1 \leqq i \leqq n, 1 \leqq j < r(i)-1\}.$$

Then $M_2 = (K_2, \Sigma_1, \Sigma_2, H_2, p_0, F_1)$ is 1-bounded, and $M_2(L) = M_1(L)$ for every language L.

LEMMA 3.2.4: *Given (ϵ-free) a-transducers M_1 and M_2, there exists an (ϵ-free) a-transducer M such that $M(L) = M_2M_1(L)$ for every language L.*

Proof: Let $M_1 = (K_1, \Sigma_1, \Sigma_2, H_1, p_0, F_1)$ and $M_2 = (K_2, \Sigma_2, \Sigma_3, H_2, q_0, F_2)$.

Suppose M_1 and M_2 are arbitrary a-transducers. By Lemma 3.2.3, we may assume that M_1 and M_2 are 1-bounded. Let $H_3 = H_1 \cup \{(p, \epsilon, \epsilon, p)/p$ in $K_1\}$ and $H_4 = H_2 \cup \{(q, \epsilon, \epsilon, q)/q$ in $K_2\}$. Then $M_3 = (K_1, \Sigma_1, \Sigma_2, H_3, p_0, F_1)$ and $M_4 = (K_2, \Sigma_2, \Sigma_3, H_4, q_0, F_2)$ are 1-bounded a-transducers, with $M_1(L) = M_3(L)$ and $M_2(L') = M_4(L')$ for all languages L and L'. Now let $K_5 = K_1 \times K_2$, $s_0 = (p_0, q_0)$, and $F_5 = F_1 \times F_2$. Let H_5 be the set of all 4-tuples $((p, q), a, b, (p', q'))$ such that a word z can be found satisfying (p, a, z, p') in H_3 and (q, z, b, q') in H_4. Let M be the a-transducer $(K_5, \Sigma_1, \Sigma_3, H_5, s_0, F_5)$. It is easily seen (Exercise 3.2.4) that $M(L) = M_4M_3(L) = M_2M_1(L)$ for every language L.

Now suppose that M_1 and M_2 are ϵ-free a-transducers. By Lemma 3.2.3, we may assume that M_1 and M_2 are 1-output. Let $K_3 = K_1 \times K_2$, $s_0 = (p_0, q_0)$, and $F_3 = F_1 \times F_2$. Let H_3 be the set of all 4-tuples $((p, q), u, v, (p', q'))$ such that either

(1) there exists z such that $(p, u, \epsilon) \overset{+}{\underset{M_1}{\vdash}} (p', \epsilon, z)$ and (q, z, v, q') is in H_2, or
(2) $p = p'$, $u = \epsilon$, and (q, ϵ, v, q') is in H_2.

Since H_2 is finite, there are only a finite number of z such that (q, z, v, q') is in H_2. Since M_1 is ϵ-free, for each such z there are only a finite number of p, u, and p' such that $(p, u, \epsilon) \overset{+}{\vdash} (p', \epsilon, z)$. Thus (1) contributes only a finite number of 4-tuples. Obviously (2) contributes only a finite number of 4-tuples, so that $M = (K_3, \Sigma_1, \Sigma_3, H_3, s_0, F_3)$ is an ϵ-free a-transducer. It is readily seen (Exercise 3.2.5) that $M(L) = M_2M_1(L)$.

We are now ready for the characterization result.

THEOREM 3.2.1: *For each family $\mathcal{L}$ of languages,*

$$\hat{\mathcal{M}}(\mathcal{L})[\mathcal{M}(\mathcal{L})] = \{h_2(h_1^{-1}(L) \cap R)/R \text{ in } \mathcal{R}, h_1 \text{ a homomorphism}, h_2 \text{ a } [\epsilon\text{-free}] \text{ homomorphism}, L \text{ in } \mathcal{L}\}$$

and is the smallest full trio [trio] containing $\mathcal{L}$.

Proof: It suffices to consider just the $\mathcal{M}(\mathcal{L})$ case.

Clearly all inverse homomorphisms and all ϵ-free homomorphisms are realized by ϵ-free a-transducers. Also, each intersection with a regular set is realized by an ϵ-free a-transducer. [For let R be a regular set. Then $R = T(A)$ for some fsa $A = (K_1, \Sigma_1, \delta, p_0, F)$. Let $M = (K_1, \Sigma_1, \Sigma_1, H, p_0, F)$, where $H = \{(p, a, a, \delta(p, a))/p$ in K_1, a in $\Sigma_1\}$. Then $M(L) = L \cap R$ for each L.] Combining the above with Lemma 3.2.4, it follows that $\mathcal{M}(\mathcal{L})$ is a trio. Let

$$\mathcal{L}' = \{h_2(h_1^{-1}(L) \cap R)/R \text{ in } \mathcal{R}, h_1 \text{ a homomorphism}, h_2 \text{ an } \epsilon\text{-free homomorphism}, L \text{ in } \mathcal{L}\}.$$

Then $\mathcal{L}' \subseteq \mathcal{M}(\mathcal{L})$. By Lemma 3.2.2, $\mathcal{M}(\mathcal{L}) \subseteq \mathcal{L}'$. Hence $\mathcal{M}(\mathcal{L}) = \mathcal{L}'$. Obviously any trio containing $\mathcal{L}$ contains $\mathcal{L}'$. Hence $\mathcal{L}' = \mathcal{M}(\mathcal{L})$ is the smallest trio containing $\mathcal{L}$.

When $\mathcal{L}$ contains exactly one language, Theorem 3.2.1 takes the following form:

COROLLARY 1: *For each nonempty language L,*[1]

$$\hat{\mathcal{M}}(L)\,[\mathcal{M}(L)] = \{h_2(h_1^{-1}(L) \cap R)/R \text{ in } \mathcal{R},\ h_1 \text{ a homomorphism},\ h_2 \text{ a [}\epsilon\text{-free] homomorphism}\}$$

and is the smallest full trio [trio] containing L.

The hypothesis that L be nonempty is required because $\mathcal{M}(\mathcal{L})$ and $\hat{\mathcal{M}}(\mathcal{L})$ are defined only for $\mathcal{L}$ a *family* of languages, i. e., $\mathcal{L}$ contains a nonempty language. Note that $\{h_2(h_1^{-1}(L) \cap R)/R$ in $\mathcal{R}$, h_1 a homomorphism, h_2 a [ϵ-free] homomorphism$\}$ is *not* a trio if $L = \emptyset$.

If $\mathcal{L}$ is a (full) trio, then the smallest (full) trio containing $\mathcal{L}$ is itself. Hence we get the following important result.

COROLLARY 2: *Each (full) trio is closed under ϵ-free (arbitrary) a-transducers.*

Using Theorem 3.2.1 we now determine the effect of the operation $\mathcal{M}$ on the two families $\{L \cup \{\epsilon\}/L \text{ in } \mathcal{L}\}$ and $\{L - \{\epsilon\}/L \text{ in } \mathcal{L}\}$.

PROPOSITION 3.2.1: (a) *For each language L,*

$$\mathcal{M}(L \cup \{\epsilon\}) = \{M(L) \cup R/M \text{ an } \epsilon\text{-free a-transducer, } R \text{ in } \mathcal{R}\}.$$

(b) *Let $\mathcal{L}$ be a family of languages and $\mathcal{L}' = \{L \cup \{\epsilon\}/L \text{ in } \mathcal{L}\}$. Then*

$$\mathcal{M}(\mathcal{L}') = \{M(L),\ M(L) \cup \{\epsilon\}/L \text{ in } \mathcal{L},\ M \text{ an } \epsilon\text{-free a-transducer}\}.$$

(c) *Let $\mathcal{L}$ and $\mathcal{L}'' = \{L - \{\epsilon\}/L \text{ in } \mathcal{L}\}$ be families of languages. Then*

$$\mathcal{M}(\mathcal{L}'') = \{M(L) - \{\epsilon\}/L \text{ in } \mathcal{L},\ M \text{ an } \epsilon\text{-free a-transducer}\}.$$

Proof: To prove (a) and (b), we first show (a) and

(b′) If $L \neq \emptyset$, then

$$\mathcal{M}(L \cup \{\epsilon\}) = \{M(L),\ M(L) \cup \{\epsilon\}/M \text{ an } \epsilon\text{-free a-transducer}\}.$$

If $L = \emptyset$ then $\mathcal{M}(L \cup \{\epsilon\}) = \mathcal{M}(\epsilon) = \mathcal{R}$ and (a) is true. Suppose $L \neq \emptyset$.

[1] We write $\hat{\mathcal{M}}(L)$ instead of $\hat{\mathcal{M}}(\{L\})$ and $\mathcal{M}(L)$ instead of $\mathcal{M}(\{L\})$.

Let

$$P(L) = \{M(L) \cup R/M \text{ an } \epsilon\text{-free a-transducer, } R \text{ in } \mathcal{R}\}.$$

By Theorem 3.2.1 and Proposition 3.1.1, with $\mathcal{L} = \mathcal{M}(L)$,

$$P(L) = \{M(L), M(L) \cup \{\epsilon\}/M \text{ an } \epsilon\text{-free a-transducer}\}.$$

By Proposition 3.1.2, $P(L)$ is a trio containing $L \cup \{\epsilon\}$. Hence $\mathcal{M}(L \cup \{\epsilon\}) \subseteq P(L)$. Consider the reverse inclusion. Since L is in $\mathcal{M}(L \cup \{\epsilon\})$, $\mathcal{M}(L) \subseteq \mathcal{M}(L \cup \{\epsilon\})$. To complete the argument it suffices to show that $\mathcal{M}(L \cup \{\epsilon\})$ is closed under union with $\{\epsilon\}$. Thus let $M = (K_1, \Sigma_1, \Sigma_2, H, p_0, F)$ be an ϵ-free a-transducer. Let q_0 be a new symbol and $M' = (K_1 \cup \{q_0\}, \Sigma_1, \Sigma_2, H', q_0, F \cup \{q_0\})$, where $H' = H \cup \{(q_0, u, v, p)/(p_0, u, v, p) \text{ in } H\}$. Then M' is ϵ-free and $M'(L \cup \{\epsilon\}) = M(L \cup \{\epsilon\}) \cup \{\epsilon\}$.

Now consider (b). If $\emptyset$ is not in $\mathcal{L}$ then (b) holds by (b′). Suppose $\emptyset$ is in $\mathcal{L}$. Let $\mathcal{L}_0' = \{L \cup \{\epsilon\}/L \text{ in } \mathcal{L}-\{\emptyset\}\}$. Then $\mathcal{M}(\mathcal{L}') = \mathcal{M}(\mathcal{L}_0' \cup \{\{\epsilon\}\}) = \mathcal{M}(\mathcal{L}_0') \cup \mathcal{M}(\{\{\epsilon\}\}) = \mathcal{M}(\mathcal{L}_0')$, since $\mathcal{M}(\{\{\epsilon\}\}) = \mathcal{R}$ and $\mathcal{R} \subseteq \mathcal{M}(\mathcal{L}_0')$. Also,

$$\begin{aligned}
&\{M(L), M(L) \cup \{\epsilon\}/L \text{ in } \mathcal{L}, M \text{ an } \epsilon\text{-free a-transducer}\}\\
&\quad = \{M(L), M(L) \cup \{\epsilon\}/L \text{ in } \mathcal{L}-\{\emptyset\}, M \text{ an } \epsilon\text{-free a-transducer}\}\\
&\quad\quad \cup \{M(\emptyset), M(\emptyset) \cup \{\epsilon\}/M \text{ an } \epsilon\text{-free a-transducer}\}\\
&\quad = \{M(L), M(L) \cup \{\epsilon\}/L \text{ in } \mathcal{L}-\{\emptyset\}, M \text{ an } \epsilon\text{-free a-transducer}\}.
\end{aligned}$$

Then

$$\begin{aligned}
\mathcal{M}(\mathcal{L}') &= \mathcal{M}(\mathcal{L}_0')\\
&= \{M(L), M(L) \cup \{\epsilon\}/L \text{ in } \mathcal{L}-\{\emptyset\}, M \text{ an } \epsilon\text{-free a-transducer}\},\\
&\qquad \text{since } \mathcal{L}-\{\emptyset\} \text{ does not contain } \emptyset,\\
&= \{M(L), M(L) \cup \{\epsilon\}/L \text{ in } \mathcal{L}, M \text{ an } \epsilon\text{-free a-transducer}\}.
\end{aligned}$$

(c) We first show that

(c′) For each language L such that $L-\{\epsilon\} \neq \emptyset$, $\mathcal{M}(L-\{\epsilon\}) = \{M(L)-\{\epsilon\}/M$ an ϵ-free a-transducer$\}$.

If L is ϵ-free, then (c′) is clearly true. Suppose L contains ϵ. Then

$$\begin{aligned}
\{M(L)/M \text{ an } \epsilon\text{-free a-transducer}\} &= \mathcal{M}(L)\\
&= \mathcal{M}((L-\{\epsilon\}) \cup \{\epsilon\})\\
&= \{M(L-\{\epsilon\}), M(L-\{\epsilon\}) \cup \{\epsilon\}/M \text{ an } \epsilon\text{-free a-transducer}\},\\
&\qquad \text{by (b′) since } L-\{\epsilon\} \neq \emptyset.
\end{aligned}$$

Thus $\mathcal{M}(L-\{\epsilon\}) = \{M(L)-\{\epsilon\}/M \text{ an } \epsilon\text{-free a-transducer}\}$.

Now consider $\mathcal{M}(\mathcal{L}'')$. If $\emptyset$ is not in $\mathcal{L}''$, then (c′) implies (c). Suppose $\mathcal{L}''$ contains $\emptyset$. If $L-\{\epsilon\} = \emptyset$ then either $L = \{\epsilon\}$ or $L = \emptyset$. In either case, $\{M(L)-\{\epsilon\}/L-\{\epsilon\} = \emptyset,\ M$ an ϵ-free a-transducer$\} \subseteq \mathcal{R}_0$. Thus

$$\begin{aligned}\mathcal{M}(\mathcal{L}'') &= \mathcal{M}(\mathcal{L}''-\{\emptyset\}) \cup \{M(\emptyset)/M \text{ an } \epsilon\text{-free a-transducer}\}\\ &= \mathcal{M}(\mathcal{L}''-\{\emptyset\})\\ &= \{M(L)-\{\epsilon\}/L \text{ in } \mathcal{L},\ L-\{\epsilon\} \neq \emptyset,\ M \text{ an } \epsilon\text{-free a-transducer}\}\\ &= \{M(L)-\{\epsilon\}/L \text{ in } \mathcal{L},\ M \text{ an } \epsilon\text{-free a-transducer}\},\\ &\qquad \text{since } \mathcal{R}_0 \subseteq \{M(L)-\{\epsilon\})/L \text{ in } \mathcal{L},\ L-\{\epsilon\} \neq \emptyset,\\ &\qquad M \text{ an } \epsilon\text{-free a-transducer}\}.\end{aligned}$$

In general, trios, semi-AFL, and AFL are not closed under erasing functions, i.e., functions whose image of non-ϵ words includes ϵ. For example, the smallest family containing $\mathcal{L}_{CS}$ and closed under arbitrary homomorphism is $\mathcal{L}_{RE}$. However, as the next result shows, a bounded amount of erasing is permitted.

Def: Let $M = (K_1, \Sigma_1, \Sigma_2, H, p_0, F)$ be an a-transducer and L a language. Then M is *ϵ-output bounded under non-ϵ input in L* if there exists an integer k with the following property: If $z_1, z_2, y, x_1, \ldots, x_n, p_1, \ldots, p_{n+1}$ are such that $(p_i, x_i, \epsilon, p_{i+1})$ is in H for all i, $1 \leqq i \leqq n$, $z_1x_1 \ldots x_nz_2$ is in L, and $(p_0, z_1x_1 \ldots x_n, \epsilon) \overset{*}{\vdash} (p_1, x_1 \ldots x_n, y)$, then $\#(\{i/x_i \neq \epsilon\}) \leqq k$.

Thus M is ϵ-output bounded under non-ϵ input in L if for some integer k, during every sequence of moves from the start state, reading a word in L, there is no sequence of moves, each having ϵ as output, in which at least $k+1$ of the moves have a non-ϵ input.

THEOREM 3.2.2: (a) *Let $\mathcal{L}$ be a trio, L be in $\mathcal{L}$, and M be an a-transducer which is ϵ-output bounded under non-ϵ input in L. Then (i) $M(L)-\{\epsilon\}$ is in $\mathcal{L}$, and (ii) $M(L)$ is in $\mathcal{L}$ if either $\mathcal{L}$ is closed under union with $\{\epsilon\}$ or if ϵ is in $M(x)$ for x in L implies $x = \epsilon$.*

(b) *Let $\mathcal{L}$ be a full trio. Then $M(L)$ is in $\mathcal{L}$ for each L in $\mathcal{L}$ and each a-transducer M.*

Proof: (b) follows immediately from Theorem 3.2.1. Consider (a). Let L be in $\mathcal{L}$ and $M = (K_1, \Sigma_1, \Sigma_2, H, p_0, F)$ an a-transducer which is ϵ-output bounded under non-ϵ input in L. Let H' be defined as follows: (p, x, w, p') is in H' if there exist $n \geqq 1$ and $p_1 = p, p_2, \ldots, p_{n+1} = p', z_1, z_2, y, x_1, \ldots, x_n, w_1, \ldots, w_n$, such that $z_1x_1 \ldots x_nz_2$ is in L, $x = x_1 \ldots x_n$, $w = w_1 \ldots w_n$, $w_j \neq \epsilon$ for exactly one j, $(p_0, z_1x_1 \ldots x_n, \epsilon) \overset{*}{\vdash} (p_1, x_1 \ldots x_n, y)$, and $(p_i, x_i,$

w_i, p_{i+1}) is in H for all i, $1 \leqq i \leqq n$. Let q_0 be a new symbol and $M_1 = (K_1 \cup \{q_0\}, \Sigma_1, \Sigma_2, H_1, q_0, F)$, where

$$H_1 = H' \cup \{(q_0, u, v, p)/(p_0, u, v, p) \text{ in } H'\}.$$

Since M is ϵ-output bounded under non-ϵ input in L, H_1 is finite. Clearly M_1 is an ϵ-free a-transducer and $M_1(L) = M(L) - \{\epsilon\}$. By Theorem 3.2.1, $M_1(L)$ is in $\mathscr{L}$. If $\mathscr{L}$ is closed under union with $\{\epsilon\}$, then $M(L)$ is in $\mathscr{L}$ since $M(L) = M_1(L)$ or $M(L) = M_1(L) \cup \{\epsilon\}$. Suppose ϵ is in $M(x)$ for x in L implies $x = \epsilon$. If ϵ is not in $M(L)$ then $M(L) = M(L) - \{\epsilon\}$. Suppose ϵ is in $M(L)$. Then $M_2 = (K_1 \cup \{q_0\}, \Sigma_1, \Sigma_2, H_1, q_0, F \cup \{q_0\})$ is an ϵ-free a-transducer and $M_2(L) = M_1(L) \cup \{\epsilon\} = M(L)$. In either case, $M(L)$ is in $\mathscr{L}$.

Theorem 3.2.2 admits of several corollaries. From Theorem 3.2.2 and from (b) of Proposition 3.2.1, we have:

COROLLARY 1: *Let L be a language containing ϵ and M be an a-transducer which is ϵ-output bounded under non-ϵ input in L. Then $M(L)$ is in $\mathscr{M}(L)$.*

An important case of an a-transducer occurs when $F = K_1$ and H is a subset of $K_1 \times \Sigma_1 \times \Sigma_2^* \times K_1$ such that (p, a, w, q) in H and (p, a, w', q') in H implies $w = w'$ and $q = q'$. This gives rise to the well-known "generalized sequential machines" from elementary formal language theory. These are defined traditionally as follows.

Def: A *gsm* (*generalized sequential machine*) is a 6-tuple $M = (K_1, \Sigma_1, \Sigma_2, \delta, \lambda, p_0)$, where

(1) K_1, Σ_1, and Σ_2 are finite sets (of *states*, *inputs*, and *outputs*, resp.),
(2) δ is a function from $K_1 \times \Sigma_1$ into K_1 (*next-state function*),
(3) λ is a function from $K_1 \times \Sigma_1$ into Σ_2^* (*output function*), and
(4) p_0 is in K_1 (*start* state).

M is *ϵ-free* if $\lambda(q, a) \neq \epsilon$ for all q in K_1 and a in Σ_1.

The functions δ and λ are extended to $K_1 \times \Sigma_1^*$ by $\delta(q, \epsilon) = q$, $\delta(q,xa) = \delta[\delta(q, x), a]$, $\lambda(q, \epsilon) = \epsilon$, and $\lambda(q, xa) = \lambda(q, x)\, \lambda[\delta(q, x), a]$ for all q in K_1, a in Σ_1, and x in Σ_1^*.

Def: For each gsm $M = (K_1, \Sigma_1, \Sigma_2, \delta, \lambda, p_0)$, the function M from Σ_1^* into Σ_2^* defined by $M(w) = \lambda(p_0, w)$ for each w in Σ_1^* is called a *gsm mapping*. The inverse of a gsm mapping is called an *inverse gsm mapping*.

Let $M = (K_1, \Sigma_1, \Sigma_2, \delta, \lambda, p_0)$ be a gsm. Let M' be the a-transducer $(K_1, \Sigma_1, \Sigma_2, H, p_0, K_1)$, where $H = \{(p, a, \lambda(p, a), \delta(p, a))/p \text{ in } K_1, a \text{ in } \Sigma_1\}$. Clearly, for all states p, q, all words w in Σ_1^*, and all words y in Σ_2^*, $(p, w, \epsilon) \vdash^* (q, \epsilon, y)$ if and only if (i) $\delta(p, w) = q$ and (ii) $y = \lambda(p, w)$. Furthermore, $M(w) = M'(w)$ for all words w. Thus a gsm may be regarded as an a-transducer.

If M is a gsm, then it has no rules in H of the form (p, ϵ, w, p'). Therefore M being ϵ-output bounded under non-ϵ input in L reduces to the following concept.

Def: Let L be a language. A gsm $M = (K_1, \Sigma_1, \Sigma_2, \delta, \lambda, p_0)$ is *ϵ-limited on L* if there exists $k \geqq 1$ such that for all w in L, if $w = xyz$ and $\lambda[\delta(p_0, x), y] = \epsilon$ for some x, y, and z, then $|y| < k$. A homomorphism h is *ϵ-limited on L* if the one-state gsm which realizes h is ϵ-limited on L, i.e., there exists $k \geqq 1$ such that for all w in L, if $w = xyz$ and $h(y) = \epsilon$, then $|y| < k$.

EXAMPLE 3.2.2: Let $L = b^2a^*b^3$. Let h be the homomorphism on $\{a, b\}^*$ defined by $h(a) = \epsilon$ and $h(b) = b$. Then h is not ϵ-limited on L since, for each $k \geqq 1$, $b^2a^{k+1}b^3$ is in L and $h(a^{k+1}) = \epsilon$.

EXAMPLE 3.2.3: Let $L = b^*ac^* \cup c^*a^2d$. Let h be the homomorphism on $\{a, b, c, d\}^*$ defined by $h(a) = \epsilon$, $h(b) = b$, $h(c) = c$, and $h(d) = d$. Then h is ϵ-limited on L since xyz in L and $h(y) = \epsilon$ implies $|y| < 3$.

COROLLARY 2: (a) *For each trio $\mathscr{L}$, each L in $\mathscr{L}$, and each gsm M (thus each homomorphism) which is ϵ-limited on L,* (i) *$M(L) - \{\epsilon\}$ is in $\mathscr{L}$, and* (ii) *$M(L)$ is in $\mathscr{L}$ if either $\mathscr{L}$ is closed under union with $\{\epsilon\}$ or if ϵ is in $M(x)$ for x in L implies $x = \epsilon$.*

(b) *Each full trio is closed under gsm mapping.*

COROLLARY 3: *Each trio is closed under inverse gsm mapping.*

Proof: Let $\mathscr{L}$ be a trio and $M = (K_1, \Sigma_1, \Sigma_2, \delta, \lambda, p_0)$ an arbitrary gsm. Let M' be the a-transducer $(K_1, \Sigma_2, \Sigma_1, H', p_0, K_1)$, where

$$H' = \{(p, \lambda(p, a), a, \delta(p, a))/p \text{ in } K_1, a \text{ in } \Sigma_1\}.$$

Obviously M' is ϵ-free, $M^{-1}(L) = M'(L)$, and $M'(L)$ is in $\mathscr{L}$ if L is in $\mathscr{L}$.

The next two corollaries concern a number of closure results.

Def: Given L_1 and L_2, let

$$L_1/L_2 = \{w/wy \text{ in } L_1 \text{ for some } y \text{ in } L_2\} \text{ and}$$
$$L_2\backslash L_1 = \{w/yw \text{ in } L_1 \text{ for some } y \text{ in } L_2\}.$$

(L_1/L_2 is called *right quotient* and $L_2\backslash L_1$ *left quotient*.)

COROLLARY 4: (a) *Let $\mathcal{L}$ be a full trio. Then L/R and $R\backslash L$ are both in $\mathcal{L}$ for each L in $\mathcal{L}$ and R in $\mathcal{R}$.*

(b) *Let $\mathcal{L}$ be a trio. Then $(a\backslash L)-\{\epsilon\}$ and $(L/a)-\{\epsilon\}$ are in $\mathcal{L}$ for each L in $\mathcal{L}$ and a in Σ_L.*

Proof: (a) Let $\Sigma_1 = \Sigma_L \cup \Sigma_R$ and c be a new symbol. For $i = 1, 2$, let $M_i = (\{p_0, p_1\}, \Sigma_1 \cup \{c\}, \Sigma_1, \delta_i, \lambda_i, p_0)$ be the gsm defined by $\delta_1(p_j, a) = \delta_2(p_j, a) = p_j$, $\delta_1(p_j, c) = \delta_2(p_j, c) = p_1$, $\lambda_1(p_0, a) = \lambda_2(p_1, a) = a$, and $\lambda_1(p_1, a) = \lambda_2(p_0, a) = \lambda_1(p_j, c) = \lambda_2(p_j, c) = \epsilon$ for all a in Σ_1 and j in $\{0, 1\}$. Let h be the homomorphism on $(\Sigma_1 \cup \{c\})^*$ defined by $h(a) = a$ for each a in Σ_1 and $h(c) = \epsilon$. Then $L/R = M_1(h^{-1}(L) \cap \Sigma_1^* cR)$ and $R\backslash L = M_2(h^{-1}(L) \cap Rc\Sigma_1^*)$. Since $\mathcal{L}$ is a full trio, L/R and $R\backslash L$ are in $\mathcal{L}$ by Theorem 3.2.2.

(b) Let M be the gsm $(K_1, \Sigma_L, \Sigma_L, \delta, \lambda, p_0)$, where $K_1 = \{p_0, p_1\}$, $\delta(p, x) = p_1$ for all p in K_1 and x in Σ_L, $\lambda(p_0, a) = \epsilon$, and $\lambda(p, y) = y$ for all $(p, y) \neq (p_0, a)$, p in K_1 and y in Σ_L. Then M is ϵ-limited on Σ_L^* and $M(L \cap a\Sigma_L^*) = a\backslash L$. Hence $M(L \cap a\Sigma_L^*)-\{\epsilon\} = (a\backslash L)-\{\epsilon\}$ is in $\mathcal{L}$ by Corollary 2.

Consider $(L/a)-\{\epsilon\}$. Now $(L/a)-\{\epsilon\} = ((a\backslash L^R)-\{\epsilon\})^R$. Since $(a\backslash L^R)-\{\epsilon\}$ is in $\mathcal{L}^R$, $((a\backslash L^R)-\{\epsilon\})^R$ is in $\mathcal{L}$.

Note that Corollary 4 cannot be strengthened to allow R in $\mathcal{L}$. For let $\mathcal{L} = \mathcal{L}_{\mathrm{CF}}$. Then $\mathcal{L}$ is a full AFL and (see Exercises 3.2.18 and 3.2.19) there exist L and R in $\mathcal{L}$ such that $R\backslash L$ and L/R are not in $\mathcal{L}$.

Open Question: Let $\mathcal{L}$ be an AFL containing $\{\epsilon\}$ and let $\mathcal{L}$ have the following property: If L is in $\mathcal{L}$ and R is in $\mathcal{R}$, then L/R is in $\mathcal{L}$. Must $\mathcal{L}$ be full?

COROLLARY 5: *Let $\mathcal{L}$ be a full trio. Then the languages $\{w \neq \epsilon/wy$ in L for some $y\}$, $\{w \neq \epsilon/yw$ in L for some $y\}$, and $\{w \neq \epsilon/uwv$ in L for some $u, v\}$ are in $\mathcal{L}$ for each L in $\mathcal{L}$.*

Proof: Let $\mathrm{Init}(L) = \{w \neq \epsilon/wy$ in L for some $y\}$, $\mathrm{Fin}(L) = \{w \neq \epsilon/yw$ in L for some $y\}$, and $\mathrm{Subw}(L) = \{w \neq \epsilon/uwv$ in L for some $u, v\}$. Then $\mathrm{Init}(L) = (L/\Sigma_1^*)-\{\epsilon\}$, $\mathrm{Fin}(L) = (\Sigma_1^*\backslash L)-\{\epsilon\}$, and $\mathrm{Subw}(L) = \mathrm{Fin}(\mathrm{Init}(L))$.

In the above corollary, $\mathrm{Init}(L)$ is the set of non-ϵ initial subwords of words in L, $\mathrm{Fin}(L)$ is the set of non-ϵ final subwords of words in L, and $\mathrm{Subw}(L)$ is the set of non-ϵ subwords of words in L.

Open Question: Let $\mathcal{L}$ be an AFL containing ϵ, and let $\mathrm{Init}(L)$ and $\mathrm{Subw}(L)$ be as in Corollary 5. Suppose $\mathcal{L}$ has the property that $\mathrm{Init}(L)$ [$\mathrm{Subw}(L)$] is in $\mathcal{L}$ for each L in $\mathcal{L}$. Does it follow that $\mathcal{L}$ is full?

We conclude this section by presenting a modification of Theorem 3.2.1. (The principal difference is that the homomorphisms h_1 and h_2 are required to be nonincreasing.) First though, we need a special type of a-transducer.

Def: An a-transducer $M = (K_1, \Sigma_1, \Sigma_2, H, p_0, F)$ is said to be ϵ-*output bounded* if there exists k such that for each sequence

$$(p_1, w_1, \epsilon) \vdash \ldots \vdash (p_{r+1}, w_{r+1}, \epsilon),$$

$r \leqq k$.

Thus an a-transducer M is ϵ-output bounded if there is some integer k such that M never has more than k consecutive moves, each having ϵ as the output.

Note that an ϵ-output bounded a-transducer is ϵ-output bounded under non-ϵ input in Σ_1^*.

LEMMA 3.2.5: *For each ϵ-free a-transducer M_1 there exists a 1-bounded, ϵ-output bounded a-transducer $M_2 = (K_2, \Sigma_1, \Sigma_2, H_2, q_0, F_2)$ such that $M_2(L) = M_1(L)$ for every language L. Furthermore, there is no element (q_0, u, ϵ, q) in H_2.*

Proof: Let $M_1 = (K_1, \Sigma_1, \Sigma_2, H_1, p_0, F_1)$. By Lemma 3.2.3, there exists a 1-output a-transducer $M_3 = (K_3, \Sigma_1, \Sigma_2, H_3, q_0, F_3)$ such that $M_3(L) = M_1(L)$ for every L. Let $H_3 = \{(p_i, u_i, v_i, p_i')/1 \leqq i \leqq n\}$. For each i, let $u_i = a_{i1}\ldots a_{ir(i)}$, each a_{ij} in Σ_1, $r(i) \geqq 0$. For each i, $r(i) \geqq 2$, let $p_{i2}, \ldots, p_{ir(i)}$ be new symbols. Let $K_2 = K_3 \cup \{p_{ij}/\text{all } i, j\}$. Let H_2 consist of the following 4-tuples (for each i):

(1) (p_i, u_i, v_i, p_i') if $r(i) \leqq 1$.

(2) $(p_i, a_{i1}, v_i, p_{i2})$, $(p_{ij}, a_{ij}, \epsilon, p_{i(j+1)})$, $2 \leqq j < r(i)$, and $(p_{ir(i)}, a_{ir(i)}, \epsilon, p_i')$, if $r(i) \geqq 2$.

Let $M_2 = (K_2, \Sigma_1, \Sigma_2, H_2, q_0, F_3)$. Clearly M_2 is 1-bounded and $M_2(L) = M_3(L)$ for every L. Now (1) introduces no ϵ-output rules, while (2) introduces at most $\max\{r(i)-1/\text{all } i\}$ ϵ-output rules which can be used in sequence. Thus M_2 is ϵ-output bounded. Clearly M_2 satisfies the last sentence of the lemma.

We are now ready for the second representation result for $\mathcal{M}(\mathcal{L})$ and $\hat{\mathcal{M}}(\mathcal{L})$.

(+)[1] THEOREM 3.2.3: *For each nonempty language L,*

(a) *$\hat{\mathcal{M}}(L \cup \{\epsilon\}) = \hat{\mathcal{M}}(L) = \{h_2(h_1^{-1}(L) \cap R)/R$ in $\mathcal{R}$, h_1 and h_2 decreasing homomorphisms$\}$.*

[1] Sections or results marked with (+) may be omitted on a first reading.

(b) $\mathscr{M}(L \cup \{\epsilon\}) = \{h_2(h_1^{-1}(L) \cap R)/R$ *in* $\mathscr{R}$, h_1 *and* h_2 *decreasing homomorphisms,* h_2 ϵ*-limited on* $R\}$.

(c) *If* $L-\{\epsilon\} \neq \emptyset$, *then*

$$\mathscr{M}(L-\{\epsilon\}) = \{h_2(h_1^{-1}(L) \cap R)/R \text{ in } \mathscr{R},\ h_1 \textit{ and } h_2 \textit{ decreasing homomorphisms, } h_2\ \epsilon\textit{-limited on } R,\ h_2^{-1}(\epsilon) \cap R = \emptyset\}$$

$$= \{L_1/L_1 \text{ in } \mathscr{M}(L \cup \{\epsilon\}),\ L_1\ \epsilon\text{-free}\}$$

$$= \{L_1-\{\epsilon\}/L_1 \text{ in } \mathscr{M}(L \cup \{\epsilon\})\}.$$

Proof: We shall only prove (b) and (c), the argument for (a) being similar to that for (b).

Consider (b). Let $\mathscr{C}(L)$ be the family of all sets of the form $h_2(h_1^{-1}(L) \cap R)$, where R is regular, h_1 is a decreasing homomorphism, and h_2 is a decreasing homomorphism which is ϵ-limited on R. By Theorem 3.2.1, $\mathscr{M}(L \cup \{\epsilon\})$ is a trio. By (b) of Proposition 3.2.1, $\mathscr{M}(L \cup \{\epsilon\})$ is closed under union with $\{\epsilon\}$. By Corollary 2 of Theorem 3.2.2, $\mathscr{M}(L \cup \{\epsilon\})$ is closed under ϵ-limited homomorphism. Hence $\mathscr{M}(L \cup \{\epsilon\})$ contains $h_2(h_1^{-1}(L) \cap R)$ for each R in $\mathscr{R}$, each decreasing homomorphism h_1, and each decreasing homomorphism h_2 which is ϵ-limited on R, thus on $h_1^{-1}(L) \cap R$.

Now let M_1 be an ϵ-free a-transducer. Then $M_1(L \cup \{\epsilon\}) = M_1(L) \cup M_1(\epsilon)$. Since $L \neq \emptyset$, $\mathscr{M}(L)$ contains $M_1(L) \cup (M_1(\epsilon)-\{\epsilon\})$ by (a) of Proposition 3.1.1. By Lemma 3.2.5, there exists a 1-bounded, ϵ-output bounded a-transducer M such that $M(L) = M_1(L) \cup (M_1(\epsilon)-\{\epsilon\})$. Let $M = (K_1, \Sigma_1, \Sigma_2, H, p_0, F_1)$. Repeat the construction of Σ_3, R_1, R_2, R_3, h_1, and h_2 as given in the proof of Lemma 3.2.2. Then $M(L) = M_1(L) \cup (M_1(\epsilon)-\{\epsilon\}) = h_2(h_1^{-1}(L) \cap R_3)$. Since M is 1-bounded, h_1 and h_2 are decreasing homomorphisms. Since M is ϵ-output bounded, h_2 is ϵ-limited on R_3. Suppose $M_1(L \cup \{\epsilon\})$ is ϵ-free. Then $M_1(L \cup \{\epsilon\}) = M_1(L) \cup (M_1(\epsilon)-\{\epsilon\}) = h_2(h_1^{-1}(L) \cap R_3)$, and $M_1(L \cup \{\epsilon\})$ is in $\mathscr{C}(L)$. Suppose $M_1(L \cup \{\epsilon\})$ contains ϵ. Then $M_1(\epsilon)$ contains ϵ since M_1 is ϵ-free. Two cases arise. Suppose L contains ϵ. Then $M_1(L \cup \{\epsilon\}) = M_1(L) \cup (M_1(\epsilon)-\{\epsilon\}) = h_2(h_1^{-1}(L) \cap R_3)$. Thus $M_1(L \cup \{\epsilon\})$ is in $\mathscr{C}(L)$. Suppose L is ϵ-free. Since $L \neq \emptyset$, there exists a Σ_L word $a_1 \ldots a_k$ in L. Let $\bar{a}_1, \ldots, \bar{a}_k$ be new symbols and $\Sigma_4 = \Sigma_3 \cup \{\bar{a}_i/1 \leqq i \leqq k\}$. Let $R_4 = R_3 \cup \{\bar{a}_1 \ldots \bar{a}_k\}$. Let h_3 and h_4 be the homomorphisms on Σ_4^* defined by $h_3(x) = h_1(x)$, $h_4(x) = h_2(x)$, $h_3(\bar{a}_i) = a_i$, and $h_4(\bar{a}_i) = \epsilon$ for all x in Σ_3 and all $\bar{a}_i$. Then $M_1(L \cup \{\epsilon\}) = h_2(h_1^{-1}(L) \cap R_3) \cup \{\epsilon\} = h_4(h_3^{-1}(L) \cap R_4)$, with h_3 and h_4 decreasing homomorphisms, and h_4 ϵ-limited on R_4. Again $M_1(L \cup \{\epsilon\})$ is in $\mathscr{C}(L)$. In all cases, therefore, $M_1(L \cup \{\epsilon\})$ is in $\mathscr{C}(L)$.

Consider (c). Let $L-\{\epsilon\} \neq \emptyset$ and let $\mathcal{C}^-(L)$ be the family of all sets of the form $h_2(h_1^{-1}(L) \cap R)$, where R is a regular set, and h_1 and h_2 are decreasing homomorphisms, with h_2 ϵ-limited on R and $h_2^{-1}(\epsilon) \cap R = \emptyset$. Let $\mathcal{L}_1 = \{L_1/L_1 \text{ in } \mathcal{M}(L \cup \{\epsilon\}),\ L_1\ \epsilon\text{-free}\}$ and $\mathcal{L}_2 = \{L_1-\{\epsilon\}/L_1 \text{ in } \mathcal{M}(L \cup \{\epsilon\})\}$. By (b), $\mathcal{C}^-(L) \subseteq \mathcal{M}(L \cup \{\epsilon\})$. By definition, $\mathcal{C}^-(L)$ is ϵ-free. Hence $\mathcal{C}^-(L) \subseteq \mathcal{L}_1$. Consider the reverse containment. Suppose L_1 is ϵ-free and in $\mathcal{M}(L \cup \{\epsilon\})$. By (b), $L_1 = h_2(h_1^{-1}(L) \cap R)$, with R in $\mathcal{R}$, and h_1 and h_2 decreasing homomorphisms, with h_2 ϵ-limited on R. Since L_1 is ϵ-free, $h_2^{-1}(\epsilon) \cap (h_1^{-1}(L) \cap R) = \emptyset$ and $L_1 = h_2\big(h_1^{-1}(L) \cap \big(R-(R \cap h_2^{-1}(\epsilon))\big)\big)$. Since R is regular, $R-(R \cap h_2^{-1}(\epsilon))$ is regular. Since h_2 is ϵ-limited on R, it is ϵ-limited on $R-(R \cap h_2^{-1}(\epsilon))$. Obviously $h_2^{-1}(\epsilon) \cap \big(R-(R \cap h_2^{-1}(\epsilon))\big) = \emptyset$. Hence L_1 is in $\mathcal{C}^-(L)$, so that $\mathcal{C}^-(L) = \mathcal{L}_1$.

To see that $\mathcal{L}_1 = \mathcal{L}_2$, note that $\mathcal{L}_1 \subseteq \mathcal{L}_2$. Since $\mathcal{M}(L \cup \{\epsilon\})$ is a trio, if L_1 is in $\mathcal{M}(L \cup \{\epsilon\})$ then $L_1-\{\epsilon\} = L_1 \cap \Sigma_{L_1}^+$ is in $\mathcal{M}(L \cup \{\epsilon\})$, thus in $\mathcal{L}_1$. Hence $\mathcal{L}_2 \subseteq \mathcal{L}_1$, whence equality.

Finally,

$$\begin{aligned}\mathcal{M}(L-\{\epsilon\}) &= \mathcal{M}((L \cup \{\epsilon\})-\{\epsilon\}) \\ &= \{M(L \cup \{\epsilon\})-\{\epsilon\}/M \text{ an } \epsilon\text{-free a-transducer}\}, \\ &\quad \text{by (c) of Proposition 3.2.1 since } L-\{\epsilon\} = \\ &\quad (L \cup \{\epsilon\})-\{\epsilon\} \neq \emptyset.\end{aligned}$$

Thus $\mathcal{M}(L-\{\epsilon\}) = \mathcal{L}_2$ and the proof is complete.

From Theorem 3.2.3, we immediately get:

(+) COROLLARY: *For each nonempty language L,*

(a) $\hat{\mathcal{M}}(L) = \{h_2(h_1^{-1}(L) \cap R)/R$ in $\mathcal{R}$, h_1 *and* h_2 *decreasing homomorphisms*$\}$.

(b) $\mathcal{M}(L) = \{h_2(h_1^{-1}(L) \cap R)/R$ in $\mathcal{R}$, h_1 *and* h_2 *decreasing homomorphisms*, h_2 *ϵ-limited on* $R\}$, *if L contains* ϵ.

(c) $\mathcal{M}(L) = \{h_2(h_1^{-1}(L) \cap R)/R$ *in* $\mathcal{R}$, h_1 *and* h_2 *decreasing homomorphisms*, h_2 *ϵ-limited on* R, $h_2^{-1}(\epsilon) \cap R = \emptyset\}$, *if L is ϵ-free.*

EXERCISE 3.2.1: Calculate $M(a^2b)$ and $M(ba)$ for $M = (K_1, \Sigma_1, \Sigma_2, H, p_2, \{p_0, p_2\})$ where K_1, Σ_1, Σ_2, and H are given in Example 3.2.1.

EXERCISE 3.2.2: Let $K_1 = \{p_0, p_1, p_2, p_3\}$, $\Sigma_1 = \{a, b\}$, $\Sigma_2 = \{c, d\}$, and $H = \{(p_0, a, c^2, p_1), (p_0, a^2, cd, p_2), (p_1, ab, c, p_1), (p_1, \epsilon, d, p_0), (p_2, \epsilon, d, p_3), (p_2, b, dc, p_1), (p_2, b^2, \epsilon, p_3), (p_3, ba, dc, p_3), (p_3, b, \epsilon, p_0)\}$.

(a) Calculate $M(a^2b)$ for $M = (K_1, \Sigma_1, \Sigma_2, H, p_0, \{p_0, p_3\})$.
(b) Calculate $M(b^2)$ and $M(ba)$ for $M = (K_1, \Sigma_1, \Sigma_2, H, p_2, \{p_1, p_2, p_3\})$.
(c) Calculate $M(bab)$ for $M = (K_1, \Sigma_1, \Sigma_2, H, p_3, \{p_1, p_3\})$.

EXERCISE 3.2.3: Let M be a 6-tuple $(K_1, \Sigma_1, \Sigma_2, H, p_0, F)$, where K_1, Σ_1, Σ_2, and F are as in an a-transducer and H is a finite set of 4-tuples, each of the form (p, U, V, q) with p, q in K_1 and U, V regular subsets of Σ_1^*, Σ_2^* resp. Let $\vdash$ be the relation on $K_1 \times \Sigma_1^* \times \Sigma_2^*$ defined by $(p, w, y) \vdash (p', w', y')$ if there exist (p, U, V, p') in H and words u in U and v in V such that $w = uw'$ and $y' = yv$. For each language L let $M(L) = \{y/(p_0, w, \epsilon) \overset{*}{\vdash} (p, \epsilon, y)$ for some p in $F\}$. For each such 6-tuple M prove there exists an a-transducer M' such that $M'(L) = M(L)$ for all languages L [Ko].

EXERCISE 3.2.4: Prove that $M(L) = M_2M_1(L)$ in the arbitrary a-transducer case in Lemma 3.2.4.

EXERCISE 3.2.5: Prove $M(L) = M_2M_1(L)$ in the ϵ-free a-transducer case in Lemma 3.2.4.

EXERCISE 3.2.6: Let $\mathcal{L}$ be a trio and L in $\mathcal{L}$. Let Σ_1 be a subset of Σ_L and π be a permutation of Σ_1. Let $P_\pi(L)$ be the language obtained in the following manner: (i) If x is in L and does not contain at least one occurrence of each symbol in Σ_1, then x is in $P_\pi(L)$. (ii) If x is in L and contains at least one occurrence of each symbol in Σ_1, then $P_\pi(L)$ contains each word obtained by replacing exactly one occurrence of each element in Σ_1 by its permutation. Prove that $P_\pi(L)$ is in $\mathcal{L}$.

EXERCISE 3.2.7: Using Theorem 3.2.1, prove (a) of Proposition 3.1.1.

EXERCISE 3.2.8: Using Theorem 3.2.1, prove (b) of Proposition 3.1.1.

EXERCISE 3.2.9: For each a-transducer M let $L_M = \bigcup_{\text{all } w} wM(w)$. Prove that the family $\{L_M/\text{all } M\}$ is
(a) A semi-AFL.
(b) Not an AFL.

EXERCISE 3.2.10: For each n-tape a-transducer $M = (K_1, (\Sigma_1, \ldots, \Sigma_n), \Sigma_{n+1}, H, p_0, F)$ let $\text{TR}(M)$, called the *transducer relation of M*, be the set of all $(w_1, \ldots, w_{n+1})$, where w_{n+1} is in $M(w_1, \ldots, w_n)$. Given $S \subseteq \Sigma_1^* \times \ldots \times \Sigma_{n+1}^*$, prove that $S = \text{TR}(M)$ for some $M = (K_1, (\Sigma_1, \ldots, \Sigma_n), \Sigma_{n+1}, H, p_0, F)$ if and only if there exists R in $\mathcal{R}$ and homomorphisms $h_1, \ldots, h_{n+1}$, each h_i from Σ_R^* into Σ_i^*, such that $S = \{(h_1(x), \ldots, h_{n+1}(x))/x \text{ in } R\}$. Furthermore, M is ϵ-free if and only if h_{n+1} is ϵ-free [Go1].

EXERCISE 3.2.11: Given $n \geqq 1$ and sets of languages $\mathcal{L}_1, \ldots, \mathcal{L}_n$ let

$$\mathcal{M}^{(n)}(\mathcal{L}_1, \ldots, \mathcal{L}_n) = \{M(L_1, \ldots, L_n)/\text{each } L_i \text{ in } \mathcal{L}_i, M \text{ an } \epsilon\text{-free } n\text{-tape a-transducer}\} \text{ and}$$

$$\hat{\mathcal{M}}^{(n)}(\mathcal{L}_1, \ldots, \mathcal{L}_n) = \{M(L_1, \ldots, L_n)/\text{each } L_i \text{ in } \mathcal{L}_i, M \text{ an } n\text{-tape a-transducer}\}.$$

Using Exercise 3.2.10, prove the following [Go1]:

(a) $\mathcal{M}^{(n)}(\mathcal{L}_1, \ldots, \mathcal{L}_n) = \{h_{n+1}(R \cap h_1^{-1}(L_1) \cap \ldots \cap h_n^{-1}(L_n))/R$ in $\mathcal{R}$, each h_i a homomorphism, h_{n+1} ϵ-free$\}$.

(b) $\hat{\mathcal{M}}^{(n)}(\mathcal{L}_1, \ldots, \mathcal{L}_n) = \{h_{n+1}(R \cap h_1^{-1}(L_1) \cap \ldots \cap h_n^{-1}(L_n))/R$ in $\mathcal{R}$, each h_i a homomorphism$\}$.

EXERCISE 3.2.12: (Continued) Given languages $L_1, \ldots, L_n$, prove that there exists a language L_0 such that[1] $\mathcal{M}^{(n)}(L_1, \ldots, L_n) = \mathcal{M}^{(1)}(L_0)$ and $\hat{\mathcal{M}}^{(n)}(L_1, \ldots, L_n) = \hat{\mathcal{M}}^{(1)}(L_0)$ [Go1].

EXERCISE 3.2.13: Prove that a gsm M is ϵ-output bounded under non-ϵ input in L if and only if M is ϵ-limited on L.

EXERCISE 3.2.14: For all words w_1 and w_2 let $\text{Overlap}(w_1, w_2) = \{uvy/w_1 = uv, w_2 = vy\}$. For all languages L_1 and L_2 let $\text{Overlap}(L_1, L_2) = \bigcup_{\substack{w_1 \text{ in } L_1 \\ w_2 \text{ in } L_2}} \text{Overlap}(w_1, w_2)$. For each semi-AFL $\mathcal{L}$ prove that

(a) Overlap (L, R) is in $\mathcal{L}$ for each L in $\mathcal{L}$ and R in $\mathcal{R}$.

(b) $\mathcal{L}$ is closed under intersection if and only if Overlap(L_1, L_2) is in $\mathcal{L}$ for all L_1, L_2 in $\mathcal{L}$.

EXERCISE 3.2.15: Let $n \geqq 2$ be an integer and $\Delta = \overbrace{\Sigma_1 \times \ldots \times \Sigma_1}^{n}$. For all $i \neq j$, $1 \leqq i, j \leqq n$, let h_{ij} be the homomorphism on Δ^* defined by $h_{ij}((a_1, \ldots, a_n)) = (a_1, \ldots, a_{i-1}, a_j, a_{i+1}, \ldots, a_n)$. Let M_1 be a gsm $(K_1, \Sigma_2, \Sigma_3, \delta, \lambda, p_0)$, where $\Sigma_3 = \Delta \cup \{h_{ij}/\text{all } i, j\}$, $|\lambda(p, a)| = 1$ for each (p, a) in $K_1 \times \Sigma_2$, and $\lambda(p_0, a)$ is in Δ for each a in Σ_2. Let f be the mapping from Σ_2^* into Δ^* defined as follows: Let $f(\epsilon) = \epsilon$. For each w in Σ_2^+ let $f(w) = z_s$, where $\lambda(p_0, w) = y_1 \ldots y_s$, each y_i in Σ_3, $z_1 = y_1$, and for each k, $1 < k \leqq s$, $z_k = z_{k-1}y_k$ if y_k is in Δ and $z_k = y_k(z_{k-1})$ if y_k is in $\{h_{ij}/\text{all } i, j\}$. Prove that there exists an a-transducer $M_2 = (K_2, \Sigma_2, \Sigma_3, H, q_0, F)$ such that $M_2(w) = f(w)$ for each w in Σ_2^* [Ni].

[1] As usual, L is identified with $\{L\}$.

EXERCISE 3.2.16: Verify each of the following [GS1]:

(a) $L/\bigcup_\alpha L_\alpha = \bigcup_\alpha (L/L_\alpha)$.

(b) $(\bigcup_\alpha L_\alpha)/L = \bigcup_\alpha (L_\alpha/L)$.

(c) $L_1/L_2L_3 = (L_1/L_3)/L_2$.

(d) $(L_1L_3)/L_2 = (L_1(L_3/L_2)) \cup (L_1/(L_2/L_3))$.

EXERCISE 3.2.17: For each a-transducer M and language L, let $M^{-1}(L) = \{x/M(x) \cap L \neq \emptyset\}$. Prove that

(a) $M^{-1}(L)$ is in $\mathscr{L}$ for each full trio $\mathscr{L}$ and L in $\mathscr{L}$.

(b) $M^{-1}(L)$ is not necessarily in $\mathscr{L}$ for an arbitrary AFL $\mathscr{L}$ and L in $\mathscr{L}$.

EXERCISE 3.2.18: Let $R = a\{b^i d^i/i > 0\}^*$ and $L = \{a^i b^{2i}/i > 0\}^*$. Prove each of the following:

(a) R and L are in $\mathscr{L}_{CF}$.

(b) $(R\backslash L) \cap b^+ = \{b^{2^n}/n > 0\}$.

(c) $R\backslash L$ is not in $\mathscr{L}_{CF}$.

EXERCISE 3.2.19: Find R and L in $\mathscr{L}_{CF}$ such that L/R is not in $\mathscr{L}_{CF}$.

EXERCISE 3.2.20: For all languages L_1 and L_2 and all symbols a and b in $\Sigma-(\Sigma_{L_1} \cup \Sigma_{L_2})$, $aL_1 \cup bL_2$ is called a *marked union* (*of* L_1 *and* L_2), and $(aL_1)^*$ a *marked∗* (*of* L_1). A *marked generalized sequential machine* (abbreviated *mgsm*) is a 7-tuple $(K_1, \Sigma_1, \Sigma_2, \$, \delta, \lambda, p_1)$, where K_1, Σ_1, Σ_2, and p_1 are as in a gsm, $\$$ is in $\Sigma-(\Sigma_1 \cup \Sigma_2)$, δ is a mapping from $K_1 \times (\Sigma_1 \cup \{\$\})$ into K_1, and λ is a mapping from $K_1 \times (\Sigma_1 \cup \{\$\})$ into $\Sigma_2^* \cup \Sigma_2^*\$$ such that $\lambda(p, a)$ is in Σ_2^* and $\lambda(p, \$)$ is in $\Sigma_2^*\$$ for each p in K_1 and a in Σ_1. The functions δ and λ are then extended to $K_1 \times (\Sigma_1 \cup \{\$\})^*$ as in a gsm. For each mgsm $S = (K_1, \Sigma_1, \Sigma_2, \$, \delta, \lambda, p_1)$, the function S^{-1} from $2^{\Sigma_2^*}$ into $2^{\Sigma_1^*}$ defined by $S^{-1}(Y) = \{x \text{ in } \Sigma_1^*/\lambda(p_1, x\$) \text{ in } Y\$\}$ is called an *inverse mgsm mapping*. An *abstract family of deterministic languages* (*AFDL*) is a family of languages closed under marked union, marked ∗, and inverse mgsm mapping. For each AFDL $\mathscr{L}$, L in $\mathscr{L}$, regular set R, finite set F, word w, and gsm S, prove that each of the following is in $\mathscr{L}$ [Ch]:

(a) $S^{-1}(L)$.

(b) $L \cap R$.

(c) $L - R$.

(d) R.
(e) $L \cup F$.
(f) L/w.
(g) $w\backslash L$.
(h) wL.
(i) Lw.

EXERCISE 3.2.21: (Continued) Prove that a family $\mathcal{L}$ of languages is an AFDL if and only if $\mathcal{L}$ is closed under marked union, marked $*$, inverse gsm mapping, and right quotient by a single symbol, i.e., L/a is in $\mathcal{L}$ for each L in $\mathcal{L}$ and a in Σ [Ch].

EXERCISE 3.2.22: Prove that for each a-transducer M there exists an a-transducer M' such that $M'(w) = \bigcup_{y \text{ in Init}'(w)} M(y)$ for each word w, where $\text{Init}'(w) = \{y/yx = w \text{ for some } x\}$.

The following notation is used in Exercises 3.2.23–3.2.25: *A family of transductions* is a pair $(\Sigma, \mathcal{T})$, or $\mathcal{T}$ when Σ is understood, where (i) $\mathcal{T}$ is a family of subsets of $\Sigma^* \times \Sigma^*$, (ii) $T \neq \emptyset$ for some T in $\mathcal{T}$, and (iii) for each T in $\mathcal{T}$, there exist finite subsets $\Sigma_1 \subseteq \Sigma$ and $\Sigma_2 \subseteq \Sigma$ such that $T \subseteq \Sigma_1^* \times \Sigma_2^*$. (Each element in $\mathcal{T}$ is called a *transduction*.) A *full abstract family of transductions* (abbreviated *full AFT*) is a family of transductions closed under the operations of union, concatenation,[1] $+$,[2] pair homomorphism,[3] inverse pair homomorphism,[4] intersection with sets of the form $R_1 \times R_2$, R_1 and R_2 regular, and segmentation.[5]

[1] The *concatenation* of transductions T_1 and T_2, written T_1T_2, is the set $\{(x_1x_2, y_1y_2)/(x_i, y_i) \text{ in } T_i, i = 1, 2\}$.

[2] If T is a transduction, then T^+ is the set $\bigcup_{i=1}^{\infty} T^i$, where $T^{j+1} = T^jT$ for each $j \geq 1$ and $T^1 = T$.

[3] Let $T \subseteq \Sigma_1^* \times \Sigma_2^*$ and h_1, h_2 homomorphisms on Σ_1^* and Σ_2^* resp. Then $(h_1, h_2)T = \{(h_1(x), h_2(y))/(x, y) \text{ in } T\}$ is called a *pair homomorphism (of T)*.

[4] Let $T \subseteq \Sigma_1^* \times \Sigma_2^*$ and h_1, h_2 homomorphisms from Σ_3^* into Σ_1^* and Σ_4^* into Σ_2^* resp. Then $(h_1^{-1}, h_2^{-1})T = \{(x, y)/(h_1(x), h_2(y)) \text{ in } T\}$ is called an *inverse pair homomorphism (of T)*.

[5] A transduction T_2 is called a *segmentation* of a transduction $T_1 \subseteq \Sigma_1^* \times \Sigma_2^*$ if (i) $T_2 \subseteq \{(x_1y_1 \ldots x_ky_k, x_1y_1 \ldots x_ky_k)/k \geq 1, \text{ each } x_i \text{ in } \Sigma_1^*, \text{ each } y_i \text{ in } \Sigma_2^*, (x_1 \ldots x_k, y_1 \ldots y_k) \text{ in } T_1\}$, and (ii) for each (x, y) in T_1, there exist $k \geq 1$, $x_1, \ldots, x_k$ in Σ_1^*, and $y_1, \ldots, y_k$ in Σ_2^* such that $x = x_1 \ldots x_k$, $y = y_1 \ldots y_k$, and $(x_1y_1 \ldots x_ky_k, x_1y_1 \ldots x_ky_k)$ is in T_2. A family $\mathcal{T}$ of transductions is said to be *closed* under segmentation if for every T_1 in $\mathcal{T}$ there is a T_2 in $\mathcal{T}$ such that T_2 is a segmentation of T_1.

EXERCISE 3.2.23: Let $\mathcal{T}$ be a full AFT, T_1 in $\mathcal{T}$, and T_2 any set formed from $\{R_1 \times R_2 / R_1, R_2 \text{ in } \mathcal{R}\}$ by a finite number of applications of union and complementation.[1] Prove each of the following transductions is in $\mathcal{T}$ [Ib2]:

(a) T_2.

(b) $T_1 \cap T_2$.

(c) $T_1 - T_2$.

(d) $T_1^{-1} = \{(y, x)/(x, y) \text{ in } T_1\}$.

(e) $T_1/T_2 = \{(x_1, y_1)/(x_1x_2, y_1y_2) \text{ in } T_1 \text{ for some } (x_2, y_2) \text{ in } T_2\}$.

(f) $\text{Init}\,(T_1) = \{(x_1, y_1)/x_1 \neq \epsilon,\ y_1 \neq \epsilon,\ (x_1x_2,\ y_1y_2) \text{ in } T_1 \text{ for some } (x_2, y_2) \text{ in } \Sigma^* \times \Sigma^*\}$.

EXERCISE 3.2.24: Prove that $\{L_1/L_1 \times L_2 \text{ in } \mathcal{T} \text{ for some } L_2\}$ is a full AFL for each full AFT $\mathcal{T}$ [Ib2].

EXERCISE 3.2.25: For each language L let $\Phi(L) = \{\alpha(L)/\alpha$ a homomorphism from Σ_L^* into $\Sigma^* \times \Sigma^*$ [2]$\}$. For each family $\mathcal{L}$ of languages, let $\Phi(\mathcal{L}) = \bigcup_{L \text{ in } \mathcal{L}} \Phi(L)$. Prove each of the following [Ib2]:

(a) $\mathcal{T} = \Phi(\{L_1/L_1 \times L_2 \text{ in } \mathcal{T} \text{ for some } L_2\})$ for each full AFT $\mathcal{T}$.

(b) $\Phi(\mathcal{L})$ is a full AFT for each full AFL $\mathcal{L}$.

3.3 Substitution

The operations considered in the previous section were essentially on a single family.[3] There are several operations of importance which involve a pair of families. In this section we focus attention on one of them, substitution. The role of substitution in language theory is so extensive that only a few preliminary results are presented now. A major treatment of the topic is given in Chapter 6.

Notation: For all sets $\mathcal{L}_1$ and $\mathcal{L}_2$ of languages, let $\hat{\text{Sub}}\,(\mathcal{L}_1, \mathcal{L}_2)$ [$\text{Sub}\,(\mathcal{L}_1, \mathcal{L}_2)$] be the set of all languages $\tau(L)$, where L is in $\mathcal{L}_1$ and τ is a [ϵ-free] substitution on Σ_L^* such that $\tau(a)$ is in $\mathcal{L}_2$ for each a in Σ_L.

[1] By *complementation* of $L_1 \times L_2$ is meant any set $(\Sigma_1^* \times \Sigma_2^*) - (L_1 \times L_2)$, where $L_1 \subseteq \Sigma_1^*$ and $L_2 \subseteq \Sigma_2^*$.

[2] α is a *homomorphism* from Σ_L^* into $\Sigma^* \times \Sigma^*$ if α maps Σ_L^* into $\Sigma^* \times \Sigma^*$ and $\alpha(uv) = \alpha(u)\,\alpha(v)$ for all u, v in Σ_L^*.

[3] We view right and left quotient here as an operation on a single family since the other family is always $\mathcal{R}$ (or $\mathcal{R}_0$).

Note that Sub $(\mathcal{L}_1, \mathcal{L}_2) = \hat{\text{Sub}}(\mathcal{L}_1, \bar{\mathcal{L}}_2)$ for all sets $\mathcal{L}_1$ and $\mathcal{L}_2$ of languages, where $\bar{\mathcal{L}}_2 = \{L \text{ in } \mathcal{L}_2/L \text{ is } \epsilon\text{-free}\}$. In particular, Sub $(\mathcal{L}_1, \mathcal{R}) = \hat{\text{Sub}}(\mathcal{L}_1, \mathcal{R}_0)$.

EXAMPLE 3.3.1: Sûb $(\mathcal{L}_{CF}, \mathcal{L}_{CF}) = \mathcal{L}_{CF}$.

EXAMPLE 3.3.2: Sûb $(\mathcal{L}_{CS}, \mathcal{R}) = \mathcal{L}_{RE}$.

EXAMPLE 3.3.3: Sub $(\mathcal{L}_{CS}, \mathcal{R}_0) = \mathcal{L}_{CS}$.

Using Sûb, we can characterize the smallest family containing $\mathcal{L}$ and closed under union, concatenation, and $+$.

PROPOSITION 3.3.1: *For each family $\mathcal{L}$, Sûb $(\mathcal{R}_0, \mathcal{L})$ [Sûb $(\mathcal{R}, \mathcal{L})$] is the smallest family containing $\mathcal{L}$ and closed under union, concatenation, and $+$ [union, concatenation, $+$,*[1] *and $*$].*

Proof: We shall present the proof for $\mathcal{R}_0$, an analogous argument holding for $\mathcal{R}$. Let $Z(\mathcal{L})$ be the smallest family containing $\mathcal{L}$ and closed under union, concatenation, and $+$. Clearly $\mathcal{L} \subseteq \hat{\text{Sub}}(\mathcal{R}_0, \mathcal{L})$. [For let L be in $\mathcal{L}$. Then $\tau(\{a\}) = L$ is in Sûb $(\mathcal{R}_0, \mathcal{L})$, where τ is the substitution on a^* defined by $\tau(a) = L$.] Since $\tau(U)^+ = \tau(U^+)$ for each language U and each substitution τ on Σ_U^*, and since U^+ is in $\mathcal{R}_0$ if U is in $\mathcal{R}_0$, Sûb $(\mathcal{R}_0, \mathcal{L})$ is closed under $+$. Consider union and concatenation of elements of Sûb $(\mathcal{R}_0, \mathcal{L})$. Let R_1 and R_2 be ϵ-free regular sets. For $i = 1, 2$, let τ_i be a substitution on $\Sigma_{R_i}^*$ such that $\tau_i(a)$ is in $\mathcal{L}$ for each a in Σ_{R_i}. By a relabelling of the elements in Σ_{R_1} if necessary, we may assume that $\Sigma_{R_1} \cap \Sigma_{R_2} = \emptyset$. Let τ_3 be the substitution on $(\Sigma_{R_1} \cup \Sigma_{R_2})^*$ defined by $\tau_3(a) = \tau_i(a)$ for each a in Σ_{R_i}, $i = 1, 2$. Then $\tau_1(R_1) \cup \tau_2(R_2) = \tau_3(R_1) \cup \tau_3(R_2) = \tau_3(R_1 \cup R_2)$ and $\tau_1(R_1)\,\tau_2(R_2) = \tau_3(R_1)\tau_3(R_2) = \tau_3(R_1R_2)$. Hence Sûb $(\mathcal{R}_0, \mathcal{L})$ is closed under union and concatenation. Therefore $Z(\mathcal{L}) \subseteq \hat{\text{Sub}}(\mathcal{R}_0, \mathcal{L})$.

To see the reverse containment, let R be in $\mathcal{R}_0$ and τ a substitution on Σ_R^* such that $\tau(a)$ is in $\mathcal{L}$ for each a in Σ_R. By definition, $\tau(a)$ is in $Z(\mathcal{L})$ for each a in Σ_R. Now τ distributes with respect to union, concatenation, and $+$, i.e., $\tau(X \cup Y) = \tau(X) \cup \tau(Y)$, $\tau(XY) = \tau(X)\tau(Y)$, and $\tau(X^+) = \tau(X)^+$. Since R is obtained from the elements $\{a\}$, a in Σ_R, by a finite number of applications of union, concatenation, and $+$, $\tau(R)$ is in $Z(\mathcal{L})$, i.e., Sûb $(\mathcal{R}_0, \mathcal{L}) \subseteq Z(\mathcal{L})$.

Since the smallest family containing a given AFL $\mathcal{L}$ and closed under union, concatenation, and $+$ is $\mathcal{L}$ itself, we get as a corollary:

[1] $+$ may be omitted.

THEOREM 3.3.1: *For each AFL* $\mathcal{L}$, *Sûb* $(\mathcal{R}_0, \mathcal{L}) = \mathcal{L}$. *For each AFL* $\mathcal{L}$ *containing* $\{\epsilon\}$, *Sûb* $(\mathcal{R}, \mathcal{L}) = \mathcal{L}$.

Theorem 3.3.1 does not necessarily hold when $\mathcal{L}$ is a semi-AFL. For let $\mathcal{L} = \mathcal{L}_{\text{lin}}$. Then Sûb $(\mathcal{R}_0, \mathcal{L})$ contains L_1L_2 for each L_1 and L_2 in $\mathcal{L}_{\text{lin}}$. Since $\mathcal{L}_{\text{lin}}$ is not closed under concatenation (Exercise 3.1.8), Sûb $(\mathcal{R}_0, \mathcal{L}) \subseteq \mathcal{L}$ is false. We shall see in Section 3.4 that Sûb $(\mathcal{R}_0, \mathcal{L}_{\text{lin}})$ is the smallest AFL containing $\mathcal{L}_{\text{lin}}$.

The parallel result to Theorem 3.3.1, with respect to substitution by ϵ-free regular sets, holds. In fact, it holds for trios. Specifically, we have:

THEOREM 3.3.2: *For each trio* $\mathcal{L}$, *Sûb* $(\mathcal{L}, \mathcal{R}_0) = \mathcal{L}$. *For each full trio* $\mathcal{L}$, *Sûb* $(\mathcal{L}, \mathcal{R}) = \mathcal{L}$.

Proof: Suppose $\mathcal{L}$ is a trio. Clearly $\mathcal{L} \subseteq$ Sûb $(\mathcal{L}, \mathcal{R}_0)$. [For let L be in $\mathcal{L}$ and τ the ϵ-free substitution on Σ_L^* defined by $\tau(a) = \{a\}$ for each a in Σ_L. Then $\tau(L) = L$ is in Sûb $(\mathcal{L}, \mathcal{R}_0)$.] Consider the reverse inclusion. Let L be in $\mathcal{L}$ and τ a substitution on Σ_L^* by ϵ-free regular sets. Thus $\tau(a) = R_a$ is in $\mathcal{R}_0$ for each a in Σ_L. For each a in Σ_L let $\bar{a}$ be a new symbol and $\Sigma_1 = \{\bar{a}/a \text{ in } \Sigma_L\}$. Let h_1 be the homomorphism on $\left(\Sigma_1 \cup \bigcup_a \Sigma_{R_a}\right)^*$ defined by $h_1(\bar{a}) = a$ for $\bar{a}$ in Σ_1 and $h_1(b) = \epsilon$ for b in $\bigcup_a \Sigma_{R_a}$. Let M be the ϵ-free a-transducer $(\{p_0\}, \Sigma_1 \cup \bigcup_a \Sigma_{R_a}, \bigcup_a \Sigma_{R_a}, H, \{p_0\})$, where

$$H = \{(p_0, b, b, p_0)/b \text{ in } \bigcup_a \Sigma_{R_a}\} \cup \{(p_0, \bar{a}b, b, p_0)/\bar{a} \text{ in } \Sigma_1,\ b \text{ in } \Sigma_{R_a}\}.$$

Let $R = \left(\bigcup_{\bar{a}} \bar{a}R_a\right)^*$. Since each R_a is ϵ-free,

$$\tau(L) = M(h_1^{-1}(L) \cap R).$$

Since R is regular, $\tau(L)$ is in $\mathcal{L}$ by Corollary 2 of Theorem 3.2.1.

Suppose $\mathcal{L}$ is a full trio. Clearly $\mathcal{L} \subseteq$ Sûb $(\mathcal{L}, \mathcal{R})$. To see the reverse inclusion, let L be in $\mathcal{L}$ and τ a substitution on Σ_L^* by regular sets. Then $\tau(a) = R_a$ is in $\mathcal{R}$ for each a in Σ_L. Let $\bar{a}$, Σ_1, and h_1 be as above. Let h_2 be the homomorphism on $\left(\Sigma_1 \cup \bigcup_a \Sigma_{R_a}\right)^*$ defined by $h_2(\bar{a}) = \epsilon$ for $\bar{a}$ in Σ_1 and $h_2(b) = b$ for b in $\bigcup_a \Sigma_{R_a}$. Then

$$\tau(L) = h_2(h_1^{-1}(L) \cap R).$$

Since $\mathcal{L}$ is a full trio, $\tau(L)$ is in $\mathcal{L}$.

We next consider a condition on a family $\mathcal{L}_2$ which guarantees that Sûb $(\mathcal{L}_1, \mathcal{L}_2)$ coincides with Sub $(\mathcal{L}_1, \mathcal{L}_2)$, $\mathcal{L}_1$ a full trio. First though, we need a preliminary result.

LEMMA 3.3.1: *For each full trio $\mathcal{L}_1$ and each family $\mathcal{L}_2$ of languages, Sûb $(\mathcal{L}_1, \mathcal{L}_2) \subseteq$ Sûb $(\mathcal{L}_1, \mathcal{L}_3)$, where $\mathcal{L}_3 = \{L-\{\epsilon\}/L$ in $\mathcal{L}_2\}$.*

Proof: Suppose L is in Sûb $(\mathcal{L}_1, \mathcal{L}_2)$. Then there exist L_1 in $\mathcal{L}_1$ and a substitution τ_1 on $\Sigma_{L_1}^*$ such that $\tau_1(a)$ is in $\mathcal{L}_2$ for each a in Σ_{L_1} and such that $L = \tau_1(L_1)$. Let τ_2 be the substitution on $\Sigma_{L_1}^*$ defined by $\tau_2(a) = \{a\}$ if $\tau_1(a)$ is ϵ-free and $\tau_2(a) = \{a, \epsilon\}$ if $\tau_1(a)$ contains ϵ. Let $L_1' = \tau_2(L_1)$. By Theorem 3.3.2, L_1' is in $\mathcal{L}_1$. Let τ_3 be the substitution on $\Sigma_{L_1}^*$ defined by $\tau_3(a) = \tau_1(a)-\{\epsilon\}$ for each a. Clearly $\tau_3(L_1') = \tau_1(L_1) = L$. Since $\tau_3(a)$ is in $\mathcal{L}_3$ for each a, L is in Sûb $(\mathcal{L}_1, \mathcal{L}_3)$.

COROLLARY: *Let $\mathcal{L}_1$ be a full trio and $\mathcal{L}_2$ a family of ϵ-free languages. Then Sûb $(\mathcal{L}_1, \mathcal{L}_2 \cup \mathcal{L}_3) =$ Sûb $(\mathcal{L}_1, \mathcal{L}_2)$, where $\mathcal{L}_3 = \{L \cup \{\epsilon\}/L$ in $\mathcal{L}_2\}$.*

Proof: Obviously Sûb $(\mathcal{L}_1, \mathcal{L}_2) \subseteq$ Sûb $(\mathcal{L}_1, \mathcal{L}_2 \cup \mathcal{L}_3)$. Since $\mathcal{L}_2$ is ϵ-free, Sûb $(\mathcal{L}_1, \mathcal{L}_2 \cup \mathcal{L}_3) \subseteq$ Sûb $(\mathcal{L}_1, \mathcal{L}_2)$ by Lemma 3.3.1, whence equality.

PROPOSITION 3.3.2: *Let $\mathcal{L}_1$ be a full trio and $\mathcal{L}_2$ a family of languages closed under $-\{\epsilon\}$. Then Sûb $(\mathcal{L}_1, \mathcal{L}_2) =$ Sub $(\mathcal{L}_1, \mathcal{L}_2)$.*

Proof: By definition, Sub $(\mathcal{L}_1, \mathcal{L}_2) \subseteq$ Sûb $(\mathcal{L}_1, \mathcal{L}_2)$. Consider the reverse containment. Let $\mathcal{L}_3 = \{L-\{\epsilon\}/L$ in $\mathcal{L}_2)$. Then $\mathcal{L}_3 \subseteq \mathcal{L}_2$ since $\mathcal{L}_2$ is closed under $-\{\epsilon\}$. Hence

$$
\begin{aligned}
\text{Sûb } (\mathcal{L}_1, \mathcal{L}_2) &\subseteq \text{Sûb } (\mathcal{L}_1, \mathcal{L}_3), \text{ by Lemma 3.3.1,}\\
&= \text{Sub } (\mathcal{L}_1, \mathcal{L}_3), \text{ since } \mathcal{L}_3 \text{ is } \epsilon\text{-free,}\\
&\subseteq \text{Sub } (\mathcal{L}_1, \mathcal{L}_2).
\end{aligned}
$$

We conclude the section by showing that in the presence of substitution closure, trios coincide with AFL.

PROPOSITION 3.3.3: *Each trio closed under ϵ-free substitution is an AFL.*

Proof: Let $\mathcal{L}$ be a trio such that Sub $(\mathcal{L}, \mathcal{L}) \subseteq \mathcal{L}$. Let $\mathcal{L}' = \{L$ in $\mathcal{L}/L$ ϵ-free$\}$. By Proposition 3.1.2, $\mathcal{L}'$ is a trio. If $\mathcal{L}$ is ϵ-free, then $\mathcal{L} = \mathcal{L}'$ and Sûb $(\mathcal{L}', \mathcal{L}') =$ Sub $(\mathcal{L}, \mathcal{L}) \subseteq \mathcal{L} = \mathcal{L}'$. Suppose $\mathcal{L}$ contains $\{\epsilon\}$. Then Sub $(\mathcal{L}', \mathcal{L}') \subseteq$ Sub $(\mathcal{L}, \mathcal{L}) \subseteq \mathcal{L}$. Since $\mathcal{L}'$ is ϵ-free, Sub $(\mathcal{L}', \mathcal{L}')$ is ϵ-free. Thus Sub $(\mathcal{L}', \mathcal{L}') \subseteq \mathcal{L}'$. In either case, Sub $(\mathcal{L}', \mathcal{L}') \subseteq \mathcal{L}'$. Since $\mathcal{L}'$ is ϵ-free, Sûb $(\mathcal{L}', \mathcal{L}') =$ Sub $(\mathcal{L}', \mathcal{L}')$. Then Sûb $(\mathcal{R}_0, \mathcal{L}') \subseteq$ Sûb $(\mathcal{L}', \mathcal{L}') =$ Sub $(\mathcal{L}', \mathcal{L}') \subseteq \mathcal{L}'$. Therefore $\mathcal{L}'$ is closed under union, concatenation, and $+$ by Proposition 3.3.1. Hence $\mathcal{L}'$ is an AFL.

If $\mathscr{L}$ is ϵ-free, then $\mathscr{L} = \mathscr{L}'$ and $\mathscr{L}$ is an AFL. Suppose $\mathscr{L}$ contains $\{\epsilon\}$. Then $\mathscr{R} \subseteq \mathscr{L}$ by Lemma 3.1.1. Let a be some symbol in Σ. Since $\{a, \epsilon\}$ is in $\mathscr{R}$, it is in $\mathscr{L}$. Let L be an arbitrary language in $\mathscr{L}'$. Let τ be the ϵ-free substitution on a^* defined by $\tau(a) = L$. Then $\tau(\{a, \epsilon\}) = L \cup \{\epsilon\}$ is in Sub $(\mathscr{L}, \mathscr{L}) \subseteq \mathscr{L}$. Hence $\mathscr{L} \subseteq \{L, L \cup \{\epsilon\}/L \text{ in } \mathscr{L}'\} \subseteq \mathscr{L}$, so $\mathscr{L} = \{L, L \cup \{\epsilon\}/L \text{ in } \mathscr{L}'\}$. Since $\mathscr{L}'$ is an AFL, $\mathscr{L}$ is an AFL by Proposition 3.1.2.

COROLLARY: *Each substitution-closed trio is an AFL.*

EXERCISE 3.3.1: Give an example of AFL $\mathscr{L}_1$ and $\mathscr{L}_2$ such that

(a) Sûb $(\mathscr{L}_1, \mathscr{L}_2) \neq$ Sûb $(\mathscr{L}_2, \mathscr{L}_1)$.

(b) Sub $(\mathscr{L}_1, \mathscr{L}_2) \neq$ Sub $(\mathscr{L}_2, \mathscr{L}_1)$. [One nontrivial example appears in [Gr2].]

EXERCISE 3.3.2: A language L is said to be a *slip language* if $\psi(L)$ is a semilinear set for some Parikh mapping ψ of Σ_L. A family of languages is said to be a *slip family* if each language in the family is a slip language. Prove the following [GS6]:

(a) If ψ is a Parikh mapping from Σ_1^* into N^n and A is a semilinear subset of N^n, then there exists a regular set $R \subseteq \Sigma_1^*$ such that $\psi(R) = A$.

(b) If $\mathscr{L}_1$ and $\mathscr{L}_2$ are slip families, then Sûb $(\mathscr{L}_1, \mathscr{L}_2)$ is a slip family. [Hint: Use (a).]

EXERCISE 3.3.3: Prove that $\tau_3(L_1') = \tau_1(L_1)$ in Lemma 3.3.1.

For each substitution τ from Σ_1^* into $2^{\Sigma_2^*}$, the *inverse of* τ, written τ^{-1}, is the function from $2^{\Sigma_2^*}$ into $2^{\Sigma_1^*}$ defined by $\tau^{-1}(Y) = \{x/\tau(x) \cap Y \neq \emptyset\}$. A trio $\mathscr{L}$ is called *quasi-full* if the trio $\{L, L \cup \{\epsilon\}/L \text{ in } \mathscr{L}\}$ is full.

EXERCISE 3.3.4: Prove that every trio is closed under τ^{-1} for each substitution τ by finite sets.

EXERCISE 3.3.5: Prove that every quasi-full AFL $\mathscr{L}$ closed under intersection is closed under τ^{-1} for each substitution τ by languages in $\mathscr{L}$.

EXERCISE 3.3.6: Prove that every quasi-full semi-AFL is closed under τ^{-1} for each substitution τ by regular sets.

EXERCISE 3.3.7: Show that Exercise 3.3.6 is no longer true if "semi-AFL" is replaced by "trio". [Hint: Consider the trio $\mathscr{L}_{ECS} \cup \mathscr{L}_{\epsilon RE}$, where $\mathscr{L}_{\epsilon RE}$ is the family of ϵ-free r.e. languages. Let L be a language in $\mathscr{L}_{\epsilon RE} - \mathscr{L}_{CS}$. Prove that there exists a context-sensitive language $L' \subseteq dc^+L$, with c and d not in Σ_L. Then examine $\tau^{-1}(L' \cup \{\epsilon\})$, where τ is the substitution on $(\Sigma_L \cup \{c\})^*$ defined by $\tau(a) = \{a\}$ for each a in Σ_L and $\tau(c) = dc^+$.]

EXERCISE 3.3.8: If $\mathcal{L}$ is a trio closed under τ^{-1} for every substitution τ by e-free regular sets, prove that $\mathcal{L}$ is quasi-full.

EXERCISE 3.3.9: Let $\mathcal{L}$ be a family of languages closed under intersection with regular sets and substitution by finite languages. For each L in $\mathcal{L}$ and R in $\mathcal{R}$, prove that

(a) L/R is in $\mathcal{L}$.

(b) $R\backslash L$ is in $\mathcal{L}$.

EXERCISE 3.3.10: A substitution τ on Σ_1^* is called *marked* if $\tau(a) \subseteq a(\Sigma-\Sigma_1)^*$ for each a in Σ_1. Let $\mathcal{L}$ be the family of all languages which contain no infinite regular set. Prove that $\mathcal{L}$ is closed under marked substitution [GGG].

3.4 (Semi-) AFL Closure

In order to obtain the smallest (semi-) AFL containing a given family $\mathcal{L}$ of languages, the (semi-) AFL operations are applied to members of $\mathcal{L}$, then the languages these operations give rise to, etc. For even the simplest $\mathcal{L}$, the resulting languages become very complicated and difficult to examine. There is a need to get different methods of obtaining this (semi-) AFL. In the present section we shall characterize this (semi-) AFL in terms of a-transducers.

Notation: For each set $\mathcal{L}$ of languages[1] let

(a) $\mathcal{S}(\mathcal{L})$ and $\hat{\mathcal{S}}(\mathcal{L})$ be the smallest semi-AFL and full semi-AFL respectively containing $\mathcal{L}$.

(b) $\mathcal{F}(\mathcal{L})$ and $\hat{\mathcal{F}}(\mathcal{L})$ be the smallest AFL and full AFL respectively containing $\mathcal{L}$.

Since the intersection of an arbitrary collection of (full) [semi-] AFL is also a (full) [semi-] AFL, each of the above exists.

In case $\mathcal{L}$ is a set of just one language, say $\mathcal{L} = \{L\}$, we write $\mathcal{O}(L)$ and $\hat{\mathcal{O}}(L)$ instead of $\mathcal{O}(\{L\})$ and $\hat{\mathcal{O}}(\{L\})$, where $\mathcal{O} = \mathcal{S}$ or $\mathcal{F}$.

Note that for $\mathcal{O} = \mathcal{S}$ or $\mathcal{F}$, $\mathcal{O}(\mathcal{L})$ $(\hat{\mathcal{O}}(\mathcal{L}))$ is the union of all families $\mathcal{O}(\mathcal{L}')$ $(\hat{\mathcal{O}}(\mathcal{L}'))$, $\mathcal{L}'$ a finite subset of $\mathcal{L}$.

We now turn to the characterization result for $\mathcal{F}(\mathcal{L})$ $(\hat{\mathcal{F}}(\mathcal{L}))$. First though, we need two lemmas.

[1] Note that whereas $\mathcal{M}(\mathcal{L})$ and $\hat{\mathcal{M}}(\mathcal{L})$ are defined only when $\mathcal{L}$ is a *family* of languages, $\mathcal{S}(\mathcal{L})$, $\hat{\mathcal{S}}(\mathcal{L})$, $\mathcal{F}(\mathcal{L})$, and $\hat{\mathcal{F}}(\mathcal{L})$ are defined when $\mathcal{L}$ is a *set* of languages.

LEMMA 3.4.1: *Let $\mathcal{L}$ be a family of languages, at least one of which contains* ϵ. *Then Sûb* $(\mathcal{R}, \mathcal{M}(\mathcal{L})) =$ *Sûb* $(\mathcal{R}_0, \mathcal{M}(\mathcal{L}))$.

Proof: Clearly Sûb $(\mathcal{R}_0, \mathcal{M}(\mathcal{L})) \subseteq$ Sûb $(\mathcal{R}, \mathcal{M}(\mathcal{L}))$. To see the reverse containment, let $L = \tau_1(R)$, where R is in $\mathcal{R}$ and τ_1 is a substitution on Σ_R^* by languages in $\mathcal{M}(\mathcal{L})$. If R is ϵ-free, then L is in Sûb $(\mathcal{R}_0, \mathcal{M}(\mathcal{L}))$. Suppose R contains ϵ. Let $R_0 = R - \{\epsilon\}$ and let b be a new symbol. By Theorem 3.2.1, $\mathcal{M}(\mathcal{L})$ is a trio containing $\mathcal{L}$. By Lemma 3.1.1, $\{\epsilon\}$ is in $\mathcal{M}(\mathcal{L})$. Let $R_1 = R_0 \cup \{b\}$ and let τ_2 be the substitution on $(\Sigma_R \cup \{b\})^*$ defined by $\tau_2(a) = \tau_1(a)$ for each a in Σ_R and $\tau_2(b) = \{\epsilon\}$. Then $\tau_2(R_1) = \tau_1(R)$, so that $\tau_1(R)$ is in Sûb $(\mathcal{R}_0, \mathcal{M}(\mathcal{L}))$.

LEMMA 3.4.2: *Let $\mathcal{L}$ be a family of languages, each of which contains* ϵ. *Then*

$$\mathcal{F}(\mathcal{L}) = \text{Sûb}(\mathcal{R}, \mathcal{M}(\mathcal{L})) \quad \text{and} \quad \hat{\mathcal{F}}(S\mathcal{L}) = \text{ûb}\,(\mathcal{R}, \hat{\mathcal{M}}(\mathcal{L})).$$

Proof: We shall present the proof for $\mathcal{F}(\mathcal{L}) =$ Sûb $(\mathcal{R}, \mathcal{M}(\mathcal{L}))$, an analogous argument holding for $\hat{\mathcal{F}}(\mathcal{L})$.

By Proposition 3.3.1, Sûb $(\mathcal{R}_0, \mathcal{M}(\mathcal{L}))$ is the smallest family containing $\mathcal{M}(\mathcal{L})$ and closed under union, concatenation, and $+$. Hence Sûb $(\mathcal{R}_0, \mathcal{M}(\mathcal{L})) \subseteq \mathcal{F}(\mathcal{M}(\mathcal{L})) \subseteq \mathcal{F}(\mathcal{F}(\mathcal{L})) = \mathcal{F}(\mathcal{L})$. Since $\mathcal{L}$ has a language containing ϵ, Sûb $(\mathcal{R}, \mathcal{M}(\mathcal{L})) =$ Sûb $(\mathcal{R}_0, \mathcal{M}(\mathcal{L}))$ by Lemma 3.4.1. Thus

$$\text{Sûb}\,(\mathcal{R}, \mathcal{M}(\mathcal{L})) = \text{Sûb}\,(\mathcal{R}_0, \mathcal{M}(\mathcal{L})) \subseteq \mathcal{F}(\mathcal{L}).$$

To complete the proof, we shall show the reverse containment.

By Proposition 3.3.1, Sûb $(\mathcal{R}, \mathcal{M}(\mathcal{L}))$ is closed under union, concatenation, and $+$. Since inverse homomorphism, intersection with a regular set, and ϵ-free homomorphism each can be realized by an ϵ-free a-transducer, it suffices to show that $\mathcal{M}(\text{Sûb}\,(\mathcal{R}, \mathcal{M}(\mathcal{L}))) \subseteq$ Sûb $(\mathcal{R}, \mathcal{M}(\mathcal{L}))$.

Let $R = T(A)$, where A is the fsa $(K_A, \Sigma_A, \delta_A, q_0, F_A)$. For each a in Σ_A let L'_a be in $\mathcal{L}$, M_a an ϵ-free a-transducer, and $L_a = M_a(L'_a)$. Let τ be the substitution on Σ_A^* defined by $\tau(a) = L_a$ for each a. Then $\tau(R)$ is in Sûb $(\mathcal{R}, \mathcal{M}(\mathcal{L}))$. Let $M = (K_M, \Sigma_1, \Sigma_2, H, p_0, F)$ be an ϵ-free a-transducer. We shall show that $M(\tau(R))$ is in Sûb $(\mathcal{R}, \mathcal{M}(\mathcal{L}))$.

Two cases arise. (The hypothesis that each language in $\mathcal{L}$ contains ϵ is used in the second case.)

(a) Suppose that $|u| \leq |v|$ for each (p, u, v, p') in H. Then by the construction in Lemma 3.2.3, we may assume without loss of generality that M is both 1-output and 1-bounded. For each p and p' in K_M let $M_{p,p'}$ be the a-transducer $(K_M, \Sigma_1, H, H_0, p, \{p'\})$, where

$$H_0 = \{(q, u, (q, u, v, q'), q')/(q, u, v, q') \text{ in } H)\}.$$

Clearly $M_{p,p'}$ is ϵ-free. (Note that $M_{p,p'}(L_a)$ is the set of all paths in M from p to p' caused by words in L_a.) By Lemma 3.2.4, there exists an ϵ-free a-transducer $M_{p,a,p'}$ so that $M_{p,a,p'}(L_a') = M_{p,p'}(L_a)$. Let h_1 be the homomorphism on H^* defined by $h_1((p, u, v, p')) = v$ for all (p, u, v, p') in H. Since M is ϵ-free, h_1 is ϵ-free. By Theorem 3.2.1, $h_1 M_{p,a,p'}(L_a') = h_1 M_{p,p'}(L_a)$ is in $\mathcal{M}(\mathcal{L})$ for each p, a, and p'. (Intuitively, $h_1 M_{p,a,p'}(L_a')$ is the set of all output words from the set of all paths in M going from p to p', caused by words in L_a.)

We are now ready to define a regular set U and a substitution τ' such that $\tau'(U) = M(\tau(R))$. Let $K_B = K_M \times K_A$, $F_B = F \times F_A$, and[1] $\Sigma_B = K_M \times \Sigma_A \times K_M$. Let B be the nondeterministic fsa[2] $(K_B, \Sigma_B, \delta_B, (p_0, q_0), F_B)$, where δ_B is defined by $\delta_B((p, q), (p, a, p')) = \{(p', \delta_A(q, a))\}$ for each (p, q) in K_B and (p, a, p') in Σ_B. Then $T(B)$ is a regular set. In particular, $T(B)$ is the set of all words

$$(p_0, a_1, p_1) \ldots (p_{n-1}, a_n, p_n)$$

such that $n \geqq 0$, p_n is in F, and $a_1 \ldots a_n$ is in R. Let τ' be the substitution on Σ_B^* defined by $\tau'((p, a, p')) = h_1 M_{p,a,p'}(L_a')$ for each (p, a, p'). Clearly $\tau'(T(B))$ is in Sûb $(\mathcal{R}, \mathcal{M}(\mathcal{L}))$. Furthermore,

$$\begin{aligned}\tau'(T(B)) &= \bigcup_{\substack{a_1 \ldots a_n \text{ in } R \\ p_n \text{ in } F}} \tau'((p_0, a_1, p_1)) \ldots \tau'((p_{n-1}, a_n, p_n)) \\ &= \bigcup_{\substack{a_1 \ldots a_n \text{ in } R \\ p_n \text{ in } F}} (h_1 M_{p_0, a_1, p_1}(L_{a_1}')) \ldots (h_1 M_{p_{n-1}, a_n, p_n}(L_{a_n}')),\end{aligned}$$

which is the set of all output words from the set of all paths in M going from p_0 to p_1, caused by input words in L_{a_1}, thence from p_1 to p_2, caused by input words in L_{a_2}, ..., thence from p_{n-1} to p_n, p_n in F, caused by words in L_{a_n}, with $a_1 \ldots a_n$ in R. This, in turn, is $M(\tau(R))$, since M is 1-bounded. (See Exercise 3.4.6.)

(b) Suppose there exist (p, u, v, p') in H such that $|u| > |v|$. Let c be a new symbol and $M_1 = (K_M, \Sigma_1, \Sigma_2 \cup \{c\}, H_1, p_0, F)$, where

$$\begin{aligned}H_1 = &\{(p, u, v, p')/(p, u, v, p') \text{ in } H, |u| \leqq |v|\} \\ &\cup \{(p, u, vc^{|u|-|v|}, p')/(p, u, v, p') \text{ in } H, |u| > |v|\}.\end{aligned}$$

Then each element (p, w, y, p') in H_1 has the property that $|w| \leqq |y|$. By (a), $M_1(\tau(R)) = \tau'(U)$ for some regular set U and some substitution τ'

[1] Remember that all symbols constructed and later used in a language are assumed to be in Σ.

[2] Note that B is not an fsa since δ_B is $\emptyset$ for certain elements in $K_B \times \Sigma_B$.

on Σ_U^* such that $\tau'(b)$ is in $\mathscr{M}(\mathscr{L})$ for each b in Σ_U, say $\tau'(b) = M_b(\bar{L}_b)$, M_b an ϵ-free a-transducer and $\bar{L}_b$ in $\mathscr{L}$. Let h_2 be the homomorphism on $(\Sigma_2 \cup \{c\})^*$ defined by $h_2(a) = a$ for a in Σ_2 and $h_2(c) = \epsilon$. Clearly $h_2\tau'(U) = h_2M_1(\tau(R)) = M(\tau(R))$. Let τ'' be the substitution on Σ_U^* defined by $\tau''(b) = h_2\tau'(b) = h_2M_b(\bar{L}_b)$ for each b in Σ_U. Then $\tau''(U) = h_2\tau'(U) = M(\tau(R))$. To complete the proof, we shall show that $\tau''(b)$ is in $\mathscr{M}(\mathscr{L})$ for each b in Σ_U.

Since $h_2\tau'(U) = h_2M_1(\tau(R)) = M(\tau(R))$ and (p, u, v, p') in H implies $v \neq \epsilon$, h_2 is ϵ-limited on $\tau'(U)$. Thus, for each b in Σ_U, h_2 is ϵ-limited on $\tau'(b) = M_b(\bar{L}_b)$. Since $\bar{L}_b \neq \emptyset$, $h_2M_b(\bar{L}_b) - \{\epsilon\}$ is in $\mathscr{M}(\bar{L}_b)$ by Corollary 2 of Theorem 3.2.2. Since $\bar{L}_b$ contains ϵ, $h_2M_b(\bar{L}_b)$ is in $\mathscr{M}(\bar{L}_b) \subseteq \mathscr{M}(\mathscr{L})$ by (a) of Proposition 3.2.1. This completes the proof.

We are now ready for the characterization of $\mathscr{F}(\mathscr{L})$ and $\hat{\mathscr{F}}(\mathscr{L})$.

THEOREM 3.4.1: *For each family $\mathscr{L}$ of languages, $\mathscr{F}(\mathscr{L}) = \hat{Sub}\,(\mathscr{R}_0, \mathscr{M}(\mathscr{L}))$ and $\hat{\mathscr{F}}(\mathscr{L}) = \hat{Sub}\,(\mathscr{R}, \hat{\mathscr{M}}(\mathscr{L})) = \hat{Sub}\,(\mathscr{R}_0, \hat{\mathscr{M}}(\mathscr{L}))$.*

Proof: We shall give the proof for $\mathscr{F}(\mathscr{L})$, an analogous, but simpler, argument holding for $\hat{\mathscr{F}}(\mathscr{L})$.

Since the theorem is true if $\mathscr{L}$ is a family of regular sets, we may assume that $\mathscr{L}$ contains some nonregular set L_0. Clearly $L_0 - \{\epsilon\} \neq \emptyset$. Let $\mathscr{L}_1 = \{L - \{\epsilon\}/L \text{ in } \mathscr{L}\}$ and $\mathscr{L}_2 = \{L \cup \{\epsilon\}/L \text{ in } \mathscr{L}\}$. Since $\mathscr{L}_1$ contains $L_0 - \{\epsilon\}$, $\mathscr{L}_1$ is a family of languages. Let $\mathscr{U}_1 = \mathscr{M}(\mathscr{L}_1)$ and $\mathscr{U}_2 = \{L \cup \{\epsilon\}/L \text{ in } \mathscr{M}(\mathscr{L}_1)\}$. Then $\mathscr{M}(\mathscr{L}_2) = \mathscr{U}_1 \cup \mathscr{U}_2$ by (b) of Proposition 3.2.1, since $\mathscr{L}_2 = \{L \cup \{\epsilon\}/L \text{ in } \mathscr{L}_1\}$.

Now consider $\mathscr{F}(\mathscr{L})$. Two cases arise.

(α) Suppose $\mathscr{L}$ is ϵ-free. Then $\mathscr{L} = \mathscr{L}_1$ and

$$\begin{aligned}
\mathscr{F}(\mathscr{L}) &= \mathscr{F}(\mathscr{L}_1)\\
&\subseteq \{L - \{\epsilon\}/L \text{ in } \mathscr{F}(\mathscr{L}_2)\}\\
&= \{L - \{\epsilon\}/L \text{ in } \hat{\text{Sub}}\,(\mathscr{R}, \mathscr{M}(\mathscr{L}_2)\}, \text{ by Lemma 3.4.2,}\\
&= \{L - \{\epsilon\}/L \text{ in } \hat{\text{Sub}}\,(\mathscr{R}, \mathscr{U}_1 \cup \mathscr{U}_2)\}\\
&= \{L - \{\epsilon\}/L \text{ in } \hat{\text{Sub}}\,(\mathscr{R}, \mathscr{U}_1)\}, \text{ by the corollary to Lemma 3.3.1,}\\
&= \{L - \{\epsilon\}/L \text{ in } \hat{\text{Sub}}\,(\mathscr{R}, \mathscr{M}(\mathscr{L}))\}, \text{ since } \mathscr{L} = \mathscr{L}_1,\\
&= \hat{\text{Sub}}\,(\mathscr{R}_0, \mathscr{M}(\mathscr{L})), \text{ since } \mathscr{M}(\mathscr{L}) \text{ is } \epsilon\text{-free,}\\
&\subseteq \mathscr{F}(\mathscr{L}).
\end{aligned}$$

Thus $\mathscr{F}(\mathscr{L}) = \hat{\text{Sub}}\,(\mathscr{R}_0, \mathscr{M}(\mathscr{L}))$.

(β) Suppose $\mathcal{L}$ has a language with ϵ in it. Then $\mathcal{M}(\mathcal{L})$ contains $\{\epsilon\}$. Now $\mathcal{F}(\mathcal{L}) = \mathcal{F}(\mathcal{L}_2)$ and

$$\begin{aligned}\mathcal{F}(\mathcal{L}_2) &= \hat{\text{Sub}}\,(\mathcal{R}, \mathcal{M}(\mathcal{L}_2)), \text{ by Lemma 3.4.2,}\\ &\subseteq \hat{\text{Sub}}\,(\mathcal{R}, \{L-\{\epsilon\}/L \text{ in } \mathcal{M}(\mathcal{L}_2)\}), \text{ by Lemma 3.3.1,}\\ &= \hat{\text{Sub}}\,(\mathcal{R}, \mathcal{M}(\mathcal{L}_1)), \text{ since } \mathcal{M}(\mathcal{L}_2) = \mathcal{U}_1 \cup \mathcal{U}_2,\\ &= \hat{\text{Sub}}\,(\mathcal{R}_0, \mathcal{M}(\mathcal{L}_1)) \cup \{L \cup \{\epsilon\}/L \text{ in } \hat{\text{Sub}}\,(\mathcal{R}_0, \mathcal{M}(\mathcal{L}_1))\}.\end{aligned}$$

Also, $\hat{\text{Sub}}\,(\mathcal{R}_0, \mathcal{M}(\mathcal{L}_1)) \subseteq \hat{\text{Sub}}\,(\mathcal{R}_0, \mathcal{M}(\mathcal{L}))$. Since $\mathcal{M}(\mathcal{L})$ contains $\{\epsilon\}$, so does $\hat{\text{Sub}}\,(\mathcal{R}_0, \mathcal{M}(\mathcal{L}))$. By Proposition 3.3.1, $\hat{\text{Sub}}\,(\mathcal{R}_0, \mathcal{M}(\mathcal{L}))$ is closed under union. Hence

$$\begin{aligned}\hat{\text{Sub}}\,(\mathcal{R}_0, \mathcal{M}(\mathcal{L}_1)) \cup \{L \cup \{\epsilon\}/L \text{ in } \hat{\text{Sub}}\,(\mathcal{R}_0, \mathcal{M}(\mathcal{L}_1))\} &\subseteq \hat{\text{Sub}}\,(\mathcal{R}_0, \mathcal{M}(\mathcal{L}))\\ &\subseteq \mathcal{F}(\mathcal{L})\\ &= \mathcal{F}(\mathcal{L}_2).\end{aligned}$$

Then $\mathcal{F}(\mathcal{L}) = \mathcal{F}(\mathcal{L}_2) = \hat{\text{Sub}}\,(\mathcal{R}_0, \mathcal{M}(\mathcal{L}))$, completing the proof.

From Theorem 3.4.1 and Proposition 3.3.1, we get

COROLLARY 1: *For each family $\mathcal{L}$ of languages,*

(a) *$\mathcal{F}(\mathcal{L})$ is the smallest family of languages containing $\mathcal{M}(\mathcal{L})$ and closed under union, concatenation, and +.*

(b) *$\hat{\mathcal{F}}(\mathcal{L})$ is the smallest family of languages containing $\hat{\mathcal{M}}(\mathcal{L})$ and closed under union, concatenation, and + (alternatively, union, concatenation, +,[1] and *).*

Thus, for each (full) trio $\mathcal{L}$, to obtain $\mathcal{F}(\mathcal{L})$ ($\hat{\mathcal{F}}(\mathcal{L})$) one merely takes the closure of $\mathcal{L}$ under union, concatenation, and +.

COROLLARY 2: *Let $\mathcal{L}$ be a full trio. Then*

$$\mathcal{F}(\mathcal{L}) = \hat{\mathcal{F}}(\mathcal{L}) = \hat{\text{Sub}}\,(\mathcal{R}_0, \mathcal{L}) = \hat{\text{Sub}}\,(\mathcal{R}, \mathcal{L}) = \text{Sub}\,(\mathcal{R}, \mathcal{L}).$$

Proof: By Theorem 3.2.1, $\mathcal{L} = \mathcal{M}(\mathcal{L}) = \hat{\mathcal{M}}(\mathcal{L})$. By Theorem 3.4.1, $\mathcal{F}(\mathcal{L}) = \hat{\text{Sub}}\,(\mathcal{R}_0, \mathcal{M}(\mathcal{L})) = \hat{\text{Sub}}\,(\mathcal{R}_0, \mathcal{L})$ and $\hat{\mathcal{F}}(\mathcal{L}) = \hat{\text{Sub}}\,(\mathcal{R}_0, \hat{\mathcal{M}}(\mathcal{L})) = \hat{\text{Sub}}\,(\mathcal{R}_0, \mathcal{L})$. Thus $\mathcal{F}(\mathcal{L}) = \hat{\mathcal{F}}(\mathcal{L}) = \hat{\text{Sub}}\,(\mathcal{R}_0, \mathcal{L}) = \hat{\text{Sub}}\,(\mathcal{R}, \mathcal{L})$. Since $L-\{\epsilon\} = L \cap \Sigma_L^+$, $\mathcal{L}$ is closed under $-\{\epsilon\}$. Thus $\hat{\text{Sub}}\,(\mathcal{R}, \mathcal{L}) = \text{Sub}\,(\mathcal{R}, \mathcal{L})$ by Proposition 3.3.2.

EXAMPLE 3.4.1: Since $\mathcal{L}_{\text{lin}}$ is a full trio, $\mathcal{F}(\mathcal{L}_{\text{lin}}) = \hat{\mathcal{F}}(\mathcal{L}_{\text{lin}}) = \hat{\text{Sub}}\,(\mathcal{R}_0, \mathcal{L}_{\text{lin}}) = \hat{\text{Sub}}\,(\mathcal{R}, \mathcal{L}_{\text{lin}}) = \text{Sub}\,(\mathcal{R}, \mathcal{L}_{\text{lin}})$.

[1] + may be omitted.

Theorem 3.4.1 gives a representation of $\mathcal{F}(\mathcal{L})$ ($\hat{\mathcal{F}}(\mathcal{L})$) in terms of $\mathcal{M}(\mathcal{L})$ ($\hat{\mathcal{M}}(\mathcal{L})$). There is an easily proved analogous representation for $\mathcal{S}(\mathcal{L})$ ($\hat{\mathcal{S}}(\mathcal{L})$).

THEOREM 3.4.2: *For each family $\mathcal{L}$ of languages,*

$$\mathcal{S}(\mathcal{L}) = \left\{ \bigcup_{i=1}^{n} M_i(L_i)/n \geqq 1,\ L_i \text{ in } \mathcal{L},\ M_i \text{ an } \epsilon\text{-free a-transducer} \right\}$$

and $$\hat{\mathcal{S}}(\mathcal{L}) = \left\{ \bigcup_{i=1}^{n} M_i(L_i)/n \geqq 1,\ L_i \text{ in } \mathcal{L},\ M_i \text{ an arbitrary a-transducer} \right\}.$$

Proof: We shall present the argument for $\mathcal{S}(\mathcal{L})$, a trivial modification holding for $\hat{\mathcal{S}}(\mathcal{L})$. Let

$$\mathcal{U}(\mathcal{L}) = \left\{ \bigcup_{i=1}^{n} M_i(L_i)/n \geqq 1,\ L_i \text{ in } \mathcal{L},\ M_i \text{ an } \epsilon\text{-free a-transducer} \right\}.$$

Obviously $\mathcal{U}(\mathcal{L})$ is a semi-AFL containing $\mathcal{L}$. Thus $\mathcal{S}(\mathcal{L}) \subseteq \mathcal{U}(\mathcal{L})$. On the other hand, $\mathcal{S}(\mathcal{L})$ contains each $M_i(L_i)$, L_i in $\mathcal{L}$, M_i an ϵ-free a-transducer. Since $\mathcal{S}(\mathcal{L})$ is closed under union, it contains each element of $\mathcal{U}(\mathcal{L})$. Thus $\mathcal{U}(\mathcal{L}) \subseteq \mathcal{S}(\mathcal{L})$,so that $\mathcal{S}(\mathcal{L}) = \mathcal{U}(\mathcal{L})$.

The analogue to Corollary 1 of Theorem 3.4.1 is:

COROLLARY 1: *For each family $\mathcal{L}$ of languages, $\mathcal{S}(\mathcal{L})$ ($\hat{\mathcal{S}}(\mathcal{L})$) is the smallest family of languages containing $\mathcal{M}(\mathcal{L})$($\hat{\mathcal{M}}(\mathcal{L})$) and closed under union.*

Thus, for each (full) trio $\mathcal{L}$, $\mathcal{S}(\mathcal{L})$ ($\hat{\mathcal{S}}(\mathcal{L})$) is obtained by taking the closure of $\mathcal{L}$ under union.

The analogue to Corollary 2 of Theorem 3.4.1 is also true.

COROLLARY 2: *For each full trio $\mathcal{L}$, $\mathcal{S}(\mathcal{L}) = \hat{\mathcal{S}}(\mathcal{L})$.*

Proof: It suffices to show that $\hat{\mathcal{S}}(\mathcal{L}) \subseteq \mathcal{S}(\mathcal{L})$. Let L be in $\hat{\mathcal{S}}(\mathcal{L})$. Then $L = \bigcup_{1}^{n} M_i(L_i)$ for some n, some $L_1, \ldots, L_n$ in $\mathcal{L}$, and some a-transducers $M_1, \ldots, M_n$. Since $\mathcal{L}$ is a full trio, $M_i(L_i)$ is in $\mathcal{L}$ for each i. Thus L is a finite union of languages in $\mathcal{L}$. Hence L is in $\mathcal{S}(\mathcal{L})$.

As an application of Theorems 3.4.1 and 3.4.2, we shall prove that the closure of a (semi-) AFL under all homomorphisms is a full (semi-) AFL. First though, we establish a lemma.

Notation: For each family $\mathcal{L}$ of languages, let

$$\mathcal{H}(\mathcal{L}) = \{h(L)/L \text{ in } \mathcal{L},\ h \text{ an } \epsilon\text{-free homomorphism on } \Sigma_L^*\}$$

and $$\hat{\mathcal{H}}(\mathcal{L}) = \{h(L)/L \text{ in } \mathcal{L},\ h \text{ an arbitrary homomorphism on } \Sigma_L^*\}.$$

LEMMA 3.4.3: *If $\mathcal{L}$ is a family of languages closed under reversal, then so is* $\hat{\mathcal{H}}(\mathcal{L})$ $(\mathcal{H}(\mathcal{L}))$.

Proof: Let $\mathcal{L}$ be closed under reversal and let L be an arbitrary element in $\hat{\mathcal{H}}(\mathcal{L})$ $(\mathcal{H}(\mathcal{L}))$. Then $L = h(L')$ for some L' in $\mathcal{L}$ and some (ϵ-free) homomorphism h on $\Sigma_{L'}^*$. Since $\mathcal{L}$ is closed under reversal, L'^R is in $\mathcal{L}$. Let h' be the (ϵ-free) homomorphism on $\Sigma_{L'}^*$, defined by $h'(a) = h(a)^R$ for each a in $\Sigma_{L'}$. Then $L^R = h'(L'^R)$, and so is in $\hat{\mathcal{H}}(\mathcal{L})$ $(\mathcal{H}(\mathcal{L}))$.

THEOREM 3.4.3: (a) *For each trio* $\mathcal{L}$, $\hat{\mathcal{H}}(\mathcal{L}) = \hat{Sub}(\mathcal{L}, \mathcal{R})$. *Furthermore,* $\hat{\mathcal{H}}(\mathcal{L})$ *is closed under reversal if* $\mathcal{L}$ *is.*

(b) *For each trio, semi-AFL, and AFL* $\mathcal{L}$, *resp.,* $\hat{\mathcal{H}}(\mathcal{L}) = \hat{O}(\mathcal{L})$, *where* $O = \mathcal{M}, \mathcal{S}$, *and* $\mathcal{F}$, *resp.*

Proof: (a) In view of Lemma 3.4.3, it suffices to show the first sentence. Since each homomorphism is a substitution by regular sets, $\hat{\mathcal{H}}(\mathcal{L}) \subseteq \hat{\text{Sub}}(\mathcal{L}, \mathcal{R})$. Consider the reverse containment. Let L be in $\mathcal{L}$ and τ a substitution of L by regular sets. Let e be a new symbol. Let τ' be the substitution on Σ_L^* defined by $\tau'(a) = (\tau(a) - \{\epsilon\}) \cup \{e/\epsilon \text{ in } \tau(a)\}$. Then $\tau'(a)$ is an ϵ-free regular set. By Theorem 3.3.2, $\tau'(L)$ is in $\hat{\text{Sub}}(\mathcal{L}, \mathcal{R}_0) \subseteq \mathcal{L}$. Let h be the homomorphism on $\Sigma_{\tau'(L)}^*$ defined by $h(b) = b$ for each b in $\Sigma_{\tau'(L)} - \{e\}$ and $h(e) = \epsilon$. Then $\tau(L) = h\tau'(L)$ is in $\hat{\mathcal{H}}(\mathcal{L})$. Thus $\hat{\text{Sub}}(\mathcal{L}, \mathcal{R}) \subseteq \hat{\mathcal{H}}(\mathcal{L})$.

(b) Suppose $\mathcal{L}$ is a trio. Obviously $\hat{\mathcal{H}}(\mathcal{L}) \subseteq \hat{\mathcal{M}}(\mathcal{L})$. Let $M = (K_1, \Sigma_1, \Sigma_2, H, p_0, F)$ be an a-transducer and L in $\mathcal{L}$. Let e be a new symbol and $M' = (K_1, \Sigma_1, \Sigma_2 \cup \{e\}, H', p_0, F)$, where

$$H' = \{(p, u, v, q) \text{ in } H/v \neq \epsilon\} \cup \{(p, u, e, q)/(p, u, \epsilon, q) \text{ in } H\}.$$

Let h be the homomorphism on $(\Sigma_2 \cup \{e\})^*$ defined by $h(a) = a$ for each a in Σ_2 and $h(e) = \epsilon$. Then $hM'(L) = M(L)$. Since M' is ϵ-free, $M'(L) \subseteq \mathcal{L}$. Thus $M(L)$ is in $\hat{\mathcal{H}}(\mathcal{L})$.

Suppose $\mathcal{L}$ is a semi-AFL. Obviously $\hat{\mathcal{H}}(\mathcal{L}) \subseteq \hat{\mathcal{S}}(\mathcal{L})$. Consider the reverse inclusion. Let L be in $\hat{\mathcal{S}}(\mathcal{L})$. By Theorem 3.4.2, $L = \bigcup_{i=1}^{n} M_i(L_i)$ for some $n \geqq 1$ and appropriate languages L_i in $\mathcal{L}$ and a-transducers M_i. From the above paragraph, $M_i(L_i) = h_i(L_i')$ for some L_i' in $\mathcal{L}$ and some homomorphism h_i. Without loss of generality, we may assume $\Sigma_{L_i'} \cap \Sigma_{L_j'} = \emptyset$ for all $i \neq j$. Since each L_i' is in the semi-AFL $\mathcal{L}$, $\bigcup_i L_i'$ is in $\mathcal{L}$. Let h be the homomorphism on $(\bigcup \Sigma_{L_i'})^*$ defined by $h(a) = h_i(a)$ for each i, $1 \leqq i \leqq n$, and each a in $\Sigma_{L_i'}$. Then $L = h(\bigcup L_i')$. Thus $\hat{\mathcal{S}}(\mathcal{L}) \subseteq \hat{\mathcal{H}}(\mathcal{L})$.

Suppose $\mathcal{L}$ is an AFL. Then $\hat{\mathcal{H}}(\mathcal{L}) \subseteq \hat{\mathcal{F}}(\mathcal{L})$. To see the reverse containment let L be in $\hat{\mathcal{F}}(\mathcal{L})$. By Theorem 3.4.1, $\hat{\mathcal{F}}(\mathcal{L}) = \hat{\text{Sub}}\ (\mathcal{R}_0, \hat{\mathcal{M}}(\mathcal{L}))$. Hence there exist R in $\mathcal{R}_0$ and a substitution τ on Σ_R^* such that $\tau(a)$ is in $\hat{\mathcal{M}}(\mathcal{L})$ for each a in Σ_R and $\tau(R) = L$. Since $\mathcal{L}$ is a trio, for each a in Σ_R there exist L_a in $\mathcal{L}$ and a homomorphism h_a such that $h_a(L_a) = \tau(a)$. We may assume that $\Sigma_{L_a} \cap \Sigma_{L_b} = \emptyset$ for all $a \neq b$ in Σ_R. Let h be the homomorphism on $\left(\bigcup_a \Sigma_{L_a}\right)^*$ defined by $h(x) = h_a(x)$ for each a in Σ_R and each x in L_a. Let τ' be the substitution on Σ_R^* defined by $\tau'(a) = L_a$ for each a in Σ_R. Then $\tau(R) = h\tau'(R)$. By Theorem 3.3.1, $\tau'(R)$ is in $\mathcal{L}$. Thus $\tau(R)$ is in $\hat{\mathcal{H}}(\mathcal{L})$, i. e., $\hat{\mathcal{F}}(\mathcal{L}) \subseteq \hat{\mathcal{H}}(\mathcal{L})$.

We conclude the section with results on AFL and semi-AFL similar to those in (b) and (c) of Proposition 3.2.1.

PROPOSITION 3.4.1: *Let $\mathcal{L}$ be a set of languages. Then for $\mathcal{O} = \mathcal{S}$ or $\mathcal{F}$,*

(a) $\mathcal{O}(\mathcal{L}') = \{U, U \cup \{\epsilon\}/U \text{ in } \mathcal{O}(\mathcal{L})\}$, *where*
$\mathcal{L}' = \{L \cup \{\epsilon\}/L \text{ in } \mathcal{L}\}$, *and*

(b) $\mathcal{O}(\mathcal{L}'') = \{U - \{\epsilon\}/U \text{ in } \mathcal{O}(\mathcal{L})\}$, *where*
$\mathcal{L}'' = \{L - \{\epsilon\}/L \text{ in } \mathcal{L}\}$.

Proof: (a) Let $P(\mathcal{L}) = \{U, U \cup \{\epsilon\}/U \text{ in } \mathcal{O}(\mathcal{L})\}$. By Proposition 3.1.2, $P(\mathcal{L})$ is a (semi-) AFL. Since $\mathcal{L} \subseteq P(\mathcal{L})$ and $\{\epsilon\}$ is in $P(\mathcal{L})$, $\mathcal{L}' \subseteq P(\mathcal{L})$. Thus $\mathcal{O}(\mathcal{L}') \subseteq P(\mathcal{L})$.

Consider the reverse containment. Obviously $\mathcal{L} \subseteq \mathcal{O}(\mathcal{L}')$ and $\{\epsilon\}$ is in $\mathcal{O}(\mathcal{L}')$. Thus $\mathcal{O}(\mathcal{L}) \subseteq \mathcal{O}(\mathcal{L}')$ and $\mathcal{O}(\mathcal{L}')$ is closed under union with $\{\epsilon\}$. Therefore $P(\mathcal{L}) \subseteq \mathcal{O}(\mathcal{L}')$.

(b) Suppose $\mathcal{L}$ is ϵ-free. Then $\mathcal{L}'' = \mathcal{L}$ and $\mathcal{O}(\mathcal{L})$ is ϵ-free. Thus $\mathcal{O}(\mathcal{L}'') = \mathcal{O}(\mathcal{L}) = \{U - \{\epsilon\}/U \text{ in } \mathcal{O}(\mathcal{L})\}$. Suppose $\mathcal{L}$ contains a language with ϵ in it. Then $\{\epsilon\}$ is in $\mathcal{O}(\mathcal{L})$. Therefore $\mathcal{O}(\mathcal{L})$ is closed under union with $\{\epsilon\}$. Let $\mathcal{L}' = \{L \cup \{\epsilon\}/L \text{ in } \mathcal{L}\}$. Since $\mathcal{L} \subseteq \mathcal{O}(\mathcal{L}')$, $\mathcal{O}(\mathcal{L}) \subseteq \mathcal{O}(\mathcal{L}')$. Since $\mathcal{L} \subseteq \mathcal{O}(\mathcal{L})$ and $\mathcal{O}(\mathcal{L})$ is closed under union with $\{\epsilon\}$, $\mathcal{L}' \subseteq \mathcal{O}(\mathcal{L})$. Thus $\mathcal{O}(\mathcal{L}') \subseteq \mathcal{O}(\mathcal{L})$, whence equality. Hence

$$\begin{aligned} \mathcal{O}(\mathcal{L}) &= \mathcal{O}(\mathcal{L}') \\ &= \{U, U \cup \{\epsilon\}/U \text{ in } \mathcal{O}(\mathcal{L}'')\}, \text{ by (a).} \end{aligned}$$

Since $\mathcal{L}''$ is ϵ-free, so is $\mathcal{O}(\mathcal{L}'')$. Thus $\mathcal{O}(\mathcal{L}'') = \{U - \{\epsilon\}/U \text{ in } \mathcal{O}(\mathcal{L})\}$.

COROLLARY: *Let $\mathcal{L}$ be a family with a language containing* ϵ, *and let* $\mathcal{O} = \mathcal{S}$ *or* $\mathcal{F}$. *Then*

(a) $\mathcal{O}(\mathcal{L}) = \mathcal{O}(\mathcal{L}')$, *where* $\mathcal{L}' = \{L \cup \{\epsilon\}/L \text{ in } \mathcal{L}\}$, *and*

(b) $\mathcal{O}(\mathcal{L}) = \{U, U \cup \{\epsilon\}/U \text{ in } \mathcal{O}(\mathcal{L}'')\}$, *where*

$\mathcal{L}'' = \{L-\{\epsilon\}/L \text{ in } \mathcal{L}\}$.

Proof: (a) Clearly $\mathcal{L} \subseteq \mathcal{O}(\mathcal{L}')$. Hence $\mathcal{O}(\mathcal{L}) \subseteq \mathcal{O}(\mathcal{L}')$. Consider the reverse containment. Since $\mathcal{L}$ has a language with ϵ in it, $\{\epsilon\}$ is in $\mathcal{O}(\mathcal{L})$. Thus $\mathcal{O}(\mathcal{L})$ is closed under union with $\{\epsilon\}$. Hence U in $\mathcal{O}(\mathcal{L})$ implies U and $U \cup \{\epsilon\}$ are in $\mathcal{O}(\mathcal{L})$. By (a) of Proposition 3.4.1, $\mathcal{O}(\mathcal{L}') \subseteq \mathcal{O}(\mathcal{L})$.

(b) Let $P(\mathcal{L}) = \{U, \ U \cup \{\epsilon\}/U \text{ in } \mathcal{O}(\mathcal{L}'')\}$. Clearly $\mathcal{L}'' \subseteq \mathcal{O}(\mathcal{L})$. Thus $\mathcal{O}(\mathcal{L}'') \subseteq \mathcal{O}(\mathcal{L})$. Since $\mathcal{L}$ has a language with ϵ in it, $\{\epsilon\}$ is in $\mathcal{O}(\mathcal{L})$. Hence $U \cup \{\epsilon\}$ is in $\mathcal{O}(\mathcal{L})$ for each U in $\mathcal{O}(\mathcal{L})$. Therefore $P(\mathcal{L}) \subseteq \mathcal{O}(\mathcal{L})$.

To see the reverse inclusion, note that

$$
\begin{aligned}
P(\mathcal{L}) &= \{U, U \cup \{\epsilon\}/U \text{ in } \mathcal{O}(\mathcal{L}'')\}, \text{ by definition,}\\
&= \{U, U \cup \{\epsilon\}/U \text{ in } \{X-\{\epsilon\}/X \text{ in } \mathcal{O}(\mathcal{L})\}\}, \text{ by (b) of Proposition 3.4.1.}
\end{aligned}
$$

Since $X = X-\{\epsilon\}$ or $X = (X-\{\epsilon\}) \cup \{\epsilon\}$, X in $\mathcal{O}(\mathcal{L})$ implies X in $P(\mathcal{L})$. Thus $\mathcal{O}(\mathcal{L}) \subseteq P(\mathcal{L})$.

Open Question: Let $\mathcal{L}$ be a family of languages closed under intersection with linear context-free languages.

(a) Is $\mathcal{F}(\mathcal{L})$ closed under intersection with linear context-free languages?

(b) Is $\hat{\mathcal{F}}(\mathcal{L})$ closed under intersection with linear context-free languages?

EXERCISE 3.4.1: Let U_1 and V_1 be infinite languages and U_2 and V_2 finite languages. Establish the following for $\mathcal{O} = \mathcal{S}$ or $\mathcal{F}$ [Rv]:

(a) $V_1 - V_2$ is in $\hat{\mathcal{O}}(U_1 - U_2)$ if V_1 is in $\hat{\mathcal{O}}(U_1)$.

(b) $V_1 - V_2$ is in $\mathcal{O}(U_1 - U_2)$ if $V_1 - V_2$ is ϵ-free and V_1 is in $\mathcal{O}(U_1)$.

EXERCISE 3.4.2: (a) Prove that $\mathcal{O}(\mathcal{L}^R) = \mathcal{O}(\mathcal{L})^R$ and $\hat{\mathcal{O}}(\mathcal{L}^R) = \hat{\mathcal{O}}(\mathcal{L})^R$ for each family $\mathcal{L}$ of languages, where $\mathcal{O} = \mathcal{M}$, $\mathcal{S}$, or $\mathcal{F}$.

(b) For $\mathcal{O} = \mathcal{M}$, $\mathcal{S}$, or $\mathcal{F}$, prove that $\mathcal{O}(\mathcal{L})$ and $\hat{\mathcal{O}}(\mathcal{L})$ are closed under reversal if $\mathcal{L}$ is.

EXERCISE 3.4.3: Let $\mathcal{L}_1$, $\mathcal{L}_2$ be families of languages and $\mathcal{L} = \mathcal{L}_1 \cup \mathcal{L}_2$. For $\mathcal{O} = \mathcal{M}$, $\mathcal{S}$, or $\mathcal{F}$ prove that $\mathcal{O}(\mathcal{L}) = \mathcal{O}(\mathcal{O}(\mathcal{L}_1) \cup \mathcal{O}(\mathcal{L}_2))$ and $\hat{\mathcal{O}}(\mathcal{L}) = \hat{\mathcal{O}}(\hat{\mathcal{O}}(\mathcal{L}_1) \cup \mathcal{O}(\mathcal{L}_2))$.

EXERCISE 3.4.4: Let M be an (ϵ-free) a-transducer. Prove that there exists a finite sequence of (ϵ-output bounded) a-transducers $M_{11}, M_{12}, \ldots, M_{r1}, M_{r2}$ such that $M(L_1L_2) = \bigcup_{i=1}^{r} M_{i1}(L_1)M_{i2}(L_2)$ for all languages L_1 and L_2.

EXERCISE 3.4.5: Let M_1, M_2, and M be (ϵ-free) a-transducers. For all languages L_1 and L_2 prove that $M(M_1(L_1)\, M_2(L_2))$ is a finite union of languages of the form $M_3(L_2)$ or $M_3(L_1)\, M_4(L_2)$, M_3 and M_4 being (ϵ-free) a-transducers.

EXERCISE 3.4.6: Prove the statement made in (a) of Lemma 3.4.2 that

$$M(\tau(R)) = \bigcup_{\substack{a_1\ldots a_n \text{ in } R \\ p_n \text{ in } F}} (h_1 M_{p_0, a_1, p_1}(L'_{a_1}))\ldots(h_1 M_{p_{n-1}, a_n, p_n}(L'_{a_n})).$$

EXERCISE 3.4.7: If $\mathcal{L}$ is a family of languages, at least one of which contains ϵ, prove that $\mathcal{F}(\mathcal{L}) = \widehat{\mathrm{Sub}}\,(\mathcal{R}, \mathcal{M}(\mathcal{L}))$.

EXERCISE 3.4.8: Prove that $\hat{\mathcal{F}}(\mathcal{L})$ is the smallest family containing $\hat{\mathcal{M}}(\mathcal{L})$ and closed under union, concatenation, and $*$ [GGr1].

EXERCISE 3.4.9: Let $\mathcal{L}_1, \ldots, \mathcal{L}_n$ be full AFL, $n \geqq 1$. Prove that $\mathcal{F}\left(\bigcup_1^n \mathcal{L}_i\right) = \hat{\mathcal{F}}\left(\bigcup_1^n \mathcal{L}_i\right)$.

EXERCISE 3.4.10: Let $\mathcal{L}$ be an AFL containing $\{\epsilon\}$ and $\mathcal{L}' = \{L/\hat{\mathcal{M}}(L) \subseteq \mathcal{L}\} \cup \{\emptyset\}$. Prove that $\mathcal{L}'$ is the largest full AFL contained in $\mathcal{L}$, i. e., that $\mathcal{L}'$ is a full AFL, $\mathcal{L}' \subseteq \mathcal{L}$, and if $\mathcal{L}'' \subseteq \mathcal{L}$ is any full AFL then $\mathcal{L}'' \subseteq \mathcal{L}'$ [GGo1].

EXERCISE 3.4.11: Let $\mathcal{L}$ be a family of languages. For each language L_1 in $\hat{\mathcal{F}}(\mathcal{L})$, prove that there exist a language L_2 in Sub $(\mathcal{R}_0, \mathcal{M}(\mathcal{L}))$ and a symbol e in Σ_{L_2} such that $L_1 = h_e(L_2)$, where h_e is the homomorphism on $\Sigma_{L_2}^*$ defined by $h(e) = \epsilon$ and $h(a) = a$ for each a in $(\Sigma_{L_2} - \{e\})^*$.

EXERCISE 3.4.12: For each set $\mathcal{L}$ of languages, prove that $\mathcal{F}(\mathcal{L}) = \widehat{\mathrm{Sub}}\,(\mathcal{R}_0, \mathcal{S}(\mathcal{L}))$ and $\hat{\mathcal{F}}(\mathcal{L}) = \mathrm{Sub}\,(\mathcal{R}, \hat{\mathcal{S}}(\mathcal{L})) = \widehat{\mathrm{Sub}}\,(\mathcal{R}_0, \hat{\mathcal{S}}(\mathcal{L}))$.

EXERCISE 3.4.13: A homomorphism h is said to be *linear decreasing* (*on a language* L) if there exists some $k > 0$, not necessarily an integer, such that $|h(w)| \geqq k|w|$ for each word w in L. For each (semi-) AFL $\mathcal{L}$, let

$$\mathcal{H}^{\mathrm{lin}}(\mathcal{L}) = \{h(L)/L \text{ in } \mathcal{L},\ h \text{ linear decreasing on } L\}.$$

Prove that $\mathcal{H}^{\text{lin}}(\mathcal{L})$ is a (semi-) AFL, closed under reversal if $\mathcal{L}$ is [GHo2].

(*)[1]EXERCISE 3.4.14: Call a function T from the positive integers to the non-negative real numbers *allowable* if $T(n_1+n_2) \leqq T(n_1)+T(n_2)$ for all n_1 and n_2. Call a homomorphism h *$T(n)$-decreasing on* L, T an allowable function and L a language, if h is defined on Σ_L^* and there exists a real number $k > 0$ such that $kT(|w|) \leqq |h(w)|$ for each non-ϵ word w in L. Prove the following: Let $\mathcal{L}_1$ be a (semi-) AFL and T an allowable function. Let $\mathcal{L}_2$ be the family of all sets of the form $h(L)$, where L is in $\mathcal{L}_1$ and h is a $T(n)$-decreasing homomorphism on L. Then $\mathcal{L}_2$ is a (semi-) AFL closed under linear-decreasing homomorphism. (See Exercise 3.4.13.) Furthermore, $\mathcal{L}_2$ is closed under reversal if $\mathcal{L}_1$ is [GHo2].

EXERCISE 3.4.15: Prove that (a) of the corollary to Proposition 3.4.1 is no longer true if $\mathcal{O} = \mathcal{M}$.

EXERCISE 3.4.16: Prove that (b) of the corollary to Proposition 3.4.1 is no longer true if $\mathcal{O} = \mathcal{M}$.

(+)3.5 One-Letter Languages

For $\mathcal{O} = \mathcal{S}$ or $\mathcal{F}$, we have already seen that if $\mathcal{L} = \mathcal{L}_{\text{ECS}}$, then $\mathcal{O}(\mathcal{L}) \subsetneq \hat{\mathcal{O}}(\mathcal{L})$. Thus there exist families of languages containing a language with ϵ such that $\mathcal{O}(\mathcal{L}) \subsetneq \hat{\mathcal{O}}(\mathcal{L})$. In this section we present an interesting, albeit special, class of families $\mathcal{L}$ such that $\mathcal{O}(\mathcal{L}) = \hat{\mathcal{O}}(\mathcal{L})$. Specifically, we show that if $\mathcal{L}$ is a family containing a language with ϵ and if there exists a letter a such that $L \subseteq a^*$ for each L in $\mathcal{L}$, then $\mathcal{O}(\mathcal{L}) = \hat{\mathcal{O}}(\mathcal{L})$. In other words, each family $\mathcal{L}$ which is over a one-letter alphabet and which has a language containing ϵ, has the property that $\mathcal{O}(\mathcal{L}) = \hat{\mathcal{O}}(\mathcal{L})$.

We first prove the following auxiliary result.

LEMMA 3.5.1: *Let a be a given symbol. For each language $L \subseteq a^*$ and each a-transducer M, there exists an ϵ-free a-transducer M' such that $M'(L) = M(L)-\{\epsilon\}$.*

Proof: Since the lemma is trivially true if $L = \emptyset$, we may assume that $L \neq \emptyset$.

Given an a-transducer $M_1 = (K_1, \{a\}, \Sigma_2, H_1, p_0, F_1)$, a sequence of elements in H_1 either of the form

$$(p_1, u_1, \epsilon, p_1), \quad \text{with} \quad u_1 \neq \epsilon,$$

[1] Difficult exercises are marked with an asterisk.

or of the form

$$(p_1, u_1, \epsilon, p_2), \ldots, (p_{n-1}, u_{n-1}, \epsilon, p_n), (p_n, u_n, \epsilon, p_1), \quad \text{with}$$

$$u_1 \ldots u_n \neq \epsilon,$$

is called an ϵ-*output loop* (*of* M_1). The states $p_1, \ldots, p_n$ are called the *states of the loop*.

To prove the lemma it suffices to show the following:

(∗) Let M_1 be an a-transducer $(K_1, \{a\}, \Sigma_2, H_1, q_0, F_1)$ with an ϵ-output loop. Then there exists a language L_2 and a regular set R_2 such that $M_1(L) = L_2 \cup R_2$ and either $L_2 = \emptyset$ or else $L_2 = M_2(L)$ for some a-transducer $M_2 = (K_2, \{a\}, \Sigma_2, H_2, q_0, F_2)$ with $K_2 \subsetneq K_1$.

For suppose (∗) holds. Let $M_1 = M$. Since K_1 is finite, by using (∗) repeatedly we obtain a finite sequence of languages $L_2, \ldots, L_t$, a finite sequence of regular sets $R_2, \ldots, R_t$, and a finite sequence of a-transducers $M_2, \ldots, M_{t-1}$, each with an ϵ-output loop, such that:

(1) $M_i(L) = L_{i+1} \cup R_{i+1}$ for $1 \leq i \leq t-1$.

(2) $L_i = M_i(L)$ for $2 \leq i \leq t-1$.

(3) Either $L_t = \emptyset$ or $L_t = M_t(L)$ for some a-transducer M_t having no ϵ-output loop.

Let $R_0 = \bigcup_2^t R_i$. Then R_0 is regular and either $M_1(L) = R_0$ or $M_1(L) = M_t(L) \cup R_0$. Suppose $M_1(L) = R_0$. By Theorems 3.2.1 and 3.1.1, there exists an ϵ-free a-transducer M' such that $M'(L) = R_0 - \{\epsilon\} = M_1(L) - \{\epsilon\}$. Suppose $M_1(L) = M_t(L) \cup R_0$. Since M_t has no ϵ-output loops, M_t is ϵ-output bounded under non-ϵ input in Σ_L^*. By Theorem 3.2.2, $M_t(L) - \{\epsilon\}$ is in $\mathcal{M}(L)$. By Theorem 3.2.1, $\mathcal{M}(L)$ is a trio. By Proposition 3.1.1, $(M_t(L) - \{\epsilon\}) \cup (R_0 - \{\epsilon\})$ is in $\mathcal{M}(L)$. Hence there exists an ϵ-free a-transducer M' such that $M'(L) = (M_t(L) - \{\epsilon\}) \cup (R_0 - \{\epsilon\}) = M(L) - \{\epsilon\}$.

We now turn to the proof of (∗). Let M_1 be the a-transducer $(K_1, \{a\}, \Sigma_2, H_1, q_0, F_1)$ with an ϵ-output loop either of the form

(4) $(p_1, u_1, \epsilon, p_1)$ and $u_1 = a^k$, $k > 0$, or

(5) $(p_1, u_1, \epsilon, p_2), \ldots, (p_{n-1}, u_{n-1}, \epsilon, p_n), (p_n, u_n, \epsilon, p_1)$ and $u_1 \ldots u_n = a^k$, $k > 0$ and $n > 0$.

We shall give the proof for (5), an analogous but simpler argument holding for (4). Let $K_0 = \{p_i / 1 \leq i \leq n\}$ and $K_2 = K_1 - K_0$. Then $K_2 \subsetneq K_1$. If q_0 is one of the p_i, then let $L_2 = \emptyset$. If q_0 is not one of the p_i, then let $M_2 = (K_2, \{a\}, \Sigma_2, H_2, q_0, F_2)$ and $L_2 = M_2(L)$, where $F_2 = F_1 \cap K_2$ and $H_2 = \{(p, u, v, q)$ in $H_1 / p, q$ in $K_2\}$.

To complete the argument for (∗), we shall exhibit a regular set R_2 such that $M_1(L) = L_2 \cup R_2$. We shall do this by constructing an a-transducer M_α such that $M_1(L) = L_2 \cup M_\alpha(L)$ and $M_\alpha(L)$ is regular. To this end, for each state p in $K_1 - \{q_0\}$ let p' be a new symbol. Let $q_0' = q_0$ if q_0 is one of the p_i, and q_0' be a new symbol otherwise. Let $K_1' = \{p'/p \text{ in } K_1\}$. Let $M_\alpha = (K_\alpha, \{a\}, \Sigma_2, H_\alpha, q_0, F_\alpha)$, where $K_\alpha = K_2 \cup K_1'$, $F_\alpha = \{p'/p \text{ in } F_1\}$, and

$$\begin{aligned} H_\alpha = &\{(p, u, v, q) \text{ in } H_1/p, q \text{ in } K_2\} \\ &\cup \{(p, u, v, q')/(p, u, v, q) \text{ in } H_1,\ p \text{ in } K_2,\ q \text{ in } K_0\} \\ &\cup \{(p', u, v, q')/(p, u, v, q) \text{ in } H_1\}. \end{aligned}$$

Clearly $M_1(L) = L_2 \cup M_\alpha(L)$. Note that

(6) If $(r_0, w_1 \ldots w_t, \epsilon) \vdash_{M_\alpha} (r_1, w_2 \ldots w_t, y_1) \vdash_{M_\alpha} \cdots \vdash_{M_\alpha} (r_t, \epsilon, y_1 \ldots y_t)$, with $r_0 = q_0$ and r_t in F_α, then one of the r_i is in $\{p'/p \text{ in } K_0\}$ and all subsequent states are in K_1'.

Now let $L_\beta = \{a^{g-jk}/a^g \text{ in } L,\ j \geqq 0,\ g-jk \geqq 0\}$. It suffices to establish that L_β is regular and that $M_\alpha(L) - \{\epsilon\} = M_\alpha(L_\beta) - \{\epsilon\}$. [For this will imply that $M_\alpha(L)$ is regular.] Consider L_β. For each i, $0 \leqq i < k$, let $U_i = L_\beta \cap \{a^j/j \equiv i \pmod k\}$. If $\{t/a^t \text{ in } L,\ t \equiv i \pmod k\}$ is finite, then so is U_i. If $\{t/a^t \text{ in } L,\ t \equiv i \pmod k\}$ is infinite, then $U_i = \{a^t/t \equiv i \pmod k\}$. In either case, U_i is regular. Hence $L_\beta = \bigcup_{i=0}^{k-1} U_i$ is regular.

Finally, we show that $M_\alpha(L) - \{\epsilon\} = M_\alpha(L_\beta) - \{\epsilon\}$. Since $L \subseteq L_\beta$, $M_\alpha(L) - \{\epsilon\} \subseteq M_\alpha(L_\beta) - \{\epsilon\}$. To see the reverse inclusion let

$$(\bar{s}_0, \bar{w}_1, \bar{y}_1, \bar{s}_1), \ldots, (\bar{s}_t, \bar{w}_{t+1}, \bar{y}_{t+1}, \bar{s}_{t+1})$$

be a sequence of elements in H_α, with $\bar{s}_0 = q_0$, $\bar{s}_{t+1}$ in F_α, $\bar{y}_1 \ldots \bar{y}_{t+1} \neq \epsilon$, and $\bar{w}_1 \ldots \bar{w}_{t+1} a^{hk}$ in L for some $h \geqq 0$. By (6), there exist i and t_1 such that $\bar{s}_{t_1} = p_i'$. Then

$$\begin{gathered} (\bar{s}_0, \bar{w}_1, \bar{y}_1, \bar{s}_1), \ldots, (\bar{s}_{t_1-1}, \bar{w}_{t_1}, \bar{y}_{t_1}, \bar{s}_{t_1}), \\ \overbrace{(p_i', u_i, \epsilon, p_{i+1}'), \ldots, (p_{i-1}', u_{i-1}, \epsilon, p_i')}^{h \text{ times}}, \\ (\bar{s}_{t_1}, \bar{w}_{t_1+1}, \bar{y}_{t_1+1}, \bar{s}_{t_1+1}), \ldots, (\bar{s}_t, \bar{w}_{t+1}, \bar{y}_{t+1}, \bar{s}_{t+1}) \end{gathered}$$

is a sequence of elements in H_α which causes a sequence of moves in M_α such that $\bar{y}_1 \ldots \bar{y}_{t+1}$ is in $M_\alpha(\bar{w}_1 \ldots \bar{w}_{t+1} a^{hk})$. Thus $M_\alpha(L_\beta) - \{\epsilon\} \subseteq M_\alpha(L) - \{\epsilon\}$.

THEOREM 3.5.1: *Let a be a given symbol and $\mathcal{L}$ a family of languages, each a subset of a^*. If $\mathcal{L}$ contains a language with ϵ, then $\mathcal{S}(\mathcal{L}) = \hat{\mathcal{S}}(\mathcal{L})$ and $\mathcal{F}(\mathcal{L}) = \hat{\mathcal{F}}(\mathcal{L})$.*

Proof: Let $\mathcal{L}$ contain a language with ϵ. It suffices to show that $\mathcal{S}(\mathcal{L}) = \hat{\mathcal{S}}(\mathcal{L})$ since, by Theorem 3.4.1, this implies that $\mathcal{F}(\mathcal{L}) = \hat{\mathcal{F}}(\mathcal{L})$. Clearly $\mathcal{S}(\mathcal{L}) \subseteq \hat{\mathcal{S}}(\mathcal{L})$. Consider the reverse containment. By Theorem 3.2.1, $\mathcal{S}(\mathcal{L})$ contains $\mathcal{M}(\mathcal{L})$. By Lemma 3.5.1, $\mathcal{S}(\mathcal{L})$ therefore contains each language $M(L)-\{\epsilon\}$, where L is in $\mathcal{L}$ and M is an arbitrary a-transducer. Since $\mathcal{L}$ contains a language with ϵ, $\mathcal{S}(\mathcal{L})$ contains $\{\epsilon\}$. Therefore $\mathcal{S}(\mathcal{L})$ contains each language $M(L)$, where L is in $\mathcal{L}$ and M is an a-transducer, i. e., $\hat{\mathcal{M}}(\mathcal{L}) \subseteq \mathcal{S}(\mathcal{L})$. Then $\mathcal{S}(\mathcal{L})$ contains $\hat{\mathcal{M}}(\mathcal{L})$ and is closed under union. By Theorem 3.4.2, $\hat{\mathcal{S}}(\mathcal{L}) \subseteq \mathcal{S}(\mathcal{L})$.

Corollary: *Let w be a given word and $\mathcal{L}$ a family of languages, each a subset of w^*. If $\mathcal{L}$ contains a language with ϵ, then $\mathcal{O}(\mathcal{L}) = \hat{\mathcal{O}}(\mathcal{L})$ for $\mathcal{O} = \mathcal{S}, \mathcal{F}$.*

Proof: Let $\mathcal{L}$ contain a language with ϵ. If $w = \epsilon$ then $\mathcal{O}(\mathcal{L}) = \mathcal{R} = \hat{\mathcal{O}}(\mathcal{L})$. Suppose $w \neq \epsilon$. Let a be a symbol in Σ and h the ϵ-free homomorphism from a^* into w^* defined by $h(a) = w$. Then $h^{-1}(\mathcal{L}) = \{h^{-1}(L)/L$ in $\mathcal{L}\}$ is a family of languages, each a subset of a^*. Furthermore, $h^{-1}(\mathcal{L})$ contains a language with ϵ. By Theorem 3.5.1, $\mathcal{O}(h^{-1}(\mathcal{L})) = \hat{\mathcal{O}}(h^{-1}(\mathcal{L}))$. Now $\mathcal{O}(h^{-1}(\mathcal{L})) \subseteq \mathcal{O}(\mathcal{L})$ and $\hat{\mathcal{O}}(h^{-1}(\mathcal{L})) \subseteq \hat{\mathcal{O}}(\mathcal{L})$. Since $\mathcal{L} = \{h(L)/L$ in $h^{-1}(\mathcal{L})\}$, $\mathcal{O}(\mathcal{L}) \subseteq \mathcal{O}(h^{-1}(\mathcal{L}))$ and $\hat{\mathcal{O}}(\mathcal{L}) \subseteq \hat{\mathcal{O}}(h^{-1}(\mathcal{L}))$. Thus $\mathcal{O}(\mathcal{L}) = \mathcal{O}(h^{-1}(\mathcal{L}))$, and $\hat{\mathcal{O}}(\mathcal{L}) = \hat{\mathcal{O}}(h^{-1}(\mathcal{L}))$. Then $\mathcal{O}(\mathcal{L}) = \mathcal{O}(h^{-1}(\mathcal{L})) = \hat{\mathcal{O}}(h^{-1}(\mathcal{L})) = \hat{\mathcal{O}}(\mathcal{L})$.

Exercise 3.5.1: Give the argument in Lemma 3.5.1 when the loop is of form (4).

Exercise 3.5.2: Let M be the a-transducer $(\{p_0, p_1\}, \{a\}, \{a\}, H, p_0, \{p_1\})$, where $H = \{(p_0, a, a, p_1), (p_1, a^2, \epsilon, p_1)\}$. Suppose there exists an ϵ-free a-transducer $M' = (K', \{a\}, \{a\}, H', q_0, F)$ such that $M'(L) = M(L)-\{\epsilon\}$ for all $L \subseteq a^*$. Let $n = \max\{|u|/(p, u, v, q)$ in $H'\}$.

(a) Prove that $|x| \geqq (|w|/n)$ for each w in a^* and x in $M'(w)$.

(b) Using (a) show that x in $M'(a^{2n+1})$ implies $|x| \geqq 2$.

(c) From the fact that $M(a^{2n+1}) = \{a\}$, show that $M'(a^{2n+1}) = \{a\}$.

(d) Using (b) and (c) show that M' does not exist. Thus infer that M' in Lemma 3.5.1 cannot be chosen independent of L.

Exercise 3.5.3: Where in the proof of Lemma 3.5.1 does the argument that M' is independent of L break down?

EXERCISE 3.5.4: Let $w_1, \ldots, w_n$ be a finite sequence of words. Show that if $\mathcal{L}$ is a family containing a language with ϵ and if $L \subseteq \bigcup_{i=1}^{n} w_i^*$ for each L in $\mathcal{L}$, then $\mathcal{O}(\mathcal{L}) = \hat{\mathcal{O}}(\mathcal{L})$ for $\mathcal{O} = \mathcal{S}$ or $\mathcal{F}$ [Ui].

EXERCISE 3.5.5: Let a be a symbol and $L \subseteq a^*$. If M is an a-transducer such that every state of M occurs in some ϵ-output loop, prove that $M(L)$ is regular [Ui].

EXERCISE 3.5.6: Let a be a given symbol. Exhibit a family $\mathcal{L}$ of languages, each a subset of a^* and one of which contains ϵ, such that $\mathcal{M}(\mathcal{L}) \neq \hat{\mathcal{M}}(\mathcal{L})$.

EXERCISE 3.5.7: Let $\mathcal{L}$ be an AFL with $\{\epsilon\}$ as a member. Let $\mathcal{L}_{\max}$ be the largest full AFL contained in $\mathcal{L}$ as guaranteed by Exercise 3.4.10. Prove that there is no language $L \subseteq a^*$, a in Σ, in $\mathcal{L} - \mathcal{L}_{\max}$.

(*) EXERCISE 3.5.8: Given distinct symbols a_1 and a_2, exhibit a language $L \subseteq a_1^* a_2^*$ such that $\mathcal{F}(L) \subsetneq \hat{\mathcal{F}}(L)$.

3.6 The Wedge Operation

The operations considered so far usually arise in a first course in automata and formal languages. In this section we introduce an operation, called "wedge", which ordinarily is not encountered at an elementary level but is important for (semi-) AFL theory. While wedge does not preserve trios, semi-AFL, or AFL, wedge followed by ϵ-free homomorphism does.

Notation: For $n \geqq 1$ and arbitrary families $\mathcal{L}_1, \ldots, \mathcal{L}_n$ of languages let

$$\mathcal{L}_1 \wedge \ldots \wedge \mathcal{L}_n = \{L_1 \cap \ldots \cap L_n / \text{each } L_i \text{ in } \mathcal{L}_i\}.$$

(The symbol "$\wedge$" is called the *wedge*.)

We frequently write $\bigwedge_{i=1}^{n} \mathcal{L}_i$ instead of $\mathcal{L}_1 \wedge \ldots \wedge \mathcal{L}_n$. Note that $\bigwedge_{i=1}^{1} \mathcal{L}_i = \mathcal{L}_1$.

Notation: For each family $\mathcal{L}$ of languages, let $\wedge \mathcal{L} = \bigcup_{n \geqq 1} \bigwedge_{i=1}^{n} \mathcal{L}_i$, where $\mathcal{L}_i = \mathcal{L}$ for each i.

The wedge operation between families of languages involves the concept of intersection of languages, one from each family. (Thus $\wedge \mathcal{L} = \{L_1 \cap \ldots \cap L_n / n \geqq 1, \text{ each } L_i \text{ in } \mathcal{L}\}$ is the intersection closure of $\mathcal{L}$.) It should not be confused with the concept of family intersection, i. e., the family $\mathcal{L}_1 \cap \ldots \cap \mathcal{L}_n = \{L/L \text{ in each } \mathcal{L}_i, 1 \leqq i \leqq n\}$. For example, if $\mathcal{L}_1 = \mathcal{R}$ and $\mathcal{L}_2 = \mathcal{L}_{\text{CF}}$, then $\mathcal{L}_1 \cap \mathcal{L}_2 = \mathcal{L}_1$ and $\mathcal{L}_1 \wedge \mathcal{L}_2 = \mathcal{L}_2$.

Observe that a family $\mathcal{L}$ being closed under wedge, i. e., $\mathcal{L} \wedge \mathcal{L} \subseteq \mathcal{L}$, is equivalent to it being closed under intersection, i. e., $L_1 \cap L_2$ is in $\mathcal{L}$ for every L_1 in $\mathcal{L}$ and L_2 in $\mathcal{L}$.

For families $\mathcal{L}_1$, $\mathcal{L}_2$, and $\mathcal{L}_3$, $\mathcal{L}_1 \wedge \mathcal{L}_2 = \mathcal{L}_2 \wedge \mathcal{L}_1$ and $(\mathcal{L}_1 \wedge \mathcal{L}_2) \wedge \mathcal{L}_3 = \mathcal{L}_1 \wedge (\mathcal{L}_2 \wedge \mathcal{L}_3) = \mathcal{L}_1 \wedge \mathcal{L}_2 \wedge \mathcal{L}_3$. Also, $\mathcal{L}_1 \cap \mathcal{L}_2 \subseteq \mathcal{L}_1$ and $\mathcal{L}_1 \cap \mathcal{L}_2 \subseteq \mathcal{L}_2$; while if $\mathcal{L}_1$ is a trio containing $\{\epsilon\}$, then $\mathcal{L}_2 \subseteq \mathcal{L}_1 \wedge \mathcal{L}_2$.

It is not necessarily true that $\mathcal{L}_1 \wedge \mathcal{L}_2$ is a trio, semi-AFL, AFL resp. if $\mathcal{L}_1$ and $\mathcal{L}_2$ are trio, semi-AFL, AFL resp.

EXAMPLE 3.6.1: Let $\mathcal{L}_1 = \mathcal{L}_2 = \mathcal{L}_{\text{CF}}$. Let $L_1 = \{ba^iba^{i+2}/i \geqq 1\}^* ba^+b$ and $L_2 = ba^2\{ba^iba^{i+2}/i \geqq 1\}^*b$. Then $L_1 \cap L_2 = \{ba^2ba^4b \ldots ba^{4k+2}b/k \geqq 0\}$. Note that the length of each word $ba^2ba^4 \ldots ba^{4k+2}b$ is the sum of the first $2k+2$ odd integers and thus is $(2k+2)^2$. Let h_1 be the ϵ-free homomorphism defined by $h_1(a) = a$ and $h_1(b) = a$. Then $h_1(L_1 \cap L_2) = \{a^{(2k+2)^2}/k \geqq 0\}$. However, $h_1(L_1 \cap L_2)$ is not in $\mathcal{L}_1 \wedge \mathcal{L}_2$. For suppose $h_1(L_1 \cap L_2) = L_3 \cap L_4$, L_3 and L_4 context free. Then $h_1(L_1 \cap L_2) = L_3 \cap L_4 \cap a^* = L_5 \cap L_6$, where $L_5 = L_3 \cap a^*$ and $L_6 = L_4 \cap a^*$ are both context free. Since context-free languages over a^* are regular, $L_5 \cap L_6$ is regular, a contradiction. Since $\mathcal{L}_1 \wedge \mathcal{L}_2$ is not closed under ϵ-free homomorphism, it is not even a trio.

While the hypotheses that $\mathcal{L}_1$ and $\mathcal{L}_2$ are (semi-) AFL do not guarantee that $\mathcal{L}_1 \wedge \mathcal{L}_2$ is a (semi-) AFL, we shall see below that they guarantee that $\mathcal{H}(\mathcal{L}_1 \wedge \mathcal{L}_2)$ is a (semi-) AFL.

LEMMA 3.6.1: *If $\mathcal{L}_1$ and $\mathcal{L}_2$ are trios, semi-AFL, and AFL, resp., then $\mathcal{H}(\mathcal{L}_1 \wedge \mathcal{L}_2)$ is a trio, semi-AFL, and AFL, resp.*

Proof: Suppose $\mathcal{L}_1$ and $\mathcal{L}_2$ are trios. Since the composition of ϵ-free homomorphisms is an ϵ-free homomorphism, $\mathcal{H}(\mathcal{L}_1 \wedge \mathcal{L}_2)$ is closed under ϵ-free homomorphism. Now let L_1 be in $\mathcal{L}_1$, L_2 in $\mathcal{L}_2$, $L = L_1 \cap L_2$, and h an ϵ-free homomorphism from Σ_L^* into Σ_1^*. Since $h(L_1 \cap L_2) \cap R = h[(L_1 \cap L_2) \cap h^{-1}(R)] = h[L_1 \cap (L_2 \cap h^{-1}(R))]$ and $h^{-1}(R)$ is regular when R is regular, $\mathcal{H}(\mathcal{L}_1 \wedge \mathcal{L}_2)$ is closed under intersection with regular sets. Consider inverse homomorphism. Let h_1 be a homomorphism from Σ_2^* into Σ_1^*. Let

$$r = \max\{|h(a)|/a \text{ in } \Sigma_L\} + \max\{|h_1(b)|/b \text{ in } \Sigma_2\}.$$

Let $\Sigma_3 = \Sigma_2 \times \left(\bigcup_{i=0}^{r} \Sigma_L^i \right)$. Let h_2 be the ϵ-free homomorphism from Σ_3^* into Σ_2^* and h_3 the homomorphism from Σ_3^* into Σ_L^* defined by $h_2((b, w)) = b$ and $h_3((b, w)) = w$ for all (b, w) in Σ_3. Let U be the set of all words in Σ_3^* of the form $(b_1, w_1) \dots (b_s, w_s)$, where $s \geqq 0$, and for each i, $1 \leqq i \leqq s$, there exists y_i such that $h_1(b_1 \dots b_i) = h(w_1 \dots w_i)\, y_i$, $|y_i| \leqq r$, and $y_s = \epsilon$.

We now show that U is regular. Let $A = (K_1, \Sigma_3, \delta, q_0, F)$ be the following fsa. For each y in Σ_1^*, $|y| \leqq r$, let $[y]$ be a new symbol and let K_1 be the set of all such $[y]$ together with a new symbol d (d is to represent the "dead" state). Let $q_0 = [\epsilon]$ and $F = \{[\epsilon]\}$. For each $[y]$ and (b, w), if there exists y' such that $yh_1(b) = h(w)\, y'$ and $|y'| \leqq r$, then let $\delta([y], (b, w)) = [y']$. If no such y' exists, then let $\delta([y], (b, w)) = d$. Let $\delta(d, (b, w)) = d$ for all (b, w). It is readily seen that $\delta(q_0, (b_1, w_1) \dots (b_s, w_s)) = [y]$ if and only if for all i, $1 \leqq i \leqq s$, $h_1(b_1 \dots b_i) = h(w_1 \dots w_i)\, y_i$, where $[y_i] = \delta(q_0, (b_1, w_1) \dots (b_i, w_i))$. From this it immediately follows that $U = T(A)$. Thus U is regular.

To complete the proof of closure under inverse homomorphism, it suffices to show that $h_1^{-1}(h(L_1 \cap L_2)) = h_2(h_3^{-1}(L_1 \cap L_2) \cap U)$. [For note that $h'^{-1}(L_1' \cap L_2') = h'^{-1}(L_1') \cap h'^{-1}(L_2')$ and $(L_1' \cap L_2') \cap R = L_1' \cap (L_2' \cap R)$. Thus $\mathscr{L}_1 \wedge \mathscr{L}_2$ is closed under inverse homomorphism and intersection with regular sets. Thus $h_3^{-1}(L_1 \cap L_2) \cap U$ is in $\mathscr{L}_1 \wedge \mathscr{L}_2$. Hence $h_1^{-1}(h(L_1 \cap L_2))$ is in $\mathscr{H}(\mathscr{L}_1 \wedge \mathscr{L}_2)$.] Let $b_1 \dots b_m$, $m \geqq 0$ and each b_i in Σ_2, be in $h_2(h_3^{-1}(L) \cap U)$. Then there exist $w_1, \dots, w_m$ such that $(b_1, w_1) \dots (b_m, w_m)$ is in $h_3^{-1}(L) \cap U$. Since $(b_1, w_1) \dots (b_m, w_m)$ is in $h_3^{-1}(L)$, $w_1 \dots w_m$ is in L. Since $(b_1, w_1) \dots (b_m, w_m)$ is in U, $h(w_1 \dots w_m) = h_1(b_1 \dots b_m)$. Thus $b_1 \dots b_m$ is in $h_1^{-1}h(L)$. Therefore $h_2(h_3^{-1}(L) \cap U) \subseteq h_1^{-1}(h(L))$. To see the reverse inclusion, assume $b_1 \dots b_m$, $m \geqq 0$ and each b_i in Σ_2, is in $h_1^{-1}h(L)$. Then there exists $a_1 \dots a_n$ in L, $n \geqq 0$ and each a_i in Σ_L, such that $h(a_1 \dots a_n) = h_1(b_1 \dots b_m)$. For each i, $1 \leqq i \leqq m$, let j_i be the largest integer $\geqq 0$ for which there exists a word y_i such that $h_1(b_1 \dots b_i) = h(a_1 \dots a_{j_i})\, y_i$. Clearly j_i and y_i exist. Then $|y_i| < \max\{|h(a)|/a \text{ in } \Sigma_L\}$ since $|y_i| \geqq \max\{|h(a)|/a \text{ in } \Sigma_L\}$ contradicts the maximality of j_i. Let $w_1 = a_1 \dots a_{j_1}$ and $w_i = a_{j_{i-1}+1} \dots a_{j_i}$, $i \geqq 2$. Now $|w_1| \leqq |h(w_1)| \leqq |h_1(b_1)| \leqq r$. Since $|h_1(b_1 \dots b_i)| = |h(a_1 \dots a_{j_i})\, y_i|$ and $|h_1(b_1 \dots b_i)\, h_1(b_{i+1})| = |h(a_1 \dots a_{j_i})\, h(w_{i+1})\, y_{i+1}|$, it follows that $|h_1(b_{i+1})| = |h(w_{i+1})| + |y_{i+1}| - |y_i|$. Hence $|h(w_{i+1})| \leqq |h_1(b_{i+1})| + |y_i|$. Since h is ϵ-free, $|w_{i+1}| \leqq |h(w_{i+1})|$. Thus

$$\begin{aligned} |w_{i+1}| &\leqq |h_1(b_{i+1})| + |y_i| \\ &\leqq \max\{|h_1(b)|/b \text{ in } \Sigma_2\} + \max\{|h(a)|/a \text{ in } \Sigma_L\} \\ &\leqq r. \end{aligned}$$

Thus $|w_i| \leqq r$ for each i. Let $x = (b_1, w_1) \ldots (b_m, w_m)$. Then x is in U, $h_3(x) = a_1 \ldots a_n$ is in $L_1 \cap L_2$, and $h_2(x) = b_1 \ldots b_m$. Therefore $b_1 \ldots b_m$ is in $h_2(h_3^{-1}(L) \cap U)$, completing the proof on inverse homomorphism.

Suppose $\mathscr{L}_1$ and $\mathscr{L}_2$ are semi-AFL. It may be assumed that $\mathscr{L}_1$ and $\mathscr{L}_2$ are both ϵ-free. [For otherwise, let $\mathscr{L}_i' = \{L \text{ in } \mathscr{L}_i / L\ \epsilon\text{-free}\}$, $i = 1, 2$. If just one of them contains a language with ϵ, then $\mathscr{L}_1 \wedge \mathscr{L}_2 = \mathscr{L}_1' \wedge \mathscr{L}_2'$, so that $\mathscr{H}(\mathscr{L}_1 \wedge \mathscr{L}_2) = \mathscr{H}(\mathscr{L}_1' \wedge \mathscr{L}_2')$. Suppose both contain languages with ϵ. Then $\mathscr{H}(\mathscr{L}_1 \wedge \mathscr{L}_2) = \{L, L \cup \{\epsilon\} / L \text{ in } \mathscr{H}(\mathscr{L}_1' \wedge \mathscr{L}_2')\}$. By Proposition 3.1.2, $\mathscr{H}(\mathscr{L}_1 \wedge \mathscr{L}_2)$ is a semi-AFL if $\mathscr{H}(\mathscr{L}_1' \wedge \mathscr{L}_2')$ is a semi-AFL.] Since $\mathscr{L}_1$ and $\mathscr{L}_2$ are trios, $\mathscr{H}(\mathscr{L}_1 \wedge \mathscr{L}_2)$ is a trio. Consider union in $\mathscr{H}(\mathscr{L}_1 \wedge \mathscr{L}_2)$. Let L_1, L_1' be in $\mathscr{L}_1$, L_2, L_2' in $\mathscr{L}_2$, and h_1, h_2 ϵ-free homomorphisms on $(\Sigma_{L_1 \cap L_2})^*$ and $(\Sigma_{L_1' \cap L_2'})^*$ resp. There is no loss of generality in assuming that $\Sigma_{L_1} \cap \Sigma_{L_1'} = \emptyset$. [For otherwise, let $\bar{x}$ be a new symbol for each element x in $\Sigma_{L_1} \cup \Sigma_{L_2}$ and let $\Sigma_0 = \{\bar{x} / x \text{ in } \Sigma_{L_1} \cap \Sigma_{L_2}\}$. Let h_3 be the homomorphism on $(\Sigma_{L_1} \cup \Sigma_{L_2})^*$ defined by $h_3(x) = \bar{x}$ for all x in $\Sigma_{L_1} \cup \Sigma_{L_2}$. Let h_4 be the ϵ-free homomorphism on Σ_0^* defined by $h_4(\bar{x}) = h_1(x)$ for all $\bar{x}$ in Σ_0. Clearly $h_3(L_1)$ is in $\mathscr{L}_1$, $h_3(L_2)$ is in $\mathscr{L}_2$, $h_3(L_1 \cap L_2) = h_3(L_1) \cap h_3(L_2)$, $\Sigma_0 = \Sigma_{h_3(L_1 \cap L_2)}$, and $h_4[h_3(L_1) \cap h_3(L_2)] = h_1(L_1 \cap L_2)$. Hence $h_3(L_1 \cap L_2)$ is in $\mathscr{L}_1 \wedge \mathscr{L}_2$, $h_4[h_3(L_1) \cap h_3(L_2)] \cup h_2(L_1' \cap L_2') = h_1(L_1 \cap L_2) \cup h_2(L_1' \cap L_2')$, and $\Sigma_{h_3(L_1)} \cap \Sigma_{L_1'} = \emptyset$.] Let h_0 be the ϵ-free homomorphism on $(\Sigma_{L_1 \cap L_2} \cup \Sigma_{L_1' \cap L_2'})^*$ defined by $h_0(x) = h_1(x)$ for all x in $\Sigma_{L_1 \cap L_2}$ and $h_0(x) = h_2(x)$ for all x in $\Sigma_{L_1' \cap L_2'}$. Since $\Sigma_{L_1} \cap \Sigma_{L_1'} = \emptyset$, h_0 is uniquely defined. Then $h_1(L_1 \cap L_2) \cup h_2(L_1' \cap L_2') = h_0[(L_1 \cap L_2) \cup (L_1' \cap L_2')]$. To complete the proof of closure under union, it suffices to show that $L = (L_1 \cap L_2) \cup (L_1' \cap L_2')$ is in $\mathscr{H}(\mathscr{L}_1 \wedge \mathscr{L}_2)$.

Let a and b be new symbols. Then $L_1 a$, $L_1' b$ are in $\mathscr{L}_1$ and $L_2 a$, $L_2' b$ are in $\mathscr{L}_2$. Thus

$$(L_1 a \cup L_1' b) \cap (L_2 a \cup L_2' b) = (L_1 \cap L_2)\, a \cup (L_1' \cap L_2')\, b$$

is in $\mathscr{L}_1 \wedge \mathscr{L}_2 \subseteq \mathscr{H}(\mathscr{L}_1 \wedge \mathscr{L}_2)$. Let h_5 be the homomorphism on $(\Sigma_{L_1 \cap L_2} \cup \Sigma_{L_1' \cap L_2'} \cup \{a, b\})^*$ defined by $h_5(a) = h_5(b) = \epsilon$ and $h_5(x) = x$ for all x in $\Sigma_{L_1 \cap L_2} \cup \Sigma_{L_1' \cap L_2'}$. Then h_5 is ϵ-limited on $(L_1 \cap L_2)\, a \cup (L_1' \cap L_2')\, b$ and $h_5[(L_1 \cap L_2)\, a \cup (L_1' \cap L_2')\, b] = L$. Since $\mathscr{L}_1$ and $\mathscr{L}_2$ are ϵ-free, L is ϵ-free, i. e., $L = L - \{\epsilon\}$. By Corollary 2 of Theorem 3.2.2, $L - \{\epsilon\} = L$ is in the trio $\mathscr{H}(\mathscr{L}_1 \wedge \mathscr{L}_2)$.

Finally, suppose that $\mathscr{L}_1$ and $\mathscr{L}_2$ are AFL. As above, it may be assumed that $\mathscr{L}_1$ and $\mathscr{L}_2$ are ϵ-free. As just shown, $\mathscr{H}(\mathscr{L}_1 \wedge \mathscr{L}_2)$ is a semi-AFL. Consider $+$. Let L_1 be in $\mathscr{L}_1$ and L_2 in $\mathscr{L}_2$. It suffices to prove that $(L_1 \cap L_2)^+$ is in $\mathscr{H}(\mathscr{L}_1 \wedge \mathscr{L}_2)$. Let a be a new symbol. Then $(L_1 a)^+$ is in $\mathscr{L}_1$ and $(L_2 a)^+$

is in $\mathcal{L}_2$. Let h be the homomorphism on $(\Sigma_{L_1} \cup \Sigma_{L_2} \cup \{a\})^*$ defined by $h(a) = \epsilon$ and $h(x) = x$ for x in $\Sigma_{L_1} \cup \Sigma_{L_2}$. Then h is ϵ-limited on $(L_1a)^+ \cap (L_2a)^+$. Also, $h((L_1a)^+ \cap (L_2a)^+) = h[((L_1 \cap L_2)\, a)^+] = h((L_1 \cap L_2)\, a)^+ = (L_1 \cap L_2)^+$. Since $\mathcal{L}_1$ and $\mathcal{L}_2$ are ϵ-free, $(L_1 \cap L_2)^+$ is ϵ-free, so $(L_1 \cap L_2)^+$ is in $\mathcal{H}(\mathcal{L}_1 \wedge \mathcal{L}_2)$.

Using the previous lemma we now establish:

THEOREM 3.6.1: *Let $\mathcal{L}_1, \ldots, \mathcal{L}_n$, $n \geqq 1$, be trios, semi-AFL, AFL, resp. Then $\mathcal{H}(\mathcal{L}_1 \wedge \ldots \wedge \mathcal{L}_n) = \mathcal{O}(\mathcal{L}_1 \wedge \ldots \wedge \mathcal{L}_n)$, $\mathcal{H}(\wedge\, \mathcal{L}_1) = \mathcal{O}(\wedge\, \mathcal{L}_1)$, $\hat{\mathcal{H}}(\mathcal{L}_1 \wedge \ldots \wedge \mathcal{L}_n) = \hat{\mathcal{O}}(\mathcal{L}_1 \wedge \ldots \wedge \mathcal{L}_n)$, and $\hat{\mathcal{H}}(\wedge\, \mathcal{L}_1) = \hat{\mathcal{O}}(\wedge\, \mathcal{L}_1)$, where $\mathcal{O} = \mathcal{M}, \mathcal{S}$, and $\mathcal{F}$, respectively.*

Proof: Consider the first equality. For $n = 1$ there is nothing to prove. For $n = 2$ the result follows from Lemma 3.6.1. Suppose $n \geqq 3$. We first show that

$$(*) \qquad \mathcal{H}(\mathcal{L}_1 \wedge \ldots \wedge \mathcal{L}_n) = \mathcal{H}(\mathcal{H}(\mathcal{L}_1 \wedge \ldots \wedge \mathcal{L}_{n-1}) \wedge \mathcal{L}_n)$$

and

$$(**) \qquad \mathcal{O}(\mathcal{L}_1 \wedge \ldots \wedge \mathcal{L}_n) = \mathcal{O}(\mathcal{H}(\mathcal{L}_1 \wedge \ldots \wedge \mathcal{L}_{n-1}) \wedge \mathcal{L}_n).$$

Since $\mathcal{L}_1 \wedge \ldots \wedge \mathcal{L}_{n-1} \subseteq \mathcal{H}(\mathcal{L}_1 \wedge \ldots \wedge \mathcal{L}_{n-1})$, the left side of $(*)$ and $(**)$ is contained in the right side of $(*)$ and $(**)$ resp. To see the reverse inclusions, it suffices to show that each element of $\mathcal{H}(\mathcal{L}_1 \wedge \ldots \wedge \mathcal{L}_{n-1}) \wedge \mathcal{L}_n$ is in $\mathcal{H}(\mathcal{L}_1 \wedge \ldots \wedge \mathcal{L}_n)$. Let L be in $\mathcal{H}(\mathcal{L}_1 \wedge \ldots \wedge \mathcal{L}_{n-1}) \wedge \mathcal{L}_n$. Then $L = h(L_1 \cap \ldots \cap L_{n-1}) \cap L_n$ for some ϵ-free homomorphism h and some L_i in $\mathcal{L}_i$, $1 \leqq i \leqq n$. Then $L = h(L_1 \cap \ldots \cap L_{n-1} \cap h^{-1}(L_n))$. Since $h^{-1}(L_n)$ is in $\mathcal{L}_n$, L is in $\mathcal{H}(\mathcal{L}_1 \wedge \ldots \wedge \mathcal{L}_n)$. Hence $(*)$ and $(**)$ are true.

Continuing by induction,

$$\begin{aligned}
\mathcal{H}(\mathcal{L}_1 \wedge \ldots \wedge \mathcal{L}_n) &= \mathcal{H}(\mathcal{H}(\mathcal{L}_1 \wedge \ldots \wedge \mathcal{L}_{n-1}) \wedge \mathcal{L}_n), \text{ by } (*),\\
&= \mathcal{H}(\mathcal{O}(\mathcal{L}_1 \wedge \ldots \wedge \mathcal{L}_{n-1}) \wedge \mathcal{L}_n), \text{ by induction},\\
&= \mathcal{O}(\mathcal{O}(\mathcal{L}_1 \wedge \ldots \wedge \mathcal{L}_{n-1}) \wedge \mathcal{L}_n), \text{ by Lemma 3.6.1},\\
&= \mathcal{O}(\mathcal{H}(\mathcal{L}_1 \wedge \ldots \wedge \mathcal{L}_{n-1}) \wedge \mathcal{L}_n), \text{ by induction},\\
&= \mathcal{O}(\mathcal{L}_1 \wedge \ldots \wedge \mathcal{L}_n), \text{ by } (**).
\end{aligned}$$

Consider the second equality. Clearly $\mathcal{H}(\wedge\, \mathcal{L}_1) \subseteq \mathcal{O}(\wedge\, \mathcal{L}_1)$. To see the reverse inclusion let L be in $\mathcal{O}(\wedge\, \mathcal{L}_1)$. Then there exists a finite subfamily $\mathcal{L}'$ of $\wedge\, \mathcal{L}_1$ such that L is in $\mathcal{O}(\mathcal{L}')$. Let $\mathcal{U}_i = \mathcal{L}_1$ for each $i \geqq 1$. Since $\wedge\, \mathcal{L}_1 = \bigcup_{j \geqq 1} (\mathcal{U}_1 \wedge \ldots \wedge \mathcal{U}_j)$ and $\mathcal{U}_1 \wedge \ldots \wedge \mathcal{U}_j \subseteq \mathcal{U}_1 \wedge \ldots \wedge \mathcal{U}_{j+1}$ for each j, $\mathscr{L}' \subseteq \mathscr{U}_1 \wedge \ldots \wedge \mathscr{U}_n$ for some n. Thus L is in $\mathcal{O}(\mathscr{L}') \subseteq \mathcal{O}\left(\bigwedge_{i=1}^{n} \mathscr{U}_i\right) = \mathscr{H}\left(\bigwedge_{i=1}^{n} \mathscr{U}_i\right) \subseteq \mathscr{H}(\wedge \mathscr{L}_1)$.

The remaining two equations follow from the first two by application of Theorem 3.4.3.

We next summarize a number of elementary properties about the wedge operation.

Notation: For each set $\mathscr{L}$ of languages let $\mathscr{M}_\cap(\mathscr{L})$, $\mathscr{S}_\cap(\mathscr{L})$, and $\mathscr{F}_\cap(\mathscr{L})$ [$\hat{\mathscr{M}}_\cap(\mathscr{L})$, $\hat{\mathscr{S}}_\cap(\mathscr{L})$, and $\hat{\mathscr{F}}_\cap(\mathscr{L})$] be the smallest [full] trio, semi-AFL, and AFL, resp. containing $\mathscr{L}$ and closed under intersection.

PROPOSITION 3.6.1: *For $m, n \geqq 1$, let $\mathscr{L}_1, \ldots, \mathscr{L}_m, \mathscr{L}_1', \ldots, \mathscr{L}_n'$ all be trios, semi-AFL, or AFL, resp., and $\mathcal{O} = \mathscr{M}, \mathscr{S}, \mathscr{F}$, resp. Then*

$$\text{(a) } \mathscr{H}\left(\bigwedge_1^m \mathscr{L}_i\right) \wedge \mathscr{H}\left(\bigwedge_1^n \mathscr{L}_j'\right) \subseteq \mathscr{H}\left(\bigwedge_1^m \mathscr{L}_i \wedge \bigwedge_1^n \mathscr{L}_j'\right)$$

and
$$\hat{\mathscr{H}}\left(\bigwedge_1^m \mathscr{L}_i\right) \wedge \hat{\mathscr{H}}\left(\bigwedge_1^n \mathscr{L}_j'\right) \subseteq \hat{\mathscr{H}}\left(\bigwedge_1^m \mathscr{L}_i \wedge \bigwedge_1^n \mathscr{L}_j'\right).$$

$$\text{(b) } \hat{\mathscr{H}}\left(\bigwedge_1^m \mathscr{L}_i\right) = \hat{\mathscr{H}}\left(\bigwedge_1^m \hat{\mathscr{H}}(\mathscr{L}_i)\right).$$

$$\text{(c) } \mathcal{O}_\cap(\mathscr{L}_1) = \mathscr{H}(\wedge \mathscr{L}_1) = \mathcal{O}(\wedge \mathscr{L}_1)$$

and
$$\hat{\mathcal{O}}_\cap(\mathscr{L}_1) = \hat{\mathscr{H}}(\wedge \mathscr{L}_1) = \hat{\mathcal{O}}(\wedge \mathscr{L}_1) = \hat{\mathcal{O}}(\wedge \hat{\mathscr{H}}(\mathscr{L}_1)) = \hat{\mathscr{H}}(\wedge \hat{\mathscr{H}}(\mathscr{L}_1))$$
$$= \hat{\mathcal{O}}_\cap(\hat{\mathscr{H}}(\mathscr{L}_1)).$$

Proof: (a) Let L_1 be in $\bigwedge^m \mathscr{L}_i$ and L_2 in $\bigwedge^n \mathscr{L}_j'$. Let h_1 and h_2 be homomorphisms, and let $L = h_1(L_1) \cap h_2(L_2)$. Then $L = h_1(L_1 \cap h_1^{-1}h_2(L_2))$. Since $\mathscr{H}(\mathscr{L}_1' \wedge \ldots \wedge \mathscr{L}_n')$ and $\hat{\mathscr{H}}(\mathscr{L}_1' \wedge \ldots \wedge \mathscr{L}_n')$ are trios by Theorem 3.6.1, $h_1^{-1}h_2(L_2) = h_3(L_2')$ for some homomorphism h_3, ϵ-free if h_2 is ϵ-free, and some set L_2' in $\mathscr{L}_1' \wedge \ldots \wedge \mathscr{L}_n'$. Then

$$L = h_1(L_1 \cap h_3(L_2')) = h_1h_3(h_3^{-1}(L_1) \cap L_2').$$

Since $h^{-1}(U_1 \cap \ldots \cap U_m) = h^{-1}(U_1) \cap \ldots \cap h^{-1}(U_m)$, $\mathscr{L}_1 \wedge \ldots \wedge \mathscr{L}_m$ is closed under inverse homomorphism. Thus L is in $\hat{\mathscr{H}}\left(\bigwedge^m \mathscr{L}_i \wedge \bigwedge^n \mathscr{L}_j'\right)$. If h_1 and h_2 are ϵ-free, then h_1h_3 is ϵ-free, so that L is in $\mathscr{H}\left(\bigwedge^m \mathscr{L}_i \wedge \bigwedge^n \mathscr{L}_j'\right)$.

(b) Clearly $\hat{\mathscr{H}}(\mathscr{L}_1) = \hat{\mathscr{H}}(\hat{\mathscr{H}}(\mathscr{L}_1))$. Continuing by induction, suppose that

$$\hat{\mathscr{H}}(\mathscr{L}_1 \wedge \ldots \wedge \mathscr{L}_{m-1}) = \hat{\mathscr{H}}[\hat{\mathscr{H}}(\mathscr{L}_1) \wedge \ldots \wedge \hat{\mathscr{H}}(\mathscr{L}_{m-1})],$$

$m \geqq 2$. Obviously $\hat{\mathscr{H}}(\mathscr{L}_1 \wedge \ldots \wedge \mathscr{L}_m) \subseteq \hat{\mathscr{H}}[\hat{\mathscr{H}}(\mathscr{L}_1) \wedge \ldots \wedge \hat{\mathscr{H}}(\mathscr{L}_m)]$. Furthermore,

$$\begin{aligned}\hat{\mathscr{H}}[\hat{\mathscr{H}}(\mathscr{L}_1) \wedge \ldots \wedge \hat{\mathscr{H}}(\mathscr{L}_m)] &\subseteq \hat{\mathscr{H}}[\hat{\mathscr{H}}(\hat{\mathscr{H}}(\mathscr{L}_1) \wedge \ldots \wedge \hat{\mathscr{H}}(\mathscr{L}_{m-1})) \wedge \hat{\mathscr{H}}(\mathscr{L}_m)] \\ &= \hat{\mathscr{H}}[\hat{\mathscr{H}}(\mathscr{L}_1 \wedge \ldots \wedge \mathscr{L}_{m-1}) \wedge \hat{\mathscr{H}}(\mathscr{L}_m)], \quad \text{by induction,} \\ &\subseteq \hat{\mathscr{H}}[\hat{\mathscr{H}}(\mathscr{L}_1 \wedge \ldots \wedge \mathscr{L}_{m-1} \wedge \mathscr{L}_m)], \quad \text{by (a),} \\ &= \hat{\mathscr{H}}(\mathscr{L}_1 \wedge \ldots \wedge \mathscr{L}_m).\end{aligned}$$

Thus $\hat{\mathscr{H}}(\mathscr{L}_1 \wedge \ldots \wedge \mathscr{L}_m) = \hat{\mathscr{H}}[\hat{\mathscr{H}}(\mathscr{L}_1) \wedge \ldots \wedge \hat{\mathscr{H}}(\mathscr{L}_m)]$.

(c) Consider the first sequence of equalities. Clearly $\mathscr{H}(\wedge \mathscr{L}_1) = \mathscr{O}(\wedge \mathscr{L}_1) \subseteq \mathscr{O}_\cap(\mathscr{L}_1)$. To get equality, it suffices to show that $\mathscr{H}(\wedge \mathscr{L}_1)$ is closed under intersection. Let $\mathscr{U}_i = \mathscr{L}_1$ for each $i \geqq 1$. Then

$$\begin{aligned}\mathscr{H}(\wedge \mathscr{L}_1) \wedge \mathscr{H}(\wedge \mathscr{L}_1) &= \bigcup_{m \geqq 1} \mathscr{H}(\mathscr{U}_1 \wedge \ldots \wedge \mathscr{U}_m) \wedge \bigcup_{n \geqq 1} \mathscr{H}(\mathscr{U}_1 \wedge \ldots \wedge \mathscr{U}_n) \\ &= \bigcup_{m,\, n \geqq 1} (\mathscr{H}(\mathscr{U}_1 \wedge \ldots \wedge \mathscr{U}_m) \wedge \mathscr{H}(\mathscr{U}_1 \wedge \ldots \wedge \mathscr{U}_n)) \\ &\subseteq \bigcup_{m,\, n \geqq 1} \mathscr{H}(\mathscr{U}_1 \wedge \ldots \wedge \mathscr{U}_{m+n}), \quad \text{by (a),} \\ &\subseteq \mathscr{H}(\wedge \mathscr{L}_1).\end{aligned}$$

For the second sequence of equalities, we have $\hat{\mathscr{O}}_\cap(\mathscr{L}_1) = \hat{\mathscr{H}}(\wedge \mathscr{L}_1) = \hat{\mathscr{O}}(\wedge \mathscr{L}_1)$ by an argument similar to the above. Replacing $\mathscr{L}_1$ by $\hat{\mathscr{H}}(\mathscr{L}_1)$, we have

$$\hat{\mathscr{O}}_\cap (\hat{\mathscr{H}}(\mathscr{L}_1)) = \hat{\mathscr{H}}(\wedge \hat{\mathscr{H}}(\mathscr{L}_1)) = \hat{\mathscr{O}}(\wedge \hat{\mathscr{H}}(\mathscr{L}_1)).$$

From (b), we readily get $\hat{\mathscr{H}}(\wedge \mathscr{L}_1) = \hat{\mathscr{H}}(\wedge \hat{\mathscr{H}}(\mathscr{L}_1))$. Hence the result.

COROLLARY: *Let $m \geqq 1$, $n \geqq 1$, and $\mathscr{L}_1, \ldots, \mathscr{L}_{m+n}$ be trios. Then*

$$\mathscr{H}\left[\mathscr{H}\left(\bigwedge_{i=1}^{m} \mathscr{L}_i\right) \wedge \bigwedge_{j=1}^{n} \mathscr{L}_{m+j}\right] = \mathscr{H}\left(\bigwedge_{1}^{m+n} \mathscr{L}_i\right)$$

and

$$\hat{\mathscr{H}}\left[\hat{\mathscr{H}}\left(\bigwedge_{i=1}^{m} \mathscr{L}_i\right) \wedge \bigwedge_{j=1}^{n} \mathscr{L}_{m+j}\right] = \hat{\mathscr{H}}\left(\bigwedge_{i=1}^{m+n} \mathscr{L}_i\right).$$

Proof: It suffices to show the $\mathscr{H}$ case, a similar argument holding for $\hat{\mathscr{H}}$

Since $\bigwedge^m \mathcal{L}_i \subseteq \mathcal{H}\left(\bigwedge^m \mathcal{L}_i\right)$,

$$\mathcal{H}\left(\bigwedge^{m+n} \mathcal{L}_i\right) \subseteq \mathcal{H}\left[\mathcal{H}\left(\bigwedge^{m} \mathcal{L}_i\right) \wedge \bigwedge_{j=1}^{n} \mathcal{L}_{m+j}\right].$$

On the other hand,

$$\begin{aligned}\mathcal{H}\left[\mathcal{H}\left(\bigwedge^{m} \mathcal{L}_i\right) \wedge \bigwedge_{j=1}^{n} \mathcal{L}_{m+j}\right] &\subseteq \mathcal{H}\left[\mathcal{H}\left(\bigwedge^{m} \mathcal{L}_i\right) \wedge \mathcal{H}\left(\bigwedge_{j=1}^{n} \mathcal{L}_{m+j}\right)\right]\\ &\subseteq \mathcal{H}\left[\mathcal{H}\left(\bigwedge^{m+n} \mathcal{L}_i\right)\right], \quad \text{by (a) of Proposition 3.6.1,}\\ &= \mathcal{H}\left(\bigwedge^{m+n} \mathcal{L}_i\right).\end{aligned}$$

Combining, we get the desired result.

We conclude the section with a relation between substitution and wedge.

THEOREM 3.6.2: *For each trio* $\mathcal{L}_1$ *and each AFL* $\mathcal{L}_2$,

(a) $\hat{Sub}\,(\mathcal{L}_1, \mathcal{L}_2) \subseteq \hat{\mathcal{H}}(\mathcal{L}_1 \wedge \mathcal{L}_2)$.

(b) $Sub\,(\mathcal{L}_1, \mathcal{L}_2) \subseteq \mathcal{H}(\mathcal{L}_1 \wedge \mathcal{L}_2)$ *if either* $\mathcal{L}_1$ *is* ϵ*-free or* $\mathcal{L}_2$ *contains* $\{\epsilon\}$.

Proof: Let L be in $\mathcal{L}_1$ and τ a substitution on Σ_L^* such that $\tau(a)$ is in $\mathcal{L}_2$ for each a in Σ_L.

(a) Let e be a new symbol. For each a in Σ_L let $\bar{a}$ be a new symbol and $\Sigma_1 = \{\bar{a}/a \text{ in } \Sigma_L\} \cup \{e\} \cup \bigcup_a \Sigma_{\tau(a)}$. Let h_1 be the homomorphism on Σ_1^* defined by $h_1(\bar{a}) = a$ for each a in Σ_L and $h_1(b) = h_1(e) = \epsilon$ for each b in $\bigcup_a \Sigma_{\tau(a)}$. Let h_2 be the homomorphism on Σ_1^* defined by $h_2(\bar{a}) = h_2(e) = \epsilon$ for each a in Σ_L and $h_2(b) = b$ for each b in $\bigcup_a \Sigma_{\tau(a)}$. Let $U = \left(\bigcup_a \bar{a}\tau(a)\right)^+ \cup \{e/\epsilon \text{ in } L\}$. Then

$$\begin{aligned}h_1^{-1}(L) = \Big\{w_0\bar{a}_1w_1\ldots\bar{a}_nw_n/a_1\ldots a_n \text{ in } L,\ n \geqq 1, \text{ each } a_i \text{ in } \Sigma_L, \text{ each}\\ w_i \text{ in } \Big(\{e\} \cup \bigcup_a \Sigma_{\tau(a)}\Big)^*\Big\} \cup \Big\{w \text{ in } \Big(\{e\} \cup \bigcup_a \Sigma_{\tau(a)}\Big)^*/\epsilon \text{ in } L\Big\},\end{aligned}$$

$$\begin{aligned}h_1^{-1}(L) \cap U = \{e/\epsilon \text{ in } L\} \cup \{\bar{a}_1w_1\ldots\bar{a}_nw_n/a_1\ldots a_n \text{ in } L,\ n \geqq 1, \text{ each}\\ a_i \text{ in } \Sigma_L, \text{ each } w_i \text{ in } \tau(a_i)\}, \text{ and}\end{aligned}$$

$$h_2[h_1^{-1}(L) \cap U] = \tau(L).$$

Since $\mathcal{L}_1$ is a trio and $\mathcal{L}_2$ is an AFL, $h_1^{-1}(L)$ is in $\mathcal{L}_1$ and U is in $\mathcal{L}_2$. Thus $\tau(L)$ is in $\hat{\mathscr{H}}(\mathcal{L}_1 \wedge \mathcal{L}_2)$.

(b) Suppose τ is an ϵ-free substitution and either $\mathcal{L}_1$ is ϵ-free or $\mathcal{L}_2$ contains $\{\epsilon\}$. For each a in Σ_L let $\bar{a}$ be a new symbol and $\Sigma_1 = \{\bar{a}/a \text{ in } \Sigma_L\} \cup \bigcup_a \Sigma_{\tau(a)}$. Let h_1 and h_2 be defined on Σ_1^* as in (a), and let $U = \left(\bigcup_a \bar{a}\,\tau(a)\right)^+ \cup \{\epsilon/\epsilon \text{ in } L\}$. Then

$$h_1^{-1}(L) = \Big\{w_0\bar{a}_1w_1\ldots\bar{a}_nw_n/a_1\ldots a_n \text{ in } L,\ n \geqq 1, \text{ each } a_i \text{ in } \Sigma_L,$$
$$\text{each } w_i \text{ in } \Big(\bigcup_a \Sigma_{\tau(a)}\Big)^*\Big\} \cup \Big\{w \text{ in } \Big(\bigcup_a \Sigma_{\tau(a)}\Big)^*/\epsilon \text{ in } L\Big\},$$

$$h_1^{-1}(L) \cap U = \{\bar{a}_1w_1\ldots\bar{a}_nw_n/a_1\ldots a_n \text{ in } L,\ n \geqq 1, \text{ each } a_i \text{ in } \Sigma_L,$$
$$\text{each } w_i \text{ in } \tau(a_i)\} \cup \{\epsilon/\epsilon \text{ in } L\}, \text{ and}$$

$$h_2(h_1^{-1}(L) \cap U) = \tau(L).$$

Since either $\mathcal{L}_1$ is ϵ-free or $\mathcal{L}_2$ contains $\{\epsilon\}$, U is in $\mathcal{L}_2$. Thus $h_1^{-1}(L) \cap U$ is in $\mathscr{H}(\mathcal{L}_1 \wedge \mathcal{L}_2)$. By Theorem 3.6.1, $\mathscr{H}(\mathcal{L}_1 \wedge \mathcal{L}_2)$ is a trio. Now h_2 is ϵ-limited on $h_1^{-1}(L) \cap U$ since each $\tau(a)$ is ϵ-free, and $h_2(x) = \epsilon$ for x in $h_1^{-1}(L) \cap U$ implies $x = \epsilon$. By Corollary 2 of Theorem 3.2.2, $h_2(h_1^{-1}(L) \cap U)$ is in $\mathscr{H}(\mathcal{L}_1 \wedge \mathcal{L}_2)$. Thus $\tau(L)$ is in $\mathscr{H}(\mathcal{L}_1 \wedge \mathcal{L}_2)$.

COROLLARY: *If an AFL is closed under intersection, then it is closed under ϵ-free substitution. If a full AFL is closed under intersection, then it is closed under arbitrary substitution.*

EXERCISE 3.6.1: Show that $\mathcal{L}_2 \subseteq \mathcal{L}_1 \wedge \mathcal{L}_2$ for every trio $\mathcal{L}_1$ containing $\{\epsilon\}$ and every family $\mathcal{L}_2$ of languages.

EXERCISE 3.6.2: (For readers familiar with semigroups.) Prove that under the operation $\wedge$, the class of all families of languages over Σ is a commutative semigroup with no identity element.

EXERCISE 3.6.3: Let $\mathcal{L}$ be a full AFL such that $\mathcal{L} \wedge \mathcal{L}_{\text{lin}} \subseteq \mathcal{L}$. Prove that $\mathcal{L}$ is closed under intersection [GHa2].

EXERCISE 3.6.4: Prove that a family $\mathcal{L}$ of languages is a full AFL if and only if $\mathcal{R}_0 \subseteq \mathcal{L}$, $\hat{\text{Sub}}(\mathcal{L}, \mathcal{R}) \subseteq \mathcal{L}$, $\hat{\text{Sub}}(\mathcal{R}_0, \mathcal{L}) \subseteq \mathcal{L}$, and $\mathcal{L} \wedge \mathcal{R} \subseteq \mathcal{L}$ [GS5].

EXERCISE 3.6.5: Using the notation of Exercise 3.2.11, prove that $\mathscr{M}^{(n)}(\mathscr{L}_1, \ldots, \mathscr{L}_n) = \mathscr{F}(\mathscr{L}_1 \wedge \ldots \wedge \mathscr{L}_n)$ and $\hat{\mathscr{M}}^{(n)}(\mathscr{L}_1, \ldots, \mathscr{L}_n) = \hat{\mathscr{F}}(\mathscr{L}_1 \wedge \ldots \wedge \mathscr{L}_n)$ for all AFL $\mathscr{L}_1, \ldots, \mathscr{L}_n$ [Go1].

EXERCISE 3.6.6: (Continued) Prove that for each AFL $\mathscr{L}$, $\mathscr{F}_\cap(\mathscr{L}) = \bigcup_{n \geqq 1} \mathscr{M}^{(n)}(\mathscr{L}_1, \ldots, \mathscr{L}_n)$ and $\hat{\mathscr{F}}_\cap(\mathscr{L}) = \bigcup_{n \geqq 1} \hat{\mathscr{M}}^{(n)}(\mathscr{L}_1, \ldots, \mathscr{L}_n)$, where $\mathscr{L}_i = \mathscr{L}$ for each i [Go1].

EXERCISE 3.6.7: Exhibit AFL $\mathscr{L}_1$ and $\mathscr{L}_2$ such that $\mathrm{Sub}(\mathscr{L}_1, \mathscr{L}_2) \subseteq \mathscr{H}(\mathscr{L}_1 \wedge \mathscr{L}_2)$ is false.

EXERCISE 3.6.8: Let $\mathscr{L}$ be a trio, let $\mathscr{L}_i = \mathscr{L}$ for each i, and let $\mathscr{L}'_k = \mathscr{H}\left(\bigwedge_{i=1}^{k} \mathscr{L}_i\right)$ for each $k \geqq 1$. Prove that $\mathscr{L}'_n = \mathscr{H}(\mathscr{L}'_{i_1} \wedge \ldots \wedge \mathscr{L}'_{i_r})$ for each $n \geqq 1$ and $i_1, \ldots, i_r > 0$ such that $i_1 + \ldots + i_r = n$.

EXERCISE 3.6.9: Let $\mathscr{L}$ be a trio, let $\mathscr{L}_i = \mathscr{L}$ for each i, and let $\mathscr{L}'_k = \mathscr{H}\left(\bigwedge_{i=1}^{k} \mathscr{L}_i\right)$ for each $k > 0$. Prove that either (i) $\mathscr{L}'_i \subsetneq \mathscr{L}'_{i+1}$ for all i, and no $\mathscr{L}'_k$ is intersection closed, or (ii) for i_0 the smallest integer r such that $\mathscr{L}'_r = \mathscr{L}'_{r+1}$ and for $j \geqq i_0$, $\mathscr{L}'_j = \mathscr{L}'_{i_0}$ and $\mathscr{L}'_j$ is intersection closed.

EXERCISE 3.6.10: (a) Prove or disprove (a) of Theorem 3.6.2 for semi-AFL $\mathscr{L}_1$ and $\mathscr{L}_2$.

(b) Prove or disprove (b) of Theorem 3.6.2 for semi-AFL $\mathscr{L}_1$ and $\mathscr{L}_2$.

The following notation is used in Exercises 3.6.11–3.6.15 below. For all languages L_1 and L_2 and for c in $\Sigma - (\Sigma_{L_1} \cup \Sigma_{L_2})$, $L_1 c L_2$ is called a *marked product*. For each language L and each c in $\Sigma - \Sigma_L$, $(Lc)^+$ is called a *marked* $+$. A family of (ϵ-free) languages closed under marked product, marked $+$, inverse homomorphism, intersection with regular sets, and union with $\{\epsilon\}$ (all but the last) is called an (ϵ-*free*) *pre-AFL*.

EXERCISE 3.6.11: Prove that $\mathscr{H}(\mathscr{L})$ is an (ϵ-free) AFL for every (ϵ-free) pre-AFL $\mathscr{L}$ [GGHo].

EXERCISE 3.6.12: Show that for all AFL $\mathscr{L}_1, \ldots, \mathscr{L}_m, \mathscr{L}$; $\bigwedge_{1}^{m} \mathscr{L}_i$ and $\wedge\, \mathscr{L}$ are each either a pre-AFL or an ϵ-free pre-AFL [GGHo].

EXERCISE 3.6.13: Prove that every (ϵ-free) pre-AFL contains all (ϵ-free) regular sets [GGHo].

EXERCISE 3.6.14: Let $\mathscr{L}$ be an AFL containing $\{\epsilon\}$ and $\mathscr{L}' = \{\Sigma_1^* - L/L$ in $\mathscr{L}, \Sigma_1 \subseteq \Sigma\}$. Prove that $\mathscr{L}'$ is a pre-AFL [GGHo]. (It was noted in Exercise 3.1.11 that $\mathscr{L}'$ need not be an AFL.)

EXERCISE 3.6.15: Let $\mathscr{L}$ be an AFL and $\mathscr{B}(\mathscr{L})$ the smallest family containing $\mathscr{L}$ and closed under union, intersection, and relative complement, where a relative complement of a language L is a set $\Sigma_1^* - L$ for which $L \subseteq \Sigma_1^*$. Prove that $\mathscr{B}(\mathscr{L})$ is a pre-AFL [GGHo].

3.7 Verifying AFL Axioms

In Theorem 3.1.2, it was proven that each family of languages closed under ϵ-free homomorphism, inverse homomorphism, intersection with regular sets, union, and $+$ is closed under concatenation, i. e., is an AFL. In the present section we consider different properties which collectively imply some AFL axioms. (The value of this type of result is that if properties $P_1, \ldots, P_k$ together imply AFL axioms $P_{k+1}, \ldots, P_{k+l}$, in certain cases it may be easier to verify properties $P_1, \ldots, P_k$ rather than $P_{k+1}, \ldots, P_{k+l}$.) Specifically, we present conditions which collectively imply (i) ϵ-free homomorphism, (ii) intersection with regular sets and union, and (iii) inverse homomorphism.

We first consider ϵ-free homomorphism.

THEOREM 3.7.1: *Each family closed under inverse homomorphism, intersection with regular sets, and length-preserving homomorphism, is closed under ϵ-free homomorphism, i. e., is a trio.*

Proof: Let $\mathscr{L}$ be such a family. Let L be in $\mathscr{L}$ and h be an ϵ-free homomorphism from Σ_L^* into Σ_1^*. For each a in Σ_L let $\bar{a}$ be a new symbol and $\bar{\Sigma}_L = \{\bar{a}/a \text{ in } \Sigma_L\}$. For each a in Σ_L let $h(a) = b_a w_a$, where b_a is in Σ_1 and w_a is in Σ_1^*. The element b_a exists since h is ϵ-free. Let h_1 and h_2 be the homomorphisms from $(\bar{\Sigma}_L \cup \Sigma_1)^*$ into Σ_L^* and $(\bar{\Sigma}_L \cup \Sigma_1)^*$ into Σ_1^* resp. defined by $h_1(\bar{a}) = a$, $h_1(x) = \epsilon$, $h_2(\bar{a}) = b_a$, and $h_2(x) = x$ for all $\bar{a}$ in $\bar{\Sigma}_L$ and x in Σ_1. Then h_2 is length preserving and

$$h(L) = h_2(h_1^{-1}(L) \cap \{\bar{a}w_a/a \text{ in } \Sigma_L\}^*).$$

Thus $h(L)$ is in $\mathscr{L}$.

We now turn to proving closure under intersection with regular sets and under union. In particular, we show that an ϵ-free family closed under concatenation, ϵ-free homomorphism, and inverse homomorphism is closed under intersection with regular sets and union. We shall establish this result in three stages, i. e., by three lemmas.

LEMMA 3.7.1: *Let $\mathcal{L}$ be a family of ϵ-free languages closed under concatenation, ϵ-free homomorphism, and inverse homomorphism. Then $\{c\}$ is in $\mathcal{L}$ for every element c in Σ.*

Proof: Let c be a given element of Σ. Let L be a nonempty language in $\mathcal{L}$. Since $\mathcal{L}$, thus L, is ϵ-free, there exists a non-ϵ word w in L. For each element a in Σ_L let $\bar{a}$ be new. Let h_1 be the homomorphism on Σ_L^* defined by $h_1(a) = \bar{a}$ for each a in Σ_L. Then h_1 is ϵ-free, so that $\bar{L} = h_1(L)$ is in $\mathcal{L}$. Since $\mathcal{L}$ is closed under concatenation, $L\bar{L}$ is in $\mathcal{L}$. Let h_2 be the homomorphism on c^* defined by $h_2(c) = wh_1(w)$. Then $h_2^{-1}(L\bar{L}) = \{c\}$ is in $\mathcal{L}$.

LEMMA 3.7.2: *Let $\mathcal{L}$ be a family of languages closed under ϵ-free homomorphism and inverse homomorphism. If cLd is in $\mathcal{L}$, with L ϵ-free and c and d two symbols not in Σ_L, then L is in $\mathcal{L}$.*

Proof: Let cLd be in $\mathcal{L}$, with L ϵ-free and c and d two symbols not in Σ_L. For all a in Σ_L let (c, a, d), (c, a), and (a, d) be new symbols. Let $\Sigma_1 = \{a, (c, a, d), (c, a), (a, d)/\text{all } a \text{ in } \Sigma_L\}$. Let h_1 be the homomorphism from Σ_1^* into $(\Sigma_L \cup \{c, d\})^*$ defined by $h_1(a) = a$, $h_1((c, a, d)) = cad$, $h_1((c, a)) = ca$, and $h_1((a, d)) = ad$ for all a in Σ_L. Let h_2 be the ϵ-free homomorphism from Σ_1^* into Σ_L^* defined by $h_2(a) = h_2((c, a, d)) = h_2((c, a)) = h_2((a, d)) = a$ for all a in Σ_L. Since L is ϵ-free, $L = h_2h_1^{-1}(cLd)$. Since $\mathcal{L}$ is closed under ϵ-free homomorphism and inverse homomorphism, L is in $\mathcal{L}$.

LEMMA 3.7.3: *Let $\mathcal{L}$ be a family of ϵ-free languages closed under concatenation, ϵ-free homomorphism, and inverse homomorphism. Then $\mathcal{L}$ is closed under intersection with regular sets, i. e., is a trio.*

Proof: Let L be in $\mathcal{L}$ and R a regular set. Then $R = T(A)$ for some fsa $A = (K_1, \Sigma_R, \delta, q_0, F)$. Let c and d be new symbols. Extend δ by letting $\delta(q_0, c) = q_0$ and $\delta(p, d) = p$ for all p in F. As usual, let $\delta(q, a_1a_2) = \delta(\delta(q, a_1), a_2)$ and $\delta(q, a_1a_2a_3) = \delta(\delta(q, a_1a_2), a_3)$ for a_1, a_2, a_3 in $\Sigma_R \cup \{c, d\}$ and q in K_1, provided the right side exists. By Lemma 3.7.1, $\{c\}$ and $\{d\}$ are in $\mathcal{L}$. Thus cLd is in $\mathcal{L}$. For all appropriate p in K_1 and a, b in $\Sigma_R \cup \{c, d\}$, let $(p, a, \delta(p, a))$, $(p, a, \delta(p, a), b, \delta(p, ab))$, and $(p, a, \delta(p, a), b, \delta(p, ab), d, \delta(p, abd))$ be new symbols. Let

$\Sigma_1 = \{(p, a, \delta(p, a))/\text{all } p, a\}$,

$\Sigma_2 = \{(p, d, p)/p \text{ in } F\} \cup \{(p, a, \delta(p, a), b, \delta(p, ab))/\text{all } p, a, b\}$, and

$$\Sigma_3 = \{(q_0, c, q_0)\} \cup \{(p, a, \delta(p, a), b, \delta(p, ab))/\text{all } p, a, b, a \neq c\}$$
$$\cup \{(p, a, \delta(p, a), b, \delta(p, ab), d, \delta(p, abd))/\text{all } p, a, b\}.$$

Let h_1 be the homomorphism from Σ_1^* into $(\Sigma_R \cup \{c, d\})^*$ defined by $h_1\big((p, a, \delta(p, a))\big) = a$ for each $(p, a, \delta(p, a))$ in Σ_1. Let $L_1 = h_1^{-1}(cLd)$. Then L_1 is in $\mathscr{L}$ and

$$L_1 = \{(q_0, c, q_0)(p_1, a_1, \delta(p_1, a_1))\ldots(p_r, a_r, \delta(p_r, a_r))(p, d, p)/$$
$$a_1\ldots a_r \text{ in } L, p \text{ in } F, \text{ each } p_i \text{ in } K_1\}.$$

Let h_2 be the ϵ-free homomorphism from Σ_2^* into Σ_1^* defined by $h_2((p, d, p))= (p, d, p)$ for each (p, d, p) in Σ_2 and

$$h_2((p, a, \delta(p, a), b, \delta(p, ab))) = (p, a, \delta(p, a))\,(\delta(p, a), b, \delta(p, ab))$$

for each $(p, a, \delta(p, a), b, \delta(p, ab))$ in Σ_2. Let $L_2 = h_2h_2^{-1}(L_1)$. Then L_2 is in $\mathscr{L}$ and is the set of all words having one of the following two forms:

(1) $(q_0, a_1, p_0)(p_0, a_2, r_0)\ldots(q_s, a_{2s+1}, p_s)(p_s, a_{2s+2}, r_s)$,
where $s \geqq 1$, $q_0 = p_0$, $a_1 = c$, $a_{2s+2} = d$, and $a_2\ldots a_{2s+1}$ is in L; or
(2) $(q_0, a_1, p_0)(p_0, a_2, r_0)\ldots(q_s, a_{2s+1}, p_s)(p_s, a_{2s+2}, r_s)\,(p_{s+1}, d, p_{s+1})$,

where $s \geqq 0$, $q_0 = p_0$, $a_1 = c$, and $a_2 \ldots a_{2s+2}$ is in L. Let h_3 be the ϵ-free homomorphism from Σ_3^* into Σ_1^* defined by

(3) $h_3((q_0, c, q_0)) = (q_0, c, q_0)$,
(4) $h_3\big((p, a, \delta(p, a), b, \delta\,(p, ab))\big) = (p, a, \delta(p, a))\,(\delta(p, a), b, \delta(p, ab))$

for each $(p, a, \delta(p, a), b, \delta(p, ab))$ in Σ_3, and

(5) $h_3\big((p, a, \delta(p, a), b, \delta(p, ab), d, \delta(p, abd))\big)$
$= (p, a, \delta(p, a))\,(\delta(p, a), b, \delta(p, ab))\,(\delta(p, ab), d, \delta(p, abd))$

for all $(p, a, \delta(p, a), b, \delta(p, ab), d, \delta(p, abd))$ in Σ_3. Let $L_3 = h_3h_3^{-1}(L_2)$. Then L_3 is in $\mathscr{L}$ and is the set of all words of the form

(6) $(q_0, c, q_0)(q_0, a_1, q_1)\ldots(q_{t-1}, a_t, q_t)(q_t, d, q_t)$,

where $a_1\ldots a_t$ is in L, q_t is in F, and $\delta(q_i, a_{i+1}) = q_{i+1}$ for all i, $0 \leqq i \leqq t-1$, i.e., $a_1\ldots a_t$ is in $L \cap R$. For consider x when $h_3h_3^{-1}(x) \neq \emptyset$, i.e., $h_3h_3^{-1}(x)= x$. If x is of the form (1), then (3), (4), (5), and the fact that $a \neq c$ for $(p, a, \delta(p,a), b, \delta(p, ab))$ in Σ_3 imply that x is of the form (6). Suppose x is of the form (2). If $s = 0$, then (5) implies x is of the form (6). If $s \geqq 1$, then (3), (4), and (5) imply x is of the form (6).

Now let h_4 be the e-free homomorphism from Σ_1^* to $(\Sigma_R \cup \{c, d\})^*$ defined by $h_4((p, a, q)) = a$ for each (p, a, q) in Σ_1. Then $L_4 = h_4(L_3)$ is in $\mathcal{L}$ and $L_4 = c(L \cap R)d$. By Lemma 3.7.2, $L \cap R$ is in $\mathcal{L}$. Hence $\mathcal{L}$ is closed under intersection with regular sets.

We are now ready for the theorem.

THEOREM 3.7.2: *Let $\mathcal{L}$ be a family of e-free languages closed under concatenation, e-free homomorphism, and inverse homomorphism. Then $\mathcal{L}$ is closed under intersection with regular sets and union, i.e., $\mathcal{L}$ is a semi-AFL.*

Proof: By Lemma 3.7.3, $\mathcal{L}$ is a trio. Consider union. Let L_1 and L_2 be in $\mathcal{L}$. If either $L_1 = \emptyset$ or $L_2 = \emptyset$, then $L_1 \cup L_2$ is obviously in $\mathcal{L}$. Suppose $L_1 \neq \emptyset$ and $L_2 \neq \emptyset$. Then there exist $w_1 \neq \epsilon$ in L_1 and $w_2 \neq \epsilon$ in L_2. Let c and d be new symbols. Let h_1 be the homomorphism on $\{c, d\}^*$ defined by $h_1(c) = w_1$ and $h_1(d) = w_1$. Since $\mathcal{L}$ is a trio, $\mathcal{L}$ is closed under intersection with regular sets. Thus $\{w_1\} = L_1 \cap \{w_1\}$ is in $\mathcal{L}$ and $h_1^{-1}(\{w_1\}) = \{c, d\}$ is in $\mathcal{L}$. Therefore $L_1\{c, d\}L_2$ is in $\mathcal{L}$. Then

$$L_1\{c, d\}L_2 \cap (w_1 c \Sigma_{L_2}^* \cup \Sigma_{L_1}^* dw_2) = w_1 cL_2 \cup L_1 dw_2$$

is in $\mathcal{L}$. For each a in Σ_{L_1} and b in Σ_{L_2}, let (a, d) and (c, b) be new symbols. Let $\Sigma_3 = \Sigma_{L_1} \cup \Sigma_{L_2} \cup \{(a, d), (c, b)/\text{all } a, b\}$. Let h_2 be the e-free homomorphism on Σ_3^* defined by $h_2(a) = a$, $h_2(b) = b$, $h_2((a, d)) = adw_2$, and $h_2((c, b)) = w_1 cb$ for all a in Σ_{L_1} and b in Σ_{L_2}. Let h_3 be the e-free homomorphism on Σ_3^* defined by $h_3(a) = a$, $h_3(b) = b$, $h_3((a, d)) = a$, and $h_3((c, b)) = b$ for all a in Σ_{L_1} and b in Σ_{L_2}. Since L_1 and L_2 are e-free,

$$h_3 h_2^{-1}(w_1 cL_2 \cup L_1 dw_2) = L_2 \cup L_1.$$

Therefore $L_1 \cup L_2$ is in $\mathcal{L}$. Hence $\mathcal{L}$ is closed under union.

As a consequence of Theorem 3.7.2, we have:

THEOREM 3.7.3: *If $\mathcal{L}$ is a family of e-free languages closed under concatenation, e-free homomorphism, inverse homomorphism, and $+$, then $\mathcal{L}$ is an AFL.*

COROLLARY: *Let $\mathcal{L}$ be a family of languages closed under concatenation, e-free homomorphism, inverse homomorphism, $+$, $-\{\epsilon\}$, and union with $\{\epsilon\}$. Then $\mathcal{L}$ is an AFL.*

Proof: Let $\mathcal{L}' = \{L - \{\epsilon\}/L \text{ in } \mathcal{L}\}$. Since $\mathcal{L}$ is closed under $-\{\epsilon\}$, $\mathcal{L}' \subseteq \mathcal{L}$. Now concatenation, e-free homomorphism, inverse homomorphism, and

+, when applied to ϵ-free languages, yield ϵ-free languages. Therefore concatenation, ϵ-free homomorphism, inverse homomorphism, and +, when applied to languages in $\mathcal{L}'$, yield ϵ-free languages in $\mathcal{L}$, thus in $\mathcal{L}'$. Obviously $\mathcal{L}'$ is a family of languages. Hence $\mathcal{L}'$ is an AFL by Theorem 3.7.3. Since $\mathcal{L}$ is closed under union with $\{\epsilon\}$,

$$\mathcal{L}'' = \{L \cup \{\epsilon\}/L \text{ in } \mathcal{L}'\} \subseteq \mathcal{L}.$$

Therefore $\mathcal{L}' \cup \mathcal{L}'' \subseteq \mathcal{L}$. From the definition of $\mathcal{L}$, $\mathcal{L} \subseteq \mathcal{L}' \cup \mathcal{L}''$, so that $\mathcal{L} = \mathcal{L}' \cup \mathcal{L}''$. By Proposition 3.1.2, $\mathcal{L}$ is an AFL.

For a more complete study of dependency and interdependency relations among the AFL axioms, the reader is referred to [GrH1].

We close the section with several conditions which together imply inverse homomorphism.

Def: A substitution τ on L is called a *star substitution* if there exists a symbol c not in Σ_L such that $\tau(a) = c^*ac^*$ for each a in Σ_L.

Thus a star substitution merely inserts arbitrarily many occurrences of a new letter before and after every symbol.

Def: A homomorphism h is said to be *symbol-limited erasing* (*on* L) if $L \subseteq (\Sigma_1\{c^i/0 \leqq i \leqq k\})^*$ for some $k \geqq 0$, with c a symbol not in Σ_1, and $h(c) = \epsilon$ and $h(a) = a$ for all a in Σ_1.

PROPOSITION 3.7.1: *Let $\mathcal{L}$ be a family of languages closed under star substitution, symbol-limited erasing homomorphism, length-preserving homomorphism, and intersection with regular sets. If $\mathcal{L}$ is closed under union with regular sets or if $\mathcal{L}$ is ϵ-free, then $\mathcal{L}$ is closed under inverse homomorphism.*

Proof: Let L be a language in $\mathcal{L}$ and h_1 a homomorphism from Σ_1^* into Σ_2^*, with $L \subseteq \Sigma_2^*$. Let $L_1 = L - \{\epsilon\}$. Since $L_1 = L \cap \Sigma_2^+$, L_1 is in $\mathcal{L}$. For each element a in Σ_1 let $\bar{a}$ be a new symbol and $\Sigma_3 = \{\bar{a}/a \text{ in } \Sigma_1\}$. Let $\Sigma_1 = \{a_1, \ldots, a_n\}$. For each i, $1 \leqq i \leqq n$, let τ_i be the star substitution on $(\Sigma_2 \cup \{\bar{a}_j/j < i\})^*$ defined by $\tau_i(x) = \bar{a}_i^* x \bar{a}_i^*$ for each x in $\Sigma_2 \cup \{\bar{a}_j/j < i\}$. Let $\tau(x) = \tau_n \ldots \tau_1(x)$ for each x in Σ_2. Then $\tau(x) = \Sigma_3^* x \Sigma_3^*$ for each x in Σ_2. Let $L_2 = \tau(L_1)$. Since τ is the composition of star substitutions, L_2 is in $\mathcal{L}$. Let $L_3 = L_2 \cap \{\bar{a}_i h_1(a_i)/1 \leqq i \leqq n\}^*$. Since $\mathcal{L}$ is closed under intersection with regular sets, L_3 is in $\mathcal{L}$. Let c be a new symbol. Let h_2 be the length-preserving homomorphism on $(\Sigma_2 \cup \Sigma_3)^*$ defined by $h_2(\bar{a}_i) = a_i$ for each $\bar{a}_i$ in Σ_3 and $h_2(b) = c$ for each b in Σ_2. Then $h_2(L_3)$ is in $\mathcal{L}$ and $h_2(L_3) \subseteq (\Sigma_1\{c^i/0 \leqq i \leqq k\})^*$, where $k = \max\{|h_1(a_i)|\,/a_i \text{ in } \Sigma_1\}$. Let h_3 be the homomorphism on $(\{c\} \cup \Sigma_1)^*$ defined by $h_3(c) = \epsilon$ and $h_3(a_i) = a_i$ for each a_i in Σ_1. Clearly h_3 is a symbol-limited erasing homomorphism on $h_2(L_3)$ and $h_3 h_2(L_3) = h_1^{-1}(L_1)$. Thus $h_1^{-1}(L_1)$ is in $\mathcal{L}$.

Suppose $\mathcal{L}$ is ϵ-free. Then $L_1 = L$ and $h_1^{-1}(L)$ is in $\mathcal{L}$. Suppose $\mathcal{L}$ is closed under union with regular sets. If L is ϵ-free, then $h_1^{-1}(L)$ is in $\mathcal{L}$. Suppose L contains ϵ. Then $L = L_1 \cup \{\epsilon\}$, so that $h_1^{-1}(L) = h_1^{-1}(L_1) \cup h_1^{-1}(\epsilon)$. Since $h_1^{-1}(\epsilon)$ is regular, $h_1^{-1}(L)$ is in $\mathcal{L}$.

COROLLARY: *If $\mathcal{L}$ is a family of languages closed under intersection with regular sets, union with regular sets, and substitution by regular sets, then $\mathcal{L}$ is closed under inverse homomorphism.*

EXERCISE 3.7.1: Extend Lemma 3.7.1 to the case where $\mathcal{L}$ is not necessarily ϵ-free.

EXERCISE 3.7.2: Give an example of a family of languages which is not an AFL but is closed under intersection with regular sets and substitution, and contains a^* for each a in Σ.

EXERCISE 3.7.3: Let $\mathcal{L}$ be a family of languages closed under substitution, star substitution, and intersection with regular sets. Prove that $\mathcal{L}$ is a full AFL if $\mathcal{L}$ contains $\{\epsilon, a\}$ for all a in Σ.

EXERCISE 3.7.4: Let $\mathcal{L}$ be a family of languages closed under arbitrary substitution and under intersection with regular sets. Prove that if $\mathcal{L}$ contains a^* for each a in Σ and also contains a language having a word with at least two different symbols, then $\mathcal{L}$ is a full AFL.

EXERCISE 3.7.5: Let $\mathcal{L}$ be an ϵ-free family closed under ϵ-free substitution, intersection with regular sets, and symbol-limited erasing homomorphism. Prove that if $\mathcal{L}$ contains $c^*a^+c^*$ for each a and c in Σ, then $\mathcal{L}$ is an AFL.

EXERCISE 3.7.6: Give an example of an ϵ-free family which (i) is not an AFL, (ii) contains a^+ for all a in Σ, and (iii) is closed under ϵ-free substitution, intersection with regular sets, and symbol-limited erasing homomorphism.

EXERCISE 3.7.7: For $n \geqq 1$ let $\mathcal{L}_n$ be the family defined in Exercise 3.1.12. Prove that $\mathcal{L}_n$ is closed under

(a) Star substitution.

(b) Symbol-limited erasing homomorphism.

[Thus $\mathcal{L}_n$ is an AFL [Ka].]

(*) EXERCISE 3.7.8: (Continued) Prove that $\mathscr{L}_n \subsetneqq \mathscr{L}_{n+1}$ for each n [Ka]. [Hint: Show that $\{a_1^k a_2^k \ldots a_{4n-2}^k / k \geqq 1\}$ is in $\mathscr{L}_{n+1} - \mathscr{L}_n$, where $a_1, \ldots, a_{4n-2}$ are distinct symbols.]

3.8 Historical References

The notion of an AFL and the idea of seriously studying formal languages via their closure properties originated in [GGr1]. The concept of a semi-AFL was introduced in [Gr3]. Properties of trios were observed in [GGr1] and [Ni], but the formal abstraction and its intensive examination were initiated here. The concept of an a-transducer was introduced in [EM] under the name "binary transduction", but its importance to formal language theory was recognized in [GGr1] and subsequent papers on AFL. The complicated idea of "ϵ-output bounded under non-ϵ input in a language" was first considered in an early version of [GGr1], but was dropped in favor of "gsm ϵ-limited on a language" in the published version. Theorems 3.1.1, 3.2.1, 3.2.2(b), 3.3.1, 3.3.2, and 3.4.1 are in [GGr1]. Theorem 3.2.1 also occurs in [Ni]. Theorem 3.2.2(a) is in an early version of [GGr1]. Theorem 3.2.3 was noted in [GGr2], and Theorem 3.5.1 in [Ui]. The wedge operation was first abstracted in [GGHo]. Also in [GGHo] are Theorem 3.6.1 and a weaker form of Theorem 3.6.2. Proposition 3.6.1 originated in [GrG]. Lemma 3.6.1 appeared in [GS3]. Theorem 3.1.2, as well as the results of Section 3.7, are in [GrH1].

CHAPTER 4

ACCEPTORS

In formal language theory one popular way to define a family of languages is by a family of acceptors. For example, pda give rise to context-free languages. In the present chapter we introduce the notion of a general family of (one-way, nondeterministic) acceptors. We do this by considering the concepts of (i) an auxiliary storage, (ii) a function g which decodes the information on the auxiliary storage, and (iii) a function f which changes the auxiliary storage. For each auxiliary storage and appropriate functions g and f, we define a family of acceptors. We then study the family of languages to which the acceptors give rise.

4.1 AFA

In this section we motivate and then formalize the notion of an "abstract family of acceptors". A number of examples of well-studied types are then presented.

Informally, we may view a type of acceptor as a device with (i) a finite number of states, (ii) a finite number of inputs, (iii) a number of auxiliary storage configurations, each of which, through appropriate coding, may be regarded as a word over an auxiliary alphabet, (iv) a start state, and (v) a set of accepting states. In addition, each type of acceptor has a uniform way of reading certain information from the auxiliary storage configuration, and a uniform way of changing the old auxiliary storage configuration to a new one. For example, in a pda the auxiliary storage configuration is the pushdown word, the uniform way of reading certain information is to pick the rightmost symbol of the pushdown word, and the uniform way to get a new pushdown word is to take the old one, delete the rightmost symbol, and concatenate to the right of the resulting word another word specified by a particular acceptor.

To abstract the notion of a family of acceptors, we specify (a) a uniform way of reading the auxiliary storage, and (b) a uniform way of changing the old storage configuration to a new one. Since we consider acceptors with an arbitrary (but finite) number of states, we assume the existence of an infinite universe K of states. Similarly, we assume the existence of an infinite universe Σ of inputs. In order to discuss auxiliary storage configurations, we assume the existence of a nonempty universe Γ (possibly finite) of auxiliary storage symbols. We specify (a) above by a function g from Γ^* into the family of finite subsets of Γ^* (to allow for nondeterministic reading). We specify (b) by a function f.

Now a new storage configuration depends on the old storage configuration as well as some information calculated by an acceptor. For example, in a pda the new storage configuration depends on the old one and a word, to be added to the old storage configuration less its rightmost symbol, determined by the pda. We abstract this additional information in the form of an "instruction". Therefore we assume the existence of a universe I of instructions. For convenience, we shall regard each instruction as an abstract symbol. The function f then maps $\Gamma^* \times I$ into $\Gamma^* \cup \{\emptyset\}$. (It turns out that f is deterministic for all the types of acceptors studied in the literature.)

We are now ready to formally define an "abstract family of (one-way, nondeterministic) acceptors". We do this in two steps. First, we define an AFA-schema, a construct which formalizes a particular type of reading and writing of the auxiliary storage. We then define an abstract family of acceptors in terms of an AFA-schema, a state universe, and an input universe.

Def: An *AFA-schema* is a 4-tuple (Γ, I, f, g), with the following properties:

(1) Γ and I are nonempty abstract sets (of *storage symbols* and *instructions*, respectively).

(2) f (the *write* function) is a mapping from $\Gamma^* \times I$ into $\Gamma^* \cup \{\emptyset\}$.

(3) g (the *read* function) is a mapping from Γ^* into the finite subsets of Γ^* such that $g(\epsilon) = \{\epsilon\}$, and ϵ is in $g(\gamma)$ if and only if $\gamma = \epsilon$.

(4) For each γ in $g(\Gamma^*)$,[1] there is an element 1_γ in I satisfying $f(\gamma', 1_\gamma) = \gamma'$ for all γ' such that $g(\gamma')$ contains γ.

(5) For each u in I, there exists a finite set $\Gamma_u \subseteq \Gamma$ with the following property: If $\Gamma_1 \subseteq \Gamma$, γ is in Γ_1^*, and $f(\gamma, u) \neq \emptyset$, then $f(\gamma, u)$ is in $(\Gamma_1 \cup \Gamma_u)^*$; that is, for each γ in Γ^*, each symbol occurring in $f(\gamma, u)$ either occurs in γ or is in Γ_u.

Intuitively, an AFA-schema is a type of auxiliary storage, i.e., memory with read function g and write function f. Condition 3 ensures that g distin-

[1] For each set A, $g(A) = \bigcup_{\gamma \text{ in } A} g(\gamma)$.

guishes the storage configuration ϵ from all other storage configurations, i.e., $g(\epsilon) \cap g(\gamma) = \emptyset$ for all $\gamma \neq \epsilon$. [Words over Γ^* are referred to as *storage*, *auxiliary storage*, *storage configurations*, or *auxiliary storage configurations*.]

The element 1_γ in (4) is an "identity" instruction. Its purpose is to give a uniform procedure for leaving the auxiliary storage invariant while an acceptor changes states or advances the input. In particular, 1_γ has the property that it leaves invariant any storage configuration γ' for which γ is in $g(\gamma')$, i. e., γ is one of the "values" of the read function acting on γ'. In general, there may be more than one element u_γ (possibly an infinite number) in I satisfying $f(\gamma', u_\gamma) = \gamma'$ for all γ' such that $g(\gamma')$ contains γ. We shall frequently be defining acceptors with special properties. Since acceptors are finitely described, we shall need a specific such u_γ for each γ. Thus the element 1_γ is to denote a specific such u_γ.

Condition 5 will be explained later.

We now define an abstract family of acceptors.

Def: An *abstract family of* (*one-way nondeterministic*) *acceptors*, abbreviated *AFA*, is an ordered pair $(\Omega, \mathcal{D})$, or $\mathcal{D}$ when Ω is understood, with the following properties:

(1) Ω is a 6-tuple $(K, \Sigma, \Gamma, I, f, g)$, where
  (a) (Γ, I, f, g) is an AFA-schema; and
  (b) K and Σ are infinite abstract sets (of *states* and *inputs*, respectively).

(2) $\mathcal{D}$ is the family of all elements (called *acceptors*) $D = (K_1, \Sigma_1, \delta, q_0, F)$, where
  (a) K_1 and Σ_1 are finite subsets of K and Σ respectively, F is a subset of K_1, and q_0 is in K_1; and
  (b) δ (the *transition* function) is a mapping from $K_1 \times (\Sigma_1 \cup \{\epsilon\}) \times g(\Gamma^*)$ into the finite subsets of $K_1 \times I$ such that the set $G_D = \{\gamma/\delta(q, a, \gamma) \neq \emptyset$ for some q and $a\}$ is finite.

Thus, an AFA is an AFA-schema and all acceptors (over a given pair of state-input alphabets) having the AFA-schema type of storage. Each acceptor has a finite number of states and input symbols. q_0 is the "start" state of the acceptor, and F is the set of "accepting" states. δ describes the moves. In order that an acceptor D be finitely specified, G_D, the subset of $g(\Gamma^*)$ on which D operates, is required to be finite by condition 2(b).

While we have defined an acceptor D, we have not indicated how it is to move under an input. Informally, D obtains information from the storage via g. (Usually g selects some subsequence $\bar{\gamma}$ (in $g(\gamma) \cap G_D$) of γ.) Based on the state, the input, and the information, D then moves to another state and gives an instruction. Based on the old storage configuration and the instruction, f determines the new storage. Formally, we have:

Notation: Let $\vdash$ be the relation on $K_1 \times \Sigma_1^* \times \Gamma^*$ defined as follows: For a in $\Sigma_1 \cup \{\epsilon\}$, $(p, aw, \gamma) \vdash (p', w, \gamma')$ if there exist $\bar{\gamma}$ and u such that $\bar{\gamma}$ is in $g(\gamma)$, (p', u) is in $\delta(p, a, \bar{\gamma})$, and $f(\gamma, u) = \gamma'$.

Consider condition 5 in the definition of an AFA-schema. Intuitively, (5) guarantees that for a given acceptor D, the auxiliary symbols used are selected from a finite alphabet.[1] In particular, let $I_1 = \{u/(p', u)$ in $\delta(p, a, \gamma)$ for some p, p', a, and $\gamma\}$ and $\Gamma_1 = \bigcup_{u \text{ in } I_1} \Gamma_u$. Then I_1 and Γ_1 are finite (since G_D is finite), and $(q_0, w, \epsilon) \overset{*}{\vdash} (q, w', y)$ implies y is in Γ_1^*. Hence an alternative approach to finitely specifying D could have been given. The sets Γ_1, I_1, and G_D could have appeared in the definition of D, δ could have been defined as a function from $K_1 \times (\Sigma_1 \cup \{\epsilon\}) \times G_D$ into $2^{K_1 \times I_1}$, and $\vdash$ could have been defined as a relation on $K_1 \times \Sigma_1^* \times \Gamma_1^*$.

The problem now arises as to the definition of when an acceptor is to accept a word. Ideally, it would be nice to define acceptance in different ways so that trios, semi-AFL, and AFL could be characterized as the families of languages "accepted" by the acceptors in AFA. However, the nondeterminism of the acceptors seems to imply closure under union for the resulting families of languages. Thus, attention will be directed only to characterizations for semi-AFL and AFL. Now historically, two methods of acceptance have been considered in the automata and formal language literature. The first, the more popular, requires that after reading the entire word the device be in an accepting state, while the second demands that the storage be empty.[2] Several methods of acceptance, based on the above two, will be presented for each AFA.

Def: Let $(\Omega, \mathcal{D})$ be an AFA and let $D = (K_1, \Sigma_1, \delta, q_0, F)$ be in $\mathcal{D}$.

(a) Let $L(D)$, called the *set accepted by D* (*by simultaneous accepting state and empty storage*), be the set of words

$$\{w \text{ in } \Sigma_1^* / (q_0, w, \epsilon) \overset{*}{\vdash} (q, \epsilon, \epsilon) \text{ for some } q \text{ in } F\}.$$

For each subset $\mathcal{E}$ of $\mathcal{D}$, let $\mathcal{L}(\mathcal{E}) = \{L(D) \mid D \text{ in } \mathcal{E}\}$.

[1] Condition 5 is no real restriction for our purposes. See Exercise 4.3.11.

[2] See Section 2.3.

(b) Let $L_f(D)$, called the *set accepted by D (by accepting state)*, be the set of words

$$\{w \text{ in } \Sigma_1^* / (q_0, w, \epsilon) \overset{*}{\vdash} (q, \epsilon, \gamma) \text{ for some } q \text{ in } F \text{ and some } \gamma \text{ in } \Gamma^*\}.$$

For each subset $\mathcal{E}$ of $\mathcal{D}$, let $\mathcal{L}_f(\mathcal{E}) = \{L_f(D) \mid D \text{ in } \mathcal{E}\}$.

We shall present below a third method of acceptance for AFA.

Notation: For each acceptor $D = (K_1, \Sigma_1, \delta, q_0, F_1)$ let $\overset{-}{\vdash}$ be the relation on $K_1 \times \Sigma_1^* \times \Gamma^*$ defined by $(p, w, \gamma) \overset{-}{\vdash} (p', w', \gamma')$ if either

(i) $(p, w, \gamma) = (p', w', \gamma')$,

(ii) $(p, w, \gamma) \vdash (p', w', \gamma')$, or

(iii) there exist $n \geqq 1$, $p_1, \ldots, p_n, \gamma_1, \ldots, \gamma_n, w_1, \ldots, w_n$ such that

$$(p, w, \gamma) \vdash (p_1, w_1, \gamma_1), (p_n, w_n, \gamma_n) \vdash (p', w', \gamma'), (p_i, w_i, \gamma_i) \vdash (p_{i+1}, w_{i+1}, \gamma_{i+1})$$

for all i, $1 \leqq i < n$, and $\gamma_i \neq \epsilon$ for all i, $1 \leqq i \leqq n$.

Thus $(p, w, \gamma) \overset{-}{\vdash} (p', w', \gamma')$ if either $(p, w, \gamma) \overset{*}{\vdash} (p', w', \gamma')$ in 0 or 1 steps, or $(p, w, \gamma) \overset{*}{\vdash} (p', w', \gamma')$ in 2 or more steps with all strictly intermediate storage configurations non-ϵ.

Def: Let $\tilde{L}(D)$, called the *set accepted by D (by simultaneous accepting state and first return to empty storage)*, be the set of words

$$\{w \text{ in } \Sigma_1^*/(q_0, w, \epsilon) \overset{-}{\vdash} (q, \epsilon, \epsilon) \text{ for some } q \text{ in } F\}.$$

For each subset $\mathcal{E}$ of $\mathcal{D}$ let $\tilde{\mathcal{L}}(\mathcal{E}) = \{\tilde{L}(D) \mid D \text{ in } \mathcal{E}\}$.

We shall see in Section 4.2 that the families of languages $\mathcal{L}(\mathcal{D})$ coincide with the full AFL, the families of languages $\mathcal{L}_f(\mathcal{D})$ with the full semi-AFL, and the families of languages $\tilde{\mathcal{L}}(\mathcal{D})$, $\mathcal{D}$ "nontrivial", also with the full semi-AFL.

One of the reasons AFA are important is that they give rise to types of acceptors which, by themselves, are of considerable interest. In presenting examples, we frequently deviate, in a nonessential way, from the definition of these devices as they appear in the literature. (The differences are usually in method of acceptance, or in the existence of a distinguished symbol leftmost on the auxiliary storage.) In addition, we occasionally present instructions as words over some alphabet, instead of as abstract symbols. This is done to stay as close as possible to the customarily-used symbolism of certain acceptors. If an instruction is given as a word w in V^* for some alphabet V, then we may formally conceive of the instruction as the abstract symbol i_w.

EXAMPLE 4.1.1: Let $\Omega_{\mathrm{PDA}} = (K, \Sigma, \Gamma, I, f, g)$, where Γ has at least two elements, $I = \Gamma^*$, $g(\epsilon) = \{\epsilon\}$, $g(yZ) = \{Z\}$, $f(\epsilon, u) = u$, and $f(yZ, u) = yu$ for all Z in Γ, y in Γ^*, and u in[1] Γ^*. Then $(\Omega_{\mathrm{PDA}}, \mathcal{D}_{\mathrm{PDA}})$ is one AFA formalization of the family of pda, and is the one we shall use throughout except where stated otherwise.

Note that in a pda, g informs the finite state control whether the auxiliary storage is empty ($g(\epsilon) = \{\epsilon\}$) and if it is nonempty, what the rightmost symbol is ($g(yZ) = \{Z\}$). The function f transforms the auxiliary storage. Note that $1_\epsilon = \epsilon$, $1_Z = Z$, $\Gamma_\epsilon = \emptyset$, and if $u = Z_1 \ldots Z_k$ is a Γ-word, then $\Gamma_u = \{Z_1, \ldots, Z_k\}$.

EXAMPLE 4.1.2: Let $\Gamma = \{Z\}$ and $I = \{0\}$. Let $f(\gamma, 0) = \gamma$ for all γ in Γ^*. Let $g(\epsilon) = \{\epsilon\}$ and $g(Z^n) = \emptyset$ for $n \geqq 1$. Clearly $\Gamma_u = \{Z\}$ for each u in I satisfies condition 5 of an AFA-schema. Note that the resulting AFA $(\Omega, \mathcal{D})$ does not depend on the auxiliary storage. In case δ is a function from $K_1 \times (\Sigma_1 \cup \{\epsilon\}) \times \{\epsilon\}$ into the (finite) subsets of $K_1 \times \{0\}$, with $\delta(q, \epsilon, \epsilon) = \emptyset$ for all q in K_1, the acceptor is a nondeterministic fsa. If, in addition, δ maps $K_1 \times \Sigma_1 \times \{\epsilon\}$ into the unit subsets of $K_1 \times \{0\}$, i.e., into the subsets of $K_1 \times \{0\}$ consisting of exactly one element, then the acceptor is an fsa. In all cases, $\mathcal{L}(\mathcal{D}) = \mathcal{L}_f(\mathcal{D}) = \mathcal{R}$ and $\tilde{\mathcal{L}}(\mathcal{D}) = \{\Sigma_1, \Sigma_1 \cup \{\epsilon\} / \text{all } \Sigma_1\}$.

EXAMPLE 4.1.3: Let $\Gamma = \{Z\}$, $I = Z^*$, $g(Z^k) = \{Z\}$ for $k \geqq 1$, and $g(\epsilon) = \{\epsilon\}$. For $k \geqq 1$ and $l \geqq 0$, let $f(\epsilon, Z^l) = Z^l$ and $f(Z^k, Z^l) = Z^{k+l-1}$. Note that δ is a function from $K_1 \times (\Sigma_1 \cup \{\epsilon\}) \times \{Z, \epsilon\}$ into the finite subsets of $K_1 \times Z^*$. Since $f(Z^k, Z) = Z^k$ for $k \geqq 1$ and $f(\epsilon, \epsilon) = \epsilon$, condition 4 of an AFA-schema is satisfied. The resulting AFA, $(\Omega_{\mathrm{C}}, \mathcal{D}_{\mathrm{C}})$, is one AFA formalization of the family of *one-way, nondeterministic 1-counters*, or *counters* for short. Let $\mathcal{L}_{\mathrm{C}} = \mathcal{L}(\mathcal{D}_{\mathrm{C}})$. Note (see Exercise 4.1.5) that Ω_{C} is obtained by letting $\Gamma = \{Z\}$ in Ω_{PDA}, i.e., $\mathcal{D}_{\mathrm{C}}$ consists of all pda in which the storage symbol alphabet consists of just one letter.

EXAMPLE 4.1.4: Let Γ contain at least three elements, one of which is the symbol $\uparrow$. Let $\bar{\Gamma} = \Gamma - \{\uparrow\}$ and $I = \bar{\Gamma}^* \cup \{-1, 0, 1\}$, where -1, 0, and 1 are new symbols. Let $g(\epsilon) = \{\epsilon\}$ and $g(\gamma_1 Z \uparrow \gamma_2) = \{Z\}$ for all γ_1, γ_2 in $\bar{\Gamma}^*$ and Z in $\bar{\Gamma}$. Let $f(\epsilon, 0) = \epsilon$ and $f(\epsilon, \gamma) = \gamma \uparrow$ for all γ in $\bar{\Gamma}^+$. For all Z_1, Z_2 in $\bar{\Gamma}$ and $\gamma_1, \gamma_2, \gamma_3, \gamma_4$ in $\bar{\Gamma}^*$, with $\gamma_3\gamma_4 \neq \epsilon$, let $f(\gamma_1 Z_1 Z_2 \uparrow \gamma_2, -1) = \gamma_1 Z_1 \uparrow Z_2 \gamma_2$, $f(\gamma_1 Z_1 \uparrow Z_2 \gamma_2, 1) = \gamma_1 Z_1 Z_2 \uparrow \gamma_2$, $f(\gamma_1 Z_1 \uparrow \gamma_2, 0) = \gamma_1 Z_1 \uparrow \gamma_2$, $f(\gamma_3 Z_1 \uparrow, \gamma_4)$

[1] The functions f and g are always to be $\emptyset$ except where otherwise stated.

$= \gamma_3\gamma_4 \upharpoonleft$, and $f(Z_1 \upharpoonleft, \epsilon) = \epsilon$. (The instruction 1 means to move right on the auxiliary storage, -1 means to move left, and 0 means to stay stationary.) The instruction 0 is a universal identity instruction. The rule $f(\epsilon, \gamma) = \gamma \upharpoonleft$ for $\gamma \neq \epsilon$ allows the pointer $\upharpoonleft$ to be added to the right of γ, and $f(Z_1 \upharpoonleft, \epsilon) = \epsilon$ allows the auxiliary storage to be reinitialized to ϵ. The resulting AFA, $(\Omega_S, \mathcal{D}_S)$, is an AFA formalization of the family of *(one-way) stack acceptors.* Let $\mathcal{L}_S = \mathcal{L}(\mathcal{D}_S)$. Thus an acceptor in $\mathcal{D}_S$ is essentially a pda which can enter and read, but not alter, the contents of the auxiliary storage.

If $f(\gamma_3 Z_1 \upharpoonleft, \gamma_4) = \gamma_3\gamma_4 \upharpoonleft$ is altered to $f(\gamma_3 Z_1 \upharpoonleft, \gamma_4) = \gamma_3 Z_1 \gamma_4 \upharpoonleft$ and the resulting function f extended so that $f(\gamma \upharpoonleft, E) = \epsilon$ for all γ in $\bar{\Gamma}^+$, where E is a new instruction, then the resulting AFA, $(\Omega_{NES}, \mathcal{D}_{NES})$, is an AFA formalization of the family of *nonerasing (one-way) stack acceptors*. Let $\mathcal{L}_{NES} = \mathcal{L}(\mathcal{D}_{NES})$. Intuitively, an acceptor in $\mathcal{D}_{NES}$ is an acceptor in $\mathcal{D}_S$ which, when it erases one symbol (as distinguished from just changing the rightmost auxiliary storage symbol), then erases the entire auxiliary storage. This is equivalent (see Exercise 4.1.8), from the languages accepted point of view, to an acceptor in $\mathcal{D}_S$ which never erases and which accepts by final state only.

EXAMPLE 4.1.5: Let Γ be a set of at least four elements, containing the special symbols β (for "blank") and $\upharpoonleft$. Let $\bar{\Gamma} = \Gamma - \{\upharpoonleft\}$ and $I = \bar{\Gamma} \cup \{e, 1, -1, 0\}$, where e, 1, -1, and 0 are new symbols. Let $g(\epsilon) = \{\epsilon\}$ and $g(\gamma_1 Z \upharpoonleft \gamma_2) = \{Z\}$ for all Z in $\bar{\Gamma}$ and γ_1, γ_2 in $\bar{\Gamma}^*$. Let $f(\epsilon, e) = \epsilon$, $f(\epsilon, 1) = \beta\upharpoonleft$, and $f(\beta^m \upharpoonleft \beta^n, e) = \epsilon$ for $m+n \geqq 1$. For all Z_1, Z_2 in $\bar{\Gamma}$ and γ_1, γ_2 in $\bar{\Gamma}^*$, let $f(\gamma_1 Z_1 \upharpoonleft \gamma_2, Z_2) = \gamma_1 Z_2 \upharpoonleft \gamma_2$, $f(\gamma_1 \upharpoonleft \gamma_2, 0) = \gamma_1 \upharpoonleft \gamma_2$, $f(\gamma_1 Z_1 \upharpoonleft \gamma_2, -1) = \gamma_1 \upharpoonleft Z_1 \gamma_2$ if $\gamma_1 \neq \epsilon$, $f(Z_1 \upharpoonleft \gamma_2, -1) = \beta \upharpoonleft Z_1 \gamma_2$, $f(\gamma_1 Z_1 \upharpoonleft Z_2 \gamma_2, 1) = \gamma_1 Z_1 Z_2 \upharpoonleft \gamma_2$, and $f(\gamma_1 Z_1 \upharpoonleft, 1) = \gamma_1 Z_1 \beta \upharpoonleft$.

Thus, the instruction Z replaces the symbol to the left of $\upharpoonleft$ by Z; -1 moves $\upharpoonleft$ left one symbol, adding β if $\upharpoonleft$ is then the leftmost symbol; 1 moves $\upharpoonleft$ right one symbol, adding β if $\upharpoonleft$ was the rightmost symbol; 0 leaves the auxiliary storage invariant; and e changes β^n, $n \geqq 0$, to ϵ. The resulting AFA, $(\Omega_{TA}, \mathcal{D}_{TA})$, is one AFA formalization of the family of nondeterministic Turing acceptors, and is the one we shall use throughout.[1] It is readily seen (Exercise 4.1.2) that $\mathcal{L}(\mathcal{D}_{TA}) = \mathcal{L}_f(\mathcal{D}_{TA}) = \tilde{\mathcal{L}}(\mathcal{D}_{TA}) = \mathcal{L}_{RE}$. Note that for an acceptor to operate, it must start by replacing the initial ϵ with $\beta\upharpoonleft$. At the

[1] By analogy with Section 2.1, a *deterministic Turing acceptor* (in $\mathcal{D}_{TA}$) is a 6-tuple $(K_1, \Sigma_1, \$, \delta, p_0, F)$, where \$ is in $\Sigma - \Sigma_1$, $(K_1, \Sigma_1 \cup \{\$\}, \delta, p_0, F)$ is in $\mathcal{D}_{TA}$, $\#(\delta(p, a, \gamma) \cup \delta(p, \epsilon, \gamma)) \leqq 1$ for each γ in $g(\Gamma^*)$, and $L(D) = \{w$ in $\Sigma_1^* / (p_0, w\$, \epsilon) \overset{*}{\vdash} (p, \epsilon, \epsilon)$ for some p in $F\}$.

end of a computation which accepts a word by empty storage, $\beta^m \upharpoonleft \beta^n$ must be replaced by ϵ.

EXERCISE 4.1.1: Prove that each of the following families is independent of the number of elements in $\bar{\Gamma}$ (as long as this number is at least two):

(a) $\mathcal{L}(\mathcal{D}_{\mathrm{PDA}})$, where $\Gamma = \bar{\Gamma}$.

(b) $\mathcal{L}(\mathcal{D}_{\mathrm{S}})$.

(c) $\mathcal{L}(\mathcal{D}_{\mathrm{NES}})$.

EXERCISE 4.1.2: Prove the following:

(a) $\mathcal{L}(\mathcal{D}_{\mathrm{PDA}})$ coincides with the family of pda languages as given in Section 2.3.

(b) $\mathcal{L}(\mathcal{D}_{\mathrm{TA}}) = \mathcal{L}_f(\mathcal{D}_{\mathrm{TA}}) = \tilde{\mathcal{L}}(\mathcal{D}_{\mathrm{TA}}) = \mathcal{L}_{\mathrm{RE}}$.

EXERCISE 4.1.3: Given a pda $D = (K_1, \Sigma_1, \delta_1, p_0, F_1)$, write $(q, w, \gamma) \overset{\Delta}{\vdash} (q', w', \gamma')$ if $(q, w, \gamma) \vdash (q', w', \gamma')$ and $\gamma' \neq \epsilon$. Let m be a positive integer. Call D *m-turn bounded* if whenever there exist $r \geqq 2$, $p_1, \ldots, p_{r+1}$, $a_1, \ldots, a_r, \gamma_1 = \epsilon$, $\gamma_2, \ldots, \gamma_{r+1}$ such that $(p_i, a_i, \gamma_i) \overset{\Delta}{\vdash} (p_{i+1}, \epsilon, \gamma_{i+1})$ for all i, $1 \leqq i < r$, and $(p_r, a_r, \gamma_r) \vdash (p_{r+1}, \epsilon, \gamma_{r+1})$, then there are at most m distinct integers i with the following property: There exists $s_i \geqq 1$ such that $|\gamma_{i+s_i}| > |\gamma_{i+s_i+1}|$ and $|\gamma_i| < |\gamma_{i+1}| = |\gamma_{i+t}|$ for all t, $1 \leqq t \leqq s_i$. In other words, D is m-turn bounded if the length of its pushdown never changes from increasing to strictly decreasing more than m times before becoming ϵ. Construct an AFA $\mathcal{D}_m$ such that $\mathcal{L}(\mathcal{D}_m)$ is the family of languages accepted by m-turn bounded pda [Gr1].

EXERCISE 4.1.4: Let $\Omega = (K, \Sigma, \Gamma, \{0, Z\}, f, g)$, where $g(\epsilon) = \{\epsilon\}$, g is arbitrary otherwise, $f(x, 0) = x$ for all x in Γ^*, $f(\epsilon, Z) = w_1$, and $f(w_i, Z) = w_{i+1}$, $1 \leqq i \leqq m$, with $w_{m+1} = \epsilon$, for some $m \geqq 1$ and distinct words $w_1, \ldots, w_m$ in Γ^+. Prove that $\mathcal{L}(\mathcal{D}) = \mathcal{L}_f(\mathcal{D}) = \tilde{\mathcal{L}}(\mathcal{D}) = \mathcal{R}$.

EXERCISE 4.1.5: Verify that the result of letting $\Gamma = \{Z\}$ in Ω_{PDA} is Ω_{C}.

EXERCISE 4.1.6: Let $\Omega = (K, \Sigma, \Gamma, I, f, g)$, where $\Gamma = \{Z_0, Z\}$, $I = \{Z, Z^{\mathrm{E}}, 0, Z_0\}$, and f and g are defined as follows (for all $i > 0$, $j \geqq 0$, and x in Γ^*): $g(\epsilon) = \{\epsilon\}$, $g(Z_0) = \{Z_0\}$, $g(Z_0Z^i) = \{Z\}$, $f(x, 0) = x$, $f(\epsilon, Z_0) = Z_0$, $f(Z_0Z^j, Z) = Z_0Z^{j+1}$, $f(Z_0Z^i, Z^{\mathrm{E}}) = Z_0Z^{i-1}$, and $f(Z_0, Z^{\mathrm{E}}) = \epsilon$. Prove that $\mathcal{L}(\mathcal{D}) = \mathcal{L}_{\mathrm{C}}$.

EXERCISE 4.1.7: Let $(\Omega, \mathcal{D})$ be the same as in Example 4.1.5, except that there is no instruction 0. (Thus $\mathcal{D}$ is technically not an AFA.) Let $\vdash$, $L(D)$, and $\mathcal{L}(\mathcal{D})$ have the same significance as in an AFA. Prove that $\mathcal{L}(\mathcal{D}) = \mathcal{L}_{\mathrm{RE}}$.

EXERCISE 4.1.8: Let Γ have an infinite number of elements. Let $\mathcal{E}$ be the family of all acceptors $D = (K_1, \Sigma_1, \delta, q_0, F)$ in $\mathcal{D}_{\mathrm{S}}$ with the following property: There is no (p, q, a, Z) in $K_1 \times K_1 \times (\Sigma_1 \cup \{\epsilon\}) \times \Gamma$ so that (q, ϵ) is in $\delta(p, a, Z)$. Prove that $\mathcal{L}_f(\mathcal{E}) = \mathcal{L}_{\mathrm{NES}}$.

EXERCISE 4.1.9: Let K, Σ, and Γ be infinite sets and let $\Gamma' = \Gamma \cup \{\uparrow_1\} \cup \{\uparrow_i, \uparrow_i' \mid i \geqq 2\}$, where $\uparrow_1, \uparrow_2, \uparrow_2', \ldots$ are new symbols. For each w in Γ^*, let u_w be a new symbol. Let $I = \{u_w / w \text{ in } \Gamma^*\} \cup \{1, l, l'\}$, where $1, l, l'$ are new symbols. Consider $\Omega = (K, \Sigma, \Gamma', I, f, g)$, where f and g are the functions defined as follows (for all w, w_1, and w_2 in Γ^*, a in Γ, and $i \geqq 1$):

(i) $f(z, 1) = z$ for all z in Γ^*,
(ii) $f(\epsilon, u_w) = w \uparrow_1$,
(iii) $f(w_1 \uparrow_1, u_{w_2}) = w_1 w_2 \uparrow_1$,
(iv) (a) $f(w \uparrow_{2i-1}, l) = w \uparrow_{2i}$,
(b) $f(w \uparrow_{2i-1}, l') = w \uparrow_{2i}'$,
(v) $f(\uparrow_{2i} w, l) = \uparrow_{2i+1} w$,
(vi) (a) $f(w_1 a \uparrow_{2i} w_2, l) = w_1 \uparrow_{2i} a w_2$,
(b) $f(w_1 \uparrow_{2i-1} a w_2, l) = w_1 a \uparrow_{2i-1} w_2$,
(vii) (a) $f(wa \uparrow_{2i}', l') = w \uparrow_{2i}'$,
(b) $f(\uparrow_{2i}', l') = \epsilon$,
(viii) $g(\epsilon) = \{\epsilon\}$,
(ix) (a) $g(w \uparrow_{2i-1}) = \{\uparrow_{2i-1}\}$,
(b) $g(\uparrow_{2i} w) = \{\uparrow_{2i}\}$,
(c) $g(\uparrow_{2i}') = \{\uparrow_{2i}'\}$,
(x) $g(w_1 a \uparrow_{2i} w_2) = \{a \uparrow_{2i}\}$,
(b) $g(wa \uparrow_{2i}') = \{a \uparrow_{2i}'\}$,
(c) $g(w_1 \uparrow_{2i-1} a w_2) = \{\uparrow_{2i-1} a\}$.

Is $(\Omega, \mathcal{D})$ an AFA? Substantiate your answer.

4.2 Full (Semi-) AFL Characterization

We now establish one of the main results of AFL theory, namely that a family $\mathcal{L}$ of languages is a full AFL if and only if $\mathcal{L} = \mathcal{L}(\mathcal{D})$ for some AFA $\mathcal{D}$. Closely connected with this result is a characterization of full semi-AFL in terms of the families $\mathcal{L}_f(\mathcal{D})$ as well as a characterization in terms of the families $\tilde{\mathcal{L}}(\mathcal{D})$.

We first consider the sufficiency for the AFL case. We shall present a sequence of preliminary results, each proving at least one of the AFL axioms for $\mathcal{L}(\mathcal{D})$.

LEMMA 4.2.1: *For each AFA $\mathcal{D}$, $\hat{Sub}$ $(\mathcal{R}_0, \mathcal{L}(\mathcal{D})) \subseteq \mathcal{L}(\mathcal{D})$.*

Proof: Let R be an ϵ-free regular set and τ a substitution on Σ_R^* such that $\tau(a)$ is in $\mathcal{L}(\mathcal{D})$ for each a in Σ_R. Let $A = (K_1, \Sigma_R, \delta_1, p_1, F_1)$ be an fsa such that[1] $R = T(A)$ and $K_1 \subseteq K$. For each a in Σ_R let $D_a = (K_a, \Sigma_a, \delta_a, p_a, F_a)$ in $\mathcal{D}$ be such that $\tau(a) = L(D_a)$. Without loss of generality, we may assume that $K_a \cap K_b = \emptyset$ for all a, b in Σ_R, $a \neq b$. We shall construct an acceptor D in $\mathcal{D}$ such that $L(D) = \tau(R)$.

Intuitively, D breaks the input word w into subwords $w_1, \ldots, w_k$, guesses in sequence that w_i is in $L(D_{a_i})$, and imitates D_{a_i} under input word w_i to check for membership of w_i in $L(D_{a_i})$. If w_i is in $L(D_{a_i})$, then D imitates by ϵ the movement of A under a_i to check the membership of $a_1 \ldots a_k$ in $T(A)$. Formally, for each a in Σ_R, p in K_a, and s in K_1 let (p, s) and $(p, \bar{s})$ be two distinct elements in $K-(K_1 \cup \bigcup_b K_b)$. Let

$$K_2 = \{p_1\} \cup \{(p, s), (p, \bar{s})/p \text{ in } \bigcup_a K_a, s \text{ in } K_1\}.$$

Let $F_2 = \bigcup_a (K_a \times F_1)$ and $D = \left(K_2, \bigcup_{a \text{ in } \Sigma_R} \Sigma_a, \delta, p_1, F_2\right)$, where δ is defined as follows:

(1) Start: $\delta(p_1, \epsilon, \epsilon) = \{((p_a, \bar{p}_1), 1_\epsilon)/a \text{ in } \Sigma_R\}$.

(2) Imitate D_a: If (p', u) is in $\delta_a(p, x, \gamma)$ for p in K_a, x in $\Sigma_a \cup \{\epsilon\}$, and γ in $g(\Gamma^*)$, then $((p', \bar{s}), u)$ is in $\delta((p, \bar{s}), x, \gamma)$ for all s in K_1.

(3) Imitate A: For all a and b in Σ_R, p in F_a, and s in K_1, $((p_b, \delta_1(s, a)), 1_\epsilon)$ is in $\delta((p, \bar{s}), \epsilon, \epsilon)$ and $((p_b, \bar{s}), 1_\epsilon)$ is in $\delta((p_b, s), \epsilon, \epsilon)$.

Let $\vdash_{D,2}$ denote a computation by a type 2 rule. It is clear that $((p, \bar{s}), xy, \gamma) \vdash_{D,2} ((p', \bar{s}), y, \gamma')$ if $(p, xy, \gamma) \vdash_{D_a} (p', y, \gamma')$ for some a in Σ_R. Suppose that $((p, \bar{s}), xy, \gamma) \vdash_{D,2} ((p', \bar{s}), y, \gamma')$. Then there exist $\bar{\gamma}$ in $g(\gamma)$ and u such that $((p', \bar{s}), u)$ is in $\delta((p, \bar{s}), x, \bar{\gamma})$ and $f(\gamma, u) = \gamma'$. This occurs if and only if (p', u) is in $\delta_a(p, x, \bar{\gamma})$ for some a in Σ_R, so that $(p, xy, \gamma) \vdash_{D_a} (p', y, \gamma')$. Hence

[1] For (nondeterministic) fsa A, we usually write $T(A)$ instead of $L(A)$. This is to indicate that the form of the nondeterministic fsa considered has no auxiliary storage, that is, is not in AFA form.

$((p, \bar{s}), xy, \gamma) \vdash_{D,2} ((p', \bar{s}), y, \gamma')$ if and only if $(p, xy, \gamma) \vdash_{D_a} (p', y, \gamma')$ for some a. Therefore, $((p_a, \bar{s}), w_1 w_2, \epsilon) \vdash^*_{D,2} ((q_a, \bar{s}), w_2, \epsilon) \vdash_D ((p_b, \delta_1(s, a)), w_2, \epsilon) \vdash_D ((p_b, \overline{\delta_1(s, a)}), w_2, \epsilon)$ if and only if $(p_a, w_1, \epsilon) \vdash^*_{D_a} (q_a, \epsilon, \epsilon)$ for some q_a in F_a. Now R is ϵ-free. Thus, w is in $\tau(R)$ if and only if there exist $k \geqq 1, a_1, \ldots, a_k$ in Σ_R and $w_1, \ldots, w_k$, each w_i in $L(D_{a_i})$ such that $a_1 \ldots a_k$ is in R and $w = w_1 \ldots w_k$. This holds if and only if for each i there exists q_i in F_{a_i} such that

$$(p_{a_i}, w_i, \epsilon) \vdash^*_{D a_i} (q_i, \epsilon, \epsilon).$$

This holds if and only if

$$\begin{aligned}
(p_1, w_1 \ldots w_k, \epsilon) &\vdash_D ((p_{a_1}, \bar{p}_1), w_1 \ldots w_k, \epsilon) \\
&\vdash^*_{D,} ((q_1, \bar{p}_1), w_2 \ldots w_k, \epsilon) \\
&\vdash_D ((p_{a_2}, \delta_1(p_1, a_1)), w_2 \ldots w_k, \epsilon) \\
&\vdash_D ((p_{a_2}, \overline{\delta_1(p_1, a_1)}), w_2 \ldots w_k, \epsilon) \\
&\cdot \quad \cdot \quad \cdot \\
&\vdash_D ((p_{a_k}, \overline{\delta_1(p_1, a_1 \ldots a_{k-1})}), w_k, \epsilon) \\
&\vdash^*_{D,2} ((q_k, \overline{\delta_1(p_1, a_1 \ldots a_{k-1})}), \epsilon, \epsilon) \\
&\vdash_D ((p_a, \delta_1(p_1, a_1 \ldots a_k)), \epsilon, \epsilon)
\end{aligned}$$

for some a in Σ_R, with $\delta_1(p_1, a_1 \ldots a_k)$ in F_1, which holds if and only if $w_1 \ldots w_k$ is in $L(D)$. Thus $\tau(R) = L(D)$ and $\tau(R)$ is in $\mathcal{L}(\mathcal{D})$, i.e., Sûb $(\mathcal{R}_0, \mathcal{L}(\mathcal{D})) \subseteq \mathcal{L}(\mathcal{D})$.

From Proposition 3.3.1 and Lemma 4.2.1, we get

COROLLARY: *For each AFA $\mathcal{D}$, $\mathcal{L}(\mathcal{D})$ is closed under union, concatenation, and +.*

LEMMA 4.2.2: *For each AFA $\mathcal{D}$, $\mathcal{L}(\mathcal{D})$ is closed under intersection with regular sets.*

Proof: Let $D = (K_1, \Sigma_1, \delta_1, p_0, F_1)$ be in $\mathcal{D}$ and $A = (K_2, \Sigma_1, \delta_2, s_0, F_2)$ an fsa. Let $K_3 = K_1 \times K_2$,[1] and $F_3 = F_1 \times F_2$. Let $D' = (K_3, \Sigma_1, \delta_3, (p_0, s_0), F_3)$, where δ_3 is defined as follows: If (p', u) is in $\delta_1(p, a, \gamma)$, a in $\Sigma_1 \cup \{\epsilon\}$, let $((p', \delta_2(s, a)), u)$ be in $\delta_3((p, s), a, \gamma)$ for each s in K_2. Clearly D' is in $\mathcal{D}$ and $L(D') = L(D) \cap T(A)$.

[1] That is, for each p in K_1 and s in K_2, (p, s) is a new symbol in K.

LEMMA 4.2.3: *For each AFA $\mathcal{D}$, $\mathcal{L}(\mathcal{D})$ is closed under inverse homomorphism.*

Proof: Let $D_1 = (K_1, \Sigma_1, \delta_1, p_0, F_1)$ be in $\mathcal{D}$ and h be a homomorphism from Σ_2^* into Σ_1^*. We shall construct an acceptor D_2 in $\mathcal{D}$ such that $L(D_2) = h^{-1}(L(D_1))$.

The idea here is that for each Σ_2-word $a_1 \ldots a_k$, D_2 imitates D_1 on $h(a_1)\ldots h(a_k)$, checking $h(a_1)\ldots h(a_k)$ for membership in $L(D_1)$. More precisely, let $n = \max\{|h(a)|/a \text{ in } \Sigma_2\}$ and $X = \{x \text{ in } \Sigma_1^*/|x| \leqq n\}$. Let $K_2 = K_1 \times X$ and $F_2 = F_1 \times \{\epsilon\}$. Let D_2 be the acceptor $(K_2, \Sigma_2, \delta_2, (p_0, \epsilon), F_2$, where δ_2 is defined as follows:

(1) For each a in Σ_2, γ in G_{D_1}, and p in K_1, let $\big((p, h(a)), 1_\gamma\big)$ be in $\delta_2((p, \epsilon), a, \gamma)$.

(2) If bx is in X, with b in $\Sigma_1 \cup \{\epsilon\}$, and (p', u) is in $\delta_1(p, b, \gamma)$, let $((p', x), u)$ be in $\delta_2((p, bx), \epsilon, \gamma)$.

Thus the rules in (1) allow D_2 to map a in Σ_2 into $h(a)$ and store $h(a)$ in its finite state control. The rules in (2) allow D_2 to imitate D_1 on $h(a)$.

Suppose $a_1 \ldots a_k$ is in $h^{-1}(L(D_1))$, with $k \geqq 1$ and each a_i in Σ_2. Then there exist $w_1, \ldots, w_k, p_1, \ldots, p_k, \gamma_0, \ldots, \gamma_k$ such that $h(a_i) = w_i$ for each i, $\gamma_0 = \gamma_k = \epsilon$, p_k is in F_1, and $(p_i, w_{i+1}, \gamma_i) \overset{*}{\underset{D_1}{\vdash}} (p_{i+1}, \epsilon, \gamma_{i+1})$ for all i, $0 \leqq i \leqq k-1$. Hence for each i, $0 \leqq i \leqq k-1$, there exist $r \geqq 0$, $q_1, \ldots, q_{r+1}$, $b_1, \ldots, b_r, v_1, \ldots, v_{r+1}$, all depending on i, such that $q_1 = p_i$, $q_{r+1} = p_{i+1}$, $v_1 = \gamma_i$, $v_{r+1} = \gamma_{i+1}$, each b_j is in $\Sigma_1 \cup \{\epsilon\}$, $h(a_{i+1}) = w_{i+1} = b_1 \ldots b_r$, and

$$(q_1, b_1 \ldots b_r, v_1) \underset{D_1}{\vdash} (q_2, b_2 \ldots b_r, v_2)$$

$$\ldots$$

$$\underset{D_1}{\vdash} (q_{r+1}, \epsilon, v_{r+1}).$$

Then there exists v_1' in $g(v_1) \cap G_{D_1}$. By (1), $((q_1, b_1 \ldots b_r), 1_{v_1})$ is in $\delta_2((q_1, \epsilon), a_{i+1}, v_1')$. Since $f(v_1, 1_{v_1'}) = v_1$,

$$((q_1, \epsilon), a_{i+1}, v_1) \underset{D_2}{\vdash} ((q_1, b_1 \ldots b_r), \epsilon, v_1).$$

For each j, $(q_j, b_j \ldots b_r, v_j) \underset{D_1}{\vdash} (q_{j+1}, b_{j+1} \ldots b_r, v_{j+1})$. Thus, there exist v_j' in $g(v_j) \cap G_{D_1}$ and u_j such that (q_{j+1}, u_j) is in $\delta_1(q_j, b_j, v_j')$ and $f(v_j, u_j) = v_{j+1}$. By (2), $((q_{j+1}, b_{j+1} \ldots b_r), u_j)$ is in $\delta_2((q_j, b_j \ldots b_r), \epsilon, v_j')$. Thus $((q_j, b_j \ldots b_r), \epsilon, v_j) \underset{D_2}{\vdash} ((q_{j+1}, b_{j+1} \ldots b_r), \epsilon, v_{j+1})$, whence $((p_i, \epsilon), a_{i+1}, \gamma_i) \overset{*}{\underset{D_2}{\vdash}} ((p_{i+1}, \epsilon), \epsilon, \gamma_{i+1})$. Thus $((p_0, \epsilon), a_1 \ldots a_k, \gamma_0) \overset{*}{\underset{D_2}{\vdash}} ((p_k, \epsilon), \epsilon, \gamma_k)$ and $a_1 \ldots a_k$ is in $L(D_2)$.

Suppose ϵ is in $h^{-1}(L(D_1))$. Then ϵ is in $L(D_1)$ and $(p_0, \epsilon, \epsilon) \overset{*}{\underset{D_1}{\vdash}} (p_1,\epsilon, \epsilon)$ for some p_1 in F_1. From this, it follows that $((p_0,\epsilon), \epsilon, \epsilon) \overset{*}{\underset{D_2}{\vdash}} ((p_1,\epsilon), \epsilon, \epsilon)$ so that ϵ is in $L(D_2)$.

Now suppose $a_1 \ldots a_k$ is in $L(D_2)$, $k \geqq 1$ and each a_i in Σ_2. Then there exist $a_1', \ldots, a_s', t_1, \ldots, t_s, v_1, \ldots, v_s$ such that each a_j' is in $\Sigma_2 \cup \{\epsilon\}$, $a_1' \ldots a_s' = a_1 \ldots a_k$, $t_1 = (p_0, \epsilon)$, t_s is in F_2, $v_1 = v_s = \epsilon$, and $(t_i, a_i', v_i) \underset{D_2}{\vdash} (t_{i+1}, \epsilon, v_{i+1})$. Let $\tau(1) < \ldots < \tau(k)$ be those integers such that $a_{\tau(j)}'$ is in Σ_2. Then $a_{\tau(j)}' = a_j$ for each j. Since δ_2 is defined by (1) and (2), $t_{\tau(j)} = (p_j, \epsilon)$ and $t_{\tau(j)+1} = (p_j, h(a_{\tau(j)}'))$ for some p_j, $1 \leqq j \leqq k$. Furthermore, for those i not in $\{\tau(1), \ldots, \tau(k)\}$, $(t_i, a_i', v_i) \underset{D_2}{\vdash} (t_{i+1}, \epsilon, v_{i+1})$ is obtained from (2). Since t_s is in F_2, $t_s = (p_{k+1}, \epsilon)$ for some p_{k+1} in F_1. Thus

$$\begin{aligned}(p_0, h(a_1)\ldots h(a_k), \epsilon) &\overset{*}{\underset{D_1}{\vdash}} (p_1, h(a_1)\ldots h(a_k), v_{\tau(1)})\\ &\overset{*}{\underset{D_1}{\vdash}} (p_2, h(a_2)\ldots h(a_k), v_{\tau(2)})\\ &\ldots\\ &\overset{*}{\underset{D_1}{\vdash}} (p_k, \epsilon, \epsilon).\end{aligned}$$

Hence $h(a_1) \ldots h(a_k) = h(a_1 \ldots a_k)$ is in $L(D_1)$, i.e., $a_1 \ldots a_k$ is in $h^{-1}(L(D_1))$.

Suppose ϵ is in $L(D_2)$. Then there exist $s \geqq 1$ and $t_1, \ldots, t_s, v_1, \ldots, v_s$ such that $t_1 = (p_0, \epsilon)$, $t_s = (p_{s-1}, \epsilon)$, with p_{s-1} in F_1, $v_1 = v_s = \epsilon$, and $(t_i, \epsilon, v_i) \underset{D_2}{\vdash} (t_{i+1}, \epsilon, v_{i+1})$ for all i, $1 \leqq i < s$. As above, it follows that $(p_0, \epsilon, \epsilon) \overset{*}{\underset{D_1}{\vdash}} (p_{s-1}, \epsilon, \epsilon)$, so that ϵ is in $h^{-1}(L(D_1))$.

The previous considerations thus show that a word w is in $h^{-1}(L(D_1))$ if and only if w is in $L(D_2)$, i.e., $L(D_2) = h^{-1}(L(D_1))$.

LEMMA 4.2.4: *For each AFA $\mathcal{D}$, $\mathcal{L}(\mathcal{D})$ is closed under homomorphism.*

Proof: Let $D_1 = (K_1, \Sigma_1, \delta_1, p_0, F_1)$ be in $\mathcal{D}$ and h be a homomorphism from Σ_1^* into Σ_2^*. We shall construct an acceptor D_2 in $\mathcal{D}$ such that $L(D_2) = h(L(D_1))$.

Informally, D_2 guesses $a_1 \ldots a_k$, verifies $a_1 \ldots a_k$ for membership in $L(D_1)$, and checks that $h(a_1) \ldots h(a_k)$ is the input word. Formally, let $n = \max\{|h(a)|/a \text{ in } \Sigma_1\}$. Let $Y = \{y \text{ in } \Sigma_2^*/|y| \leqq n\}$, $K_2 = (K_1 \times \Sigma_1 \times Y) \cup (K_1 \times \{\epsilon\} \times \{\epsilon\})$, and $F_2 = F_1 \times \{\epsilon\} \times \{\epsilon\}$. Let $D_2 = (K_2, \Sigma_2, \delta_2, (p_0, \epsilon, \epsilon), F_2)$, where δ_2 is defined as follows:

(1) For each γ in G_{D_1}, p in K_1, and a in Σ_1, let $((p, a, h(a)), 1_\gamma)$ be in $\delta_2((p, \epsilon, \epsilon), \epsilon, \gamma)$.

(2) For all p in K_1, a in Σ_1, γ in G_{D_1}, and by in Y, with b in Σ_2, let $((p, a, y), 1_\gamma)$ be in $\delta_2((p, a, by), b, \gamma)$.

(3) For a in $\Sigma_1 \cup \{\epsilon\}$ and p in K_1, if (p', u) is in $\delta_1(p, a, \gamma)$ let $((p', \epsilon, \epsilon), u)$ be in $\delta_2((p, a, \epsilon), \epsilon, \gamma)$.

Thus D_2 guesses $h(a)$ by (1), verifies $h(a)$ on the input tape by (2), and imitates D_1 by (3). It is readily seen that $h(L(D_1)) \subseteq L(D_2)$. To see the reverse inclusion, suppose w is in $L(D_2)$. Then there exist $t_1, \ldots, t_{s+1}$ in K_2, $b_1, \ldots, b_s$ in $\Sigma_2 \cup \{\epsilon\}$, and $v_1, \ldots, v_{s+1}$ such that $t_1 = (p_0, \epsilon, \epsilon)$, t_{s+1} is in F_2, $w = b_1 \ldots b_s$, $v_1 = v_{s+1} = \epsilon$, and

$$(t_1, b_1 \ldots b_s, v_1) \vdash_{\overline{D_2}} \ldots \vdash_{\overline{D_2}} (t_{s+1}, \epsilon, v_{s+1}).$$

Let $\tau(1) < \ldots < \tau(k)$ be those integers such that $t_{\tau(j)} = (p_{j-1}, \epsilon, \epsilon)$ for some p_{j-1} in K_1. Since t_{s+1} is in F_2, $\tau(k) = s+1$. For $1 \leqq j < k$, either $t_{\tau(j)+1} = (p_{j-1}, a_j, h(a_j))$ for some a_j in Σ_1 or $t_{\tau(j)+1} = t_{\tau(j+1)} = (p_j, a_j, h(a_j))$, where $a_j = \epsilon$. From (2), it then follows that $w = b_1 \ldots b_s = h(a_1) \ldots h(a_{k-1})$ and $(p_i, a_{i+1} \ldots a_{k-1}, v_{\tau(i+1)}) \vdash_{\overline{D_1}} (p_{i+1}, a_{i+2} \ldots a_{k-1}, v_{\tau(i+2)})$ for all i, $0 \leqq i \leqq k-2$. Thus w is in $h(L(D_1))$ and $L(D_2) \subseteq h(L(D_1))$.

From the corollary to Lemma 4.2.1, and from Lemmas 4.2.2, 4.2.3, and 4.2.4 we get:

THEOREM 4.2.1: *$\mathcal{L}(\mathcal{D})$ is a full AFL for every AFA $\mathcal{D}$.*

We now consider the converse of Theorem 4.2.1. Specifically, we show that if $\mathcal{L}$ is a full AFL then there exists an AFA $\mathcal{D}$ such that $\mathcal{L} = \mathcal{L}(\mathcal{D})$. To do this we first associate with each family $\mathcal{L}_1$ of languages an AFA $\mathcal{D}(\mathcal{L}_1)$. Then we show that $\mathcal{L}(\mathcal{D}(\mathcal{L}_1))$ is the smallest full AFL containing $\mathcal{L}_1$. Thus $\mathcal{L}(\mathcal{D}(\mathcal{L}_1)) = \mathcal{L}_1$ if $\mathcal{L}_1$ is a full AFL.

Turning to the AFA $\mathcal{D}(\mathcal{L}_1)$ we have:

Notation: Let $\mathcal{L}_1 = \{L_i / i \text{ in } \mathcal{I}\}$ be a family of languages over Σ, where $\mathcal{I}$ is an index set disjoint from $\Sigma \cup \{\epsilon\}$. Then $(\Omega, \mathcal{D}(\mathcal{L}_1))$ denotes the AFA in which $\Gamma = \Sigma$, $I = \mathcal{I} \cup \Sigma \cup \{\epsilon\}$, K is the set of positive integers,[1] and f and g are defined as follows: $g(\epsilon) = \{\epsilon\}$, $g(\gamma Z) = \{Z\}$ for all γ in Σ^* and Z in Σ, $f(\gamma, Z) = \gamma Z$ for all γ in Σ^* and Z in $\Sigma \cup \{\epsilon\}$, and $f(\gamma, i) = \epsilon$ for all i in $\mathcal{I}$ and γ in L_i.

By Theorem 4.2.1, $\mathcal{L}(\mathcal{D}(\mathcal{L}_1))$ is a full AFL.

We are now ready for the converse to Theorem 4.2.1. That is, we now show that for each full AFL $\mathcal{L}$, there exists an AFA $\mathcal{D}$ such that $\mathcal{L}(\mathcal{D}) = \mathcal{L}$.

THEOREM 4.2.2: *For each family $\mathcal{L}_1$, $\mathcal{L}(\mathcal{D}(\mathcal{L}_1)) = \hat{\mathcal{F}}(\mathcal{L}_1)$.*

[1] We shall only need the fact that K is infinite.

Proof: For each i in $\mathcal{I}$ let $D_i = (\{p_0, p_1\}, \Sigma_{L_i}, \delta_i, p_0, \{p_1\})$ be the acceptor in $\mathcal{D}(\mathcal{L}_1)$ where $\delta_i(p_0, \epsilon, \epsilon) = \delta_i(p_0, \epsilon, Z) = \{(p_1, i)\}$ and $\delta_i(p_0, Z, Y) = \{(p_0, Z)\}$ for all Z in Σ_{L_i} and Y in $\Sigma_{L_i} \cup \{\epsilon\}$. Clearly $L(D_i) = L_i$. Thus L_i is in $\mathcal{L}(\mathcal{D}(\mathcal{L}_1))$. Therefore $\mathcal{L}(\mathcal{D}(\mathcal{L}_1))$ is a full AFL containing $\mathcal{L}_1$, so that $\hat{\mathcal{F}}(\mathcal{L}_1) \subseteq \mathcal{L}(\mathcal{D}(\mathcal{L}_1))$.

To complete the argument we show the reverse inclusion. Let $D = (K_1, \Sigma_1, \delta, p_0, F_1)$ be in $\mathcal{D}(\mathcal{L}_1)$. For each p and p' in K_1, let

$$L_{pp'} = \{w \text{ in } \Sigma_1^*/(p, w, \epsilon) \stackrel{*}{\vdash} (p', \epsilon, \epsilon)\}$$

and let $\alpha(p, p')$ be a new symbol in $\Sigma - \Sigma_1$. Let R be the set

$$\{\alpha(p_0, p)/p \text{ in } F_1\} \cup \\ \{\alpha(p_0, p_{i_1})\alpha(p_{i_1}, p_{i_2})\ldots\alpha(p_{i_n}, p)/n \geqq 1, p_i \text{ in } K_1, p \text{ in } F_1\}.$$

It follows readily from Lemma 3.2.1 that R is a regular set. Clearly $L(D) = \tau(R)$, where τ is the substitution defined by $\tau(\alpha(p, p')) = L_{pp'}$ for each $\alpha(p, p')$. Since $\hat{\mathcal{F}}(\mathcal{L}_1)$ is a full AFL, it follows from Theorem 3.3.1 that $\hat{\mathcal{F}}(\mathcal{L}_1)$ is closed under substitution into any regular set. Thus $L(D)$ is in $\hat{\mathcal{F}}(\mathcal{L}_1)$ if $L_{pp'}$ is in $\hat{\mathcal{F}}(\mathcal{L}_1)$ for every p and p' in K_1.

Let p and p' be given. For each i in $\mathcal{I}$, q, a, and γ such that $\gamma \neq \epsilon$ and (p', i) is in $\delta(q, a, \gamma)$ let $L_{i, q, a, \gamma}$ be the set of all words ya such that $(p, ya, \epsilon) \stackrel{*}{\vdash} (q, a, \gamma''\gamma)$ for some $\gamma''\gamma$ in L_i. Then

$$L_{pp'} = \bigcup_{i, q, a, \gamma} L_{i, q, a, \gamma} \cup Q,$$

where Q is the finite set $\{\epsilon/p = p'\} \cup \{b/(p, b, \epsilon) \vdash (p', \epsilon, \epsilon)\}$. Since there are only a finite number of $L_{i, q, a, \gamma}$ it suffices to show that each $L_{i, q, a, \gamma}$ is in $\hat{\mathcal{F}}(\mathcal{L}_1)$.

Let i, q, a, and γ be given. Let $\bar{p}'$ be a new symbol. Let $D_{i, q, a, \gamma} = (K_1 \cup \{\bar{p}'\}, \Sigma_1, \delta', p, \{\bar{p}'\})$, where δ' is the function of i, q, a, and γ defined as follows:

(1) If (q_2, u) is in $\delta(q_1, b, \gamma''')$, with u not in $\mathcal{I}$ and $(u, \gamma''') \neq (\epsilon, \epsilon)$, let (q_2, u) be in $\delta'(q_1, b, \gamma''')$.

(2) $(\bar{p}', i)$ is in $\delta'(q, a, \gamma)$.

Since (2) is the only rule of the form (q_2, u) in $\delta'(q_1, b, \gamma''')$, with u in $\mathcal{I}$, it follows that $L(D_{i, q, a, \gamma}) = L_{i, q, a, \gamma}$.

Let $\Delta = \{u \neq i/(q_2, u) \text{ in } \delta'(q_1, b, \gamma'') \text{ for some } q_1, q_2, b, \gamma''\}$. Let M (depending on p, p', i, q, a, γ) be the a-transducer $(K_2, \Delta, \Sigma_1, H, (p, \epsilon), \{(q, \gamma)\})$, where $K_2 = K_1 \times (\Delta \cup \{\epsilon\})$ and

$$H = \{((q_1, \gamma_1), u, b, (q_2, u))/u \neq \epsilon, u \neq i, (q_2, u) \text{ in } \delta'(q_1, b, \gamma_1)\} \\ \cup \{((q_1, \gamma_1), u, b, (q_2, \gamma_1))/u = \epsilon, (q_2, u) \text{ in } \delta'(q_1, b, \gamma_1)\}.$$

Then

$$M(L_i \cap \Delta^*)a = \{ya/(p, ya, \epsilon) \overset{*}{\vdash} (q, a, \gamma''\gamma), \gamma''\gamma \text{ in } L_i\} = L_{i,q,a,\gamma}.$$

Since L_i is in $\hat{\mathcal{F}}(\mathcal{L}_1)$, so is $L_i \cap \Delta^*$. By Theorem 3.2.1, $M(L_i \cap \Delta^*)$, thus $M(L_i \cap \Delta^*)\, a = L_{i,q,a,\gamma}$, is in $\hat{\mathcal{F}}(\mathcal{L}_1)$.

Combining Theorems 4.2.1 and 4.2.2 we get:

THEOREM 4.2.3: *$\mathcal{L}$ is a full AFL if and only if $\mathcal{L} = \mathcal{L}(\mathcal{D})$ for some AFA $\mathcal{D}$. Furthermore, $\mathcal{D}$ may always be assumed to be over a countably infinite state alphabet.*

We next present two characterizations for a family $\mathcal{L}$ of languages to be a full semi-AFL.

Notation: For each AFA $(\Omega, \mathcal{D})$, with $\Omega = (K, \Sigma, \Gamma, I, f, g)$, using induction extend the function f from $\Gamma^* \times I$ to $\Gamma^* \times I^+$ by letting $f(\gamma, u'u) = f(f(\gamma, u'), u)$ for each γ in Γ^*, u' in I^+, and u in I.

Thus $f(\gamma, u_1 \dots u_n)$, $n \geqq 1$, each u_i in I, is the end result of starting with γ on the storage tape and applying $u_1, \dots, u_n$ in sequence.

Def: An AFA-schema (Γ, I, f, g) is said to be *nontrivial* if there exists $n \geqq 2$ and $u_1, \dots, u_n$ in I such that $f(\epsilon, u_1) \neq \epsilon$, $f(\epsilon, u_1 \dots u_n) = \epsilon$, and $gf(\epsilon, u_1 \dots u_i) \neq \emptyset$ for each i, $1 \leqq i < n$. An AFA-schema is called *trivial* if it is not nontrivial. An AFA is said to be *nontrivial* (*trivial*) if its AFA-schema is nontrivial (trivial).

Thus, an AFA-schema is nontrivial if there is some computation whose storage starts at ϵ, becomes non-ϵ, and ultimately returns to ϵ. The condition that $gf(\epsilon, u_1 \dots u_i) \neq \emptyset$ is to guarantee that the computation does not block because of the reading function.

THEOREM 4.2.4: *The following three statements are equivalent*:

(a) *$\mathcal{L}$ is a full semi-AFL.*

(b) *$\mathcal{L} = \tilde{\mathcal{L}}(\mathcal{D})$ for some nontrivial AFA $\mathcal{D}$.*

(c) *$\mathcal{L} = \mathcal{L}_f(\mathcal{D})$ for some AFA $\mathcal{D}$.*

The proof is a variation of Theorem 4.2.3 and is left to the reader. [See Exercises 4.2.9 and 4.2.10.]

There are a number of definitions, notations, lemmas, theorems, propositions, and corollaries about AFA which are intended to hold for the languages defined by some of the following methods of acceptance: (i) simultaneous final state and return to ϵ, (ii) simultaneous final state and first return to ϵ (with all AFA nontrivial), and (iii) final state. The only methods of acceptance considered are (i), (i) and (ii), (i) and (iii), and (i), (ii), and (iii). All AFL mentioned in conjunction with the first method of acceptance are replaced by semi-AFL when with the second or third method. Rather than present each variation in explicit form, we shall place the symbols "($\sim$)", "(f)", or "($\sim, f$)" in front of case (i) when case (ii), case (iii), or cases (ii) and (iii) respectively, are also intended. (For example, Theorems 4.2.3 and 4.2.4 would now be written as "($\sim, f$) A family $\mathcal{L}$ of languages is a full AFL if and only if $\mathcal{L} = \mathcal{L}(\mathcal{D})$ for some AFA $\mathcal{D}$.") Moreover, if the statement under examination requires a proof, then the argument will just be given for case (i), with the remaining cases usually left for the formal exercises.

Theorem 4.2.3 asserts that the families of languages obtained from families of one-way nondeterministic acceptors (with acceptance by simultaneous accepting states and empty storage) coincide with full AFL. It is shown in [Ch] that those families of languages obtained from families of one-way "deterministic" acceptors coincide with the AFDL as defined in Exercise 3.2.20. In the same spirit, a characterization of those families of languages obtained from families of "two-way deterministic" acceptors appears in [AU]. At present, there is no known characterization of families of languages obtained from families of "two-way nondeterministic" acceptors.

($\sim, f$) *Open Problem*: Characterize those full AFL $\mathcal{L}$ for which there exists an AFA $\mathcal{D}$, with I finite, such that $\mathcal{L} = \mathcal{L}(\mathcal{D})$. [A characterization of those $\mathcal{L}$ for which there exists an AFA $\mathcal{D}$, with both I and $g(\Gamma^*)$ finite, such that $\mathcal{L} = \mathcal{L}(\mathcal{D})$, is given in Section 5.2.]

EXERCISE 4.2.1: Give an acceptor proof that $\hat{\text{Sub}}\,(\mathcal{L}(\mathcal{D}), \mathcal{R}) \subseteq \mathcal{L}(\mathcal{D})$.

EXERCISE 4.2.2: Let $n \geqq 0$ and $D = (K_1, \Sigma_1, \delta, q_0, F)$ be an acceptor such that for each w_1, w_2 in Σ_1^*, γ in Γ^*, q' in K_1, and q'' in F, if $(q_0, w_1w_2, \epsilon) \overset{*}{\vdash} (q', w_2, \gamma) \overset{*}{\vdash} (q'', \epsilon, \epsilon)$ then $|\gamma| \leqq n$. Prove that $L(D)$ is regular.

EXERCISE 4.2.3: Let f be such that there exists an integer n with the property that if $f(\gamma, u) \neq \emptyset$, then $|\gamma| \leqq n$. Prove that $\mathcal{L}(\mathcal{D}) = \mathcal{R}$.

EXERCISE 4.2.4: For $i = 1, 2$, let $(\Omega_i, \mathcal{D}_i)$, $\Omega_i = (K, \Sigma, \Gamma_i, I_i, f_i, g_i)$ be AFA, with $\Gamma_1 \cap \Gamma_2 = \emptyset$ and $I_1 \cap I_2 = \emptyset$. Let $(\Omega, \mathcal{D})$, $\Omega = (K, \Sigma, \Gamma_1 \cup \Gamma_2, I_1 \cup I_2, f, g)$, be the AFA where f and g are defined by $f(\gamma, u) = f_i(\gamma, u)$ and $g(\gamma) = g_i(\gamma)$ for each (γ, u) in $\Gamma_i^* \times I_i$, $i = 1, 2$. Prove that $\mathcal{L}(\mathcal{D}) = \hat{\mathcal{F}}(\mathcal{L}(\mathcal{D}_1) \cup \mathcal{L}(\mathcal{D}_2))$.

EXERCISE 4.2.5: Let $(\Omega, \mathcal{D})$, $\Omega = (K, \Sigma, \Gamma, I, f, g)$, be an AFA, with Γ finite, h a decreasing homomorphism from Γ^* into Γ^*, and $I' = I \cup \{h\}$. Let f' be the function from $\Gamma^* \times I'$ into $\Gamma^* \cup \{\emptyset\}$ defined by $f'(\gamma, u) = f(\gamma, u)$ and $f'(\gamma, h) = h(\gamma)$ for all γ in Γ^* and u in I. Consider $(\Omega', \mathcal{D}')$, where $\Omega' = (K, \Sigma, \Gamma, I', f', g)$. Prove that

(a) $\mathcal{L}(\mathcal{D}) = \mathcal{L}(\mathcal{D}')$ when $\mathcal{D} = \mathcal{D}_{\text{PDA}}$.

(b) If h is allowed to be an arbitrary homomorphism, then (a) need not hold.

(c) $\mathcal{L}(\mathcal{D}) = \mathcal{L}(\mathcal{D}')$ when $\mathcal{D} = \mathcal{D}_{\text{S}}$.

EXERCISE 4.2.6: Let $L_0 = \{wcw^R/w \text{ in } \{a, b\}^*\}$.

(a) Prove that $\mathcal{L}_{\text{lin}} = \hat{\mathcal{S}}(L_0)$ and $\hat{\mathcal{F}}(\mathcal{L}_{\text{lin}}) = \hat{\mathcal{F}}(L_0)$.

(b) Let K be an infinite set. Let ξ be a new symbol and Γ an infinite set containing ξ. Let $I = (\Gamma - \{\xi\})^*$. Consider $(\Omega, \mathcal{D})$, $\Omega = (K, \Sigma, \Gamma, I, f, g)$, where f and g are defined as follows (for all w in $(\Gamma - \{\xi\})^*$, y in $(\Gamma - \{\xi\})^+$, and Y, Z in $\Gamma - \{\xi\}$):

(i) $g(\epsilon) = \{\epsilon\}$ and $g(wZ) = g(\xi wZ) = \{Z\}$.

(ii) $f(wZ, y) = wy$, $f(\epsilon, w) = w$, $f(\xi wZ, Y) = \xi wY$, and $f(\xi Z, \epsilon) = f(Z, \epsilon) = \epsilon$.

(iii) $f(wZ, \epsilon) = f(\xi wZ, \epsilon) = \xi w$ for $w \neq \epsilon$.

Intuitively, $\mathcal{D}$ is a 1-turn (bounded) pda AFA, that is, each D in $\mathcal{D}$ makes at most one turn. [See Exercise 4.1.3.] Prove that $\hat{\mathcal{S}}(L_0) = \tilde{\mathcal{L}}(\mathcal{D})$ and $\hat{\mathcal{F}}(L_0) = \mathcal{L}(\mathcal{D})$.

EXERCISE 4.2.7: Prove that $\tilde{\mathcal{L}}(\mathcal{D}) = \{\Sigma_1, \Sigma_1 \cup \{\epsilon\}/\Sigma_1 \subseteq \Sigma\}$ and $\mathcal{L}(\mathcal{D}) = \mathcal{R}$ for each trivial AFA.

EXERCISE 4.2.8: Exhibit a trivial AFA $\mathcal{D}$ such that $\mathcal{L}_f(\mathcal{D}) \neq \mathcal{R}$ and $\mathcal{L}_f(\mathcal{D})$ is a full semi-AFL.

EXERCISE 4.2.9: Verify that (a) and (b) of Theorem 4.2.4 are equivalent.

EXERCISE 4.2.10: Verify that (a) and (c) of Theorem 4.2.4 are equivalent.

EXERCISE 4.2.11: Prove that $\mathcal{L}(\mathcal{D}) = \hat{\mathcal{F}}(\tilde{\mathcal{L}}(\mathcal{D}))$ for each AFA $\mathcal{D}$.

EXERCISE 4.2.12: Given $m > 0$, let $\mathcal{D}_m$ be the AFA of m-turn bounded pda as specified in Exercise 4.1.3.

(a) Prove that $\tilde{\mathcal{L}}(\mathcal{D}_m) \neq \mathcal{L}(\mathcal{D}_m)$.

(b) Is $\tilde{\mathcal{L}}(\mathcal{D}_m) = \mathcal{L}_f(\mathcal{D}_m)$?

EXERCISE 4.2.13: Let $n \geqq 2$ and ϱ be a function from $\{1, \ldots, n\}$ into $\{1, R\}$ such that $\varrho(1) = 1$. Let K, Σ, and Γ be infinite sets and let $\Gamma_\varrho = \Gamma \cup \{\uparrow_1, \ldots, \uparrow_n\}$, where $\uparrow_1, \ldots, \uparrow_n$ are new symbols. For each w in Γ^* let u_w be a new symbol. Let $I = \{u_w/w \text{ in } \Gamma^*\} \cup \{1, v, v', E\}$, where $1, v, v'$, and E are new symbols. Let $(\Omega_\varrho, \mathcal{D}_\varrho)$ be the AFA where $\Omega_\varrho = (K, \Sigma, \Gamma_\varrho, I, f_\varrho, g_\varrho)$ and f_ϱ and g_ϱ are the functions defined as follows (for all w in Γ^*, w' in Γ^*, a in Γ, $1 \leqq i < n$, and $1 \leqq j \leqq n$):

(i) $f_\varrho(z, 1) = z$ for all z in Γ_ϱ^*.

(ii) $f_\varrho(\epsilon, u_w) = w \uparrow_1$.

(iii) $f_\varrho(w \uparrow_1, u_{w'}) = ww' \uparrow_1$.

(iv) (α) $f_\varrho(w \uparrow_i, v) = \uparrow_{i+1} w$ if $\varrho(i) = \varrho(i+1) = 1$.
(β) $f_\varrho(w \uparrow_i, v') = w \uparrow_{i+1}$ if $\varrho(i) = 1$ and $\varrho(i+1) = R$.
(γ) $f_\varrho(\uparrow_i w, v') = w \uparrow_{i+1}$ if $\varrho(i) = \varrho(i+1) = R$.
(δ) $f_\varrho(\uparrow_i w, v) = \uparrow_{i+1} w$ if $\varrho(i) = R$ and $\varrho(i+1) = 1$.

(v) (α) $f_\varrho(w \uparrow_i aw', E) = wa \uparrow_i w'$ if $\varrho(i) = 1$.
(β) $f_\varrho(wa \uparrow_i w', E) = w \uparrow_i aw'$ if $\varrho(i) = R$.

(vi) (α) $f_\varrho(\uparrow_n aw, E) = \uparrow_n w$ if $\varrho(n) = 1$.
(β) $f_\varrho(wa \uparrow_n, E) = w \uparrow_n$ if $\varrho(n) = R$.

(vii) $f_\varrho(\uparrow_n, E) = \epsilon$.

(viii) $g_\varrho(\epsilon) = \{\epsilon\}$.

(ix) (α) $g_\varrho(w \uparrow_j) = \{\uparrow_j\}$ if $\varrho(j) = 1$.
(β) $g_\varrho(\uparrow_j w) = \{\uparrow_j\}$ if $\varrho(j) = R$.

(x) (α) $g_\varrho(w \uparrow_j aw') = \{\uparrow_j a\}$ if $\varrho(j) = 1$.
(β) $g_\varrho(wa \uparrow_j w') = \{a \uparrow_j\}$ if $\varrho(j) = R$.

Let $\mathcal{R}_\varrho$ be the family of all sets of the form

$$\{(h_1(w))^{\varrho(1)} \ldots (h_n(w))^{\varrho(n)}/w \text{ in } U\},$$

where U is in $\mathcal{R}$ and $h_1, \ldots, h_n$ are homomorphisms on Σ_U^*. Prove the following [GS6]:

(a) $\hat{\mathcal{F}}(\mathcal{R}_\varrho) \subseteq \mathcal{L}(\mathcal{D}_\varrho)$.

(b) $\mathcal{L}(\mathcal{D}_\varrho) \subseteq \hat{\mathcal{F}}(\mathcal{R}_\varrho)$.

The following terminology is used in Exercises 4.2.14–4.2.16. An *abstract family of (one-way nondeterministic) transducers* (abbreviated AFTR) is a pair $(\Omega, \mathcal{K})$, with Ω a 6-tuple $(K, \Sigma, \Gamma, I, f, g)$ as in an AFA and $\mathcal{K}$ the family of all elements (called *transducers*) $M = (K_1, \Sigma_1, \Sigma_2, \delta, p_0, F)$ having the properties: (i) K_1, Σ_1, Σ_2, p_0, and F are as in an a-transducer, and (ii) δ is a function from $K_1 \times (\Sigma_1 \cup \{\epsilon\}) \times g(\Gamma^*)$ into the finite subsets of $K_1 \times I \times \Sigma_2^*$ such that the set $G_M = \{\gamma / \delta(q, a, \gamma) \neq \emptyset$ for some q and $a\}$ is finite. For each transducer $M = (K_1, \Sigma_1, \Sigma_2, \delta, p_0, F)$ let $\vdash$ be the relation on $K_1 \times \Sigma_1^* \times \Gamma^* \times \Sigma_2^*$ defined by $(p, aw, \gamma, x) \vdash (p', w, \gamma', xy)$, a in $\Sigma_1 \cup \{\epsilon\}$, if there exist $\bar{\gamma}$ and u such that $\bar{\gamma}$ is in $g(\gamma)$, (p', u, y) is in $\delta(p, a, \bar{\gamma})$, and $f(\gamma, u) = \gamma'$. Let $T(M) = \{(w, y)/(w, y)$ in $\Sigma_1^* \times \Sigma_2^*$, $(p_0, w, \epsilon, \epsilon) \overset{*}{\vdash} (p, \epsilon, \epsilon, y)$ for some p in $F\}$ and $\mathcal{T}(\mathcal{K}) = \{T(M)/M$ in $\mathcal{K}\}$.

EXERCISE 4.2.14: Let $(\Omega, \mathcal{K})$ be an AFTR and $T \subseteq \Sigma_1^* \times \Sigma_2^*$ in $\mathcal{T}(\mathcal{K})$. If h is a homomorphism on Σ_1^*, prove that $\{(h(x), y)/(x, y)$ in $T\}$ is in $\mathcal{T}(\mathcal{K})$ [Ib2].

EXERCISE 4.2.15: Let $(\Omega, \mathcal{K})$ be an AFTR and $(\Omega, \mathcal{D})$ an AFA. Using the notation in Exercise 3.2.25, prove that $\Phi(\mathcal{L}(\mathcal{D})) = \mathcal{T}(\mathcal{K})$ [Ib2].

EXERCISE 4.2.16: Let $\mathcal{T}$ be a family of transductions. Prove that $\mathcal{T} = \mathcal{T}(\mathcal{K})$ for some AFTR $(\Omega, \mathcal{K})$ if and only if $\mathcal{T}$ is a full AFT as defined prior to Exercise 3.2.23 [Ib2].

4.3 Quasi-Realtime Acceptors

In an arbitrary acceptor there may be no integer k such that the number of consecutive ϵ-moves never exceeds k. [For consider a pda $(K_1, \Sigma_1, \delta, p_0, F)$ having $\delta(p_0, \epsilon, \epsilon) = \{(p_0, 1_\epsilon)\}$. Then $(p_0, \epsilon, \epsilon) \overset{k}{\vdash} (p_0, \epsilon, \epsilon)$ for each $k \geq 0$.] In the present section acceptors having such an integer are examined. These devices, called "quasi-realtime acceptors", are then used to characterize those (semi-) AFL containing $\{\epsilon\}$.

$(\sim, f)$ *Def*: Let k be a nonnegative integer and $\mathcal{D}$ an AFA. Let $\mathcal{D}_k^t$ be the set of all D in $\mathcal{D}$ such that $(p, \epsilon, \gamma) \overset{l}{\underset{D}{\vdash}} (p', \epsilon, \gamma')$ implies $l \leq k$. Let[1] $\mathcal{L}^t(\mathcal{D}) = \bigcup_{k=0}^{\infty} \mathcal{L}(\mathcal{D}_k^t)$. Each D in $\bigcup_{k=0}^{\infty} \mathcal{D}_k^t$ is called a *quasi-realtime acceptor*, and each L in $\mathcal{L}^t(\mathcal{D})$ is called a *quasi-realtime language*.

Thus D is in $\mathcal{D}_k^t$ if it never has more than k consecutive ϵ-moves.

[1] The remaining two cases are: $\tilde{\mathcal{L}}^t(\mathcal{D}) = \bigcup_{k=0}^{\infty} \tilde{\mathcal{L}}(\mathcal{D}_k^t)$ and $\mathcal{L}_f^t(\mathcal{D}) = \bigcup_{k=0}^{\infty} \mathcal{L}_f(\mathcal{D}_k^t)$.

Note that $\{\epsilon\}$ is in $\mathcal{L}(\mathcal{D}_0^t)$ and thus is in $\mathcal{L}^t(\mathcal{D})$. [See Exercise 4.3.1.]

EXAMPLE 4.3.1: Let Γ contain at least three elements, one of which is $\uparrow$. Let $\bar{\Gamma} = \Gamma - \{\uparrow\}$ and $I = (\{\epsilon\} \cup (\bar{\Gamma}^* \uparrow \bar{\Gamma}^*)) \times (\{\epsilon\} \cup (\bar{\Gamma}^* \uparrow \bar{\Gamma}^*))$. Let $g(\epsilon) = \{\epsilon\}$ and

$$g(w) = \{\gamma_1 \uparrow \gamma_2 / w = \gamma_3 \gamma_1 \uparrow \gamma_2 \gamma_4 \text{ for some } \gamma_3 \text{ and } \gamma_4\}$$

for all w in $\bar{\Gamma}^* \uparrow \bar{\Gamma}^*$. For each $w_1, w_2, \gamma_1, \gamma_2, \gamma_3$, and γ_4 in $\bar{\Gamma}^*$, let $f(\epsilon, (\epsilon, \epsilon)) = \epsilon$, $f(\epsilon, (\epsilon, \gamma_3 \uparrow \gamma_4)) = \gamma_3 \uparrow \gamma_4$, $f(\gamma_1 \uparrow \gamma_2, (\gamma_1 \uparrow \gamma_2, \epsilon)) = \epsilon$, and

$$f(w_1 \gamma_1 \uparrow \gamma_2 w_2, (\gamma_1 \uparrow \gamma_2, \gamma_3 \uparrow \gamma_4)) = w_1 \gamma_3 \uparrow \gamma_4 w_2.$$

The AFA $(\Omega, \mathcal{D})$ obtained is that of the (one-way) *list-storage* acceptors. It can be shown that $\mathcal{L}(\mathcal{D}_0^t) = \mathcal{L}^t(\mathcal{D})$. [See Exercise 4.3.2.] Thus $\mathcal{D}$ consists of all acceptors in which the auxiliary storage is changed by productions essentially of the form $\gamma_1 \uparrow \gamma_2 \rightarrow \gamma_3 \uparrow \gamma_4$.

We first show that $\mathcal{L}^t(\mathcal{D})$ is an AFL containing $\{\epsilon\}$.

LEMMA 4.3.1: *Sûb* $(\mathcal{R}, \mathcal{L}^t(\mathcal{D})) \subseteq \mathcal{L}^t(\mathcal{D})$.

Proof: We first note that for each D in $\mathcal{D}_k^t$ there exists D' in $\mathcal{D}_k^t$ such that $L(D') = L(D) - \{\epsilon\}$. (For let $D = (K_1, \Sigma_1, \delta_1, p_0, F_1)$ be in $\mathcal{D}_k^t$. Let $D' = (K_1', \Sigma_1, \delta_1', (p_0, 0), F_1)$ where $K_1' = K_1 \cup (K_1 \times \{0, 1, \ldots, k\})$ and δ_1' is defined as follows: For each (p, a, γ) in $K_1 \times (\Sigma_1 \cup \{\epsilon\}) \times G_D$, $\delta_1'(p, a, \gamma) = \delta_1(p, a, \gamma)$, $((p', i+1), \gamma')$ is in $\delta_1'((p, i), \epsilon, \gamma)$ for all i, $0 \leqq i < k$, if (p', γ') is in $\delta_1(p, \epsilon, \gamma)$, and (p', γ') is in $\delta_1'((p, i), a, \gamma)$ for all i, $0 \leqq i \leqq k$, if $a \neq \epsilon$ and (p', γ') is in $\delta_1(p, a, \gamma)$. Then D' is in $\mathcal{D}_k^t$ and $L(D') = L(D) - \{\epsilon\}$.)

Now let R be in $\mathcal{R}$ and τ be a substitution such that $\tau(a)$ is in $\mathcal{L}^t(\mathcal{D})$ for each a in Σ_R. Since $\mathcal{R}$ is a full AFL and $\mathcal{L}^t(\mathcal{D})$ is closed under $-\{\epsilon\}$, we may assume by Proposition 3.3.2 that τ is an ϵ-free substitution. For each a in Σ_R, there exist an integer k_a and an acceptor D_a in $\mathcal{D}_{k_a}^t$ such that $\tau(a) = L(D_a)$. Let $k = \max \{k_a / a \text{ in } \Sigma_R\}$. Repeat the construction given in Lemma 4.2.1, except that $F_2 = \bigcup_a (K_a \times F_1) \cup \{p_1 / \epsilon \text{ in } R\}$. Clearly $L(D) = \tau(R)$. Since each $L(D_a)$ is ϵ-free, no p_a is in F_a. It is readily seen that in each sequence of configurations, at most one application of rule 1 is used, followed by at least one type 2 rule, followed by at least one and at most two type 3 rules, followed by at least one type 2 rule, etc. Since each $L(D_a)$ is ϵ-free, a type 1 or type 3 rule, followed by consecutive type 2 rules, followed by a type 3 rule, must contain a non-ϵ type 2 rule. Since each D_a is in $\mathcal{D}_{k_a}^t$, there are at most $k_a \leqq k$ consecutive type 2 ϵ-rules. Thus, the maximum number of consecutive ϵ-rules that can be applied in a computation is k (type 2 rules)+2 (type 3 rules)+k (type 2 rules), i.e., $2k+2$ ϵ-rules. Thus D is in $\mathcal{D}^t_{2k+2}$, so that $L(D)$ is in $\mathcal{L}^t(\mathcal{D})$.

($\sim$, f) THEOREM 4.3.1: *For each AFA $\mathcal{D}$, $\mathcal{L}^t(\mathcal{D})$ is an AFL containing* $\{\epsilon\}$.

Proof: As noted prior to Lemma 4.3.1, $\mathcal{L}^t(\mathcal{D})$ contains $\{\epsilon\}$.

By Lemma 4.3.1 and Proposition 3.3.1, $\mathcal{L}^t(\mathcal{D})$ is closed under union, concatenation, and $+$.

Consider intersection with regular sets. Examining the proof of Lemma 4.2.2, we see that the ϵ-rules in D' are exactly those in D. Thus D' is in $\mathcal{D}^t_k$ if D is in $\mathcal{D}^t_k$.

Consider inverse homomorphism. Examining the proof of Lemma 4.2.3, we see that the ϵ-rules in D_2 arise by imitating the movement of D_1 for $h(a)$. Let D_1 be in $\mathcal{D}^t_{k_1}$. Let $k_2 = \max\{|h(a)|/a \text{ in } \Sigma_2\}$. If $h(a) = b_1 \ldots b_r$, $r \geqq 0$, each b_i in Σ_1, then b_1 is read in at most k_1+1 moves, b_1b_2 in at most $2(k_1+1)$ moves, $\ldots$, and $b_1 \ldots b_r$ in at most $r(k_1+1)$ moves. In addition, there may be k_1 ϵ-moves after b_r. Thus there are at most $(r+1)(k_1+1) \leqq (k_2+1)(k_1+1)$ consecutive ϵ-moves in D_2. Thus D_2 is in $\mathcal{D}^t_{(k_2+1)(k_1+1)}$, so that $\mathcal{L}^t(\mathcal{D})$ is closed under inverse homomorphism.

Consider ϵ-free homomorphism. Thus examine the proof of Lemma 4.2.4 for the case when D_1 is in $\mathcal{D}^t_k$ and the homomorphism is ϵ-free. Since the homomorphism is ϵ-free, an application of a type 1 rule must be followed by one or more applications of type 2 rules, that is, by an application of a non-ϵ-rule. When no further applications of type 2 rules can be used, type 3 rules must then be used. Type 3 rules can be applied at most $k+1$ consecutive times (once from (p, a, ϵ) to (p', ϵ, ϵ) and at most k times from (p', ϵ, ϵ) to $(p'', \epsilon, \epsilon)$). When type 3 rules can no longer be applied, then only a type 1 rule can be applied. Thus D_2 is in $\mathcal{D}^t_{k+2}$, so that $\mathcal{L}^t(\mathcal{D})$ is closed under ϵ-free homomorphism.

Hence $\mathcal{L}^t(\mathcal{D})$ is an AFL containing $\{\epsilon\}$.

We now consider the converse of Theorem 4.3.1. In particular, we shall find that for each family $\mathcal{L}_1$ of languages the smallest AFL containing $\mathcal{L}_1$ and $\{\epsilon\}$ is $\mathcal{L}^t(\mathcal{D}(\mathcal{L}_1))$.

($\sim$, f) LEMMA 4.3.2: *For each family $\mathcal{L}_1$ of languages,* $\mathcal{F}(\mathcal{L}_1 \cup \{\{\epsilon\}\}) = \mathcal{L}^t(\mathcal{D}(\mathcal{L}_1))$.

Proof: For each language L_i in $\mathcal{L}_1$, the acceptor D_i constructed in Theorem 4.2.2 is in $\mathcal{D}^t_1(\mathcal{L}_1)$. Thus $L_i = L(D_i)$ is in $\mathcal{L}^t(\mathcal{D}(\mathcal{L}_1))$. Since $\{\epsilon\}$ is in

$\mathcal{L}^t(\mathcal{D}(\mathcal{L}_1))$, $\mathcal{L}^t(\mathcal{D}(\mathcal{L}_1))$ is an AFL containing $\mathcal{L}_1 \cup \{\{\epsilon\}\}$. Hence $\mathcal{F}(\mathcal{L}_1 \cup \{\{\epsilon\}\}) \subseteq \mathcal{L}^t(\mathcal{D}(\mathcal{L}_1))$.

Consider the reverse inclusion. Let $D = (K_1, \Sigma_1, \delta, p_0, F_1)$ be in $\mathcal{D}_k^t(\mathcal{L}_1)$. We use the notation of Theorem 4.2.2. Since $\mathcal{F}(\mathcal{L}_1 \cup \{\{\epsilon\}\})$ is an AFL containing $\{\epsilon\}$, it is closed under substitution into any regular set. Thus we have to show that $L_{pp'}$ in $\mathcal{L}^t(\mathcal{D}(\mathcal{L}_1))$ is in $\mathcal{F}(\mathcal{L}_1 \cup \{\{\epsilon\}\})$. This, in turn, reduces to proving that $L_{i,q,a,\gamma}$ is in $\mathcal{F}(\mathcal{L}_1 \cup \{\{\epsilon\}\})$. Clearly $D_{i,q,a,\gamma}$ is in $\mathcal{D}_k^t(\mathcal{L}_1)$ for some k. Now the a-transducer M has ϵ-output only if $\delta'(q_1, \epsilon, \gamma_1) \neq \emptyset$. By hypothesis, there are at most k consecutive ϵ-moves in $D_{i,q,a,\gamma}$. Thus M has at most k consecutive moves with ϵ as output. By Theorem 3.2.2, $M(L_i \cap \Delta^*)$, thus $M(L_i \cap \Delta^*)\, a = L_{i,q,a,\gamma}$, is in $\mathcal{F}(\mathcal{L}_1 \cup \{\{\epsilon\}\})$. Hence $\mathcal{L}^t(\mathcal{D}(\mathcal{L}_1)) \subseteq \mathcal{F}(\mathcal{L}_1 \cup \{\{\epsilon\}\})$, whence equality.

Combining Theorem 4.3.1 and Lemma 4.3.2, we have

$(\sim, f)$ THEOREM 4.3.2: *A family $\mathcal{L}$ of languages is an AFL containing $\{\epsilon\}$ if and only if $\mathcal{L} = \mathcal{L}^t(\mathcal{D})$ for some AFA $\mathcal{D}$.*

Theorems 4.2.3, 4.2.4 and 4.3.2 exhibit basic connections between formal languages and AFA theory:

$(\sim, f)$ (1) A family $\mathcal{L}$ of languages is a full AFL if and only if $\mathcal{L} = \mathcal{L}(\mathcal{D})$ for some AFA $\mathcal{D}$; and

$(\sim, f)$ (2) A family $\mathcal{L}$ of languages is an AFL containing $\{\epsilon\}$ if and only if $\mathcal{L} = \mathcal{L}^t(\mathcal{D})$ for some AFA $\mathcal{D}$.

Thus AFL, semi-AFL,[1] full AFL, and full semi-AFL are natural objects to study if one is interested in families of languages defined by types of one-way acceptors.

An AFA $\mathcal{D}$ gives rise to two AFL, namely $\mathcal{L}^t(\mathcal{D})$ and $\mathcal{L}(\mathcal{D})$. It is natural to inquire into the relationship between these AFL. The following result indicates that there is a very fundamental one.

$(\sim, f)$ THEOREM 4.3.3: *For each AFA $\mathcal{D}$, $\hat{\mathcal{H}}(\mathcal{L}(\mathcal{D}_0^t)) = \hat{\mathcal{H}}(\mathcal{L}^t(\mathcal{D})) = \mathcal{L}(\mathcal{D})$.*

Proof: Since $\mathcal{L}(\mathcal{D}_0^t) \subseteq \mathcal{L}^t(\mathcal{D}) \subseteq \mathcal{L}(\mathcal{D})$ and $\mathcal{L}(\mathcal{D})$ is a full AFL, $\hat{\mathcal{H}}(\mathcal{L}(\mathcal{D}_0^t)) \subseteq \hat{\mathcal{H}}(\mathcal{L}^t(\mathcal{D})) \subseteq \hat{\mathcal{H}}(\mathcal{L}(\mathcal{D})) = \mathcal{L}(\mathcal{D})$. It thus suffices to show that $\mathcal{L}(\mathcal{D}) \subseteq \hat{\mathcal{H}}(\mathcal{L}(\mathcal{D}_0^t))$.

[1] Strictly speaking, AFL and semi-AFL containing $\{\epsilon\}$. The inclusion or exclusion of ϵ in languages is of no real consequence, by Proposition 3.1.2. For to each (semi-)AFL $\mathcal{L}_1$, the family $\{L, L \cup \{\epsilon\}/L \text{ in } \mathcal{L}_1\}$ is a (semi-)AFL containing $\{\epsilon\}$; and to each (semi-) AFL $\mathcal{L}_2$ containing $\{\epsilon\}$, the family $\{L/L \text{ in } \mathcal{L}_2, L\ \epsilon\text{-free}\}$ is an ϵ-free (semi-)AFL and coincides with the family $\{L - \{\epsilon\}/L \text{ in } \mathcal{L}_2\}$.

Let $D_1 = (K_1, \Sigma_1, \delta_1, p_0, F)$ be an acceptor in $\mathcal{D}$. Let e be a new symbol and $\Sigma_2 = \Sigma_1 \cup \{e\}$. Let $D_2 = (K_1, \Sigma_2, \delta_2, p_0, F)$ be the acceptor where δ_2 is defined by $\delta_2(q, a, \gamma) = \delta_1(q, a, \gamma)$ and $\delta_2(q, e, \gamma) = \delta_1(q, \epsilon, \gamma)$ for each q in K_1, a in Σ_1, and γ in $g(\Gamma^*)$. Clearly D_2 is in $\mathcal{D}_0^t$. Let h be the homomorphism on Σ_2^* defined by $h(a) = a$ for each a in Σ_1 and $h(e) = \epsilon$. Then $h(L(D_2)) = L(D_1)$, so that $\mathcal{L}(\mathcal{D}) \subseteq \hat{\mathcal{H}}(\mathcal{L}(\mathcal{D}_0^t))$.

We conclude the section with some examples.

EXAMPLE 4.3.2: Let $\mathcal{D} = \mathcal{D}_{\text{PDA}}$. Then $\mathcal{L}(\mathcal{D}_0^t) = \mathcal{L}_{\text{CF}}$.[1] Thus $\mathcal{L}^t(\mathcal{D}) = \mathcal{L}(\mathcal{D}) = \mathcal{L}_{\text{CF}}$.

EXAMPLE 4.3.3: It can be shown [Gr2] that $\mathcal{L}^t(\mathcal{D}_{\text{S}}) \neq \mathcal{L}(\mathcal{D}_{\text{S}})$.

EXAMPLE 4.3.4: It can be shown [Gr2] that $\mathcal{L}^t(\mathcal{D}_{\text{NES}}) \neq \mathcal{L}(\mathcal{D}_{\text{NES}})$.

Open Problem: Find reasonable conditions on a full AFL $\mathcal{L}$ which guarantee the existence of an infinite number of AFL $\mathcal{L}'$ such that $\hat{\mathcal{H}}(\mathcal{L}') = \mathcal{L}$.

Open Problem: What can be said about the family of those AFL $\mathcal{L}$ containing $\{\epsilon\}$ with the property that $\hat{\mathcal{H}}(\mathcal{L}) = \mathcal{L}_{\text{RE}}$?

EXERCISE 4.3.1: Prove that $\{\epsilon\}$ is in $\mathcal{L}(\mathcal{D}_0^t)$ for each AFA $\mathcal{D}$.

EXERCISE 4.3.2: Show that $\mathcal{L}(\mathcal{D}_0^t) = \mathcal{L}^t(\mathcal{D})$ in Example 4.3.1.

EXERCISE 4.3.3: Let $\mathcal{D}$ be an AFA. Show that $\mathcal{L}(\mathcal{D}_0^t)$ is closed under union, concatenation, $+$, intersection with regular sets, and ϵ-free homomorphism.

EXERCISE 4.3.4: Find an AFA $\mathcal{D}$ such that $\mathcal{L}(\mathcal{D}_0^t)$ is not closed under inverse homomorphism and thus is not an AFL.

EXERCISE 4.3.5: For each $D = (K_1, \Sigma_1, \delta, p_0, F)$ and $k \geqq 0$, let $L(k, D)$ be the set of all words w with the following property: There exists a sequence $(p_0, w, \epsilon) \vdash \ldots \vdash (p, \epsilon, \epsilon)$, p in F, which has at most k consecutive ϵ-moves. Prove that $\{L(k, D)/\text{all } k, D\} = \mathcal{L}^t(\mathcal{D})$.

EXERCISE 4.3.6: Prove that $\mathcal{L}^t(\mathcal{D}_{\text{C}}) = \mathcal{L}(\mathcal{D}_{\text{C}})$.

[1] See Section 2.3.

EXERCISE 4.3.7: Let $L_1 = \{wcw^R/w \text{ in } \{a, b\}^*\} \cup \{\epsilon\}$.

(a) Show that $\mathcal{S}(L_1) = \mathcal{L}_{\text{lin}}$ and $\mathcal{F}(L_1) = \mathcal{F}(\mathcal{L}_{\text{lin}})$. Using Exercise 4.2.6, infer that $\mathcal{S}(L_1) = \hat{\mathcal{S}}(\{wcw^R/w \text{ in } \{a, b\}^*\})$ and $\mathcal{F}(L_1) = \hat{\mathcal{F}}(\{wcw^R/w \text{ in } \{a, b\}^*)$.

(b) Show that $\mathcal{S}(L_1) = \tilde{\mathcal{L}}^t(\mathcal{D})$ and $\mathcal{F}(L_1) = \mathcal{L}^t(\mathcal{D})$, where $\mathcal{D}$ is the AFA in Exercise 4.2.6.

EXERCISE 4.3.8: Prove that a family $\mathcal{L}$ of languages is a semi-AFL containing $\{\epsilon\}$ if and only if $\mathcal{L} = \mathcal{L}_f^t(\mathcal{D})$ for some AFA $\mathcal{D}$.

EXERCISE 4.3.9: Prove that a family $\mathcal{L}$ of languages is a semi-AFL containing $\{\epsilon\}$ if and only if $\mathcal{L} = \tilde{\mathcal{L}}^t(\mathcal{D})$ for some nontrivial AFA $\mathcal{D}$.

EXERCISE 4.3.10: Prove that $\tilde{\mathcal{L}}^t(\mathcal{D}_{\text{PDA}}) = \mathcal{L}^t(\mathcal{D}_{\text{PDA}})$.

EXERCISE 4.3.11: Let $(\Omega, \mathcal{D})$, $\Omega = (K, \Sigma, \Gamma, I, f, g)$, have all the axioms of an AFA except condition 5 of an AFA-schema. In addition, suppose that $\Gamma = \{Z_i/i \text{ in } B\}$ where $B \subseteq N$. Let $\Gamma' = \{a, b\}$. Let $h(\epsilon) = \epsilon$, $h(Z_i) = ba^ib$ for each Z_i in Γ, and $h(Y_1 \ldots Y_r) = h(Y_1) \ldots h(Y_r)$ for all $r \geqq 1$ and each $Y_1, \ldots, Y_r$ in Γ. Let g' and f' be the functions on Γ'^* and $\Gamma'^* \times I$ defined by $g'(\gamma) = hg[h^{-1}(\gamma)]$ and $f'(\gamma, u) = hf(h^{-1}(\gamma), u)$ for each γ in Γ'^* and u in I. Prove the following:

(a) $(\Omega', \mathcal{D}')$, $\Omega' = (K, \Sigma, \Gamma', I, f', g')$, is an AFA.
(b) $\mathcal{L}(\mathcal{D}') = \mathcal{L}(\mathcal{D})$ and $\mathcal{L}^t(\mathcal{D}') = \mathcal{L}^t(\mathcal{D})$.
(c) $\tilde{\mathcal{L}}(\mathcal{D}') = \tilde{\mathcal{L}}(\mathcal{D})$ and $\tilde{\mathcal{L}}^t(\mathcal{D}') = \tilde{\mathcal{L}}^t(\mathcal{D})$.
(d) $\mathcal{L}_f(\mathcal{D}') = \mathcal{L}_f(\mathcal{D})$ and $\mathcal{L}_f^t(\mathcal{D}') = \mathcal{L}_f^t(\mathcal{D})$.

[Thus, condition 5 in the definition of an AFA schema imposes no real limitation as far as the ability to define (semi-) AFL.]

(+)4.4 Tape and Time Restrictions

We now consider acceptors which have a restriction on either the length of the auxiliary storage (tape-restriction) or on the number of steps required to process the input (time-restriction). Under appropriate hypotheses, the languages defined by the tape-restricted acceptors and those by the time-restricted acceptors each form a (semi-) AFL containing $\{\epsilon\}$.

$(\sim, f)$ *Notation*: Let T be a nondecreasing function from N into N. An acceptor $D = (K_1, \Sigma_1, \delta_1, p_0, F)$ in $\mathcal{D}$ is said to be in[1] $\mathcal{D}_{T(n)}$ if, for all w in Σ_1^*, p in K_1, and γ in Γ^*, $(p_0, w, \epsilon) \overset{*}{\vdash} (p, \epsilon, \gamma)$ implies $|\gamma| \leqq T(|w|)$. For each positive integer k, let $T_k(n) = T(kn)$ and let $\mathcal{L}_{T(n)}(\mathcal{D}) = \bigcup_{k \geqq 1} \mathcal{L}(\mathcal{D}_{T_k(n)})$.

Thus $\mathcal{D}_{T(n)}$ is the set of acceptors in $\mathcal{D}$ whose last auxiliary storage in "processing" a word w is bounded by $T(|w|)$. Actually (see Exercise 4.4.1), $\mathcal{D}_{T(n)}$ is the set of acceptors such that any auxiliary storage occurring while partially processing w is bounded by $T(|w|)$.

We now show that $\mathcal{L}_{T(n)}(\mathcal{D})$ is an AFL for each function T.

$(\sim, f)$ THEOREM 4.4.1: *For each nondecreasing function T, $\mathcal{L}_{T(n)}(\mathcal{D})$ is an AFL containing $\{\epsilon\}$.*

Proof: Clearly $\mathcal{L}_{T(n)}(\mathcal{D})$ contains $\{\epsilon\}$.

Consider substitution into the ϵ-free regular sets. That is, let R be in $\mathcal{R}_0$ and τ a substitution such that for each a in Σ_R, $\tau(a) = L(D_a)$, D_a in $\mathcal{D}_{T_{k_a}(n)}$ for some $k_a \geqq 1$. Let D be as given in Lemma 4.2.1. The ϵ-rules either simulate those in D_a or do not affect the length of the auxiliary storage. Since T is nondecreasing, and D imitates some D_a and leaves D_a only when the auxiliary storage is ϵ, D is in $\mathcal{D}_{T_k(n)}$ where $k = \max\{k_a / a \text{ in } \Sigma_1\}$. Thus $\mathcal{L}_{T(n)}(\mathcal{D})$ is closed under union, concatenation, and $+$.

Next consider intersection with regular sets as given in the proof of Lemma 4.2.2. Since $((p_0, s_0), w, \epsilon) \underset{D'}{\overset{*}{\vdash}} ((p, s), \epsilon, \gamma)$ implies $(p_0, w, \epsilon) \underset{D}{\overset{*}{\vdash}} (p, \epsilon, \gamma)$, D in $\mathcal{D}_{T_k(n)}$ implies D' is in $\mathcal{D}_{T_k(n)}$. Thus $\mathcal{L}_{T(n)}(\mathcal{D})$ is closed under intersection with regular sets.

Turning to inverse homomorphism, consider the proof in Lemma 4.2.3. Now $((p_0, \epsilon), w, \epsilon) \underset{D_2}{\overset{*}{\vdash}} ((p, x), \epsilon, \gamma)$ implies x is a final subword of $h(w)$ and $(p_0, h(w), \epsilon) \underset{D_1}{\overset{*}{\vdash}} (p, x, \gamma)$. Thus, if D_1 is in $\mathcal{D}_{T_{k_1}(n)}$ and $k_2 = \max\{1, |h(b)| / b \text{ in } \Sigma_2\}$, then

$$\begin{aligned} |\gamma| &\leqq T_{k_1}(|h(w)| - |x|) \\ &\leqq T_{k_1}(|h(w)|) \\ &\leqq T_{k_1}(k_2 |w|) = T_{k_1 k_2}(|w|). \end{aligned}$$

Hence D_2 is in $\mathcal{D}_{T_{k_1 k_2}(n)}$, i. e., $L(D_2)$ is in $\mathcal{L}_{T(n)}(\mathcal{D})$.

[1] Mathematically speaking, the symbolism $\mathcal{D}_T$ is preferred to that of $\mathcal{D}_{T(n)}$. However, in view of the numerous subscripts and superscripts attached to $\mathcal{D}$, it seems better to add the extra symbols "(n)". A similar comment holds for $\mathcal{D}^{T(n)}$, defined later in the section.

Finally, consider closure under ϵ-free homomorphism. In the proof of Lemma 4.2.4, if $((p_0, \epsilon, \epsilon), w, \epsilon) \overset{*}{\underset{D_2}{\vdash}} ((p, \epsilon, \epsilon), \epsilon, \gamma)$ then there exists w' in Σ_1^* such that $h(w') = w$ and $(p_0, w', \epsilon) \overset{*}{\underset{D_1}{\vdash}} (p, \epsilon, \gamma)$; and if $((p_0, \epsilon, \epsilon), w, \epsilon) \overset{*}{\underset{D_2}{\vdash}} ((p, a, y), \epsilon, \gamma)$, a in Σ_1, then there exists w' in Σ_1^* such that $h(w'a) = wy$, $h(w')$ is an initial subword of w, and $(p_0, w', \epsilon) \overset{*}{\underset{D_1}{\vdash}} (p, \epsilon, \gamma)$. Since h is an ϵ-free homomorphism, $|w'| \leqq |h(w')|$. If D_1 is in $\mathcal{D}_{T_{k_1}(n)}$, then

$$|\gamma| \leqq T(k_1|w'|) \leqq T(k_1|h(w')|) \leqq T(k_1\,|w|),$$

so that D_2 is also in $\mathcal{D}_{T_{k_1}(n)}$.

Hence $\mathcal{L}_{T(n)}(\mathcal{D})$ is an AFL.

Above we examined acceptors with a limitation on the total length of storage tape used. We now consider acceptors with a restriction on the total number of moves made. This should not be confused with the notion of quasi-realtime, which only places a bound on the number of consecutive ϵ-moves.

$(\sim, f)$ *Notation*: Let T be a nondecreasing function from N into N. An acceptor $D = (K_1, \Sigma_1, \delta, p_0, F)$ in $\mathcal{D}$ is said to be in $\mathcal{D}^{T(n)}$ if for all w in Σ_1^*, $(p_0, w, \epsilon) \overset{m}{\vdash} (p, \epsilon, \gamma)$ implies $m \leqq T(|w|)$. For each positive integer k, let $T_k(n) = T(kn)$ and let $\mathcal{L}^{T(n)}(\mathcal{D}) = \bigcup_{k \geqq 1} \mathcal{L}(\mathcal{D}^{T_k(n)})$.

Thus D is in $\mathcal{D}^{T(n)}$ if each word of length n can be "processed" in at most $T(n)$ moves. Actually (see Exercise 4.4.17), $\mathcal{D}^{T(n)}$ is the set of acceptors such that at most $T(n)$ moves are used in partially processing each word of length n.

Since $(p_0, w, \epsilon) \overset{m}{\vdash} (p, \epsilon, \gamma)$ implies $|w| \leqq m$, it is necessary to assume $T(n) \geqq n$ for all n to avoid the family consisting of just the empty set and $\{\epsilon\}$.

$(\sim, f)$ THEOREM 4.4.2: *Let T be a nondecreasing function such that $T(n) \geqq n$ and $T(n_1+n_2) \geqq T(n_1)+T(n_2)$ for all n, n_1, and n_2. Then $\mathcal{L}^{T(n)}(\mathcal{D})$ is an AFL containing* $\{\epsilon\}$.

Proof: Clearly $\mathcal{L}^{T(n)}\mathcal{D})$ contains $\{\epsilon\}$.

Since $T(n_1)+T(n_2) \leqq T(n_1+n_2)$, it follows that $2T(0) = T(0)+T(0) \leqq T(0)$. Hence $T(0) \leqq 0$, so that $T(0) = 0$. For each D in $\mathcal{D}^{T_k(n)}$, there exists D' in $\mathcal{D}^{T_k(n)}$ such that $L(D') = L(D)-\{\epsilon\}$. (For let $D = (K_1, \Sigma_1, \delta, p_0, F)$. Since $T(|\epsilon|) = T(0) = 0$, there is no p and γ such that $(p_0, \epsilon, \epsilon) \vdash (p, \epsilon, \gamma)$. Without loss of generality we may therefore assume that $\delta(p_0, \epsilon, \epsilon) = \emptyset$. Let q_0 be a new symbol and $D' = (K_1 \cup \{q_0\}, \Sigma_1, \delta', q_0, F)$, where $\delta'(p, a, \gamma) = \delta(p, a, \gamma)$ and $\delta'(q_0, a, \gamma) = \delta(p_0, a, \gamma)$ for each p in K_1, a in $\Sigma_1 \cup \{\epsilon\}$, and γ in $g(\Gamma^*)$. Then $L(D') = L(D)-\{\epsilon\}$ and D' is in $\mathcal{D}^{T_k(n)}$.) Also, for each D

in $\mathcal{D}^{T_k(n)}$ there exists D' in $\mathcal{D}^{T_k(n)}$ such that $L(D') = L(D) \cup \{\epsilon\}$. (For let $D = (K_1, \Sigma_1, \delta, p_0, F)$ and q_0 be a new symbol. Let $D' = (K_1 \cup \{q_0\}, \Sigma_1, \delta', q_0, F \cup \{q_0\})$, with δ' as above. Then $L(D') = L(D) \cup \{\epsilon\}$ and D' is in $\mathcal{D}^{T_k(n)}$.)

Consider Sûb $(\mathcal{R}, \mathcal{L}^{T(n)}(\mathcal{D}))$. Since $\mathcal{R}$ is a full AFL and $\mathcal{L}^{T(n)}(\mathcal{D})$ is closed under $-\{\epsilon\}$, Sûb $(\mathcal{R}, \mathcal{L}^{T(n)}(\mathcal{D}))$ = Sub $(\mathcal{R}, \mathcal{L}^{T(n)}(\mathcal{D}))$ by Proposition 3.3.2. Let R be in $\mathcal{R}$ and τ be a substitution on Σ_R^* such that for each a in Σ_R, $\tau(a) = L(D_a)$ and is ϵ-free, with D_a in $\mathcal{D}^{T_{k_a}(n)}$ for some $k_a \geqq 1$. Since $\tau(R) = \tau(R-\{\epsilon\}) \cup \{\epsilon\}$ if R contains ϵ, and since Sûb $(\mathcal{R}, \mathcal{L}^{T(n)}(\mathcal{D}))$ is closed under $\cup\{\epsilon\}$, we may assume that for no a in Σ_R is ϵ in $L(D_a) \cup R$. Let $k = \max\{k_a/a \text{ in } \Sigma_R\}$. Then $T(k_a n) \leqq T(kn)$ for all n and all k_a, since T is nondecreasing. Let $A = (K_1, \Sigma_1, \delta_1, p_1, F_1)$, $D_a = (K_a, \Sigma_a, \delta_a, p_a, F_a)$, K_2, and F_2 be as in Lemma 4.2.1. Let $D = \left(K_2, \bigcup_{a \text{ in } \Sigma_R} \Sigma_a, \delta, p_1, F_2\right)$, where δ is defined as follows for a in Σ_R and x in $(\Sigma_a \cup \{\epsilon\})$:

(1) If (p', u) is in $\delta_a(p_a, x, \epsilon)$, let $((p', \bar{p}_1), u)$ be in $\delta(p_1, x, \epsilon)$.

(2) If (p', u) is in $\delta_a(p, x, \gamma)$ for p in K_a, then $((p', \bar{s}), u)$ is in $\delta((p, \bar{s}), x, \gamma)$ for all s in K_1.

(3) For all b in Σ_R, p in F_a, and s in K_1, $((p_b, \delta_1(s, a), 1_\epsilon)$ is in $\delta\big((p, \bar{s}), \epsilon, \epsilon\big)$ and $((p_b, \bar{s}), 1_\epsilon)$ is in $\delta((p_b, s), \epsilon, \epsilon)$.

By the argument in Lemma 4.2.1, using the fact that ϵ is in no $R \cup L(D_a)$, it follows that $\tau(R) = L(D)$. For w in $\left(\bigcup_a \Sigma_a\right)^*$, if $(p_1, w, \epsilon) \mathrel{\vdash\!\frac{m}{D}} (q, \epsilon, \gamma)$, then there exist $r, w_1, \ldots, w_r$ such that $w = w_1 \ldots w_r$, each w_i in $\Sigma_{a(i)}^+$ for some $a(i)$. Now

$$
\begin{aligned}
m &\leqq 3|w| + \sum_1^r T(k_{a(i)}|w_i|) \\
&\leqq 3|w| + \sum_1^r T(k|w_i|) \\
&\leqq T(3|w|) + T(k|w|), \text{ since } T(n) \geqq n \text{ and } T(n_1) + T(n_2) \leqq T(n_1 + n_2), \\
&\leqq T((k+3)|w|).
\end{aligned}
$$

Therefore $L(D)$ is in $\mathcal{L}^{T(n)}$.

The proof of Lemma 4.2.2 introduces no new ϵ-rules. Therefore $\mathcal{L}^{T(n)}(\mathcal{D})$ is closed under intersection with regular sets.

Consider inverse homomorphism. Let D_1 in $\mathcal{D}^{T_k(n)}$, h, and D_2 be as in Lemma 4.2.3. Let $r = \max\{|h(a)|/a \text{ in } \Sigma_2\}$. Suppose $((p_0, \epsilon), w, \epsilon) \mathrel{\vdash\!\frac{m}{D_2}} ((p, \epsilon), \epsilon, \gamma)$. Then $m \leqq |w| + t$, where $(p_0, h(w), \epsilon) \mathrel{\vdash\!\frac{t}{D_1}} (p, \epsilon, \gamma)$. Since

$t \leqq T(k \mid h(w) \mid) \leqq T(kr|w|)$,

$$m \leqq |w|+T(kr|w|) \leqq T((kr+1)|w|).$$

Therefore $L(D_2)$ is in $\mathscr{L}^{T(n)}(\mathscr{D})$.

Consider ϵ-free homomorphism. Let D_1 in $\mathscr{D}^{T_k(n)}$, h an ϵ-free homomorphism, Y, and F_2 be as in Lemma 4.2.4. Let $r = \max\{|h(a)|/a \text{ in } \Sigma_1\}$ and D_2 as in Lemma 4.2.4. Suppose

$$((p_0, \epsilon, \epsilon), w, \epsilon) \mid\frac{m}{D_2}\ (q, \epsilon, \gamma).$$

Then

$$\begin{aligned} m &\leqq |w|+r|w|+T(k|w|) \\ &\leqq T((r+1+k)|w|). \end{aligned}$$

Thus D_2 is in $\mathscr{D}^{T_{r+1+k}(n)}$, so that $\mathscr{L}^{T(n)}(\mathscr{D})$ is closed under ϵ-free homomorphism. Hence $\mathscr{L}^{T(n)}(\mathscr{D})$ is an AFL.

EXERCISE 4.4.1: For each nondecreasing function T, prove that $\mathscr{D}_{T(n)}$ is the set of acceptors $(K_1, \Sigma_1, \delta, p_0, F)$ such that for each p in K_1, w and w' in Σ_1^*, and γ in Γ^*, $|\gamma| \leqq T(|w|)$ if $(p_0, w, \epsilon) \mid\frac{*}{}\ (p, w', \gamma)$.

EXERCISE 4.4.2: Let $\mathscr{D} = \mathscr{D}_{TA}$ and $T(n) = n$ for each $n \geqq 0$. Prove that

(a) $\mathscr{L}(\mathscr{D}_{T_k(n)}) = \mathscr{L}(\mathscr{D}_{T(n)})$ for each $k \geqq 1$.

(b) $\mathscr{L}(\mathscr{D}_{T(n)}) = \mathscr{L}_{ECS}$.

EXERCISE 4.4.3: Let T be a nondecreasing function. Prove that $\mathscr{L}(\mathscr{D}_{T(n)})$ has all the properties of a full AFL except inverse homomorphism.

EXERCISE 4.4.4: Let $\mathscr{D} = \mathscr{D}_{TA}$. Let L be a language in $\mathscr{L}(\mathscr{D}_{2^{4n}})-\mathscr{L}(\mathscr{D}_{2^n})$. (It is known [SHL; Sa] that L exists.)

(a) Prove that there exists L' in $\mathscr{L}(\mathscr{D}_{2^{4n}})-\mathscr{L}(\mathscr{D}_{2^n})$ such that $L' \subseteq (\Sigma_L^4)^*$.

(b) Let $\Sigma_1 = \Sigma_L \times \Sigma_L \times \Sigma_L \times \Sigma_L$. Let h be the homomorphism on Σ_1^* defined by $h((a_1, a_2, a_3, a_4)) = a_1a_2a_3a_4$ for all (a_1, a_2, a_3, a_4) in Σ_1. Prove that $h^{-1}(L')$ is not in $\mathscr{L}(\mathscr{D}_{2^{4n}})$. Thus infer that $\mathscr{L}(\mathscr{D}_{2^{4n}})$ is not closed under inverse homomorphism.

EXERCISE 4.4.5: Let $T(n) = n$. Prove that $\mathscr{H}^{\text{lin}}(\mathscr{L}^t(\mathscr{D})) = \mathscr{L}_{T(n)}(\mathscr{D})$ for each AFA $\mathscr{D}$, $\mathscr{H}^{\text{lin}}$ as in Exercise 3.4.13.

EXERCISE 4.4.6: For each nontrivial AFA $\mathscr{D}$ and each nondecreasing function T, prove that $\tilde{\mathscr{L}}_{T(n)}(\mathscr{D})$ is a semi-AFL containing $\{\epsilon\}$.

EXERCISE 4.4.7: For each AFA $\mathcal{D}$ and each nondecreasing function T, prove that $\bigcup_{k \geqq 1} \mathcal{L}_f(\mathcal{D}_{T_k(n)})$ is a semi-AFL containing $\{\epsilon\}$.

EXERCISE 4.4.8: Let $T(n)$ be a nondecreasing function. For each $D = (K_1, \Sigma_1, \delta, p_0, F)$ in $\mathcal{D}$ and $k \geqq 0$, let $L(k, D)$ be the set of all w with the following property: There exists a sequence $(p_0, w, \epsilon) = (p_0, w_0, \gamma_0) \vdash \ldots \vdash (p_r, w_r, \gamma_r) = (p_r, \epsilon, \epsilon)$, p_r in F, such that $|\gamma_i| \leqq T(k|w|)$ for each i.

(a) Is the family $\{L(k, D)/\text{all } k, D\}$ an AFL?

(b) If it is, does it coincide with $\mathcal{L}_{T(n)}(\mathcal{D})$?

EXERCISE 4.4.9: Let $T(n)$ be a nondecreasing function. For each $D = (K_1, \Sigma_1, \delta, p_0, F)$ in $\mathcal{D}$ and $k \geqq 0$, let $L(k, D)$ be the set of all w with the following property: For each sequence $(p_0, w, \epsilon) = (p_0, w_0, \gamma_0) \vdash \ldots \vdash (p_r, w_r, \gamma_r) = (p_r, \epsilon, \epsilon)$, with p_r in F, $|\gamma_i| \leqq T(k|w|)$ for each i.

(a) Is the family $\{L(k, D)/ \text{all } k, D\}$ an AFL?

(b) If it is, does it coincide with $\mathcal{L}_{T(n)}(\mathcal{D})$?

EXERCISE 4.4.10: Let T be a nondecreasing function from N into N such that $T(n) \geqq n$ for all $n \geqq n_T$, n_T some integer. Let L be a language. A homomorphism h on Σ_L^* is said to be *T-bounded on L* if there exists some $k > 0$ such that $|w| \leqq k\,T(|h(w)|)$ for all words w in L. For each family $\mathcal{L}$ of languages let $\mathcal{H}_T(\mathcal{L}) = \{h(L)/L \text{ in } \mathcal{L}, h \text{ a homomorphism } T\text{-bounded on } L\}$. Let $\mathcal{D} = \mathcal{D}_{\text{TA}}$. Prove the following [BGW]:

(a) $\mathcal{H}_T(\mathcal{L}_{\text{CS}}) = \{L(D)/D \text{ in } \mathcal{D}_{T(n)}\}$.

(b) $\mathcal{H}_T(\mathcal{U}) = \{L(D)/D \text{ deterministic, } D \text{ in } \mathcal{D}_{T(n)}\}$, where $\mathcal{U}$ is the family of deterministic lba languages.

EXERCISE 4.4.11: Find (if there are any) a full AFL $\mathcal{L}$, AFA $\mathcal{D}_1$ and $\mathcal{D}_2$, and T satisfying the hypotheses of Theorem 4.4.2 such that $\mathcal{L} = \mathcal{L}(\mathcal{D}_1) = \mathcal{L}(\mathcal{D}_2)$ and $\mathcal{L}^{T(n)}(\mathcal{D}_1) \neq \mathcal{L}^{T(n)}(\mathcal{D}_2)$.

In Exercises 4.4.12–4.4.16 let T be a nondecreasing function such that $T(n) \geqq n$ and $T(n_1+n_2) \geqq T(n_1)+T(n_2)$ for all n, n_1, and n_2.

EXERCISE 4.4.12: Show that $\mathcal{L}^{T(n)}(\mathcal{D})$ is closed under linear-decreasing homomorphism[1] for each AFA $\mathcal{D}$. [Hint: It suffices to consider a linear-decreasing homomorphism h on $(\Sigma_1 \cup \{c\})^*$, c not in Σ_1, such that $h(a) = a$ for all a in Σ_1 and $h(c) = \epsilon$.]

[1] The notion of a linear-decreasing homomorphism is defined in Exercise 3.4.13.

EXERCISE 4.4.13: For each AFA $\mathcal{D}$, $D = (K_1, \Sigma_1, \delta, p_0, F)$, and $k \geqq 0$, let $L(k, D)$ be the set of all w with the following property: There exists a sequence $(p_0, w, \epsilon) \vdash \ldots \vdash (p, \epsilon, \epsilon)$, of length r, p in F, such that $r \leqq T(k|w|)$.

(a) Is $\{L(k, D)/\text{all } k, D \text{ in } \mathcal{D}\}$ an AFL?

(b) If it is, does it coincide with $\mathcal{L}^{T(n)}(\mathcal{D})$?

EXERCISE 4.4.14: For each AFA $\mathcal{D}$, $D = (K_1, \Sigma_1, \delta, p_0, F)$ in $\mathcal{D}$, and $k \geqq 0$, let $L(k, D)$ be the set of all w with the following property: If $(p_0, w, \epsilon) \vdash \ldots \vdash (p, \epsilon, \epsilon)$, p in F, is a sequence of length r, then $r \leqq T(k|w|)$.

(a) Is $\{L(k, D)/\text{all } k, D \text{ in } \mathcal{D}\}$ an AFL?

(b) If it is, does it coincide with $\mathcal{L}^{T(n)}(\mathcal{D})$?

EXERCISE 4.4.15: Prove that $\tilde{\mathcal{L}}^{T(n)}(\mathcal{D})$ is a semi-AFL containing $\{\epsilon\}$, for every nontrivial AFA $\mathcal{D}$.

EXERCISE 4.4.16: Prove that $\mathcal{L}_f^{T(n)}(\mathcal{D})$ is a semi-AFL containing $\{\epsilon\}$ for each AFA $\mathcal{D}$.

EXERCISE 4.4.17: Prove that $\mathcal{D}^{T(n)}$ is the set of acceptors $(K_1, \Sigma_1, \delta, p_0, F)$ such that for each p in K_1, w and w' in Σ_1^*, and γ in Γ^*, $m \leqq T(|w|)$ if $(p_0, w, \epsilon) \overset{m}{\vdash} (p, w', \gamma)$.

4.5 Multitape AFA

Thus far, we have discussed acceptors in which each configuration of the auxiliary storage is a word over an auxiliary alphabet. There are numerous automata in which each configuration of the auxiliary storage is a finite sequence of words, each word over an auxiliary alphabet. Such devices are called "multitape" acceptors. While a multitape acceptor can be simulated by a single-tape acceptor, for certain purposes it is preferable not to do so. In the present section we formulate the notion of a multitape (storage) acceptor and show its relation to single-tape acceptors.

Def: A *multitape AFA* is an ordered pair $(\Omega, \mathcal{D})$, or $\mathcal{D}$ when Ω is understood, with the following properties:

(1) Ω is a 5-tuple $(K, \Sigma, \mathcal{A}, \prec, \mu)$, where

(a) $\mathcal{A}$ is a nonempty index set and $\prec$ is a simple order on $\mathcal{A}$.

(b) μ is a function on $\mathcal{A}$ such that for each α in $\mathcal{A}$, $\mu(\alpha) = (\Gamma_\alpha, I_\alpha, f_\alpha, g_\alpha)$ is an AFA-schema.

(c) K and Σ are infinite abstract sets (of *states* and *inputs*, respectively).

(2) $\mathcal{D}$ is the family of all 6-tuples $D = (K_1, \Sigma_1, \delta, q_0, F, \nu)$, called *multitape acceptors*, where

(a) $\nu = (\alpha_1, \ldots, \alpha_k)$, k finite and $k \neq 0$, α_i in $\mathcal{A}$ for each i, and $\alpha_j \prec \alpha_{j+1}$ for each j, $1 \leqq j < k$.

(b) K_1 and Σ_1 are finite subsets of K and Σ, respectively, F is a subset of K_1, and q_0 is in K_1.

(c) δ is a function from $K_1 \times (\Sigma_1 \cup \{\epsilon\}) \times (g_{\alpha_1}(\Gamma^*_{\alpha_1}) \times \ldots \times g_{\alpha_k}(\Gamma^*_{\alpha_k}))$ into the finite subsets of $K_1 \times (I_{\alpha_1} \times \ldots \times I_{\alpha_k})$ such that

$$G_D = \{(\gamma_1, \ldots, \gamma_k) / \delta(q, a, (\gamma_1, \ldots, \gamma_k)) \neq \emptyset \text{ for some } (q, a) \text{ in } K_1 \times (\Sigma_1 \cup \{\epsilon\})\}$$

is finite.

As in an AFA, K is the set of all possible "states" and Σ the set of all possible "inputs". $\mathcal{A}$ is an index set for the various types of auxiliary storage and is finite in many cases. μ is the function which assigns a type of auxiliary storage to each α in $\mathcal{A}$. Each multitape acceptor has a finite number of states and input symbols, a "start" state q_0, and a set F of "accepting" states. Each multitape acceptor has a finite number of tapes, with ν indicating the indices. The role of $\prec$ is to impose some order, just as in a cartesian product of sets there is a first coordinate, second coordinate, etc.[1] (Thus a multitape AFA is essentially an ordered collection of AFA-schema together with all multitape acceptors having only the designated AFA-schema as types of storage.) Finally, each multitape acceptor has a "move" or "transition function" δ. In order that an acceptor D be finitely specified, G_D, the subset of $g_{\alpha_1}(\Gamma^*_{\alpha_1}) \times \ldots \times g_{\alpha_k}(\Gamma^*_{\alpha_k})$ on which D operates, is required to be finite. Still to be explained is how the multitape acceptor moves with respect to its auxiliary tapes.

As in an AFA, for each α in $\mathcal{A}$ and γ in $g_\alpha(\Gamma^*_\alpha)$ there may be more than one element $u_{\alpha,\gamma}$ in I_α satisfying $f_\alpha(\gamma', u_{\alpha,\gamma}) = \gamma'$ for all γ' such that $g_\alpha(\gamma')$ contains γ. Hence we have:

Notation: For each α in $\mathcal{A}$ and each γ in $g_\alpha(\Gamma^*_\alpha)$, $1(\alpha, \gamma)$ denotes a specific element in I_α satisfying $f_\alpha(\gamma', 1(\alpha, \gamma)) = \gamma'$ for all γ' such that $g_\alpha(\gamma')$ contains γ. In case $\gamma = \epsilon$, $1(\alpha, \epsilon)$ is abbreviated 1_α.

[1] The order in which a device displays its tapes in an arbitrary multitape AFA is immaterial. However, the order does become crucial when considering certain subfamilies of multitape AFA, such as the family of nested multitape acceptors in Section 6.2.

The movement of a multitape acceptor is analogous to that of an acceptor in an AFA. In effect, the tapes are to be read and changed simultaneously via the g_α and f_α functions, with the transition function δ depending on all the tapes involved.

Def: Let $D = (K_1, \Sigma_1, \delta, q_0, F, v)$ be a multitape acceptor, with $v = (\alpha_1, \ldots, \alpha_k)$. A *configuration* is a triple $C = (q, w, (\gamma_1, \ldots, \gamma_k))$, where q is in K_1, w is in Σ_1^*, and each γ_i is in $\Gamma_{\alpha_i}^*$.

Notation: Let $\vdash$ be the relation on configurations defined as follows: For a in $\Sigma_1 \cup \{\epsilon\}$ and w in Σ_1^*, $(q, aw, (\gamma_1, \ldots, \gamma_k)) \vdash (q', w, (\gamma_1', \ldots, \gamma_k'))$ if there exist $\bar{\gamma}_1, \ldots, \bar{\gamma}_k$, each $\bar{\gamma}_i$ in $g_{\alpha_i}(\gamma_i)$, such that $(q', (u_1, \ldots, u_k))$ is in $\delta(q, a, (\bar{\gamma}_1, \ldots, \bar{\gamma}_k))$ and $f_{\alpha_i}(\gamma_i, u_i) = \gamma_i'$ for each i.

For each multitape AFA $\mathcal{D}$ and each $v = (\alpha_1, \ldots, \alpha_k)$, we shall be interested in those multitape acceptors with auxiliary storage tapes v, i. e., all multitape acceptors with the same auxiliary storage tapes.

Notation: For each multitape AFA $\mathcal{D}$ and each v, let $\mathcal{D}_v$ be the family of all $D = (K_1, \Sigma_1, \delta, q_0, F, v)$ in $\mathcal{D}$.

The language defined by a multitape acceptor is the obvious one.

$(\sim, f)$ *Notation*: For each $D = (K_1, \Sigma_1, \delta, q_0, F, v)$ in $\mathcal{D}$, let[1]

$$L(D) = \{w/(q_0, w, (\epsilon, \ldots, \epsilon)) \overset{*}{\underset{D}{\vdash}} (q, \epsilon, (\epsilon, \ldots, \epsilon)) \text{ for some } q \text{ in } F\}.$$

Let $\mathcal{L}(\mathcal{D}) = \{L(D)/D \text{ in } \mathcal{D}\}$ and for each v, $\mathcal{L}(\mathcal{D}_v) = \{L(D)/D \text{ in } \mathcal{D}_v\}$.

The companion acceptors and languages for the notion of "quasi-real-time" are the following:

$(\sim, f)$ *Def*: An acceptor D in $\mathcal{D}$ is *quasi-realtime* if there exists an integer $m \geqq 0$ such that for all configurations $C = (q, \epsilon, (\gamma_1, \ldots, \gamma_k))$ and $C' = (q', \epsilon, (\gamma_1', \ldots, \gamma_k'))$, $C \overset{n}{\vdash} C'$ implies $n \leqq m$. Let

$$\mathcal{L}^t(\mathcal{D}_v) = \{L(D)/D \text{ in } \mathcal{D}_v \text{ is quasi-realtime}\}$$

[1] The related concepts $\tilde{L}(D)$, $\tilde{\mathcal{L}}(\mathcal{D})$, $L_f(D)$, and $\mathcal{L}_f(\mathcal{D})$ are as follows: Call a multitape AFA $(\Omega, \mathcal{D})$, $\Omega = (K, \Sigma, \mathcal{A}, \prec, \mu)$, *nontrivial* if for some α in $\mathcal{A}$, $(\Gamma_\alpha, I_\alpha, f_\alpha, g_\alpha)$ is nontrivial. Define $(p, w, (\gamma_1, \ldots, \gamma_k)) \overset{-}{\underset{D}{\vdash}} (q, \epsilon, (\gamma_1', \ldots, \gamma_k'))$ if $(p, w, (\gamma_1, \ldots, \gamma_k)) \overset{*}{\underset{D}{\vdash}} (q, \epsilon, (\gamma_1', \ldots, \gamma_k'))$ in 0 or 1 steps, or in 2 or more steps with all strictly intermediate storage configurations not $(\epsilon, \ldots, \epsilon)$. For each $D = (K_1, \Sigma_1, \delta, q_0, F, v)$ in $\mathcal{D}$ let $\tilde{L}(D) = \{w/(q_0, w, (\epsilon, \ldots, \epsilon)) \overset{-}{\vdash} (q, \epsilon, (\epsilon, \ldots, \epsilon)) \text{ for some } q \text{ in } F\}$ and $\tilde{\mathcal{L}}(\mathcal{D}) = \{\tilde{L}(D)/D \text{ in } \mathcal{D}\}$. Let $L_f(D) = \{w/(q_0, w, (\epsilon, \ldots, \epsilon)) \overset{*}{\vdash} (q, \epsilon, (\gamma_1, \ldots, \gamma_k)) \text{ for some } q \text{ in } F\}$ and $\mathcal{L}_f(\mathcal{D}) = \{L_f(D)/D \text{ in } \mathcal{D}\}$.

and

$$\mathcal{L}^t(\mathcal{D}) = \{L(D)/D \text{ in } \mathcal{D} \text{ is quasi-realtime}\}.$$

Note (see Exercise 4.5.1) that $(\sim, f)$ $\mathcal{L}(\mathcal{D}) = \bigcup_{\text{all } \nu} \mathcal{L}(\mathcal{D}_\nu)$ and $\mathcal{L}^t(\mathcal{D}) = \bigcup_{\text{all } \nu} \mathcal{L}^t(\mathcal{D}_\nu)$ for each multitape AFA $\mathcal{D}$.

If $\nu_1 = (\alpha_1, \ldots, \alpha_k)$, $\nu_2 = (\beta_1, \ldots, \beta_l)$, $A = \{\alpha_1, \ldots, \alpha_k\}$, $B = \{\beta_1, \ldots, \beta_l\}$, and $A \subseteq B$, then $\mathcal{D}_{\nu_1}$ can be "embedded" in $\mathcal{D}_{\nu_2}$ in the following sense: Each D in $\mathcal{D}_{\nu_1}$ may be identified with the multitape acceptor D' in $\mathcal{D}_{\nu_2}$ which consists of (i) the tapes of D, and (ii) the tapes in $B - A$, with ϵ on them, acting under the identity instruction (i. e., 1_{β_i}). D' behaves "essentially" the same as D, is quasi-realtime if and only if D is, and is such that $L(D') = L(D)$. Thus $(\sim, f)$ $\mathcal{L}(\mathcal{D}_{\nu_1}) \subseteq \mathcal{L}(\mathcal{D}_{\nu_2})$ and $\mathcal{L}^t(\mathcal{D}_{\nu_1}) \subseteq \mathcal{L}^t(\mathcal{D}_{\nu_2})$. In particular, if $\mathcal{A}$ is finite, say $\mathcal{A} = \{\alpha_1, \ldots, \alpha_k\}$, then $\mathcal{L}(\mathcal{D}) = \mathcal{L}(\mathcal{D}_\nu)$ and $\mathcal{L}^t(\mathcal{D}) = \mathcal{L}^t(\mathcal{D}_\nu)$ where $\nu = (\alpha_1, \ldots, \alpha_k)$. A single-tape AFA, i. e., a multitape AFA with just one tape, is identified with the obvious AFA. That is, the multitape AFA $(\Omega, \mathcal{D})$, where $\Omega = (K, \Sigma, \mathcal{A}, \prec, \mu)$, $\mathcal{A} = \{\alpha_1\}$, and $\mathcal{D} = \{D = (K_1, \Sigma_1, \delta, q_0, F, \nu)/\text{all } D\}$, is identified with the AFA $(\Omega', \mathcal{D}')$, where $\Omega' = (K, \Sigma, \Gamma, I, f, g)$, $\mathcal{D}' = \{D' = (K_1, \Sigma_1, \delta, q_0, F)/\text{all } D'\}$ and $\mu(\alpha_1) = (\Gamma, I, f, g)$.

EXAMPLE 4.5.1: Let $\mathcal{A} = \{\alpha_1, \alpha_2\}$ and $\mu(\alpha_1) = \mu(\alpha_2)$ be a pushdown schema. Then $\mathcal{L}(\mathcal{D})$ is the family of all languages accepted by 2-pushdown tape acceptors, i. e., those acceptors with exactly two storage tapes, each a pushdown. It will be shown in Lemma 4.7.1 that $\mathcal{L}(\mathcal{D}) = \mathcal{L}_{\text{RE}}$.

Clearly multitape AFA are not AFA, although AFA may be regarded as a special case of multitape AFA. However, as is now shown, multitape AFA are equivalent (from the point of view of sets accepted) to AFA.

$(\sim, f)$ LEMMA 4.5.1: *For each multitape AFA $(\Omega, \mathcal{D})$, there exists an AFA $(\bar{\Omega}, \bar{\mathcal{D}})$ such that $\mathcal{L}(\bar{\mathcal{D}}) = \mathcal{L}(\mathcal{D})$ and $\mathcal{L}^t(\bar{\mathcal{D}}) = \mathcal{L}^t(\mathcal{D})$.*

Proof: Intuitively, $\bar{\Omega}$ is to be the AFA obtained by taking the tapes of each finite set of tapes and juxtaposing them in the obvious order, with appropriate separators. Formally, let $\Omega = (K, \Sigma, \mathcal{A}, \prec, \mu)$ and $\mu(\alpha) = (\Gamma_\alpha, I_\alpha, f_\alpha, g_\alpha)$ for each α. Let ξ be a new symbol not in $\bigcup_{\alpha \text{ in } \mathcal{A}} \Gamma_\alpha$. For each $\nu = (\alpha_1, \ldots, \alpha_k)$ and for each $(u_1, \ldots, u_k)$ in $I_{\alpha_1} \times \ldots \times I_{\alpha_k}$, let $\sigma(\nu)$ and $\sigma(\nu, (u_1, \ldots, u_k))$ be new symbols. Let

$$\bar{\Gamma} = \bigcup_{\alpha \text{ in } \mathcal{A}} \Gamma_\alpha \cup \{\xi\} \cup \{\sigma(\nu)/\text{all } \nu\}$$

and

$$\bar{I} = \{\sigma(v, (u_1, \ldots, u_k))/\text{all } v \text{ and } (u_1, \ldots, u_k)\} \cup \{\sigma(v)/\text{all } v\} \cup \{\epsilon\}.$$

For $(\gamma_1, \ldots, \gamma_k)$ in $\Gamma^*_{\alpha_1} \times \ldots \times \Gamma^*_{\alpha_k}$ and $v = (\alpha_1, \ldots, \alpha_k)$, let

$$\bar{g}(\sigma(v)\xi\gamma_1\xi \ldots \gamma_k) = \sigma(v)\xi g_{\alpha_1}(\gamma_1)\, \xi \ldots g_{\alpha_k}(\gamma_k).$$

Let $\bar{g}(\epsilon) = \{\epsilon\}$. For each $v = (\alpha_1, \ldots, \alpha_k)$, each $(u_1, \ldots, u_k)$ in $I_{\alpha_1} \times \ldots \times I_{\alpha_k}$, and each $(\gamma_1, \ldots, \gamma_k)$ in $\Gamma^*_{\alpha_1} \times \ldots \times \Gamma^*_{\alpha_k}$, let $\bar{f}(\epsilon, \sigma(v)) = \sigma(v)\xi^k$, $\bar{f}(\sigma(v)\xi^k, \epsilon) = \epsilon$, $\bar{f}(\epsilon, \epsilon) = \epsilon$, and

$$\bar{f}\big(\sigma(v)\xi\gamma_1\xi \ldots \gamma_k, \sigma(v, (u_1, \ldots, u_k))\big) = \sigma(v)\, \xi\bar{\gamma}_1\xi \ldots \bar{\gamma}_k,$$

where $\bar{\gamma}_i = f_{\alpha_i}(\gamma_i, u_i)$ for each i.

We first note the following (for $v = (\alpha_1, \ldots, \alpha_k)$):

(1) $\bar{f}\big(\sigma(v)\, \xi\gamma_1 \ldots \xi\gamma_k, \sigma(v, (1(\alpha_1, \gamma_1'), \ldots, 1(\alpha_k, \gamma_k')))\big) = \sigma(v)\, \xi\gamma_1 \ldots \xi\gamma_k$ for all $\sigma(v)\, \xi\gamma_1 \ldots \xi\gamma_k$ such that $\bar{g}(\sigma(v)\, \xi\gamma_1 \ldots \xi\gamma_k)$ contains $\sigma(v)\, \xi\gamma_1' \ldots \xi\gamma_k'$.

(2) For all γ, $\bar{f}(\gamma, \sigma(v))$ is in $\{\sigma(v), \xi\}^* \cup \{\emptyset\}$ and $\bar{f}(\gamma, \epsilon)$ is either ϵ or $\emptyset$. For each $(u_1, \ldots, u_k)$ in $I_{\alpha_1} \times \ldots \times I_{\alpha_k}$ and $\Gamma_{u_1}, \ldots, \Gamma_{u_k}$ as in (5) of the definition of an AFA-schema, $\Gamma_{\sigma(v,(u_1, \ldots, u_k))} = \bigcup_{i=1}^{k} \Gamma_{u_i} \cup \{\sigma(v), \xi\}$. Hence $(\bar{\Gamma}, \bar{I}, \bar{f}, \bar{g})$ is an AFA-schema.

Consider $\mathscr{L}(\bar{\mathscr{D}})$ and $\mathscr{L}^t(\bar{\mathscr{D}})$. Suppose that $D = (K_1, \Sigma_1, \delta, q_0, F, v)$ is an arbitrary multitape acceptor in $\mathscr{D}$. Let $\bar{q}_0$ and $\bar{r}_0$ be new symbols in K and $\bar{D} = (\bar{K}_1, \Sigma_1, \bar{\delta}, \bar{q}_0, \{\bar{r}_0\})$ the acceptor in $\bar{\mathscr{D}}$, where $\bar{K}_1 = K_1 \cup \{\bar{q}_0, \bar{r}_0\}$ and $\bar{\delta}$ is defined as follows:

(3) $\big(q', \sigma(v, (u_1, \ldots, u_k))\big)$ is in $\bar{\delta}(q, a, \sigma(v)\, \xi\gamma_1\xi \ldots \gamma_k)$ if $(q', (u_1, \ldots, u_k))$ is in $\delta(q, a, (\gamma_1, \ldots, \gamma_k))$.

(4) $(\bar{r}_0, \epsilon)$ is in $\bar{\delta}(p, \epsilon, \sigma(v)\xi^k)$ if p is in F.

(5) $\bar{\delta}(\bar{q}_0, \epsilon, \epsilon) = \{(q_0, \sigma(v))\}$.

Clearly $L(\bar{D}) = L(D)$ and $\bar{D}$ is quasi-realtime if D is quasi-realtime. Thus, $\mathscr{L}(\mathscr{D}) \subseteq \mathscr{L}(\bar{\mathscr{D}})$ and $\mathscr{L}^t(\mathscr{D}) \subseteq \mathscr{L}^t(\bar{\mathscr{D}})$.

Now let $\bar{D} = (\bar{K}_1, \Sigma_1, \bar{\delta}, \bar{q}_0, \bar{F})$ be in $\bar{\mathscr{D}}$. Note that many different $\sigma(v)$ might appear in $\bar{D}$. Let

$$Q = \{v/(\bar{q}', \sigma(v)) \text{ in } \bar{\delta}(\bar{q}, a, \epsilon) \text{ for some } \bar{q} \text{ and } a\}.$$

We may assume that if $\big(\bar{q}', \sigma(v_1, (u_1, \ldots, u_k))\big)$ is in $\bar{\delta}(\bar{q}, a, \sigma(v_2)\, \xi\gamma_1\xi \ldots \gamma_k)$, then $v_1 = v_2 = (\alpha_1, \ldots, \alpha_k)$, where u_i is in I_{α_i} and γ_i is in $g_{i\alpha}(\Gamma^*_{\alpha_i})$ for each i, $1 \leqq i \leqq k$, and v_1 is in Q. (For no other type of rule can be applied in the $\vdash$ relation.) Since Q is finite, there exists some $v_0 = (\alpha_1, \ldots, \alpha_n)$ such that if v is in Q, then $v = (\alpha_{j_1}, \ldots, \alpha_{j_k})$ for some $1 \leqq j_1 < \ldots < j_k \leqq n$. Let

$K_1 = \bar{K}_1 \times (Q \cup \{\epsilon\})$. Let $D = (K_1, \Sigma_1, \delta, (\bar{q}_0, \epsilon), \bar{F} \times \{\epsilon\}, v_0)$ be the acceptor in $\mathcal{D}$, where δ is defined as follows (for arbitrary $v = (\alpha_{j_1}, \ldots, \alpha_{j_k})$):

(6) $((\bar{q}', \epsilon), (1_{\alpha_1}, \ldots, 1_{\alpha_n}))$ is in $\delta((\bar{q}, \epsilon), a, (\epsilon, \ldots, \epsilon))$ if $(\bar{q}', \epsilon)$ is in $\bar{\delta}(\bar{q}, a, \epsilon)$.

(7) $((\bar{q}', \epsilon), (1_{\alpha_1}, \ldots, 1_{\alpha_n}))$ is in $\delta((\bar{q}, v), a, (\epsilon, \ldots, \epsilon))$ if $(\bar{q}', \epsilon)$ is in $\bar{\delta}(\bar{q}, a, \sigma(v)\xi^k)$.

(8) $((\bar{q}', v), (1_{\alpha_1}, \ldots, 1_{\alpha_n}))$ is in $\delta((\bar{q}, \epsilon), a, (\epsilon, \ldots, \epsilon))$ if $(\bar{q}', \sigma(v))$ is in $\bar{\delta}(\bar{q}, a, \epsilon)$.

(9) $((\bar{q}', v), (u_1', \ldots, u_n'))$ is in $\delta((\bar{q}, v), a, (\gamma_1', \ldots, \gamma_n'))$ if $(\bar{q}', \sigma(v, (u_{j_1}, \ldots, u_{j_k})))$ is in $\bar{\delta}(\bar{q}, a, \sigma(v)\, \xi\gamma_{j_1}\xi \ldots \gamma_{j_k})$, where γ_{j_s} is in $g_{\alpha_{j_s}}(\Gamma^*_{\alpha_{j_s}})$ for each s, $u_i' = u_{j_t}$ and $\gamma_i' = \gamma_{j_t}$ if $i = j_t$, and $u_i' = 1_{\alpha_i}$ and $\gamma_i' = \epsilon$ if i is not in $\{j_1, \ldots, j_k\}$.

It is readily seen that $L(D) = L(\bar{D})$ and D is quasi-realtime if $\bar{D}$ is quasi-realtime. Thus $\mathcal{L}(\bar{\mathcal{D}}) \subseteq \mathcal{L}(\mathcal{D})$ and $\mathcal{L}^t(\bar{\mathcal{D}}) \subseteq \mathcal{L}^t(\mathcal{D})$, whence equality in both cases.

Thus, considered as families of recognition devices, multitape AFA are no more powerful than AFA.

Since each $\mathcal{D}_v$ may be regarded as a multitape AFA, we have:

$(\sim, f)$ COROLLARY: *For each multitape AFA $\mathcal{D}$ and each v, there exists an AFA $(\bar{\Omega}, \mathcal{D})$ such that $\mathcal{L}(\bar{\mathcal{D}}) = \mathcal{L}(\mathcal{D}_v)$ and $\mathcal{L}^t(\bar{\mathcal{D}}) = \mathcal{L}^t(\mathcal{D}_v)$.*

From Lemma 4.5.1 and Theorems 4.2.1, 4.3.1 and 4.3.3, we get:

$(\sim, f)$ THEOREM 4.5.1: *For each multitape AFA $\mathcal{D}$, $\mathcal{L}^t(\mathcal{D})$ and $\mathcal{L}(\mathcal{D})$ are AFL containing $\{\epsilon\}$, with $\mathcal{L}(\mathcal{D})$ being full. Furthermore, $\hat{\mathcal{H}}(\mathcal{L}^t(\mathcal{D})) = \mathcal{L}(\mathcal{D})$.*

Since each $\mathcal{D}_v$ may be regarded as a multitape AFA, we have:

$(\sim, f)$ COROLLARY: *For each multitape AFA $\mathcal{D}$ and each v, $\mathcal{L}^t(\mathcal{D}_v)$ and $\mathcal{L}(\mathcal{D}_v)$ are AFL containing $\{\epsilon\}$, with $\mathcal{L}(\mathcal{D}_v)$ being full. Furthermore, $\hat{\mathcal{H}}(\mathcal{L}^t(\mathcal{D}_v)) = \mathcal{L}(\mathcal{D}_v)$.*

EXAMPLE 4.5.2: Let $\Omega_C = (K, \Sigma, \Gamma, I, f, g)$. For each positive integer n let $\Omega(n) = (K, \Sigma, \mathcal{A}(n), \prec_n, \mu_n)$, where $\mathcal{A}(n) = \{1, \ldots, n\}$ and $\mu_n(i) = (\Gamma, I, f, g)$ for each i. Then $(\Omega(n), \mathcal{D}(n))$ is called the *multitape AFA of n-counters*. For each n, let $\mathcal{C}_n = \mathcal{L}^t(\mathcal{D}(n))$, so that $\mathcal{C}_n \subseteq \mathcal{C}_{n+1}$. Let $L_n = \{a_1^{i_1} \ldots a_n^{i_n} c\, a_n^{i_n} \ldots a_1^{i_1} / \text{each } i_j \geqq 1\}$ for each n, where $a_1, \ldots, a_n, c$ are distinct symbols. Clearly L_n is in $\mathcal{C}_n$. (See Exercise 4.5.2.) We shall show that L_{n+1} is not in $\mathcal{C}_n$, so that $\mathcal{C}_n \subsetneqq \mathcal{C}_{n+1}$.

Let n be fixed and suppose that L_{n+1} is in $\mathcal{C}_n$. Then there exist $k \geqq 0$ and a multitape acceptor[1] $D = (K_1, \Sigma_1, \delta, p_0, F)$ in $\mathcal{D}_k^t(n)$ such that $L_{n+1} = L(D)$.

[1] We shall omit the component v in the description of a specific acceptor whenever v is obvious.

Without loss of generality, we may assume that each instruction in (Γ, I, f, g) increases the length of the auxiliary storage by at most one. Let $r = \#(K_1)$. Let s_0 be a positive integer such that $s_0^{n+1} > r((k+1)(n+1)s_0+k)^n$. The integer s_0 exists since, for fixed n, k, and r, the function s^{n+1} grows faster than the function $r((k+1)(n+1)s+k)^n$. Let $U(s_0) = \{a_1^{i_1} \ldots a_{n+1}^{i_{n+1}}/1 \leq i_j \leq s_0$ for each $j\}$. For each word w in $U(s_0)$, wcw^R is in $L(D)$. Hence there exist p_w, p'_w, and γ_w such that

$$(p_0, wcw^R, (\epsilon, \ldots, \epsilon)) \overset{*}{\vdash} (p_w, cw^R, \gamma_w) \overset{*}{\vdash} (p'_w, \epsilon, (\epsilon, \ldots, \epsilon)),$$

with p'_w in F. Note that $(p_{w_1}, \gamma_{w_1}) \neq (p_{w_2}, \gamma_{w_2})$ for $w_1 \neq w_2$. [For suppose $(p_{w_1}, \gamma_{w_1}) = (p_{w_2}, \gamma_{w_2})$ for some $w_1 \neq w_2$. Then $(p_0, w_1cw_2^R, (\epsilon, \ldots, \epsilon)) \overset{*}{\vdash} (p_{w_1}, cw_2^R, \gamma_{w_1}) = (p_{w_2}, cw_2^R, \gamma_{w_2}) \overset{*}{\vdash} (p'_{w_2}, \epsilon, (\epsilon, \ldots, \epsilon))$, so that $w_1cw_2^R$ is in $L(D)$, a contradiction.] Since there are s_0^{n+1} words in $U(s_0)$, there are s_0^{n+1} different pairs (p_w, γ_w). We shall show that there are at most $r((k+1)(n+1)s_0+k)^n$ different (p_w, γ_w), thereby effecting a contradiction.

To see this let w be in $U(s_0)$. Then $(p_0, w, (\epsilon, \ldots, \epsilon)) \overset{*}{\vdash} (p_w, \epsilon, \gamma_w)$, with γ_w of the form $(a^{w(1)}, \ldots, a^{w(n)})$. Since $|w| \leq (n+1)s_0$, since there are at most k consecutive ϵ-moves, and since each instruction increases the length of each auxiliary storage tape by at most one, it follows that $w(i) \leq (k+1)(n+1)s_0+k$ for each word w and each i. Hence there are at most $((k+1)(n+1)s_0+k)^n$ different γ_w and thus at most $r((k+1)(n+1)s_0+k)^n$ different pairs (p_w, γ_w).

Open Problem: Let $\mathcal{D}$ be the AFA of 1-stack counters.[1] By a long, complicated argument, it can be shown [GR2] that $\mathcal{L}^t(\mathcal{D}) = \mathcal{L}(\mathcal{D})$. Find a reasonably simple proof of this fact.

EXERCISE 4.5.1: Prove that $\mathcal{L}(\mathcal{D}) = \bigcup_{\text{all } \nu} \mathcal{L}(\mathcal{D}_\nu)$ and $\mathcal{L}^t(\mathcal{D}) = \bigcup_{\text{all } \nu} \mathcal{L}^t(\mathcal{D}_\nu)$ for each multitape AFA $\mathcal{D}$.

EXERCISE 4.5.2: Prove that L_n in Example 4.5.2 is in $\mathcal{C}_n$.

EXERCISE 4.5.3: Let $L = \{wcw^R/w \text{ in } \{a, b\}^*\}$.

(a) Prove that L is not in $\bigcup_{n \geq 1} \mathcal{C}_n$.

(b) Using (a) and Exercise 4.3.6, show that L is in $\mathcal{L}_{\text{CF}} - \mathcal{L}_{\text{C}}$.

EXERCISE 4.5.4: Let $\Omega = (K, \Sigma, \Gamma, I, f, g)$, where $\Gamma = \{a, ⥣\}$, $I = \{a, a^{\text{E}}, a^{®}, a^{\text{L}}, a^{\text{B}}, 0\}$ and f and g are defined as follows (for all x, y in a^*): $g(\epsilon) = \{\epsilon\}$,

[1] See Exercise 4.5.4 for the definition of a 1-stack counter.

$g(x\uparrow y) = \{a\}$ if $xy \neq \epsilon$, $f(\epsilon, 0) = \epsilon$, $f(x\uparrow y, 0) = x\uparrow y$, $f(\epsilon, a) = a\uparrow$, $f(xa\uparrow, a) = xaa\uparrow$, $f(xaa\uparrow, a^{E}) = xa\uparrow$, $f(a\uparrow, a^{E}) = \epsilon$, $f(xa\uparrow y, a^{L}) = x\uparrow ay$, $f(x\uparrow ay, a^{®}) = xa\uparrow y$, and $f(\uparrow ax, a^{B}) = a\uparrow x$. Then $(\Omega, \mathcal{D})$ is one particular AFA formulation for the family of *1-stack counters.* (The instruction a means add a to the stack if at the right end, a^{E} means erase a from the stack if at the right end, a^{L} means move left over a, $a^{®}$ means move right over a, and a^{B} means move right over a if the pointer is at the left end of the stack.) For each positive integer n let $(\Omega(n), \mathcal{D}(n))$ be the AFA of *n-stack counters.* That is, $\Omega(n) = (K, \Sigma, \mathcal{A}(n), \prec_n, \mu_n)$, where $\mathcal{A}(n) = \{1, \ldots, n\}$ and $\mu_n(i)$ is a 1-stack counter AFA. For each n, let $\mathcal{S}_n = \mathcal{L}^t(\mathcal{D}(n))$. Prove that $\mathcal{S}_n \subsetneq \mathcal{S}_{n+1}$ for each n [BGi]. [Hint: Show that $L_{n+1} = \{wcw^R/w \text{ in } U_{n+1}\}$ is in $\mathcal{S}_{n+1} - \mathcal{S}_n$, where $U_{n+1} = \{a^{k_1}b^{m_1}\ldots a^{k_{n+1}}b^{m_{n+1}}/1 \leqq m_j \leqq k_j \text{ for each } j\}$.]

EXERCISE 4.5.5: Using the symbolism in Exercise 4.5.4 prove the following [BGi]:

(a) For each $n \geqq 1$, L_n is in $\mathcal{C}_{2n} - \mathcal{S}_n$, where $L_n = \{wcw^R/w \text{ in } U_n\}$ and $U_n = \{a^{i_1}ba^{i_2}\ldots ba^{i_{2n}}/\text{each } i_j \geqq 1\}$.

(b) $\mathcal{S}_n \subseteq \mathcal{C}_{2n}$ for each n.

(c) $\bigcup_{i \geqq 1} \mathcal{S}_i = \bigcup_{j \geqq 1} \mathcal{C}_j$.

(d) There are no i and j such that $\mathcal{S}_i = \mathcal{C}_j$.

(e) For each k and m, Sub $(\mathcal{C}_k, \mathcal{C}_k) \subseteq \mathcal{C}_m$ is false.

(f) For each k and m, Sub $(\mathcal{S}_k, \mathcal{S}_k) \subseteq \mathcal{S}_m$ is false.

EXERCISE 4.5.6: Prove that for each nontrivial multitape AFA $\mathcal{D}$, there exists a nontrivial AFA $\overline{\mathcal{D}}$ such that $\tilde{\mathcal{L}}(\overline{\mathcal{D}}) = \tilde{\mathcal{L}}(\mathcal{D})$.

EXERCISE 4.5.7: Prove that for each multitape AFA $\mathcal{D}$, there exists an AFA $\overline{\mathcal{D}}$ such that $\mathcal{L}_f(\overline{\mathcal{D}}) = \mathcal{L}_f(\mathcal{D})$.

The following terminology is used in Exercises 4.5.8–4.5.10. A *structured storage abstract family of acceptors*, abbreviated SS-AFA, is an ordered pair $(\Omega, \mathcal{D})$ with the following properties:

(a) Ω is a 7-tuple $(K, \Sigma, S, \Gamma, I, f, g)$, where (i) K and Σ are infinite abstract sets; (ii) S, Γ, and I are abstract sets (of *storage space elements*, *storage symbols*, and *instructions*, respectively), with S countable; (iii) f is a mapping from $\tilde{\Gamma}^S \times I$ into $\tilde{\Gamma}^S \cup \{\emptyset\}$, $\tilde{\Gamma}^S$ denoting the set of all functions each of which maps some finite subset of S into Γ; (iv) g is a mapping from $\tilde{\Gamma}^S$ into the finite subsets of $\tilde{\Gamma}^S$ such that $g(\tilde{\epsilon}) = \{\tilde{\epsilon}\}$, and $\tilde{\epsilon}$ is in $g(\tau)$ implies

$\tau = \tilde{\epsilon}$, $\tilde{\epsilon}$ denoting the unique[1] function from $\emptyset$ to Γ; (v) for each τ in $g(\widetilde{\Gamma^S})$, there is an element 1_τ in I satisfying $f(\tau', 1_\tau) = \tau'$ for all τ' such that $g(\tau')$ contains τ; and (vi) for each u in I, there exists a finite set $\Gamma_u \subseteq \Gamma$ with the property that if $\Gamma_1 \subseteq \Gamma$, τ is in $\widetilde{\Gamma_1^S}$, and $f(\tau, u) \neq \emptyset$, then $f(\tau, u)$ is in $(\widetilde{\Gamma_1 \cup \Gamma_u})^S$.

(b) $\mathcal{D}$ is the family of all elements (called *SS-acceptors*) $D = (K_1, \Sigma_1, \delta, q_0, F)$, where (i) K_1 and Σ_1 are finite subsets of K and Σ respectively, F is a subset of K_1, and q_0 is in K_1; and (ii) δ is a mapping from $K_1 \times (\Sigma_1 \cup \{\epsilon\}) \times g(\widetilde{\Gamma^S})$ into the finite subsets of $K_1 \times I$ such that the set $G_D = \{\tau / \delta(q, a, \tau) \neq \emptyset$ for some q and $a\}$ is finite.

Let $\vdash$ be the relation on $K_1 \times \Sigma_1^* \times \widetilde{\Gamma^S}$ defined as follows: For a in $\Sigma_1 \cup \{\epsilon\}$, write $(p, aw, \tau) \vdash (p', w, \tau')$ if there exist $\bar{\tau}$ and u such that $\bar{\tau}$ is in $g(\tau)$, (p', u) is in $\delta(p, a, \bar{\tau})$, and $f(\tau, u) = \tau'$. For each $D = (K_1, \Sigma_1, \delta, q_0, F)$ let $L(D) = \{w \text{ in } \Sigma_1^* / (q_0, w, \epsilon) \overset{*}{\vdash} (q, \epsilon, \epsilon)$ for some q in $F\}$ and let $\mathcal{L}(\mathcal{D}) = \{L(D)/D \text{ in } \mathcal{D}\}$. For each integer k, let $\mathcal{D}_k^t$ be the set of all D in $\mathcal{D}$ such that $(p, \epsilon, \tau) \overset{m}{\vdash} (p', \epsilon, \tau')$ implies $m \leq k$. Let $\mathcal{L}^t(\mathcal{D}) = \bigcup_{k=0}^{\infty} \{L(D)/D \text{ in } \mathcal{D}_k^t\}$.

EXERCISE 4.5.8: Prove that for each AFA $(\Omega, \mathcal{D})$ there exists an SS-AFA $(\Omega', \mathcal{D}')$ such that $\mathcal{L}(\mathcal{D}') = \mathcal{L}(\mathcal{D})$ and $\mathcal{L}^t(\mathcal{D}') = \mathcal{L}^t(\mathcal{D})$ [GaG].

EXERCISE 4.5.9: Prove that for each SS-AFA $(\Omega, \mathcal{D})$ there exists an AFA $(\Omega', \mathcal{D}')$ such that $\mathcal{L}(\mathcal{D}') = \mathcal{L}(\mathcal{D})$ and $\mathcal{L}^t(\mathcal{D}') = \mathcal{L}^t(\mathcal{D})$ [GaG].

EXERCISE 4.5.10: Show that a multitape AFA is a special instance of an SS-AFA [GaG].

4.6 Multitape AFA and Intersection

In Section 3.6, we introduced a "wedge" operator $\wedge$ for families of languages. We now define a "wedge" operator $\wedge$ between multitape AFA, and establish a representation theorem for $\mathcal{H}(\mathcal{L}^t(\mathcal{D}_1) \wedge \mathcal{L}^t(\mathcal{D}_2))$ and $\hat{\mathcal{H}}(\mathcal{L}(\mathcal{D}_1) \wedge \mathcal{L}(\mathcal{D}_2))$ in terms of $\mathcal{D}_1$ and $\mathcal{D}_2$. This leads to a representation of $\mathcal{L}^t(\mathcal{D}_\nu)$ and $\mathcal{L}(\mathcal{D}_\nu)$, $\mathcal{D}$ a multitape AFA and $\nu = (\alpha_1, \ldots, \alpha_k)$, in terms of the $\mathcal{L}^t(\mathcal{D}_{\alpha_i})$ and $\mathcal{L}(\mathcal{D}_{\alpha_i})$.

[1] Given Γ_1 and Γ_2, we identify $\tilde{\epsilon}_{\Gamma_1}$ with $\tilde{\epsilon}_{\Gamma_2}$, where $\tilde{\epsilon}_{\Gamma_i}$ is the function from $\emptyset$ to Γ_i, $i = 1, 2$.

Notation: Let $\mathcal{B}$ be an abstract set, $<_{\mathcal{B}}$ a simple order on $\mathcal{B}$, and $\{(\Omega_\beta, \mathcal{D}_\beta)/\beta$ in $\mathcal{B}\}$ a family of multitape AFA, with $\Omega_\beta = (K, \Sigma, \mathcal{A}_\beta, <_\beta, \mu_\beta)$ for each β. Then $\bigwedge_{\mathcal{B}} \mathcal{D}_\beta$ is the multitape AFA $\left(\Omega, \bigwedge_{\mathcal{B}} \mathcal{D}_\beta\right)$, where $\Omega = (K, \Sigma, \mathcal{A}, <, \mu)$ is defined as follows:

(1) $\mathcal{A} = \bigcup_{\beta \text{ in } \mathcal{B}} (\mathcal{A}_\beta \times \{\beta\})$.

(2) $\mu(\alpha, \beta) = \mu_\beta(\alpha)$ for each β in $\mathcal{B}$ and each α in $\mathcal{A}_\beta$.

(3) $(\alpha, \beta) < (\alpha', \beta')$ if either $\beta = \beta'$ and $\alpha <_\beta \alpha'$, or $\beta <_{\mathcal{B}} \beta'$.

If $\mathcal{B}$ is a finite set $\mathcal{B} = \{\beta_1, \ldots, \beta_n\}$ and $<_{\mathcal{B}}$ is the order on $\mathcal{B}$ as given, then $\bigwedge_{\mathcal{B}} \mathcal{D}_\beta$ is written as $\bigwedge_{1 \leq i \leq n} \mathcal{D}_{\beta_i}$ or $\mathcal{D}_{\beta_1} \wedge \ldots \wedge \mathcal{D}_{\beta_n}$.

Obviously the set of words accepted by $\bigwedge_{\mathcal{B}} \mathcal{D}_\beta$ is independent of the order $<_{\mathcal{B}}$ on $\mathcal{B}$.

Frequently $\mathcal{B}$ is a subset of the integers. In this case, unless stated otherwise, $<_{\mathcal{B}}$ is the natural order of the integers.

If the $\mathcal{A}_\beta$ are pairwise disjoint, then we may identify each (α, β) with α and write $\mathcal{A}$ as $\bigcup_{\beta \text{ in } \mathcal{B}} \mathcal{A}_\beta$. In the sequel, we shall always assume (without loss of generality) that the $\mathcal{A}_\beta$ are pairwise disjoint.

Note that $(\mathcal{D}_1 \wedge \mathcal{D}_2) \wedge \mathcal{D}_3 = \mathcal{D}_1 \wedge (\mathcal{D}_2 \wedge \mathcal{D}_3)$ for all multitape AFA $\mathcal{D}_1$, $\mathcal{D}_2$, and $\mathcal{D}_3$.

For each multitape AFA $(\Omega, \mathcal{D})$, with $\Omega = (K, \Sigma, \mathcal{A}, <, \mu)$, $\mathcal{D}$ may be identified with[1] $\bigwedge_{\mathcal{A}} \mathcal{D}_\alpha$. For example, if $\mathcal{D}$ is the multitape AFA of 2-pushdown tape acceptors, then $\mathcal{D} = \mathcal{D}_{\text{PDA}} \wedge \mathcal{D}_{\text{PDA}}$.

We now turn to evaluating $\mathcal{L}(\mathcal{D}_1 \wedge \ldots \wedge \mathcal{D}_n)$ and $\mathcal{L}^t(\mathcal{D}_1 \wedge \ldots \wedge \mathcal{D}_n)$ in terms of the $\mathcal{D}_i$. In particular, we shall see that $\mathcal{L}(\mathcal{D}_1 \wedge \ldots \wedge \mathcal{D}_n) = \hat{\mathcal{H}}(\mathcal{L}(\mathcal{D}_1) \wedge \ldots \wedge \mathcal{L}(\mathcal{D}_n))$ and $\mathcal{L}^t(\mathcal{D}_1 \wedge \ldots \wedge \mathcal{D}_n) = \mathcal{H}(\mathcal{L}^t(\mathcal{D}_1) \wedge \ldots \wedge \mathcal{L}^t(\mathcal{D}_n))$. Expressed otherwise, the family of those sets accepted by at least one (quasi-realtime) acceptor in the multitape AFA $\mathcal{D}_1 \wedge \ldots \wedge \mathcal{D}_n$ coincides with the family of (ϵ-free) homomorphic images of the languages in $\mathcal{L}(\mathcal{D}_1) \wedge \ldots \wedge \mathcal{L}(\mathcal{D}_n)$ ($\mathcal{L}^t(\mathcal{D}_1) \wedge \ldots \wedge \mathcal{L}^t(\mathcal{D}_n)$). First though, we prove two lemmas.

$(\sim, f)$ LEMMA 4.6.1: *For all multitape AFA $\mathcal{D}_1$ and $\mathcal{D}_2$,*

$$\mathcal{L}(\mathcal{D}_1) \wedge \mathcal{L}(\mathcal{D}_2) \subseteq \mathcal{L}(\mathcal{D}_1 \wedge \mathcal{D}_2)$$

and

$$\mathcal{L}^t(\mathcal{D}_1) \wedge \mathcal{L}^t(\mathcal{D}_2) \subseteq \mathcal{L}^t(\mathcal{D}_1 \wedge \mathcal{D}_2).$$

[1] For α in $\mathcal{A}$, we identify $\mathcal{D}_\alpha$ with $\mathcal{D}_{(\alpha)}$.

Proof: For each i, let $\Omega_i = (K, \Sigma, \mathcal{A}_i, \prec_i, \mu_i)$ and let $D_i = (K_i, \Sigma_i, \delta_i, q_i, F_i, \nu_i)$ be in $\mathcal{D}_i$, with $\nu_1 = (\alpha_1, \ldots, \alpha_k)$ and $\nu_2 = (\beta_1, \ldots, \beta_l)$. We shall construct an acceptor D_3 in $\mathcal{D}_1 \wedge \mathcal{D}_2$ such that $L(D_3) = L(D_1) \cap L(D_2)$.

Informally, the working tapes of D_3 are the tapes of D_1 followed by those of D_2. The states of D_3 are formed by the usual cross product construction. When reading an input of $\Sigma_1 \cap \Sigma_2$, D_3 imitates the action of D_1 on the $\mathcal{D}_1$-tapes and the action of D_2 on the $\mathcal{D}_2$-tapes. Under ϵ, D_3 imitates either D_1 or D_2 on the appropriate tapes. Thus, D_3 simultaneously performs the computations of D_1 and D_2 and therefore accepts the intersection $L(D_1) \cap L(D_2)$. Formally, let $\nu_3 = (\alpha_1, \ldots, \alpha_k, \beta_1, \ldots, \beta_l)$, $K_3 = K_1 \times K_2$, and $F_3 = F_1 \times F_2$. Let $D_3 = (K_3, \Sigma_1 \cap \Sigma_2, \delta_3, (q_1, q_2), F_3, \nu_3)$, where δ_3 is defined as follows:

(1) If a is in $\Sigma_1 \cap \Sigma_2$, $(q', (u_1, \ldots, u_k))$ is in $\delta_1(q, a, (\gamma_1, \ldots, \gamma_k))$ and $(p', (\bar{u}_1, \ldots, \bar{u}_l))$ is in $\delta_2(p, a, (\gamma_1', \ldots, \gamma_l'))$, let $((q', p'), (u_1, \ldots, u_k, \bar{u}_1, \ldots, \bar{u}_l))$ be in $\delta_3((q, p), a, (\gamma_1, \ldots, \gamma_k, \gamma_1', \ldots, \gamma_l'))$.

(2) If $(q', (u_1, \ldots, u_k))$ is in $\delta_1(q, \epsilon, (\gamma_1, \ldots, \gamma_k))$, then for all $(\gamma_1', \ldots, \gamma_l')$ in G_{D_2} and p in K_2 let $\big((q', p), (u_1, \ldots, u_k, 1(\beta_1, \gamma_1'), \ldots, 1(\beta_l, \gamma_l'))\big)$ be in $\delta_3((q, p,), \epsilon, (\gamma_1, \ldots, \gamma_k, \gamma_1', \ldots, \gamma_l'))$.

(3) If $(p', (u_1', \ldots, u_l'))$ is in $\delta_2(p, \epsilon, (\gamma_1', \ldots, \gamma_l'))$, then for all $(\gamma_1, \ldots, \gamma_k)$ in G_{D_1} and all q in K_1 let $((q, p'), (1(\alpha_1, \gamma_1), \ldots, 1(\alpha_k, \gamma_k), u_1', \ldots, u_l'))$ be in $\delta_3((q, p), \epsilon, (\gamma_1, \ldots, \gamma_k, \gamma_1', \ldots, \gamma_l'))$.

Clearly $L(D_3) = L(D_1) \cap L(D_2)$ and D_3 is quasi-realtime if and only if D_1 and D_2 are quasi-realtime. Hence the result.

(f) LEMMA 4.6.2: *For all multitape AFA $\mathcal{D}_1$ and $\mathcal{D}_2$,*

(a) $\mathcal{H}(\mathcal{L}^t(\mathcal{D}_1) \wedge \mathcal{L}^t(\mathcal{D}_2)) = \mathcal{L}^t(\mathcal{D}_1 \wedge \mathcal{D}_2)$

and

(b) $\hat{\mathcal{H}}(\mathcal{L}(\mathcal{D}_1) \wedge \mathcal{L}(\mathcal{D}_2)) = \hat{\mathcal{H}}(\mathcal{L}^t(\mathcal{D}_1) \wedge \mathcal{L}^t(\mathcal{D}_2)) = \mathcal{L}(\mathcal{D}_1 \wedge \mathcal{D}_2)$.

Proof: For each i, let $\Omega_i = (K, \Sigma, \mathcal{A}_i, \prec_i, \mu_i)$.

Consider (a). By Lemma 4.6.1 and Theorem 4.5.1,

$$\mathcal{H}(\mathcal{L}^t(\mathcal{D}_1) \wedge \mathcal{L}^t(\mathcal{D}_2)) \subseteq \mathcal{H}[\mathcal{L}^t(\mathcal{D}_1 \wedge \mathcal{D}_2)] = \mathcal{L}^t(\mathcal{D}_1 \wedge \mathcal{D}_2).$$

To see the reverse containment, let $D = (K_1, \Sigma_1, \delta, q_0, F, \nu)$ be a quasi-realtime multitape acceptor in $\mathcal{D}_1 \wedge \mathcal{D}_2$, with $\nu = (\alpha_1, \ldots, \alpha_k, \beta_1, \ldots, \beta_l)$, $\alpha_1, \ldots, \alpha_k$ in $\mathcal{A}_1$, and $\beta_1, \ldots, \beta_l$ in $\mathcal{A}_2$. Let $L = L(D)$. For each $q, a, \gamma_1, \ldots, \gamma_{k+l}$ such that $\#\big(\delta(q, a, (\gamma_1, \ldots, \gamma_{k+l}))\big) > 0$ and each m, $1 \leqq m \leqq \#\big(\delta(q, a, (\gamma_1, \ldots, \gamma_{k+l}))\big)$ let $(q, a, (\gamma_1, \ldots, \gamma_{k+l}), m)$ be a new element of Σ. Let Σ_2 be the set of all such $(q, a, (\gamma_1, \ldots, \gamma_{k+l}), m)$. Clearly Σ_2 is finite. Let c be a new element of Σ. Let h_1 and h_2 be the homomorphisms on Σ_2^* and $(\Sigma_1 \cup \{c\})^*$, respectively, defined by $h_1\big((q, a, (\gamma_1, \ldots, \gamma_{k+l}), m)\big) = a$ for each $(q, a,$

$(\gamma_1, \ldots, \gamma_{k+l}), m)$ in Σ_2, $a \neq \epsilon$, $h_1((q, \epsilon, (\gamma_1, \ldots, \gamma_{k+l}), m)) = c$ for each $(q, \epsilon, (\gamma_1, \ldots, \gamma_{k+l}), m)$ in Σ_2, $h_2(a) = a$ for each a in Σ_1, and $h_2(c) = \epsilon$. We shall show that there exist L_1 in $\mathscr{L}^t(\mathscr{D}_1)$ and L_2 in $\mathscr{L}^t(\mathscr{D}_2)$ such that $L = h_2h_1(L_1 \cap L_2)$ and h_2 is ϵ-limited on $h_1(L_1 \cap L_2)$. By Theorem 3.6.1, $\mathscr{H}(\mathscr{L}^t(\mathscr{D}_1) \wedge \mathscr{L}^t(\mathscr{D}_2))$ is an AFL and contains $\{\epsilon\}$. By Corollary 2 of Theorem 3.2.2, it will then follow that $h_2h_1(L_1 \cap L_2)$ is in $\mathscr{H}(\mathscr{L}^t(\mathscr{D}_1) \wedge \mathscr{L}^t(\mathscr{D}_2))$.

For $i = 1, 2$, let $D_i = (K_1, \Sigma_2, \delta_i, q_0, F, v_i)$, where $v_1 = (\alpha_1, \ldots, \alpha_k)$, $v_2 = (\beta_1, \ldots, \beta_l)$, and δ_1 and δ_2 are defined as follows: For each $(q, a, (\gamma_1, \ldots, \gamma_{k+l}), m)$ in Σ_2, let the elements of $\delta(q, a, (\gamma_1, \ldots, \gamma_{k+l}))$ be simply ordered in some way. If $(q', (u_1, \ldots, u_{k+l}))$ is the m-th member of $\delta(q, a, (\gamma_1, \ldots, \gamma_{k+l}))$, let

$$\delta_1(q, (q, a, (\gamma_1, \ldots, \gamma_{k+l}), m), (\gamma_1, \ldots, \gamma_k)) = \{(q', (u_1, \ldots, u_k))\}$$

and

$$\delta_2(q, (q, a, (\gamma_1, \ldots, \gamma_{k+l}), m), (\gamma_{k+1}, \ldots, \gamma_{k+l})) = \{(q', (u_{k+1}, \ldots, u_{k+l}))\}.$$

Let $L_1 = L(D_1)$ and $L_2 = L(D_2)$. Since D_1 and D_2 have no ϵ-moves, L_1 is in $\mathscr{L}^t(\mathscr{D}_1)$ and L_2 is in $\mathscr{L}^t(\mathscr{D}_2)$. Clearly $L \subseteq h_2h_1(L_1 \cap L_2)$. [Informally, the vocabulary of L_1 and L_2 consists of symbols which encode single moves of D. Each acceptor D_i for L_i imitates the action of D on the $\mathscr{D}_i$-tapes, ignoring the other tapes. A word is in L_i whenever it encodes actions of D going from the initial to an accepting state while causing the $\mathscr{D}_i$-tapes to go from empty storage back to empty storage. Thus a word is in $L_1 \cap L_2$ whenever it encodes an accepting computation of D. The homomorphisms h_1 and h_2 merely extract the input from the encoding of a computation.]

Consider the reverse containment. If ϵ is in $L_1 \cap L_2$, then q_0 is in F and ϵ is in L. Suppose $w \neq \epsilon$ is in $L_1 \cap L_2$, with $|w| = n$. Then $w = w_1 \ldots w_n$, where $w_i = (p_i, a_i, (\gamma_{i1}, \ldots, \gamma_{i(k+l)}), m_i)$ for some p_i in K_1, a_i in $\Sigma_1 \cup \{\epsilon\}$, $(\gamma_{i1}, \ldots, \gamma_{i(k+l)})$ in G_D, and $1 \leqq m_i \leqq \#(\delta(p_i, a_i, (\gamma_{i1}, \ldots, \gamma_{i(k+l)})))$, $1 \leqq i \leqq n$. For each i, let $(p_i', (u_{i1}, \ldots, u_{i(k+l)}))$ be the m_i-th element of $\delta(p_i, a_i, (\gamma_{i1}, \ldots, \gamma_{i(k+l)}))$. By definition of $\vdash$, δ_1, and δ_2, it follows that $p_1 = q_0$, $p_{r+1} = p_r'$, $1 \leqq r < n$, and p_n' is in F. Furthermore, there exist $y_{11}, \ldots, y_{1(k+l)}, y_{21}, \ldots, y_{2(k+l)}, \ldots, y_{n(k+l)}$ such that $y_{11} = \ldots = y_{1(k+l)} = \epsilon$, $y_{(i+1)j} = f_{\alpha_j}(y_{ij}, u_{ij})$ and $\epsilon = f_{\alpha_j}(y_{nj}, u_{nj})$ for $1 \leqq i < n$, $1 \leqq j \leqq k$, $y_{(i+1)(k+j)} = f_{\beta_j}(y_{i(k+j)}, u_{i(k+j)})$ and $\epsilon = f_{\beta_j}(y_{n(k+j)}, u_{n(k+j)})$ for $1 \leqq i < n$, $1 \leqq j \leqq l$, γ_{ij} is in $g_{\alpha_j}(y_{ij})$ for $1 \leqq i \leqq n$, $1 \leqq j \leqq k$, and γ_{ij} is in $g_{\beta_j}(y_{ij})$ for $1 \leqq i \leqq n$, $k+1 \leqq j \leqq k+l$. Let $p_{n+1} = p_n'$ and $y_{(n+1)1} = \ldots =$

$y_{(n+1)(k+l)} = \epsilon$. Then

$$(p_i, a_i, (y_{i1}, \ldots, y_{i(k+l)})) \underset{D}{\vdash} (p_{i+1}, \epsilon, (y_{(i+1)1}, \ldots, y_{(i+1)(k+l)}))$$

for $1 \leqq i \leqq n$, so that $a_1 \ldots a_n = h_2h_1(w)$ is in L. Therefore $h_2h_1(L_1 \cap L_2) = L$. Furthermore, if $h_2h_1(w_r \ldots w_{r+s}) = \epsilon$, then $h_1(w_r \ldots w_{r+s}) = c^{s+1}$ and $a_r = \ldots = a_{r+s} = \epsilon$. Then

$$(p_r, \epsilon, (y_{r1}, \ldots, y_{r(k+l)})) \overset{s+1}{\underset{D}{\vdash}} (p_{r+s+1}, \epsilon, (y_{(r+s+1)1}, \ldots, y_{(r+s+1)(k+l)})).$$

Since D is quasi-realtime, there exists an integer t such that for all configurations $C = (q, \epsilon, (y_1, \ldots, y_{k+l}))$ and $C' = (q', \epsilon, (y_1', \ldots, y_{k+l}'))$ of D, $C \overset{i}{\vdash} C'$ implies $i \leqq t$. Hence $s+1 \leqq t$. Therefore h_2 is ϵ-limited on $h_1(L_1 \cap L_2)$.

Consider (b). Then

$$\begin{aligned}
\mathscr{L}(\mathscr{D}_1 \wedge \mathscr{D}_2) &= \hat{\mathscr{H}}(\mathscr{L}^t(\mathscr{D}_1 \wedge \mathscr{D}_2)), \quad \text{by Theorem 4.5.1,}\\
&= \hat{\mathscr{H}}[\mathscr{H}(\mathscr{L}^t(\mathscr{D}_1) \wedge \mathscr{L}^t(\mathscr{D}_2))], \quad \text{by (a) above,}\\
&= \hat{\mathscr{H}}(\mathscr{L}^t(\mathscr{D}_1) \wedge \mathscr{L}^t(\mathscr{D}_2)), \quad \text{since } \hat{\mathscr{H}}\mathscr{H} = \hat{\mathscr{H}},\\
&= \hat{\mathscr{H}}(\hat{\mathscr{H}}(\mathscr{L}^t(\mathscr{D}_1)) \wedge \hat{\mathscr{H}}(\mathscr{L}^t(\mathscr{D}_2))),\\
&\qquad \text{by (b) of Proposition 3.6.1,}\\
&= \hat{\mathscr{H}}(\mathscr{L}(\mathscr{D}_1) \wedge \mathscr{L}(\mathscr{D}_2)), \quad \text{by Theorem 4.5.1.}
\end{aligned}$$

Open Question: Is it true that for all nontrivial multitape AFA $\mathscr{D}_1$ and $\mathscr{D}_2$, $\hat{\mathscr{H}}(\tilde{\mathscr{L}}(\mathscr{D}_1) \wedge \tilde{\mathscr{L}}(\mathscr{D}_2)) = \tilde{\mathscr{L}}(\mathscr{D}_1 \wedge \mathscr{D}_2)$? [See Exercise 4.6.1.]

(*f*) THEOREM 4.6.1: *For* $n \geqq 1$ *and all multitape AFA* $\mathscr{D}_1, \ldots, \mathscr{D}_n$,

(a) $\mathscr{H}(\mathscr{L}^t(\mathscr{D}_1) \wedge \ldots \wedge \mathscr{L}^t(\mathscr{D}_n)) = \mathscr{L}^t(\mathscr{D}_1 \wedge \ldots \wedge \mathscr{D}_n)$

and

$$\begin{aligned}
\text{(b) } \hat{\mathscr{H}}(\mathscr{L}(\mathscr{D}_1) \wedge \ldots \wedge \mathscr{L}(\mathscr{D}_n)) &= \hat{\mathscr{H}}(\mathscr{L}^t(\mathscr{D}_1) \wedge \ldots \wedge \mathscr{L}^t(\mathscr{D}_n))\\
&= \mathscr{L}(\mathscr{D}_1 \wedge \ldots \wedge \mathscr{D}_n).
\end{aligned}$$

Proof: For each i, let $\Omega_i = (K, \Sigma, \mathscr{A}_i, \prec_i, \mu_i)$.

(a) Clearly $\mathscr{H}(\mathscr{L}^t(\mathscr{D}_1)) = \mathscr{L}^t(\mathscr{D}_1)$, so that (a) is true for $n = 1$. Continuing by induction suppose the theorem is true for $n-1$, $n \geqq 2$. Then

$$\begin{aligned}
\mathscr{L}^t(\mathscr{D}_1 \wedge \ldots \wedge \mathscr{D}_n) &= \mathscr{L}^t((\mathscr{D}_1 \wedge \ldots \wedge \mathscr{D}_{n-1}) \wedge \mathscr{D}_n)\\
&= \mathscr{H}(\mathscr{L}^t(\mathscr{D}_1 \wedge \ldots \wedge \mathscr{D}_{n-1}) \wedge \mathscr{L}^t(\mathscr{D}_n)),\\
&\qquad \text{by Lemma 4.6.2,}\\
(1) \qquad &= \mathscr{H}[\mathscr{H}(\mathscr{L}^t(\mathscr{D}_1) \wedge \ldots \wedge \mathscr{L}^t(\mathscr{D}_{n-1})) \wedge \mathscr{L}^t(\mathscr{D}_n)],\\
&\qquad \text{by induction.}
\end{aligned}$$

Now

$$\begin{aligned}
&\mathscr{H}[\mathscr{H}(\mathscr{L}^t(\mathscr{D}_1) \wedge \ldots \wedge \mathscr{L}^t(\mathscr{D}_{n-1})) \wedge \mathscr{L}^t(\mathscr{D}_n)] = \\
&\quad = \mathscr{H}[\mathscr{H}(\mathscr{L}^t(\mathscr{D}_1) \wedge \ldots \wedge \mathscr{L}^t(\mathscr{D}_{n-1})) \wedge \mathscr{H}(\mathscr{L}^t(\mathscr{D}_n))], \quad \text{by Theorem 4.5.1,} \\
&\quad \subseteq \mathscr{H}[\mathscr{H}(\mathscr{L}^t(\mathscr{D}_1) \wedge \ldots \wedge \mathscr{L}^t(\mathscr{D}_{n-1}) \wedge \mathscr{L}^t(\mathscr{D}_n))], \quad \text{by (a) of Proposition 3.6.1,} \\
&\quad = \mathscr{H}(\mathscr{L}^t(\mathscr{D}_1) \wedge \ldots \wedge \mathscr{L}^t(\mathscr{D}_n)), \quad \text{since } \mathscr{H}\mathscr{H} = \mathscr{H}, \\
&\quad \subseteq \mathscr{H}[\mathscr{H}(\mathscr{L}^t(\mathscr{D}_1) \wedge \ldots \wedge \mathscr{L}^t(\mathscr{D}_{n-1})) \wedge \mathscr{L}^t(\mathscr{D}_n)], \\
&\qquad \text{since } \mathscr{L}^t(\mathscr{D}_1) \wedge \ldots \wedge \mathscr{L}^t(\mathscr{D}_{n-1}) \subseteq \mathscr{H}(\mathscr{L}^t(\mathscr{D}_1) \wedge \ldots \wedge \mathscr{L}^t(\mathscr{D}_{n-1})).
\end{aligned}$$

Hence,

(2)

$$\mathscr{H}[\mathscr{H}(\mathscr{L}^t(\mathscr{D}_1) \wedge \ldots \wedge \mathscr{L}^t(\mathscr{D}_{n-1})) \wedge \mathscr{L}^t(\mathscr{D}_n)] = \mathscr{H}(\mathscr{L}^t(\mathscr{D}_1) \wedge \ldots \wedge \mathscr{L}^t(\mathscr{D}_n)).$$

Combining (1) and (2), we get

$$\mathscr{H}(\mathscr{L}^t(\mathscr{D}_1) \wedge \ldots \wedge \mathscr{L}^t(\mathscr{D}_n)) = \mathscr{L}^t(\mathscr{D}_1 \wedge \ldots \wedge \mathscr{D}_n).$$

(b) $\hat{\mathscr{H}}(\mathscr{L}(\mathscr{D}_1) \wedge \ldots \wedge \mathscr{L}(\mathscr{D}_n)) =$

$$\begin{aligned}
&= \hat{\mathscr{H}}[\hat{\mathscr{H}}(\mathscr{L}^t(\mathscr{D}_1)) \wedge \ldots \wedge \hat{\mathscr{H}}(\mathscr{L}^t(\mathscr{D}_n))], \quad \text{by Theorem 4.5.1,} \\
&= \hat{\mathscr{H}}(\mathscr{L}^t(\mathscr{D}_1) \wedge \ldots \wedge \mathscr{L}^t(\mathscr{D}_n)), \quad \text{by (b) of Proposition 3.6.1,} \\
&= \hat{\mathscr{H}}[\mathscr{H}(\mathscr{L}^t(\mathscr{D}_1) \wedge \ldots \wedge \mathscr{L}^t(\mathscr{D}_n))], \quad \text{since } \hat{\mathscr{H}}\mathscr{H} = \hat{\mathscr{H}}, \\
&= \hat{\mathscr{H}}(\mathscr{L}^t(\mathscr{D}_1 \wedge \ldots \wedge \mathscr{D}_n)), \quad \text{by (a) above,} \\
&= \mathscr{L}(\mathscr{D}_1 \wedge \ldots \wedge \mathscr{D}_n), \quad \text{by Theorem 4.5.1.}
\end{aligned}$$

COROLLARY: *For each multitape AFA* $\mathscr{D}$ *and each* $v = (\alpha_1, \ldots, \alpha_k)$, $\mathscr{L}^t(\mathscr{D}_v) = \mathscr{H}(\mathscr{L}^t(\mathscr{D}_{\alpha_1}) \wedge \ldots \wedge \mathscr{L}^t(\mathscr{D}_{\alpha_k}))$ *and* $\mathscr{L}(\mathscr{D}_v) = \hat{\mathscr{H}}(\mathscr{L}(\mathscr{D}_{\alpha_1}) \wedge \ldots \wedge \mathscr{L}(\mathscr{D}_{\alpha_k}))$.

EXAMPLE 4.6.1: The family $\mathscr{L}_l$ of *list* languages is defined as the family of ϵ-free languages in $\mathscr{L}^t(\mathscr{D}_{\text{PDA}} \wedge \mathscr{D}_{\text{PDA}})$. Since $\mathscr{L}^t(\mathscr{D}_{\text{PDA}} \wedge \mathscr{D}_{\text{PDA}})$ is an AFL, $\mathscr{L}_l$ is an AFL by Proposition 3.1.2. By Theorem 4.6.1, $\mathscr{L}^t(\mathscr{D}_{\text{PDA}} \wedge \mathscr{D}_{\text{PDA}}) = \mathscr{H}(\mathscr{L}^t(\mathscr{D}_{\text{PDA}}) \wedge \mathscr{L}^t(\mathscr{D}_{\text{PDA}}))$. Let $\mathscr{L}_1$ be the ϵ-free languages in $\mathscr{L}^t(\mathscr{D}_{\text{PDA}})$. Clearly $\mathscr{L}_l = \mathscr{H}(\mathscr{L}_1 \wedge \mathscr{L}_1)$. Let $\mathscr{L}_{\epsilon\text{CF}}$ be the family of ϵ-free context-free languages. Since $\mathscr{L}_{\text{CF}} = \mathscr{L}^t(\mathscr{D}_{\text{PDA}})$, $\mathscr{L}_{\epsilon\text{CF}} = \mathscr{L}_1$. Therefore $\mathscr{L}_l = \mathscr{H}(\mathscr{L}_{\epsilon\text{CF}} \wedge \mathscr{L}_{\epsilon\text{CF}})$.

Open Question: Is $\mathscr{H}(\mathscr{L}^t(\mathcal{D}_{\text{PDA}}) \wedge \mathscr{L}^t(\mathcal{D}_{\text{PDA}})) = \mathscr{H}(\mathscr{L}^t(\mathcal{D}_{\text{PDA}}) \wedge \mathscr{L}^t(\mathcal{D}_{\text{PDA}}) \wedge \mathscr{L}^t(\mathcal{D}_{\text{PDA}}))$ [BGr]?

Theorem 4.6.1 relates the intersection of languages from a given finite number of AFL to the wedge operator for AFA. The next result relates the arbitrary (but finite) intersection of languages in an AFL to an "infinite wedge" operator.

Notation: For each AFA $\mathcal{D}$ let $\wedge\mathcal{D}$ be the multitape AFA $\bigwedge_{\mathcal{A}} \mathcal{D}_n$, where $\mathcal{A} = \{i/i \geqq 1\}$ and $\mathcal{D}_i = \mathcal{D}$ for each i.

(*f*) THEOREM 4.6.2: *For each AFA* $\mathcal{D}$,

(a) $\mathscr{L}^t(\wedge \mathcal{D}) = \mathscr{H}(\wedge \mathscr{L}^t(\mathcal{D})) = \mathscr{F}_\cap(\mathscr{L}^t(\mathcal{D}))$, *and*

(b) $\mathscr{L}(\wedge \mathcal{D}) = \hat{\mathscr{H}}(\wedge \mathscr{L}(\mathcal{D})) = \hat{\mathscr{H}}(\wedge \mathscr{L}^t(\mathcal{D})) = \hat{\mathscr{F}}_\cap(\mathscr{L}(\mathcal{D}))$
$= \hat{\mathscr{F}}_\cap(\mathscr{L}^t(\mathcal{D}))$.

Proof: (a) By (c) of Proposition 3.6.1, $\mathscr{H}(\wedge \mathscr{L}^t(\mathcal{D})) = \mathscr{F}_\cap(\mathscr{L}^t(\mathcal{D}))$. Suppose that $\Omega = (K, \Sigma, \Gamma, I, f, g)$. Then $\wedge\mathcal{D}$ is the multitape AFA $(\bar{\Omega}, \bar{\mathcal{D}})$, where $\bar{\Omega} = (K, \Sigma, \mathcal{A}, \prec, \mu)$, $\mathcal{A} = \{i/i \geqq 1\}$, $\prec = <$, and $\mu(i) = (\Gamma, I, f, g)$ for each i. For each n let $\mathcal{D}^{(n)} = \bar{\mathcal{D}}_{(1, \ldots, n)}$. Then $\mathscr{L}^t(\wedge \mathcal{D}) = \bigcup_{\text{all } \nu} \mathscr{L}^t(\bar{\mathcal{D}}_\nu)$. Clearly $\mathscr{L}^t(\bar{\mathcal{D}}_\nu) = \mathscr{L}^t(\bar{\mathcal{D}}_{\nu'})$ if the number of coordinates in ν and ν' are the same. Thus $\mathscr{L}^t(\wedge\mathcal{D}) = \bigcup_{n \geqq 1} \mathscr{L}^t(\mathcal{D}^{(n)})$. Now $\mathcal{D}^{(n)}$ may be regarded as the n-tape AFA $\bar{\mathcal{D}}_1 \wedge \ldots \wedge \bar{\mathcal{D}}_n$. By Theorem 4.6.1, therefore, $\mathscr{L}^t(\mathcal{D}^{(n)}) = \mathscr{H}(\mathscr{L}^t(\bar{\mathcal{D}}_1) \wedge \ldots \wedge \mathscr{L}^t(\bar{\mathcal{D}}_n))$. Thus $\mathscr{L}^t(\mathcal{D}^{(n)}) \subseteq \mathscr{H}(\wedge \mathscr{L}^t(\mathcal{D}))$. Hence $\mathscr{L}^t(\wedge \mathcal{D}) = \bigcup_{n \geqq 1} \mathscr{L}^t(\mathcal{D}^{(n)}) \subseteq \mathscr{H}(\wedge \mathscr{L}^t(\mathcal{D}))$. On the other hand, if L is in $\mathscr{H}(\wedge \mathscr{L}^t(\mathcal{D}))$, then $L = h(L_1 \cap \ldots \cap L_n)$ for some ϵ-free homomorphism h, some $n \geqq 1$, and some languages $L_1, \ldots, L_n$ in $\mathscr{L}^t(\mathcal{D})$. Then $L_1 \cap \ldots \cap L_n$ is in $\mathscr{L}^t(\bar{\mathcal{D}}_1) \wedge \ldots \wedge \mathscr{L}^t(\bar{\mathcal{D}}_n)$, so that $L = h(L_1 \cap \ldots \cap L_n)$ is in $\mathscr{H}(\mathscr{L}^t(\bar{\mathcal{D}}_1) \wedge \ldots \wedge \mathscr{L}^t(\bar{\mathcal{D}}_n)) = \mathscr{L}^t(\mathcal{D}^{(n)})$. Therefore $\mathscr{H}(\wedge \mathscr{L}^t(\mathcal{D})) \subseteq \bigcup_n \mathscr{L}^t(\mathcal{D}^{(n)}) = \mathscr{L}^t(\wedge \mathcal{D})$, whence equality.

(b) Since

$$\begin{aligned}
\mathscr{L}(\wedge \mathcal{D}) &= \hat{\mathscr{H}}(\mathscr{L}^t(\wedge \mathcal{D})), && \text{by Theorem 4.5.1,}\\
&= \hat{\mathscr{H}}(\mathscr{H}(\wedge \mathscr{L}^t(\mathcal{D}))), && \text{by (a) above,}\\
&= \hat{\mathscr{H}}(\wedge \mathscr{L}^t(\mathcal{D})), && \text{because } \hat{\mathscr{H}}\mathscr{H} = \hat{\mathscr{H}},\\
&= \hat{\mathscr{F}}_\cap(\mathscr{L}^t(\mathcal{D})), && \text{by (c) of Proposition 3.6.1,}
\end{aligned}$$

it follows that $\mathcal{L}(\wedge \mathcal{D}) = \mathcal{H}(\wedge \mathcal{L}^t(\mathcal{D})) = \mathcal{F}_\cap(\mathcal{L}^t(\mathcal{D}))$. Since

$$\begin{aligned}\mathcal{L}(\wedge \mathcal{D}) &= \hat{\mathcal{H}}(\wedge \mathcal{L}^t(\mathcal{D}))\\ &= \hat{\mathcal{H}}(\wedge \hat{\mathcal{H}}(\mathcal{L}^t(\mathcal{D}))), \quad \text{by (c) of Proposition 3.6.1,}\\ &= \hat{\mathcal{H}}(\wedge \mathcal{L}(\mathcal{D})), \quad \text{by Theorem 4.5.1,}\\ &= \hat{\mathcal{F}}_\cap(\mathcal{L}(\mathcal{D})), \quad \text{by (c) of Proposition 3.6.1,}\end{aligned}$$

the remaining equalities follow.

Using the previous result, we now present a characterization of a (full) AFL closed under intersection.

$^{(+)}$(*f*) THEOREM 4.6.3: *A family $\mathcal{L}$ of languages is a (full) AFL containing $\{\epsilon\}$ and closed under intersection if and only if there exists a multitape AFA $(\Omega, \mathcal{D})$, $\Omega = (K, \Sigma, \mathcal{A}, <, \mu)$, such that $\mathcal{L} = \mathcal{L}^t(\mathcal{D})$ ($\mathcal{L} = \mathcal{L}(\mathcal{D})$), $\mathcal{A}$ is infinite, and $\mu(\alpha) = \mu(\beta)$ for all α and β in $\mathcal{A}$.*

Proof: Suppose $(\Omega, \mathcal{D})$ is a multitape AFA such that $\mathcal{L} = \mathcal{L}^t(\mathcal{D})$ ($\mathcal{L} = \mathcal{L}(\mathcal{D})$), $\mathcal{A}$ is infinite, and $\mu(\alpha) = \mu(\beta)$ for all α and β in $\mathcal{A}$. Clearly $\mathcal{L}$ contains $\{\epsilon\}$. Now $\mathcal{L}^t(\mathcal{D}) = \bigcup_{\text{all } \nu} \mathcal{L}^t(\mathcal{D}_\nu)$ and $\mathcal{L}(\mathcal{D}) = \bigcup_{\text{all } \nu} \mathcal{L}(\mathcal{D}_\nu)$. Since $\mathcal{L}^t(\mathcal{D}_\nu) = \mathcal{L}^t(\mathcal{D}_{\nu'})$ and $\mathcal{L}(\mathcal{D}_\nu) = \mathcal{L}(\mathcal{D}_{\nu'})$ if the number of coordinates in ν and ν' are the same, there is no loss of generality in assuming $\mathcal{A} = \{i/i \geqq 1\}$. Then $\mathcal{D} = \wedge \mathcal{D}_1$. The "if" then follows from Theorem 4.6.2.

Consider the "only if". Suppose $\mathcal{L}$ is a (full) AFL containing $\{\epsilon\}$ and closed under intersection. Then there exists an AFA $\mathcal{D}_1$ such that $\mathcal{L}^t(\mathcal{D}_1) = \mathcal{L}(\mathcal{L}(\mathcal{D}_1) = \mathcal{L})$. Since $\mathcal{L}$ is a (full) AFL closed under intersection, $\mathcal{L} = \mathcal{F}_\cap(\mathcal{L}) = \mathcal{F}_\cap(\mathcal{L}^t(\mathcal{D}_1))$ $(\mathcal{L} = \hat{\mathcal{F}}_\cap(\mathcal{L}) = \hat{\mathcal{F}}_\cap(\mathcal{L}(\mathcal{D}_1)))$. By Theorem 4.6.2, $\mathcal{F}_\cap(\mathcal{L}^t(\mathcal{D}_1)) = \mathcal{L}^t(\wedge\mathcal{D}_1)$ $(\hat{\mathcal{F}}_\cap(\mathcal{L}(\mathcal{D}_1)) = \mathcal{L}(\wedge\mathcal{D}_1))$, whence the result.

EXAMPLE 4.6.2: By Theorem 4.6.3,

(a) $\bigcup_{n \geqq 1} \mathcal{C}_n$ is closed under intersection.

(b) $\mathcal{L}^t(\wedge\mathcal{D}_{\text{PDA}})$ is closed under intersection.

Open Question: Is it true for each nontrivial AFA $\mathcal{D}$ that $\tilde{\mathcal{L}}^t(\wedge\mathcal{D}) = \mathcal{H}(\wedge \tilde{\mathcal{L}}^t(\mathcal{D})) = \mathcal{S}_\cap(\tilde{\mathcal{L}}^t(\mathcal{D}))$?

Open Question: Is it true that a family $\mathcal{L}$ of languages is a semi-AFL containing $\{\epsilon\}$ and closed under intersection if and only if there exists a multitape AFA $(\Omega, \mathcal{D})$, $\Omega = (K, \Sigma, \mathcal{A}, <, \mu)$, such that $\mathcal{L} = \tilde{\mathcal{L}}^t(\mathcal{D})$, $\mathcal{A}$ is infinite, and $\mu(\alpha) = \mu(\beta)$ for all α and β in $\mathcal{A}$?

EXERCISE 4.6.1: Prove that $\tilde{\mathcal{L}}(\mathcal{D}_1) \wedge \tilde{\mathcal{L}}(\mathcal{D}_2) \subseteq \tilde{\mathcal{L}}(\mathcal{D}_1 \wedge \mathcal{D}_2)$ for all non-trivial multitape AFA $\mathcal{D}_1$ and $\mathcal{D}_2$.

EXERCISE 4.6.2: Prove that $\mathcal{L}_f(\mathcal{D}_1) \wedge \mathcal{L}_f(\mathcal{D}_2) \subseteq \mathcal{L}_f(\mathcal{D}_1 \wedge \mathcal{D}_2)$ for all multitape AFA $\mathcal{D}_1$ and $\mathcal{D}_2$.

EXERCISE 4.6.3: Prove that $\hat{\mathcal{H}}(\mathcal{L}_f(\mathcal{D}_1) \wedge \mathcal{L}_f(\mathcal{D}_2)) = \mathcal{L}_f(\mathcal{D}_1 \wedge \mathcal{D}_2)$ for all multitape AFA $\mathcal{D}_1$ and $\mathcal{D}_2$.

EXERCISE 4.6.4: Prove that $\mathcal{L}_l$ coincides with the ϵ-free languages accepted by some quasi-realtime list-storage acceptor.

EXERCISE 4.6.5: for $i \geqq 1$, let $\mathcal{D}_i = \mathcal{D}_{\text{PDA}}$. Prove the following [BGr]:

(a) $\mathcal{H}\left(\bigwedge_{i=1}^{4} \mathcal{L}^t(\mathcal{D}_i)\right) = \mathcal{H}\left(\bigwedge_{i=1}^{n} \mathcal{L}^t(\mathcal{D}_i)\right), \quad n \geqq 5.$

(b) $\mathcal{H}\left(\bigwedge_{i=1}^{3} \mathcal{L}^t(\mathcal{D}_i)\right) = \mathcal{H}\left(\bigwedge_{i=1}^{4} \mathcal{L}^t(\mathcal{D}_i)\right).$

EXERCISE 4.6.6: Prove that $\mathcal{H}(\mathcal{L}_f^t(\mathcal{D}_1) \wedge \ldots \wedge \mathcal{L}_f^t(\mathcal{D}_n)) = \mathcal{L}_f^t(\mathcal{D}_1 \wedge \ldots \wedge \mathcal{D}_n)$ for all $n \geqq 1$ and multitape AFA $\mathcal{D}_1, \ldots, \mathcal{D}_n$.

EXERCISE 4.6.7: Prove that $\bigcup_{n \geqq 1} \mathcal{C}_n \subsetneqq \mathcal{L}_{\text{ECS}}$.

EXERCISE 4.6.8: Prove that $\mathcal{L}^t(\mathcal{D}_{\text{TA}}) \subseteq \mathcal{L}^t(\mathcal{D}_{\text{PDA}} \wedge \mathcal{D}_{\text{PDA}})$.

EXERCISE 4.6.9: Prove that $\mathcal{L}^t(\wedge \mathcal{D}_{\text{TA}}) = \mathcal{L}^t(\wedge \mathcal{D}_{\text{PDA}}) = \mathcal{L}^t(\mathcal{D}_{\text{PDA}} \wedge \mathcal{D}_{\text{PDA}} \wedge \mathcal{D}_{\text{PDA}})$ [BGr].

EXERCISE 4.6.10: For each AFA $\mathcal{D}$, show that $\mathcal{L}_f^t(\wedge \mathcal{D}) = \mathcal{H}(\wedge \mathcal{L}_f^t(\mathcal{D})) = \mathcal{S}_\cap(\mathcal{L}_f^t(\mathcal{D}))$.

EXERCISE 4.6.11: Prove that a family $\mathcal{L}$ of languages is a semi-AFL containing $\{\epsilon\}$ and closed under intersection if and only if there exists a multitape AFA $(\Omega, \mathcal{D})$, $\Omega = (K, \Sigma, \mathcal{A}, \prec, \mu)$, such that $\mathcal{L} = \mathcal{L}_f^t(\mathcal{D})$, $\mathcal{A}$ is infinite, and $\mu(\alpha) = \mu(\beta)$ for all α and β in $\mathcal{A}$.

4.7 Full AFL of Multitape AFA

In this section we shall show that $\hat{\mathscr{H}}(\mathscr{F}(L_0) \wedge \mathscr{F}(L_0)) = \mathscr{L}_{\mathrm{RE}}$, where $L_0 = \{a^n b^n / n \geqq 1\}$. Now most of the commonly encountered AFL $\mathscr{L}$ have the property that $\mathscr{F}(L_0) \subseteq \mathscr{L} \subseteq \mathscr{L}_{\mathrm{RE}}$. If $\mathscr{L}_1$ and $\mathscr{L}_2$ are any such AFL, then $\mathscr{L}_{\mathrm{RE}} = \hat{\mathscr{H}}(\mathscr{F}(L_0) \wedge \mathscr{F}(L_0)) \subseteq \hat{\mathscr{H}}(\mathscr{L}_1 \wedge \mathscr{L}_2) \subseteq \hat{\mathscr{H}}(\mathscr{L}_{\mathrm{RE}} \wedge \mathscr{L}_{\mathrm{RE}}) = \mathscr{L}_{\mathrm{RE}}$, so that $\hat{\mathscr{H}}(\mathscr{L}_1 \wedge \mathscr{L}_2) = \mathscr{L}_{\mathrm{RE}}$. In view of Theorem 4.6.1, the previous sentence may be rephrased as follows: For most of the common two (or more) storage-tape AFA $\mathscr{D}$, $\mathscr{L}(\mathscr{D}) = \mathscr{L}_{\mathrm{RE}}$.

In order to derive the result on $\hat{\mathscr{H}}(\mathscr{F}(L_0) \wedge \mathscr{F}(L_0))$, $L_0 = \{a^n b^n / n \geqq 1\}$, we shall need three lemmas. The first says that each r.e. set can be simulated by a 2-pushdown tape acceptor. The second says that each 2-pushdown tape acceptor can be simulated by a 4-counter. The third lemma asserts that each 4-counter can be simulated by a 2-counter.

LEMMA 4.7.1: $\mathscr{L}_{\mathrm{RE}} = \hat{\mathscr{H}}(\mathscr{L}_{\mathrm{CF}} \wedge \mathscr{L}_{\mathrm{CF}})$.

Proof: First note that

$$\begin{aligned}\hat{\mathscr{H}}(\mathscr{L}_{\mathrm{CF}} \wedge \mathscr{L}_{\mathrm{CF}}) &\subseteq \hat{\mathscr{H}}(\mathscr{L}_{\mathrm{ECS}} \wedge \mathscr{L}_{\mathrm{ECS}}) \\ &= \hat{\mathscr{H}}(\mathscr{L}_{\mathrm{ECS}}), \text{ since } \mathscr{L}_{\mathrm{ECS}} \text{ is closed under intersection,} \\ &= \mathscr{L}_{\mathrm{RE}}.\end{aligned}$$

Consider the reverse containment. Let L be an arbitrary r. e. set. It suffices to construct a 2-pushdown tape acceptor B such that $L = L(B)$. Since L is r. e., there exists a Turing acceptor $A = (K_A, \Sigma_1, \delta_A, p_1, F)$ such that $L = L(A)$. Let W be the set of all symbols not $\uparrow$ which occur on the storage tape of A. Since there are only a finite number of instructions occurring in A, we may assume W is finite. We shall construct a 2-pushdown tape acceptor B such that, except for a few exceptional cases, if $\gamma_1 \uparrow \gamma_2$ is the storage tape of A then (γ_1, γ_2^R) is the pair of storage tapes of B.

For each state q in K_A let $\bar{q}$ be a new symbol. Let B be the 2-pushdown tape acceptor $(K_B, \Sigma_1, \delta_B, p_1, F)$, where $K_B = \{q, \bar{q} / q \text{ in } K_A\}$ and δ_B is defined as follows (for all Z_1, Z_2 in W; Y_1, Y_2 in $W \cup \{\epsilon\}$; q, p in K_A; and x in $\Sigma_1 \cup \{\epsilon\}$):

(1) If (q, e) is in $\delta_A(p, x, \epsilon)$, let $(q, (\epsilon, \epsilon))$ be in $\delta_B(p, x, (\epsilon, \epsilon))$.
[Thus (ϵ, ϵ) in B simulates ϵ in A.]

(2) If $(q, 1)$ is in $\delta_A(p, x, \epsilon)$, let $(q, (\beta, \epsilon))$ be in $\delta_B(p, x, (\epsilon, \epsilon))$.
[Thus (β, ϵ) simulates $\beta \uparrow$.]

(3) If (q, Z_2) is in $\delta_A(p, x, Z_1)$, let $(q, (Z_2, 1_{Y_2}))$ be in $\delta_B(p, x, (Z_1, Y_2))$. [If $(p, x, \gamma_1 Z_1 \uparrow \gamma_2) \vdash_{\overline{A}} (q, \epsilon, \gamma_1 Z_2 \uparrow \gamma_2)$, then $(p, x, (\gamma_1 Z_1, \gamma_2^R)) \vdash_{\overline{B}} (q, \epsilon, (\gamma_1 Z_2, \gamma_2^R))$.]

(4) If $(q, 0)$ is in $\delta_A(p, x, Y_1)$, let $(q, (1_{Y_1}, 1_{Y_2}))$ be in $\delta_B(p, x, (Y_1, Y_2))$. [If $(p, x, \gamma_1 Y_1 \uparrow \gamma_2) \vdash_{\overline{A}} (q, \epsilon, \gamma_1 Y_1 \uparrow \gamma_2)$, then $(p, x, (\gamma_1 Y_1, \gamma_2^R)) \vdash_{\overline{B}} (q, \epsilon, (\gamma_1 Y_1, \gamma_2^R))$.]

(5) If $(q, 1)$ is in $\delta_A(p, x, Z_1)$, let $(q, (Z_1 Z_2, \epsilon))$ be in $\delta_B(p, x, (Z_1, Z_2))$ and $(q, (Z_1\beta, \epsilon))$ in $\delta_B(p, x, (Z_1, \epsilon))$.
[If $(p, x, \gamma_1 Z_1 \uparrow Z_2\gamma_2) \vdash_{\overline{A}} (q, \epsilon, \gamma_1 Z_1 Z_2 \uparrow \gamma_2)$, then $(p, x, (\gamma_1 Z_1, \gamma_2^R Z_2)) \vdash_{\overline{B}} (q, \epsilon, (\gamma_1 Z_1 Z_2, \gamma_2^R))$. If $(p, x, \gamma_1 Z_1 \uparrow) \vdash_{\overline{A}} (q, \epsilon, \gamma_1 Z_1 \beta \uparrow)$, then $(p, x, (\gamma_1 Z_1, \epsilon)) \vdash_{\overline{B}} (q, \epsilon, (\gamma_1 Z_1 \beta, \epsilon))$.]

(6) If $(q, -1)$ is in $\delta_A(p, x, Z_1)$, let $(q, (\epsilon, Y_2 Z_1))$ be in $\delta_B(p, x, (Z_1, Y_2))$ and $(q, (\beta, Z_1))$ in $\delta_B(q, \epsilon, (\epsilon, Z_1))$.
[If $(p, x, \gamma_1 Z_1 \uparrow \gamma_2) \vdash_{\overline{A}} (q, \epsilon, \gamma_1 \uparrow Z_1 \gamma_2), \gamma_1 \neq \epsilon$, then $(p, x, (\gamma_1 Z_1, \gamma_2^R)) \vdash_{\overline{B}} (q, \epsilon, (\gamma_1, \gamma_2^R Z_1))$. If $(p, x, Z_1 \uparrow \gamma_2) \vdash_{\overline{A}} (q, \epsilon, \beta \uparrow Z_1 \gamma_2)$, then $(p, x, (Z_1, \gamma_2^R)) \overset{*}{\vdash_{\overline{B}}} (q, \epsilon, (\beta, \gamma_2^R Z_1))$.]

(7) Suppose (q, e) is in $\delta_A(p, x, \beta)$. Let

(a) $(\bar{q}, (\epsilon, \epsilon))$ be in $\delta_B(p, x, (\beta, \beta))$.
(b) $(\bar{q}, (\epsilon, \epsilon))$ be in $\delta_B(p, x, (\beta, \epsilon))$.
(c) $(\bar{q}, (\epsilon, \epsilon))$ be in $\delta_B(\bar{q}, \epsilon, (\beta, \beta))$.
(d) $(\bar{q}, (\epsilon, \epsilon))$ be in $\delta_B(\bar{q}, \epsilon, (\epsilon, \beta))$.
(e) $(\bar{q}, (\epsilon, \epsilon))$ be in $\delta_B(\bar{q}, \epsilon, (\beta, \epsilon))$.
(f) $(q, (\epsilon, \epsilon))$ be in $\delta_B(\bar{q}, \epsilon, (\epsilon, \epsilon))$.

[If $(p, x, \beta^m \uparrow \beta^n) \vdash (q, \epsilon, \epsilon)$, $m \geqq 1$, then $(p, x, (\beta^m, \beta^n)) \overset{*}{\vdash} (q, \epsilon, (\epsilon, \epsilon))$.]

Clearly $L(B) = L(A)$ and the proof is complete.

$(\sim, f)$ LEMMA 4.7.2: *For each pda D_1, there exists a 2-counter D_2 such that $L(D_2) = L(D_1)$.*

Proof: By recoding the pushdown alphabet and adding additional states, we may assume that (i) the pushdown alphabet of D_1 has just the two symbols 1 and 2, and (ii) each instruction either adds exactly one symbol to the storage or deletes one symbol. Thus $D_1 = (K_1, \Sigma_1, \delta_1, p_1, F_1)$ contains rules only of the following form (where Y and Z are in $\{1, 2\}$, x is in $\Sigma_1 \cup \{\epsilon\}$, and p and q are in K_1): (q, ZY) in $\delta_1(p, x, Z)$, (q, Y) in $\delta_1(p, x, \epsilon)$, and (q, ϵ) in $\delta_1(p, x, Z)$. Since each pushdown symbol is either 1 or 2, each storage word $Z_1 \ldots Z_m$ may be uniquely represented by the number $n(Z_1 \ldots Z_m) = Z_m + Z_{m-1}3 + \ldots Z_1 3^{m-1}$ if $m \geqq 1$ and $n(\epsilon) = 0$. Note that for each W in $\{1, 2\}^*$ and Y in $\{1, 2\}$,

$(*)$ $n(WY) = 3n(W) + Y$.

For each p in K_1 let $\bar{p}$ be a new symbol and $\bar{K}_1 = \{\bar{p}/p \text{ in } K_1\}$. Let $K_2 = (K_1 \times \{\epsilon, 1, 2, 3, 4, 5\}) \cup (\bar{K}_1 \times \{\epsilon, 1, 2\}) \cup (K_1 \times \{1, 2\} \times \{1, 2\})$. We shall construct a 2-counter $D_2 = (K_2, \Sigma_1, \delta_2, (p_1, \epsilon), F_2)$, where $F_2 = F_1 \times \{\epsilon\}$ and a is the only symbol in the storage alphabet of D_2. The acceptor D_2 will be seen to have the property that for each word w in Σ_1^*, each Z_i in $\{1, 2\}$, and each $m \geqq 0$,

(**) $(p_1, w, \epsilon) \overset{*}{\underset{D_1}{\vdash}} (p, \epsilon, Z_1 \ldots Z_m)$ if and only if $((p_1, \epsilon), w, (\epsilon, \epsilon)) \overset{*}{\underset{D_2}{\vdash}} ((\bar{p}, Z_m), \epsilon, (\epsilon, a^{n(Z_1 \ldots Z_{m-1})})) \overset{*}{\underset{D_2}{\vdash}} ((p, Z_m), \epsilon, (a^{n(Z_1 \ldots Z_{m-1})}, \epsilon))$, with $Z_1 \ldots Z_{m-1} = Z_m = \epsilon$ if $m = 0$.

Thus D_2 simulates D_1 with $Z_1 \ldots Z_m$ on the auxiliary storage by remembering Z_m in the state and representing $Z_1 \ldots Z_{m-1}$ by $a^{n(Z_1 \ldots Z_{m-1})}$ on the first counter. Each move of D_1 which adds a symbol Y to the auxiliary storage is simulated in D_2 by multiplying the counter by 3, adding a^{Z_m} to the resulting counter, and inserting Y into the state. If D_1 erases Z_m, then D_2 divides the length of its counter by 3 and puts the remainder, Z_{m-1}, into the state. To construct D_2 we thus have to show how to multiply by 3 and divide by 3 in a 2-counter.

The function δ_2 is defined as follows (where Y and Z are in $\{1, 2\}$, x is in $\Sigma_1 \cup \{\epsilon\}$, and p and q are in K_1):

(1) Suppose (q, Y) is in $\delta_1(p, x, \epsilon)$. Let $((\bar{q}, Y), (\epsilon, \epsilon))$ be in $\delta_2((p, \epsilon), x, (\epsilon, \epsilon))$. [By (1) and (3b) below, if $(p, x, \epsilon) \underset{D_1}{\vdash} (q, \epsilon, Y)$ then $((p, \epsilon), x, (\epsilon, \epsilon)) \underset{D_2}{\vdash} ((\bar{q}, Y), \epsilon, (\epsilon, \epsilon)) \underset{D_2}{\vdash} ((q, Y), \epsilon, (\epsilon, \epsilon))$.]

(2) Suppose (q, ZY) is in $\delta_1(p, x, Z)$. Let

(a) $((q, Y, Z), (a, \epsilon))$ be in $\delta_2((p, Z), x, (a, \epsilon))$ and $((q, Y, Z), (\epsilon, \epsilon))$ in $\delta_2((p, Z), x, (\epsilon, \epsilon))$.

(b) $((q, Y, Z), (\epsilon, a^3))$ be in $\delta_2((q, Y, Z), \epsilon, (a, \epsilon))$ and $((q, Y, Z), (\epsilon, a^4))$ in $\delta_2((q, Y, Z), \epsilon, (a, a))$.

[By (a) and (b) of (2), if $(p, x, WZ) \underset{D_1}{\vdash} (q, \epsilon, WZY)$, then $((p, Z), x, (a^{n(W)}, \epsilon)) \overset{*}{\underset{D_2}{\vdash}} ((q, Y, Z), \epsilon, (\epsilon, a^{3n(W)}))$.]

(c) $((\bar{q}, Y), (\epsilon, a^Z))$ be in $\delta_2((q, Y, Z), \epsilon, (\epsilon, \epsilon))$ and $((\bar{q}, Y), (\epsilon, a^{Z+1}))$ in $\delta_2((q, Y, Z), \epsilon, (\epsilon, a))$.

[By (c) of (2), $((q, Y, Z), \epsilon, (\epsilon, a^{3n(W)})) \overset{*}{\underset{D_2}{\vdash}} ((\bar{q}, Y), \epsilon, (\epsilon, a^{n(WZ)}))$. Thus, if $(p, x, WZ) \underset{D_1}{\vdash} (q, \epsilon, WZY)$, then $((p, Z), x, (a^{n(W)}, \epsilon)) \overset{*}{\underset{D_2}{\vdash}} ((\bar{q}, Y), \epsilon, (\epsilon, a^{n(WZ)}))$.]

(3) (a) $((\bar{q}, Y), (a, \epsilon))$ is in $\delta_2((\bar{q}, Y), \epsilon, (\epsilon, a))$ and $((\bar{q}, Y), (a^2, \epsilon))$ is in $\delta_2((\bar{q}, Y), \epsilon, (a, a))$.

(b) $((q, Y), (a, \epsilon))$ is in $\delta_2((\bar{q}, Y), \epsilon, (a, \epsilon))$ and $((q, Y), (\epsilon, \epsilon))$ is in $\delta_2((\bar{q}, Y), \epsilon, (\epsilon, \epsilon))$.

[By (3), $((\bar{q}, Y), \epsilon, (\epsilon, a^{n(W)})) \vdash_{D_2}^{*} ((q, Y), \epsilon, (a^{n(W)}, \epsilon))$.]

(4) Suppose (q, ϵ) is in $\delta_1(p, x, Z)$. Let

(a) $((\bar{q}, \epsilon), (\epsilon, \epsilon))$ be in $\delta_2((p, Z), x, (\epsilon, \epsilon))$ and $((q, \epsilon), (\epsilon, \epsilon))$ in $\delta_2((\bar{q}, \epsilon), \epsilon, (\epsilon, \epsilon))$.

[By (a) of (4), if $(p, x, Z) \vdash_{D_1} (q, \epsilon, \epsilon)$ then $((p, Z), x, (\epsilon, \epsilon)) \vdash_{D_2} ((\bar{q}, \epsilon), \epsilon, (\epsilon, \epsilon)) \vdash_{D_2} ((q, \epsilon), \epsilon, (\epsilon, \epsilon))$.]

(b) $((q, 3), (a, \epsilon))$ be in $\delta_2((p, Z), x, (a, \epsilon))$.

(c) $((q, 4), (\epsilon, \epsilon))$ be in $\delta_2((q, 3), \epsilon, (a, \epsilon))$ and $((q, 4), (\epsilon, a))$ in $\delta_2((q, 3), \epsilon, (a, a))$.

(d) $((q, 5), (\epsilon, \epsilon))$ be in $\delta_2((q, 4), \epsilon, (a, \epsilon))$ and $((q, 5), (\epsilon, a))$ in $\delta_2((q, 4), \epsilon, (a, a))$.

(e) $((q, 3), (\epsilon, a))$ be in $\delta_2((q, 5), \epsilon, (a, \epsilon))$ and $((q, 3), (\epsilon, a^2))$ in $\delta_2((q, 5), \epsilon, (a, a))$.

(f) $((\bar{q}, 1), (\epsilon, \epsilon))$ be in $\delta_2((q, 4), \epsilon, (\epsilon, \epsilon))$ and $((\bar{q}, 1), (\epsilon, a))$ in $\delta_2((q, 4), \epsilon, (\epsilon, a))$.

(g) $((\bar{q}, 2), (\epsilon, \epsilon))$ be in $\delta_2((q, 5), \epsilon, (\epsilon, \epsilon))$ and $((\bar{q}, 2), (\epsilon, a))$ in $\delta_2((q, 5), \epsilon, (\epsilon, a))$.

[By $(b)-(g)$ of (4), if $(p, x, WYZ) \vdash_{D_1} (q, \epsilon, WY)$ then $((p, Z), x, (a^{n(WY)}, \epsilon)) \vdash_{D_2}^{*} ((\bar{q}, Y), \epsilon, (\epsilon, a^{n(W)}))$. By (3), $((\bar{q}, Y), \epsilon, (\epsilon, a^{n(W)})) \vdash_{D_2}^{*} ((q, Y), \epsilon, (a^{n(W)}, \epsilon))$. Thus $((p, Z), x, (a^{n(WY)}, \epsilon)) \vdash_{D_2}^{*} ((q, Y), \epsilon, (a^{n(W)}, \epsilon))$.]

By construction of δ_2, it is clear that if $(p_1, w, \epsilon) \vdash_{D_1}^{*} (p, \epsilon, Z_1 \ldots Z_m)$, $m \geqq 0$, then $((p_1, \epsilon), w, (\epsilon, \epsilon)) \vdash_{D_2}^{*} ((\bar{p}, Z_m), \epsilon, (\epsilon, a^{n(Z_1 \ldots Z_{m-1})})) \vdash_{D_2}^{*} ((p, Z_m), \epsilon, (a^{n(Z_1 \ldots Z_{m-1})}, \epsilon))$. A straightforward case analysis shows that the other half of (**) also holds. (See Exercise 4.7.1.) From (**), it immediately follows that $L(D_1) = L(D_2)$.

$(\sim, f)$ COROLLARY: $\mathscr{L}_{RE} = \mathscr{L}(\mathscr{D}_C \wedge \mathscr{D}_C \wedge \mathscr{D}_C \wedge \mathscr{D}_C)$.

Proof:
$$\begin{aligned} \mathscr{L}_{RE} &= \hat{\mathscr{H}}(\mathscr{L}(\mathscr{D}_{PDA}) \wedge \mathscr{L}(\mathscr{D}_{PDA})), && \text{by Lemma 4.7.1,}\\ &\subseteq \hat{\mathscr{H}}(\mathscr{L}(\mathscr{D}_C \wedge \mathscr{D}_C) \wedge \mathscr{L}(\mathscr{D}_C \wedge \mathscr{D}_C)), && \text{by Lemma 4.7.2,}\\ &= \mathscr{L}((\mathscr{D}_C \wedge \mathscr{D}_C) \wedge (\mathscr{D}_C \wedge \mathscr{D}_C)), && \text{by Theorem 4.6.1,}\\ &= \mathscr{L}(\mathscr{D}_C \wedge \mathscr{D}_C \wedge \mathscr{D}_C \wedge \mathscr{D}_C). \end{aligned}$$

On the other hand,

$$\begin{aligned} \mathscr{L}(\mathscr{D}_C \wedge \mathscr{D}_C \wedge \mathscr{D}_C \wedge \mathscr{D}_C) &= \hat{\mathscr{H}}(\mathscr{L}(\mathscr{D}_C) \wedge \mathscr{L}(\mathscr{D}_C) \wedge \mathscr{L}(\mathscr{D}_C) \wedge \mathscr{L}(\mathscr{D}_C)),\\ &\qquad \text{by Theorem 4.6.1,}\\ &\subseteq \hat{\mathscr{H}}(\mathscr{L}_{ECS} \wedge \mathscr{L}_{ECS} \wedge \mathscr{L}_{ECS} \wedge \mathscr{L}_{ECS})\\ &\subseteq \hat{\mathscr{H}}(\mathscr{L}_{ECS})\\ &= \mathscr{L}_{RE}. \end{aligned}$$

We now strengthen the above corollary.

$(\sim, f)$ LEMMA 4.7.3: $\mathscr{L}_{\mathrm{RE}} = \mathscr{L}(\mathscr{D}_{\mathrm{C}} \wedge \mathscr{D}_{\mathrm{C}} \wedge \mathscr{D}_{\mathrm{C}} \wedge \mathscr{D}_{\mathrm{C}}) = \mathscr{L}(\mathscr{D}_{\mathrm{C}} \wedge \mathscr{D}_{\mathrm{C}})$.

Proof: Obviously $\mathscr{L}(\mathscr{D}_{\mathrm{C}} \wedge \mathscr{D}_{\mathrm{C}}) \subseteq \mathscr{L}(\mathscr{D}_{\mathrm{C}} \wedge \mathscr{D}_{\mathrm{C}} \wedge \mathscr{D}_{\mathrm{C}} \wedge \mathscr{D}_{\mathrm{C}}) = \mathscr{L}_{\mathrm{RE}}$. It thus suffices to show that $\mathscr{L}(\mathscr{D}_{\mathrm{C}} \wedge \mathscr{D}_{\mathrm{C}} \wedge \mathscr{D}_{\mathrm{C}} \wedge \mathscr{D}_{\mathrm{C}}) \subseteq \mathscr{L}(\mathscr{D}_{\mathrm{C}} \wedge \mathscr{D}_{\mathrm{C}})$. Let L be in $\mathscr{L}(\mathscr{D}_{\mathrm{C}} \wedge \mathscr{D}_{\mathrm{C}} \wedge \mathscr{D}_{\mathrm{C}} \wedge \mathscr{D}_{\mathrm{C}})$. Then $L = L(D_1)$ for some 4-counter $D_1 = (K_1, \Sigma_1, \delta_1, p_1, F_1)$. By adding extra states if necessary, we may assume that each move of D_1 (i) changes only one of the counters, and (ii) either increases or decreases that counter by one symbol.

For all (m_1, m_2, m_3, m_4) in N^4 let $n(m_1, m_2, m_3, m_4) = 2^{m_1}3^{m_2}5^{m_3}7^{m_4}$. The function n clearly is one to one. Also, $n(m_1, m_2, m_3, m_4)$ is a (positive) multiple of 2, 3, 5, and 7, resp., if and only if $m_1 > 0$, $m_2 > 0$, $m_3 > 0$, and $m_4 > 0$, resp. For each i in N, let $s(i) = 0$ if $i = 0$ and $s(i) = 1$ if $i > 0$. We shall construct a 2-counter $D_2 = (K_2, \Sigma_1, \delta_2, p_1, \{p_0\})$, with $((K_1 \times \{0, 1\} \times \{0, 1\} \times \{0, 1\} \times \{0, 1\}) \cup K_1) \subseteq K_2$ and p_0 a symbol not in K_1, having the following two properties:

(1) $(p_1, w, (\epsilon, \epsilon, \epsilon, \epsilon)) \overset{*}{\underset{D_1}{\vdash}} (p, \epsilon, (a^{m_1}, a^{m_2}, a^{m_3}, a^{m_4}))$, p in K_1, if and only if $(p_1, w, (\epsilon, \epsilon)) \overset{*}{\underset{D_2}{\vdash}} \big((p, s(m_1), s(m_2), s(m_3), s(m_4)), \epsilon, (a^{n(m_1, \ldots, m_4)}, \epsilon)\big)$.

(2) $((p, 0, 0, 0, 0), \epsilon, (a^{n(0, 0, 0, 0)}, \epsilon)) \underset{D_2}{\vdash} (p_0, \epsilon, (\epsilon, \epsilon))$ for all p in F_1. From this, it will follow that $L(D_1) = L(D_2)$, whence L is in $\mathscr{L}(\mathscr{D}_{\mathrm{C}} \wedge \mathscr{D}_{\mathrm{C}})$.

We first note the following. The proof of Lemma 4.7.2 shows that for a given positive integer π and all positive integers m there exists a 2-counter subroutine, i.e., a sequence of moves, which

(3) changes the counters configuration (a^m, ϵ) into $(a^{\pi m}, \epsilon)$,

and another subroutine which

(4) changes the counters configuration $(a^{\pi m}, \epsilon)$ into (a^m, ϵ).

By a simple modification of these subroutines, it is easy to verify that there exist subroutines which

(5) change the counters configuration (a^m, ϵ) into (a^{k_2}, a^{k_1}), where $m = \pi k_1 + k_2$, $0 \leqq k_2 < \pi$, and

(6) change the counters configuration (a^{k_2}, a^{k_1}), $0 \leqq k_2 < \pi$, into $(a^{\pi k_1 + k_2}, \epsilon)$.

[For (5), we erase counter 1 π times and add symbol a to counter 2, erase counter 1 π times and add symbol a to counter 2, etc. Simultaneously, we remember in the state how many erasings of counter 1 since the last time the symbol a was added to counter 2. When counter 1 is empty, k_2 is in the state and a^{k_1} on counter 2. We then add the symbol a k_2 times to counter 1, arriving at the counters configuration (a^{k_2}, a^{k_1}). For (6), we essentially reverse the procedure for (5).]

More formally, let $\pi_1 = 2$, $\pi_2 = 3$, $\pi_3 = 5$, and $\pi_4 = 7$. Let i be in $\{1, 2, 3, 4\}$ and 0_i and 1_i denote any two vectors in $\{0, 1\}\times\{0, 1\}\times\{0, 1\}\times\{0, 1\}$ which differ only in that the i-th coordinate of 0_i is 0 and the i-th coordinate of 1_i is 1. Let x be an arbitrary element of $\Sigma_1 \cup \{\epsilon\}$, m_1, m_2, m_3, m_4 nonnegative integers, and p and q states in K_1. Let $l = n(m_1, m_2, m_3, m_4)$. Let $(p, 0_i)$, $(p, 1_i)$, $(q, 0_i)$, $(q, 1_i)$, $(q_i, 0, 0_i)$, $(q_i, 1, 1_i)$, and $(q_i, 2, 0_i)$ be new symbols representing states in D_2. Using (3)–(6) it is straightforward to show that a 2-counter $D_2 = (K_2, \Sigma_1, \delta_2, p_1, \{p_0\})$ can be constructed having just the following properties:

(7) $(p_1, \epsilon, (\epsilon, \epsilon)) \vdash_{D_2} ((p_1, 0, 0, 0, 0), \epsilon, (a^{n(0,0,0,0)}, \epsilon))$ and, for each p in F_1,

$$((p, 0, 0, 0, 0), \epsilon, (a^{n(0,0,0,0)}, \epsilon)) \vdash_{D_2} (p_0, \epsilon, (\epsilon, \epsilon)).$$

(8) Suppose that under x, D_1 in one step adds the symbol a to the i-th storage, and goes from state p to state q.

(a) If $m_i = 0$, then let

$$((p, 0_i), x, (a^l, \epsilon)) \overset{*}{\vdash}_{D_2} ((q, 1_i), \epsilon, (a^{\pi_i l}, \epsilon)).$$

(b) If $m_i > 0$, then let

$$((p, 1_i), x, (a^l, \epsilon)) \overset{*}{\vdash}_{D_2} ((q, 1_i), \epsilon, (a^{\pi_i l}, \epsilon)).$$

(9) Suppose that under x, D_1 in one step erases the symbol a from the i-th storage, and goes from p to q. Suppose that $m_i > 0$.

(a) Then $((p, 1_i), x, (a^l, \epsilon)) \overset{*}{\vdash}_{D_2} ((q_i, 0, 0_i), \epsilon, (a^{l/\pi_i}, \epsilon))$.

(b) If l/π_i is a multiple of π_i, then let

$$((q_i, 0, 0_i), \epsilon, (a^{l/\pi_i}, \epsilon)) \overset{*}{\vdash}_{D_2} ((q_i, 1, 1_i), \epsilon, (\epsilon, a^{l/\pi_i\pi_i}))$$
$$\overset{*}{\vdash}_{D_2} ((q, 1_i), \epsilon, (a^{l/\pi_i}, \epsilon)).$$

(c) If l/π_i is not a multiple of π_i, then let

$$((q_i, 0, 0_i), \epsilon, (a^{l/\pi_i}, \epsilon)) \overset{*}{\vdash}_{D_2} ((q_i, 2, 0_i), \epsilon, (a^{k_2}, a^{k_1}))$$
$$\overset{*}{\vdash}_{D_2} ((q, 0_i), \epsilon, (a^{l/\pi_i}, \epsilon)),$$

where $l/\pi_i = \pi_i k_1 + k_2$, $0 \leq k_2 < \pi_i$.

[Intuitively, the components 1_i and 0_i are used to denote that the length of the non-ϵ counter is or is not, respectively, a multiple of π_i.]

From (7), (8), and (9), it follows that (1) and (2) hold.

We are now ready for the main result of the section.

THEOREM 4.7.1: *For* $L_0 = \{a^n b^n / n \geqq 1\}$, $\hat{\mathscr{H}}(\mathscr{F}(L_0) \wedge \mathscr{F}(L_0)) = \mathscr{L}_{\mathrm{RE}}$.

Proof: Clearly $\hat{\mathscr{H}}(\mathscr{F}(L_0) \wedge \mathscr{F}(L_0)) \subseteq \mathscr{L}_{\mathrm{RE}}$. It thus suffices to show the reverse containment. Thus let L be an arbitrary r.e. set. By Lemma 4.7.3, there exists a 2-counter $D = (K_1, \Sigma_L, \delta, q_0, F_1)$ such that $L = L(D)$. Without loss of generality, we may assume that each move of the 2-counter either adds or erases a from exactly one of the counters. We may also assume that q_0 is not in F_1 and that $K_1 \cap \Sigma_L = \emptyset$. Let c be a new symbol. Let W be the set of all words of the form $u_0 \ldots u_k$, where $k \geqq 1$, $u_i = q_i c^{2^{m_i} 3^{n_i}} x_{i+1} q_{i+1} c^{2^{m_{i+1}} 3^{n_{i+1}}}$, q_{k+1} is in F_1, $m_0 = n_0 = m_{k+1} = n_{k+1} = 0$, and

$$(q_i, x_{i+1}, (a^{m_i}, a^{n_i})) \underset{D}{\vdash} (q_{i+1}, \epsilon, (a^{m_{i+1}}, a^{n_{i+1}}))$$

for each i, $0 \leqq i \leqq k$. Let h be the homomorphism on $(K_1 \cup \Sigma_L \cup \{c\})^*$ defined by $h(q) = h(c) = \epsilon$ for all q in K_1, and $h(x) = x$ for all x in Σ_L. Obviously $L = h(W)$ since q_0 is not in F_1 and each move either adds or erases the symbol a from exactly one counter.

To complete the proof we shall show that $W = L_1 \cap L_2$ for some L_1 and L_2 in $\mathscr{F}(L_0)$. For each rule $\mu: (q, (y_1, y_2))$ in $\delta(p, x, (z_1, z_2))$, with p and q in K_1, x in $\Sigma_L \cup \{\epsilon\}$, y_1 and y_2 in $\{\epsilon, a, a^2\}$, and z_1 and z_2 in $\{\epsilon, a\}$, let S_μ be the following set:

(1) If μ is either $(q, (a, \epsilon))$ in $\delta(p, x, (\epsilon, \epsilon))$ or $(q, (a, a))$ in $\delta(p, x, (\epsilon, a))$ or $(q, (a^2, \epsilon))$ in $\delta(p, x, (a, \epsilon))$ or $(q, (a^2, a))$ in $\delta(p, x, (a, a))$, then let $S_\mu = \{pc^r xqc^{2r} / r \geqq 1\}$.
[This case covers the situation where the symbol a is added to the first storage.]

(2) If μ is either $(q, (\epsilon, a))$ in $\delta(p, x, (\epsilon, \epsilon))$ or $(q, (a, a))$ in $\delta(p, x, (a, \epsilon))$ or $(q, (\epsilon, a^2))$ in $\delta(p, x, (\epsilon, a))$ or $(q, (a, a^2))$ in $\delta(p, x, (a, a))$, then let $S_\mu = \{pc^r xqc^{3r} / r \geqq 1\}$.
[This case covers the situation where a is added to the second storage.]

(3) If μ is either $(q, (\epsilon, \epsilon))$ in $\delta(p, x, (a, \epsilon))$ or $(q, (\epsilon, a))$ in $\delta(p, x, (a, a))$ then let $S_\mu = \{pc^{2r} xqc^r / r \geqq 1\}$.
[This case covers the situation where a is erased from the first storage.]

(4) If μ is either $(q, (\epsilon, \epsilon))$ in $\delta(p, x, (\epsilon, a))$ or $(q, (a, \epsilon))$ in $\delta(p, x, (a, a))$ then let $S_\mu = \{pc^{3r} xqc^r / r \geqq 1\}$.
[This case covers the situation where a is erased from the second storage.]
Let $S = \bigcup_{\text{all } \mu} S_\mu$. Since each S_μ is in $\mathscr{F}(L_0)$, so is S. Let $L_1 = S^+$, $V = \{qc^r qc^r / q \text{ in } K_1, r \geqq 1\}$, and

$$L_2 = q_0 c(\Sigma_L V \cup V)^+ (\Sigma_L F_1 c \cup F_1 c).$$

Clearly L_1 and L_2 are in $\mathcal{F}(L_0)$, and $W = L_1 \cap L_2$.

COROLLARY: *If $\mathcal{L}_1$ and $\mathcal{L}_2$ are AFL containing $\{a^nb^n/n \geqq 1\}$, then $\mathcal{L}_{RE} \subseteq \hat{\mathcal{H}}(\mathcal{L}_1 \wedge \mathcal{L}_2)$.*

It can be shown [BB] that for $L_0 = \{a^nb^n/n \geqq 1\}$, $\hat{\mathcal{H}}(\mathcal{S}(L_0) \wedge \mathcal{S}(L_0)) \supsetneq \mathcal{L}_{RE}$. In fact, it is proved in [BB] that $\hat{\mathcal{H}}(\mathcal{S}(L_0) \wedge \mathcal{S}(L_0)) \subsetneq \mathcal{L}_{ECS}$.

EXERCISE 4.7.1: Verify the remaining part of (∗∗) in Lemma 4.7.2.

EXERCISE 4.7.2: Construct δ_2 for a 2-counter which realizes (9) in Lemma 4.7.3.

EXERCISE 4.7.3: For each pda D_1, prove that there exists a 2-counter

(a) D_2 such that $\tilde{L}(D_2) = \tilde{L}(D_1)$.

(b) D_3 such that $L_f(D_3) = L_f(D_1)$.

EXERCISE 4.7.4: Prove that

(a) $\mathcal{L}_{RE} = \tilde{\mathcal{L}}(\mathcal{D}_C \wedge \mathcal{D}_C \wedge \mathcal{D}_C \wedge \mathcal{D}_C)$.

(b) $\mathcal{L}_{RE} = \mathcal{L}_f(\mathcal{D}_C \wedge \mathcal{D}_C \wedge \mathcal{D}_C \wedge \mathcal{D}_C)$.

EXERCISE 4.7.5: Prove that

(a) $\mathcal{L}_{RE} = \tilde{\mathcal{L}}(\mathcal{D}_C \wedge \mathcal{D}_C)$.

(b) $\mathcal{L}_{RE} = \mathcal{L}_f(\mathcal{D}_C \wedge \mathcal{D}_C)$.

EXERCISE 4.7.6: For each x in $\Sigma_L \cup \{\epsilon\}$, show that $\{pc^{3r}xqc^r/r \geqq 1\}$ is in $\mathcal{F}(L_0)$, the notation as in Theorem 4.7.1.

EXERCISE 4.7.7: Let $\mathcal{L}$ be a full AFL closed under intersection with linear context-free languages. Prove that $\mathcal{L}_{RE} \subseteq \mathcal{L}$ [GHa2].

EXERCISE 4.7.8: Let $\mathcal{L}$ be a full AFL containing $\{a^nb^n/n \geqq 1\}$ and closed under[1] τ^{-1} for every substitution τ by languages in $\mathcal{L}$. Let ϱ be the function on $\{a, b\}^*$ defined by $\varrho(\epsilon) = 1$, $\varrho(ua) = 2\varrho(u)+1$, and $\varrho(ub) = 2\varrho(u)+2$ for all u in $\{a, b\}^*$. Prove the following:

(a) $\{wc^{\varrho(w)}/w \text{ in } \{a, b\}^*\}$ and $\{d^{\varrho(w)}w/w \text{ in } \{a, b\}^*\}$ are in $\mathcal{L}$. [Hint: For the first language, consider $\tau^{-1}(\{a^ib^i/i \geqq 1\}^+) \cap d\{a, b\}^*c^*$, where τ is the

[1] See the definitions prior to Exercise 3.3.4.

substitution on $\{a, b, c, d\}^*$ defined by $\tau(a) = \{b^i a^{2i+1}/i \geqq 1\}$, $\tau(b) = \{b^i a^{2i+2}/i \geqq 1\}$, $\tau(c) = \{b\}$, and $\tau(d) = \{a\}$.]

(b) $\{wcw/w \text{ in } \Sigma_0^*\}$ is in $\mathscr{L}$ for each Σ_0 and each symbol c not in Σ_0. [Hint: Consider $\tau^{-1}(\{uc^{\varrho(u)}d^{\varrho(v)}v/u,\ v \text{ in } \{a, b\}^*\})$, where τ is the substitution on $\{a, b, c\}^*$ defined by $\tau(a) = \{a\}$, $\tau(b) = \{b\}$, and $\tau(c) = \{c^n d^n/n \geqq 1\}$.]

(c) $\{sutcsvtc/s, t \text{ in } \Sigma_0^*\}$ is in $\mathscr{L}$ for each Σ_0, symbol c not in Σ_0, and u, v in Σ_0^*.

(d) Let $G = (V, \Sigma_1, P, \sigma)$ be an arbitrary phrase structure grammar, with $V \cap P = \emptyset$. Let c be a new symbol. Then

$$L(G) = h(\tau^{-1}(\{wcwc/w \text{ in } V^*\}^*) \cap \sigma P^* \Sigma_1^* c),$$

where h is the homomorphism and τ the substitution on $(P \cup \Sigma_1 \cup \{\sigma, c\})^*$ defined by $h(u \to v) = h(\sigma) = h(c) = \epsilon$, $h(x) = x$, $\tau(u \to v) = \{sutcsvtc/s, t \text{ in } V^*\}$, $\tau(x) = \{x\}$, $\tau(\sigma) = \{\sigma c\}$, and $\tau(c) = \{c\}$, for each $u \to v$ in P and x in Σ_1. Thus infer that $\mathscr{L}_{\text{RE}} \subseteq \mathscr{L}$.

EXERCISE 4.7.9: Prove that $\mathscr{L}_{\text{RE}} \subseteq \hat{\mathscr{F}}_\cap(L)$ for each infinite subset L of $\{a^n b^n/n \geqq 0\}$ [GGo2].

EXERCISE 4.7.10: For each language $L \subseteq a^* b^*$ and each $i \geqq 0$, let $L_i = \{b^j/ a^i b^j \text{ in } L\}$. Suppose that $\bigcup_{i=0}^{\infty} L_i$ is infinite and there exists a positive integer k such that $\#(L_i) \leqq k$ for all i. Prove that $\mathscr{L}_{\text{RE}} \subseteq \hat{\mathscr{F}}_\cap(L)$ [GGo2].

EXERCISE 4.7.11: Let $L = \{a^{n_i}/i \geqq 0\}$ be an infinite language. Prove that $\mathscr{L}_{\text{RE}} \subseteq \hat{\mathscr{F}}_\cap(L)$ if $\liminf_{i \to \infty} (n_{i+1}/n_i) > 1$ [GGo2].

4.8 Reversal

In the current section a condition on an AFA$\mathscr{D}$ is presented which guarantees that $(\sim)\mathscr{L}^t(\mathscr{D})$ and $\mathscr{L}(\mathscr{D})$ are closed under reversal. Using this condition, many well-known (semi-) AFL can be shown to be closed under reversal.

Def: An AFA $(\Omega, \mathscr{D})$, with $\Omega = (K, \Sigma, \Gamma, I, f, g)$, is said to be *reversible* if the following condition holds: For each u in I and ξ in $g(\Gamma^*)$, there exists $v_{u,\xi}$ in I so that for each γ and γ', ξ in $g(\gamma)$, $f(\gamma, u) = \gamma'$ if and only if $f(\gamma', v_{u,\xi}) = \gamma$.

EXAMPLE 4.8.1: Let K, Σ, and Γ be infinite sets. Let $I = \{0, E_Z/Z \text{ in } \Gamma\} \cup \Gamma$, where E_Z is a new symbol for each Z in Γ. Let $(\Omega, \mathcal{D})$ be the AFA where $f(\gamma, 0) = \gamma$, $f(\gamma Z, E_Z) = \gamma$, $f(\gamma, Z) = \gamma Z$, $g(\epsilon) = \{\epsilon\}$, and $g(\gamma Z) = \{Z\}$ for each γ in Γ^* and Z in Γ. Then $\mathcal{D}$ is reversible, and, with trivial variation, is the AFA of pushdown acceptors.

($\sim$) THEOREM 4.8.1: *For each reversible AFA $\mathcal{D}$, $\mathcal{L}(\mathcal{D})$ and $\mathcal{L}^t(\mathcal{D})$ are both closed under reversal.*

Proof: Let D_1 be in $\mathcal{D}$. An acceptor D_2 in $\mathcal{D}$ will be exhibited such that $L(D_2) = (L(D_1))^R$. In effect, D_2 will be the acceptor obtained by "running D_1 backwards".

Let $D_1 = (K_1, \Sigma_1, \delta_1, p_1, F_1)$. Without loss of generality, we may assume that $F_1 = \{d\}$ and $\delta_1(d, a, \xi) = \emptyset$ for each a and ξ. We may also assume that G_{D_1} contains ϵ. [Otherwise, $L(D_1) = \emptyset$ or $L(D_1) = \{\epsilon\}$, and there is nothing to prove.] For each (u, ξ) in $I \times g(\Gamma^*)$, let

$$\begin{aligned} H_{u,\xi} &= gf(g^{-1}(\xi), u) \cap G_{D_1} \\ &= \{\xi'/\delta_1(q, a, \xi') \neq \emptyset \text{ for some } q \text{ and } a,\ \xi' \text{ in } g(f(\gamma, u)), \\ &\qquad \xi \text{ in } g(\gamma) \text{ for some } \gamma\}, \end{aligned}$$

where $g^{-1}(\xi) = \{\gamma \text{ in } \Gamma^*/\xi \text{ in } g(\gamma)\}$. Since G_{D_1} is finite, $H_{u,\xi}$ is finite (possibly empty). Let D_2 be the acceptor $(K_2, \Sigma_1, \delta_2, (d, \epsilon), \{(p_1, \epsilon)\})$, where $K_2 = K_1 \times G_{D_1}$ and δ_2 is defined as follows: If (p, u) is in $\delta_1(q, a, \xi)$, then let $((q, \xi), v_{u,\xi})$ be in $\delta_2((p, \xi'), a, \xi')$ for all ξ' in $H_{u,\xi}$.

Since K_1 and G_{D_1} are both finite, K_2 is finite and D_2 is an acceptor. The fact that $L(D_2) = (L(D_1))^R$ and the fact that D_1 is in $\mathcal{D}_l^t$ for some l if and only if D_2 is in $\mathcal{D}_l^t$ for some l is an immediate consequence of the following:

Let $k \geqq 1$ and $w_1, \ldots, w_k$ be in $\Sigma_1 \cup \{\epsilon\}$. Let $q_0, \ldots, q_k$ be in K_1 and $\gamma_0, \ldots, \gamma_k$ in Γ^*. Then

(1) $(q_0, w_k \ldots w_1, \gamma_0) \vdash_{D_1} (q_1, w_{k-1} \ldots w_1, \gamma_1) \vdash_{D_1} \cdots \vdash_{D_1} (q_k, \epsilon, \gamma_k)$,
with $g(\gamma_k) \cap G_{D_1} \neq \emptyset$,
if and only if

(2) $((q_k, \xi_k), w_1 \ldots w_k, \gamma_k) \vdash_{D_2} \cdots \vdash_{D_2} ((q_0, \xi_0), \epsilon, \gamma_0)$
for some ξ_0 in $g(\gamma_0) \cap G_{D_1}, \ldots, \xi_k$ in $g(\gamma_k) \cap G_{D_1}$.

To see that (1) implies (2), we use induction on k. The case for $k = 1$ is trivial and is subsumed in the case $k = m+1$ given below. Suppose (1) implies (2) for $k \leqq m$. Consider $k = m+1$. Suppose (1) holds for $k = m+1$. Then we have

(3) $(q_0, w_{m+1}, \gamma_0) \vdash_{D_1} (q_1, \epsilon, \gamma_1)$ and

(4) $(q_1, w_m \ldots w_1, \gamma_1) \vdash_{D_1} \cdots \vdash_{D_1} (q_{m+1}, \epsilon, \gamma_{m+1})$,
with $g(\gamma_1) \cap G_{D_1} \neq \emptyset$ and $g(\gamma_{m+1}) \cap G_{D_1} \neq \emptyset$. From (4) and induction,
(5) $((q_{m+1}, \xi_{m+1}), w_1 \ldots w_m, \gamma_{m+1}) \overset{*}{\vdash}_{D_2} ((q_1, \xi_1), \epsilon, \gamma_1)$,
with ξ_i in $g(\gamma_i) \cap G_{D_1}$, $1 \leqq i \leqq m+1$. From (3), there exist ξ_0 in $g(\gamma_0) \cap G_{D_1}$ and (q_1, u_1) in $\delta_1(q_0, w_{m+1}, \xi_0)$ such that $f(\gamma_0, u_1) = \gamma_1$. Then ξ_1 is in H_{u_1, ξ_0}. By construction of D_2 we have
(6) $((q_0, \xi_0), v_{u_1, \xi_0})$ is in $\delta_2((q_1, \xi_1), w_{m+1}, \xi_1)$.
By definition of reversible,
(7) $f(\gamma_1, v_{u_1, \xi_0}) = \gamma_0$.
From (6) and (7), we have
(8) $((q_1, \xi_1), w_{m+1}, \gamma_1) \vdash_{D_2} ((q_0, \xi_0), \epsilon, \gamma_0)$.
Combining (5) and (8), we get (2) for $k = m+1$.

Using induction we now show that (2) implies (1). Suppose $k = 1$. Then
(9) $((q_1, \xi_1), w_1, \gamma_1) \vdash_{D_2} ((q_0, \xi_0), \epsilon, \gamma_0)$
for some ξ_0 in $g(\gamma_0) \cap G_{D_1}$ and some ξ_1 in $g(\gamma_1) \cap G_{D_1}$. Then
(10) $((q_0, \xi_0), v)$ is in $\delta_2((q_1, \xi_1), w_1, \bar{\xi})$ and
(11) $f(\gamma_1, v) = \gamma_0$
for some $\bar{\xi}$ in $g(\gamma_1)$ and some v in I. By construction of δ_2, $\bar{\xi} = \xi_1$. By (10) and the definition of δ_2, $v = v_{u, \xi_0}$ for some u in I satisfying the condition of reversibility such that
(12) (q_1, u) is in $\delta_1(q_0, w_1, \xi_0)$.
From (11) and the definition of reversibility,
(13) $f(\gamma_0, u) = \gamma_1$.
From (12), (13), ξ_0 in $g(\gamma_0)$, and ξ_1 in $g(\gamma_1) \cap G_{D_1}$, we have
(14) $(q_0, w_1, \gamma_0) \vdash_{D_1} (q_1, \epsilon, \gamma_1)$,
with $g(\gamma_1) \cap G_{D_1} \neq \emptyset$, i.e., (1) holds.

Assume (2) implies (1) for $1 \leqq k \leqq m$. Consider $k = m+1$. Then
(15) $((q_{m+1}, \xi_{m+1}), w_1, \gamma_{m+1}) \vdash_{D_2} ((q_m, \xi_m), \epsilon, \gamma_m)$ and
(16) $((q_m, \xi_m), w_2 \ldots w_{m+1}, \gamma_m) \overset{*}{\vdash}_{D_2} ((q_0, \xi_0), \epsilon, \gamma_0)$
for some ξ_0 in $g(\gamma_0) \cap G_{D_1}, \ldots, \xi_{m+1}$ in $g(\gamma_{m+1}) \cap G_{D_1}$. By induction, we get
(17) $(q_m, w_1, \gamma_m) \vdash_{D_1} (q_{m+1}, \epsilon, \gamma_{m+1})$ and
(18) $(q_0, w_{m+1} \ldots w_2, \gamma_0) \overset{*}{\vdash}_{D_1} (q_m, \epsilon, \gamma_m)$,
with $g(\gamma_{m+1}) \cap G_{D_1} \neq \emptyset$. Hence $(q_0, w_{m+1} \ldots w_1, \gamma_0) \overset{*}{\vdash}_{D_1} (q_{m+1}, \epsilon, \gamma_{m+1})$, with $g(\gamma_{m+1}) \cap G_{D_1} \neq \emptyset$, i. e., (1) holds, thereby completing the proof.

There are no known necessary and sufficient conditions on an AFA $\mathcal{D}$ in order for $\mathcal{L}(\mathcal{D})$ (or $\mathcal{L}^t(\mathcal{D})$) to be closed under reversal.

($\sim$) *Open Problem*: Find a necessary and sufficient condition on an AFA $\mathcal{D}$ such that $\mathcal{L}(\mathcal{D})$ (or $\mathcal{L}^t(\mathcal{D})$) is closed under reversal.

EXERCISE 4.8.1: Using Theorem 4.8.1, prove that each of the following AFL are closed under reversal:

(a) $\mathscr{L}_S$.

(b) The list-storage acceptor languages.

(c) $\mathscr{L}_C$.

EXERCISE 4.8.2: Prove that $\hat{\mathscr{F}}(\{a^n b^m/n > m \geqq 0\})$ is not closed under reversal [GGr1].

EXERCISE 4.8.3: Prove the following [Og, a; Og, b]:

(a) $\{a^{n^2} b^n/n \geqq 1\}$ is in $\mathscr{L}_{NES}$.

(*) (b) $\{b^n a^{n^2}/n \geqq 1\}$ is not in $\mathscr{L}_{NES}$. Thus infer that $\mathscr{L}_{NES}$ is not closed under reversal, and that $\hat{\mathscr{F}}(\{a^{n^2} b^n/n \geqq 1\})$ is not closed under reversal.

EXERCISE 4.8.4: Using Exercise 4.8.3, exhibit a reversible AFA$\mathscr{D}$ such that $\mathscr{L}_f(\mathscr{D})$ is not closed under reversal.

EXERCISE 4.8.5: Let $(\Omega, \mathscr{D})$, with $\Omega = (K, \Sigma, \Gamma, I, f, g)$, be an AFA satisfying the following:

($*$) There exists a one-to-one function h from Γ^* into Γ^* such that (i) $gh(\gamma) = hg(\gamma)$ for all γ in Γ^*, (ii) $h(\epsilon) = \epsilon$, and (iii) for each u in I and ξ in $g(\Gamma^*)$, there exists $v_{u,\xi}$ in I so that for each γ and γ', ξ in $g(\gamma)$, $f(\gamma, u) = \gamma'$ if and only if $f(h(\gamma'), v_{u,\xi}) = h(\gamma)$.

Prove that $\mathscr{L}(\mathscr{D})$ ($\mathscr{L}^t(\mathscr{D})$) is closed under reversal [GHa2].

EXERCISE 4.8.6: Let $\mathscr{L}$ be a (full) AFL which contains $\{\epsilon\}$, is closed under reversal, and is closed under intersection with linear context-free languages. Prove that there exists an AFA$\mathscr{D}$ satisfying ($*$) of Exercise 4.8.5 such that $\mathscr{L} = \mathscr{L}^t(\mathscr{D})$($\mathscr{L} = \mathscr{L}(\mathscr{D})$) [GHa2]. [Hint: Modify the proofs of Theorems 4.2.3 and 4.3.2.]

EXERCISE 4.8.7: Let $G = (V, \Sigma_1, P, \sigma)$, where $\Sigma_1 = \{a, b, c\}$, $V - \Sigma_1 = \{\sigma, \xi\}$, and $P = \{\sigma \to a\sigma\xi, \sigma \to a\xi, \xi \to b\xi c, \xi \to bc\}$. Using the terminology of Exercise 3.1.10, prove the following [Wa]:

(a) $L(G) = \{a^n b^{k_1} c^{k_1} \ldots b^{k_n} c^{k_n}/n \geqq 1, \text{ each } k_i \geqq 1\}$.

(b) $L(G)$ is not left derivation bounded.

(c) $L(G)^R$ is left derivation bounded. Thus infer that the AFL of left derivation bounded languages is not closed under reversal.

EXERCISE 4.8.8: Verify that $\tilde{\mathscr{L}}(\mathscr{D})$ and $\tilde{\mathscr{L}}^t(\mathscr{D})$ are both closed under reversal for every reversible AFA$\mathscr{D}$.

4.9 Historical References

The idea of constructing a model for a family of acceptors by considering all acceptors with specified read-write functions comes from [GGr1]. A different model for families of acceptors, called "closed classes of balloon automata", was introduced in [HU2]. The balloon automaton model was published about a year earlier than the AFA model. By one of those occasional scientific coincidences, however, both models were formulated about the same time, namely the summer of 1966. It turns out that closed classes of one-way nondeterministic balloon automata are equivalent, from the point of view of languages accepted, to AFA.

The contents of Sections 4.1, 4.2, and 4.3, with the exception of AFA-schema, occur in [GGr1]. Theorem 4.4.1 also is in [GGr1]. The concept of an AFA-schema, as well as the material in Sections 4.5 and 4.6, are in [GrG]. The fact that $\mathscr{L}_{RE} = \mathscr{L}(\mathscr{D}_C \wedge \mathscr{D}_C)$, i. e., that the family of 2-counter languages coincides with $\mathscr{L}_{RE}$, was known well before the advent of AFL theory, appearing in [Mi]. Theorem 4.7.1 was established in [HH]. Theorem 4.8.1 originated in [GHa2].

CHAPTER 5

PRINCIPAL (SEMI-)AFL

One way to define a specific (semi-) AFL is by means of an AFA. Another is by specifying a certain family of languages and considering the smallest (semi-) AFL containing this family. The simplest case of the latter situation is when the given family of languages contains exactly one language. Such (semi-) AFL are called principal and form the subject of the present chapter.

5.1 Elementary Results

In the present section we introduce some basic terminology about principal (semi-) AFL and then prove a few elementary results.

We start with the formal definition of a principal (semi-) AFL.

Def: Let $\mathcal{L}$ be a family of languages. If there exists a language L such that $\mathcal{L} = \mathcal{F}(L)$ ($\mathcal{L} = \hat{\mathcal{F}}(L)$) then $\mathcal{L}$ is said to be a (*full*) *principal AFL* and L a (*full*) *AFL generator* of $\mathcal{L}$. If $\mathcal{F}$ is replaced by $\mathcal{S}$ then $\mathcal{L}$ is said to be a (*full*) *principal semi-AFL* and L a (*full*) *semi-AFL generator* of $\mathcal{L}$. If $\mathcal{L}$ is not (full) principal, then it is called *nonprincipal* (*non-full-principal*).

The modifier "(semi-) AFL" is omitted from "(semi-) AFL generator" when no confusion can arise.

The notion of a (full) principal trio as a (full) trio generated by a single language is superfluous and thus omitted. In particular, it will be seen later (Proposition 5.1.1) that such trios coincide with (full) principal semi-AFL.

Each (semi-) AFL that is full and principal is full principal. For, if $\mathcal{L} = \mathcal{O}(L)$ and $\mathcal{L}$ is full, then $\mathcal{L} = \hat{\mathcal{O}}(L)$, $\mathcal{O} = \mathcal{S}$ or $\mathcal{F}$.

It will be seen later[1] that each AFL $\mathcal{L}$ is (full) principal if and only if $\mathcal{L}$ is a (full) principal semi-AFL, although not every (full) AFL generator is a (full) semi-AFL generator.

[1] See the corollary to Theorem 5.4.1.

It is known [Ui] that there exist full principal AFL which are nonprincipal. In view of the previous paragraph, such AFL are full principal semi-AFL which are nonprincipal semi-AFL.

The simplest way to illustrate a [full] principal (semi-) AFL is to take an arbitrary language and consider the [full] (semi-) AFL it generates. Thus $\mathcal{S}(\{a^n b^n/n \geqq 1\})$ is a principal semi-AFL, and $\hat{\mathcal{F}}(\{a^i b^j c^k/0 \leqq i \leqq k,\ j \geqq 1,\ k \geqq 3\})$ is a full principal AFL. There are also natural examples. $\mathcal{R}$ is a [full] principal AFL and a [full] principal semi-AFL, with each regular set a full (semi-) AFL generator and each regular set containing ϵ a (semi-) AFL generator. $\mathcal{R}_0$ is a principal (semi-) AFL, with each ϵ-free regular set a (semi-) AFL generator. We shall see that many well-known families of languages are principal (semi-) AFL and/or full principal (semi-) AFL.

EXAMPLE 5.1.1: Let W_2 be the Dyck set on $\{a, b\}$. Let $n \geqq 1$ and U the Dyck set on $\{a_1, \ldots, a_n\}$. Let h be the homomorphism on $\{a_1, \ldots, a_n, a_1^{\mathrm{E}}, \ldots, a_n^{\mathrm{E}}\}^*$ defined by $h(a_i) = a^i b$ and $h(a_i^{\mathrm{E}}) = b^{\mathrm{E}}(a^{\mathrm{E}})^i$ for each i. Then $h^{-1}(W_2) = U$. Thus each Dyck set is of the form $h^{-1}(W_2)$ for some ϵ-free homomorphism h. Now the Chomsky–Schutzenberger Theorem asserts that given Σ_1 there exist Σ_2, a Dyck set $U \subseteq \Sigma_2^*$, and a homomorphism h_1 from Σ_2^* onto Σ_1^* such that for each context-free language $L \subseteq \Sigma_1^*$ a regular set $R \subseteq \Sigma_2^*$ can be found satisfying $L = h_1(U \cap R)$. Since U is of the form $h_2^{-1}(W_2)$ for some homomorphism h_2, $L = h_1(h_2^{-1}(W_2) \cap R)$. Therefore L is in $\hat{\mathcal{M}}(W_2)$. Since W_2 is context free, $\hat{\mathcal{F}}(W_2) \subseteq \mathcal{L}_{\mathrm{CF}}$. Hence

$$\mathcal{L}_{\mathrm{CF}} \subseteq \hat{\mathcal{M}}(W_2) \subseteq \hat{\mathcal{S}}(W_2) \subseteq \hat{\mathcal{F}}(W_2) \subseteq \mathcal{L}_{\mathrm{CF}},$$

so that $\mathcal{L}_{\mathrm{CF}} = \hat{\mathcal{M}}(W_2) = \hat{\mathcal{S}}(W_2) = \hat{\mathcal{F}}(W_2)$. Thus $\mathcal{L}_{\mathrm{CF}}$ is a full principal (semi-) AFL, fully generated by W_2. We shall see in Example 5.3.1 that $\mathcal{L}_{\mathrm{CF}}$ is a principal (semi-) AFL, with W_2 a generator.

EXAMPLE 5.1.2: By Exercises 4.2.6 and 4.3.7, $\hat{\mathcal{F}}(\mathcal{L}_{\mathrm{lin}}) = \hat{\mathcal{F}}(L_0) = \mathcal{F}(L_1)$, where $L_0 = \{wcw^R/w \text{ in } \{a, b\}^*\}$ and $L_1 = L_0 \cup \{\epsilon\}$. Thus $\hat{\mathcal{F}}(\mathcal{L}_{\mathrm{lin}})$ is both principal and full principal.

EXAMPLE 5.1.3: We now show that $\mathcal{L}_{\mathrm{CS}}$ is a principal AFL [We]. We do this by exhibiting an lba B with the following property: For each lba A there exists a regular set R_A and an ϵ-free a-transducer M_A such that $M_A(T(B) \cap R_A) = T(A)$.

Let a, b, -1, 0, 1, p_1, m_1, m_2, m_3, m_4, and m_5 be fixed symbols. We start by defining an "encoding" over $\{-1, 0, 1, a, b, m_1, m_2\}$ for each lba $A = (K_1, \Sigma_1, W_1, \delta_1, p_1, F_1)$. Without loss of generality we may assume that $K_1 \cap W_1 = \emptyset$, $(K_1 \cup W_1) \cap \{a, b, -1, 0, 1, m_1, m_2, m_3, m_4, m_5\} = \emptyset$, and $F_1 = \{p_2\}$. Let $p_1, \ldots, p_r$ be the elements of K_1, $a_1, \ldots, a_s$ the elements of Σ_1, and $b_1, \ldots, b_t$ the elements of $W_1 - \Sigma_1$. Let

$$U = \{(p, c, p', c', d)/(p', c', d) \text{ in } \delta(p, c) \text{ for some } p \text{ in } K_1 \text{ and } c \text{ in } W_1\}$$

and let $u_1, \ldots, u_y$ be the elements of U. Let h_{1A} be the homomorphism on $(\{-1, 0, 1\} \cup K_1 \cup W_1)^*$ defined by $h_{1A}(-1) = -1$, $h_{1A}(0) = 0$, $h_{1A}(1) = 1$, $h_{1A}(a_i) = ab^{3i}a$ for all i, $1 \leqq i \leqq s$, $h_{1A}(b_j) = ab^{3j+1}a$ for all j, $1 \leqq j \leqq t$, and $h_{1A}(p_k) = ab^{3k+2}a$ for all k, $1 \leqq k \leqq r$. For each $u = (p, c, p', c', d)$ in U let

$$C(u) = h_{1A}(p)\, h_{1A}(c)\, h_{1A}(p')\, h_{1A}(c')\, h_{1A}(d).$$

Let

$$C(A) = m_2 m_1\, C(u_1)\, m_1\, C(u_2) \ldots m_1\, C(u_y)\, m_1 m_2.$$

The encoding $C(A)$ contains the salient information about A. In particular, the subwords $C(u_i)$ can be determined. Given $C(u_i)$, the code for the present state, present work symbol, next state, overprint symbol, and direction of A can be ascertained. Note also that the code words for elements in Σ_1 and $W_1 - \Sigma_1$ can be differentiated. Let h_{2A} be the homomorphism on $(W_1 \cup K_1)^*$ defined by $h_{2A}(e) = h_{1A}(e)\, m_3^{|C(A)| - |h_{1A}(e)|}$ for each e in $W_1 \cup K_1$. Thus $|h_{2A}(e)| = |C(A)|$ for each e in $W_1 \cup K_1$. It is to be understood that the e-free homomorphisms h_{1A} and h_{2A} are given with each lba A.

We now define the desired lba $B = (K_2, \Sigma_2, W_2, \delta_2, p_1, \{p_2\})$, where $\Sigma_2 = \{a, b, -1, 0, 1, m_1, m_2, m_3, m_4, m_5\}$. We shall describe how B operates on words in the set

$$I_A(e)\{C(A) m_5 h_{2A}(e') m_4 m_3^{|C(A)|} m_5 / e' \text{ in } \Sigma_1\}^*,$$

where A is an lba, e is in Σ_1, and $I_A(e) = C(A)\, m_5 h_{2A}(e)\, m_4 h_{2A}(p_1)\, m_5$. (The manner in which B operates on other words in Σ_2^+ is immaterial.) B operates in cycles. At the beginning of each cycle, the tape of B consists of a sequence of blocks, each of the form

(i) $C(A)\, m_5 h_{2A}(e)\, m_4 h_{2A}(q)\, m_5$, e in W_1 and q in K_1, or

(ii) $C(A)\, m_5 h_{2A}(e)\, m_4 m_3^{|C(A)|} m_5$, e in W_1,

with exactly one type (i) block in the sequence. From the nature of the markers $m_1, \ldots, m_5$, a block on the tape is a subword of the form $m_2 \alpha m_2 m_5 \beta m_5$, where α contains no m_2 and β contains no m_5. At the beginning of each cycle,

B is positioned at the leftmost symbol of the unique type (i) block $C(A)\, m_5\, h_{2A}(e)\, m_4 h_{2A}(q)\, m_5$. (Intuitively, B simulates A at state q reading symbol e.) Then B nondeterministically selects some subword

$$C(u_i) = h_{1A}(p)\, h_{1A}(c)\, h_{1A}(p')\, h_{1A}(c')\, h_{1A}(d)$$

of $C(A)$ and, by standard lba techniques (see Exercise 5.1.8), determines if $h_{1A}(p) = h_{1A}(q)$ and $h_{1A}(c) = h_{1A}(e)$. If agreement occurs, then B overprints $h_{2A}(e)$ with $h_{2A}(c')$ and $h_{2A}(q)$ with $m_3^{|C(A)|}$. Then B moves out of the block in the direction of A, as given by $h_{1A}(d)$. If B goes off the tape at the right end and $h_{1A}(p') = h_{1A}(p_2)$ then B accepts. (This corresponds to A going off the right end of its tape in an accepting state.) If B goes off the tape at the right end and $h_{1A}(p') \neq h_{1A}(p_2)$, then B does not accept. If B does not go off the tape, then B enters a block, overprints in that block $m_3^{|C(A)|}$ with $h_{2A}(p')$, goes to the leftmost symbol in that block, and is ready to begin the cycle again.

For each lba A let

$$R_A = \bigcup_{e \text{ in } \Sigma_1} I_A(e)\{C(A)\, m_5 h_{2A}(e')\, m_4 m_3^{|C(A)|} m_5 / e' \text{ in } \Sigma_1\}^*,$$

where $I_A(e) = C(A) m_5 h_{2A}(e) m_4 h_{2A}(p_1)\, m_5$. Clearly R_A is regular. Let M_A be the ϵ-free a-transducer $(\{p_0\}, \Sigma_2, \Sigma_1, H_A, p_0, \{p_0\})$, where

$$H_A = \{(p_0, I_A(e), e, p_0), (p_0, C(A)\, m_5 h_{2A}(e)\, m_4 m_3^{|C(A)|} m_5, e, p_0)/e \text{ in } \Sigma_1\}.$$

Clearly $M_A(T(B) \cap R_A) = T(A)$, completing the argument.

An obvious generalization of (full) principal AFL or semi-AFL is "(full) finitely generated", i. e., $\mathcal{L} = \mathcal{F}(\mathcal{U})$ or $\mathcal{L} = \mathcal{S}(\mathcal{U})$ ($\mathcal{L} = \hat{\mathcal{F}}(\mathcal{U})$ or $\mathcal{L} = \hat{\mathcal{S}}(\mathcal{U})$) for some finite family $\mathcal{U}$. We shall see below that such AFL, respectively semi-AFL, coincide with (full) principal AFL, respectively (full) principal semi-AFL.

LEMMA 5.1.1: *Let L_1 and L_2 be languages and c be a symbol not in $\Sigma_{L_1} \cup \Sigma_{L_2}$. Then for $\mathcal{O} = \mathcal{S}$ or $\mathcal{F}$, $\hat{\mathcal{O}}(\{L_1, L_2\}) = \hat{\mathcal{O}}(L_1 \cup cL_2)$ and $\mathcal{O}(\{L_1, L_2\}) = \mathcal{O}(L)$, where $L = L_1 \cup cL_2 \cup (L_2 \cap \{\epsilon\})$.*

Proof: We give the proof for $\mathcal{O}(\{L_1, L_2\})$, the argument for $\hat{\mathcal{O}}(\{L_1, L_2\})$ being similar.

Since L is in $\mathcal{O}(\{L_1, L_2\})$, $\mathcal{O}(L) \subseteq \mathcal{O}(\{L_1, L_2\})$. It thus suffices to show that L_1 and L_2 are in $\mathcal{O}(L)$. If L_1 contains ϵ, then $L_1 = L \cap \Sigma_{L_1}^*$. Otherwise,

$L_1 = L \cap \Sigma_{L_1}^+$. In either case, L_1 is in $\mathcal{O}(L)$. Let h be the homomorphism on $(\Sigma_{L_2} \cup \{c\})^*$ defined by $h(c) = \epsilon$ and $h(a) = a$ for each a in Σ_{L_2}. Then $L_2 = h(L \cap c\Sigma_{L_2}^*)$.

Now h is ϵ-limited on $c\Sigma_{L_2}^*$ and hence on $L \cap c\Sigma_{L_2}^*$. Therefore $L_2 - \{\epsilon\}$ is in $\mathcal{O}(L)$ by Corollary 2 of Theorem 3.2.2. If L_2 contains ϵ, then so does L and hence $\{\epsilon\} = L \cap \{\epsilon\}$ is in $\mathcal{O}(L)$. Then $L_2 = (L_2 - \{\epsilon\}) \cup \{\epsilon\}$ is in $\mathcal{O}(L)$. If L_2 does not contain ϵ, then $L_2 = L_2 - \{\epsilon\}$ is in $\mathcal{O}(L)$. In either case, L_2 is in $\mathcal{O}(L)$ and the proof is complete.

THEOREM 5.1.1: *A (semi-) AFL $\mathcal{L}$ is [full] principal if and only if there exists a finite family $\mathcal{U}$ of languages such that $\mathcal{L} = \mathcal{O}(\mathcal{U})$ $[\mathcal{L} = \hat{\mathcal{O}}(\mathcal{U})]$, $\mathcal{O} = \mathcal{S}$ or $\mathcal{F}$.*

Proof: The "only if" is trivial. Thus consider the "if". It suffices to consider the $\mathcal{O}$ case.

By induction, assume that $\mathcal{O}(\{L_1, \ldots, L_m\})$ is principal for $m \geqq 1$ and each $L_1, \ldots, L_m$. Consider $\mathcal{O}(\{L_1, \ldots, L_{m+1}\})$ for arbitrary $L_1, \ldots, L_{m+1}$. Then

$$\begin{aligned} \mathcal{O}(\{L_1, \ldots, L_{m+1}\}) &= \mathcal{O}(\mathcal{O}(\{L_1, \ldots, L_m\}) \cup \mathcal{O}(L_{m+1})), \quad \text{by Exercise 3.4.3,} \\ &= \mathcal{O}(\mathcal{O}(L_1') \cup \mathcal{O}(L_{m+1})) \text{ for some } L_1', \quad \text{by induction,} \\ &= \mathcal{O}(\{L_1', L_{m+1}\}), \quad \text{by Exercise 3.4.3,} \\ &= \mathcal{O}(L_1'') \text{ for some } L_1'', \quad \text{by Lemma 5.1.1.} \end{aligned}$$

Thus $\mathcal{O}(\{L_1, \ldots, L_{m+1}\})$ is principal and the induction is extended.

COROLLARY: *Let $\mathcal{L}_1, \ldots, \mathcal{L}_n$ be (full) principal AFL, resp. (full) principal semi-AFL. Then so is $\mathcal{O}(\mathcal{L}_1 \cup \ldots \cup \mathcal{L}_n)$ $(\hat{\mathcal{O}}(\mathcal{L}_1 \cup \ldots \cup \mathcal{L}_n))$ for $\mathcal{O} = \mathcal{F}$, resp. $\mathcal{S}$.*

Consider the existence of nonprincipal and non-full-principal AFL. Suppose Σ is countable. Then the family of regular subsets of Σ^* is countable and the family of homomorphisms defined on finite subsets of Σ^* is countable. Now let L be a given language. Each member of $\hat{\mathcal{F}}(L)$ $(\mathcal{F}(L))$ is the last element of some sequence $L_1, \ldots, L_r$ for some r, where each L_i, $1 \leqq i \leqq r$, is either (i) L; (ii) an (ϵ-free) regular set; (iii) $L_j \cap R$ for some $j < i$ and some regular set R; (iv) $L_{j_1} \cup L_{j_2}$ or $L_{j_1}L_{j_2}$ for some $j_1 < i$ and $j_2 < i$; (v) L_j^+ for some $j < i$; (vi) $h^{-1}(L_j)$ for some $j < i$ and some homomorphism h; or (vii) $h(L_j)$ for some $j < i$ and some (ϵ-free) homomorphism h. Thus every member of $\hat{\mathcal{F}}(L)$ $(\mathcal{F}(L))$ can be obtained from L by a finite number of operations, each chosen from a countable collection of operations. Hence $\mathcal{F}(L)$ and $\hat{\mathcal{F}}(L)$ are countable. In other words, if Σ is countable then no uncountable AFL over Σ is either principal or full principal. A similar statement also holds for semi-AFL.

EXAMPLE 5.1.4: Let $\mathcal{L}$ be the family of all languages over a countable alphabet Σ. Clearly $\mathcal{L}$ is a full (semi-) AFL and uncountable. Hence $\mathcal{L}$ is nonprincipal and non-full-principal.

Another situation yielding a nonprincipal (non-full-principal) [semi-] AFL is the following result:

LEMMA 5.1.2: *Let* $\{\mathcal{L}_\alpha/\alpha \text{ in } A\}$ *be an infinite chain of (full) [semi-] AFL, with no largest element. Then* $\bigcup_\alpha \mathcal{L}_\alpha$ *is a nonprincipal (non-full-principal) (full) [semi-] AFL.*

Proof: Obviously $\mathcal{L} = \bigcup_\alpha \mathcal{L}_\alpha$ is a (full) [semi-] AFL. Suppose that $\mathcal{L}$ is (full) principal. Then $\mathcal{L} = \mathcal{O}(L)$ ($\mathcal{L} = \hat{\mathcal{O}}(L)$) for some L, where $\mathcal{O} = \mathcal{F}[\mathcal{S}]$. Since L is in $\bigcup_\alpha \mathcal{L}_\alpha$, there exists some α in A such that L is in $\mathcal{L}_\alpha$. Since the chain has no largest element, there exists some β in A so that $\mathcal{L}_\alpha \subsetneq \mathcal{L}_\beta$. Then $\mathcal{L} = \mathcal{O}(L)$ ($\mathcal{L} = \hat{\mathcal{O}}(L)$) $\subseteq \mathcal{L}_\alpha \subsetneq \mathcal{L}_\beta \subseteq \mathcal{L}$, a contradiction.

From Lemma 5.1.2 and Theorem 5.1.1, we obtain the following characterization result.

THEOREM 5.1.2: *Let* $\mathcal{L}$ *be a countable (full) [semi-] AFL. Then* $\mathcal{L}$ *is nonprincipal (non-full-principal) if and only if there exists an infinite sequence of (full) [semi-] AFL,* $\mathcal{L}_1, \ldots, \mathcal{L}_n, \ldots$ *such that* $\mathcal{L} = \bigcup_n \mathcal{L}_n$ *and* $\mathcal{L}_n \subsetneq \mathcal{L}_{n+1}$ *for each n.*

Proof: By Lemma 5.1.2, it suffices to consider the "only if". Suppose $\mathcal{L}$ is nonprincipal (non-full-principal). Since $\mathcal{L}$ is countable, $\mathcal{L}-\{\emptyset\} = \{L_1, \ldots, L_n, \ldots\}$. Let $i_1 = 1$. Let $\mathcal{O} = \mathcal{S}$ or $\mathcal{F}$. Continuing by induction, for each $m < r$ suppose that the positive integer i_m exists and that $\mathcal{L}_m = \mathcal{O}(\{L_{i_1}, \ldots, L_{i_m}\})$ ($\mathcal{L}_m = \hat{\mathcal{O}}(\{L_{i_1}, \ldots, L_{i_m}\})$). Furthermore, suppose $\mathcal{L}_m \subsetneq \mathcal{L}_{m+1}$ for each m, $1 \leqq m < r-1$. Since $\mathcal{L}$ is not (full) principal, thus by Theorem 5.1.1, not (full) finitely generated, there exists a smallest integer i_r such that L_{i_r} is not in $\mathcal{L}_{r-1}$. Let $\mathcal{L}_r = \mathcal{O}(\{L_{i_1}, \ldots, L_{i_r}\})$ ($\mathcal{L} = \hat{\mathcal{O}}(\{L_{i_1}, \ldots, L_{i_r}\})$). Then L_{i_r} is in $\mathcal{L}_r - \mathcal{L}_{r-1}$, so that $\mathcal{L}_{r-1} \subsetneq \mathcal{L}_r$. Thus the induction is extended. By the method of construction, $L_1, \ldots, L_n$ are in $\mathcal{L}_n$ for each n. Hence $\mathcal{L} = \bigcup_{m \geqq 1} \mathcal{L}_m$.

REMARK: The method of proof of Theorem 5.1.2 also shows that each $\mathscr{L}_n$ can be assumed (full) principal. In other words, let $\mathscr{L}$ be a countable (full) [semi-] AFL. Then $\mathscr{L}$ is nonprincipal (non-full-principal) if and only if there exists an infinite sequence $\mathscr{L}_1, \ldots, \mathscr{L}_n, \ldots$ of (full) principal [semi-]AFL such that $\mathscr{L} = \bigcup_n \mathscr{L}_n$ and $\mathscr{L}_n \subsetneqq \mathscr{L}_{n+1}$ for each n.

Theorem 5.1.2 is the most important method we have for showing that a particular [semi-] AFL is nonprincipal (non-full-principal). There are two difficulties associated with applying it to a given [semi-] AFL $\mathscr{L}$. These are

(i) Finding a property about positive integers so that each language satisfies this property for at least one integer n and, for each n, all languages with this property for n form a [semi-] AFL $\mathscr{L}_n$.

(ii) Proving that for the $\mathscr{L}_1, \ldots, \mathscr{L}_n, \ldots$ obtained in (i), $\mathscr{L}_n \subsetneqq \mathscr{L}_{n+1}$ for each n.

Item (ii) is usually the more difficult.

EXAMPLE 5.1.5: As shown in Example 4.5.2, $\mathscr{C}_n \subsetneqq \mathscr{C}_{n+1}$. Hence $\bigcup_n \mathscr{C}_n$ is a nonprincipal AFL.

EXAMPLE 5.1.6: For each $m \geqq 1$ let $\mathscr{L}_m$ be the full AFL of m-turn bounded pda languages. [See Exercise 4.1.3.] It can be shown [Gr1] that $\mathscr{L}_m \subsetneqq \mathscr{L}_{m+1}$ for each m. Hence $\mathscr{L} = \bigcup_m \mathscr{L}_m$, the so-called *finite-turn pda languages*, is a full AFL which is not (full) principal.

Open Problem: Is $\mathscr{L}_S$ a principal AFL?

We conclude the section by showing that each (full) principal semi-AFL $\mathscr{S}(L)$ ($\hat{\mathscr{S}}(L)$) is the smallest (full) trio containing L. In view of Theorem 3.2.1, it suffices to show that $\mathscr{S}(L) = \mathscr{M}(L)$ ($\hat{\mathscr{S}}(L) = \hat{\mathscr{M}}(L)$).

PROPOSITION 5.1.1: *For each nonempty language L, $\mathscr{S}(L) = \mathscr{M}(L)$ and $\hat{\mathscr{S}}(L) = \hat{\mathscr{M}}(L)$.*

Proof: Clearly we need only consider the semi-AFL case. Obviously $\mathscr{M}(L) \subseteq \mathscr{S}(L)$. To see the reverse containment, it suffices to show that $\mathscr{M}(L)$ is closed under union. Let $M_1 = (K_1, \Sigma_1, \Sigma_2, H_1, p_0, F_1)$ and $M_2 = (K_2, \Sigma_1, \Sigma_2, H_2, q_0, F_2)$ be ϵ-free a-transducers. Without loss of generality, we may assume that $K_1 \cap K_2 = \emptyset$. Let r_0 be a new symbol. Let $M_3 = (K_3, \Sigma_1, \Sigma_2, H_3, r_0, F_3)$, where $K_3 = K_1 \cup K_2 \cup \{r_0\}$, $F_3 = F_1 \cup F_2 \cup \{r_0/p_0$ in F_1

or q_0 in $F_2\}$, and

$$H_3 = H_1 \cup H_2 \cup \{(r_0, u, v, p)/(p_0, u, v, p) \text{ in } H_1\} \cup \{(r_0, u, v, q)/(q_0, u, v, q) \text{ in } H_2\}.$$

Then M_3 is an ϵ-free a-transducer and $M_3(L) = M_1(L) \cup M_2(L)$. Thus $\mathcal{M}(L)$ is closed under union.

REMARK: Proposition 5.1.1 cannot be extended to a finite family of languages. [See Exercise 5.1.20.]

EXERCISE 5.1.1: Prove that each (full) principal [semi-] AFL has an infinite number of (full) generators.

EXERCISE 5.1.2: Let $L_0 = \{ww^R/w \text{ in } \{a, b\}^*\}$. Prove that
(a) $\mathcal{L}_{\text{lin}} = \mathcal{S}(L_0) = \hat{\mathcal{S}}(L_0)$.
(b) $\mathcal{F}(\mathcal{L}_{\text{lin}}) = \mathcal{F}(L_0) = \hat{\mathcal{F}}(L_0)$.

EXERCISE 5.1.3: Prove that $\mathcal{L}_{\text{rec}}$ is not a principal AFL [GGr2].

EXERCISE 5.1.4: Prove that a (full) principal [semi-] AFL is closed under reversal if and only if there exists a (full) generator L such that $L = L^R$.

EXERCISE 5.1.5: Let $\mathcal{L}$ be a (full) [semi-] AFL containing a largest proper (full) [semi-] AFL. Prove that $\mathcal{L}$ is (full) principal [GS7].

EXERCISE 5.1.6: Let $\{L_i\}_{i \geqq 1}$ be a sequence of languages. Show that there exists a principal (semi-) AFL $\mathcal{L}$ such that $\{L_i/i \geqq 1\} \subseteq \mathcal{L}$.

EXERCISE 5.1.7: Let W_1 be the Dyck set on $\{a\}$. Prove the following:
(a) $\mathcal{M}(Y) = \mathcal{M}(W_1)$, where $Y = \{\epsilon\} \cup \{w \text{ in } W_1/w \text{ not in } (W_1-\{\epsilon\})\{a, a^E\}^+\}$.
(b) $\mathcal{M}(W_1) \neq \mathcal{F}(W_1)$ [GGr1].
(c) $\hat{\mathcal{M}}(W_1) \neq \hat{\mathcal{F}}(W_1)$ [GGr1].

EXERCISE 5.1.8: Show how B determines if $h_{1A}(p) = h_{1A}(q)$ and $h_{1A}(c) = h_{1A}(e)$ in Example 5.1.3.

EXERCISE 5.1.9: Verify that $M_A(T(B) \cap R_A) = T(A)$ in Example 5.1.3.

EXERCISE 5.1.10: Prove that the family of deterministic lba languages is a principal AFL [We].

The following terminology is used in Exercises 5.1.11–5.1.13. Let $\mathcal{D} = \mathcal{D}_{TA}$ and let T be a nondecreasing function from **N** into **N**. Then T is said to be *constructable* if there exists a deterministic Turing acceptor $D = (K_1, \Sigma_1, \delta, p_0, F_1)$ in $\mathcal{D}_{T(n)}$[1] such that for each w in Σ_1^*, $(p_0, w, \epsilon) \overset{*}{\vdash} (p, \epsilon, \gamma Z \uparrow)$ for some p in K_1, γ in Γ^*, and Z in Γ, where $|\gamma Z| = T(|w|)$ and $\delta(p, \epsilon, Z) = \emptyset$. T is said to be *superadditive* if $T(m)+T(n) \leqq T(m+n)$ for all m and n. T is said to be *semihomogeneous* if for each positive integer k_1 there exists a positive integer k_2 such that $T(k_1 m) \leqq k_2 T(m)$ for all m.

EXERCISE 5.1.11: Let T be constructable and superadditive. Furthermore, suppose $T(m) \geqq m$ for all m. Prove [BGIW] that

(a) $\mathcal{L}(\mathcal{D}_{T(n)})$ is principal if it is an AFL.

(b) $\{L(D)/D$ deterministic, D in $\mathcal{D}_{T(n)}\}$ is principal if it is an AFL.

EXERCISE 5.1.12: Let T be constructable, superadditive, and semihomogeneous. Furthermore, suppose $T(m) \geqq m$ for all m. Prove [BGIW] that

(a) $\mathcal{L}(\mathcal{D}_{T(n)})$ is a principal AFL.

(b) $\{L(D)/D$ deterministic, D in $\mathcal{D}_{T(n)}\}$ is a principal AFL.

EXERCISE 5.1.13: Let T be constructable and $T(rm) \geqq rT(m)$ for all positive integers r and m. Prove [GR1] that

(a) $\mathcal{F}(\mathcal{L}(\mathcal{D}_{T(n)}))$ is a principal AFL and has a language in $\mathcal{L}(\mathcal{D}_{T(n)})$ as a generator.

(b) $\mathcal{F}(\mathcal{U})$ is a principal AFL and has a language in $\mathcal{U}$ as a generator, where $\mathcal{U} = \{L(D)/D$ deterministic, D in $\mathcal{D}_{T(n)}\}$.

[If a pushdown tape is added to a Turing acceptor, then the resulting two-tape device is called an auxiliary pushdown machine, APDM [Co]. Let tape bounds on an APDM refer only to the Turing tape (so that there is no restriction on the pushdown tape). Then the results of Exercises 5.1.11–5.1.13 can be extended to the case where $\mathcal{D}$ is the family of APDM [BGW; GR1]. Using Exercises 5.1.11–5.1.13 and the extensions to APDM, the following results are noted [BGIW; BGW; GR1]: (i) The family of (deterministic) [nonerasing] "two-way" stack-acceptor languages is a principal AFL; (ii) The family of "writing" pushdown-acceptor languages is a principal AFL; and (iii) The smallest AFL containing the (deterministic) "two-way" pushdown-acceptor languages is a principal AFL.]

[1] See Section 4.4.

EXERCISE 5.1.14: Let $L_1 \neq \emptyset$ and $L_2 \neq \emptyset$. Prove that $L_1cL_2 \cup ((L_1 \cup L_2) \cap \{\epsilon\})$ generates $\mathcal{F}(\{L_1, L_2\})$ and L_1cL_2 fully generates $\hat{\mathcal{F}}(\{L_1, L_2\})$, where c is a symbol not in $\Sigma_{L_1} \cup \Sigma_{L_2}$.

EXERCISE 5.1.15: Let $\mathcal{L}$ be a semi-AFL and $\mathcal{L}_1, \ldots, \mathcal{L}_n$ trios. Suppose that $\mathcal{L} \subseteq \bigcup_{i=1}^{n} \mathcal{L}_i$. Prove that $\mathcal{L} \subseteq \mathcal{L}_i$ for some i.

EXERCISE 5.1.16: Let $\mathcal{L}$ be a (full) principal AFL, respectively (full) principal semi-AFL, and let $\mathcal{L} = \mathcal{O}(\mathcal{U})(\hat{\mathcal{O}}(\mathcal{U}))$, $\mathcal{O} = \mathcal{F}$, resp. $\mathcal{S}$. Prove that $\mathcal{L} = \mathcal{O}(\mathcal{U}')(\mathcal{L} = \hat{\mathcal{O}}(\mathcal{U}'))$ for some finite subset $\mathcal{U}'$ of $\mathcal{U}$.

EXERCISE 5.1.17: Let $\mathcal{L}$ be a full principal AFL and $\mathcal{U}$ a family of languages such that $\hat{\mathcal{F}}(\mathcal{U}) = \mathcal{L}$. Show that there exists a language L in $\mathcal{F}(\mathcal{U})$ such that $\hat{\mathcal{F}}(L) = \mathcal{L}$.

EXERCISE 5.1.18: Let $\mathcal{L}$ be a (full) principal semi-AFL. Prove that there exists a language L in $\mathcal{L}$ such that $\mathcal{L}$ is the family of all languages $M(L)$, where $M = (K_1, \Sigma_1, \Sigma_2, H, p_0, F)$ is an ϵ-free a-transducer (arbitrary a-transducer), $H \subseteq K_1 \times \Sigma_1 \times \Sigma_2^* \times K_1$.

EXERCISE 5.1.19: Using Exercise 3.2.12, prove that $\mathcal{M}^{(n)}(L_1, \ldots, L_n)$ and $\hat{\mathcal{M}}^{(n)}(L_1, \ldots, L_n)$ are closed under union for all $L_1, \ldots, L_n$ [Go1].

EXERCISE 5.1.20: (a) Exhibit two incomparable full principal AFL.

(b) Let $\mathcal{L}_1 = \hat{\mathcal{F}}(L_1)$ and $\mathcal{L}_2 = \hat{\mathcal{F}}(L_2)$ be two incomparable full principal AFL. Prove that $\mathcal{M}(\mathcal{L}) \subsetneq \mathcal{S}(\mathcal{L})$ and $\hat{\mathcal{M}}(\mathcal{L}) \subsetneq \hat{\mathcal{S}}(\mathcal{L})$, where $\mathcal{L} = \{L_1, L_2\}$. [This, with (a), shows that Proposition 5.1.1 cannot be extended to a finite family of languages.]

5.2 AFA Characterization

Since (semi-) AFL containing ϵ may be characterized in terms of AFA, it is reasonable to seek an AFA characterization for principal (semi-) AFL. In the present section we provide such a characterization.

Def: An AFA $(\Omega, \mathcal{D})$, $\Omega = (K, \Sigma, \Gamma, I, f, g)$, is said to be *finitely encoded* if I and $g(\Gamma^*)$ are both finite.

We shall show that ($\sim$) an AFL $\mathcal{L}$ containing $\{\epsilon\}$ is (full) principal if and only if $\mathcal{L} = \mathcal{L}^t(\mathcal{D})(\mathcal{L} = \mathcal{L}(\mathcal{D}))$ for some finitely encoded AFA $\mathcal{D}$. We need three lemmas to accomplish this.

($\sim$) LEMMA 5.2.1: *For each (full) principal AFL $\mathcal{L}$ containing $\{\epsilon\}$, there exists a finitely encoded AFA $\mathcal{D}$ such that $\mathcal{L} = \mathcal{L}^t(\mathcal{D})(\mathcal{L} = \mathcal{L}(\mathcal{D}))$.*

Proof: We shall prove the result for full principal AFL, an analogous result holding for arbitrary principal AFL.

Since $\mathcal{L}$ is full principal and thus full, $\mathcal{L} = \mathcal{L}(\mathcal{D}')$ for some AFA $(\Omega', \mathcal{D}')$, with $\Omega' = (K, \Sigma, \Gamma', I', f', g')$. Since $\mathcal{L}$ is full principal, $\mathcal{L} = \hat{\mathcal{F}}(L)$ for some L in $\mathcal{L}(\mathcal{D}')$. Then $L = L(D)$ for some acceptor $D = (K_1, \Sigma_1, \delta, q_0, F)$. Let

$$I = \{u \text{ in } I'/(p, u) \text{ in } \delta(q, a, \gamma) \text{ for some } p, q, a, \gamma\} \cup \{1_\gamma/\gamma \text{ in } G_D\}.$$

Since δ is finite-valued and G_D is finite, I is finite. Let Γ be the smallest subset of Γ' such that $\Gamma'_u \subseteq \Gamma$ for each u in I and such that $G_D \subseteq \Gamma^*$. Clearly Γ exists and is finite. Let f be the restriction of f' to $\Gamma^* \times I$. Let g be the function on Γ^* defined by $g(\gamma) = g'(\gamma) \cap G_D$ for each γ in Γ^*. Let $(\Omega, \mathcal{D})$ be the AFA where $\Omega = (K, \Sigma, \Gamma, I, f, g)$. Then D is in $\mathcal{D}$. Hence $\mathcal{L}(\mathcal{D})$ is a full AFL containing L. Also, $\mathcal{L}(\mathcal{D}) \subseteq \mathcal{L}(\mathcal{D}')$. [See Exercise 5.2.1.] Thus $\hat{\mathcal{F}}(L) \subseteq \mathcal{L}(\mathcal{D}) \subseteq \mathcal{L}(\mathcal{D}') = \hat{\mathcal{F}}(L)$, so that $\mathcal{L} = \mathcal{L}(\mathcal{D}') = \mathcal{L}(\mathcal{D})$. Since $g(\Gamma^*) \subseteq G_D$ and I are both finite, $\mathcal{D}$ is finitely encoded.

($\sim$) REMARK: The proof of Lemma 5.2.1 actually shows the following result: Let $\Omega' = (K, \Sigma, \Gamma', I', f', g')$. If $\mathcal{L}^t(\mathcal{D}')(\mathcal{L}(\mathcal{D}'))$ is (full) principal, then there exists a finitely encoded AFA $\mathcal{D}$, with $\Omega = (K, \Sigma, \Gamma, I, f, g)$, having the following properties:

(i) $\mathcal{L}(\mathcal{D}) = \mathcal{L}(\mathcal{D}')(\mathcal{L}^t(\mathcal{D}) = \mathcal{L}^t(\mathcal{D}'))$,
(ii) $\Gamma \subseteq \Gamma'$ and $I \subseteq I'$,
(iii) f is the function f' restricted to $\Gamma^* \times I$,
(iv) for each u in I, $\Gamma_u = \Gamma'_u \cap \Gamma$, and
(v) there exists $H' \subseteq \Gamma'^*$ such that $g(\gamma) = g'(\gamma) \cap H'$ for all γ in Γ^*.

The next lemma concerns special sets and is used in the proof of the characterization result.

($\sim$) *Notation*: Let $(\Omega, \mathcal{D})$ be a finitely encoded AFA. Let $L_{\mathcal{D}}$ denote the set of all words in[1] $(g(\Gamma^*) \times I)^*$ of the form ϵ or

$$(\gamma_1, u_1) \ldots (\gamma_n, u_n),$$

[1] Since $g(\Gamma^*) \times I$ is to be used as an alphabet for words, $g(\Gamma^*) \times I$ is assumed to be a subset of Σ.

where $\gamma_1 = \epsilon$, (γ_i, u_i) is in $g(\Gamma^*)\times I$, γ_{i+1} is in $gf(\epsilon, u_1 \ldots u_i)$ for each i, $1 \leqq i \leqq n$, and $\gamma_{n+1} = \epsilon$.[1]

Thus, in addition to ϵ, $L_{\mathcal{D}}$ contains the encoding of each sequence $\gamma_1, u_1, \ldots, \gamma_n, u_n, \gamma_{n+1}$, where $u_1, \ldots, u_n$ are instructions and $\gamma_1, \ldots, \gamma_{n+1}$ are the consecutive (under the instructions) storage information configurations, with $\gamma_1 = \gamma_{n+1} = \epsilon$. In other words, $L_{\mathcal{D}}$ represents the behavior of the sequence of storage information configurations, interspersed with appropriate instructions, during each possible accepting computation.

($\sim$) LEMMA 5.2.2: *For each finitely encoded AFA $\mathcal{D}$, $L_{\mathcal{D}}$ is in $\mathcal{L}^t(\mathcal{D})$.*

Proof: Let $D = (\{q_1\}, g(\Gamma^*)\times I, \delta, q_1, \{q_1\})$, where δ is defined by $\delta(q_1, (\gamma, u), \gamma) = \{(q_1, u)\}$ for each (γ, u) in $g(\Gamma^*)\times I$. Clearly D is in $\mathcal{D}_0^t$ and $L_{\mathcal{D}} = L(D)$. Thus $L_{\mathcal{D}}$ is in $\mathcal{L}^t(\mathcal{D})$.

The following symbolism is used only in the remainder of this section.

Notation: Given $L_{\mathcal{D}}$, let Δ be a finite nonempty subset of Σ such that $\Delta \cap (g(\Gamma^*)\times I) = \emptyset$. Let h_Δ be the homomorphism on $(\Delta \cup (g(\Gamma^*)\times I))^*$ defined by $h_\Delta(a) = \epsilon$ for each a in Δ and $h_\Delta(a) = a$ for each a in $g(\Gamma^*)\times I$. Let $\bar{h}_\Delta$ be the homomorphism on $(\Delta \cup (g(\Gamma^*)\times I))^*$ defined by $\bar{h}_\Delta(a) = a$ for each a in Δ and $\bar{h}_\Delta(a) = \epsilon$ for each a in $g(\Gamma^*)\times I$.

Thus the homomorphism h_Δ preserves elements of $g(\Gamma^*)\times I$ and erases all elements of Δ. The homomorphism $\bar{h}_\Delta$ preserves elements of Δ and erases all elements of $g(\Gamma^*)\times I$.

Notation: Let $\mathcal{D}$ be a finitely encoded AFA and $D = (K_1, \Delta, \delta, q_0, F_1)$ an acceptor in $\mathcal{D}$. For each state p in K_1 let $\bar{p}$ be a new symbol. Let σ be a new symbol. Denote by R_D the language generated by the right-linear context-free grammar $(V, (g(\Gamma^*)\times I) \cup \Delta, P_D, \sigma)$, where

$$V = \{\bar{p}/p \text{ in } K_1\} \cup \Delta \cup (g(\Gamma^*)\times I) \cup \{\sigma\} \quad \text{and}$$

$$P_D = \{\sigma \to \bar{q}_0\} \cup \{\bar{q} \to a(\gamma, u)\,\bar{q}'/(q', u) \text{ in } \delta(q, a, \gamma)\} \cup \{\bar{q} \to \epsilon/q \text{ in } F_1\}.$$

Thus the set R_D consists of all words of the form

$$a_1(\gamma_1, u_1)\ldots a_n(\gamma_n, u_n),$$

[1] The analogue to $L_{\mathcal{D}}$ for the $\sim$ case is as follows: Let $(\Omega, \mathcal{D})$ be a finitely encoded AFA. Let $\tilde{L}_{\mathcal{D}}$ denote the set of all words in $(g(\Gamma^*)\times I)^*$ of the form ϵ or $(\gamma_1, u_1) \ldots (\gamma_n, u_n)$, where $\gamma_1 = \epsilon$, u_1 is in I, (γ_i, u_i) is in $g(\Gamma^+)\times I$ for each i, $2 \leqq i \leqq n$, γ_{i+1} is in $gf(\epsilon, u_1 \ldots u_i)$ for each i, $1 \leqq i \leqq n$, and $\gamma_{n+1} = \epsilon$. There is no analogue to $L_{\mathcal{D}}$ for the f case.

where D has a sequence of states $q_0, \ldots, q_n$, with q_n in F_1 and (q_i, u_i) in $\delta(q_{i-1}, a_i, \gamma_i)$ for all i, $1 \leqq i \leqq n$.

Since R_D is generated by a right-linear context-free grammar, it is a regular set.

The next lemma states that if D is an acceptor, over an alphabet disjoint from $g(\Gamma^*)\times I$, in a finitely encoded AFA, then $L(D)$ can be expressed as the homomorphic image of the intersection of (a) a regular set which encodes the finite state control of D, and (b) a member of $\{h^{-1}(L_{\mathcal{D}})/h$ a homomorphism$\}$.

($\sim$) LEMMA 5.2.3: *For each finitely encoded AFA* $\mathcal{D}$ *and each* $D = (K_1, \Delta, \delta, q_0, F_1)$ *in* $\mathcal{D}$, $L(D) = \bar{h}_\Delta(h_\Delta^{-1}(L_{\mathcal{D}}) \cap R_D)$. *Moreover, if* D *is quasi-realtime, then* $\bar{h}_\Delta$ *is* ϵ*-limited on* $h_\Delta^{-1}(L_{\mathcal{D}}) \cap R_D$.

Proof: Informally, $L_{\mathcal{D}}$ contains all words $(\gamma_1, u_1)\ldots(\gamma_n, u_n)$, where ϵ, $f(\epsilon, u_1), \ldots, f(\epsilon, u_1\ldots u_n) = \epsilon$ is a sequence of auxiliary storage configurations for some possible accepting computation of some acceptor of $\mathcal{D}$ and γ_{i+1} is in $gf(\epsilon, u_1\ldots u_i)$ for all i, $1 \leqq i \leqq n$, $\gamma_1 = \gamma_{n+1} = \epsilon$. Also, $h_\Delta^{-1}(L_{\mathcal{D}})$ is $L_{\mathcal{D}}$ with all possible words of Δ^* inserted at all points. The set R_D consists of all words

$$a_1(\gamma_1, u_1)\ldots a_n(\gamma_n, u_n),$$

where D has a sequence of states $q_0, \ldots, q_n$, q_n an accepting state, with (q_i, u_i) in $\delta(q_{i-1}, a_i, \gamma_i)$ for all i, $1 \leqq i \leqq n$. Thus $h_\Delta^{-1}(L_{\mathcal{D}}) \cap R_D$ combines both auxiliary storage and state transition restrictions. The homomorphism $\bar{h}_\Delta$ then erases all symbols not the input of a computation, thus leaving $L(D)$.

Formally, we first prove that $L(D) \subseteq \bar{h}_\Delta(h_\Delta^{-1}(L_{\mathcal{D}}) \cap R_D)$. Thus let w be in $L(D)$. Suppose $w = \epsilon$ and q_0 is in F_1. Then $\sigma \Rightarrow \bar{q}_0 \Rightarrow \epsilon$, so that ϵ is in R_D. Since ϵ is in $L_{\mathcal{D}}$, it is in $h_\Delta^{-1}(L_{\mathcal{D}})$, hence in $h_\Delta^{-1}(L_{\mathcal{D}}) \cap R_D$. Therefore ϵ is in $\bar{h}_\Delta(h_\Delta^{-1}(L_{\mathcal{D}}) \cap R_D)$. Now suppose either $w = \epsilon$ and q_0 is not in F_1, or else $w \neq \epsilon$. Then there exist $n \geqq 1$, $a_1, \ldots, a_n$ in $\Delta \cup \{\epsilon\}$, $p_1, \ldots, p_n$ in K_1, with p_n in F_1, and $y_1, \ldots, y_n$ in Γ^* such that $y_1 = \epsilon$,

$$\begin{aligned}(q_0, a_1\ldots a_n, y_1) &\vdash (p_1, a_2\ldots a_n, y_2)\\ &\cdots\\ &\vdash (p_{n-1}, a_n, y_n)\\ &\vdash (p_n, \epsilon, \epsilon),\end{aligned}$$

and $w = a_1\ldots a_n$. Hence there exist $u_1, \ldots, u_n$ in I and $\gamma_2, \ldots, \gamma_n$ in G_D such that $f(\epsilon, u_1) = y_2$, $f(y_i, u_i) = y_{i+1}$ for all i, $2 \leqq i \leqq n-1$, $f(y_n, u_n) = \epsilon$, γ_i in $g(y_i)$ for all i, $2 \leqq i \leqq n$, (p_1, u_1) in $\delta(q_0, a_1, \epsilon)$, and (p_{i+1}, u_{i+1}) in

$\delta(p_i, a_{i+1}, \gamma_{i+1})$ for all i, $1 \leqq i \leqq n-1$. For each i, $1 \leqq i \leqq n-1$, since $y_{i+1} = f(\epsilon, u_1 \ldots u_i)$ and $\epsilon = f(\epsilon, u_1 \ldots u_n)$, it follows that γ_{i+1} is in $gf(\epsilon, u_1 \ldots u_i)$ and $\{\epsilon\} = gf(\epsilon, u_1 \ldots u_n)$. Therefore

$$(\gamma_1, u_1) \ldots (\gamma_n, u_n)$$

is in $L_{\mathcal{D}}$, where $\gamma_1 = \epsilon$. Hence the word

$$w' = a_1(\gamma_1, u_1) \ldots a_n(\gamma_n, u_n)$$

is in $h_\Delta^{-1}(L_{\mathcal{D}})$. Obviously w' is in R_D, so that w' is in $h_\Delta^{-1}(L_{\mathcal{D}}) \cap R_D$, and $w = \bar{h}_\Delta(w')$. Thus $L(D) \subseteq \bar{h}_\Delta(h_\Delta^{-1}(L_{\mathcal{D}}) \cap R_D)$.

To see the reverse inclusion, let w be in $\bar{h}_\Delta(h_\Delta^{-1}(L_{\mathcal{D}}) \cap R_D)$. Suppose $w = \epsilon$ and ϵ is in R_D. Since any application of a rule $\bar{q} \to a(\gamma, u)\bar{q}'$ introduces the terminal symbol (γ, u), if ϵ is in R_D then q_0 is in F_1. Thus ϵ is in $L(D)$. Now suppose either $w = \epsilon$ and ϵ is not in R_D, or else $w \neq \epsilon$. Then there exist $n \geqq 1$, $u_1, \ldots, u_n$ in I, $\gamma_1, \ldots, \gamma_n$ in $g(\Gamma^*)$, $\gamma_1 = \epsilon$, and $a_1, \ldots, a_n$ in $\Delta \cup \{\epsilon\}$ such that the word $w' = a_1(\gamma_1, u_1) \ldots a_n(\gamma_n, u_n)$ is in $h_\Delta^{-1}(L_{\mathcal{D}}) \cap R_D$ and $w = a_1 \ldots a_n = \bar{h}_\Delta(w')$. Since w' is in $h_\Delta^{-1}(L_{\mathcal{D}})$, $\epsilon = f(\epsilon, u_1 \ldots u_n)$ and there exist $y_1 = \epsilon, \ldots, y_n$ such that $y_{i+1} = f(\epsilon, u_1 \ldots u_i)$ and γ_{i+1} is in $g(y_{i+1})$ for each i, $1 \leqq i \leqq n-1$. Since w' is in R_D, there exist $p_1, \ldots, p_n$ such that $\bar{q}_0 \to a_1(\gamma_1, u_1)\bar{p}_1$, $\bar{p}_i \to a_{i+1}(\gamma_{i+1}, u_{i+1})\bar{p}_{i+1}$ for each i, $1 \leqq i \leqq n-1$, and $\bar{p}_n \to \epsilon$. It follows from the definition of R_D that p_n is in F_1, (p_1, u_1) is in $\delta(q_0, a_1, \epsilon)$, and (p_{i+1}, u_{i+1}) is in $\delta(p_i, a_{i+1}, \gamma_{i+1})$ for each i, $1 \leqq i \leqq n-1$. Hence

$$\begin{aligned}(q_0, a_1 \ldots a_n, \epsilon) &\vdash (p_1, a_2 \ldots a_n, y_2)\\ &\ldots\\ &\vdash (p_{n-1}, a_n, y_n)\\ &\vdash (p_n, \epsilon, \epsilon),\end{aligned}$$

so that $w = a_1 \ldots a_n$ is in $L(D)$. Then $\bar{h}_\Delta(h_\Delta^{-1}(L_{\mathcal{D}}) \cap R_D) \subseteq L(D)$, whence $L(D) = \bar{h}_\Delta(h_\Delta^{-1}(L_{\mathcal{D}}) \cap R_D)$.

Suppose that D is quasi-realtime. Then there exists $k \geqq 0$ such that D has at most k consecutive ϵ-moves. Thus, for each word $w = a_1 \ldots a_n$ in $L(D)$, at most k consecutive a_i can be ϵ. Hence $\bar{h}_\Delta$ maps at most $2k+1$ consecutive symbols of w' into ϵ. Therefore $\bar{h}_\Delta$ is ϵ-limited on $h_\Delta^{-1}(L_{\mathcal{D}}) \cap R_D$, completing the proof.

We need one more lemma.

($\sim$) LEMMA 5.2.4: *For each finitely encoded AFA $\mathcal{D}$, $\mathcal{L}(\mathcal{D}) = \hat{\mathcal{M}}(L_{\mathcal{D}}) = \hat{\mathcal{F}}(L_{\mathcal{D}})$ and $\mathcal{L}^t(\mathcal{D}) = \mathcal{M}(L_{\mathcal{D}}) = \mathcal{F}(L_{\mathcal{D}})$.*

Proof: By Lemma 5.2.2, $L_{\mathcal{D}}$ is in $\mathcal{L}^t(\mathcal{D}) \subseteq \mathcal{L}(\mathcal{D})$. Since $\mathcal{L}(\mathcal{D})$ is a full AFL, $\hat{\mathcal{M}}(L_{\mathcal{D}}) \subseteq \hat{\mathcal{F}}(L_{\mathcal{D}}) \subseteq \mathcal{L}(\mathcal{D})$. Consider the reverse containment. Let L be in $\mathcal{L}(\mathcal{D})$. For each a in Σ_L, let $\bar{a}$ be a new element in $\Sigma-((g(\Gamma^*)\times I) \cup \Sigma_L)$. Let $\Delta = \{\bar{a}/a \text{ in } \Sigma_L\}$ and let α_Δ be the homomorphism from Σ_L^* onto Δ^* defined by $\alpha_\Delta(a) = \bar{a}$ for each a in Σ_L. Then $(g(\Gamma^*)\times I) \cap \Delta = \emptyset$ and $\alpha_\Delta(L)$ is in $\mathcal{L}(\mathcal{D})$. Let $D = (K_1, \Delta, \delta, q_0, F_1)$ be an acceptor in $\mathcal{D}$ such that $L(D) = \alpha_\Delta(L)$. By Lemma 5.2.3, $\alpha_\Delta(L) = \bar{h}_\Delta(h_\Delta^{-1}(L_{\mathcal{D}}) \cap R_D)$. Since R_D is regular, $\alpha_\Delta(L)$ is in $\hat{\mathcal{M}}(L_{\mathcal{D}})$. Hence $L = \alpha_\Delta^{-1}(\alpha_\Delta(L))$ is in $\hat{\mathcal{M}}(L_{\mathcal{D}}) \subseteq \hat{\mathcal{F}}(L_{\mathcal{D}})$, so that $\hat{\mathcal{M}}(L_{\mathcal{D}}) = \mathcal{L}(\mathcal{D})$.

Now consider $\mathcal{M}(L_{\mathcal{D}})$. Since $\mathcal{M}(L_{\mathcal{D}}) \subseteq \mathcal{F}(L_{\mathcal{D}}) \subseteq \mathcal{L}^t(\mathcal{D})$, it suffices to show the reverse containment. We use the notation in the preceding paragraph. Let L be in $\mathcal{L}^t(\mathcal{D})$. Since α_Δ is an ϵ-free homomorphism, $\alpha_\Delta(L)$ is in $\mathcal{L}^t(\mathcal{D})$. Thus $\alpha_\Delta(L) = L(D)$ for some quasi-realtime acceptor D. By Lemma 5.2.3, $\alpha_\Delta(L) = \bar{h}_\Delta(h_\Delta^{-1}(L_{\mathcal{D}}) \cap R_D)$ and $\bar{h}_\Delta$ is ϵ-limited on $h_\Delta^{-1}(L_{\mathcal{D}}) \cap R_D$. Hence $\alpha_\Delta(L)-\{\epsilon\}$ is in $\mathcal{M}(L_{\mathcal{D}})$. By Proposition 5.1.1, $\mathcal{M}(L_{\mathcal{D}})$ is closed under union with $\{\epsilon\}$. [For $L_{\mathcal{D}}$ contains ϵ, so that $\mathcal{M}(L_{\mathcal{D}})$ contains $\{\epsilon\}$.] Thus $\alpha_\Delta(L)$ is in $\mathcal{M}(L_{\mathcal{D}})$. Therefore $L = \alpha_\Delta^{-1}\alpha_\Delta(L)$ is in $\mathcal{M}(L_{\mathcal{D}})$, so that $\mathcal{L}^t(\mathcal{D}) \subseteq \mathcal{M}(L_{\mathcal{D}}) \subseteq \mathcal{F}(L_{\mathcal{D}})$. Thus $\mathcal{L}^t(\mathcal{D}) = \mathcal{M}(L_{\mathcal{D}}) = \mathcal{F}(L_{\mathcal{D}})$.

($\sim$) COROLLARY: *For each finitely encoded AFA $\mathcal{D}$,*
$\mathcal{L}(\mathcal{D}) = \{h_2(h_1^{-1}(L_{\mathcal{D}}) \cap R)/R$ *in* $\mathcal{R}$, h_1 *and* h_2 *homomorphisms*$\}$ *and*
$\mathcal{L}^t(\mathcal{D}) = \{h_2(h_1^{-1}(L_{\mathcal{D}}) \cap R)/R$ *in* $\mathcal{R}$, h_1 *and* h_2 *homomorphisms*, h_2 ϵ-*free*$\}$.

The corollary to Lemma 5.2.4 resembles the Chomsky – Schutzenberger characterization of the pda languages ($= \mathcal{L}_{CF}$) given in Example 5.1.1, namely that $\mathcal{L}_{CF}$ is the family of all languages of the form $h_2(h_1^{-1}(W_2) \cap R)$, where h_1 and h_2 are homomorphisms, R is a regular set, and $W_2 \subseteq \{a_1, a_1^E, a_2, a_2^E\}^*$ is the Dyck set on two letters. We shall explore this resemblance further in Section 5.3.

Combining Lemmas 5.2.1 and 5.2.4, we have the following characterization of a (full) principal AFL containing $\{\epsilon\}$.

($\sim$) THEOREM 5.2.1: *An AFL $\mathcal{L}$ containing $\{\epsilon\}$ is (full) principal if and only if there exists some finitely encoded AFA $\mathcal{D}$ such that $\mathcal{L} = \mathcal{L}^t(\mathcal{D})$ ($\mathcal{L} = \mathcal{L}(\mathcal{D})$), in which case $\mathcal{L} = \mathcal{F}(L_{\mathcal{D}}) = \mathcal{M}(L_{\mathcal{D}})$ ($\mathcal{L} = \hat{\mathcal{F}}(L_{\mathcal{D}}) = \hat{\mathcal{M}}(L_{\mathcal{D}})$).*

We conclude the section with several applications of Theorem 5.2.1 to known AFL.

EXAMPLE 5.2.1: Let $\mathcal{D}$ be the AFA where $\Gamma = \{a, b\}$, $I = \{\epsilon\} \cup \Gamma \cup \Gamma^2$, $g(\epsilon) = \{\epsilon\}$, $g(ya) = \{a\}$, $g(yb) = \{b\}$, $f(\epsilon, u) = u$, and $f(ya, u) = yu = f(yb, u)$ for all y in Γ^* and u in I. Clearly $\mathcal{D}$ is a finitely encoded AFA and contains only pda. Now every context-free language is accepted by a pda which (α) has at most two storage symbols, and (β) never increases the length of the auxiliary storage by more than one. Thus $\mathcal{L}(\mathcal{D}) = \mathcal{L}_{CF}$. Theorem 5.2.1 then provides another proof that $\mathcal{L}_{CF}$ is a full principal AFL.

Consider the quasi-realtime case. Every context-free language is accepted by a pda with no ϵ-moves, thus by a pda in $(\mathcal{D}_{PDA})_0^t$. Therefore $\mathcal{L}_{CF} = \mathcal{L}^t(\mathcal{D}_{PDA})$. Moreover, for every quasi-realtime pda D there clearly is a quasi-realtime pda D' in $\mathcal{D}$ such that $L(D) = L(D')$. Thus $\mathcal{L}_{CF} = \mathcal{L}^t(\mathcal{D}_{PDA}) = \mathcal{L}^t(\mathcal{D})$. By Theorem 5.2.1, $\mathcal{L}_{CF}$ is a principal AFL.

EXAMPLE 5.2.2: Let $\mathcal{D}$ be the AFA where $\Gamma = \{a, b, \uparrow\}$, $\Gamma_1 = \{a, b\}$, $I = \Gamma_1^2 \cup \Gamma_1 \cup \{\epsilon, -1, 0, 1\}$, and f and g as in $\mathcal{D}_S$. Clearly $\mathcal{D}$ is finitely encoded. It is easy to see that for every one-way stack acceptor D there is a one-way stack acceptor D' satisfying (α) and (β) in Example 5.2.1 and such that $L(D') = L(D)$. Furthermore, D' is quasi-realtime if D is. Hence $\mathcal{L}(\mathcal{D}) = \mathcal{L}(\mathcal{D}_S)$ and $\mathcal{L}^t(\mathcal{D}) = \mathcal{L}^t(\mathcal{D}_S)$. Therefore $\mathcal{L}(\mathcal{D}_S)$ is full principal and $\mathcal{L}^t(\mathcal{D}_S)$ principal. It can be shown [Gr2] that $\mathcal{L}^t(\mathcal{D}_S)$ is *not* full and thus not full principal.

Analogous results hold for $\mathcal{L}(\mathcal{D}_{NES})$ and $\mathcal{L}^t(\mathcal{D}_{NES})$.

EXAMPLE 5.2.3: Let $\mathcal{D}_{NSA}$ be the AFA defined as follows. Let $\bar{\Gamma}$ be an infinite set such that $\bar{\Gamma} \cap \{\uparrow, ¢, \$, -1, 0, 1\} = \emptyset$, and let $\Gamma = \bar{\Gamma} \cup \{\uparrow, ¢, \$\}$. For notational convenience, the symbol \$ is always to be appended to the symbol immediately to its left if there is such a symbol, and the subword \$\$ is always to be excluded. Thus $Z\$$, Z in $\bar{\Gamma} \cup \{¢\}$, is really $Z_\$$, a new symbol; and $u\$$, $u = Z_1 \dots Z_m$, $m \geqq 1$, each Z_i in $\Gamma - \{\uparrow\}$, $Z_m \neq \$$, is really $Z_1 \dots Z_{m-1} Z_{m\$}$. Let $I = \bar{\Gamma}^*\$ \cup ¢\bar{\Gamma}^*\$ \cup \{e\} \cup \{-1, 0, 1\}$. Let g be defined by $g(\epsilon) = \{\epsilon\}$, $g(xZ\uparrow y) = \{Z\}$, and $g(xZ\$\uparrow y) = \{Z\$\}$ for all Z in $\bar{\Gamma} \cup \{¢\}$ and x, y in $(\Gamma - \{\uparrow\})^*$. Let f be defined as follows (for all xy in $(\Gamma - \{\uparrow\})^*$, $x \neq \epsilon$, and u in $\bar{\Gamma}^*$):

(a) $f(\epsilon, ¢u\$) = ¢u\$\uparrow$ and $f(xZ\uparrow y, ¢u\$) = x¢u\$\uparrow Zy$ for all Z in $\bar{\Gamma} \cup \bar{\Gamma}\$$.

(b) $f(xZ\$\uparrow y, u\$) = xu\$\uparrow y$ for all Z in $\bar{\Gamma}$.

(c) $f(x¢\$\uparrow Zy, e) = xZ\uparrow y$ and $f(¢\$\uparrow, e) = \epsilon$ for all Z in $\bar{\Gamma} \cup \bar{\Gamma}\$$.

(d) $f(xZ\$\uparrow y, -1) = x\uparrow Z\$y$ and $f(xZ\uparrow y, -1) = x\uparrow Zy$ for all Z in $\bar{\Gamma} \cup \{¢\}$.

(e) $f(xZ\uparrow y, 0) = xZ\uparrow y$ for all Z in Γ.

(f) $f(y'Y\uparrow Zy, 1) = y'YZ\uparrow y$ and $f(y'Y\uparrow Z\$y, 1) = y'YZ\$\uparrow y$ for all Y, Z in $\bar{\Gamma} \cup \{¢\}$ and y' in $(\Gamma - \{\uparrow\})^*$.

The family $\mathcal{D}_{\mathrm{NSA}}$ is called the AFA of *nested stack acceptors* [Ah2] and $\mathcal{L}_{\mathrm{NSA}} = \mathcal{L}(\mathcal{D}_{\mathrm{NSA}})$ the family of *nested stack-acceptor languages.*

Intuitively, a nested stack acceptor is a stack acceptor (conditions (d), (e), and (f)) which embeds stacks within stacks (conditions (a), (b), and (c)) to arbitrary depth in a special way, each stack being bounded on the left by ¢ and on the right by $Z\$$, Z some symbol in $\bar{\Gamma}$. Call the symbol immediately to the left of $\uparrow$ the *active* symbol. When a new stack is embedded, the new stack is placed between the active symbol and the symbol immediately to its left. The rightmost symbol in the embedded stack then becomes the active symbol. A stack may be removed when it is empty, i. e., is ¢$ and the active symbol. When this happens the symbol immediately to the right of the eliminated stack becomes the active symbol. As in a stack acceptor, the pointer can stay stationary, move left, or move right, except that it cannot go right when the active symbol is of the form $Z\$$, i. e., is the rightmost symbol of a stack. It can move left of a ¢ symbol except when that occurrence is the leftmost symbol of the auxiliary storage.

Now let $\mathcal{D}'$ be the AFA where $\Gamma' = \{a, b, ¢, \$, \uparrow, -1, 0, 1\}$,

$$I' = \{¢u\$/|u| \leqq 2, u \text{ in } \{a, b\}^*\} \cup \{e, -1, 0, 1\} \cup \{u\$/|u| \leqq 2, u \text{ in } \{a, b\}^*\},$$

and f' and g' are the same as f and g, respectively, in $\mathcal{D}_{\mathrm{NSA}}$. Then $\mathcal{D}'$ is finitely encoded, $\mathcal{L}(\mathcal{D}_{\mathrm{NSA}}) = \mathcal{L}(\mathcal{D}')$, and $\mathcal{L}^t(\mathcal{D}_{\mathrm{NSA}}) = \mathcal{L}^t(\mathcal{D}')$. [See Exercise 5.2.10.] Consequently, the family of all nested stack acceptor languages is a full principal AFL and the family of all quasi-realtime nested stack acceptor languages is a principal AFL.

EXAMPLE 5.2.4: It is noted in Exercise 5.2.11 that $\mathcal{L}_{\mathrm{RE}}$ is a full principal AFL. Consider the problem of whether $\mathcal{L}_{\mathrm{RE}}$ is a principal AFL. Let $\Delta = \{a_1, \ldots, a_i, \ldots\}$ be a countably infinite subset of Σ.[1] For each $n \geqq 1$ let $\Delta_n = \{a_1, \ldots, a_n\}$ and let h_n be the homomorphism on Δ_n^* defined by $h_n(a_i) = a_1^i a_2$ for each i, $1 \leqq i \leqq n$. Let $\mathcal{L}$ be the family of r. e. languages over Δ. Let $L_1, \ldots, L_i, \ldots$ be an effective enumeration of the languages in $\mathcal{L}$ such that $L_n \subseteq \Delta_n^*$ for each n. Then

$$L = \{\epsilon\} \cup \{a_1^n a_2 h_n(w)/w \text{ in } L_n, n \geqq 1\}$$

is an r. e. subset of $\{a_1, a_2\}^*$. For each n, let M_n be a gsm, ϵ-limited on $L \cap a_1^n a_2 \Delta_2^*$, which maps $a_1^n a_2$ into ϵ and then decodes $a_1^i a_2$ into a_i, for each i,

[1] Remember that there is no assumption that Σ is *countably* infinite

$1 \leqq i \leqq n$. Clearly $L_n = M_n(L \cap a_1^n a_2 \Delta_2^*)$. Now $L \cap a_1^n a_2 \Delta_2^*$ is in $\mathcal{F}(L)$. By Theorem 3.2.2, L_n is in $\mathcal{F}(L)$ since $\mathcal{F}(L)$ contains $\{\epsilon\}$. Therefore $\mathcal{L} \subseteq \mathcal{F}(L)$. Now let L' be an arbitrary language in $\mathcal{L}_{\text{RE}}$. Let $n(L') = \#(\Sigma_{L'})$. Let h be a one-to-one function from $\Sigma_{L'}$ onto $\{a_1, \ldots, a_{n(L')}\}$. Extend h to be a homomorphism from $\Sigma_{L'}^*$ onto $\{a_1, \ldots, a_{n(L')}\}^*$. Clearly h^{-1} is a homomorphism from $\{a_1, \ldots, a_{n(L')}\}^*$ onto $\Sigma_{L'}^*$. Then $h(L')$ is in $\mathcal{L} \subseteq \mathcal{F}(L)$. Hence $L' = h^{-1}(h(L'))$ is in $\mathcal{F}(L)$. Therefore $\mathcal{L}_{\text{RE}} \subseteq \mathcal{F}(L)$. Since the reverse containment is obvious, $\mathcal{F}(L) = \mathcal{L}_{\text{RE}}$, i. e., $\mathcal{L}_{\text{RE}}$ is a principal AFL.

EXERCISE 5.2.1: Prove that $\mathcal{L}(\mathcal{D}) \subseteq \mathcal{L}(\mathcal{D}')$ in Lemma 5.2.1.

EXERCISE 5.2.2: Prove that for each (full) principal semi-AFL $\mathcal{L}$ containing $\{\epsilon\}$, there exists a finitely encoded nontrivial AFA $\mathcal{D}$ such that $\mathcal{L} = \tilde{\mathcal{L}}^t(\mathcal{D})$ $(\mathcal{L} = \tilde{\mathcal{L}}(\mathcal{D}))$.

EXERCISE 5.2.3: Prove that $\tilde{L}_{\mathcal{D}}$ is in $\tilde{\mathcal{L}}^t(\mathcal{D})$ for each nontrivial, finitely encoded AFA $\mathcal{D}$.

The following terminology is used in Exercises 5.2.4–5.2.7. An AFA $\mathcal{D}$, with $\Omega = (K, \Sigma, \Gamma, I, f, g)$, is said to be *finitely* (t-) *encodable* if there exists a finitely encoded AFA $\mathcal{D}'$, with $\Omega' = (K', \Sigma, \Gamma', I', f', g')$, satisfying the following properties: (a) $\mathcal{L}(\mathcal{D}) = \mathcal{L}(\mathcal{D}')(\mathcal{L}^t(\mathcal{D}) = \mathcal{L}^t(\mathcal{D}'))$; (b) $K' \subseteq K$, $\Gamma' \subseteq \Gamma$, and $I' \subseteq I$; (c) f' is the function f restricted to $\Gamma'^* \times I'$; (d) for each u in I', $\Gamma'_u = \Gamma_u \cap \Gamma'$; and (e) there exists $H \subseteq \Gamma^*$ such that $g'(\gamma) = g(\gamma) \cap H$ for all γ in Γ'^*.

EXERCISE 5.2.4: For each AFA $\mathcal{D}$, prove that $\mathcal{L}(\mathcal{D})(\mathcal{L}^t(\mathcal{D}))$ is full principal (principal) if and only if $\mathcal{D}$ is finitely (t-) encodable [GGr2].

EXERCISE 5.2.5: Prove the following [GGr2]:

(a) A full AFL $\mathcal{L}$ is full principal if and only if $\mathcal{D}$ is finitely encodable for every AFA $\mathcal{D}$ such that $\mathcal{L} = \mathcal{L}(\mathcal{D})$.

(b) An AFL $\mathcal{L}$ containing $\{\epsilon\}$ is principal if and only if $\mathcal{D}$ is finitely t-encodable for every AFA $\mathcal{D}$ such that $\mathcal{L} = \mathcal{L}^t(\mathcal{D})$.

EXERCISE 5.2.6: Prove that an AFL $\mathcal{L}$ (containing $\{\epsilon\}$) is full principal (principal) if and only if $\mathcal{L} = \mathcal{L}(\mathcal{D})(\mathcal{L} = \mathcal{L}^t(\mathcal{D}))$ for some finitely (t-) encodable AFA $\mathcal{D}$ [GGr2].

EXERCISE 5.2.7: Prove that a full AFL $\mathcal{L}$ is principal if and only if there exists a finitely t-encodable AFA $\mathcal{D}$ such that $\mathcal{L} = \mathcal{L}(\mathcal{D}) = \mathcal{L}^t(\mathcal{D})$ [GGr2].

EXERCISE 5.2.8: Show that $\tilde{L}(D) = \bar{h}_\Delta(h_\Delta^{-1}(\tilde{L}_{\mathcal{D}}) \cap R_D)$ for each nontrivial, finitely encoded AFA $\mathcal{D}$ and each $D = (K_1, \Delta, \delta, q_0, F_1)$ in $\mathcal{D}$.

EXERCISE 5.2.9: For each nontrivial, finitely encoded AFA $\mathcal{D}$, show that $\tilde{\mathcal{L}}(\mathcal{D}) = \hat{\mathcal{M}}(\tilde{L}_{\mathcal{D}}) = \hat{\mathcal{F}}(\tilde{L}_{\mathcal{D}})$ and $\tilde{\mathcal{L}}'(\mathcal{D}) = \mathcal{M}(\tilde{L}_{\mathcal{D}}) = \mathcal{F}(\tilde{L}_{\mathcal{D}})$.

EXERCISE 5.2.10: Show that $\mathcal{L}(\mathcal{D}') = \mathcal{L}(\mathcal{D}_{\mathrm{NSA}})$ and $\mathcal{L}'(\mathcal{D}') = \mathcal{L}'(\mathcal{D}_{\mathrm{NSA}})$ in Example 5.2.3.

EXERCISE 5.2.11: Give an AFA proof that $\mathcal{L}_{\mathrm{RE}}$ is a full principal AFL [GGr2].

EXERCISE 5.2.12: Prove that $\mathcal{L}_{\mathrm{NSA}}$ is closed under reversal [Ah1].

EXERCISE 5.2.13: Prove that $\mathcal{L}_{\mathrm{NSA}}$ is substitution closed [Ah1].

EXERCISE 5.2.14: Let $\mathcal{L}_{\mathrm{CRE}}$ be the family of languages L such that $\Sigma_L^* - L$ is in $\mathcal{L}_{\mathrm{RE}}$. Prove the following [Ui]:
(a) $\mathcal{L}_{\mathrm{CRE}}$ is a principal AFL.
(b) $\mathcal{L}_{\mathrm{CRE}}$ is not a full AFL.

5.3 Generators from Finitely Encoded AFA

If a (semi-) AFL is defined by a (nontrivial) finitely encoded AFA, it is natural to look to the AFA for a generator for the (semi-) AFL. As proved in Theorem 5.2.1, $L_{\mathcal{D}}(\tilde{L}_{\mathcal{D}})$ is one such generator. In $L_{\mathcal{D}}(\tilde{L}_{\mathcal{D}})$, each non-$\epsilon$ word is of the form $(\gamma_1, u_1)\ldots(\gamma_n, u_n)$, with γ_i in $g(\Gamma^*)$ and u_i in I. Words of this form are extremely complicated to handle in explicit examples because of the presence of the $g(\Gamma^*)$-component. We thus seek a more tractable generator from the AFA. In particular, we shall consider the set obtained from the words in $L_{\mathcal{D}}(\tilde{L}_{\mathcal{D}})$ by eliminating the $g(\Gamma^*)$-component. For the AFL case, in addition to considering the set of the words $u_1\ldots u_n$, we also examine a closely related set. These two languages will provide us with specific (full) generators for many important (full) principal AFL.

The two languages[1] to be studied are the following:

[1] In the semi-AFL case, only one language, $\tilde{L}'_{\mathcal{D}}$, is to be studied.

($\sim$) *Notation*: For each finitely encoded AFA$\mathcal{D}$ let

$$L'_{\mathcal{D}} = \{\epsilon\} \cup \{u_1 \ldots u_n / n \geqq 1, f(\epsilon, u_1 \ldots u_n) = \epsilon\} \quad \text{and}$$

$$\tilde{L}'_{\mathcal{D}} = \{\epsilon\} \cup \{u_1 \ldots u_n / f(\epsilon, u_1 \ldots u_n) = \epsilon \neq f(\epsilon, u_1 \ldots u_i) \text{ for all } i < n, n \geqq 1\}.$$

In other words, $L'_{\mathcal{D}}$ is the set of all words over the instruction alphabet which transform the empty storage to the empty storage. $\tilde{L}'_{\mathcal{D}}$ is the set of all "first return empty storage to empty storage" words over the instruction alphabet, that is, $\tilde{L}'_{\mathcal{D}} = \{\epsilon\} \cup \text{Min}\,(L'_{\mathcal{D}} - \{\epsilon\})$, where

$$\text{Min}\,(X) = \{x \text{ in } X / yz = x \text{ and } y \text{ in } X \text{ imply } y = x\}.$$

Note (see Exercise 5.3.1) that $L'_{\mathcal{D}} = \tilde{L}'^{+}_{\mathcal{D}}$.

For technical reasons, when discussing $L'_{\mathcal{D}}$ and $\tilde{L}'_{\mathcal{D}}$ it is convenient to require $\mathcal{D}$ to have the following property:

Def: An AFA$\mathcal{D}$ is said to be *reduced* if for each x in Γ^*, $g(x) \neq \emptyset$ if and only if $f(x, u) \neq \emptyset$ for some u in I.

There exist some elementary relations in generative capacity between $L'_{\mathcal{D}}$, $\tilde{L}'_{\mathcal{D}}$, and $L_{\mathcal{D}}$.

($\sim$) PROPOSITION 5.3.1: *For each reduced, finitely encoded AFA* $\mathcal{D}$,
(a) $\mathcal{F}(L'_{\mathcal{D}}) \subseteq \mathcal{F}(\tilde{L}'_{\mathcal{D}}) \subseteq \mathcal{F}(L_{\mathcal{D}}) = \mathcal{L}^t(\mathcal{D})$, *and*
(b) $\hat{\mathcal{F}}(L'_{\mathcal{D}}) \subseteq \hat{\mathcal{F}}(\tilde{L}'_{\mathcal{D}}) \subseteq \hat{\mathcal{F}}(L_{\mathcal{D}}) = \mathcal{L}(\mathcal{D})$.

Proof: We consider just (a), the argument for (b) being analogous. By Theorem 5.2.1, $\mathcal{F}(L_{\mathcal{D}}) = \mathcal{L}^t(\mathcal{D})$. Since $L'_{\mathcal{D}} = \tilde{L}'^{+}_{\mathcal{D}}$, $\mathcal{F}(L'_{\mathcal{D}}) \subseteq \mathcal{F}(\tilde{L}'_{\mathcal{D}})$. To see that $\mathcal{F}(\tilde{L}'_{\mathcal{D}}) \subseteq \mathcal{F}(L_{\mathcal{D}})$, let h be the ϵ-free homomorphism on $(g(\Gamma^*) \times I)^*$ defined by $h((\gamma, u)) = u$ for all (γ, u) in $g(\Gamma^*) \times I$. Since $\mathcal{D}$ is reduced,

$$\tilde{L}'_{\mathcal{D}} = h\big(L_{\mathcal{D}} \cap [\{\epsilon\} \cup (\{\epsilon\} \times I)(g(\Gamma^+) \times I)^*]\big).$$

Thus $\tilde{L}'_{\mathcal{D}}$ is in $\mathcal{F}(L_{\mathcal{D}})$, and $\mathcal{F}(\tilde{L}'_{\mathcal{D}}) \subseteq \mathcal{F}(L_{\mathcal{D}})$.

There exist reduced $\mathcal{D}$ (see Exercise 5.3.4) such that $\mathcal{F}(L'_{\mathcal{D}}) \neq \mathcal{L}^t(\mathcal{D})$ ($\hat{\mathcal{F}}(L'_{\mathcal{D}}) \neq \mathcal{L}(\mathcal{D})$). There also exist reduced $\mathcal{D}$ (see Exercise 5.3.12) such that $\mathcal{F}(\tilde{L}'_{\mathcal{D}}) = \mathcal{L}^t(\mathcal{D})(\hat{\mathcal{F}}(\tilde{L}'_{\mathcal{D}}) = \mathcal{L}(\mathcal{D}))$ but $\mathcal{F}(L'_{\mathcal{D}}) \neq \mathcal{L}^t(\mathcal{D})(\hat{\mathcal{F}}(L'_{\mathcal{D}}) \neq \mathcal{L}(\mathcal{D}))$.

In dealing with specific $\tilde{L}'_{\mathcal{D}}$ and $L'_{\mathcal{D}}$, we frequently encounter instructions u with the property that $f(x, u) = x$ for all "accessible" x. (Eliminating all words containing such instructions often results in languages which are easier to treat or describe.) This leads to the following concepts.

Def: Given a reduced AFA$\mathcal{D}$, a word x in Γ^* is said to be *accessible* if either $x = \epsilon$ or there exist $n \geqq 1$ and instructions $u_1, \ldots, u_n$ such that $f(\epsilon, u_1 \ldots u_n) = x$.

Def: Given a reduced AFA$\mathcal{D}$, an instruction u is said to be a *universal identity* if $f(x, u) = x$ for all accessible x such that $g(x) \neq \emptyset$. Let I_{U} be the set of all universal identities.

Thus a universal identity serves as a multiplicative identity for subwords of words in $\tilde{L}'_{\mathcal{D}}$ and $L'_{\mathcal{D}}$, $\mathcal{D}$ reduced and finitely encoded.

The basic useful fact about universal identities is expressed in the following result.

PROPOSITION 5.3.2: *For each reduced, finitely encoded AFA$\mathcal{D}$,*
(a) $\mathcal{M}(L'_{\mathcal{D}}) = \mathcal{M}(L'_{\mathcal{D}} \cap (I - I_{\mathrm{U}})^*)$ *and* $\mathcal{M}(\tilde{L}'_{\mathcal{D}}) = \mathcal{M}(\tilde{L}'_{\mathcal{D}} \cap (I - I_{\mathrm{U}})^*)$; *and*
(b) $\hat{\mathcal{M}}(L'_{\mathcal{D}}) = \hat{\mathcal{M}}(L'_{\mathcal{D}} \cap (I - I_{\mathrm{U}})^*)$ *and* $\hat{\mathcal{M}}(\tilde{L}'_{\mathcal{D}}) = \hat{\mathcal{M}}(\tilde{L}'_{\mathcal{D}} \cap (I - I_{\mathrm{U}})^*)$.

Proof: It suffices to prove (a).

By Theorem 3.2.1, $\mathcal{M}(L'_{\mathcal{D}} \cap (I - I_{\mathrm{U}})^*) \subseteq \mathcal{M}(L'_{\mathcal{D}})$ and $\mathcal{M}(\tilde{L}'_{\mathcal{D}} \cap (I - I_{\mathrm{U}})^*) \subseteq \mathcal{M}(\tilde{L}'_{\mathcal{D}})$. Let h be the homomorphism on I^* defined by $h(u) = u$ for each u in $I - I_{\mathrm{U}}$ and $h(u) = \epsilon$ for each u in I_{U}. Then $L'_{\mathcal{D}} = h^{-1}(L'_{\mathcal{D}} \cap (I - I_{\mathrm{U}})^*)$. (See Exercise 5.3.6.) Hence $\mathcal{M}(L'_{\mathcal{D}}) \subseteq \mathcal{M}(L'_{\mathcal{D}} \cap (I - I_{\mathrm{U}})^*)$, whence equality. Also (see Exercise 5.3.6),

$$\tilde{L}'_{\mathcal{D}} = h^{-1}(\tilde{L}'_{\mathcal{D}} \cap (I - I_{\mathrm{U}})^*) \cap (I \cup \{\epsilon\} \cup (I - I_{\mathrm{U}}) I^*(I - I_{\mathrm{U}})),$$

i. e., no word of length at least two can begin or end in a universal identity. Thus $\mathcal{M}(\tilde{L}'_{\mathcal{D}}) \subseteq \mathcal{M}(\tilde{L}'_{\mathcal{D}} \cap (I - I_{\mathrm{U}})^*)$, whence equality.

By Proposition 5.3.2 and by Theorem 3.4.1, we have:

COROLLARY: *For each reduced, finitely encoded AFA$\mathcal{D}$,*
(a) $\mathcal{F}(L'_{\mathcal{D}}) = \mathcal{F}(L'_{\mathcal{D}} \cap (I - I_{\mathrm{U}})^*)$ *and* $\mathcal{F}(\tilde{L}'_{\mathcal{D}}) = \mathcal{F}(\tilde{L}'_{\mathcal{D}} \cap (I - I_{\mathrm{U}})^*)$; *and*
(b) $\hat{\mathcal{F}}(L'_{\mathcal{D}}) = \hat{\mathcal{F}}(L'_{\mathcal{D}} \cap (I - I_{\mathrm{U}})^*)$ *and* $\hat{\mathcal{F}}(\tilde{L}'_{\mathcal{D}}) = \hat{\mathcal{F}}(\tilde{L}'_{\mathcal{D}} \cap (I - I_{\mathrm{U}})^*)$.

We now turn to presenting a ($\sim$) necessary and sufficient condition for $\mathcal{F}(\tilde{L}'_{\mathcal{D}}) = \mathcal{L}^t(\mathcal{D})(\hat{\mathcal{F}}(\tilde{L}'_{\mathcal{D}}) = \mathcal{L}(\mathcal{D}))$.

We shall need the following auxiliary AFA.

Notation: Let $(\Omega, \mathcal{D})$, $\Omega = (K, \Sigma, \Gamma, I, f, g)$, be a finitely encoded AFA and 0 a new symbol. For each word α in $g(\Gamma^+)$ if $g(\Gamma^+) \neq \emptyset$, and for each symbol

α in Γ if[1] $g(\Gamma^+) = \emptyset$, let $(\Omega_\alpha, \mathcal{D}_\alpha)$ be the AFA $\Omega_\alpha = (K, \Sigma, \Gamma_\alpha, I_\alpha, f_\alpha, g_\alpha)$, where $\Gamma_\alpha = \Gamma$, $I_\alpha = I \cup \{0\}$, and f_α and g_α are defined as follows: For all x in Γ^* and all u in I, let $f_\alpha(x, u) = f(x, u)$ and, if $g(x) \neq \emptyset$, $f_\alpha(x, 0) = x$. Let $g_\alpha(\epsilon) = \{\epsilon\}$, and for all x in Γ^+ satisfying $g(x) \neq \emptyset$ let $g_\alpha(x) = \{\alpha\}$.

Thus f_α is essentially the same as f. The only role g has is to distinguish between the two situations where the auxiliary storage is empty and where it is not. The inclusion of the universal identity 0 in I_α is to ensure the existence of an identity element satisfying condition 4 in the definition of an AFA-schema.

In each acceptor in $\mathcal{D}_\alpha$ the transitions depend only on (the states, the inputs, and) whether or not the storage is empty. The transitions do not depend on any other information obtained from the storage. One AFA which already has this property is $\mathcal{D}_C$.

Note that $\mathcal{D}_\alpha$ is reduced if $\mathcal{D}$ is reduced.

In general, α is to be assumed specified when Ω_α or $\mathcal{D}_\alpha$ is written.

The ($\sim$) necessary and sufficient condition for $\mathcal{F}(\tilde{L}'_{\mathcal{D}})$ and $\mathcal{L}^t(\mathcal{D})$ ($\hat{\mathcal{F}}(\tilde{L}'_{\mathcal{D}})$ and $\mathcal{L}(\mathcal{D})$) to coincide is that $L_{\mathcal{D}}$ be in $\mathcal{L}^t(\mathcal{D}_\alpha)(\mathcal{L}(\mathcal{D}_\alpha))$. First though, a preliminary result is needed.

($\sim$) LEMMA 5.3.1: *For each reduced, finitely encoded AFA $\mathcal{D}$, $\mathcal{F}(\tilde{L}'_{\mathcal{D}}) = \mathcal{L}^t(\mathcal{D}_\alpha)$.*

Proof: Let $D = (\{p_0, p_1\}, I, \delta, p_0, \{p_1\})$ be the quasi-realtime acceptor in $\mathcal{D}_\alpha$ in which δ is defined by $\delta(p_0, \epsilon, \epsilon) = \{(p_1, 1_\epsilon)\}$, $\delta(p_0, u, \epsilon) = \{(p_1, u)\}$ and $\delta(p_1, u, \alpha) = \{(p_1, u)\}$ for each u in I. From the fact that $\mathcal{D}$ is reduced, it follows (see Exercise 5.3.8) that $L(D) = \tilde{L}'_{\mathcal{D}}$. Thus $\mathcal{F}(\tilde{L}'_{\mathcal{D}}) \subseteq \mathcal{L}^t(\mathcal{D}_\alpha)$.

To see the reverse inclusion let c and d be new symbols. Let h be the homomorphism on $(I \cup (\{c\} \times I) \cup (I \times \{d\}) \cup (\{c\} \times I \times \{d\}))^*$ defined by $h((c, u)) = cu$, $h((u, d)) = ud$, $h(u) = u$, and $h((c, u, d)) = cud$ for each u in I. Let τ be the ϵ-free substitution on $(I \cup (\{c\} \times I) \cup (I \times \{d\}) \cup (\{c\} \times I \times \{d\}))^*$ defined by $\tau((c, u)) = (\epsilon, 0)^*(\epsilon, u)$, $\tau(u) = (\alpha, 0)^*(\alpha, u)$, $\tau((u, d)) = (\alpha, 0)^*(\alpha, u)(\epsilon, 0)^*$, and $\tau((c, u, d)) = (\epsilon, 0)^*(\epsilon, u)(\epsilon, 0)^*$ for each u in I. Then (see Exercise 5.3.9)

$$L_{\mathcal{D}_\alpha} = \tau\big(h^{-1}((c\tilde{L}'_{\mathcal{D}}d)^*)\big) \cup (\epsilon, 0)^*.$$

Since $\tau(a)$ is an ϵ-free regular set for each a in $I \cup (\{c\} \times I) \cup (I \times \{d\}) \cup (\{c\} \times I \times \{d\})$, $\tau\big(h^{-1}((c\tilde{L}'_{\mathcal{D}}d)^*)\big)$ is in $\mathcal{F}(\tilde{L}'_{\mathcal{D}})$ by Theorem 3.3.2. Since $\mathcal{F}(\tilde{L}'_{\mathcal{D}})$ contains $\{\epsilon\}$, it contains each regular set and thus $(\epsilon, 0)^*$. Hence $L_{\mathcal{D}_\alpha}$ is in $\mathcal{F}(\tilde{L}'_{\mathcal{D}})$, so that $\mathcal{L}^t(\mathcal{D}_\alpha) = \mathcal{F}(L_{\mathcal{D}_\alpha}) \subseteq \mathcal{F}(\tilde{L}'_{\mathcal{D}})$.

[1] α exists in this case since $\Gamma \neq \emptyset$ by condition 1 in the definition of an AFA schema.

REMARK: Intuitively, $L_{\mathcal{D}_\alpha}$ is in $\mathcal{F}(\tilde{L}'_{\mathcal{D}})$ because all the occurrences of (ϵ, u) in words of $L_{\mathcal{D}_\alpha}$ can be obtained from the occurrences of c in $(c\tilde{L}'_{\mathcal{D}}d)^*$. On the other hand, there exist $\mathcal{D}_\alpha$ such that $L_{\mathcal{D}_\alpha}$ is not in $\mathcal{F}(L'_{\mathcal{D}})$ (see Exercise 5.3.12), the reason being that for such a $\mathcal{D}_\alpha$, no AFL generator of $\mathcal{F}(L'_{\mathcal{D}})$ can yield all occurrences of (ϵ, u) in words of $L_{\mathcal{D}_\alpha}$.

We are now ready for the $(\sim)$ necessary and sufficient condition that $\mathcal{F}(\tilde{L}'_{\mathcal{D}}) = \mathcal{L}^t(\mathcal{D})(\hat{\mathcal{F}}(\tilde{L}'_{\mathcal{D}}) = \mathcal{L}(\mathcal{D}))$.

$(\sim)$ THEOREM 5.3.1: *For each reduced, finitely encoded AFA* $\mathcal{D}$, $\mathcal{F}(\tilde{L}'_{\mathcal{D}}) = \mathcal{L}^t(\mathcal{D})$ $(\hat{\mathcal{F}}(\tilde{L}'_{\mathcal{D}}) = \mathcal{L}(\mathcal{D}))$ *if and only if* $L_{\mathcal{D}}$ *is in* $\mathcal{L}^t(\mathcal{D}_\alpha) = \mathcal{F}(L_{\mathcal{D}_\alpha})$ $(\mathcal{L}(\mathcal{D}_\alpha) = \hat{\mathcal{F}}(L_{\mathcal{D}_\alpha}))$.

Proof: We shall establish the result for the $\mathcal{F}(\tilde{L}'_{\mathcal{D}}) = \mathcal{L}^t(\mathcal{D})$ case, the argument for $\hat{\mathcal{F}}(\tilde{L}'_{\mathcal{D}}) = \mathcal{L}(\mathcal{D})$ being a trivial modification.

Suppose that $\mathcal{F}(\tilde{L}'_{\mathcal{D}}) = \mathcal{L}^t(\mathcal{D})$. Then $\mathcal{F}(L_{\mathcal{D}}) = \mathcal{L}^t(\mathcal{D}) = \mathcal{F}(\tilde{L}'_{\mathcal{D}}) = \mathcal{L}^t(\mathcal{D}_\alpha)$, the last equality by Lemma 5.3.1. Hence $L_{\mathcal{D}}$ is in $\mathcal{L}^t(\mathcal{D}_\alpha)$.

Now suppose that $L_{\mathcal{D}}$ is in $\mathcal{L}^t(\mathcal{D}_\alpha)$, that is, $\mathcal{F}(L_{\mathcal{D}}) \subseteq \mathcal{L}^t(\mathcal{D}_\alpha)$. Then

$$\begin{aligned} \mathcal{F}(\tilde{L}'_{\mathcal{D}}) &\subseteq \mathcal{F}(L_{\mathcal{D}}), && \text{by Proposition 5.3.1,} \\ &\subseteq \mathcal{L}^t(\mathcal{D}_\alpha), \\ &= \mathcal{F}(\tilde{L}'_{\mathcal{D}}), && \text{by Lemma 5.3.1.} \end{aligned}$$

Thus $\mathcal{F}(\tilde{L}'_{\mathcal{D}}) = \mathcal{L}^t(\mathcal{D})$.

$(\sim)$ COROLLARY: *Let* $\mathcal{D}$ *be a reduced, finitely encoded AFA and* $\#(g(\{x/x$ *accessible*$\})) \leqq 2$. *Then* $\mathcal{F}(\tilde{L}'_{\mathcal{D}}) = \mathcal{L}^t(\mathcal{D})$ *and* $\hat{\mathcal{F}}(\tilde{L}'_{\mathcal{D}}) = \mathcal{L}(\mathcal{D})$.

Proof: Let $P = g(\{x/x$ accessible$\})$. Then $\#(P) \leqq 2$. Since $g(\epsilon) = \{\epsilon\}$, $\#(P) \geqq 1$. If $\#(P) = 1$, then $g(x) = \emptyset$ for all accessible $x \neq \epsilon$. Then

$$\begin{aligned} L_{\mathcal{D}} &= \{\epsilon\} \cup \{(\epsilon, u_1)\ldots(\epsilon, u_n)/gf(\epsilon, u_1\ldots u_i) = \{\epsilon\} \text{ for each } i\} \\ &= L_{\mathcal{D}_\alpha} \cap (\{\epsilon\}\times I)^*. \end{aligned}$$

Suppose $\#(P) = 2$. Then there exists α in Γ^+ such that $g(x) = \{\alpha\}$ for all accessible $x \neq \epsilon$ satisfying $g(x) \neq \emptyset$. It is readily seen that $L_{\mathcal{D}} = L_{\mathcal{D}_\alpha} \cap (\{\epsilon, \alpha\}\times I)^*$. (See Exercise 5.3.11.) In each case, therefore, $L_{\mathcal{D}}$ is in $\mathcal{F}(L_{\mathcal{D}_\alpha})$. By Theorem 5.3.1, $\mathcal{F}(\tilde{L}'_{\mathcal{D}}) = \mathcal{L}^t(\mathcal{D})$, whence $\hat{\mathcal{F}}(\tilde{L}'_{\mathcal{D}}) = \mathcal{L}(\mathcal{D})$.

We now turn to a $(\sim)$ sufficiency condition for $\mathcal{F}(\tilde{L}'_{\mathcal{D}}) = \mathcal{F}(L'_{\mathcal{D}}) = \mathcal{L}^t(\mathcal{D})$ for a reduced, finitely encoded AFA $\mathcal{D}$. The condition is that for each γ in $g(\Gamma^+)$, there exist instructions $u_1, \ldots, u_{n_\gamma}$ so that $f(x, u_1\ldots u_{n_\gamma}) = \emptyset$

for all accessible x, γ not in $g(x)$, and $f(x, u_1 \ldots u_{n_\gamma}) = x$ for all accessible x, γ in $g(x)$.

LEMMA 5.3.2: *Let $\mathcal{D}$ be a reduced, finitely encoded AFA with the following property: There exists a finite subset S of I^+ such that*

(a) *$f(\epsilon, \sigma) = \emptyset$ for each σ in S;*

(b) *for each accessible x in Γ^+, $f(x, \sigma) = x$ for some σ in S; and*

(c) *for each accessible x in Γ^+ and each σ in S, if $f(x, \sigma) \neq \emptyset$ then $f(x, \sigma) = x$.*

Then $\tilde{L}'_{\mathcal{D}}$ is in $\mathcal{M}(L'_{\mathcal{D}})$ and $\mathcal{F}(L'_{\mathcal{D}}) = \mathcal{F}(\tilde{L}'_{\mathcal{D}})$.

Proof: Suppose that $S = \emptyset$. By (b), there is no accessible x in Γ^+. Thus $f(\epsilon, u)$ is either empty or is ϵ for each u in I. Then $\tilde{L}'_{\mathcal{D}} = L'_{\mathcal{D}} \cap (\{\epsilon\} \cup I)$, so that $\tilde{L}'_{\mathcal{D}}$ is in $\mathcal{M}(L'_{\mathcal{D}})$.

Suppose that $S \neq \emptyset$. Let M be the ϵ-free a-transducer $(\{p_0, p_1\}, I, I, H, p_0, \{p_0, p_1\})$, where

$$H = \{(p_0, u\sigma, u, p_0)/u \text{ in } I, \sigma \text{ in } S\} \cup \{(p_0, u, u, p_1)/u \text{ in } I\}.$$

Hence for u in I^*,

(1) if $(p_0, u, \epsilon) \overset{*}{\vdash} (p_1, \epsilon, v)$, then $u = u_1u_2 \ldots u_{2n-1}$ and $v = u_1u_3 \ldots u_{2n-1}$ for some $n \geqq 1$, with $u_1, u_3, \ldots, u_{2n-1}$ in I and $u_2, u_4, \ldots, u_{2n-2}$ in S.

By (1), (a), and (c),

(2) $M(L'_{\mathcal{D}}) \subseteq \tilde{L}'_{\mathcal{D}}$.

Let $Z(\epsilon) = \epsilon$. For each $u = u_1 \ldots u_n$ in $\tilde{L}'_{\mathcal{D}}$, $n \geqq 1$ and each u_i in I, let

$$Z(u) = \{u_1\sigma_1u_2\sigma_2 \ldots \sigma_{n-1}u_n/\text{each } \sigma_i \text{ in } S, f(\epsilon, u_1\sigma_1u_2 \ldots \sigma_{n-1}u_n) \neq \emptyset\}.$$

By (c),

(3) $Z(u) \subseteq L'_{\mathcal{D}}$.

By (b) and the definition of M,

(4) $\{u\} \subseteq M(Z(u))$.

By (4), (3), and (2),

(5) $\tilde{L}'_{\mathcal{D}} \subseteq M\left(\bigcup_{u \text{ in } \tilde{L}'_{\mathcal{D}}} Z(u)\right) \subseteq M(L'_{\mathcal{D}}) \subseteq \tilde{L}'_{\mathcal{D}}$,

so that $\tilde{L}'_{\mathcal{D}} = M(L'_{\mathcal{D}})$. Then $\mathcal{F}(\tilde{L}'_{\mathcal{D}}) \subseteq \mathcal{F}(\mathcal{M}(L'_{\mathcal{D}})) = \mathcal{F}(L'_{\mathcal{D}})$. Since $\mathcal{F}(L'_{\mathcal{D}}) \subseteq \mathcal{F}(\tilde{L}'_{\mathcal{D}})$, equality occurs.

$(\sim)$[1] THEOREM 5.3.2: *Let $\mathcal{D}$ be a reduced, finitely encoded AFA with the following property: For each γ in $g(\Gamma^+)$ there exist $n_\gamma \geqq 1$ and instructions $u_1, \ldots, u_{n_\gamma}$ such that for all accessible x, (i) if γ is not in $g(x)$ then $f(x, u_1 \ldots u_{n_\gamma})$*

[1] See Exercise 5.3.22 for the statement of the $\sim$ case.

$= \emptyset$, *and* (ii) *if* γ *is in* $g(x)$ *then* $f(x, u_1 \ldots u_{n_\gamma}) = x$. *Then* $\mathscr{F}(\tilde{L}'_{\mathcal{D}}) = \mathscr{F}(L'_{\mathcal{D}}) = \mathscr{L}^t(\mathcal{D})$ *and* $\hat{\mathscr{F}}(\tilde{L}'_{\mathcal{D}}) = \hat{\mathscr{F}}(L'_{\mathcal{D}}) = \mathscr{L}(\mathcal{D})$.

Proof: It suffices to show only $\mathscr{F}(\tilde{L}'_{\mathcal{D}}) = \mathscr{F}(L'_{\mathcal{D}}) = \mathscr{L}^t(\mathcal{D})$. We first establish that $\mathscr{F}(\tilde{L}'_{\mathcal{D}}) = \mathscr{L}^t(\mathcal{D})$. By Theorem 5.3.1 it is enough to verify that $L_{\mathcal{D}}$ is in $\mathscr{L}^t(\mathcal{D}_\alpha)$. This will be done by exhibiting a quasi-realtime acceptor D in $\mathcal{D}_\alpha$ such that $L_{\mathcal{D}} = L(D)$.

Intuitively, for each γ in $g(\Gamma^+)$, $u_1, \ldots, u_{n_\gamma}$ is a test sequence which determines if γ is a legitimate value for $g(x)$. This sequence causes a block if γ is not in $g(x)$ and returns the storage x to x if γ is in $g(x)$. The acceptor D will read an input symbol (γ, u) from the start state and move to a special state $(\gamma, u, 1)$, producing the instruction u_1. Under a sequence of ϵ-moves, D will produce the instructions $u_2, \ldots, u_{n_\gamma}$, finally moving back to the start state. Thus D will be able to read (γ, u) and return to the start state if γ is in $g(x)$.

Formally, let

$$K_1 = \{q_0\} \cup \{(\gamma, u, i)/(\gamma, u) \text{ in } g(\Gamma^*)\times I,\ i \text{ in } \{1, \ldots, n_\gamma\}\}$$

and $D = (K_1, g(\Gamma^*)\times I, \delta, q_0, \{q_0\})$, where δ is defined as follows (for all γ in $g(\Gamma^+)$, $u_1, \ldots, u_{n_\gamma}$ satisfying the hypotheses, and u in I):

(1) $\delta(q_0, (\epsilon, u), \epsilon) = \{(q_0, u)\}$.

[By (1), $(q_0, (\epsilon, u), \epsilon) \vdash (q_0, \epsilon, f(\epsilon, u))$ if $f(\epsilon, u) \neq \emptyset$.]

(2) $\delta(q_0, (\gamma, u), \alpha) = \{((\gamma, u, 1), u_1)\}$.

[By (2), for $\gamma \neq \epsilon$ and $x \neq \epsilon$, $(q_0, (\gamma, u), x) \vdash ((\gamma, u, 1), \epsilon, f(x, u_1))$ if $f(x, u_1) \neq \emptyset$.]

(3) $\delta((\gamma, u, i), \epsilon, \alpha) = \delta((\gamma, u, i), \epsilon, \epsilon) = \{((\gamma, u, i+1), u_{i+1})\}$ for each i, $1 \leqq i < n_\gamma$.

[By (3) and the fact that $\mathcal{D}$ is reduced, $((\gamma, u, 1), \epsilon, f(x, u_1)) \overset{*}{\vdash} ((\gamma, u, n_\gamma), \epsilon, f(x, u_1 \ldots u_{n_\gamma}))$ if $f(x, u_1 \ldots u_{n_\gamma}) \neq \emptyset$.]

(4) $\delta((\gamma, u, n_\gamma), \epsilon, \alpha) = \delta((\gamma, u, n_\gamma), \epsilon, \epsilon) = \{(q_0, u)\}$.

[By (4), $((\gamma, u, n_\gamma), \epsilon, x) \vdash (q_0, \epsilon, f(x, u))$.]

Intuitively, (1) checks to see if the storage is ϵ. (2) and (3) apply $u_1, \ldots, u_{n_\gamma}$ to see if γ is in $g(x)$. Note that D blocks if γ is not in $g(x)$. If γ is in $g(x)$, then (2) and (3), in sequence, apply $u_1, \ldots, u_{n_\gamma}$ to transform x to x. Finally, (4) changes the storage x to $f(x, u)$.

Clearly D is a quasi-realtime acceptor in $\mathcal{D}_\alpha$. Furthermore, $L(D) = L_{\mathcal{D}}$. Hence $\mathscr{F}(\tilde{L}'_{\mathcal{D}}) = \mathscr{L}^t(\mathcal{D})$.

To complete the proof, we now show that $\mathscr{F}(\tilde{L}'_{\mathcal{D}}) = \mathscr{F}(L'_{\mathcal{D}})$. There is no loss in generality in assuming that $g(x) \neq \emptyset$ for each accessible x in Γ^*.

[For consider the AFA $(\Omega', \mathcal{D}')$, where $\Omega' = (K, \Sigma, \Gamma, I, f', g')$ is defined as follows: Let $g'(\epsilon) = \{\epsilon\}$. For each u in I let $f'(\epsilon, u) = f(\epsilon, u)$ if there exist $n \geqq 1$, $v_1, \ldots, v_n$ in I such that $v_1 = u$ and $f(\epsilon, v_1 \ldots v_n) = \epsilon$, and let $f'(\epsilon, u) = \emptyset$ otherwise. For each x in Γ^+ and u in I, let $g'(x) = g(x)$ and $f'(x, u) = f(x, u)$ if there exist $n \geqq 2$, $v_1, \ldots, v_n$ in I, and i_0, $1 \leqq i_0 < n$, such that $f(\epsilon, v_1 \ldots v_{i_0}) = x$, $v_{i_0+1} = u$, and $f(\epsilon, v_1 \ldots v_n) = \epsilon$. Let $f'(x, u) = \emptyset$ otherwise and let $g'(x) = \emptyset$ if there is no u in I such that $f'(x, u) \neq \emptyset$. Since $\mathcal{D}$ is reduced, so is $\mathcal{D}'$. Clearly $\tilde{L}'_{\mathcal{D}} = \tilde{L}'_{\mathcal{D}'}$, $L'_{\mathcal{D}} = L'_{\mathcal{D}'}$, $\mathcal{L}^t(\mathcal{D}) = \mathcal{L}^t(\mathcal{D}')$, $\mathcal{L}(\mathcal{D}) = \mathcal{L}(\mathcal{D}')$, $g'(x) \neq \emptyset$ for each accessible x, and f' and g' satisfy the hypotheses of the theorem.] For each γ in $g(\Gamma^+)$ let $u_1, \ldots, u_{n_\gamma}$ be as in the hypothesis and let $\sigma_\gamma = u_1 \ldots u_{n_\gamma}$. Let S be the set of words σ_γ. Since $\mathcal{D}$ is a finitely encoded AFA, $g(\Gamma^*)$ is finite. Thus S is a finite subset of I^+. Since ϵ is not in $g(\Gamma^+)$, $f(\epsilon, \sigma_\gamma) = \emptyset$ for each σ_γ in S. Suppose that $x \neq \epsilon$ is accessible. By hypothesis, if γ is not in $g(x)$ then $f(x, \sigma_\gamma) = \emptyset$ and if γ is in $g(x)$ then $f(x, \sigma_\gamma) = x$. Since x is accessible, $g(x) \neq \emptyset$. Hence there exist γ in $g(x)$. Then $f(x, \sigma_\gamma) = x$. Therefore the hypotheses of Lemma 5.3.2 are satisfied, so that $\mathcal{F}(L'_{\mathcal{D}}) = \mathcal{F}(\tilde{L}'_{\mathcal{D}})$.

The application of Theorem 5.3.2 occurs most frequently for the case when $n_\gamma = 2$ for each γ. In this situation, Theorem 5.3.2 reduces to the following:

($\sim$) COROLLARY: *Let $\mathcal{D}$ be a reduced, finitely encoded AFA with the following property: For each γ in $g(\Gamma^+)$ there exist instructions u_γ and v_γ such that for all accessible x,* (i) *if γ is not in $g(x)$ then $f(x, u_\gamma v_\gamma) = \emptyset$, and* (ii) *if γ is in $g(x)$ then $f(x, u_\gamma v_\gamma) = x$. Then $\mathcal{F}(\tilde{L}'_{\mathcal{D}}) = \mathcal{F}(L'_{\mathcal{D}}) = \mathcal{L}^t(\mathcal{D})$ and $\hat{\mathcal{F}}(\tilde{L}'_{\mathcal{D}}) = \hat{\mathcal{F}}(L'_{\mathcal{D}}) = \mathcal{L}(\mathcal{D})$.*

EXAMPLE 5.3.1: Let $\Omega = (K, \Sigma, \Gamma, I, f, g)$, where $\Gamma = \{a_1, a_2\}$, $I = \Gamma \cup \{0, a_1^E, a_2^E\}$, and f and g are defined as follows (for all x in Γ^* and i in $\{1, 2\}$): $f(x, 0) = x$, $f(x, a_i) = xa_i$, $f(xa_i, a_i^E) = x$, $g(\epsilon) = \{\epsilon\}$, and $g(xa_i) = \{a_i\}$. Then $(\Omega, \mathcal{D})$ is another AFA formalization for the family of pda. Clearly $\mathcal{D}$ is reduced and finitely encoded. For $\gamma = a_i$, let $u_\gamma = a_i^E$ and $v_\gamma = a_i$. Then a_i is in $g(y)$ if and only if $y = xa_i$ for some x. Hence $f(y, a_i^E a_i) = y$ if a_i is in $g(y)$ and $f(y, a_i^E a_i) = \emptyset$ if a_i is not in $g(y)$. By the corollary to Theorem 5.3.2, $\mathcal{F}(L'_{\mathcal{D}}) = \mathcal{L}^t(\mathcal{D})$ and $\hat{\mathcal{F}}(L'_{\mathcal{D}}) = \mathcal{L}(\mathcal{D})$. By Proposition 5.3.2, $\mathcal{F}(L'_{\mathcal{D}} \cap (I - I_U)^*) = \mathcal{F}(L'_{\mathcal{D}})$ and $\hat{\mathcal{F}}(L'_{\mathcal{D}} \cap (I - I_U)^*) = \hat{\mathcal{F}}(L'_{\mathcal{D}})$. Thus $L'_{\mathcal{D}} \cap (I - I_U)^*$, the Dyck set W_2 on two letters, is a generator for the quasi-realtime pda languages ($= \mathcal{L}_{CF}$) and a full generator for the pda languages ($= \mathcal{L}_{CF}$).

EXAMPLE 5.3.2: Let $\Omega = (K, \Sigma, \Gamma, I, f, g)$, where $\Gamma = \{a_1, a_2, \uparrow\}$, $I = \{a_1, a_2, a_1^E, a_2^E, a_1^{®}, a_2^{®}, a_1^L, a_2^L, 0\}$, and f and g are defined as follows (for all x, y in $\{a_1, a_2\}^*$, a, b in $\{a_1, a_2\}$, and i in $\{1, 2\}$): $g(\epsilon) = \{\epsilon\}$, $g(xa\uparrow) = \{a\uparrow\}$, $g(\uparrow by) = \{\uparrow b\}$, $g(xa\uparrow by) = \{a\uparrow, \uparrow b\}$, $f(\epsilon, 0) = \epsilon$, $f(x\uparrow y, 0) = x\uparrow y$ for $xy \neq \epsilon$, $f(\epsilon, a) = a\uparrow$, $f(xa\uparrow, b) = xab\uparrow$, $f(xaa_i\uparrow, a_i^E) = xa\uparrow$, $f(a_i\uparrow, a_i^E) = \epsilon$, $f(xa_i\uparrow y, a_i^L) = x\uparrow a_i y$, and $f(x\uparrow a_i y, a_i^{®}) = xa_i\uparrow y$. Then $(\Omega, \mathcal{D})$ is a reduced, finitely encoded AFA formulation for the family of stack acceptors, $\mathcal{L}^t(\mathcal{D}) = \mathcal{L}^t(\mathcal{D}_S)$, and $\mathcal{L}(\mathcal{D}) = \mathcal{L}(\mathcal{D}_S)$. (See Exercise 5.3.21.) (The instruction a_i means add a_i to the stack if at the right end, a_i^E means erase a_i from the stack if at the right end reading a_i, a_i^L means move left over a_i, and $a_i^{®}$ means move right over a_i.) If $\gamma = a_i\uparrow$, let $u_\gamma = a_i^L$ and $v_\gamma = a_i^{®}$. If $\gamma = \uparrow a_i$, let $u_\gamma = a_i^{®}$ and $v_\gamma = a_i^L$. Then the above corollary is satisfied, so that $\tilde{L}'_{\mathcal{D}}$ and $L'_{\mathcal{D}}$ are both (full) generators for $\mathcal{L}^t(\mathcal{D}_S)$ $(\mathcal{L}(\mathcal{D}_S))$. Hence $L'_{\mathcal{D}} \cap (I-\{0\})^*$ is a (full) generator for $\mathcal{L}^t(\mathcal{D}_S)(\mathcal{L}(\mathcal{D}_S))$. This language is the set of all words w in $(I-\{0\})^*$ such that $\uparrow\upharpoonright w \overset{*}{\Longrightarrow} \uparrow\upharpoonright$, $\upharpoonright$ a new symbol, by the following set of general Post productions (for $\underline{P}_1$ and $\underline{P}_2$ over $\{a_1, a_2, a_1^E, a_2^E\}^*$ and $\underline{P}_3$ over $(I-\{0\})^*$):

$$\{\underline{P}_1 a\uparrow \underline{P}_2 \upharpoonright a^L \underline{P}_3 \to \underline{P}_1\uparrow a\underline{P}_2\upharpoonright \underline{P}_3,\ \underline{P}_1\uparrow a\underline{P}_2\upharpoonright a^{®}\underline{P}_3 \to \underline{P}_1 a\uparrow \underline{P}_2\upharpoonright \underline{P}_3,$$
$$\underline{P}_1 a\uparrow\upharpoonright a^E \underline{P}_3 \to \underline{P}_1\uparrow\upharpoonright \underline{P}_3,\ \underline{P}_1\uparrow\upharpoonright a\underline{P}_3 \to \underline{P}_1 a\uparrow\upharpoonright \underline{P}_3 / a \text{ in } \{a_1, a_2\}\}.$$

EXAMPLE 5.3.3: Let $N' = \{1, 2, \ldots\}$ and m and n be in N'. Let $H_m = (a_1^* a_2^*)^r$ for $m = 2r$ and $H_m = (a_1^* a_2^*)^r a_1^*$ for $m = 2r+1$. Let $(\Omega_{m,n}, \mathcal{D}_{m,n})$, $\Omega_{m,n} = (K, \Sigma, \Gamma_{m,n}, I, f_{m,n}, g_{m,n})$, be the AFA where $\Gamma_{m,n} = \{a_1, a_2, Z_0\} \cup \{(+, j), (-, j)/1 \leq j \leq n\}$, $I = \{a_1, a_2, a_1^E, a_2^E, 0, Z_0\}$, and $f_{m,n}$ and $g_{m,n}$ are defined as follows $\Big($for all i in $\{1, 2\}$, j in $\{1, \ldots, n\}$, k in $\{1, \ldots, n-1\}$, xa_i in H_m, and y in $H_m \cup \bigcup_{j=1}^{n} (-, j)H_m \cup \bigcup_{k=1}^{n-1} (+, k)(H_m - \{\epsilon\})\Big)$: $f_{m,n}(x, a_i) = xa_i$, $f_{m,n}(xa_i, a_i^E) = (-, 1)x$, $f_{m,n}((-, j)xa_i, a_i^E) = (-, j)x$, $f_{m,n}((-, j), Z_0) = \epsilon$, $f_{m,n}((-, k)x, a_i) = (+, k)xa_i$, $f_{m,n}((+, k)x, a_i) = (+, k)xa_i$, $x \neq \epsilon$, $f_{m,n}((+, k)xa_i, a_i^E) = (-, k+1)x$, $f_{m,n}(y, 0) = y$, $g_{m,n}(\epsilon) = \{\epsilon\}$, $g_{m,n}(xa_i) = \{a_i\}$, $g_{m,n}((-, j)xa_i) = \{a_i\}$, $g_{m,n}((-, j)) = \{Z_0\}$, and $g_{m,n}((+, k)xa_i) = \{a_i\}$. Then $(\Omega_{m,n}, \mathcal{D}_{m,n})$ is a reduced, finitely encoded AFA formalization for the family of *(m, n)-bounded pda*. It is easy to see that each acceptor $D = (K_1, \Sigma_1, \delta, q_0, F)$ in $\mathcal{D}_{m,n}$ is a pda and each computation $(p_0, w_0, \gamma_0) \vdash \ldots \vdash (p_s, w_s, \gamma_s)$, with $\gamma_0 = \epsilon$, has the properties that (i) it never changes from increasing to decreasing more than n times before reinitializing the auxiliary storage to ϵ; and (ii) each γ_i is of the form x, $(-, j)x$, or $(+, j)x$ for some x in H_m. It is readily verified that there is no sequence $u_1, \ldots, u_s$

of instructions (other than 0, ..., 0) such that $f_{m,n}(x, u_1 \ldots u_s) = x$ for all x satisfying a_1 in $g_{m,n}(x)$. [See Exercise 5.3.25.] Hence, Theorem 5.3.2 cannot be applied.

EXERCISE 5.3.1: Prove that $L'_{\mathcal{D}} = \tilde{L}'^{+}_{\mathcal{D}}$.

EXERCISE 5.3.2: Let $(\Omega, \mathcal{D})$ be an AFA and $\Omega' = (K, \Sigma, \Gamma, I, f', g')$, where f' and g' are defined as follows: For each x in Γ^*, if $g(x) \neq \emptyset$ and $f(x, u) \neq \emptyset$ for some u in I then let $g'(x) = g(x)$ and $f'(x, v) = f(x,v)$ for all v in I. Otherwise, let $g'(x) = f'(x, v) = \emptyset$ for all v in I. Prove each of the following [GGr3]:

(a) $(\Omega', \mathcal{D}')$ is a reduced AFA, nontrivial if $(\Omega, \mathcal{D})$ is nontrivial.
(b) $\mathcal{D}'$ is finitely encoded if $\mathcal{D}$ is finitely encoded.
(c) $\mathcal{L}^t(\mathcal{D}') = \mathcal{L}^t(\mathcal{D})$ and $\mathcal{L}(\mathcal{D}') = \mathcal{L}(\mathcal{D})$.
(d) $\tilde{\mathcal{L}}^t(\mathcal{D}') = \tilde{\mathcal{L}}^t(\mathcal{D})$ and $\tilde{\mathcal{L}}(\mathcal{D}') = \tilde{\mathcal{L}}(\mathcal{D})$.

EXERCISE 5.3.3: Must $\mathcal{F}(\tilde{L}'_{\mathcal{D}}) \subseteq \mathcal{F}(L_{\mathcal{D}})$ hold if $\mathcal{D}$ is not reduced? [Justify your answer.]

EXERCISE 5.3.4: Let $\Omega = (K, \Sigma, \Gamma, I, f, g)$, where $\Gamma = \{Z\}$, $I = \{0, Z, E\}$, and f and g are defined as follows (for all x in Z^*): $f(x, 0) = x$, $f(x, Z) = xZ$, $f(x, E) = \epsilon$, $g(\epsilon) = \{\epsilon\}$, $g(Z^n) = Z$ if n is not a square, and $g(Z^n) = Z^2$ if $n > 0$ is a square. Prove the following:

(a) $\mathcal{D}$ is a reduced, finitely encoded AFA.
(b) $\mathcal{F}(\tilde{L}'_{\mathcal{D}}) = \hat{\mathcal{F}}(\tilde{L}'_{\mathcal{D}}) = \mathcal{R}$.
(c) $\{a^{n^2}/n \geqq 1\}$ is in $\mathcal{L}^t(\mathcal{D})$. Hence infer that $\mathcal{F}(L'_{\mathcal{D}}) \subseteq \mathcal{F}(\tilde{L}'_{\mathcal{D}}) \neq \mathcal{L}^t(\mathcal{D})$ and $\hat{\mathcal{F}}(L'_{\mathcal{D}}) \subseteq \hat{\mathcal{F}}(\tilde{L}'_{\mathcal{D}}) \neq \mathcal{L}(\mathcal{D})$.

EXERCISE 5.3.5: Let $\Omega = (K, \Sigma, \Gamma, I, f, g)$, where $\Gamma = \{a, b\}$, $I = \{a, b, E, 0\}$, and f and g are defined for all x in Γ^* by $f(x,0) = x$, $f(x, a) = xa$, $f(x, b) = xb$, $f(xa, E) = f(xb, E) = x$, $g(\epsilon) = \{\epsilon\}$, $g(xa) = \{a\}$, and $g(xb) = \{b\}$. Show the following [GGr3]:

(a) $(\Omega, \mathcal{D})$ is a reduced, finitely encoded AFA formalization for the family of pda.
(b) $\tilde{L}'_{\mathcal{D}}$ is the set of all words w in I^* such that $\#_E(w) = \#_a(w) + \#_b(w)$ and $\#_E(x) < \#_a(x) + \#_b(x)$ for each proper initial subword x of w.
(c) $\tilde{L}'_{\mathcal{D}}$ is a counter language.
(d) $\mathcal{F}(\tilde{L}'_{\mathcal{D}}) \neq \mathcal{L}^t(\mathcal{D})$.

EXERCISE 5.3.6: Let h be as in Proposition 5.3.2. Prove each of the following:

(a) $L'_{\mathcal{D}} = h^{-1}(L'_{\mathcal{D}} \cap (I-I_U)^*)$ and $\tilde{L}'_{\mathcal{D}} = h^{-1}(\tilde{L}'_{\mathcal{D}} \cap (I-I_U)^*) \cap (I \cup \{\epsilon\} \cup (I-I_U)I^*(I-I_U))$.

(b) $h(L'_{\mathcal{D}}) = L'_{\mathcal{D}} \cap (I-I_U)^*$ and $h(\tilde{L}'_{\mathcal{D}}) = \tilde{L}'_{\mathcal{D}} \cap (I-I_U)^*$.

EXERCISE 5.3.7: Let $\mathcal{D}$ be a reduced, finitely encoded AFA with the following property: There exists a finite subset J of I^+ such that for each accessible x in Γ^+ and each u in I^+, $f(x, u) = \epsilon$ if and only if $f(x, u) \neq \emptyset$ and u is of the form u_1u_2 for some u_2 in J. Prove that $\mathcal{F}(\tilde{L}'_{\mathcal{D}}) = \mathcal{F}(L'_{\mathcal{D}})$ [GGr3].

EXERCISE 5.3.8: Verify that $L(D) = \tilde{L}'_{\mathcal{D}}$ in Lemma 5.3.1.

EXERCISE 5.3.9: Prove that $L_{\mathcal{D}_\alpha} = \tau\big(h^{-1}((c\tilde{L}'_{\mathcal{D}}d)^*)\big) \cup (\epsilon, 0)^*$ in Lemma 5.3.1.

EXERCISE 5.3.10: Prove that $\mathcal{S}(\tilde{L}'_{\mathcal{D}}) = \tilde{\mathcal{L}}^t(\mathcal{D}_\alpha)$ for each nontrivial, reduced, finitely encoded AFA $\mathcal{D}$.

EXERCISE 5.3.11: Verify that $L_{\mathcal{D}} = L_{\mathcal{D}_\alpha} \cap (\{\epsilon, \alpha\} \times I)^*$ in the corollary to Theorem 5.3.1.

EXERCISE 5.3.12: Let $\Omega = (K, \Sigma, \Gamma, I, f, g)$, where $\Gamma = \{Y, Z\}$, $I = \{0, a, b\}$, and f and g are defined as follows: $g(\epsilon) = \{\epsilon\}$, $g(x) = \{Y\}$ for all x in Γ^+, $f(x, 0) = x$ for all x in Γ^*, $f(Y^n, a) = Y^{n+1}$ for $n \geqq 0$, $f(Y^{n+1}, b) = f(ZY^{n+1}, b) = ZY^n$ for $n \geqq 1$, and $f(ZY, b) = f(Y, b) = f(\epsilon, b) = \epsilon$. Let $L_1 = \{\epsilon, b\} \cup \{a^nb^n/n \geqq 1\}$, $L'_1 = \{a^nb^n/n \geqq 0\}$, $L_2 = (\{a^nb^m/m \geqq n \geqq 0\})^*$, and $L'_2 = \{a^nb^m/m \geqq n \geqq 0\}$. Show each of the following [GGr3]:

(a) $\mathcal{D}$ is a reduced, finitely encoded AFA.

(b) $\mathcal{F}(\tilde{L}'_{\mathcal{D}}) = \mathcal{F}(L_1) = \mathcal{L}^t(\mathcal{D}) = \mathcal{F}(L'_1)$.

(c) $\hat{\mathcal{F}}(L_1)$ is closed under reversal.

(d) $\mathcal{F}(L'_{\mathcal{D}}) = \mathcal{F}(L_2) = \mathcal{F}(L'_2) = \mathcal{F}(L'_{\mathcal{D}} \cap (I-\{0\})^*)$.

(e) Use Exercise 4.8.2 to show that $\hat{\mathcal{F}}(L'_2)$ is not closed under reversal.

Then infer that $\mathcal{L}(\mathcal{D}) = \hat{\mathcal{F}}(\tilde{L}'_{\mathcal{D}}) = \hat{\mathcal{F}}(L_1) \neq \hat{\mathcal{F}}(L_2) = \hat{\mathcal{F}}(L'_{\mathcal{D}})$, whence $\mathcal{L}^t(\mathcal{D}) = \mathcal{F}(\tilde{L}'_{\mathcal{D}}) \neq \mathcal{F}(L'_{\mathcal{D}})$. Also, infer that for no $\mathcal{D}_\alpha$ is $L_{\mathcal{D}_\alpha}$ in $\mathcal{F}(L'_{\mathcal{D}})$.

EXERCISE 5.3.13: Show that for each nontrivial, reduced, finitely encoded AFA $\mathcal{D}$, $\mathcal{S}(\tilde{L}'_{\mathcal{D}}) = \tilde{\mathcal{L}}^t(\mathcal{D})$ $(\hat{\mathcal{S}}(\tilde{L}'_{\mathcal{D}}) = \tilde{\mathcal{L}}(\mathcal{D}))$ if and only if $\tilde{L}_{\mathcal{D}}$ is in $\tilde{\mathcal{L}}^t(\mathcal{D}_\alpha) = \mathcal{S}(\tilde{L}_{\mathcal{D}_\alpha})(\tilde{\mathcal{L}}(\mathcal{D}_\alpha) = \hat{\mathcal{S}}(\tilde{L}_{\mathcal{D}_\alpha}))$.

EXERCISE 5.3.14: Show that for each nontrivial, reduced, finitely encoded

AFA$\mathcal{D}$, if $\#(g(\{x/x \text{ accessible}\})) \leqq 2$, then $\mathcal{S}(\tilde{L}'_{\mathcal{D}}) = \tilde{\mathcal{L}}^t(\mathcal{D})$ and $\hat{\mathcal{S}}(\tilde{L}'_{\mathcal{D}}) = \tilde{\mathcal{L}}(\mathcal{D})$.

EXERCISE 5.3.15: Prove that the Dyck set on one letter is a (full) generator for $\mathcal{L}^t(\mathcal{D}_C)$ ($\mathcal{L}(\mathcal{D}_C)$) [GGr3].

EXERCISE 5.3.16: Let $\Sigma_1 = \{a_1, a_2, a_1^{®}, a_2^{®}, a_1^{L}, a_2^{L}\}$, and let E, $\uparrow$, and $\upharpoonright$ be three symbols not in Σ_1. Let L be the set containing ϵ and all words wE in Σ_1^+E, where $\uparrow \upharpoonright w \overset{*}{\Longrightarrow} y \uparrow \upharpoonright$ for some y in $\{a_1, a_2\}^+$ by the following set of general Post productions ($\underline{P}_1$ and $\underline{P}_2$ are over $\{a_1, a_2\}^*$, and $\underline{P}_3$ is over Σ_1^*):

$$\{\underline{P}_1 a \uparrow \underline{P}_2 \upharpoonright a^{L} \underline{P}_3 \rightarrow \underline{P}_1 \uparrow a \underline{P}_2 \upharpoonright \underline{P}_3,\ \underline{P}_1 \uparrow a \underline{P}_2 \upharpoonright a^{®} \underline{P}_3 \rightarrow \underline{P}_1 a \uparrow \underline{P}_2 \upharpoonright \underline{P}_3,$$
$$\underline{P}_1 \uparrow \upharpoonright a \underline{P}_3 \rightarrow \underline{P}_1 a \uparrow \upharpoonright \underline{P}_3 / a \text{ in } \{a_1, a_2\}\}.$$

Prove that L is a (full) generator for $\mathcal{L}^t(\mathcal{D}_{\text{NES}})$ ($\mathcal{L}(\mathcal{D}_{\text{NES}})$) [GGr3].

EXERCISE 5.3.17: Let L be the set of all words w in $\{a, a^{E}, a^{L}, a^{®}, a^{B}\}^*$ such that (i) $\#_a(w) = \#_{a^E}(w)$ and $\#_{a^L}(w) = \#_{a^®}(w) + \#_{a^B}(w)$, and (ii) for each initial subword x of w, (a) $0 \leqq \#_{a^L}(x) - (\#_{a^®}(x) + \#_{a^B}(x)) \leqq \#_a(x) - \#_{a^E}(x)$, (b) if $x = ya$ or $x = ya^{E}$ then $\#_{a^L}(x) = \#_{a^®}(x) + \#_{a^B}(x)$, and (c) if $x = ya^{B}$ then $\#_{a^L}(y) - ((\#_{a^®}(y) + \#_{a^B}(y)) = \#_a(y) - \#_{a^E}(y)$. Prove that L is a generator for the quasi-realtime 1-stack counter languages. [See Exercise 4.5.4.]

EXERCISE 5.3.18: Let $\Omega = (K, \Sigma, \Gamma, I, f, g)$, where $\Gamma = \{a, \upharpoonleft\}$, $I = \{a, a^{®}, a^{L}, a^{B}, 0, E\}$, g is defined as in Exercise 4.5.4, and f is defined as follows: f on $\Gamma^* \times (I - \{E\})$ is as in Exercise 4.5.4 and $f(xa\upharpoonleft, E) = \epsilon$ for all x in a^*. Then $(\Omega, \mathcal{D})$ is a reduced, finitely encoded AFA formulation for the family of *nonerasing 1-stack counters*. Let L be the set containing ϵ and all words wE, w a word in $\{a, a^{®}, a^{L}, a^{B}\}^+$ such that (i) $\#_{a^L}(w) = \#_{a^®}(w) + \#_{a^B}(w)$, and (ii) for each initial subword x of w, (a) $0 \leqq \#_{a^L}(x) - (\#_{a^®}(x) + \#_{a^B}(x)) \leqq \#_a(x)$, (b) if $x = ya$ then $\#_{a^L}(x) = \#_{a^®}(x) + \#_{a^B}(x)$, and (c) if $x = ya^{B}$, then $\#_{a^L}(y) - (\#_{a^®}(y) + \#_{a^B}(y)) = \#_a(y)$. Prove that L is a full generator for $\mathcal{L}(\mathcal{D})$.

EXERCISE 5.3.19: Let $N' = \{1, 2, \ldots\}$, ω be a symbol not in N', and m be in $N' \cup \{\omega\}$. Let $H_\omega = \{a_1, a_2\}^*$, $H_m = (a_1^* a_2^*)^r$ for $m = 2r$, and $H_m = (a_1^* a_2^*)^r a_1^*$ for $m = 2r + 1$. Let $\Omega_{m,\omega} = (K, \Sigma, \Gamma, I, f_{m,\omega}, g)$, where $\Gamma = \{a_1, a_2\}$, $I = \{a_1, a_2, a_1^{E}, a_2^{E}, 0\}$, and $f_{m,\omega}$ and g are defined as follows (for all x in H_m,

i in $\{1, 2\}$, and y, ya_i in H_m): $g(\epsilon) = \{\epsilon\}$, $g(ya_i) = \{a_i\}$, $f_{m,\omega}(x, 0) = x$, $f_{m,\omega}(y, a_i) = ya_i$, and $f_{m,\omega}(ya_i, a_i^{\mathrm{E}}) = y$. Then $\mathcal{D}_{m,\omega}$ is a reduced, finitely encoded AFA for the family of (m, ω)-*bounded pda*. Prove that $L'_{\mathcal{D}_{m,\omega}} \cap (I-\{0\})^*$ is a full generator for $\mathcal{L}(\mathcal{D}_{m,\omega})$. Give a description of $L'_{\mathcal{D}_{m,\omega}} \cap (I-\{0\})^*$ [GGr3].

EXERCISE 5.3.20: Describe a full generator for $\mathcal{L}_{\mathrm{NSA}}$.

EXERCISE 5.3.21: Verify that $\mathcal{L}^t(\mathcal{D}) = \mathcal{L}^t(\mathcal{D}_{\mathrm{S}})$ and $\mathcal{L}(\mathcal{D}) = \mathcal{L}(\mathcal{D}_{\mathrm{S}})$ in Example 5.3.2.

EXERCISE 5.3.22: Let $\mathcal{D}$ be a reduced, nontrivial, finitely encoded AFA with the following property: For each γ in $g(\Gamma^+)$ there exist $n_\gamma \geqq 1$ and instructions $u_1, \ldots, u_{n_\gamma}$ such that for all accessible x, (i) if γ is not in $g(x)$, then $f(x, u_1 \ldots u_{n_\gamma}) = \emptyset$, (ii) if γ is in $g(x)$ then $f(x, u_1 \ldots u_{n_\gamma}) = x$, with $f(x, u_1 \ldots u_i) \neq \epsilon$ for each i, $1 \leqq i < n_\gamma$. Prove that $\mathcal{S}(\tilde{L}'_{\mathcal{D}}) = \tilde{\mathcal{L}}^t(\mathcal{D})$ and $\hat{\mathcal{S}}(\tilde{L}'_{\mathcal{D}}) = \tilde{\mathcal{L}}(\mathcal{D})$.

EXERCISE 5.3.23: Using Exercise 5.3.22, verify that the Dyck set W_2 on two letters is a semi-AFL generator for $\mathcal{L}_{\mathrm{CF}}$.

EXERCISE 5.3.24: Verify that $\tilde{L}'_{\mathcal{D}} \cap (I-\{0\})^*$, $\tilde{L}'_{\mathcal{D}}$ as in Example 5.3.2, is a semi-AFL generator for $\mathcal{L}^t(\mathcal{D}_{\mathrm{S}})$.

EXERCISE 5.3.25: Verify that in Example 5.3.3 there is no sequence $u_1, \ldots, u_s$ of instructions (other than $0, \ldots, 0$) such that $f_{m,n}(x, u_1 \ldots u_s) = x$ for all x satisfying a_1 in $g_{m,n}(x)$.

5.4 Representation Theorems

By definition, $\mathcal{F}(L)$ and $\hat{\mathcal{F}}(L)$ are the smallest AFL and full AFL, resp., containing L. As such, each set L' in $\mathcal{F}(L)$ ($\hat{\mathcal{F}}(L)$) is obtained from L by a finite number of applications of the closure operations of a (full) AFL. By Theorem 3.4.1, if $L \neq \emptyset$ then L' is obtained from the languages in the (full) semi-AFL $\mathcal{M}(L)$ ($\hat{\mathcal{M}}(L)$) by a finite number of applications of union, concatenation, and $+$. In the present section, we give two "simpler" representations for each such language. Specifically, we first show that $\mathcal{F}(L) = \mathcal{M}((Lc)^*)$ or $\mathcal{F}(L) = \mathcal{M}((Lc)^+)$, according as L contains ϵ or is ϵ-free, and

$\hat{\mathcal{F}}(L) = \hat{\mathcal{M}}((Lc)^*)$, with c a symbol not in Σ_L. We then prove that each language in $\mathcal{F}(L)$ [$\hat{\mathcal{F}}(L)$] can be represented in terms of $(Lc)^*$, decreasing homomorphism, inverse homomorphism, and intersection with regular sets. We conclude the section with a representation of certain (full) principal AFL as (full) principal semi-AFL $\mathcal{M}(L)$ ($\hat{\mathcal{M}}(L)$) for particular L.

Turning to the first representation theorem, we have the following preliminary result:

LEMMA 5.4.1: *For each language L and each symbol c not in* Σ_L, $\mathcal{M}((Lc)^*)$ *and* $\hat{\mathcal{M}}((Lc)^*)$ *are closed under* $+$; *and if* $L \neq \emptyset$, *then* $\mathcal{M}((Lc)^+)$ *is closed under* $+$.

Proof: It suffices to give the proof for $\mathcal{M}((Lc)^*)$.

Let $M_1 = (K_1, \Sigma_1, \Sigma_2, H_1, p_0, F_1)$ be an ϵ-free a-transducer. By Lemma 3.2.5, there exists a 1-bounded ϵ-output bounded a-transducer $M_2 = (K_2, \Sigma_1, \Sigma_2, H_2, q_0, F_2)$ such that $M_2(U) = M_1(U)$ for all languages U. Furthermore, there is no element (q_0, u, ϵ, q) in H_2. For each q in K_2 let $\bar{q}$ be a new symbol. Let $M_3 = (K_3, \Sigma_1, \Sigma_2, H_3, q_0, F_2)$, where $K_3 = K_2 \cup \{\bar{q}/q \text{ in } K_2\}$ and H_3 contains all 4-tuples of the following form:

(1) (q_1, u, v, q_2) if (q_1, u, v, q_2) is in H_2.
(2) (q_1, c, v, q_0) if (q_1, c, v, q_2) is in H_2 for some q_2 in F_2.
(3) $(q_1, c, v, \bar{q}_2)$ if (q_1, c, v, q_2) is in H_2.
(4) $(\bar{q}_1, \epsilon, v, \bar{q}_2)$ if (q_1, ϵ, v, q_2) is in H_2.
(5) $(\bar{q}_1, \epsilon, v, q_0)$ if (q_1, ϵ, v, q_2) is in H_2 and q_2 is in F_2.

Informally, the a-transducer M_3 operates as follows. On reading the last c in a word of the form $w_1cw_2c \ldots w_rc$, M_3 either simulates M_2 (by (1)), or resets to q_0 if M_2 goes to an accepting state (by (2)), or simulates M_2 in marked states so that if ϵ-moves take M_2 to an accepting state then M_3 resets to q_0 (by (4) and (5)). Clearly $M_3((Lc)^*) = M_2((Lc)^*)^+$. Since M_2 is ϵ-output bounded and no (q_0, u, ϵ, q) is in H_3, M_3 is ϵ-output bounded. Since $\mathcal{M}((Lc)^*)$ is closed under union with $\{\epsilon\}$, $M_3((Lc)^*)$ is in $\mathcal{M}((Lc)^*)$ by Theorem 3.2.2. [In the $\mathcal{M}((Lc)^+)$ case, $M_3((Lc)^+)-\{\epsilon\}$ is in $\mathcal{M}((Lc)^+)$. Since H_3 contains no element (q_0, u, ϵ, q), $M_3((Lc)^+)-\{\epsilon\} = M_3((Lc)^+)$.]

We are now ready for the first representation result.

THEOREM 5.4.1: *Let L be a language and c a symbol not in* Σ_L. *Then* $\mathcal{F}(L \cup \{\epsilon\}) = \mathcal{M}((Lc)^*)$ *and* $\hat{\mathcal{F}}(L) = \hat{\mathcal{M}}((Lc)^*)$. *If* $L \neq \emptyset$ *then* $\mathcal{F}(L-\{\epsilon\}) = \mathcal{M}((Lc)^+)$.

Proof: It suffices to consider the argument for $\mathcal{F}(L \cup \{\epsilon\})$. Since $(Lc)^*$ is in $\mathcal{F}(L \cup \{\epsilon\})$, $\mathcal{M}((Lc)^*) \subseteq \mathcal{F}(L \cup \{\epsilon\})$. Consider the reverse containment. Obviously there exists an ϵ-free a-transducer M_1 such that $M_1((Lc)^*) = L \cup \{\epsilon\}$. Therefore $L \cup \{\epsilon\}$ is in $\mathcal{M}((Lc)^*)$. By Theorem 3.2.1, $\mathcal{M}((Lc)^*)$ is a trio. Since $\mathcal{M}((Lc)^*)$ is closed under union by Proposition 5.1.1 and under $+$ by Lemma 5.4.1, it is an AFL by Theorem 3.1.2. Since $L \cup \{\epsilon\}$ is in $\mathcal{M}((Lc)^*)$, it follows that $\mathcal{F}(L \cup \{\epsilon\}) \subseteq \mathcal{M}((Lc)^*)$. Hence $\mathcal{F}(L \cup \{\epsilon\}) = \mathcal{M}((Lc)^*)$.

COROLLARY: *A (full) AFL $\mathcal{L}$ is (full) principal if and only if $\mathcal{L}$ is a (full) principal semi-AFL.*

Proof: The if is trivial. Consider the only if. Let $\mathcal{L} = \mathcal{F}(L)$ $(\hat{\mathcal{F}}(L))$. We may assume $L \neq \emptyset$ since otherwise $\mathcal{L} = \mathcal{R}_0(\mathcal{R})$ and the only if is satisfied. By Theorem 5.4.1, if L contains ϵ then $\mathcal{F}(L) = \mathcal{M}((Lc)^*)$, and if L is ϵ-free then $\mathcal{F}(L) = \mathcal{M}((Lc)^+)$. Hence $\mathcal{F}(L)$ is a principal semi-AFL, with $(Lc)^*$ a generator in the former case and $(Lc)^+$ a generator in the latter case. Since $\hat{\mathcal{F}}(L) = \hat{\mathcal{M}}((Lc)^*)$, $\hat{\mathcal{F}}(L)$ is a full semi-AFL with $(Lc)^*$ as a full generator.

The second representation result is as follows.

(+) THEOREM 5.4.2: *Let L be a language and c a symbol not in Σ_L. Then*

(a) $\hat{\mathcal{F}}(L) = \{h_2(h_1^{-1}((Lc)^*) \cap R)/R$ *in* $\mathcal{R}$, h_1 *and* h_2 *decreasing homomorphisms*$\}$.

(b) $\mathcal{F}(L \cup \{\epsilon\}) = \{h_2(h_1^{-1}((Lc)^*) \cap R)/R$ *in* $\mathcal{R}$, h_1 *and* h_2 *decreasing homomorphisms*, h_2 ϵ*-limited on* $R\}$.

(c) $\mathcal{F}(L-\{\epsilon\}) = \{h_2(h_1^{-1}((Lc)^*) \cap R)/R$ *in* $\mathcal{R}$, h_1 *and* h_2 *decreasing homomorphisms*, h_2 ϵ*-limited on* R, $h_2^{-1}(\epsilon) \cap R = \emptyset\}$,

and, if $L \neq \emptyset$,

$\mathcal{F}(L-\{\epsilon\}) = \{h_2(h_1^{-1}((Lc)^+) \cap R)/R$ *in* $\mathcal{R}$, h_1 *and* h_2 *decreasing homomorphisms*, h_2 ϵ*-limited on* R, $h_2^{-1}(\epsilon) \cap R = \emptyset\}$.

Proof: (a) and (b) follow immediately from Theorem 5.4.1 and Theorem 3.2.3.

Consider (c). If $L = \{\epsilon\}$, then (c) holds since $\mathcal{F}(L-\{\epsilon\})$ and the other two sets in the equations are all $\mathcal{R}_0$. If $L = \emptyset$, then the two sets in the first equation are also $\mathcal{R}_0$. Thus suppose $L-\{\epsilon\} \neq \emptyset$. The second equation then follows from Theorems 5.4.1 and 3.2.3. Consider the first equation. Let $\mathcal{U}(L)$ be the right side of the first equation. From (b), $\mathcal{U}(L) \subseteq \mathcal{F}(L \cup \{\epsilon\})$.

Now

$$\mathcal{F}(L-\{\epsilon\}) = \mathcal{F}((L \cup \{\epsilon\})-\{\epsilon\})$$
$$= \{U-\{\epsilon\}/U \text{ in } \mathcal{F}(L \cup \{\epsilon\})\}, \quad \text{by (b) of Proposition 3.4.1,}$$
$$= \{U \text{ in } \mathcal{F}(L \cup \{\epsilon\})/U \text{ is } \epsilon\text{-free}\}, \quad \text{by Proposition 3.1.2.}$$

Since each language in $\mathcal{U}(L)$ is e-free, $\mathcal{U}(L) \subseteq \mathcal{F}(L-\{\epsilon\})$. To see the reverse containment, let U be in $\mathcal{F}(L-\{\epsilon\})$. Since $\mathcal{F}(L-\{\epsilon\}) \subseteq \mathcal{F}(L \cup \{\epsilon\})$, $U = h_2(h_1^{-1}((Lc)^*) \cap R)$ for some regular set R and some decreasing homomorphisms h_1 and h_2, where h_2 is e-limited on R. Let $R' = R-(h_2^{-1}(\epsilon) \cap R)$. Clearly R' is regular, h_2 is e-limited on R', and $h_2^{-1}(\epsilon) \cap R' = \emptyset$. Then $U = h_2(h_1^{-1}((Lc)^*) \cap R) = h_2(h_1^{-1}((Lc)^*) \cap R') \cup V$, where $V = h_2(h_1^{-1}((Lc)^*) \cap (h_2^{-1}(\epsilon) \cap R))$. Since V is either $\{\epsilon\}$ or $\emptyset$ and U is e-free, $V = \emptyset$. Hence $U = h_2(h_1^{-1}((Lc)^*) \cap R')$, so that U is in $\mathcal{U}(L)$, i. e., $\mathcal{F}(L-\{\epsilon\}) \subseteq \mathcal{U}(L)$, whence equality.

Consider $\mathcal{L}_{CF}$. For $\mathcal{D}$ the AFA of pda given in Example 5.3.1 and W_2 the Dyck set over $\{a, b\}$,

$$\mathcal{L}(\mathcal{D}) = \mathcal{L}_{CF}$$
$$= \{h_2(h_1^{-1}(W_2) \cap R)/R \text{ in } \mathcal{R},\ h_1 \text{ and } h_2 \text{ homomorphisms}\},$$
by the Chomsky – Schutzenberger Theorem,[1]
$$= \hat{\mathcal{M}}(W_2), \quad \text{by Theorem 3.2.1,}$$
$$= \hat{\mathcal{M}}(L'_{\mathcal{D}} \cap (I-I_U)^*)$$
$$= \hat{\mathcal{M}}(L'_{\mathcal{D}}).$$

Thus $\mathcal{L}(\mathcal{D}) = \hat{\mathcal{M}}(L'_{\mathcal{D}})$. We now turn to a generalization of this fact, namely, we determine conditions on a finitely encoded AFA $\mathcal{D}$ such that

$$\mathcal{L}^t(\mathcal{D}) = \{h_2(h_1^{-1}(L'_{\mathcal{D}} \cap (I-I_U)^*) \cap R)/R \text{ regular, } h_1 \text{ and } h_2 \text{ homomorphisms, with } h_2\ \epsilon\text{-free}\}$$
$$= \mathcal{M}(L'_{\mathcal{D}} \cap (I-I_U)^*), \quad \text{by Theorem 3.2.1,}$$
$$= \mathcal{M}(L'_{\mathcal{D}}), \quad \text{by Proposition 5.3.2;}$$

and the obvious analogue for $\mathcal{L}(\mathcal{D})$.

In order to obtain this representation result, we shall need an auxiliary concept and three lemmas. The auxiliary notion is that of an acceptor in which each move depends only on the state and the input. The first lemma

[1] See Example 5.1.1.

asserts that each language defined by such a quasi-realtime acceptor is in $\mathcal{M}(L'_{\mathcal{D}})$.

Def: An acceptor $(K_1, \Sigma_1, \delta, q_0, F)$ in a finitely encoded AFA$\mathcal{D}$ is said to be *storage independent* if $\delta(p, a, \gamma_1) = \delta(p, a, \gamma_2)$ for all p in K_1, γ_1 and γ_2 in $g(\Gamma^*)$, and a in $\Sigma_1 \cup \{\epsilon\}$. Let

$$\mathcal{L}^{\beta}(\mathcal{D}) = \{L(D)/D \text{ in } \mathcal{D},\ D \text{ quasi-realtime and storage independent}\}.$$

LEMMA 5.4.2: *$\mathcal{L}^{\beta}(\mathcal{D}) \subseteq \mathcal{M}(L'_{\mathcal{D}})$ for each reduced, finitely encoded AFA$\mathcal{D}$.*

Proof: Let $D = (K_1, \Sigma_1, \delta, q_0, F)$ be quasi-realtime and storage independent. Let M be the a-transducer $(K_1, I, \Sigma_1, H, q_0, F)$, where

$$H = \{(q, u, a, p)/(p, u) \text{ in } \delta(q, a, \gamma) \text{ for all } \gamma \text{ in } g(\Gamma^*)\}.$$

Since D is quasi-realtime, M is ϵ-output bounded under non-ϵ input in I^* and thus ϵ-output bounded under non-ϵ input in $L'_{\mathcal{D}}$. From the fact that $\mathcal{D}$ is reduced it follows that $L(D) = M(L'_{\mathcal{D}})$. Since ϵ is in $L'_{\mathcal{D}}$, $M(L'_{\mathcal{D}})$ is in $\mathcal{M}(L'_{\mathcal{D}})$ by Corollary 1 of Theorem 3.2.2.

The remaining two lemmas present a condition which guarantees that[1] $\tilde{L}_{\mathcal{D}}$ is in $\mathcal{M}(L'_{\mathcal{D}})$ and $\tilde{\mathcal{L}}^{t}(\mathcal{D}) \subseteq \mathcal{M}(L'_{\mathcal{D}})$.

LEMMA 5.4.3: *Let $\mathcal{D}$ be a reduced, finitely encoded AFA with the following property: For each γ in $g(\Gamma^+)$ there exist $n_\gamma \geqq 1$ and instructions $u_1, \ldots, u_{n_\gamma}$ such that for all accessible x,* (i) *if γ is not in $g(x)$ then $f(x, u_1 \ldots u_{n_\gamma}) = \emptyset$, and* (ii) *if γ is in $g(x)$ then $f(x, u_1 \ldots u_{n_\gamma}) = x$. Then $\tilde{L}_{\mathcal{D}}$ is in $\mathcal{M}(L'_{\mathcal{D}})$.*

Proof: Let $D = (K_1, g(\Gamma^*) \times I, \delta, q_0, \{q_0\})$ be the acceptor in $\mathcal{D}_\alpha$ defined in Theorem 5.3.2 such that $L(D) = L_{\mathcal{D}}$. Let $\bar{D}$ be the acceptor $(K_1, g(\Gamma^*) \times I, \bar{\delta}, q_0, \{q_0\})$ in $\mathcal{D}$, where $\bar{\delta}(q, x, \gamma) = \delta(q, x, \alpha) \cup \delta(q, x, \epsilon)$ for all q in K_1, x in $(g(\Gamma^*) \times I) \cup \{\epsilon\}$, and γ in $g(\Gamma^*)$. Then $\bar{D}$ is quasi-realtime storage-independent, and $L(\bar{D}) = L(D) = L_{\mathcal{D}}$. Therefore $L_{\mathcal{D}}$ is in $\mathcal{L}^{\beta}(\mathcal{D})$. By Lemma 5.4.2, $L_{\mathcal{D}}$ is in $\mathcal{M}(L'_{\mathcal{D}})$. Then

$$\tilde{L}_{\mathcal{D}} = L_{\mathcal{D}} \cap [\{\epsilon\} \cup (\{\epsilon\} \times I)(g(\Gamma^+) \times I)^*]$$

is in $\mathcal{M}\mathcal{M}(L'_{\mathcal{D}}) = \mathcal{M}(L'_{\mathcal{D}})$.

LEMMA 5.4.4: *For each $\mathcal{D}$ satisfying the hypotheses of Lemma 5.4.3, $\tilde{\mathcal{L}}^{t}(\mathcal{D}) \subseteq \mathcal{M}(L'_{\mathcal{D}})$.*

[1] For the specification of $\tilde{L}_{\mathcal{D}}$, see the second footnote in the notation for $L_{\mathcal{D}}$.

Proof: Suppose $\mathcal{D}$ is trivial. Then $\tilde{\mathcal{L}}^t(\mathcal{D})$ is a family of finite sets and $\tilde{\mathcal{L}}^t(\mathcal{D}) \subseteq \mathcal{R} = \mathcal{M}(L'_{\mathcal{D}})$. Suppose $\mathcal{D}$ is nontrivial. Then

$$\begin{aligned}\tilde{\mathcal{L}}^t(\mathcal{D}) &= \mathcal{M}(\tilde{L}_{\mathcal{D}}), && \text{by the} \sim \text{version of Lemma 5.2.4,}\\ &\subseteq \mathcal{M}\mathcal{M}(L'_{\mathcal{D}}), && \text{by Lemma 5.4.3,}\\ &\subseteq \mathcal{M}(L'_{\mathcal{D}}).\end{aligned}$$

From Lemma 5.4.4, we obtain our final representation result.

THEOREM 5.4.3: *Let $\mathcal{D}$ satisfy the hypotheses of Lemma 5.4.3. Suppose further that $\tilde{\mathcal{L}}^t(\mathcal{D}) = \mathcal{L}^t(\mathcal{D})$. Then $\mathcal{L}^t(\mathcal{D}) = \mathcal{M}(L'_{\mathcal{D}})$ and $\mathcal{L}(\mathcal{D}) = \hat{\mathcal{M}}(L'_{\mathcal{D}})$.*

Proof:
$$\begin{aligned}\mathcal{L}^t(\mathcal{D}) &= \tilde{\mathcal{L}}^t(\mathcal{D})\\ &\subseteq \mathcal{M}(L'_{\mathcal{D}}), && \text{by Lemma 5.4.4,}\\ &\subseteq \mathcal{L}^t(\mathcal{D}), && \text{by Proposition 5.3.1.}\end{aligned}$$

Thus $\mathcal{L}^t(\mathcal{D}) = \mathcal{M}(L'_{\mathcal{D}})$. From this it follows that $\mathcal{L}(\mathcal{D}) = \hat{\mathcal{M}}(L'_{\mathcal{D}})$.

Two AFA satisfying Theorem 5.4.3 are given in Exercise 5.4.7.

EXERCISE 5.4.1: Prove that $\mathcal{L}_{\text{LDB}}$ is a non-full-principal AFL, where $\mathcal{L}_{\text{LDB}}$ is given in Exercise 3.1.10.

Exercises 5.4.2 and 5.4.3 employ the notation of Exercise 3.2.11.

EXERCISE 5.4.2: Let $L_1, \ldots, L_n$ be languages, with c not in $\bigcup_1^n \Sigma_{L_i}$. Prove the following [Go1]:

(a) $\hat{\mathcal{M}}^{(n)}((L_1c)^*, \ldots, (L_nc)^*) = \hat{\mathcal{F}}(\hat{\mathcal{F}}(L_1) \wedge \ldots \wedge \hat{\mathcal{F}}(L_n))$.

(b) $\mathcal{M}^{(n)}((L_1c)^*, \ldots, (L_nc)^*) = \mathcal{F}(\mathcal{F}(L_1 \cup \{\epsilon\}) \wedge \ldots \wedge \mathcal{F}(L_n \cup \{\epsilon\}))$.

(c) $\mathcal{M}^{(n)}((L_1c)^+, \ldots, (L_nc)^+) = \mathcal{F}(\mathcal{F}(L_1 - \{\epsilon\}) \wedge \mathcal{F}(L_2) \wedge \ldots \wedge \mathcal{F}(L_n))$,

if $L_i \neq \emptyset$ for each i.

EXERCISE 5.4.3: Let L be a language and c not in Σ_L. Prove the following [Go1]:

(a) $\hat{\mathcal{F}}_\cap(L) = \bigcup_{n \geqq 1} \hat{\mathcal{M}}^{(n)}((Lc)^*, \ldots, (Lc)^*)$.

(b) $\mathcal{F}_\cap(L \cup \{\epsilon\}) = \bigcup_{n \geqq 1} \mathcal{M}^{(n)}((Lc)^*, \ldots, (Lc)^*)$.

(c) $\mathcal{F}_\cap(L - \{\epsilon\}) = \bigcup_{n \geqq 1} \mathcal{M}^{(n)}((Lc)^+, \ldots, (Lc)^+)$, if $L \neq \emptyset$.

EXERCISE 5.4.4:[1] Let $\mathscr{L}_1$ be the family of all recursive subsets of a^*. Suppose that $\mathscr{L}$ is an AFL satisfying $\mathscr{L}_1 \subseteq \mathscr{L} \subseteq \mathscr{L}_{\text{REC}}$ and $\mathscr{L} = \mathscr{F}(L)$ for some L.

(a) Use Theorem 5.4.1 to show that the languages in $\mathscr{L}$, thus $\mathscr{L}_1$, can be effectively enumerated by deterministic Turing acceptors which halt.

(b) Use a diagonalization argument to show that such an enumeration of $\mathscr{L}_1$ is impossible. Thus infer [Ui] that $\mathscr{L}$ is not principal.

EXERCISE 5.4.5: Prove that $\mathscr{L}^{\beta}(\mathscr{D}) = \mathscr{M}(L'_{\mathscr{D}})$ for each reduced, finitely encoded AFA $\mathscr{D}$ with a universal identity element [GGr3].

EXERCISE 5.4.6: Prove that $\tilde{L}_{\mathscr{D}}$ is in $\mathscr{L}^{\beta}(\mathscr{D})$ if $\mathscr{D}$ satisfies the hypotheses of Lemma 5.4.3 [GGr3].

EXERCISE 5.4.7: In each of the following AFA, show that $\tilde{\mathscr{L}}^t(\mathscr{D}) = \mathscr{L}^t(\mathscr{D})$ [GGr3]. Also describe $L'_{\mathscr{D}}$.

(a) $\mathscr{D}$ as in Example 5.3.1.

(b) $\mathscr{D}$ as in Example 5.3.2.

EXERCISE 5.4.8: Show that each of the following AFA does not satisfy the hypotheses of Theorem 5.4.3.

(a) $\mathscr{D}_{\text{C}}$ [Bo2].

(b) The AFA of 1-stack counters [GGr3]. (See Exercise 4.5.4.)

(c) The AFA of nonerasing 1-stack counters [GGr3]. (See Exercise 5.3.18.)

EXERCISE 5.4.9: Let $(\Omega, \mathscr{D})$ be the following modified version of $\mathscr{D}_{\text{C}}$. Let $\Gamma = \{a_1, Z_0\}$, $I = \{0, Z_0, a_1, a_1^{\text{E}}\}$, and for $n \geqq 1$, let $g(\epsilon) = \{\epsilon\}, g(Z_0) = \{Z_0\}$, $g(Z_0 a_1^n) = a_1$, $f(w, 0) = w$ for w in Γ^*, $f(\epsilon, a_1) = Z_0 a_1$, $f(Z_0 a_1^m, a_1) = Z_0 a_1^{m+1}$, $m \geqq 0$, $f(Z_0 a_1^n, a_1^{\text{E}}) = Z_0 a_1^{n-1}$, and $f(Z_0, Z_0) = \epsilon$. Prove the following [GGr3]:

(a) $\mathscr{D}$ satisfies the hypotheses of Theorem 5.4.3.

(b) $\mathscr{L}^t(\mathscr{D}) = \tilde{\mathscr{L}}^t(\mathscr{D}) = \mathscr{F}(\tilde{L}'_{\mathscr{D}})$.

(c) $\mathscr{M}(\tilde{L}'_{\mathscr{D}}) \neq \mathscr{F}(\tilde{L}'_{\mathscr{D}})$.

[1] An elementary knowledge of recursive function theory is assumed here.

5.5 The Wedge Operator

We now study the wedge operator on principal (semi-) AFL. In particular, we present an algebraic proof that $\mathscr{H}(\mathscr{L}_1 \wedge \mathscr{L}_2)[\hat{\mathscr{H}}(\mathscr{L}_1 \wedge \mathscr{L}_2)]$ is a [full] principal (semi-) AFL if $\mathscr{L}_1$ and $\mathscr{L}_2$ are [full] principal (semi-) AFL. Furthermore, using a new operation we exhibit a [full] generator for the resulting [full] principal (semi-) AFL which depends on the given [full] generators for $\mathscr{L}_1$ and $\mathscr{L}_2$.

Notation: For all languages L_1 and L_2 let

$$\text{Shuf}(L_1, L_2) = \{w_1 y_1 \ldots w_n y_n / w_1 \ldots w_n \text{ in } L_1,\ y_1 \ldots y_n \text{ in } L_2,\ n \geqq 1\}.$$

LEMMA 5.5.1: *Let L_1 and L_2 be languages such that $\Sigma_{L_1} \cap \Sigma_{L_2} = \emptyset$. Then for $L = \text{Shuf}(L_1, L_2)$,*

(a) $\hat{\mathscr{M}}(L_1) \wedge \hat{\mathscr{M}}(L_2) \subseteq \hat{\mathscr{M}}(L)$ *if* $L_1 \neq \emptyset$ *and* $L_2 \neq \emptyset$,

(b) $\mathscr{M}(L_1 \cup \{\epsilon\}) \wedge \mathscr{M}(L_2 \cup \{\epsilon\}) \subseteq \mathscr{M}(L \cup \{\epsilon\})$, *and*

(c) $\mathscr{M}(L_1 - \{\epsilon\}) \wedge \mathscr{M}(L_2 - \{\epsilon\}) \subseteq \mathscr{M}(L - \{\epsilon\})$ *if* $L_1 - \{\epsilon\} \neq \emptyset$ *and* $L_2 - \{\epsilon\} \neq \emptyset$.

Proof: We shall show (c), the proofs for (a) and (b) being similar.

Assume that $L_1 - \{\epsilon\} \neq \emptyset$ and $L_2 - \{\epsilon\} \neq \emptyset$. [These assumptions are used only to ensure that $\mathscr{M}(L_1 - \{\epsilon\})$ and $\mathscr{M}(L_2 - \{\epsilon\})$ are defined.] Let $L' = \text{Shuf}(L_1 - \{\epsilon\}, L_2 - \{\epsilon\})$. Note that $L' \neq \emptyset$. We first show that

(1) $\mathscr{M}(L') = \mathscr{M}(L - \{\epsilon\})$.

To see this first suppose L_1 and L_2 are ϵ-free. Then $L' = L = L - \{\epsilon\}$, so that $\mathscr{M}(L') = \mathscr{M}(L - \{\epsilon\})$. Next, suppose that L_1 contains ϵ but L_2 does not. Then $L' = (L - \{\epsilon\}) \cap (\Sigma_L^* - \Sigma_{L_2}^+)$, so that $\mathscr{M}(L') \subseteq \mathscr{M}(L - \{\epsilon\})$. Now $L - \{\epsilon\} = L' \cup L_2$ and L' is in $\mathscr{M}(L')$. It suffices to show that L_2 is in $\mathscr{M}(L')$. [For $\mathscr{M}(L')$ is a semi-AFL by Proposition 5.1.1. Then $L - \{\epsilon\} = L' \cup L_2$ is in $\mathscr{M}(L')$, so that $\mathscr{M}(L - \{\epsilon\}) \subseteq \mathscr{M}(L')$, whence $\mathscr{M}(L - \{\epsilon\}) = \mathscr{M}(L')$.] To this end let w be a word in $L_1 - \{\epsilon\}$. Since $L_1 - \{\epsilon\} \neq \emptyset$, w exists. Let h_0 be the homomorphism on Σ_L^* defined by $h_0(x) = \epsilon$ for each x in Σ_{L_1} and $h_0(x) = x$ for each x in Σ_{L_2}. Then $L_2 = L_2 - \{\epsilon\} = h_0(L' \cap w\Sigma_{L_2}^+)$. Since h_0 is ϵ-limited on $L' \cap w\Sigma_{L_2}^+$, $L_2 = L_2 - \{\epsilon\}$ is in $\mathscr{M}(L' \cap w\Sigma_{L_2}^+)$ by Corollary 2 of Theorem 3.2.2. Since $L' \cap w\Sigma_{L_2}^+$ is in $\mathscr{M}(L')$, L_2 is in $\mathscr{M}(L')$. Thus $\mathscr{M}(L') = \mathscr{M}(L - \{\epsilon\})$. An analogous argument holds if L_2 contains ϵ, but L_1 does not. Finally, suppose that L_1 and L_2 both contain ϵ. Then $L' = (L - \{\epsilon\}) \cap (\Sigma_L^+ -$

$(\Sigma_{L_1}^+ \cup \Sigma_{L_2}^+))$, so that $\mathcal{M}(L') \subseteq \mathcal{M}(L-\{\epsilon\})$. Now $L-\{\epsilon\} = L' \cup (L_1-\{\epsilon\}) \cup (L_2-\{\epsilon\})$, and L', $L_1-\{\epsilon\}$, and $L_2-\{\epsilon\}$ are in $\mathcal{M}(L')$ by an argument analogous to the above. Since $M(L')$ is a semi-AFL, $L-\{\epsilon\}$ is in $\mathcal{M}(L')$, whence $\mathcal{M}(L-\{\epsilon\}) \subseteq \mathcal{M}(L')$. Thus $\mathcal{M}(L-\{\epsilon\}) = \mathcal{M}(L')$.

We next note that

(2) $h_1^{-1}(L_1-\{\epsilon\}) \cap h_2^{-1}(L_2-\{\epsilon\})$ is in $\mathcal{M}(L')$ for all homomorphisms h_1 and h_2.

For let h_1 and h_2 be homomorphisms from Σ_1^* into $\Sigma_{L_1}^*$ and Σ_2^* into $\Sigma_{L_2}^*$, resp. Let h_3 be the homomorphism on $(\Sigma_1 \cap \Sigma_2)^*$ defined by $h_3(a) = h_1(a)\, h_2(a)$ for each a in $\Sigma_1 \cap \Sigma_2$. Consider $h_1^{-1}(L_1-\{\epsilon\}) \cap h_2^{-1}(L_2-\{\epsilon\})$ and $h_3^{-1}(L')$. Clearly ϵ is not in

$$h_1^{-1}(L_1-\{\epsilon\}) \cup h_2^{-1}(L_2-\{\epsilon\}) \cup h_3^{-1}(L').$$

Let $a_1 \ldots a_k$ be a $\Sigma_1 \cap \Sigma_2$-word. Then $a_1 \ldots a_k$ is in $h_1^{-1}(L_1-\{\epsilon\}) \cap h_2^{-1}(L_2-\{\epsilon\})$ if and only if $h_1(a_1) \ldots h_1(a_k)$ is in $L_1-\{\epsilon\}$ and $h_2(a_1) \ldots h_2(a_k)$ is in $L_2-\{\epsilon\}$. Since $\Sigma_{L_1} \cap \Sigma_{L_2} = \emptyset$, this occurs if and only if

$$h_1(a_1)\, h_2(a_1) \ldots h_1(a_k)\, h_2(a_k) = h_3(a_1) \ldots h_3(a_k)$$

is in L', and hence $a_1 \ldots a_k$ is in $h_3^{-1}(L')$. Thus $h_1^{-1}(L_1-\{\epsilon\}) \cap h_2^{-1}(L_2-\{\epsilon\}) = h_3^{-1}(L')$ and thus is in $\mathcal{M}(L')$.

We next observe that

(3) if L_3 is a language in $\mathcal{M}(L_1-\{\epsilon\})$, then $L_3 \cap h_3^{-1}(L_2-\{\epsilon\})$ is in $\mathcal{M}(L-\{\epsilon\})$ for every homomorphism h_3.

For let $L_3 = M(L_1-\{\epsilon\})$ for some ϵ-free a-transducer M. By Corollary 1 to Theorem 3.2.1, $M(L_1-\{\epsilon\}) = h_2(h_1^{-1}(L_1-\{\epsilon\}) \cap R)$ for some R in $\mathcal{R}$, homomorphism h_1, and ϵ-free homomorphism h_2. Let $h_4 = h_3h_2$. Then

$$\begin{aligned} L_3 \cap h_3^{-1}(L_2-\{\epsilon\}) &= h_2(h_1^{-1}(L_1-\{\epsilon\}) \cap R) \cap h_3^{-1}(L_2-\{\epsilon\}) \\ &= h_2(h_1^{-1}(L_1-\{\epsilon\}) \cap R \cap h_2^{-1}h_3^{-1}(L_2-\{\epsilon\})) \\ &= h_2(h_1^{-1}(L_1-\{\epsilon\}) \cap h_4^{-1}(L_2-\{\epsilon\}) \cap R). \end{aligned}$$

By (2) and (1), $h_1^{-1}(L_1-\{\epsilon\}) \cap h_4^{-1}(L_2-\{\epsilon\})$ is in $\mathcal{M}(L-\{\epsilon\})$. Thus $h_2(h_1^{-1}(L_1-\{\epsilon\}) \cap h_4^{-1}(L_2-\{\epsilon\}) \cap R) = L_3 \cap h_3^{-1}(L_2-\{\epsilon\})$ is in $\mathcal{M}(L-\{\epsilon\})$.

We are now ready to consider $\mathcal{M}(L_1-\{\epsilon\}) \wedge \mathcal{M}(L_2-\{\epsilon\})$. Let L_4 be in $\mathcal{M}(L_1-\{\epsilon\})$ and L_5 in $\mathcal{M}(L_2-\{\epsilon\})$. By Corollary 1 to Theorem 3.2.1, $L_5 = h_6(h_5^{-1}(L_2-\{\epsilon\}) \cap R_1)$, where h_5 and h_6 are homomorphisms, with h_6

ϵ-free, and R_1 in $\mathcal{R}$. Now

$$\begin{aligned} L_4 \cap L_5 &= L_4 \cap h_6(h_5^{-1}(L_2-\{\epsilon\}) \cap R_1) \\ &= h_6(h_6^{-1}(L_4) \cap h_5^{-1}(L_2-\{\epsilon\}) \cap R_1). \end{aligned}$$

Since $\mathcal{M}(L_1-\{\epsilon\})$ is a semi-AFL, $h_6^{-1}(L_4) \cap R_1$ is in $\mathcal{M}(L_1-\{\epsilon\})$. By (3), $(h_6^{-1}(L_4) \cap R_1) \cap h_5^{-1}(L_2-\{\epsilon\})$ is in $\mathcal{M}(L-\{\epsilon\})$, whence $h_6(h_6^{-1}(L_4) \cap R_1 \cap h_5^{-1}(L_2-\{\epsilon\})) = L_4 \cap L_5$ is in $\mathcal{M}(L-\{\epsilon\})$.

THEOREM 5.5.1: *Let L_1 and L_2 be nonempty languages. Let h and h' be one-to-one, length-preserving homomorphisms on $\Sigma_{L_1}^*$ and $\Sigma_{L_2}^*$ resp., such that $\Sigma_{h(L_1)} \cap \Sigma_{h'(L_2)} = \emptyset$. Let c_1 and c_2 be two new symbols. Then*

(a) $\mathcal{H}(\mathcal{F}(L_1) \wedge \mathcal{F}(L_2)) = \mathcal{F}(Shuf((h(L_1)c_1)^+, (h'(L_2)c_2)^+))$ *if L_1 or L_2 is ϵ-free,*

(b) $\mathcal{H}(\mathcal{F}(L_1) \wedge \mathcal{F}(L_2)) = \mathcal{F}(Shuf((h(L_1)c_1)^*, (h'(L_2)c_2)^*))$ *if L_1 and L_2 contain ϵ,*

(c) $\hat{\mathcal{H}}(\mathcal{F}(L_1) \wedge \mathcal{F}(L_2)) = \hat{\mathcal{F}}(Shuf((h(L_1)c_1)^*, (h'(L_2)c_2)^*))$,

(d) $\mathcal{H}(\mathcal{S}(L_1) \wedge \mathcal{S}(L_2)) = \mathcal{S}(Shuf(h(L_1), h'(L_2)))$, *and*

(e) $\hat{\mathcal{H}}(\mathcal{S}(L_1) \wedge \mathcal{S}(L_2)) = \hat{\mathcal{S}}(Shuf(h(L_1), h'(L_2)))$.

Proof: Since $\mathcal{O}(L) = \mathcal{O}(h''(L))$ and $\hat{\mathcal{O}}(L) = \hat{\mathcal{O}}(h''(L))$, $\mathcal{O} = \mathcal{S}$ or $\mathcal{F}$, for each language L and each one-to-one, length-preserving homomorphism h'' on Σ_L^*, it suffices to assume that h and h' are the identity functions and $\Sigma_{L_1} \cap \Sigma_{L_2} = \emptyset$.

(a) Let L_1 or L_2 be ϵ-free and $L = \text{Shuf}((L_1c_1)^+, (L_2c_2)^+)$. For i in $\{1, 2\}$, let h_i be the homomorphism on $(\Sigma_{L_1} \cup \Sigma_{L_2} \cup \{c_1, c_2\})^*$ defined by $h_i(a) = a$ for a in $\Sigma_{L_i} \cup \{c_i\}$ and $h_i(a) = \epsilon$ otherwise. Then $L = h_1^{-1}((L_1c_1)^+) \cap h_2^{-1}((L_2c_2)^+)$ since $(\Sigma_{L_1} \cup \{c_1\}) \cap (\Sigma_{L_2} \cup \{c_2\}) = \emptyset$. Hence L is in $\mathcal{F}(L_1) \wedge \mathcal{F}(L_2) \subseteq \mathcal{H}(\mathcal{F}(L_1) \wedge \mathcal{F}(L_2))$. Therefore $\mathcal{F}(L) \subseteq \mathcal{H}(\mathcal{F}(L_1) \wedge \mathcal{F}(L_2))$.

Consider the reverse containment. First suppose that L_1 and L_2 are ϵ-free. By Theorem 5.4.1, $\mathcal{M}((L_ic_i)^+) = \mathcal{F}(L_i-\{\epsilon\}) = \mathcal{F}(L_i)$ for each i. Then

$$\begin{aligned} \mathcal{F}(L_1) \wedge \mathcal{F}(L_2) &= \mathcal{M}((L_1c_1)^+) \wedge \mathcal{M}((L_2c_2)^+) \\ &\subseteq \mathcal{M}(L-\{\epsilon\}), \quad \text{by (c) of Lemma 5.5.1}, \\ &= \mathcal{M}(L), \quad \text{since } L \text{ is } \epsilon\text{-free}, \\ &\subseteq \mathcal{F}(L). \end{aligned}$$

Hence $\mathcal{H}(\mathcal{F}(L_1) \wedge \mathcal{F}(L_2)) \subseteq \mathcal{F}(L)$.

Next, suppose that L_1 is ϵ-free and L_2 contains ϵ. If $L_2 = \{\epsilon\}$, then, as is easily seen (Exercise 5.5.2), (a) is true. Suppose $L_2 - \{\epsilon\} \neq \emptyset$. Then

$$\begin{aligned}\mathscr{H}(\mathscr{F}(L_1) \wedge \mathscr{F}(L_2)) &= \mathscr{H}(\mathscr{F}(L_1) \wedge \mathscr{F}(L_2 - \{\epsilon\})), && \text{by (b) of Proposition 3.4.1 since } L_1 \text{ is } \epsilon\text{-free,}\\ &\subseteq \mathscr{F}\big(\mathrm{Shuf}\,((L_1c_1)^+, ((L_2-\{\epsilon\})c_2)^+)\big), && \text{since } L_1 \text{ and } L_2-\{\epsilon\} \text{ are } \epsilon\text{-free,}\\ &\subseteq \mathscr{F}\big(\mathrm{Shuf}\,((L_1c_1)^+, (L_2c_2)^+)\big), && \text{since } ((L_2-\{\epsilon\})c_2)^+ \subseteq (L_2c_2)^+.\end{aligned}$$

A similar argument arises if L_1 contains ϵ and L_2 is ϵ-free.

(b) An argument similar to that in the first part of (a) shows that $\mathscr{F}(\mathrm{Shuf}((L_1c_1)^*, (L_2c_2)^*)) \subseteq \mathscr{H}(\mathscr{F}(L_1) \wedge \mathscr{F}(L_2))$. Consider the reverse containment. By Theorem 5.4.1, $\mathscr{M}((L_ic_i)^*) = \mathscr{F}(L_i)$ for each i. Then

$$\begin{aligned}\mathscr{F}(L_1) \wedge \mathscr{F}(L_2) &= \mathscr{M}((L_1c_1)^*) \wedge \mathscr{M}((L_2c_2)^*)\\ &\subseteq \mathscr{M}\big(\mathrm{Shuf}\,((L_1c_1)^*, (L_2c_2)^*)\big), && \text{by (b) of Lemma 5.5.1,}\\ &\subseteq \mathscr{F}\big(\mathrm{Shuf}\,((L_1c_1)^*, (L_2c_2)^*)\big).\end{aligned}$$

Hence $\mathscr{H}(\mathscr{F}(L_1) \wedge \mathscr{F}(L_2)) \subseteq \mathscr{F}\big(\mathrm{Shuf}((L_1c_1)^*, (L_2c_2)^*)\big)$.

(c) If L_1 and L_2 both contain ϵ, then

$$\begin{aligned}\hat{\mathscr{H}}(\mathscr{F}(L_1) \wedge \mathscr{F}(L_2)) &= \hat{\mathscr{H}}\big(\mathscr{H}(\mathscr{F}(L_1) \wedge \mathscr{F}(L_2))\big)\\ &= \hat{\mathscr{H}}\big(\mathscr{F}(\mathrm{Shuf}\,((L_1c_1)^*, (L_2c_2)^*))\big), && \text{by (b),}\\ &= \hat{\mathscr{F}}\big(\mathrm{Shuf}\,((L_1c_1)^*, (L_2c_2)^*)\big).\end{aligned}$$

Suppose L_1 or L_2 does not contain ϵ. Then

$$\begin{aligned}\hat{\mathscr{H}}(\mathscr{F}(L_1) \wedge \mathscr{F}(L_2)) &= \hat{\mathscr{H}}\big(\mathscr{H}(\mathscr{F}(L_1) \wedge \mathscr{F}(L_2))\big)\\ &= \hat{\mathscr{H}}\big(\mathscr{F}(\mathrm{Shuf}\,((L_1c_1)^+, (L_2c_2)^+))\big), && \text{by (a),}\\ &= \hat{\mathscr{F}}\big(\mathrm{Shuf}\,((L_1c_1)^+, (L_2c_2)^+)\big).\end{aligned}$$

Since $\mathrm{Shuf}((L_1c_1)^*, (L_2c_2)^*) = (L_1c_1)^+ \cup (L_2c_2)^+ \cup \{\epsilon\} \cup \mathrm{Shuf}((L_1c_1)^+, (L_2c_2)^+)$ and $\mathrm{Shuf}((L_1c_1)^+, (L_2c_2)^+) = \mathrm{Shuf}((L_1c_1)^*, (L_2c_2)^*) \cap R$, where R is the regular set $(\Sigma_{L_1} \cup \Sigma_{L_2} \cup \{c_1, c_2\})^+ - ((\Sigma_{L_1}^* c_1)^+ \cup (\Sigma_{L_2}^* c_2)^+)$, it follows that $\hat{\mathscr{F}}\big(\mathrm{Shuf}((L_1c_1)^+, (L_2c_2)^+)\big) = \hat{\mathscr{F}}\big(\mathrm{Shuf}((L_1c_1)^*, (L_2c_2)^*)\big)$.

(d) Let $L = \mathrm{Shuf}(L_1, L_2)$. For i in $\{1, 2\}$ let h_i be the homomorphism on $(\Sigma_{L_1} \cup \Sigma_{L_2})^*$ defined by $h_i(a) = a$ for a in Σ_{L_i} and $h_i(a) = \epsilon$ otherwise.

Then $L = h_1^{-1}(L_1) \cap h_2^{-1}(L_2)$ since $\Sigma_{L_1} \cap \Sigma_{L_2} = \emptyset$. Therefore L is in $\mathcal{S}(L_1) \wedge \mathcal{S}(L_2) \subseteq \mathcal{H}(\mathcal{S}(L_1) \wedge \mathcal{S}(L_2))$, so that $\mathcal{S}(L) \subseteq \mathcal{H}(\mathcal{S}(L_1) \wedge \mathcal{S}(L_2))$.

Consider the reverse inclusion. It suffices to show that $\mathcal{S}(L_1) \wedge \mathcal{S}(L_2) \subseteq \mathcal{S}(L)$, since semi-AFL are closed under ϵ-free homomorphism. Suppose L_1 is ϵ-free and $L_2 = \{\epsilon\}$. Then $\mathcal{S}(L_1) \wedge \mathcal{S}(L_2) = \mathcal{S}(L_1) \wedge \mathcal{R} = \mathcal{S}(L_1) = \mathcal{S}(L)$. A similar situation occurs if $L_1 = \{\epsilon\}$ and L_2 is ϵ-free. Suppose L_1 or L_2 is ϵ-free and the other language is not $\{\epsilon\}$. Then

$$\begin{aligned}\mathcal{S}(L_1) \wedge \mathcal{S}(L_2) &= \mathcal{S}(L_1-\{\epsilon\}) \wedge \mathcal{S}(L_2-\{\epsilon\})\\ &= \mathcal{M}(L_1-\{\epsilon\}) \wedge \mathcal{M}(L_2-\{\epsilon\})\\ &\subseteq \mathcal{M}(L-\{\epsilon\}), \quad \text{by (c) of Lemma 5.5.1,}\\ &\subseteq \mathcal{M}(L)\\ &= \mathcal{S}(L).\end{aligned}$$

Suppose L_1 and L_2 both contain ϵ. Then

$$\begin{aligned}\mathcal{S}(L_1) \wedge \mathcal{S}(L_2) &= \mathcal{M}(L_1) \wedge \mathcal{M}(L_2)\\ &\subseteq \mathcal{M}(L), \quad \text{by (b) of Lemma 5.5.1,}\\ &= \mathcal{S}(L).\end{aligned}$$

In all cases, therefore, $\mathcal{S}(L_1) \wedge \mathcal{S}(L_2) \subseteq \mathcal{S}(L)$.

(e) This follows from (d) by (b) of Theorem 3.4.3.

Corollary 1: *If $\mathcal{L}_1$ and $\mathcal{L}_2$ are (full) principal* [*semi-*] *AFL, then so is $\mathcal{H}(\mathcal{L}_1 \wedge \mathcal{L}_2)$ $(\hat{\mathcal{H}}(\mathcal{L}_1 \wedge \mathcal{L}_2))$.*

From the corollary to Proposition 3.6.1, $\mathcal{H}(\mathcal{L}_1 \wedge \ldots \wedge \mathcal{L}_n) = \mathcal{H}(\mathcal{H}(\mathcal{L}_1 \wedge \ldots \wedge \mathcal{L}_{n-1}) \wedge \mathcal{L}_n)$ and $\hat{\mathcal{H}}(\mathcal{L}_1 \wedge \ldots \wedge \mathcal{L}_n) = \hat{\mathcal{H}}(\hat{\mathcal{H}}(\mathcal{L}_1 \wedge \ldots \wedge \mathcal{L}_{n-1}) \wedge \mathcal{L}_n)$ for semi-AFL $\mathcal{L}_1, \ldots, \mathcal{L}_n$, $n \geqq 3$. Thus, by a simple induction, we have

Corollary 2: *If $\mathcal{L}_1, \ldots, \mathcal{L}_n$ are (full) principal* [*semi-*] *AFL, then so is $\mathcal{H}(\mathcal{L}_1 \wedge \ldots \wedge \mathcal{L}_n)$ $(\hat{\mathcal{H}}(\mathcal{L}_1 \wedge \ldots \wedge \mathcal{L}_n))$.*

By Theorem 3.6.1, $\mathcal{H}(\wedge\mathcal{L})$ $(\hat{\mathcal{H}}(\wedge\mathcal{L}))$ is a (full) AFL if $\mathcal{L}$ is a (full) AFL. As noted in Section 4.7, $\hat{\mathcal{H}}(\mathcal{L}_1 \wedge \mathcal{L}_2)$ is usually $\mathcal{L}_{RE}$ (and thus full principal) for AFL $\mathcal{L}_1$ and $\mathcal{L}_2$. Thus $\hat{\mathcal{H}}(\wedge\mathcal{L})$ is often $\mathcal{L}_{RE}$, and hence full principal, for an AFL $\mathcal{L}$. On the other hand, $\mathcal{H}(\wedge\mathcal{L})$ is not necessarily principal even if $\mathcal{L}$ is principal. For example, suppose that $\mathcal{L} = \mathcal{C}_1$. Then $\mathcal{L}$ is principal by Exercise 5.3.15. Let $\mathcal{L}_1 = \mathcal{C}_1$ and $\mathcal{L}_{n+1} = \mathcal{L}_n \wedge \mathcal{L}_1$ for each $n \geqq 1$.

Then $\mathcal{H}(\mathcal{L}_n) = \mathcal{C}_n$. As noted in Example 4.5.2, $\mathcal{C}_n \subsetneq \mathcal{C}_{n+1}$ for each n. Consequently, $\mathcal{H}(\wedge\mathcal{L}) = \bigcup_n \mathcal{H}(\mathcal{L}_n)$ is not principal by Lemma 5.1.2.

Open Question: Does there exist a principal (semi-) AFL $\mathcal{L}$ such that $\hat{\mathcal{H}}(\wedge\mathcal{L})$ is not a full principal semi-AFL?

Open Question: Do there exist two full principal AFL $\mathcal{L}_1$ and $\mathcal{L}_2$ such that $\mathcal{L}_1 \cap \mathcal{L}_2$ is not full principal?

EXERCISE 5.5.1: Prove that $\text{Shuf}(L_1 \cup L_2, L_1' \cup L_2') = \bigcup_{i,j \text{ in } \{1,2\}} \text{Shuf}(L_i, L_j')$.

EXERCISE 5.5.2: Verify (a) of Theorem 5.5.1 for the case when L_1 is ϵ-free and $L_2 = \{\epsilon\}$.

EXERCISE 5.5.3: Verify directly that if $L_1 \neq \emptyset$, $L_2 = \{\epsilon\}$, and c_1 and c_2 are new symbols, then $\mathcal{H}(\mathcal{F}(L_1) \wedge \mathcal{F}(L_2)) = \mathcal{F}(\text{Shuf}((L_1c_1)^+, (L_2c_2)^+))$.

Let $\text{Shuf}(\mathcal{L}_1, \mathcal{L}_2) = \{\text{Shuf}(L_1, L_2)/L_1 \text{ in } \mathcal{L}_1, L_2 \text{ in } \mathcal{L}_2\}$ for all families of languages $\mathcal{L}_1$ and $\mathcal{L}_2$.

EXERCISE 5.5.4: Show that $\text{Shuf}(\mathcal{L}_1, \mathcal{L}_2) = \text{Shuf}(\mathcal{L}_2, \mathcal{L}_1)$.

EXERCISE 5.5.5: Prove that $\text{Shuf}(\text{Shuf}(\mathcal{L}_1, \mathcal{L}_2), \mathcal{L}_3) = \text{Shuf}(\mathcal{L}_1, \text{Shuf}(\mathcal{L}_2, \mathcal{L}_3))$.

EXERCISE 5.5.6: Prove that a trio $\mathcal{L}$ is closed under intersection if and only if it is closed under Shuf, i.e., $\text{Shuf}(\mathcal{L}, \mathcal{L}) \subseteq \mathcal{L}$.

EXERCISE 5.5.7: Show that $\text{Shuf}(\mathcal{L}, \mathcal{R}) \subseteq \mathcal{L}$ for each trio $\mathcal{L}$.

EXERCISE 5.5.8: Prove that $\mathcal{M}(\mathcal{L}_1 \wedge \mathcal{L}_2) = \mathcal{M}(\text{Shuf}(\mathcal{L}_1, \mathcal{L}_2))$ for all trios $\mathcal{L}_1$ and $\mathcal{L}_2$.

EXERCISE 5.5.9: Show that $\mathcal{F}(\mathcal{L}_1 \wedge \mathcal{L}_2) \neq \mathcal{F}(\text{Shuf}(\mathcal{L}_1, \mathcal{L}_2))$ for $\mathcal{L}_1 = \mathcal{L}_{\text{CF}}$ and $\mathcal{L}_2 = \{\{a\}\}$. From this, infer that the hypothesis in Exercise 5.5.8 that $\mathcal{L}_1$ and $\mathcal{L}_2$ are trios cannot be arbitrarily removed.

EXERCISE 5.5.10: Prove that $\mathcal{L}_{\text{RE}} \cap \mathcal{L}_{\text{CRE}}$ is not principal, where $\mathcal{L}_{\text{CRE}} = \{L/\Sigma_L^* - L \text{ is in } \mathcal{L}_{\text{RE}}\}$ [Ui]. [This example shows that the intersection of principal AFL need not be principal.]

EXERCISE 5.5.11: Using Theorem 5.2.1, Theorem 4.6.1, and Lemma 4.5.1, prove that $\hat{\mathscr{H}}(\mathscr{L}_1 \wedge \mathscr{L}_2)$ is a full principal AFL if $\mathscr{L}_1$ and $\mathscr{L}_2$ are full principal AFL.

EXERCISE 5.5.12: Using Exercise 4.6.5, show that $\mathscr{H}(\wedge \mathscr{L}_{CF})$ is principal.

(+)5.6 Some Nonprincipal (Semi-)AFL

We have already given some examples of (semi-)AFL which are either not principal or not full principal. Here we present three full (semi-)AFL which are not (full) principal. To avoid straying too far from our main development, we shall just establish the key points in the argument, leaving the proofs of auxiliary results as exercises.

We now introduce the notion of a "semilinear set of type p". This concept will play a major role in our discussion.

Def: A linear subset A of N^q is said to be of *type* p, $p \geqq 0$, if there exist elements $v, v_1, \ldots, v_m$ in N^q such that each v_i has at most p nonzero coordinates and such that $A = \left\{ v + \sum_{i=1}^{m} k_i v_i / \text{each } k_i \text{ in } N \right\}$. A semilinear set is said to be of *type* p if it can be represented as a finite union of linear sets, each of type p.

Note that in the above definition, v may have more than p nonzero coordinates.

EXAMPLE 5.6.1: Let $p_1 = (2, 3, 0, 4)$, $p_2 = (0, 2, 1, 0)$, $p_3 = (1, 0, 1, 0)$, $p_4 = (0, 1, 1, 6)$, and $p_5 = (1, 1, 0, 0)$. Let $A = \left\{ (1, 2, 3, 2) + \sum_{i=1}^{4} k_i p_i / \text{each } k_i \text{ in } N \right\}$ and $B = \{(2, 2, 3, 0) + k(1, 1, 0, 0)/k \text{ in } N\}$. Then $A \cup B$ is semilinear of type 3.

We summarize a number of elementary facts about subsets of type p.

LEMMA 5.6.1:

(a) *If A is a semilinear set of type p, then A is also of type p' for every $p' \geqq p$.*

(b) *A semilinear set is of type 0 if and only if it is finite.*

(c) *Each semilinear subset of N^q is of type q.*

(d) *If A and B are semilinear subsets of N^q of type p, then so are $A \cup B$ and $A + B = \{x + y / x \text{ in } A, y \text{ in } B\}$.*

Notation: In this section $a_1, \ldots, a_q$ denote distinct symbols of Σ.

Def: A language $L \subseteq a_1^* \ldots a_q^*$ is said to be *linear*, *semilinear*, or *semilinear of type p*, respectively, if[1] $\psi(L)$ is linear, semilinear, or semilinear of type p, resp.

It is known [GS2] that a language $L \subseteq a_1^* \ldots a_q^*$ is regular if and only if it is semilinear of type 1.

It is known [Gi] that a context-free subset of $a_1^* \ldots a_q^*$ is semilinear of type 2.

From Lemma 5.6.1, there immediately follows:

LEMMA 5.6.2:

(a) *If $A \subseteq a_1^* \ldots a_q^*$ and $B \subseteq a_1^* \ldots a_q^*$ are semilinear languages of type p, then $A \cup B$ is semilinear of type p.*

(b) *If $AB \subseteq a_1^* \ldots a_q^*$ and if A, B are semilinear of type p, then AB is semilinear of type p.*

Def: For each $n \geqq 1$ and each function ϱ from $\{1, \ldots, n\}$ into $\{1, R\}$, let $\mathcal{R}_\varrho$, called the *homomorphic replication of $\mathcal{R}$ of type ϱ*, be the family of all languages of the form

$$\{h_1^{\varrho(1)}(w) \ldots h_n^{\varrho(n)}(w)/w \text{ in } U\},$$

where U is in $\mathcal{R}$, there exist Σ_2 and homomorphisms $h_1, \ldots, h_n$ from Σ_U^* into Σ_2^*, and $h_i^{\varrho(i)}(w) = (h_i(w))^{\varrho(i)}$ for each i.

Thus the purpose of ϱ is to indicate whether the i-th homomorphic image of a word is reversed or not.

EXAMPLE 5.6.2: Let $\varrho(1) = 1$ and $\varrho(2) = R$. Then $\mathcal{R}_\varrho$ is the family of all languages of the form $\{h_1(w)(h_2(w))^R/w \text{ in } U\}$, where U is in $\mathcal{R}$ and h_1 and h_2 are homomorphisms on Σ_U^*.

We shall first show that $\bigcup_\varrho \hat{\mathcal{O}}(\mathcal{R}_\varrho) = \hat{\mathcal{O}}\left(\bigcup_\varrho \mathcal{R}_\varrho\right)$, $\mathcal{O} = \mathcal{S}$ or $\mathcal{F}$,[2] and is not (full) principal. To do this we shall need three lemmas. The first asserts that for ϱ a function from $\{1, \ldots, n\}$ into $\{1, R\}$, each language in $\mathcal{R}_\varrho$ which is a subset of $a_1^* \ldots a_q^*$ for some $q \geqq 1$ is semilinear of type n. The second lemma extends the first to languages in $\hat{\mathcal{F}}(\mathcal{R}_\varrho)$. The third asserts that a certain semilinear language of type $n+1$ is not in $\hat{\mathcal{F}}(\mathcal{R}_\varrho)$.

[1] ψ is the Parikh mapping from $a_1^* \ldots a_q^*$ into N^q. See Section 1.2.

[2] Actually, $\hat{\mathcal{S}}(\mathcal{R}_\varrho) = \mathcal{R}_\varrho$, a fact noted in Exercise 5.6.11.

LEMMA 5.6.3: *Each language in* $\mathcal{R}_\varrho$ *which is a subset of* $a_1^*\ldots a_q^*$ *for some* $q \geqq 1$ *is semilinear of type* n, *where* ϱ *is defined from* $\{1, \ldots, n\}$ *into* $\{1, R\}$

Proof: Let U be a regular set and let $h_1, \ldots, h_n$ be homomorphisms from Σ_U^* into $\{a_1, \ldots, a_q\}^*$. For each $L \subseteq \Sigma_U^*$ let $L_\varrho = \{h_1^{\varrho(1)}(w)\ldots h_n^{\varrho(n)}(w)/w \text{ in } L\}$. Suppose that $U_\varrho \subseteq a_1^*\ldots a_q^*$. We shall show that U_ϱ is semilinear of type n.

To do this, we examine ϱ when applied to the union, concatenation, and $*$ of certain semilinear languages of type n. Specifically, we consider four cases.

(a) Suppose $L \subseteq \Sigma_U^*$ is finite and $L_\varrho \subseteq a_1^*\ldots a_q^*$. Then L_ϱ is finite. Hence L_ϱ is of type 0, and thus of type n.

(b) Suppose that $L \subseteq \Sigma_U^*$, $L_1 \subseteq \Sigma_U^*$, and $(L \cup L_1)_\varrho \subseteq a_1^*\ldots a_q^*$. Then $L_\varrho \subseteq a_1^*\ldots a_q^*$ and $L_{1\varrho} \subseteq a_1^*\ldots a_q^*$ since $L_\varrho \cup L_{1\varrho} = (L \cup L_1)_\varrho$. Furthermore, if L_ϱ and $L_{1\varrho}$ are semilinear of type n, then $L_\varrho \cup L_{1\varrho} = (L \cup L_1)_\varrho$ is semilinear of type n.

(c) Suppose $L \subseteq \Sigma_U^*$, $L_1 \subseteq \Sigma_U^*$, and $(LL_1)_\varrho \subseteq a_1^*\ldots a_q^*$. Then $L_\varrho \subseteq a_1^*\ldots a_q^*$ and $L_{1\varrho} \subseteq a_1^*\ldots a_q^*$. [For let w be in L and w_1 in L_1. Then $h_1^{\varrho(1)}(w)\ldots h_n^{\varrho(n)}(w)$ is in L_ϱ and $h_1^{\varrho(1)}(w_1)\ldots h_n^{\varrho(n)}(w_1)$ is in $L_{1\varrho}$. Now $h_1^{\varrho(1)}(ww_1)\ldots h_n^{\varrho(n)}(ww_1)$ is in $a_1^*\ldots a_q^*$ and, for each i, $h_i(ww_1) = h_i(w)\,h_i(w_1)$ and $(h_i(ww_1))^R = (h_i(w_1))^R (h_i(w))^R$. Therefore $h_1^{\varrho(1)}(w)\ldots h_n^{\varrho(n)}(w)$ is in $a_1^*\ldots a_q^*$ and $h_1^{\varrho(1)}(w_1)\ldots h_n^{\varrho(n)}(w_1)$ is in $a_1^*\ldots a_q^*$.] Furthermore, suppose L_ϱ and $L_{1\varrho}$ are semilinear languages of type n. Then $(LL_1)_\varrho$ is also semilinear of type n because $\psi((LL_1)_\varrho) = \psi(L_\varrho)+\psi(L_{1\varrho})$.

(d) Suppose $L \subseteq \Sigma_U^*$ and $(L^*)_\varrho \subseteq a_1^*\ldots a_q^*$. Then $L_\varrho \subseteq a_1^*\ldots a_q^*$. Assume there exist words w in L and y in L and integers i, s_1, and s_2, $s_1 < s_2$, such that $h_i^{\varrho(i)}(w)$ contains an occurrence of a_{s_1} and $h_i^{\varrho(i)}(y)$ an occurrence of a_{s_2}. Thus $h_1^{\varrho(1)}(yw)\ldots h_n^{\varrho(n)}(yw)$ is not in $a_1^*\ldots a_q^*$. Since y and w are in L, $h_1^{\varrho(1)}(yw)\ldots h_n^{\varrho(n)}(yw)$ is in $(L^*)_\varrho \subseteq a_1^*\ldots a_q^*$, a contradiction. Hence for each i there exists p_i, $1 \leqq p_i \leqq q$, such that $h_i(L) \subseteq a_{p_i}^*$, whence $h_i(L^*) \subseteq a_{p_i}^*$. Clearly $1 \leqq p_1 \leqq \ldots \leqq p_n \leqq q$. Thus the only coordinates in each vector of $\psi((L^*)_\varrho)$ which can be nonzero are $p_1, \ldots, p_n$. Now suppose that L_ϱ is semilinear. Obviously L_ϱ must be of type n. Then $(L^*)_\varrho$ is linear. [To see this let $L_\varrho = A_1 \cup \ldots \cup A_t$, where each A_i is linear. For each i let w_i, v_{i1}, $\ldots, v_{im(i)}$ be elements of N^q such that $A_i = \{w_i+k_1v_{i1}+\ldots+k_{m(i)}v_{im(i)}/\text{each } k_i \text{ in } N\}$. Let $\{y_1, \ldots, y_s\} = \{w_i, v_{i1}, \ldots, v_{im(i)}/1 \leqq i \leqq t\}$. Then $\psi((L^*)_\varrho) = \{(0, \ldots, 0)+k_1y_1+\ldots+k_sy_s/\text{each } k_i \text{ in } N\}$.] Since each vector in $\psi((L^*)_\varrho)$ can only have the $p_1, \ldots, p_n$ coordinates nonzero, $(L^*)_\varrho$ is of type n.

Now consider the regular set U. Since U is regular, there exist s and a sequence of sets $U_1, \ldots, U_s$ such that $U_s = U$, each U_i is either a finite subset of Σ_U^* or is obtained from the sets $U_1, \ldots, U_{i-1}$ by one application of union, concatenation, or $*$. Since $U_\varrho \subseteq a_1^* \ldots a_q^*$, we may assume by (a)–(d) that $(U_i)_\varrho \subseteq a_1^* \ldots a_q^*$ for each i. By (a), each finite $(U_i)_\varrho$ is semilinear of type n. By (b), (c), and (d), $(U_i)_\varrho$ is semilinear of type n for each i. Hence U_ϱ is semilinear of type n and the lemma is proved.

LEMMA 5.6.4: *Each language in $\hat{\mathcal{F}}(\mathcal{R}_\varrho)$ which is a subset of $a_1^* \ldots a_q^*$ for some $q \geqq 1$ is semilinear of type n, where ϱ is defined from $\{1, \ldots, n\}$ into $\{1, R\}$.*

Proof: By Exercise 5.6.11, $\mathcal{R}_\varrho$ is a full semi-AFL. Thus $\hat{\mathcal{F}}(\mathcal{R}_\varrho) = \hat{\text{Sub}}(\mathcal{R}_0, \mathcal{R}_\varrho)$, i.e., $\hat{\mathcal{F}}(\mathcal{R}_\varrho)$ is obtained from the languages of $\mathcal{R}_\varrho$ by closure under union, concatenation, and $+$. Hence we consider three cases.

(a) If $L_1 \cup L_2 \subseteq a_1^* \ldots a_q^*$, then $L_1 \subseteq a_1^* \ldots a_q^*$ and $L_2 \subseteq a_1^* \ldots a_q^*$. Furthermore, if L_1 and L_2 are semilinear languages of type n, then so is $L_1 \cup L_2$.

(b) If $L_1L_2 \subseteq a_1^* \ldots a_q^*$, then $L_1 \subseteq a_1^* \ldots a_q^*$ and $L_2 \subseteq a_1^* \ldots a_q^*$. Furthermore, if L_1 and L_2 are semilinear languages of type n, then so is L_1L_2.

(c) If $L^+ \subseteq a_1^* \ldots a_q^*$, then $L \subseteq a_i^*$ for some i. Furthermore, if L is semilinear, then L^+ is semilinear and of type 1.

It follows from (a), (b), and (c) that the languages in $\hat{\mathcal{F}}(\mathcal{R}_\varrho)$ contained in $a_1^* \ldots a_q^*$ are generated from the languages in $\mathcal{R}_\varrho$ contained in $a_1^* \ldots a_q^*$ by union, concatenation, and $+$. By Lemma 5.6.3, the languages in $\mathcal{R}_\varrho$ contained in $a_1^* \ldots a_q^*$ are semilinear of type n. By (a), (b), and (c), it then follows that each language in $\hat{\mathcal{F}}(\mathcal{R}_\varrho)$ contained in $a_1^* \ldots a_q^*$ is semilinear of type n.

LEMMA 5.6.5: *Let ϱ be a function from $\{1, \ldots, n\}$ into $\{1, R\}$. Then $\{a_1^t \ldots a_{n+1}^t / t \geqq 0\}$ is a semilinear language of type $n+1$ which is not in $\hat{\mathcal{F}}(\mathcal{R}_\varrho)$.*

Proof: Obviously $L_0 = \{a_1^t \ldots a_{n+1}^t / t \geqq 0\}$ is semilinear of type $n+1$. By Lemma 5.6.4, each language in $\hat{\mathcal{F}}(\mathcal{R}_\varrho)$ contained in $a_1^* \ldots a_q^*$ for some $q \geqq 1$, is semilinear of type n. To complete the proof, it suffices to show that L_0 is not semilinear of type n.

Suppose the contrary, i.e., L_0 is of type n. Then $A = \psi(L_0)$ is of type n. Hence $A = A_1 \cup \ldots \cup A_r$ for linear sets $A_1, \ldots, A_r$, each A_i a linear set of type n. Since A is infinite and r is finite, there exists an integer s such that A_s is infinite. Let $A_s = \{x/x = v + k_1v_1 + \ldots + k_mv_m$, each k_i in $N\}$, each v_i with at most n nonzero coordinates. Since A_s is infinite, we may assume that $v_1 \neq (0, \ldots, 0)$. Then $v + v_1 \neq v + 2v_1$. Since v_1 has at most n nonzero coordinates, there exists an integer i such that the i-th coordinate of v_1 is 0.

Then $v+v_1$ and $v+2v_1$ have the same i-th coordinate. Since $v+v_1 = (t_1, \ldots, t_1)$ and $v+2v_1 = (t_2, \ldots, t_2)$ for some t_1 and t_2, it follows that $t_1 = t_2$. Thus $v+v_1 = v+2v_1$, a contradiction.

We are now ready to show that $\hat{\mathcal{S}}\left(\bigcup_\varrho \mathcal{R}_\varrho\right)$ and $\hat{\mathcal{F}}\left(\bigcup_\varrho \mathcal{R}_\varrho\right)$ are not (full) principal.

THEOREM 5.6.1: *For* $\mathcal{O} = \mathcal{S}$ *or* $\mathcal{F}$, $\hat{\mathcal{O}}\left(\bigcup_\varrho \mathcal{R}_\varrho\right) = \bigcup_\varrho \hat{\mathcal{O}}(\mathcal{R}_\varrho)$ *and is not (full) principal.*

Proof: Since $\hat{\mathcal{O}}(\mathcal{R}_\varrho) \subseteq \hat{\mathcal{O}}\left(\bigcup_\varrho \mathcal{R}_\varrho\right)$ for each ϱ, $\bigcup_\varrho \hat{\mathcal{O}}(\mathcal{R}_\varrho) \subseteq \hat{\mathcal{O}}\left(\bigcup_\varrho \mathcal{R}_\varrho\right)$. To demonstrate the reverse containment, it suffices to show that

($*$) given ϱ_1 and ϱ_2, there exists ϱ_3 such that $\hat{\mathcal{O}}(\mathcal{R}_{\varrho_1}) \cup \hat{\mathcal{O}}(\mathcal{R}_{\varrho_2}) \subseteq \hat{\mathcal{O}}(\mathcal{R}_{\varrho_3})$.

For assume that ($*$) holds. Clearly $\bigcup_\varrho \hat{\mathcal{O}}(\mathcal{R}_\varrho)$ is closed under intersection with regular sets, homomorphism, inverse homomorphism, and, for $\mathcal{O} = \mathcal{F}$, +. Let L_1 and L_2 be arbitrary languages in $\bigcup_\varrho \hat{\mathcal{O}}(\mathcal{R}_\varrho)$. Then L_1 is in $\hat{\mathcal{O}}(\mathcal{R}_{\varrho_1})$ and L_2 is in $\hat{\mathcal{O}}(\mathcal{R}_{\varrho_2})$ for some ϱ_1 and ϱ_2. By ($*$), there exists ϱ_3 such that $\hat{\mathcal{O}}(\mathcal{R}_{\varrho_1}) \cup \hat{\mathcal{O}}(\mathcal{R}_{\varrho_2}) \subseteq \hat{\mathcal{O}}(\mathcal{R}_{\varrho_3})$. Thus L_1 and L_2 are in $\hat{\mathcal{O}}(\mathcal{R}_{\varrho_3})$. Then $L_1 \cup L_2$ is in $\hat{\mathcal{O}}(\mathcal{R}_{\varrho_3})$, hence in $\bigcup_\varrho \hat{\mathcal{O}}(\mathcal{R}_\varrho)$. Therefore $\bigcup_\varrho \hat{\mathcal{O}}(\mathcal{R}_\varrho)$ is a full (semi-)AFL. Since $\bigcup_\varrho \mathcal{R}_\varrho \subseteq \bigcup_\varrho \hat{\mathcal{O}}(\mathcal{R}_\varrho)$, $\hat{\mathcal{O}}\left(\bigcup_\varrho \mathcal{R}_\varrho\right) \subseteq \bigcup_\varrho \hat{\mathcal{O}}(\mathcal{R}_\varrho)$.

Suppose ϱ_1 is defined on $\{1, \ldots, n\}$ and ϱ_2 on $\{1, \ldots, m\}$. Let ϱ_3 be defined on $\{1, \ldots, n+m\}$ by $\varrho_3(i) = \varrho_1(i)$ for $1 \leqq i \leqq n$ and $\varrho_3(i) = \varrho_2(i-n)$ for $n+1 \leqq i \leqq n+m$. Clearly $\mathcal{R}_{\varrho_1} \cup \mathcal{R}_{\varrho_2} \subseteq \mathcal{R}_{\varrho_3}$, so that

$$\hat{\mathcal{O}}(\mathcal{R}_{\varrho_1}) \cup \hat{\mathcal{O}}(\mathcal{R}_{\varrho_2}) \subseteq \hat{\mathcal{O}}(\mathcal{R}_{\varrho_1} \cup \mathcal{R}_{\varrho_2}) \subseteq \hat{\mathcal{O}}(\mathcal{R}_{\varrho_3}).$$

It remains to show that $\bigcup_\varrho \hat{\mathcal{O}}(\mathcal{R}_\varrho)$ is not (full) principal. Since $\bigcup_\varrho \hat{\mathcal{O}}(\mathcal{R}_\varrho)$ is a full (semi-) AFL, it suffices to show that $\bigcup_\varrho \hat{\mathcal{O}}(\mathcal{R}_\varrho)$ is not full principal. Thus let L be an arbitrary language in $\bigcup_\varrho \hat{\mathcal{O}}(\mathcal{R}_\varrho)$. Then L is in $\hat{\mathcal{O}}(\mathcal{R}_{\varrho_0})$ for some ϱ_0. Let ϱ_0 be defined from $\{1, \ldots, n\}$ into $\{1, R\}$. By Lemma 5.6.5, $L_0 = \{a_1^t \ldots a_{n+1}^t / t \geqq 0\}$ is a semilinear language of type $n+1$ which is not in $\hat{\mathcal{O}}(\mathcal{R}_{\varrho_0})$. Obviously L_0 is in $\bigcup_\varrho \hat{\mathcal{O}}(\mathcal{R}_\varrho)$. Hence $\hat{\mathcal{O}}(L) \subseteq \hat{\mathcal{O}}(\mathcal{R}_{\varrho_0}) \subsetneqq \bigcup_\varrho \hat{\mathcal{O}}(\mathcal{R}_\varrho)$, so that $\bigcup_\varrho \hat{\mathcal{O}}(\mathcal{R}_\varrho)$ is not full principal.

We now exhibit another full (semi-) AFL which is not (full) principal.

THEOREM 5.6.2: *For* $\mathcal{O} = \mathcal{S}$ *or* $\mathcal{F}$, $\hat{\mathcal{O}}(\mathcal{L}_{SL})$ *is not (full) principal, where* $\mathcal{L}_{SL}$ *is the family of all semilinear languages contained in* $a_1^* \dots a_q^*$ *for some* $q \geqq 1$.

Proof: We first show that

$$(*) \qquad \mathcal{L}_{SL} \subseteq \bigcup_{\varrho} \mathcal{R}_{\varrho}.$$

Thus let L be a semilinear language contained in $a_1^* \dots a_q^*$ for some $q \geqq 1$ and let ϱ be the function on $\{1, \dots, q\}$ defined by $\varrho(i) = 1$ for each i. To show $(*)$ it suffices to verify that

$$(**) \qquad L \text{ is in } \mathcal{R}_{\varrho}.$$

Let $A = \psi(L)$. Note that $\mathcal{R}_{\varrho}$ is closed under union. [Let L_1 and L_2 be in $\mathcal{R}_{\varrho}$. Then there exist L_3 and L_4 in $\mathcal{R}$, $\Sigma_{L_3} \cap \Sigma_{L_4} = \emptyset$, homomorphisms $h_{31}, \dots, h_{3q}$ on $\Sigma_{L_3}^*$, and homomorphisms $h_{41}, \dots, h_{4q}$ on $\Sigma_{L_4}^*$ such that $L_1 = \{h_{31}^{\varrho(1)}(w) \dots h_{3q}^{\varrho(q)}(w)/w \text{ in } L_3\}$ and $L_2 = \{h_{41}^{\varrho(1)}(w) \dots h_{4q}^{\varrho(q)}(w)/w \text{ in } L_4\}$. Let $h_{11}, \dots, h_{1q}$ be the homomorphisms on $(\Sigma_{L_3} \cup \Sigma_{L_4})^*$ defined by $h_{1i}(a) = h_{3i}(a)$ for each a in Σ_{L_3} and $h_{1i}(a) = h_{4i}(a)$ for each a in Σ_{L_4}, $1 \leqq i \leqq q$. Then $L_3 \cup L_4$ is in $\mathcal{R}$ and $L_1 \cup L_2 = \{h_{11}^{\varrho(1)}(w) \dots h_{1q}^{\varrho(q)}(w)/w \text{ in } L_3 \cup L_4\}$. Thus $L_1 \cup L_2$ is in $\mathcal{R}_{\varrho}$.] Hence, without loss of generality, we may assume that L is linear. Then $A = \left\{w + \sum_{i=1}^{s} k_i v_i / \text{each } k_i \text{ in } N\right\}$ for some $w, v_1, \dots, v_s$ in N^q. Let $w = (w_1, \dots, w_q)$ and $v_i = (v_{i1}, \dots, v_{iq})$ for each i. Let $b, b_1, \dots, b_s$ be new symbols and $U = bb_1^* \dots b_s^*$. For each j, $1 \leqq j \leqq q$, let h_j be the homomorphism on $\{b, b_1, \dots, b_s\}^*$ defined by $h_j(b) = a_j^{w_j}$ and $h_j(b_i) = a_j^{v_{ij}}$ for each i, $1 \leqq i \leqq s$. Then $L = \{h_1^{\varrho(1)}(w) \dots h_q^{\varrho(q)}(w)/w \text{ in } U\}$ is in $\mathcal{R}_{\varrho}$, so that $(**)$ holds.

Now let L be in $\hat{\mathcal{O}}(\mathcal{L}_{SL})$. Then L is in $\bigcup_{\varrho} \hat{\mathcal{O}}(\mathcal{R}_{\varrho})$, so that L is in $\hat{\mathcal{O}}(\mathcal{R}_{\varrho})$ for some ϱ, ϱ a function from $\{1, \dots, q\}$ into $\{1, R\}$. Let $L_0 = \{a_1^t \dots a_{q+1}^t / t \geqq 0\}$. By Lemma 5.6.5, L_0 is not in $\hat{\mathcal{F}}(\mathcal{R}_{\varrho})$. Therefore L_0 is neither in $\mathcal{F}(L)$ nor in $\hat{\mathcal{F}}(L)$. Obviously L_0 is in $\mathcal{L}_{SL}$. Thus $\mathcal{O}(L) \neq \hat{\mathcal{O}}(\mathcal{L}_{SL})$ and $\hat{\mathcal{O}}(L) \neq \hat{\mathcal{O}}(\mathcal{L}_{SL})$. Since L is an arbitrary element of $\hat{\mathcal{O}}(\mathcal{L}_{SL})$, $\hat{\mathcal{O}}(\mathcal{L}_{SL})$ is not (full) principal.

By a modification of the above argument, we get:

THEOREM 5.6.3: *For* $\mathcal{O} = \mathcal{S}$ *or* $\mathcal{F}$, $\hat{\mathcal{O}}(\mathcal{L})$ *is not (full) principal, where* $\mathcal{L}$ *is the family of all languages of the form* $\{a_1^t \dots a_q^t / t \geqq 0\}$, *with* $q \geqq 1$.

EXERCISE 5.6.1: Prove (a) of Lemma 5.6.1.

EXERCISE 5.6.2: Prove (b) of Lemma 5.6.1.

EXERCISE 5.6.3: Prove (c) of Lemma 5.6.1.

EXERCISE 5.6.4: Prove (d) of Lemma 5.6.1.

EXERCISE 5.6.5: Write $\mathcal{R}_\varrho$ when
(a) $\varrho(1) = R$, $\varrho(2) = 1$, and $\varrho(3) = R$.
(b) $\varrho(1) = 1$, $\varrho(2) = 1$, $\varrho(3) = R$, and $\varrho(4) = R$.

EXERCISE 5.6.6: Prove Theorem 5.6.3.

The following terminology is used in Exercises 5.6.7–5.6.20. For each family $\mathcal{L}$, $n \geqq 1$, and function ϱ from $\{1, \ldots, n\}$ into $\{1, R\}$, let $\mathcal{L}_\varrho$ be the family of all languages of the form $\{(h_1(w))^{\varrho(1)} \ldots (h_n(w))^{\varrho(n)}/w \text{ in } L\}$, where L is in $\mathcal{L}$ and $h_1, \ldots, h_n$ are homomorphisms on Σ_L^*. Let $\mathcal{O} = \mathcal{S}$ or $\mathcal{F}$.

In Exercises 5.6.7–5.6.15 let $\mathcal{L}$ be a full slip (semi-)AFL,[1] $n \geqq 1$, and ϱ be a function from $\{1, \ldots, n\}$ into $\{1, R\}$.

EXERCISE 5.6.7: Prove that $\mathcal{L}_\varrho$ is a slip family [GS6].

EXERCISE 5.6.8: Prove that $\mathcal{L}_\varrho$ is closed under union [GS6].

(*) EXERCISE 5.6.9: Prove that $\mathcal{L}_\varrho$ is closed under intersection with regular sets [GS6].

EXERCISE 5.6.10: Prove that Sûb $(\mathcal{L}_\varrho, \mathcal{R}) \subseteq \mathcal{L}_\varrho$ [GS6].

EXERCISE 5.6.11: Prove that $\mathcal{L}_\varrho$ is a full semi-AFL. [Hint: Use Exercises 5.6.8, 5.6.9, and 5.6.10, in conjunction with Proposition 3.7.1.]

EXERCISE 5.6.12: For $n \geqq 1$, prove that $\mathcal{L}_\varrho$ cannot be an AFL.

EXERCISE 5.6.13: Show that $\mathcal{F}(\mathcal{L}_\varrho) = \hat{\mathcal{F}}(\mathcal{L}_\varrho)$ [GS6].

EXERCISE 5.6.14: Show that $\mathcal{F}(\mathcal{L}_\varrho)$ is a full slip AFL [GS6].

EXERCISE 5.6.15: Prove that $\bigcup_\varrho \mathcal{O}(\mathcal{L}_\varrho)$ is a full slip (semi-)AFL [GS6].

(*)EXERCISE 5.6.16: Suppose $\mathcal{L} = \hat{\mathcal{F}}(L_0)$, and b, c, and d are three symbols not in Σ_{L_0}. Let τ be the substitution on $2^{(\Sigma_{L_0} \cup \{d\})^*}$ defined by $\tau(a) = \{b, c\}^* a$

[1] A *slip (semi-)AFL* is a slip family (see Exercise 3.3.2) which is a (semi-)AFL.

$\{b, c\}^*$ for each a in $\Sigma_{L_0} \cup \{d\}$. Let $n \geqq 1$ and let ϱ be a function from $\{1, \ldots, n\}$ into $\{1, R\}$. Let $\varphi_1, \ldots, \varphi_n$ be the homomorphisms from $(\Sigma_{L_0} \cup \{b, c, d\})^*$ into $((\Sigma_{L_0} \cup \{b, c, d\}) \times \{1, \ldots, n\})^*$ defined by $\varphi_i(a) = (a, i)$ for all a in $\Sigma_{L_0} \cup \{b, c, d\}$ and all i. Prove [GS6] that $\hat{\mathscr{F}}(\mathscr{L}_\varrho) = \hat{\mathscr{F}}(L_1)$, where

$$L_1 = \{(\varphi_1(w))^{\varrho(1)} \ldots (\varphi_n(w))^{\varrho(n)}/w \text{ in } \tau((L_0 d)^*)\}.$$

In Exercises 5.6.17–5.6.20, $\mathscr{L}$ denotes $\mathscr{L}_{CF}$.

EXERCISE 5.6.17: Given positive integers n and q, a language L is said to have *property* $P(n, q)$ if each word w in L, $|w| > n$, is of the form $w = x_1 y_1 \ldots x_{2q} y_{2q} x_{2q+1}$, where each x_i and y_j is in Σ_L^*, $y_1 \ldots y_{2q} \neq \epsilon$, $|y_i| \leqq n$ for each i, and $x_1 y_1^m x_2 \ldots x_{2q} y_{2q}^m x_{2q+1}$ is in L for each $m \geqq 1$. Let ϱ be a function from $\{1, \ldots, q\}$ into $\{1, R\}$. Prove the following [Ib3]:

(a) Each L in $\mathscr{L}_\varrho$ has property $P(n, q)$ for some n. [Hint: Use the Bar-Hillel, Perles, and Shamir Lemma.]

(b) Each L in $\hat{\mathscr{F}}(\mathscr{L}_\varrho)$ has property $P(n, q)$ for some n. [Hint: Use (a).]

EXERCISE 5.6.18: For each $q \geqq 1$ and function ϱ from $\{1, \ldots, q\}$ into $\{1, R\}$, prove that $\{a_1^m \ldots a_{2q+1}^m / m \geqq 1\}$ is not in $\hat{\mathscr{F}}(\mathscr{L}_\varrho)$ [Ib3].

EXERCISE 5.6.19: For each $q \geqq 1$ let ϱ_q be the function from $\{1, \ldots, q\}$ into $\{1, R\}$ defined by $\varrho_q(i) = 1$ for each i. Prove that $\bigcup_{q \geqq 1} \hat{\mathscr{O}}(\mathscr{L}_{\varrho_q})$ is a full (semi-) AFL which is not full principal [Ib3].

EXERCISE 5.6.20: Prove that $\bigcup_{\varrho} \hat{\mathscr{O}}(\mathscr{L}_\varrho)$ is a full (semi-)AFL which is not full principal [Ib3].

5.7 Historical References

The initial paper on principal AFL was [GGr2].[1] It contained the material in Sections 5.1, 5.2, and 5.5, as well as Theorems 5.4.1 and 5.4.2. The coinage of the term "finitely encoded" was in [Gr4]. Theorem 5.4.3 and the contents of Section 5.3 are in [GGr3]. The results of Section 5.6 are in [GS6].

[1] Although [We] was published first, it was written after, and in response to a question raised in, [GGr2].

CHAPTER 6

SUBSTITUTION

In Section 3.3 we briefly discussed substitution in connection with families of languages. We now return to this topic and devote the present chapter to its study. In particular, we shall see that Sub $(\mathcal{L}_1, \mathcal{L}_2)$ (Sûb $(\mathcal{L}_1, \mathcal{L}_2)$) is a (full) [semi-]AFL if $\mathcal{L}_1$ and $\mathcal{L}_2$ are, and give an AFA representation for it. In case $\mathcal{L}_1$ and $\mathcal{L}_2$ are (full) principal, Sub $(\mathcal{L}_1, \mathcal{L}_2)$ (Sûb $(\mathcal{L}_1, \mathcal{L}_2)$) is also (full) principal and a (full) generator for it is exhibited in terms of the (full) generators for $\mathcal{L}_1$ and $\mathcal{L}_2$. Several notions of substitution closure are examined and shown to coincide for structures of interest. The chapter concludes with a consideration of substitution-closed full principal AFL.

6.1 Substitution of (Semi-)AFL

We now consider the substitution of one (semi-) AFL into another (semi-) AFL. We shall prove the important fact that the resulting family of languages is also a (semi-) AFL.

In order to establish the above result we need a lemma asserting that under a certain mild condition, substitution is an "associative" operation.

Def: A family $\mathcal{L}$ of languages is said to be *symmetric* if $h(L)$ is in $\mathcal{L}$ for each L in $\mathcal{L}$ and each one-to-one, length-preserving homomorphism h from Σ_L^* into Σ^*.

In particular, each trio is a symmetric family of languages.

LEMMA 6.1.1: *Let $\mathcal{L}_1$, $\mathcal{L}_2$, and $\mathcal{L}_3$ be families of languages, with $\mathcal{L}_2$ symmetric. Then*

(a) *Sub $(\mathcal{L}_1$, Sub $(\mathcal{L}_2, \mathcal{L}_3))$ = Sub (Sub $(\mathcal{L}_1, \mathcal{L}_2), \mathcal{L}_3)$ and*
(b) *Sûb $(\mathcal{L}_1$, Sûb $(\mathcal{L}_2, \mathcal{L}_3))$ = Sûb (Sûb $(\mathcal{L}_1, \mathcal{L}_2), \mathcal{L}_3)$.*

Proof: We shall present the argument for (b), the one for (a) being similar.

Given L_1 in $\mathcal{L}_1$, let τ_2 be a substitution of L_1 by languages in $\mathcal{L}_2$ and τ_3 a substitution of $\tau_2(L_1)$ by languages in $\mathcal{L}_3$. Then $\tau_3(\tau_2(L_1)) = \tau'(L_1)$, where τ' is the substitution such that $\tau'(a) = \tau_3(\tau_2(a))$ for each a in Σ_{L_1}. Since $\tau_2(a)$ is in $\mathscr{L}_2$ and τ_3 is a substitution by languages in $\mathscr{L}_3$, $\tau_3(\tau_2(a))$ is in $\hat{\text{Sub}}(\mathscr{L}_2, \mathscr{L}_3)$. Therefore τ' is a substitution by languages in $\hat{\text{Sub}}(\mathscr{L}_2, \mathscr{L}_3)$, so that

$$\hat{\text{Sub}}(\hat{\text{Sub}}(\mathscr{L}_1, \mathscr{L}_2), \mathscr{L}_3) \subseteq \hat{\text{Sub}}(\mathscr{L}_1, \hat{\text{Sub}}(\mathscr{L}_2, \mathscr{L}_3)).$$

To see the reverse inclusion, let L_1 be in $\mathscr{L}_1$ and τ' a substitution of L_1 by languages in $\hat{\text{Sub}}(\mathscr{L}_2, \mathscr{L}_3)$. Then for each a in Σ_{L_1}, $\tau'(a) = \tau_{3,a}(L_{2,a})$, where $L_{2,a}$ is in $\mathscr{L}_2$ and $\tau_{3,a}$ is a substitution on $\Sigma^*_{L_{2,a}}$ by languages in $\mathscr{L}_3$. Since $\mathscr{L}_2$ is symmetric and Σ is infinite, we may assume that

$$(*) \qquad \Sigma_{L_{2,a}} \cap \Sigma_{L_{2,a'}} = \emptyset \quad \text{for all } a \text{ and } a',\ a \neq a'.$$

Let $\Sigma_4 = \bigcup_a \Sigma_{L_{2,a}}$. Let τ_3 be the substitution on Σ_4^* defined by $\tau_3(b) = \tau_{3,a}(b)$ for each a in Σ_{L_1} and b in $\Sigma_{L_{2,a}}$. By $(*)$, τ_3 is uniquely defined. Let τ_2 be the substitution of L_1 by languages in $\mathscr{L}_2$ defined by $\tau_2(a) = L_{2,a}$ for each a in Σ_{L_1}. Then $\tau'(L_1) = \tau_3\tau_2(L_1)$. Thus $\tau'(L_1)$ is in $\hat{\text{Sub}}(\hat{\text{Sub}}(\mathscr{L}_1, \mathscr{L}_2), \mathscr{L}_3)$. Therefore

$$\hat{\text{Sub}}(\mathscr{L}_1, \hat{\text{Sub}}(\mathscr{L}_2, \mathscr{L}_3)) \subseteq \hat{\text{Sub}}(\hat{\text{Sub}}(\mathscr{L}_1, \mathscr{L}_2), \mathscr{L}_3),$$

whence equality.

REMARK: Note that the symmetric condition in the hypothesis is not used in proving either $\hat{\text{Sub}}(\hat{\text{Sub}}(\mathscr{L}_1, \mathscr{L}_2), \mathscr{L}_3) \subseteq \hat{\text{Sub}}(\mathscr{L}_1, \hat{\text{Sub}}(\mathscr{L}_2, \mathscr{L}_3))$ or $\text{Sub}(\text{Sub}(\mathscr{L}_1, \mathscr{L}_2), \mathscr{L}_3) \subseteq \text{Sub}(\mathscr{L}_1, \text{Sub}(\mathscr{L}_2, \mathscr{L}_3))$.

We are now ready for the main result of the section.

THEOREM 6.1.1: *Let $\mathscr{L}_1$ and $\mathscr{L}_2$ both be trios, semi-AFL, or AFL. Then*

(a) $\text{Sub}(\mathscr{L}_1, \mathscr{L}_2)$ is a trio, semi-AFL, or AFL, resp.

(b) $\hat{\text{Sub}}(\mathscr{L}_1, \mathscr{L}_2)$ is a trio, semi-AFL, or AFL, resp. Furthermore, if $\mathscr{L}_2$ contains $\{\epsilon\}$, then

$$\hat{\text{Sub}}(\mathscr{L}_1, \mathscr{L}_2) = \hat{\text{Sub}}(\hat{\mathscr{H}}(\mathscr{L}_1), \mathscr{L}_2) = \text{Sub}(\hat{\mathscr{H}}(\mathscr{L}_1), \mathscr{L}_2).$$

(c) $\hat{\text{Sub}}(\mathscr{L}_1, \mathscr{L}_2)$ is a full trio, semi-AFL, or AFL, resp. if $\mathscr{L}_2$ is full; and $\hat{\text{Sub}}(\mathscr{L}_1, \mathscr{L}_2) = \text{Sub}(\mathscr{L}_1, \mathscr{L}_2)$ if $\mathscr{L}_1$ is also full.

Proof: (a) It suffices to assume that $\mathscr{L}_1$ is ϵ-free. [For suppose $\mathscr{L}_1$ contains $\{\epsilon\}$. Clearly $\text{Sub}(\mathscr{L}_1, \mathscr{L}_2) = \{L, L \cup \{\epsilon\}/L \text{ in } \text{Sub}(\mathscr{L}_1', \mathscr{L}_2)\} \cup \text{Sub}(\mathscr{L}_1'', \mathscr{L}_2)$ if $\mathscr{L}_1$ is a trio and $\text{Sub}(\mathscr{L}_1, \mathscr{L}_2) = \{L, L \cup \{\epsilon\}/L \text{ in } \text{Sub}(\mathscr{L}_1', \mathscr{L}_2)\}$ if

$\mathscr{L}_1$ is an AFL or semi-AFL, where $\mathscr{L}_1' = \{L \text{ in } \mathscr{L}_1/L \text{ } \epsilon\text{-free}, L \cup \{\epsilon\} \text{ in } \mathscr{L}_1\}$ and $\mathscr{L}_1'' = \{L \text{ in } \mathscr{L}_1/L \text{ } \epsilon\text{-free}\}$. By Proposition 3.1.2, $\mathscr{L}_1''$ is a trio. Obviously $\{L, L \cup \{\epsilon\}/L, L \cup \{\epsilon\} \text{ in } \mathscr{L}_1\}$, therefore $\mathscr{L}_1'$, is a trio, semi-AFL, or AFL if $\mathscr{L}_1$ is a trio, semi-AFL, or AFL, resp. By Proposition 3.1.2, $\{L, L \cup \{\epsilon\}/L$ in Sub $(\mathscr{L}_1', \mathscr{L}_2)\}$ will be a trio, semi-AFL, or AFL, resp. if Sub $(\mathscr{L}_1', \mathscr{L}_2)$ is a trio, semi-AFL, or AFL, resp. Thus Sub $(\mathscr{L}_1, \mathscr{L}_2)$ will be a (semi-)AFL if Sub $(\mathscr{L}_1', \mathscr{L}_2)$ is a (semi-)AFL, and, by Exercise 3.1.3, Sub $(\mathscr{L}_1, \mathscr{L}_2)$ will be a trio if Sub $(\mathscr{L}_1', \mathscr{L}_2)$ and Sub $(\mathscr{L}_1'', \mathscr{L}_2)$ are trios.] Hence Sub $(\mathscr{L}_1, \mathscr{L}_2)$ is a family of ϵ-free languages. Let L_1 be a language in $\mathscr{L}_1$ and τ_1 an ϵ-free substitution on $\Sigma_{L_1}^*$ such that $\tau_1(a)$ is in $\mathscr{L}_2$ for all a in Σ_{L_1}.

Consider intersection with regular sets. Let R be a regular set. We shall show that $\tau_1(L_1) \cap R$ is in Sub $(\mathscr{L}_1, \mathscr{L}_2)$. Clearly we may assume $\Sigma_{\tau_1(L_1)} \cap \Sigma_{L_1} = \emptyset$. Since $\tau_1(L_1)$ is ϵ-free, $\tau_1(L_1) \cap R = \tau_1(L_1) \cap (R - \{\epsilon\})$. Thus we may assume that R is ϵ-free. Let τ_2 be the ϵ-free substitution on $\Sigma_{L_1}^*$ defined by $\tau_2(a) = a\tau_1(a)$ for each a in Σ_{L_1}. Let h be the homomorphism on $(\Sigma_{L_1} \cup \Sigma_{\tau_1(L_1)})^*$ defined by $h(a) = \epsilon$ for each a in Σ_{L_1} and $h(b) = b$ for each b in $\Sigma_{\tau_1(L_1)}$. Then $\tau_1 = h\tau_2$ and

$$\tau_1(L_1) \cap R = h\tau_2(L_1) \cap R = h(\tau_2(L_1) \cap h^{-1}(R)).$$

Since R is regular, $h^{-1}(R)$ is regular. Thus there exists an fsa $A = (K_1, \Sigma_{L_1} \cup \Sigma_{\tau_1(L_1)}, \delta, p_0, F)$ such that $T(A) = h^{-1}(R)$. Since R is ϵ-free, so is $h^{-1}(R)$. Let

$$R' = \{(p_0, a_1, p_1)\ldots(p_{m-1}, a_m, p_m)/m \geqq 1, \text{ each } p_i \text{ in } K_1, p_m \text{ in } F, \text{ each } a_j \text{ in } \Sigma_{L_1}\}.$$

By Lemma 3.2.1, R' is regular.

For each a in Σ_{L_1} and each p and q in K_1 let

$$R(p, a, q) = \{w \text{ in } \Sigma_{\tau_1(L_1)}^* / \delta(p, aw) = q\}.$$

Then $R(p, a, q)$ is regular (since $R(p, a, q) = T(B)$, where B is the fsa $(K_1, \Sigma_{\tau_1(L_1)}, \delta, \delta(p, a), \{q\})$). Let τ_3 be the ϵ-free substitution on $(K_1 \times \Sigma_{L_1} \times K_1)^*$ defined by $\tau_3((p, a, q)) = aR(p, a, q)$ for each (p, a, q) in $K_1 \times \Sigma_{L_1} \times K_1$. Then $\tau_3(R')$ is the subset of $h^{-1}(R)$ consisting of all words that do not begin with a symbol of $\Sigma_{\tau_1(L_1)}$. Since $\tau_2(L_1)$ contains no word beginning with a symbol of $\Sigma_{\tau_1(L_1)}$, $\tau_2(L_1) \cap h^{-1}(R) = \tau_2(L_1) \cap \tau_3(R')$.

Let τ' be the ϵ-free substitution on $\Sigma_{L_1}^*$ defined by $\tau'(a) = K_1 \times \{a\} \times K_1$ for each a in Σ_{L_1} and τ'' the ϵ-free substitution on $(K_1 \times \Sigma_{L_1} \times K_1)^*$ defined by $\tau''((p, a, q)) = \tau_2(a)$ for each (p, a, q). Then $\tau_2 = \tau''\tau'$, so that

$$\tau_2(L_1) \cap h^{-1}(R) = \tau''\tau'(L_1) \cap \tau_3(R').$$

Let τ_3'' be the ϵ-free substitution on $(K_1 \times \Sigma_{L_1} \times K_1)^*$ defined by

$$\begin{aligned}\tau_3''((p, a, q)) &= \tau''((p, a, q)) \cap \tau_3((p, a, q)) \\ &= a\tau_1(a) \cap aR(p, a, q)\end{aligned}$$

for each (p, a, q). It is easily seen (Exercise 6.1.4) that $\tau''\tau'(L_1) \cap \tau_3(R') = \tau_3''(\tau'(L_1) \cap R')$. Therefore

$$\begin{aligned}\tau_1(L_1) \cap R &= h(\tau_2(L_1) \cap h^{-1}(R)) \\ &= h(\tau''\tau'(L_1) \cap \tau_3(R')) \\ &= h\tau_3''(\tau'(L_1) \cap R').\end{aligned}$$

Now $\tau'(L_1)$ is in Sub $(\mathcal{L}_1, \mathcal{R}_0)$. Thus $\tau'(L_1)$ is in $\mathcal{L}_1$ by Theorem 3.3.2. Then $\tau'(L_1) \cap R'$ is in $\mathcal{L}_1$. The composite $h\tau_3''$ is an ϵ-free substitution on $(K_1 \times \Sigma_{L_1} \times K_1)^*$ such that $h\tau_3''((p, a, q)) = h(a\tau_1(a) \cap aR(p, a, q)) = \tau_1(a) \cap R(p, a, q)$ for each (p, a, q). Since $\tau_1(a)$ is in $\mathcal{L}_2$ and $R(p, a, q)$ is in $\mathcal{R}$, $\tau_1(L_1) \cap R = h\tau_3''(\tau'(L_1) \cap R')$ is in Sub $(\mathcal{L}_1, \mathcal{L}_2)$.

Consider ϵ-free homomorphism. We shall prove the stronger result that $h(L)$ is in Sub $(\mathcal{L}_1, \mathcal{L}_2)$ for each L in Sub $(\mathcal{L}_1, \mathcal{L}_2)$ and each homomorphism h, ϵ-limited on L, such that $h(L)$ is ϵ-free. Accordingly, let h be an ϵ-limited homomorphism on $\tau_1(L_1)$ such that $h(\tau_1(L_1))$ is ϵ-free. Let $\Sigma_1 = \{a \text{ in } \Sigma_{\tau_1(L_1)}/ h(a) = \epsilon\}$. Let h_1 be the homomorphism on $\Sigma_{L_1}^*$ defined, for each a in Σ_{L_1}, by $h_1(a) = \epsilon$ if $\tau_1(a) \subseteq \Sigma_1^+$ and $h_1(a) = a$ otherwise. Since h is ϵ-limited on $\tau_1(L_1)$, h_1 is ϵ-limited on L_1. Since $h(\tau_1(L_1))$ is ϵ-free, $h_1(L_1)$ is ϵ-free. Hence $h_1(L_1)$ is in $\mathcal{L}_1$ by Corollary 2 of Theorem 3.2.2. Let τ_2 be the substitution on $\Sigma_{h_1(L_1)}^*$ defined by $\tau_2(a) = h(\tau_1(a) - \Sigma_1^+)$ for each a in $\Sigma_{h_1(L_1)}$. Clearly $\tau_1(a) - \Sigma_1^+$ is in $\mathcal{L}_2$ and $\tau_2(a)$ is ϵ-free for each a. Since h is ϵ-limited on $\tau_1(L_1)$, h is ϵ-limited on each $\tau_1(a)$. Hence each $\tau_2(a)$ is in $\mathcal{L}_2$ by Corollary 2 of Theorem 3.2.2. Therefore $\tau_2(h_1(L_1))$ is in Sub $(\mathcal{L}_1, \mathcal{L}_2)$. Since $\tau_2(h_1(L_1)) = h\tau_1(L_1)$ (see Exercise 6.1.5), $h\tau_1(L_1)$ is in Sub $(\mathcal{L}_1, \mathcal{L}_2)$.

Consider inverse homomorphism. Since

$$\begin{aligned}\text{Sub}\,(\text{Sub}\,(\mathcal{L}_1, \mathcal{L}_2,), \mathcal{R}_0) &= \text{Sub}\,(\mathcal{L}_1, \text{Sub}\,(\mathcal{L}_2, \mathcal{R}_0)), \quad \text{by Lemma 6.1.1,} \\ &= \text{Sub}\,(\mathcal{L}_1, \mathcal{L}_2),\end{aligned}$$

Sub $(\mathcal{L}_1, \mathcal{L}_2)$ is closed under substitution by ϵ-free regular sets. Thus Sub $(\mathcal{L}_1, \mathcal{L}_2)$ is closed under star substitution. As proved above, Sub $(\mathcal{L}_1, \mathcal{L}_2)$ is closed under ϵ-limited homomorphism. Thus Sub $(\mathcal{L}_1, \mathcal{L}_2)$ is closed under symbol-limited erasing homomorphism and length-preserving homomorphism. As proved above, Sub $(\mathcal{L}_1, \mathcal{L}_2)$ is also closed under intersection with regular sets. Since Sub $(\mathcal{L}_1, \mathcal{L}_2)$ is ϵ-free, it follows from

Proposition 3.7.1 that Sub $(\mathscr{L}_1, \mathscr{L}_2)$ is closed under inverse homomorphism. Therefore Sub $(\mathscr{L}_1, \mathscr{L}_2)$ is a trio.

Suppose $\mathscr{L}_1$ and $\mathscr{L}_2$ are semi-AFL. Consider union. Let L_2 be in $\mathscr{L}_1$ and τ_2 an ϵ-free substitution on $\Sigma_{L_2}^*$ such that $\tau_2(a)$ is in $\mathscr{L}_2$ for each a in Σ_{L_2}. Without loss of generality we may assume that $\Sigma_{L_1} \cap \Sigma_{L_2} = \emptyset$. [Otherwise, for each b in Σ_{L_2} let $\bar{b}$ be a new symbol. Let $\Sigma_0 = \{\bar{b}/b \text{ in } \Sigma_{L_2}\}$ and let h_0 be the ϵ-free homomorphism on $\Sigma_{L_2}^*$ which maps each b in Σ_{L_2} into $\bar{b}$. Let $\bar{\tau}_2$ be the substitution on Σ_0^* defined by $\bar{\tau}_2(\bar{b}) = \tau_2(b)$ for each b in Σ_0. Then $h_0(L_2)$ is in $\mathscr{L}_1$, $\Sigma_{L_1} \cap \Sigma_0 = \emptyset$, and $\tau_1(L_1) \cup \tau_2(L_2) = \tau_1(L_1) \cup \bar{\tau}_2(h_0(L_2))$.] Let τ_3 be the substitution on $(\Sigma_{L_1} \cup \Sigma_{L_2})^*$ defined by $\tau_3(a) = \tau_1(a)$ for each a in Σ_{L_1} and $\tau_3(b) = \tau_2(b)$ for each b in Σ_{L_2}. Then $\tau_1(L_1) \cup \tau_2(L_2) = \tau_3(L_1 \cup L_2)$. Since $L_1 \cup L_2$ is in $\mathscr{L}_1$ and τ_3 is ϵ-free, Sub $(\mathscr{L}_1, \mathscr{L}_2)$ is closed under union, i.e., Sub $(\mathscr{L}_1, \mathscr{L}_2)$ is a semi-AFL.

Suppose that $\mathscr{L}_1$ and $\mathscr{L}_2$ are AFL. By Theorem 3.1.2, it suffices to show that Sub $(\mathscr{L}_1, \mathscr{L}_2)$ is closed under $+$. However, this follows from the fact that $\tau_1(L_1)^+ = \tau_1(L_1^+)$.

(b) Suppose $\mathscr{L}_2$ is ϵ-free. Then $\hat{\text{Sub}}\,(\mathscr{L}_1, \mathscr{L}_2) = \text{Sub}\,(\mathscr{L}_1, \mathscr{L}_2)$, so that $\hat{\text{Sub}}\,(\mathscr{L}_1, \mathscr{L}_2)$ is a trio, semi-AFL, or AFL, resp. by (a).

Suppose $\mathscr{L}_2$ contains $\{\epsilon\}$. Obviously $\hat{\text{Sub}}\,(\mathscr{L}_1, \mathscr{L}_2) \subseteq \hat{\text{Sub}}\,(\hat{\mathscr{H}}(\mathscr{L}_1), \mathscr{L}_2)$. To see the reverse containment, let L_1 be in $\mathscr{L}_1$, h a homomorphism from $\Sigma_{L_1}^*$ into Σ_2^*, and τ a substitution on Σ_2^* such that $\tau(a)$ is in $\mathscr{L}_2$ for each a in Σ_2. Let c be a new symbol and τ' the substitution on $(\Sigma_2 \cup \{c\})^*$ defined by $\tau'(a) = \tau(a)$ for each a in Σ_2 and $\tau'(c) = \{\epsilon\}$. Let h' be the homomorphism on $\Sigma_{L_1}^*$ defined, for each a in Σ_{L_1}, by (i) $h'(a) = h(a)$ if $h(a) \neq \epsilon$, and (ii) $h'(a) = c$ if $h(a) = \epsilon$. Since h' is ϵ-free, $h'(L_1)$ is in $\mathscr{L}_1$. Clearly $\tau(h(L_1)) = \tau'(h'(L_1))$ and hence is in $\hat{\text{Sub}}\,(\mathscr{L}_1, \mathscr{L}_2)$. Thus $\hat{\text{Sub}}\,(\hat{\mathscr{H}}(\mathscr{L}_1), \mathscr{L}_2) \subseteq \hat{\text{Sub}}\,(\mathscr{L}_1, \mathscr{L}_2)$, whence equality. Finally, since $\hat{\mathscr{H}}(\mathscr{L}_1)$ is a full trio, $\hat{\text{Sub}}\,(\hat{\mathscr{H}}(\mathscr{L}_1), \mathscr{L}_2) = \text{Sub}\,(\hat{\mathscr{H}}(\mathscr{L}_1), \mathscr{L}_2)$ by Proposition 3.3.2. By (a), Sub $(\hat{\mathscr{H}}(\mathscr{L}_1), \mathscr{L}_2)$ is a trio, semi-AFL, or AFL, resp.

(c) Suppose $\mathscr{L}_2$ is full. By (b), $\hat{\text{Sub}}\,(\mathscr{L}_1, \mathscr{L}_2)$ is a trio, semi-AFL, or AFL, resp. Now

$$\begin{aligned} \hat{\mathscr{H}}(\hat{\text{Sub}}(\mathscr{L}_1, \mathscr{L}_2)) &\subseteq \hat{\text{Sub}}\,(\hat{\text{Sub}}\,(\mathscr{L}_1, \mathscr{L}_2), \mathscr{R}) \\ &= \hat{\text{Sub}}\,(\mathscr{L}_1, \hat{\text{Sub}}\,(\mathscr{L}_2, \mathscr{R})), \quad \text{by Lemma 6.1.1,} \\ &= \hat{\text{Sub}}\,(\mathscr{L}_1, \mathscr{L}_2), \quad \text{by Theorem 3.3.2 since } \mathscr{L}_2 \text{ is full.} \end{aligned}$$

Then $\hat{\text{Sub}}\,(\mathscr{L}_1, \mathscr{L}_2)$ is closed under arbitrary homomorphism and so is full. If, in addition, $\mathscr{L}_1$ is also full, then $\hat{\text{Sub}}\,(\mathscr{L}_1, \mathscr{L}_2) = \text{Sub}\,(\mathscr{L}_1, \mathscr{L}_2)$ by (b) (or by Proposition 3.3.2).

Theorem 6.1.1 has several simple consequences.

Notation: Let $\mathcal{L}_1, \ldots, \mathcal{L}_n$ be a finite sequence of sets of languages. Let $\text{Sub}(\mathcal{L}_1) = \hat{\text{Sub}}(\mathcal{L}_1) = \mathcal{L}_1$. By induction, for each k, $3 \leqq k \leqq n$, let $\text{Sub}(\mathcal{L}_1, \ldots, \mathcal{L}_k) = \text{Sub}(\text{Sub}(\mathcal{L}_1, \ldots, \mathcal{L}_{k-1}), \mathcal{L}_k)$ and $\hat{\text{Sub}}(\mathcal{L}_1, \ldots, \mathcal{L}_k) = \hat{\text{Sub}}(\hat{\text{Sub}}(\mathcal{L}_1, \ldots, \mathcal{L}_{k-1}), \mathcal{L}_k)$.

If the $\mathcal{L}_i$ are all symmetric, as for example when they are trios, then by Lemma 6.1.1, $\text{Sub}(\mathcal{L}_1, \ldots, \mathcal{L}_k) = \text{Sub}(\mathcal{L}_1, \text{Sub}(\mathcal{L}_2, \ldots, \mathcal{L}_k)) = \text{Sub}(\mathcal{L}_1, \text{Sub}(\mathcal{L}_2, \ldots, \mathcal{L}_{k-1}), \mathcal{L}_k)$ etc. Similar equalities hold for $\hat{\text{Sub}}(\mathcal{L}_1, \ldots, \mathcal{L}_k)$.

COROLLARY 1: *Let $\mathcal{L}_1, \ldots, \mathcal{L}_n$ all be trios, semi-AFL, or AFL. Then*

(a) *$\text{Sub}(\mathcal{L}_1, \ldots, \mathcal{L}_n)$ is a trio, semi-AFL, or AFL, resp.*

(b) *$\hat{\text{Sub}}(\mathcal{L}_1, \ldots, \mathcal{L}_n)$ is a trio, semi-AFL, or AFL, resp. Furthermore, if $\mathcal{L}_1, \ldots, \mathcal{L}_n$ are full, then $\text{Sub}(\mathcal{L}_1, \ldots, \mathcal{L}_n) = \hat{\text{Sub}}(\mathcal{L}_1, \ldots, \mathcal{L}_n)$.*

(c) *$\hat{\text{Sub}}(\mathcal{L}_1, \ldots, \mathcal{L}_n)$ is full if $\mathcal{L}_n$ is full.*

COROLLARY 2: *For all trios $\mathcal{L}_1$ and $\mathcal{L}_2$,*

$$\begin{aligned} \text{Sub}(\hat{\mathcal{H}}(\mathcal{L}_1), \hat{\mathcal{H}}(\mathcal{L}_2)) = \hat{\text{Sub}}(\hat{\mathcal{H}}(\mathcal{L}_1), \hat{\mathcal{H}}(\mathcal{L}_2)) &= \hat{\mathcal{H}}(\hat{\text{Sub}}(\mathcal{L}_1, \mathcal{L}_2)) \\ &= \hat{\mathcal{H}}(\text{Sub}(\mathcal{L}_1, \mathcal{L}_2)). \end{aligned}$$

Proof: By Proposition 3.3.2, $\text{Sub}(\hat{\mathcal{H}}(\mathcal{L}_1), \hat{\mathcal{H}}(\mathcal{L}_2)) = \hat{\text{Sub}}(\hat{\mathcal{H}}(\mathcal{L}_1), \hat{\mathcal{H}}(\mathcal{L}_2))$. Next,

$$\begin{aligned} \hat{\mathcal{H}}(\hat{\text{Sub}}(\mathcal{L}_1, \mathcal{L}_2)) &= \hat{\text{Sub}}(\hat{\text{Sub}}(\mathcal{L}_1, \mathcal{L}_2), \mathcal{R}), && \text{by Theorem 3.4.3,} \\ &= \hat{\text{Sub}}(\mathcal{L}_1, \hat{\text{Sub}}(\mathcal{L}_2, \mathcal{R})), && \text{by Lemma 6.1.1,} \\ &= \hat{\text{Sub}}(\mathcal{L}_1, \hat{\mathcal{H}}(\mathcal{L}_2)), && \text{by Theorem 3.4.3,} \\ &= \hat{\text{Sub}}(\hat{\mathcal{H}}(\mathcal{L}_1), \hat{\mathcal{H}}(\mathcal{L}_2)), && \text{by (b) of Theorem 6.1.1.} \end{aligned}$$

Consider the last equality. Obviously, $\hat{\mathcal{H}}(\text{Sub}(\mathcal{L}_1, \mathcal{L}_2)) \subseteq \hat{\mathcal{H}}(\hat{\text{Sub}}(\mathcal{L}_1, \mathcal{L}_2))$. To see the reverse containment, let L_1 be in $\mathcal{L}_1$, τ a substitution on $\Sigma_{L_1}^*$ such that $\tau(a)$ is in $\mathcal{L}_2$ for each a in Σ_{L_1}, and h a homomorphism on $\Sigma_{\tau(L_1)}^*$. Let e be a new symbol. Let τ' be the ϵ-free substitution on $\Sigma_{L_1}^*$ defined by $\tau'(a) = (\tau(a) - \{\epsilon\}) \cup \{e/\epsilon \text{ in } \tau(a)\}$ for each a in Σ_{L_1}. Clearly each $\tau'(a)$ is in $\mathcal{L}_2$, so that $\tau'(L_1)$ is in $\text{Sub}(\mathcal{L}_1, \mathcal{L}_2)$. Let h' be the homomorphism on $(\Sigma_{\tau(L_1)} \cup \{e\})^*$ defined by $h'(a) = h(a)$ for a in $\Sigma_{\tau(L_1)}$ and $h'(e) = \epsilon$. Clearly $h'\tau'(L_1) = h\tau(L_1)$ so that $\hat{\mathcal{H}}(\hat{\text{Sub}}(\mathcal{L}_1, \mathcal{L}_2)) \subseteq \hat{\mathcal{H}}(\text{Sub}(\mathcal{L}_1, \mathcal{L}_2))$.

REMARKS: (1) $\hat{\text{Sub}}(\mathcal{L}_1, \mathcal{L}_2)$ is not necessarily full even if $\mathcal{L}_2$ contains $\{\epsilon\}$.

For let $\mathcal{L}_1 = \mathcal{R}$ and $\mathcal{L}_2 = \mathcal{L}_{\text{ECS}}$. Then $\hat{\text{Sub}}(\mathcal{L}_1, \mathcal{L}_2) = \mathcal{L}_{\text{ECS}}$, which is not full.

(2) It is not true, in general, that $\text{Sub}(\mathcal{L}_1, \ldots, \mathcal{L}_n) = \hat{\text{Sub}}(\mathcal{L}_1, \ldots, \mathcal{L}_n)$ for arbitrary AFL $\mathcal{L}_1, \ldots, \mathcal{L}_n$. For let $n \geqq 3$, $\mathcal{L}_1 = \ldots = \mathcal{L}_{n-2} = \mathcal{R}$, and $\mathcal{L}_{n-1} = \mathcal{L}_n = \mathcal{L}_{\text{ECS}}$. Then $\text{Sub}(\mathcal{L}_1, \ldots, \mathcal{L}_n) = \mathcal{L}_{\text{ECS}}$ and $\hat{\text{Sub}}(\mathcal{L}_1, \ldots, \mathcal{L}_n) = \hat{\text{Sub}}(\mathcal{L}_1, \ldots, \mathcal{L}_{n-2}, \hat{\text{Sub}}(\mathcal{L}_{n-1}, \mathcal{L}_n)) = \mathcal{L}_{\text{RE}}$.

EXERCISE 6.1.1: Show that the symmetric condition in Lemma 6.1.1 cannot always be removed and still have $\hat{\text{Sub}}(\mathcal{L}_1, \hat{\text{Sub}}(\mathcal{L}_2, \mathcal{L}_3)) \subseteq \hat{\text{Sub}}(\hat{\text{Sub}}(\mathcal{L}_1, \mathcal{L}_2), \mathcal{L}_3)$.

EXERCISE 6.1.2: Let $\mathcal{L}_1$ be a semi-AFL and $\mathcal{L}_2$ a family of languages. Prove that $\hat{\text{Sub}}(\mathcal{L}_1, \mathcal{L}_2)$ is closed under union.

EXERCISE 6.1.3: Let $\mathcal{L}_1$ be an AFL and $\mathcal{L}_2$ a family of languages. Prove that $\hat{\text{Sub}}(\mathcal{L}_1, \mathcal{L}_2)$ is closed under union, concatenation, and $+$.

EXERCISE 6.1.4: Prove that $\tau''\tau'(L_1) \cap \tau_3(R') = \tau_3''(\tau'(L_1) \cap R')$ in (a) of Theorem 6.1.1.

EXERCISE 6.1.5: Prove that $\tau_2 h_1(L_1) = h\tau_1(L_1)$ in (a) of Theorem 6.1.1.

EXERCISE 6.1.6: Let $\mathcal{L}$ be ϵ-free and let $\mathcal{L}_i = \mathcal{L}$ for each i. Prove that $\text{Sub}(\mathcal{L}_1, \ldots, \mathcal{L}_n) = \hat{\text{Sub}}(\mathcal{L}_1, \ldots, \mathcal{L}_n)$.

In the exercises below let $\mathcal{F}_0$ be the family of all finite, ϵ-free subsets of Σ^*.

EXERCISE 6.1.7: Prove that $\hat{\text{Sub}}(\mathcal{L}_1, \mathcal{L}_2) \wedge \mathcal{R} \subseteq \hat{\text{Sub}}(\hat{\text{Sub}}(\mathcal{L}_1, \mathcal{F}_0) \wedge \mathcal{R}, \mathcal{L}_2 \wedge \mathcal{R})$ for all families $\mathcal{L}_1$ and $\mathcal{L}_2$ of languages [GS5].

EXERCISE 6.1.8: Prove that $\hat{\text{Sub}}(\mathcal{L}_1 \wedge \mathcal{R}, \mathcal{L}_2 \wedge \mathcal{R}) \subseteq \mathcal{H}[\hat{\text{Sub}}(\hat{\text{Sub}}(\mathcal{L}_1, \mathcal{F}_0), \mathcal{L}_2 \cup \mathcal{F}_0) \wedge \mathcal{R}]$ for all families $\mathcal{L}_1$ and $\mathcal{L}_2$ of languages [GS5].

EXERCISE 6.1.9: Let $\mathcal{L}_1$ and $\mathcal{L}_2$ be families of languages. Let $\mathcal{F}_0 \subseteq \mathcal{L}_2$ and $\hat{\text{Sub}}(\mathcal{F}_0, \mathcal{L}_2) \subseteq \mathcal{L}_2$. If $\mathcal{L}_1$ has a language containing a non-ϵ word, prove that $\mathcal{L}_2 \subseteq \hat{\mathcal{F}}[\hat{\text{Sub}}(\mathcal{L}_1, \mathcal{L}_2)]$ [GS5].

EXERCISE 6.1.10: Let $\mathcal{L}_1$ and $\mathcal{L}_2$ be families of languages, with $\mathcal{L}_1$ having a language containing a non-ϵ word. Prove that

(a) $\hat{\mathscr{M}}(\hat{\text{Sub}}(\mathscr{L}_1, \mathscr{L}_2)) \subseteq \hat{\text{Sub}}(\mathscr{T}(\mathscr{L}_1), \hat{\mathscr{M}}(\mathscr{L}_2))$, where $\mathscr{T}(\mathscr{L}_1) = \{\tau(L) \cap R/L$ in $\mathscr{L}_1$, R in $\mathscr{R}$, τ a substitution by finite sets$\}$ [Le, a].

(b) $\hat{\text{Sub}}(\mathscr{L}_1, \mathscr{L}_2)$ is a full AFL using (a), where $\mathscr{L}_1$ and $\mathscr{L}_2$ are full AFL [Le, a].

EXERCISE 6.1.11: Let $\mathscr{L}_1$ be a substitution-closed family of languages such that $\mathscr{T}(\mathscr{L}_1) \subseteq \mathscr{L}_1$, $\mathscr{T}(\mathscr{L}_1)$ as in Exercise 6.1.10. Furthermore, suppose $\mathscr{L}_1$ has a language with a non-ϵ word. For each family $\mathscr{L}_2$ of languages prove that $\mathscr{N}(\mathscr{L}_2) \subseteq \hat{\text{Sub}}(\mathscr{L}_1, \hat{\mathscr{M}}(\mathscr{L}_2))$, where $\mathscr{N}(\mathscr{L}_2)$ is the smallest family $\mathscr{L}$ of languages containing $\mathscr{L}_2$ such that $\hat{\mathscr{M}}(\mathscr{L}) \subseteq \mathscr{L}$ and $\hat{\text{Sub}}(\mathscr{L}_1, \mathscr{L}) \subseteq \mathscr{L}$ [Le, a].

EXERCISE 6.1.12: For each family $\mathscr{L}$ of languages let $\text{OP}(\mathscr{L}) = \{L/\hat{\text{Sub}}(L, \mathscr{L}) \subseteq \mathscr{L}\}$. Prove that $\text{OP}(\mathscr{L}) \subseteq \mathscr{L}$ and is a substitution-closed full AFL for every full AFL $\mathscr{L}$ [Le, a].

EXERCISE 6.1.13: Let $\mathscr{L}$ be a family containing at least one language with a non-ϵ word such that $\mathscr{L} \wedge \mathscr{R} \subseteq \mathscr{L}$ and $\hat{\text{Sub}}(\mathscr{L}, \mathscr{F}_0) \subseteq \mathscr{L}$. Prove the following [GS6]:

(a) $\hat{\mathscr{F}}(\mathscr{L}) = \hat{\text{Sub}}(\hat{\text{Sub}}(\mathscr{R}_0, \mathscr{L}), \mathscr{R})$.

(b) $\hat{\mathscr{F}}(\mathscr{L})$ is a slip[1] AFL if $\mathscr{L}$ is a slip AFL.

EXERCISE 6.1.14: Prove that there is a largest slip AFL [GS 6]. [Hint: Use Exercise 6.1.13.]

EXERCISE 6.1.15: Define the *commutative closure* of a language L as the set $c(L)$ consisting of all words which are permutations of words in L. That is, ϵ is in $c(L)$ if ϵ is in L; and for $m \geqq 1$, each a_i in Σ, $a_1 \ldots a_m$ is in $c(L)$ if there is a permutation π of $\{1, \ldots, m\}$ such that $a_{\pi(1)} \ldots a_{\pi(m)}$ is in L. The *commutative closure* of a family $\mathscr{L}$ is defined as the family $c(\mathscr{L}) = \{c(L)/L$ in $\mathscr{L}\}$. Using Exercise 6.1.13, prove that $\hat{\mathscr{F}}(c(\mathscr{R})) = \hat{\mathscr{F}}(\mathscr{L}_0)$ and is a slip AFL, where $\mathscr{L}_0 = \mathscr{H}(c(\mathscr{R}) \wedge \mathscr{R})$ [GS6].

EXERCISE 6.1.16: (Continued) Prove that $\hat{\mathscr{F}}(c(\mathscr{L})) = \hat{\mathscr{F}}(c(\mathscr{R}))$ for each slip AFL $\mathscr{L}$ [GS6]. [Hint: Use (a) of Exercise 3.3.2.]

The following notation is used in Exercises 6.1.17–6.1.21. Let τ be a substitution on Σ_1^*. Let $\tau^{(1)}$ be the substitution on $\left(\Sigma_1 \cup \bigcup_a \Sigma_{\tau(a)}\right)^*$ defined

[1] See the notation prior to Exercise 5.6.7.

by $\tau^{(1)}(a) = \tau(a)$ for each a in Σ_1 and $\tau^{(1)}(b) = \{b\}$ for each b in $\bigcup_a \Sigma_{\tau(a)} - \Sigma_1$. Let $\tau^{(\infty)}$ be the substitution on $\left(\Sigma_1 \cup \bigcup_a \Sigma_{\tau(a)}\right)^*$ defined by $\tau^{(\infty)}(c) = \bigcup_{n \geqq 1} \tau^{(n)}(c)$, where $\tau^{(n+1)}(c) = \tau^{(1)}(\tau^{(n)}(c))$ for each $n \geqq 1$ and each c in $\Sigma_1 \cup \bigcup_a \Sigma_{\tau(a)}$. Then $\tau^{(\infty)}$ is called an *iterated* substitution. If a is in $\tau(a)$ for each a in Σ_1, then $\tau^{(\infty)}$ is called a *nested* iterated substitution.

EXERCISE 6.1.17: Call a language L *unitary* if $|w| \leqq 1$ for all w in L. Let $\mathscr{L}$ be a family of languages containing at least one nonunitary set and closed under intersection with regular sets, union with unitary sets, and nested iterated substitution. Prove that $\mathscr{L}$ is a substitution-closed full AFL [Gr4]. [An $\mathscr{L}$ with the above properties is called a *superAFL.*]

EXERCISE 6.1.18: Prove that $\mathscr{L}_{CF} \subseteq \mathscr{L}$ for each superAFL $\mathscr{L}$ [Gr4]. [Hint: Prove that $\mathscr{L}$ contains the Dyck set over two letters.]

EXERCISE 6.1.19: Prove that $\mathscr{L}_{CF}$ is a superAFL [Kr].

EXERCISE 6.1.20: Prove that $\mathscr{L}_{CF}$ is not closed under iterated substitution [Gr4].

EXERCISE 6.1.21: Prove that $\mathscr{L}_{NSA}$ is a superAFL [Gr4].

6.2 AFA Representation of Substitution

Earlier, we gave a device representation for the wedge of two (semi-) AFL, i. e., for (semi-) AFL $\mathscr{L}_1$ and $\mathscr{L}_2$ we presented a multitape AFA representation for $\mathscr{H}(\mathscr{L}_1 \wedge \mathscr{L}_2)$ in terms of AFA representing $\mathscr{L}_1$ and $\mathscr{L}_2$. In this section we seek a device representation for the substitution of one AFL into another. We achieve this goal with two representations, one a "nested" multitape AFA and the other a particular single-tape AFA.

We first consider "nested" multitape AFA. In the course of arguing that it represents substitution of AFL, we introduce the second family of devices. Each of the two families plays a role in showing that the other represents substitution.

Intuitively, a multitape acceptor is "nested" if (i) each move can change at most one storage tape, and (ii) all tapes to the right of this one are ϵ. In order to express these two conditions in the formalism of multitape acceptors we need to distinguish identity instructions in multitape acceptors. More precisely, we have

Notation: Let $(\Omega, \mathcal{D})$ be a multitape AFA, with $\Omega = (K, \Sigma, \mathcal{A}, \prec, \mu)$ and $\mu(\alpha) = (\Gamma_\alpha, I_\alpha, f_\alpha, g_\alpha)$ for each α in $\mathcal{A}$. For each α in $\mathcal{A}$ and each γ in $g_\alpha(\Gamma_\alpha^*)$, let $\psi_\alpha(\gamma) = \{u \text{ in } I_\alpha / f_\alpha(\gamma', u) = \gamma' \text{ for all } \gamma' \text{ in } g_\alpha^{-1}(\gamma)\}$, where $g_\alpha^{-1}(\gamma) = \{\gamma'' / \gamma$ in $g_\alpha(\gamma'')\}$.

For each α in $\mathcal{A}$ and γ in $g_\alpha(\Gamma_\alpha^*)$, $\psi_\alpha(\gamma) \neq \emptyset$ since $1(\alpha, \gamma)$ is in $\psi_\alpha(\gamma)$.

We are now able to define a "nested" multitape AFA.

Def: A *nested multitape AFA* is a pair $(\Omega, \mathcal{D}^{\mathrm{N}})$, where

(1) $(\Omega, \mathcal{D})$ is a multitape AFA, with $\Omega = (K, \Sigma, \mathcal{A}, \prec, \mu)$, and

(2) $\mathcal{D}^{\mathrm{N}}$ is the set of all $D = (K_1, \Sigma_1, \delta, q_0, F, (\alpha_1, \ldots, \alpha_k))$ in $\mathcal{D}$ with the following property (for arbitrary q', q in K_1, a in $\Sigma_1 \cup \{\epsilon\}$, $(u_1, \ldots, u_k)$ in $I_{\alpha_1} \times \ldots \times I_{\alpha_k}$, and $(\gamma_1, \ldots, \gamma_k)$ in G_D): If $(q', (u_1, \ldots, u_k))$ is in $\delta(q, a, (\gamma_1, \ldots, \gamma_k))$ and u_l is not in $\psi_{\alpha_l}(\gamma_l)$ for some l, then u_i is in $\psi_{\alpha_i}(\gamma_i)$ for all $i \neq l$ and $\gamma_i = \epsilon$ for all $i > l$.

Each D in $\mathcal{D}^{\mathrm{N}}$ is called a *nested* acceptor.

$(\sim, f)$ *Notation*: Let $\mathcal{L}(\mathcal{D}^{\mathrm{N}}) = \{L(D)/D \text{ in } \mathcal{D}^{\mathrm{N}}\}$ and $\mathcal{L}^t(\mathcal{D}^{\mathrm{N}}) = \{L(D)/D$ in $\mathcal{D}^{\mathrm{N}}$ and D quasi-realtime$\}$.

Note that if D is nested and $(q, a, (\gamma_1, \ldots, \gamma_k)) \vdash (q', \epsilon, (\gamma_1', \ldots, \gamma_k'))$, then there is at most one l with $\gamma_l \neq \gamma_l'$, *and* either $l = k$ or $\gamma_i = \epsilon = \gamma_i'$ for $i > l$. Thus at most one tape of D is changed and all tapes to the right of it are inactive, i.e., are ϵ.

The meaning of the term "nested" becomes clearer if we consider some familiar AFA. Suppose an acceptor such as a pda, a Turing acceptor, or a one-way stack acceptor has the storage configuration depicted in Fig. 1,

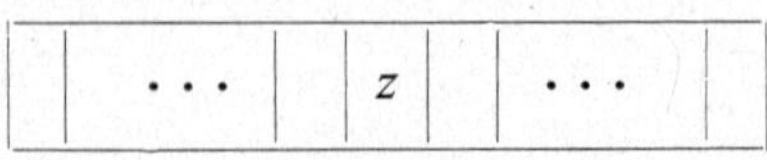

FIG. 1.

that is, a tape with a read-write head which affects exactly one symbol of the storage tape. This type of configuration is usually reflected in the formalism by a pointer symbol, $\uparrow$, and the definition $g(xZ\uparrow y) = \{Z\}$, where Z is a symbol and x and y are words which may have restrictions. (For example, $y = \epsilon$ in a pda.) In these cases, activating a tape is equivalent to inserting a new tape, initially ϵ, enclosed in markers – say matched brackets – where the read-write head is. The nesting condition says that the head cannot leave the bracketed tape until the bracketed tape becomes ϵ. This is equivalent to preventing the multitape AFA from changing a tape until all tapes to the right are inactive. Restricting the device to n tapes is equivalent to restricting the depth of the nesting of brackets to n.

From the definition, it is clear that $\mathcal{D} = \mathcal{D}^{N}$ for each single-tape AFA and $\mathcal{D}^{N} \subseteq \mathcal{D}$ otherwise. In general, a nested multitape AFA need not be a multitape AFA as defined in Section 4.5. To motivate the use of the word "AFA" after "nested multitape", we now show that a nested multitape AFA is equivalent (from the sets accepted point of view) to a single-tape AFA.

($\sim$,f) LEMMA 6.2.1: *For each nested multitape AFA* $(\Omega, \mathcal{D}^{N})$, *there exists a single-tape AFA* $(\bar{\Omega}, \bar{\mathcal{D}})$ *such that* $\mathcal{L}^{t}(\bar{\mathcal{D}}) = \mathcal{L}^{t}(\mathcal{D}^{N})$ *and* $\mathcal{L}(\bar{\mathcal{D}}) = \mathcal{L}(\mathcal{D}^{N})$.

Proof: Intuitively, $(\bar{\Omega}, \bar{D})$ is to be the single-tape AFA obtained by taking the tapes of each finite set of tapes and placing them on one tape, in order, with appropriate separators, and then applying the nesting condition.

Formally, let $\Omega = (K, \Sigma, \mathcal{A}, \prec, \mu)$ and let ξ be a new symbol not in $\bigcup_{\alpha \text{ in } \mathcal{A}} \Gamma_\alpha$. For each $v = (\alpha_1, \ldots, \alpha_k)$, l, $1 \leqq l \leqq k$, and u in I_{α_l}, let $\sigma(v)$ and $\sigma(v, l, u)$ be new symbols. Let $\bar{\Gamma} = \bigcup_{\alpha} \Gamma_\alpha \cup \{\xi\} \cup \{\sigma(v)/\text{all } v\}$ and

$$\bar{I} = \{\sigma(v, l, u)/v = (\alpha_1, \ldots, \alpha_k), 1 \leqq l \leqq k, u \text{ in } I_{\alpha_l}\} \cup \{\sigma(v)/\text{all } v\} \cup \{\epsilon\}.$$

For $v = (\alpha_1, \ldots, \alpha_k)$ and for $(\gamma_1, \ldots, \gamma_k)$ in $\Gamma^*_{\alpha_1} \times \ldots \times \Gamma^*_{\alpha_k}$, let

$$\bar{g}(\sigma(v)\,\xi\gamma_1\xi\ldots\gamma_k) = \sigma(v)\,\xi g_{\alpha_1}(\gamma_1)\,\xi\ldots g_{\alpha_k}(\gamma_k).$$

Let $\bar{g}(\epsilon) = \{\epsilon\}$. For $v = (\alpha_1, \ldots, \alpha_k)$, let $\bar{f}(\epsilon, \sigma(v)) = \sigma(v)\,\xi^k$, $\bar{f}(\sigma(v)\,\xi^k, \epsilon) = \epsilon$, and $\bar{f}(\epsilon, \epsilon) = \epsilon$. For $v = (\alpha_1, \ldots, \alpha_k)$, $(\gamma_1, \ldots, \gamma_k)$ in $\Gamma^*_{\alpha_1} \times \ldots \times \Gamma^*_{\alpha_k}$, l such that either $l = k$ or $\gamma_i = \epsilon$ for all $i > l$, and u in I_{α_l}, let

$$\bar{f}(\sigma(v)\,\xi\gamma_1\xi\ldots\gamma_k, \sigma(v, l, u)) = \sigma(v)\,\xi\gamma'_1\xi\ldots\gamma'_k,$$

where $\gamma'_i = \gamma_i$ for all i, $i \neq l$, and $\gamma'_l = f_{\alpha_l}(\gamma_l, u)$. By the same reasoning as in Lemma 4.5.1, $(\bar{\Gamma}, \bar{I}, \bar{f}, \bar{g})$ is an AFA-schema. Let $\bar{\Omega} = (K, \Sigma, \bar{\Gamma}, \bar{I}, \bar{f}, \bar{g})$.

Let $D = (K_1, \Sigma_1, \delta, q_0, F, v)$ be in $\mathcal{D}^{N}$. Let $\bar{q}_0$ and r_0 be new symbols in K and $\bar{D} = (K_1 \cup \{\bar{q}_0, r_0\}, \Sigma_1, \bar{\delta}, \bar{q}_0, \{r_0\})$, where $\bar{\delta}$ is defined as follows (for each q in K_1, a in $\Sigma_1 \cup \{\epsilon\}$, and γ_i in $g_{\alpha_i}(\Gamma^*_{\alpha_i})$ for all i, $1 \leqq i \leqq k$):

(1) $\bar{\delta}(\bar{q}_0, \epsilon, \epsilon) = \{(q_0, \sigma(v))\}$.

(2) (r_0, ϵ) is in $\bar{\delta}(p, \epsilon, \sigma(v)\,\xi^k)$ for each p in F.

(3) $\bar{\delta}(q, a, \sigma(v)\,\xi\gamma_1\xi\ldots\gamma_k)$ contains $(q', \sigma(v, l, u_l))$ if $(q', (u_1, \ldots, u_k))$ is in $\delta(q, a, (\gamma_1, \ldots, \gamma_k))$ and l is such that $1 \leqq l \leqq k$, u_i is in $\psi_{\alpha_i}(\gamma_i)$ for all $i \neq l$, $1 \leqq i \leqq k$, and $\gamma_i = \epsilon$ for all i, $l < i \leqq k$.

Clearly $L(D) = L(\bar{D})$ and $\bar{D}$ is quasi-realtime if D is.
Now let $\bar{D} = (K_1, \Sigma_1, \delta, q_0, F)$ be in $\mathcal{D}$. Let

$$Q = \{v/(q', \sigma(v)) \text{ in } \delta(q, a, \epsilon) \text{ for some } q \text{ in } K_1 \text{ and } a \text{ in } \Sigma_1 \cup \{\epsilon\}\}.$$

As in the proof of Lemma 4.5.1, we may assume that there exists $v_0 = (\alpha_1, \ldots, \alpha_n)$ such that $v = (\alpha_{j_1}, \ldots, \alpha_{j_k})$ for some $1 \leqq j_1 < \ldots < j_k \leqq n$ if v is in Q. We may also assume that if $(q', \sigma(v_1, l, u))$ is in $\delta(q, a, \sigma(v_2)\xi\gamma_1\xi\ldots\gamma_k)$, then $v_1 = v_2 = (\alpha_{j_1}, \ldots, \alpha_{j_k})$ is in Q, u is in $I_{\alpha_{j_l}}$, γ_i is in $g_{\alpha_{j_i}}(\Gamma^*_{\alpha_{j_i}})$ for $1 \leqq i \leqq k$, and $\gamma_i = \epsilon$ for $i > l$. Let $D = (K_1 \times (Q \cup \{\epsilon\}), \Sigma_1, \delta_1, (q_0, \epsilon), F \times \{\epsilon\}, v_0)$, where δ_1 is defined as follows (for arbitrary q in K_1, $v = (\alpha_{j_1}, \ldots, \alpha_{j_k})$, a in $\Sigma_1 \cup \{\epsilon\}$, and γ_{j_i} in $g_{\alpha_{j_i}}(\Gamma^*_{\alpha_{j_i}})$ for all i, $1 \leqq i \leqq k$):

(4) $((q', \epsilon), (1_{\alpha_1}, \ldots, 1_{\alpha_n}))$ is in $\delta_1((q, \epsilon), a, (\epsilon, \ldots, \epsilon))$ if (q', ϵ) is in $\delta(q, a, \epsilon)$.

(5) $((q', \epsilon), (1_{\alpha_1}, \ldots, 1_{\alpha_n}))$ is in $\delta_1((q, v), a, (\epsilon, \ldots, \epsilon))$ if (q', ϵ) is in $\delta(q, a, \sigma(v)\xi^k)$.

(6) $((q', v), (1_{\alpha_1}, \ldots, 1_{\alpha_n}))$ is in $\delta_1((q, \epsilon), a, (\epsilon, \ldots, \epsilon))$ if $(q', \sigma(v))$ is in $\delta(q, a, \epsilon)$.

(7) $((q', v), (u_1', \ldots, u_n'))$ is in $\delta_1((q, v), a, (\gamma_1', \ldots, \gamma_n'))$ if $(q', \sigma(v, l, u))$ is in $\delta(q, a, \sigma(v)\xi\gamma_{j_1}\xi\ldots\gamma_{j_k})$, where $\gamma_{j_i} = \epsilon$ for all $i > l$, $u_{j_i}' = 1(\alpha_{j_i}, \gamma_{j_i})$ for all $i \neq l$, $u_{j_l}' = u$, and $\gamma_j' = \epsilon$ and $u_j' = 1_{\alpha_j}$ for all j not in $\{j_1, \ldots, j_k\}$.

Then $L(D) = L(\bar{D})$ and D is quasi-realtime if $\bar{D}$ is.

From Lemma 6.2.1, Theorem 4.2.3, and Theorem 4.3.2, there immediately follows:

$(\sim, f)$ THEOREM 6.2.1: *For each nested multitape AFA $\mathcal{D}^{\mathrm{N}}$, $\mathcal{L}(\mathcal{D}^{\mathrm{N}})$ is a full AFL and $\mathcal{L}^t(\mathcal{D}^{\mathrm{N}})$ is an AFL containing $\{\epsilon\}$.*

In order to prove that nested multitape AFA provide a representation for substitution, we need two lemmas on inclusion which together imply equality. These two lemmas, Lemmas 6.2.2 and 6.2.6, play the same role for substitution that Lemmas 4.6.1 and 4.6.2 do for wedge.

$(\sim, f)$ LEMMA 6.2.2: *For all multitape AFA $\mathcal{D}_1$ and $\mathcal{D}_2$,*

$$Sub\,[\mathcal{L}^t(\mathcal{D}_1^{\mathrm{N}}), \mathcal{L}^t(\mathcal{D}_2^{\mathrm{N}})] \subseteq \mathcal{L}^t((\mathcal{D}_1 \wedge \mathcal{D}_2)^{\mathrm{N}}) \text{ and}$$
$$Sub\,[\mathcal{L}(\mathcal{D}_1^{\mathrm{N}}), \mathcal{L}(\mathcal{D}_2^{\mathrm{N}})] = S\hat{u}b\,[\mathcal{L}(\mathcal{D}_1^{\mathrm{N}}), \mathcal{L}(\mathcal{D}_2^{\mathrm{N}})] \subseteq \mathcal{L}((\mathcal{D}_1 \wedge \mathcal{D}_2)^{\mathrm{N}}).$$

Proof: By Theorem 6.2.1, $\mathcal{L}(\mathcal{D}_1^{\mathrm{N}})$ and $\mathcal{L}(\mathcal{D}_2^{\mathrm{N}})$ are full AFL. By Proposition 3.3.2, Sub $[\mathcal{L}(\mathcal{D}_1^{\mathrm{N}}), \mathcal{L}(\mathcal{D}_2^{\mathrm{N}})] =$ Sûb $[\mathcal{L}(\mathcal{D}_1^{\mathrm{N}}), \mathcal{L}(\mathcal{D}_2^{\mathrm{N}})]$.

Let $\Omega_i = (K, \Sigma, \mathcal{A}_i, \prec_i, \mu_i)$ for $i = 1, 2$. Let $D_1 = (K_1, \Sigma_1, \delta_1, q_0, F_1, \nu_1)$ be in $\mathcal{D}_1^{\mathrm{N}}$ and for each a in Σ_1 let $D_a = (K_a, \Sigma_a, \delta_a, q_a, F_a, \nu_a)$ be in $\mathcal{D}_2^{\mathrm{N}}$ such that $L(D_a)$ is ϵ-free. We may assume that $K_1 \cap K_a = K_a \cap K_b = \emptyset$ for all a and $b, a \neq b$, in Σ_1. Let $\nu_1 = (\alpha_1, \ldots, \alpha_k)$. By extending each ν_a if necessary, we may assume that there exists $\nu_2 = (\beta_1, \ldots, \beta_l)$ such that $\nu_a = \nu_2$ for all a in Σ_1. Let τ be the ϵ-free substitution on Σ_1^* defined by $\tau(a) = L(D_a)$ for each a in Σ_1. We shall construct an acceptor D_3 in $(\mathcal{D}_1 \wedge \mathcal{D}_2)^{\mathrm{N}}$ such that $L(D_3) = \tau(L(D_1))$.

Informally, D_3 combines D_1 and the D_a as follows: D_3 uses the $\mathcal{D}_1$-tapes to check membership in $L(D_1)$. To see if a subword is in $\tau(a)$, a in Σ_1, D_3 uses the $\mathcal{D}_2$-tapes. If a subword is in $\tau(a)$ then the $\mathcal{D}_2$-tapes become empty and D_3 uses the $\mathcal{D}_1$-tapes to imitate the action of D_1 under a. Since $\tau(\varepsilon) = \{\varepsilon\}$, D_3 imitates an ε-rule of D_1 whenever the $\mathcal{D}_2$-tapes are empty.

Formally, let $D_3 = (K_3, \bigcup_{a \text{ in } \Sigma_1} \Sigma_a, \delta_3, q_0, F_1, \nu_3)$, where $K_3 = K_1 \cup \bigcup_{a \text{ in } \Sigma_1} (K_1 \times K_a)$, $\nu_3 = (\alpha_1, \ldots, \alpha_k, \beta_1, \ldots, \beta_l)$, and δ_3 is defined as follows (for each q in K_1, a in Σ_1, and $(\gamma_1, \ldots, \gamma_k)$ in G_{D_1}):

(1) Let $(q', (u_1, \ldots, u_k, 1_{\beta_1}, \ldots, 1_{\beta_l}))$ be in $\delta_3(q, \epsilon, (\gamma_1, \ldots, \gamma_k, \epsilon, \ldots, \epsilon))$ if $(q', (u_1, \ldots, u_k))$ is in $\delta_1(q, \epsilon, (\gamma_1, \ldots, \gamma_k))$.

(2) Let $((q, q_a), (1(\alpha_1, \gamma_1), \ldots, 1(\alpha_k, \gamma_k), 1_{\beta_1}, \ldots, 1_{\beta_l}))$ be in $\delta_3(q, \epsilon, (\gamma_1, \ldots, \gamma_k, \epsilon, \ldots, \epsilon))$.

(3) Let $((q, q'), (1(\alpha_1, \gamma_1), \ldots, 1(\alpha_k, \gamma_k), u_1, \ldots, u_l))$ be in $\delta_3((q, p), b, (\gamma_1, \ldots, \gamma_k, \gamma'_1, \ldots, \gamma'_l))$ if $(p', (u_1, \ldots, u_l))$ is in $\delta_a(p, b, (\gamma'_1, \ldots, \gamma'_l))$, where p is in K_a, b in Σ_a, and $(\gamma'_1, \ldots, \gamma'_l)$ in G_{D_a}.

(4) Let $(q', (u_1, \ldots, u_k, 1_{\beta_1}, \ldots, 1_{\beta_l}))$ be in $\delta_3((q, p), \epsilon, (\gamma_1, \ldots, \gamma_k, \epsilon, \ldots, \epsilon))$ if p is in F_a and $(q', (u_1, \ldots, u_k))$ is in $\delta_1(q, a, (\gamma_1, \ldots, \gamma_k))$.

Clearly $L(D_3) = \tau(L(D_1))$. Since D_1 and the D_a are nested, so is D_3. If D_1 and the D_a are quasi-realtime, then D_3 is quasi-realtime. (For if D_1 has at most k_1 consecutive ϵ-moves and each D_a at most k_a, then D_3 has at most $2\max\{k_a/\text{all } a\} + k_1 + 2$ consecutive ϵ-moves.)

The argument for Lemma 6.2.6 is rather involved and requires three preliminary lemmas as well as a different kind of AFA with "nests".

Notation: For $i = 1, 2$, let $(\Omega_i, \mathcal{D}_i)$ be the (single-tape) AFA $(K, \Sigma, \Gamma_i, I_i, f_i, g_i)$. Let ξ be a symbol not in $\Gamma_1 \cup \Gamma_2$ and let PUSH and POP be two symbols not in $I_1 \cup I_2$. Then $\mathcal{D}_1 \sigma \mathcal{D}_2$ denotes the (single-tape) AFA $(K, \Sigma, \Gamma_1 \cup \Gamma_2 \cup \{\xi\}, I_1 \cup I_2 \cup \{\text{PUSH}, \text{POP}\}, f_0, g_0)$, where f_0 and g_0 are defined by $f_0(x, u) = f_1(x, u)$, $f_0(x, \text{PUSH}) = x\xi$, $f_0(x\xi y, v) = x\xi f_2(y, v)$, $f_0(x\xi, \text{POP}) = x$, $g_0(x) = g_1(x)$, $g_0(x\xi z) = g_2(z)$, and $g_0(x\xi) = \{\xi\}$ for all x in Γ_1^*, y in Γ_2^*, z in Γ_2^+, u in I_1, and v in I_2.

Note that the instruction **PUSH** places a separator between the $\mathcal{D}_1$-tape and the $\mathcal{D}_2$-tape, and **POP** erases that symbol. The auxiliary storage of $\mathcal{D}_1\sigma\mathcal{D}_2$ mimics that of $\mathcal{D}_1$ until a PUSH is employed. Then the $\mathcal{D}_1\sigma\mathcal{D}_2$-storage simulates that of $\mathcal{D}_2$ until a POP is employed when the $\mathcal{D}_2$-storage is empty. At that time the $\mathcal{D}_1\sigma\mathcal{D}_2$-storage goes back to mimicking $\mathcal{D}_1$ etc.

We shall show that $\mathcal{L}^t(\mathcal{D}_1\sigma\mathcal{D}_2)(\mathcal{L}(\mathcal{D}_1\sigma\mathcal{D}_2))$ is a subset of Sub $(\mathcal{L}^t(\mathcal{D}_1), \mathcal{L}^t(\mathcal{D}_2))$ $(\text{Sub}(\mathcal{L}(\mathcal{D}_1), \mathcal{L}(\mathcal{D}_2)))$ and contains $\mathcal{L}^t((\mathcal{D}_1\wedge\mathcal{D}_2)^{\text{N}})(\mathcal{L}((\mathcal{D}_1\wedge\mathcal{D}_2)^{\text{N}}))$.

Notation: Let $D = (K_1, \Sigma_1, \delta, q_0, F)$ be in $\mathcal{D}_1\sigma\mathcal{D}_2$. Let $\vdash_{\overline{1,D}}$ be the relation on $K_1\times\Sigma_1^*\times\Gamma_1^*$ defined by $(q_1, w_1, x_1) \vdash_{\overline{1,D}} (q_2, w_2, x_2)$ if x_1, x_2 is in Γ_1^* and $(q_1, w_1, x_1) \vdash_{\overline{D}} (q_2, w_2, x_2)$. Let $\vdash_{\overline{2,D}}$ be the relation on $K_1\times\Sigma_1^*\times(\Gamma_1\cup\Gamma_2 \cup \{\xi\})^*$ defined by $(q_1, w_1, x_1\xi y) \vdash_{\overline{2,D}} (q_2, w_2, x_2\xi y_2)$ if $(q_1, w_1, x_1\xi y_1) \vdash_{\overline{D}} (q_2, w_2, x_2\xi y_2)$.

Thus $\vdash_{\overline{1,D}}$ describes the movements of D when the storage tapes are in Γ_1^* and $\vdash_{\overline{2,D}}$ describes the movements of D when the tapes are of the form $x\xi y$, x in Γ_1^* and y in Γ_2^*.

Clearly, for any D in $\mathcal{D}_1\sigma\mathcal{D}_2$, $(q, w, x\xi y) \vdash^{*}_{\overline{2,D}} (q', w', x'\xi y')$ if and only if $x = x'$ and $(q, w, \xi y) \vdash^{*}_{\overline{2,D}} (q', w', \xi y')$.

We first need a lemma which allows us to consider only members of $\mathcal{D}_1\sigma\mathcal{D}_2$ such that at least one input symbol is read whenever the second nest is "pushed open" and later "popp d shut".

($\sim, f$) LEMMA 6.2.3:[1] *For all AFA $\mathcal{D}_1$ and $\mathcal{D}_2$ and all D in $\mathcal{D}_1\sigma\mathcal{D}_2$, there exists $\bar{D}$ in $\mathcal{D}_1\sigma\mathcal{D}_2$ such that*

(a) $L(\bar{D}) = L(D)$,

(b) *$\bar{D}$ is quasi-realtime if D is, and*

(c) *if $(q, w, x) \vdash_{\overline{D}} (q', w', x\xi) \vdash^{*}_{\overline{2,D}} (p, w'', x\xi) \vdash_{\overline{D}} (p', \epsilon, x)$, then $w \neq \epsilon$.*

Proof: Let $D = (K_1, \Sigma_1, \delta, q_0, F)$. Let $S = \{(p, q)/(p, \epsilon, \xi) \vdash^{*}_{\overline{2,D}} (p', \epsilon, \xi) \vdash (q, \epsilon, \epsilon)$ for some $p'\}$. (Thus S contains all (p, q) such that for some p', $(p, \epsilon, \xi) \vdash^{*}_{\overline{2,D}} (p', \epsilon, \xi)$ and (q, POP) is in $\delta(p', \epsilon, \xi)$.) For each q in K_1, let $(q, 1)$ be new and let $\bar{K}_1 = K_1 \cup \{(q, 1)/q \text{ in } K_1\}$. Let $\bar{D} = (\bar{K}_1, \Sigma_1, \bar{\delta}, q_0, F)$, where $\bar{\delta}$ is defined as follows (for all p in K_1, q' in K_1, a in $\Sigma_1 \cup \{\epsilon\}$, γ in $(\Gamma_1 \cup \Gamma_2 \cup \{\xi\})^*$, and u in $I_1 \cup I_2$):

(1) Suppose (q', u) is in $\delta(p, a, \gamma)$.

 (a) Then (q', u) is in $\bar{\delta}(p, a, \gamma)$.

 (b) If $a \neq \epsilon$, then (q', u) is in $\bar{\delta}((p, 1), a, \gamma)$.

 (c) If $a = \epsilon$, then $((q', 1), u)$ is in $\bar{\delta}((p, 1), a, \gamma)$.

[1] See Exercise 6.2.7 for the $\sim$ case.

(2) Suppose (q', PUSH) is in $\delta(p, a, \gamma)$.

(a) If $a \neq \epsilon$, then (q', PUSH) is in $\bar{\delta}(p, a, \gamma)$.

(b) If $a = \epsilon$, then $((q', 1), \text{PUSH})$ is in $\bar{\delta}(p, a, \gamma)$ and $(q, 1_\gamma)$ is in $\bar{\delta}(p, \epsilon, \gamma)$ for all q satisfying (q', q) in S.

(3) Suppose (q, POP) is in $\delta(p, a, \xi)$.

(a) Then (q, POP) is in $\bar{\delta}(p, a, \xi)$.

(b) If $a \neq \epsilon$, then (q, POP) is in $\bar{\delta}((p, 1), a, \xi)$.

Intuitively, D in a state q is simulated by $\bar{D}$ in state q until a PUSH is applied. If the input is non-ϵ then D in a state q continues to be simulated by $\bar{D}$ in state q. If the input is ϵ, then D in a state q is simulated by $\bar{D}$ in state $(q, 1)$ until a non-ϵ input occurs. At that time, D in a state q is again simulated by $\bar{D}$ in state q. In addition, $(p, \epsilon, \gamma) \vdash_{D} (q', \epsilon, \gamma\xi) \overset{*}{\vdash}_{D} (q'', \epsilon, \gamma\xi) \vdash_{D} (q, \epsilon, \gamma)$ is simulated by $(p, \epsilon, \gamma) \vdash_{\bar{D}} (q, \epsilon, \gamma)$.

More specifically, by (2b), (1b), (1c), and (3b), each state $(q, 1)$ represents q and the fact that a symbol in Σ_1 has not been read since PUSH was last applied. The only computations of D omitted in $\bar{D}$ are those involved in

$$(p, \epsilon, x) \vdash_{D} (q', \epsilon, x\xi) \overset{*}{\vdash}_{2, D} (p', \epsilon, x\xi) \vdash_{D} (q, \epsilon, x).$$

Here (q', q) is in S, so that (2b) is applicable. It readily follows that (a) holds. By (2b), $(q, \epsilon, x) \vdash_{\bar{D}} (\bar{q}, \epsilon, x\xi)$ implies $\bar{q} = (q', 1)$ for some q'. By (1), (2), and (3), POP cannot be applied until some symbol in Σ_1 is read. Hence (c) is satisfied. Finally, each new ϵ-rule introduced in $\bar{D}$ which does not directly mimic an ϵ-rule in D is of the type (2b). Each such rule corresponds to some (q, q') in S, which in turn, corresponds to at least one ϵ-rule in D. Hence $\bar{D}$ is quasi-realtime if D is.

We now show that $\mathcal{L}^t(\mathcal{D}_1\sigma\mathcal{D}_2)$ $(\mathcal{L}(\mathcal{D}_1\sigma\mathcal{D}_2))$ is a subset of Sub $(\mathcal{L}^t(\mathcal{D}_1), \mathcal{L}^t(\mathcal{D}_2))$ $(\text{Sub}\ (\mathcal{L}(\mathcal{D}_1), \mathcal{L}(\mathcal{D}_2)))$.

$(\sim, f)$ LEMMA 6.2.4: *For all AFA $\mathcal{D}_1$ and $\mathcal{D}_2$, $\mathcal{L}^t(\mathcal{D}_1\sigma\mathcal{D}_2) \subseteq$ Sub $(\mathcal{L}^t(\mathcal{D}_1), \mathcal{L}^t(\mathcal{D}_2))$ and $\mathcal{L}(\mathcal{D}_1\sigma\mathcal{D}_2) \subseteq$ Sub $(\mathcal{L}(\mathcal{D}_1), \mathcal{L}(\mathcal{D}_2))$.*

Proof: Let $D = (K_1, \Sigma_1, \delta, q_0, F)$ be a (quasi-realtime) acceptor in $\mathcal{D}_1\sigma\mathcal{D}_2$. Without loss of generality we may assume that D satisfies condition (c) of Lemma 6.2.3. For each p and q in K_1 and γ in $G_D \cap g_1(\Gamma_1^*)$, let $\langle p, \gamma, q\rangle$ be a new symbol in Σ and let Σ_2 be the set of all $\langle p, \gamma, q\rangle$. Clearly Σ_2 is finite. Let τ be the substitution on $(\Sigma_1 \cup \Sigma_2)^*$ defined by $\tau(a) = \{a\}$ for each a in Σ_1 and

$$\tau(\langle p, \gamma, q\rangle) = \{aw'/(p', w', \xi) \overset{*}{\vdash}_{2, D} (q', w'', \xi) \vdash_{D} (q, \epsilon, \epsilon) \text{ and } (p', \text{PUSH}) \text{ is in } \delta(p, a, \gamma) \text{ for some } p', q' \text{ in } K_1, a \text{ in } \Sigma_1 \cup \{\epsilon\}, \text{ and } w', w'' \text{ in } \Sigma_1^*\}$$

for each $\langle p, \gamma, q\rangle$. By condition (c) of Lemma 6.2.3, τ is ϵ-free. We shall demonstrate the lemma by proving that $\tau(a)$ is in $\mathcal{L}(\mathcal{D}_2)$ ($\mathcal{L}^t(\mathcal{D}_2)$) for each a in $\Sigma_1 \cup \Sigma_2$ and then exhibiting a language L in $\mathcal{L}(\mathcal{D}_1)$ ($\mathcal{L}^t(\mathcal{D}_1)$) such that $L(D) = \tau(L)$.

Consider $\tau(a)$ for a in $\Sigma_1 \cup \Sigma_2$. For each a in Σ_1, $\tau(a) = \{a\}$ is an ϵ-free regular set and hence in $\mathcal{L}(\mathcal{D}_2)$ ($\mathcal{L}^t(\mathcal{D}_2)$). Suppose $\langle p, \gamma, q\rangle$ is in Σ_2. Let $(p, 1)$ and $(q, 2)$ be new symbols in K. Let $K_{p,\gamma,q} = K_1 \cup \{(p, 1), (q, 2)\}$. Let $D_{p,\gamma,q}$ be the acceptor $(K_{p,\gamma,q}, \Sigma_1, \delta_{p,\gamma,q}, (p, 1), \{(q, 2)\})$ in $\mathcal{D}_2$, where $\delta_{p,\gamma,q}$ is defined as follows (for all p', q' in K_1 and a in $\Sigma_1 \cup \{\epsilon\}$):

(1) If (q', PUSH) is in $\delta(p, a, \gamma)$, let $(q', 1_\epsilon)$ be in $\delta_{p,\gamma,q}((p, 1), a, \epsilon)$.

(2) If (q', u) is in $\delta(p', a, \bar{\gamma})$, u in I_2 and $\bar{\gamma}$ in $g_2(\Gamma_2^*)$, let (q', u) be in $\delta_{p,\gamma,q}$ $(p', a, \bar{\gamma})$.

(3) If (q, POP) is in $\delta(p', a, \xi)$, let $((q, 2), 1_\epsilon)$ be in $\delta_{p,\gamma,q}(p', a, \epsilon)$.

Note that $D_{p,\gamma,q}$ is quasi-realtime if D is. Clearly $L(D_{p,\gamma,q}) = \tau(\langle p, \gamma, q\rangle)$. Therefore $\tau(\langle p, \gamma, q\rangle)$ is in $\mathcal{L}(\mathcal{D}_2)$ ($\mathcal{L}^t(\mathcal{D}_2)$).

Now let $L_1 = \{w/(q_0, w, \epsilon) \overset{*}{\underset{1,D}{\vdash}} (\bar{p}, \epsilon, \epsilon)$ for some $\bar{p}$ in $F\}$. Let L_2 be the set of all words of the form

$$w_1 \langle p_1, \gamma_1, q_1\rangle w_2 \langle p_2, \gamma_2, q_2\rangle \ldots w_n \langle p_n, \gamma_n, q_n\rangle w_{n+1},$$

$n \geqq 1$, having the property that there exist $\bar{p}$ in F and $x_1, \ldots, x_n$ in Γ_1^* such that $(q_0, w_1, \epsilon) \overset{*}{\underset{1,D}{\vdash}} (p_1, \epsilon, x_1)$, $(q_n, w_{n+1}, x_n) \overset{*}{\underset{1,D}{\vdash}} (\bar{p}, \epsilon, \epsilon)$, and (q_i, w_{i+1}, x_i) $\overset{*}{\underset{1,D}{\vdash}} (p_{i+1}, \epsilon, x_{i+1})$ for all i, $1 \leqq i < n$, with γ_j in $g_1(x_j)$ for all j, $1 \leqq j \leqq n$. Let $L = L_1 \cup L_2$. Evidently $\tau(L_1) = L_1 \subseteq L(D)$. If $(p', w', \xi) \overset{*}{\underset{2,D}{\vdash}} (q', w'', \xi)$, then as noted earlier, $(p', w', x\xi) \overset{*}{\underset{2,D}{\vdash}} (q', w'', x\xi)$ for each x in Γ_1^*. Thus, if

$$w_1 \langle p_1, \gamma_1, q_1\rangle w_2 \ldots \langle p_n, \gamma_n, q_n\rangle w_{n+1}$$

is in L and y_i is in $\tau(\langle p_i, \gamma_i, q_i\rangle)$ for all i, $1 \leqq i \leqq n$, then $w_1 y_1 w_2 \ldots y_n w_{n+1}$ is in $L(D)$. Hence

(4) $\tau(L) \subseteq L(D)$.

To see the reverse containment, suppose w is in $L(D)$. Either w is in L_1 or there exist $w_1, \ldots, w_{n+1}$, $\langle p_1, \gamma_1, q_1\rangle, \ldots, \langle p_n, \gamma_n, q_n\rangle$, $y_1, \ldots, y_n$ such that $w = w_1 y_1 \ldots w_n y_n w_{n+1}$,

$$w_1 \langle p_1, \gamma_1, q_1\rangle \ldots w_n \langle p_n, \gamma_n, q_n\rangle w_{n+1}$$

is in L, and y_i is in $\tau(\langle p_i, \gamma_i, q_i\rangle)$ for all i, $1 \leqq i \leqq n$. Hence,

(5) $L(D) \subseteq \tau(L)$.

Combining (4) and (5), we get

(6) $L(D) = \tau(L)$.

To complete the proof that $L(D)$ is in Sub $(\mathcal{L}(\mathcal{D}_1), \mathcal{L}(\mathcal{D}_2))$ $\big(\text{Sub}(\mathcal{L}^t(\mathcal{D}_1), \mathcal{L}^t(\mathcal{D}_2))\big)$, it suffices to show that L is in $\mathcal{L}(\mathcal{D}_1)$ $(\mathcal{L}^t(\mathcal{D}_1))$. Let $\bar{D} = (K_1, \Sigma_1 \cup \Sigma_2, \bar{\delta}, q_0, F)$ be the acceptor in $\mathcal{D}_1$, where $\bar{\delta}$ is defined as follows:

(7) If (q', u) is in $\delta(q, a, \gamma)$, with q in K_1, a in $\Sigma_1 \cup \{\epsilon\}$, γ in $g_1(\Gamma_1^*)$, and u in I_1, let (q', u) be in $\bar{\delta}(q, a, \gamma)$.

(8) If $\langle p, \gamma, q\rangle$ is in Σ_2, let $(q, 1_\gamma)$ be in $\bar{\delta}(p, \langle p, \gamma, q\rangle, \gamma)$.

For each w in Σ_1^*, $(p, w, x) \overset{*}{\underset{\bar{D}}{\vdash}} (p', \epsilon, x')$ if and only if $(p, w, x) \overset{*}{\underset{1, D}{\vdash}} (p', \epsilon, x')$. From this it readily follows that $L = L(\bar{D})$. Since the only ϵ-rules in $\bar{D}$ are also in D, $\bar{D}$ is quasi-realtime if D is. Therefore L is in $\mathcal{L}(\mathcal{D}_1)$ $(\mathcal{L}^t(\mathcal{D}_1))$, completing the proof.

We next show that $\mathcal{L}((\mathcal{D}_1 \wedge \mathcal{D}_2)^{\text{N}}) \subseteq \mathcal{L}(\mathcal{D}_1 \sigma \mathcal{D}_2)$ $\big(\mathcal{L}^t((\mathcal{D}_1 \wedge \mathcal{D}_2)^{\text{N}}) \subseteq \mathcal{L}^t(\mathcal{D}_1 \sigma \mathcal{D}_2)\big)$. The main problem in deriving this result is that in instantaneous description $(q, w, (x, x'))$, $x' \neq \epsilon$, an acceptor in $(\mathcal{D}_1 \wedge \mathcal{D}_2)^{\text{N}}$ knows $g_1(x)$ whereas in instantaneous description $(q, w, x\xi x')$, $x' \neq \epsilon$, an acceptor in $\mathcal{D}_1 \sigma \mathcal{D}_2$ does not know $g_1(x)$. For an acceptor in either $(\mathcal{D}_1 \wedge \mathcal{D}_2)^{\text{N}}$ or $\mathcal{D}_1 \sigma \mathcal{D}_2$, x will not change during a computation on the $\mathcal{D}_2$-tape, but, since g_1 is multivalued, γ_1 in the rule $(q', (u, v))$ in $\delta(q, a, (\gamma_1, \gamma_2))$ of an acceptor in $(\mathcal{D}_1 \wedge \mathcal{D}_2)^{\text{N}}$ can change. We shall remedy this situation by guessing, just before opening the $\mathcal{D}_2$-nest, which possible γ_1 in $g_1(x)$ will be used in the computation on the $\mathcal{D}_2$-tape.

$(\sim, f)$ LEMMA 6.2.5: *For all AFA $\mathcal{D}_1$ and $\mathcal{D}_2$,*

$$\mathcal{L}^t((\mathcal{D}_1 \wedge \mathcal{D}_2)^{\text{N}}) \subseteq \mathcal{L}^t(\mathcal{D}_1 \sigma \mathcal{D}_2) \text{ and } \mathcal{L}((\mathcal{D}_1 \wedge \mathcal{D}_2)^{\text{N}}) \subseteq \mathcal{L}(\mathcal{D}_1 \sigma \mathcal{D}_2).$$

Proof: Let $D = (K_1, \Sigma_1, \delta, q_0, F, (1, 2))$ be an acceptor in $(\mathcal{D}_1 \wedge \mathcal{D}_2)^{\text{N}}$. Let

$$G_1 = \{\gamma_1/(\gamma_1, \gamma_2) \text{ in } G_D \text{ for some } \gamma_2\} \text{ and}$$

$$G_2 = \{\gamma_2/(\gamma_1, \gamma_2) \text{ in } G_D \text{ for some } \gamma_1\}.$$

Without loss of generality we may assume that (ϵ, ϵ) is in G_D, so that G_1 contains ϵ. Let $\mathcal{G} = \{G \neq \emptyset / G \subseteq G_1\}$ and $I' = \{v \text{ in } I_2/(q', (u, v)) \text{ in } \delta(q, a, (\gamma_1, \gamma_2)) \text{ for some } q', q \text{ in } K_1, a \text{ in } \Sigma_1 \cup \{\epsilon\}, u \text{ in } I_1, (\gamma_1, \gamma_2) \text{ in } G_D\}$. For each q in K_1, G in $\mathcal{G}$, and v in I', let $(q, G, 0)$, $(q, G, 1)$, and (q, G, v) be new symbols in K, where 0 and 1 are not symbols in I'. Let $\bar{D} = (K_2, \Sigma_1, \bar{\delta}, q_0, F)$ be the acceptor in $\mathcal{D}_1 \sigma \mathcal{D}_2$ where

$$K_2 = K_1 \cup \{(q, G, 0), (q, G, 1), (q, G, v)/q \text{ in } K_1, G \text{ in } \mathcal{G}, v \text{ in } I'\}$$

and $\bar{\delta}$ is defined as follows (for all q, q' in K_1, a in $\Sigma_1 \cup \{\epsilon\}$, u in I_1, v in I_2, G in $\mathcal{G}$, γ_1 in Γ_1^*, and γ_2 in Γ_2^*):

(1) (q', u) is in $\bar{\delta}(q, a, \gamma_1)$ if $(q', (u, v))$ is in $\delta(q, a, (\gamma_1, \epsilon))$ and v is in[1] $\psi_2(\epsilon)$.

(2) $((q, \{\gamma_1\}, 0), 1(1, \gamma_1))$ is in $\bar{\delta}(q, \epsilon, \gamma_1)$ for all γ_1 in G_1.

(3) $((q, G \cup \{\gamma_1\}, 0), 1(1, \gamma_1))$ is in $\bar{\delta}((q, G, 0), \epsilon, \gamma_1)$ for all γ_1 in $G_1 - G$. [By (2) and (3), $(q, \epsilon, x) \overset{*}{\underset{\bar{D}}{\vdash}} ((q, G, 0), \epsilon, x)$, where x is in Γ_1^* and G is a nonempty subset of $g_1(x) \cap G_1$.]

(4) $((q', G, v), \text{PUSH})$ is in $\bar{\delta}((q, G, 0), a, \gamma_1)$ and $((q', G, 1), v)$ is in $\bar{\delta}((q', G, v), \epsilon, \xi)$, if $(q', (u, v))$ is in $\delta(q, a, (\gamma_1, \epsilon))$, v is not in $\psi_2(\epsilon)$, and γ_1 is in G.

[By (4), $((q, G, 0), a, x) \underset{\bar{D}}{\vdash} ((q', G, v), \epsilon, x\xi) \underset{\bar{D}}{\vdash} ((q', G, 1), \epsilon, x\xi f_2(\epsilon, v))$, if $(q, a, (x, \epsilon)) \underset{D}{\vdash} (q', \epsilon, (x, f_2(\epsilon, v)))$, with $f(\epsilon, v) \neq \epsilon$.]

(5) $((q', G, 1), v)$ is in $\bar{\delta}((q, G, 1), a, \gamma_2)$ if $(q', (u, v))$ is in $\delta(q, a, (\gamma_1, \gamma_2))$, γ_1 is in G, and $\gamma_2 \neq \epsilon$.

[By (5), $((q, G, 1), a, x\xi x') \underset{\bar{D}}{\vdash} ((q', G, 1), \epsilon, x\xi f_2(x', v))$ if $(q, a, (x, x')) \underset{D}{\vdash} (q', \epsilon, (x, f_2(x', v)))$, with $(q', (u, v))$ in $\delta(q, a, (\gamma_1, \gamma_2))$, γ_1 in $g_1(x)$, γ_2 in $g_2(x')$, u in $\psi_1(\gamma_1)$, γ_1 in G, and $\gamma_2 \neq \epsilon$.]

(6) (q, POP) is in $\bar{\delta}((q, G, 1), \epsilon, \xi)$.

[By (6), $((q, G, 1), \epsilon, x\xi) \underset{\bar{D}}{\vdash} (q, \epsilon, x)$.]

Informally, $\bar{D}$ operates as follows. While D is computing on the $\mathcal{D}_1$-tape, $\bar{D}$ imitates D by type 1 rules. At some point, $\bar{D}$ guesses that D wants to open a $\mathcal{D}_2$-nest. Then $\bar{D}$ uses type 2 and type 3 rules to guess all possible γ_1 in $g_1(x)$ that D will need, and uses type 4 rules to open its $\mathcal{D}_2$-nest. While in the $\mathcal{D}_2$-nest, $\bar{D}$ imitates D by type 5 rules. $\bar{D}$ checks to see that it has the correct γ_1 in $g_1(x)$ in the G-component of its state. Whenever the $\mathcal{D}_2$-nest is empty, $\bar{D}$ can close it by a type 6 rule and start imitating D on the $\mathcal{D}_1$-tape again. By a straightforward argument, it can be formally shown that $L(\bar{D}) = L(D)$. We omit the details.

Finally, the only new ϵ-rules in $\bar{D}$ not having a direct counterpart in D are types 2, 3, and 6. Now type 2 and 3 rules can only be applied at most $\#(G_1)$ consecutive times. A type 6 rule cannot be applied twice in a row. Furthermore, a type 6 rule can be applied only after at least one occurrence of a type 4 rule and then a type 5 rule. Suppose D is quasi-realtime, so that D has at most k_1 consecutive ϵ-moves for some k_1. Then $\bar{D}$ has at most $(\#(G_1)+2)(k_1+1)$ consecutive ϵ-moves and hence is quasi-realtime. Thus $\mathcal{L}((\mathcal{D}_1 \wedge \mathcal{D}_2)^{\text{N}}) \subseteq \mathcal{L}(\mathcal{D}_1 \sigma \mathcal{D}_2)$ and $\mathcal{L}^t((\mathcal{D}_1 \wedge \mathcal{D}_2)^{\text{N}}) \subseteq \mathcal{L}^t(\mathcal{D}_1 \sigma \mathcal{D}_2)$.

[1] Recall that $\psi_2(\epsilon) = \{v \text{ in } I_2/f_2(\gamma', v) = \gamma' \text{ for all } \gamma' \text{ in } g_2^{-1}(\epsilon)\} = \{v \text{ in } I_2/f_2(\epsilon, v) = \epsilon\}$.

We are now to prove the reverse containment of Lemma 6.2.2.

$(\sim, f)$ LEMMA 6.2.6: *For all multitape AFA* $\mathcal{D}_1$ *and* $\mathcal{D}_2$,

$$\mathcal{L}^t((\mathcal{D}_1 \wedge \mathcal{D}_2)^N) \subseteq Sub\,(\mathcal{L}^t(\mathcal{D}_1^N), \mathcal{L}^t(\mathcal{D}_2^N)) \quad and$$
$$\mathcal{L}((\mathcal{D}_1 \wedge \mathcal{D}_2)^N) \subseteq Sub\,(\mathcal{L}(\mathcal{D}_1^N), \mathcal{L}(\mathcal{D}_2^N)) = S\hat{u}b\,(\mathcal{L}(\mathcal{D}_1^N), \mathcal{L}(\mathcal{D}_2^N)).$$

Proof: By Theorem 6.2.1 and by (b) of Theorem 6.1.1, $\text{Sub}(\mathcal{L}(\mathcal{D}_1^N), \mathcal{L}(\mathcal{D}_2^N)) = \text{S\^ub}\,(\mathcal{L}(\mathcal{D}_1^N), \mathcal{L}(\mathcal{D}_2^N))$.

We shall give the argument for $\mathcal{L}^t((\mathcal{D}_1 \wedge \mathcal{D}_2)^N) \subseteq \text{Sub}(\mathcal{L}^t(\mathcal{D}_1^N), \mathcal{L}^t(\mathcal{D}_2^N))$, the same proof holding for $\mathcal{L}((\mathcal{D}_1 \wedge \mathcal{D}_2)^N) \subseteq \text{Sub}\,(\mathcal{L}(\mathcal{D}_1^N), \mathcal{L}(\mathcal{D}_2^N))$. By Lemma 6.2.1, there exist single tape AFA $\overline{\mathcal{D}}_1$ and $\overline{\mathcal{D}}_2$ such that $\mathcal{L}^t(\overline{\mathcal{D}}_1) = \mathcal{L}^t(\mathcal{D}_1^N)$ and $\mathcal{L}^t(\overline{\mathcal{D}}_2) = \mathcal{L}^t(\mathcal{D}_2^N)$. From the definitions of $\wedge$ and $\mathcal{D}^N$ and from the method of proof of Lemma 6.2.1, it is obvious that $\mathcal{L}^t((\mathcal{D}_1 \wedge \mathcal{D}_2)^N) \subseteq \mathcal{L}^t((\overline{\mathcal{D}}_1 \wedge \overline{\mathcal{D}}_2)^N)$. Then

$$\begin{aligned}
\mathcal{L}^t((\mathcal{D}_1 \wedge \mathcal{D}_2)^N) &\subseteq \mathcal{L}^t((\overline{\mathcal{D}}_1 \wedge \overline{\mathcal{D}}_2)^N) \\
&\subseteq \mathcal{L}^t(\overline{\mathcal{D}}_1 \sigma \overline{\mathcal{D}}_2), \quad \text{by Lemma 6.2.5,} \\
&\subseteq \text{Sub}\,(\mathcal{L}^t(\overline{\mathcal{D}}_1), \mathcal{L}^t(\overline{\mathcal{D}}_2)), \quad \text{by Lemma 6.2.4,} \\
&= \text{Sub}\,(\mathcal{L}^t(\mathcal{D}_1^N), \mathcal{L}^t(\mathcal{D}_2^N)).
\end{aligned}$$

The next lemma combines the two previous main inclusions and gives a representation result for consecutive substitutions by a finite sequence of AFL.

$(\sim, f)$ LEMMA 6.2.7: *Let* $\mathcal{D}_1, \ldots, \mathcal{D}_n$ *be multitape AFA, with* $n \geqq 2$. *Then*

$$\mathcal{L}^t((\mathcal{D}_1 \wedge \ldots \wedge \mathcal{D}_n)^N) = Sub(\mathcal{L}^t(\mathcal{D}_1^N), \ldots, \mathcal{L}^t(\mathcal{D}_n^N)) \quad and$$

$$\begin{aligned}
\mathcal{L}((\mathcal{D}_1 \wedge \ldots \wedge \mathcal{D}_n)^N) &= S\hat{u}b\,(\mathcal{L}(\mathcal{D}_1^N), \ldots, \mathcal{L}(\mathcal{D}_n^N)) \\
&= Sub\,(\mathcal{L}(\mathcal{D}_1^N), \ldots, \mathcal{L}(\mathcal{D}_n^N)) \\
&= S\hat{u}b\,\big(\mathcal{L}^t(\mathcal{D}_1^N), Sub\,(\mathcal{L}(\mathcal{D}_2^N), \ldots, \mathcal{L}(\mathcal{D}_n^N))\big).
\end{aligned}$$

Proof: Suppose $n = 2$. By Lemmas 6.2.2 and 6.2.6, $\mathcal{L}^t((\mathcal{D}_1 \wedge \mathcal{D}_2)^N) = \text{Sub}\,(\mathcal{L}^t(\mathcal{D}_1^N), \mathcal{L}^t(\mathcal{D}_2^N))$ and $\text{Sub}\,(\mathcal{L}(\mathcal{D}_1^N), \mathcal{L}(\mathcal{D}_2^N)) = \text{S\^ub}\,(\mathcal{L}(\mathcal{D}_1^N), \mathcal{L}(\mathcal{D}_2^N)) = \mathcal{L}((\mathcal{D}_1 \wedge \mathcal{D}_2)^N)$. Then

$$\begin{aligned}
\mathcal{L}((\mathcal{D}_1 \wedge \mathcal{D}_2)^N) &= \text{Sub}\,(\mathcal{L}(\mathcal{D}_1^N), \mathcal{L}(\mathcal{D}_2^N)) = \text{S\^ub}\,(\mathcal{L}(\mathcal{D}_1^N), \mathcal{L}(\mathcal{D}_2^N)) \\
&= \text{S\^ub}\,\big(\hat{\mathcal{H}}(\mathcal{L}^t(\mathcal{D}_1^N)), \mathcal{L}(\mathcal{D}_2^N)\big), \quad \text{by Lemma 6.2.1 and Theorem 4.3.3,} \\
&= \text{S\^ub}\,(\mathcal{L}^t(\mathcal{D}_1^N), \mathcal{L}(\mathcal{D}_2^N)), \quad \text{by Theorem 6.1.1.}
\end{aligned}$$

Continuing by induction, suppose the result is true for $n = k \geqq 2$. Consider $n = k+1$. Then

$$\mathcal{L}^t((\mathcal{D}_1 \wedge \ldots \wedge \mathcal{D}_{k+1})^{\mathrm{N}}) = \mathrm{Sub}\left(\mathcal{L}^t((\mathcal{D}_1 \wedge \ldots \wedge \mathcal{D}_k)^{\mathrm{N}}), \mathcal{L}^t(\mathcal{D}_{k+1}^{\mathrm{N}})\right),$$

since the lemma is true for $n = 2$,

$$= \mathrm{Sub}\left(\mathrm{Sub}\,(\mathcal{L}^t(\mathcal{D}_1^{\mathrm{N}}), \ldots, \mathcal{L}^t(\mathcal{D}_k^{\mathrm{N}})), \mathcal{L}^t(\mathcal{D}_{k+1}^{\mathrm{N}})\right),$$

by induction,

$$= \mathrm{Sub}\,(\mathcal{L}^t(\mathcal{D}_1^{\mathrm{N}}), \ldots, \mathcal{L}^t(\mathcal{D}_{k+1}^{\mathrm{N}})).$$

Similarly,

$$\mathcal{L}((\mathcal{D}_1 \wedge \ldots \wedge \mathcal{D}_{k+1})^{\mathrm{N}}) = \mathrm{Sub}\,(\mathcal{L}(\mathcal{D}_1^{\mathrm{N}}), \ldots, \mathcal{L}(\mathcal{D}_{k+1}^{\mathrm{N}})) \quad \text{and}$$
$$\mathcal{L}((\mathcal{D}_1 \wedge \ldots \wedge \mathcal{D}_{k+1})^{\mathrm{N}}) = \mathrm{S\hat{u}b}\,(\mathcal{L}(\mathcal{D}_1^{\mathrm{N}}), \ldots, \mathcal{L}(\mathcal{D}_{k+1}^{\mathrm{N}})).$$

Also,

$$\mathcal{L}((\mathcal{D}_1 \wedge \ldots \wedge \mathcal{D}_{k+1})^{\mathrm{N}}) = \mathrm{S\hat{u}b}\left(\mathcal{L}(\mathcal{D}_1^{\mathrm{N}}), \mathcal{L}((\mathcal{D}_2 \wedge \ldots \wedge \mathcal{D}_{k+1})^{\mathrm{N}})\right),$$

since the lemma is true for $n = 2$,

$$= \mathrm{S\hat{u}b}\left(\hat{\mathcal{H}}(\mathcal{L}^t(\mathcal{D}_1^{\mathrm{N}})), \mathcal{L}((\mathcal{D}_2 \wedge \ldots \wedge \mathcal{D}_{k+1})^{\mathrm{N}})\right),$$

by Lemma 6.2.1 and Theorem 4.3.3,

$$= \mathrm{S\hat{u}b}\left(\mathcal{L}^t(\mathcal{D}_1^{\mathrm{N}}), \mathcal{L}((\mathcal{D}_2 \wedge \ldots \wedge \mathcal{D}_{k+1})^{\mathrm{N}})\right), \quad \text{by Theorem 6.1.1},$$
$$= \mathrm{S\hat{u}b}\left(\mathcal{L}^t(\mathcal{D}_1^{\mathrm{N}}), \mathrm{Sub}\,(\mathcal{L}(\mathcal{D}_2^{\mathrm{N}}), \ldots, \mathcal{L}(\mathcal{D}_{k+1}^{\mathrm{N}}))\right), \quad \text{by induction.}$$

Hence the result.

Since $\mathcal{D}^{\mathrm{N}} = \mathcal{D}$ for each AFA$\mathcal{D}$, we immediately get:

$(\sim, f)$ THEOREM 6.2.2: *Let $\mathcal{D}_1, \ldots, \mathcal{D}_n$ be AFA, with $n \geqq 2$. Then*

$$\mathcal{L}^t((\mathcal{D}_1 \wedge \ldots \wedge \mathcal{D}_n)^{\mathrm{N}}) = \mathit{Sub}\,(\mathcal{L}^t(\mathcal{D}_1), \ldots, \mathcal{L}^t(\mathcal{D}_n))$$

and

$$\mathcal{L}((\mathcal{D}_1 \wedge \ldots \wedge \mathcal{D}_n)^{\mathrm{N}}) = \mathit{S\hat{u}b}\,(\mathcal{L}(\mathcal{D}_1), \ldots, \mathcal{L}(\mathcal{D}_n))$$
$$= \mathit{Sub}\,(\mathcal{L}(\mathcal{D}_1), \ldots, \mathcal{L}(\mathcal{D}_n))$$
$$= \mathit{S\hat{u}b}\left(\mathcal{L}^t(\mathcal{D}_1), \mathit{Sub}\,(\mathcal{L}(\mathcal{D}_2), \ldots, \mathcal{L}(\mathcal{D}_n))\right).$$

We now turn to a second representation of substitution by devices. To do this we generalize the operation of σ between AFA.

Notation: For $n \geqq 2$ and $i = 1, \ldots, n$ let $(\Omega_i, \mathcal{D}_i)$ be the AFA $(K, \Sigma, \Gamma_i, I_i, f_i, g_i)$. Let ξ be a symbol not in $\bigcup_i \Gamma_i$ and let PUSH and POP be two symbols not in $\bigcup_i I_i$. Then $\mathcal{D}_1\sigma\ldots\sigma\mathcal{D}_n$ denotes the AFA $\Big(K, \Sigma, \bigcup_i \Gamma_i \cup \{\xi\}, \bigcup_i I_i$

$\cup$ {PUSH, POP}, $f, g)$, where f and g are defined as follows (for each $i \geqq 2$, $j \geqq 1$, x_j in Γ_j^*, z_j in Γ_j^+, and u_j in I_j): $f(x_1, u_1) = f_1(x_1, u_1)$, $f(x_1\xi x_2 \ldots \xi x_i, u_i) = x_1\xi x_2 \ldots \xi f_i(x_i, u_i)$, $f(x_1, \text{PUSH}) = x_1\xi$, $f(x_1\xi, \text{POP}) = x_1$, $f(x_1\xi x_2 \ldots \xi x_i, \text{PUSH}) = x_1\xi x_2 \ldots \xi x_i \xi$ and $f(x_1\xi x_2 \ldots \xi x_i \xi, \text{POP}) = x_1\xi x_2 \ldots \xi x_i$, $i < n$, $g(x_1) = g_1(x_1)$, $g(x_1\xi x_2 \ldots \xi z_i) = g_i(z_i)$, and $g(x_1\xi x_2 \ldots \xi) = \{\xi\}$.

For $n \geqq 3$, $\mathcal{D} = \mathcal{D}_1\sigma \ldots \sigma\mathcal{D}_n$ is not identical to $\mathcal{D}' = ((\ldots((\mathcal{D}_1\sigma\mathcal{D}_2)\sigma\mathcal{D}_3)\ldots)\sigma\mathcal{D}_n)$, or any other grouping $\mathcal{D}'$ of the $\mathcal{D}_1, \ldots, \mathcal{D}_n$ in the order given. Nevertheless, it is easily seen (Exercise 6.2.15) that $\mathcal{L}^t(\mathcal{D}) = \mathcal{L}^t(\mathcal{D}')$ and $\mathcal{L}(\mathcal{D}) = \mathcal{L}(\mathcal{D}')$.

We now have a second representation theorem for substitution.

($\sim, f$) THEOREM 6.2.3: *Let $\mathcal{D}_1, \ldots, \mathcal{D}_n$ be AFA, with $n \geqq 2$. Then*

$$\mathcal{L}^t(\mathcal{D}_1\sigma \ldots \sigma\mathcal{D}_n) = Sub\,(\mathcal{L}^t(\mathcal{D}_1), \ldots, \mathcal{L}^t(\mathcal{D}_n))$$

and

$$\mathcal{L}(\mathcal{D}_1\sigma \ldots \sigma\mathcal{D}_n) = Sub\,(\mathcal{L}(\mathcal{D}_1), \ldots, \mathcal{L}(\mathcal{D}_n)).$$

Proof: We shall give the argument for $\mathcal{L}^t(\mathcal{D}_1\sigma \ldots \sigma\mathcal{D}_n)$, an analogous proof holding for $\mathcal{L}(\mathcal{D}_1\sigma \ldots \sigma\mathcal{D}_n)$.

Consider $n = 2$. Then

$$\begin{aligned} \mathcal{L}^t((\mathcal{D}_1 \wedge \mathcal{D}_2)^{\mathrm{N}}) &\subseteq \mathcal{L}^t(\mathcal{D}_1\sigma\mathcal{D}_2), && \text{by Lemma 6.2.5,} \\ &\subseteq \text{Sub}\,(\mathcal{L}^t(\mathcal{D}_1), \mathcal{L}^t(\mathcal{D}_2)), && \text{by Lemma 6.2.4,} \\ &\subseteq \mathcal{L}^t((\mathcal{D}_1 \wedge \mathcal{D}_2)^{\mathrm{N}}), && \text{by Lemma 6.2.2.} \end{aligned}$$

Hence $\mathcal{L}^t(\mathcal{D}_1\sigma\mathcal{D}_2) = \text{Sub}\,(\mathcal{L}^t(\mathcal{D}_1), \mathcal{L}^t(\mathcal{D}_2))$.

Continuing by induction, suppose the theorem is true for $n = k \geqq 2$. Then

$$\begin{aligned} \mathcal{L}^t(\mathcal{D}_1\sigma \ldots \sigma\mathcal{D}_{k+1}) &= \mathcal{L}^t((\mathcal{D}_1\sigma \ldots \sigma\mathcal{D}_k)\sigma\mathcal{D}_{k+1}), && \text{since the theorem is true for } n = 2, \\ &= \text{Sub}\,(\mathcal{L}^t(\mathcal{D}_1\sigma \ldots \sigma\mathcal{D}_k), \mathcal{L}^t(\mathcal{D}_{k+1})), && \text{by induction,} \\ &= \text{Sub}\,(\text{Sub}\,(\mathcal{L}^t(\mathcal{D}_1), \ldots, \mathcal{L}^t(\mathcal{D}_k)), \mathcal{L}^t(\mathcal{D}_{k+1})), && \text{by induction,} \\ &= \text{Sub}\,(\mathcal{L}^t(\mathcal{D}_1), \ldots, \mathcal{L}^t(\mathcal{D}_{k+1})). \end{aligned}$$

Hence the theorem.

EXERCISE 6.2.1: For each nontrivial multitape AFA $\mathcal{D}$, prove that $\tilde{\mathcal{L}}(\mathcal{D}^{\mathrm{N}})$ is a full semi-AFL and $\tilde{\mathcal{L}}^t(\mathcal{D}^{\mathrm{N}})$ is a semi-AFL containing $\{\epsilon\}$.

EXERCISE 6.2.2: For each multitape AFA$\mathcal{D}$, prove that $\mathcal{L}_f(\mathcal{D}^{\mathrm{N}})$ is a full semi-AFL and $\mathcal{L}_f^t(\mathcal{D}^{\mathrm{N}})$ is a semi-AFL containing $\{\epsilon\}$.

EXERCISE 6.2.3: Show that a nested multitape AFA is a special instance of an[1] SS-AFA [GaG].

EXERCISE 6.2.4: Prove that Sub $[\tilde{\mathcal{L}}^t(\mathcal{D}_1^{\mathrm{N}}), \tilde{\mathcal{L}}^t(\mathcal{D}_2^{\mathrm{N}})] \subseteq \tilde{\mathcal{L}}^t((\mathcal{D}_1 \wedge \mathcal{D}_2)^{\mathrm{N}})$ and Sub $[\tilde{\mathcal{L}}(\mathcal{D}_1^{\mathrm{N}}), \tilde{\mathcal{L}}(\mathcal{D}_2^{\mathrm{N}})] =$ Sûb $[\tilde{\mathcal{L}}(\mathcal{D}_1^{\mathrm{N}}), \tilde{\mathcal{L}}(\mathcal{D}_2^{\mathrm{N}})] \subseteq \tilde{\mathcal{L}}((\mathcal{D}_1 \wedge \mathcal{D}_2)^{\mathrm{N}})$ for all nontrivial multitape AFA $\mathcal{D}_1$ and $\mathcal{D}_2$.

EXERCISE 6.2.5: Prove that Sub$[\mathcal{L}_f^t(\mathcal{D}_1^{\mathrm{N}}), \mathcal{L}_f^t(\mathcal{D}_2^{\mathrm{N}})] \subseteq \mathcal{L}_f^t((\mathcal{D}_1 \wedge \mathcal{D}_2)^{\mathrm{N}})$ and Sub $[\mathcal{L}_f(\mathcal{D}_1^{\mathrm{N}}), \mathcal{L}_f(\mathcal{D}_2^{\mathrm{N}})] =$ Sûb $[\mathcal{L}_f(\mathcal{D}_1^{\mathrm{N}}), \mathcal{L}_f(\mathcal{D}_2^{\mathrm{N}})] \subseteq \mathcal{L}_f((\mathcal{D}_1 \wedge \mathcal{D}_2)^{\mathrm{N}})$ for all multitape AFA $\mathcal{D}_1$ and $\mathcal{D}_2$.

EXERCISE 6.2.6: Prove that for all AFA $\mathcal{D}_1$ and $\mathcal{D}_2$ and each D in $\mathcal{D}_1\sigma\mathcal{D}_2$, there exists $\bar{D}$ in $\mathcal{D}_1\sigma\mathcal{D}_2$ such that (a) $L_f(\bar{D}) = L_f(D)$, (b) $\bar{D}$ is quasi-realtime if D is, and (c) if $(q, w, x) \vdash_{\bar{D}} (q', w', x\xi) \overset{*}{\vdash}_{2,\bar{D}} (p, w'', x\xi) \vdash_{\bar{D}} (p', \epsilon, x)$, then $w \neq \epsilon$.

EXERCISE 6.2.7: Let $\mathcal{D}_1$ and $\mathcal{D}_2$ be nontrivial AFA. Write $(p, w, x\xi) \overset{+-}{\vdash}_{2,D} (p', w'$, $x\xi$), if $(p, w, x\xi) \overset{+}{\vdash}_{2,D} (p', w', x\xi)$ by a sequence of configurations, only the first and last having $x\xi$ as the auxiliary storage component. Prove that for each D in $\mathcal{D}_1\sigma\mathcal{D}_2$, there exists $\bar{D}$ in $\mathcal{D}_1 \sigma \mathcal{D}_2$ such that (a) $\tilde{L}(\bar{D}) = \tilde{L}(D)$, (b) $\bar{D}$ is quasi-realtime if D is, (c) if $(q, w, \epsilon) \overset{*}{\vdash}_{\bar{D}} (q', w', x\xi y)$ then $x \neq \epsilon$, (d) if $(q, w, x) \vdash_{\bar{D}} (q', w', x\xi) \overset{*}{\vdash}_{2,\bar{D}} (p, w'', x\xi) \vdash_{\bar{D}} (p', \epsilon, x)$, then $w \neq \epsilon$, and (e) if $(q, w, x) \vdash_{\bar{D}} (q', w', x\xi) \overset{+-}{\vdash}_{2,\bar{D}} (p, w'', x\xi)$ then there is no p' and w''' such that $(p, w'', x\xi) \overset{+-}{\vdash}_{2,D} (p', w''', x\xi)$.

EXERCISE 6.2.8: Prove that $\mathcal{L}_f^t(\mathcal{D}_1\sigma\mathcal{D}_2) \subseteq$ Sub $(\mathcal{L}_f^t(\mathcal{D}_1), \mathcal{L}_f^t(\mathcal{D}_2))$ and $\mathcal{L}_f(\mathcal{D}_1\sigma\mathcal{D}_2) \subseteq$ Sub $(\mathcal{L}_f(\mathcal{D}_1), \mathcal{L}_f(\mathcal{D}_2))$ for all AFA $\mathcal{D}_1$ and $\mathcal{D}_2$.

EXERCISE 6.2.9: Prove that $\tilde{\mathcal{L}}^t(\mathcal{D}_1\sigma\mathcal{D}_2) \subseteq$ Sub $(\tilde{\mathcal{L}}^t(\mathcal{D}_1), \tilde{\mathcal{L}}^t(\mathcal{D}_2))$ and $\tilde{\mathcal{L}}(\mathcal{D}_1\sigma\mathcal{D}_2) \subseteq$ Sub $(\tilde{\mathcal{L}}(\mathcal{D}_1), \tilde{\mathcal{L}}(\mathcal{D}_2))$ for all nontrivial AFA $\mathcal{D}_1$ and $\mathcal{D}_2$.

EXERCISE 6.2.10: Prove that $\mathcal{L}_f^t((\mathcal{D}_1 \wedge \mathcal{D}_2)^{\mathrm{N}}) \subseteq \mathcal{L}_f^t(\mathcal{D}_1\sigma\mathcal{D}_2)$ and $\mathcal{L}_f((\mathcal{D}_1 \wedge \mathcal{D}_2)^{\mathrm{N}}) \subseteq \mathcal{L}_f(\mathcal{D}_1\sigma\mathcal{D}_2)$ for all AFA $\mathcal{D}_1$ and $\mathcal{D}_2$.

EXERCISE 6.2.11: Prove that $\tilde{\mathcal{L}}^t((\mathcal{D}_1 \wedge \mathcal{D}_2)^{\mathrm{N}}) \subseteq \tilde{\mathcal{L}}^t(\mathcal{D}_1\sigma\mathcal{D}_2)$ and $\tilde{\mathcal{L}}((\mathcal{D}_1 \wedge \mathcal{D}_2)^{\mathrm{N}}) \subseteq \tilde{\mathcal{L}}(\mathcal{D}_1\sigma\mathcal{D}_2)$ for all nontrivial AFA $\mathcal{D}_1$ and $\mathcal{D}_2$.

EXERCISE 6.2.12: Prove that $\mathcal{L}_f^t((\mathcal{D}_1 \wedge \mathcal{D}_2)^{\mathrm{N}}) \subseteq$ Sub$(\mathcal{L}_f^t(\mathcal{D}_1^{\mathrm{N}}), \mathcal{L}_f^t(\mathcal{D}_2^{\mathrm{N}}))$ and $\mathcal{L}_f((\mathcal{D}_1 \wedge \mathcal{D}_2)^{\mathrm{N}}) \subseteq$ Sub $(\mathcal{L}_f(\mathcal{D}_1^{\mathrm{N}}), \mathcal{L}_f(\mathcal{D}_2^{\mathrm{N}}))$ for all multitape AFA $\mathcal{D}_1$ and $\mathcal{D}_2$.

[1] See the terminology prior to Exercise 4.5.8.

EXERCISE 6.2.13: Prove that $\tilde{\mathcal{L}}^t((\mathcal{D}_1 \wedge \mathcal{D}_2)^N) \subseteq \text{Sub}(\tilde{\mathcal{L}}^t(\mathcal{D}_1^N), \tilde{\mathcal{L}}^t(\mathcal{D}_2^N))$ and $\tilde{\mathcal{L}}((\mathcal{D}_1 \wedge \mathcal{D}_2)^N) \subseteq \text{Sub}(\tilde{\mathcal{L}}(\mathcal{D}_1^N), \tilde{\mathcal{L}}(\mathcal{D}_2^N))$ for all nontrivial multitape AFA $\mathcal{D}_1$ and $\mathcal{D}_2$.

EXERCISE 6.2.14: Use Theorem 6.2.2 to prove that $\text{Sub}(\mathcal{L}_1, \ldots, \mathcal{L}_n)$ is an AFL if $\mathcal{L}_1, \ldots, \mathcal{L}_n$ are AFL, $n \geqq 2$.

EXERCISE 6.2.15: Prove that $\mathcal{L}^t(\mathcal{D}_1\sigma\ldots\sigma\mathcal{D}_n) = \mathcal{L}^t((\ldots((\mathcal{D}_1\sigma\mathcal{D}_2)\sigma\mathcal{D}_3)\ldots)\sigma\mathcal{D}_n)$ for all AFA $\mathcal{D}_1, \ldots, \mathcal{D}_n$.

EXERCISE 6.2.16: Prove that $\tilde{\mathcal{L}}^t(\mathcal{D}_1\sigma\ldots\sigma\mathcal{D}_n) = \tilde{\mathcal{L}}^t(\ldots((\mathcal{D}_1\sigma\mathcal{D}_2)\ldots)\sigma\mathcal{D}_n)$ for $n \geqq 2$ and all nontrivial AFA $\mathcal{D}_1, \ldots, \mathcal{D}_n$.

6.3 Substitution Closure

Given a family $\mathcal{L}$ of languages, we now examine the smallest family of languages containing $\mathcal{L}$ and closed under substitution or under ϵ-free substitution. We also consider the smallest (full) AFL containing $\mathcal{L}$ and closed under [ϵ-free] substitution. We then study relations between the different types of substitution closure when $\mathcal{L}$ is a trio or a full trio.

Notation: For each family $\mathcal{L}$ let $\hat{\sigma}(\mathcal{L})$ ($\sigma(\mathcal{L})$) be the smallest family containing $\mathcal{L}$ and closed under (ϵ-free) substitution.

Since (i) the family of all languages contains $\mathcal{L}$ and is closed under (ϵ-free) substitution, and (ii) the intersection of an arbitrary collection of families, each of which contains $\mathcal{L}$ and is closed under (ϵ-free) substitution, is also a family containing $\mathcal{L}$ and closed under (ϵ-free) substitution, $\sigma(\mathcal{L})$ and $\hat{\sigma}(\mathcal{L})$ both exist.

We now introduce some additional concepts for a family $\mathcal{L}$ and then connect them with $\sigma(\mathcal{L})$, $\hat{\sigma}(\mathcal{L})$.

Notation: For each family $\mathcal{L}$ of languages let $\text{Sub}_0(\mathcal{L}, \mathcal{L}) = \widehat{\text{Sub}}_0(\mathcal{L}, \mathcal{L}) = \mathcal{L}$ and, by induction, $\text{Sub}_{k+1}(\mathcal{L}, \mathcal{L}) = \text{Sub}\left[\mathcal{L}, \bigcup_{i=0}^{k} \text{Sub}_i(\mathcal{L}, \mathcal{L})\right]$ and $\widehat{\text{Sub}}_{k+1}(\mathcal{L}, \mathcal{L}) = \widehat{\text{Sub}}\left[\mathcal{L}, \bigcup_{i=0}^{k} \widehat{\text{Sub}}_i(\mathcal{L}, \mathcal{L})\right]$ for each $k \geqq 0$. Let $\text{Sub}_\infty(\mathcal{L}, \mathcal{L}) = \bigcup_{i=0}^{\infty} \text{Sub}_i(\mathcal{L}, \mathcal{L})$ and $\widehat{\text{Sub}}_\infty(\mathcal{L}, \mathcal{L}) = \bigcup_{i=0}^{\infty} \widehat{\text{Sub}}_i(\mathcal{L}, \mathcal{L})$.

The following lemma will be used several times in this section.

LEMMA 6.3.1: (a) *For each family* $\mathcal{L}$ *of languages,* $Sub_k(\mathcal{L}, \mathcal{L}) \subseteq Sub_{k+1}(\mathcal{L}, \mathcal{L})$ *and* $\hat{Sub}_k(\mathcal{L}, \mathcal{L}) \subseteq \hat{Sub}_{k+1}(\mathcal{L}, \mathcal{L})$ *for all* $k \geqq 1$. *If* $\mathcal{L}$ *is a trio, then* $Sub_0(\mathcal{L}, \mathcal{L}) \subseteq Sub_1(\mathcal{L}, \mathcal{L})$ *and* $\hat{Sub}_0(\mathcal{L}, \mathcal{L}) \subseteq \hat{Sub}_1(\mathcal{L}, \mathcal{L})$.

(b) *Let* $\mathcal{L}$ *be a trio and* $\mathcal{L}_i = \mathcal{L}$ *for all* $i \geqq 1$. *Then* $Sub_k(\mathcal{L}, \mathcal{L}) = Sub(\mathcal{L}_1, \ldots, \mathcal{L}_{k+1})$ *and* $\hat{Sub}_k(\mathcal{L}, \mathcal{L}) = \hat{Sub}(\mathcal{L}_1, \ldots, \mathcal{L}_{k+1})$ *for all* $k \geqq 0$.

Proof: We shall give the argument for Sub_k, an analogous proof holding for $\hat{\mathrm{Sub}}_k$.

(a) For $k \geqq 1$,

$$\begin{aligned}\mathrm{Sub}_k(\mathcal{L}, \mathcal{L}) &= \mathrm{Sub}\left(\mathcal{L}, \bigcup_{i=0}^{k-1} \mathrm{Sub}_i(\mathcal{L}, \mathcal{L})\right)\\ &\subseteq \mathrm{Sub}\left(\mathcal{L}, \bigcup_{i=0}^{k} \mathrm{Sub}_i(\mathcal{L}, \mathcal{L})\right)\\ &= \mathrm{Sub}_{k+1}(\mathcal{L}, \mathcal{L}).\end{aligned}$$

Suppose $\mathcal{L}$ is a trio. For each L in $\mathcal{L} = \mathrm{Sub}_0(\mathcal{L}, \mathcal{L})$ let σ_L be the substitution on Σ_L^* defined by $\sigma_L(a) = \{a\}$ for each a in Σ_L. Then σ_L is ϵ-free. Since $\mathcal{L}$ is a trio, $\sigma_L(a)$ is in $\mathcal{L}$ for each a in Σ_L. Thus $\sigma_L(L) = L$ is in $\mathrm{Sub}(\mathcal{L}, \mathcal{L}) = \mathrm{Sub}\left[\mathcal{L}, \bigcup_{i=0}^{0} \mathrm{Sub}_i(\mathcal{L}, \mathcal{L})\right] = \mathrm{Sub}_1(\mathcal{L}, \mathcal{L})$.

(b) Since $\mathrm{Sub}_0(\mathcal{L}, \mathcal{L}) = \mathcal{L} = \mathrm{Sub}(\mathcal{L}) = \mathrm{Sub}(\mathcal{L}_1)$, (b) is true for $k = 0$. Continuing by induction, suppose (b) is true for $k \geqq 0$. Then

$$\begin{aligned}\mathrm{Sub}_{k+1}(\mathcal{L}, \mathcal{L}) &= \mathrm{Sub}\left(\mathcal{L}, \bigcup_{i=0}^{k} \mathrm{Sub}_i(\mathcal{L}, \mathcal{L})\right)\\ &= \mathrm{Sub}(\mathcal{L}_1, \mathrm{Sub}_k(\mathcal{L}, \mathcal{L})), \quad \text{by (a)},\\ &= \mathrm{Sub}(\mathcal{L}_1, \mathrm{Sub}(\mathcal{L}_2, \ldots, \mathcal{L}_{k+2})), \quad \text{by induction},\\ &= \mathrm{Sub}(\mathrm{Sub}(\mathcal{L}_1, \ldots, \mathcal{L}_{k+1}), \mathcal{L}_{k+2})\\ &= \mathrm{Sub}(\mathcal{L}_1, \ldots, \mathcal{L}_{k+2}).\end{aligned}$$

Hence the induction is extended, and (b) is true.

REMARK: It is not always true that $\mathrm{Sub}_0(\mathcal{L}, \mathcal{L}) \subseteq \mathrm{Sub}_1(\mathcal{L}, \mathcal{L})$ and $\hat{\mathrm{Sub}}_0(\mathcal{L}, \mathcal{L}) \subseteq \hat{\mathrm{Sub}}_1(\mathcal{L}, \mathcal{L})$. For let $\mathcal{L} = \{\{ab\}\}$. Then $\mathrm{Sub}_0(\mathcal{L}, \mathcal{L}) = \hat{\mathrm{Sub}}_0(\mathcal{L}, \mathcal{L}) = \{\{ab\}\}$ and $\mathrm{Sub}_1(\mathcal{L}, \mathcal{L}) = \hat{\mathrm{Sub}}_1(\mathcal{L}, \mathcal{L}) = \{\{abab\}\}$.

PROPOSITION 6.3.1: *For each family* $\mathcal{L}$ *of languages*

(a) $\sigma(\mathcal{L})[\hat{\sigma}(\mathcal{L})]$ *is the smallest family* $\mathcal{L}'$ *containing* $\mathcal{L}$ *such that* $Sub(\mathcal{L}, \mathcal{L}') \subseteq \mathcal{L}'[\hat{Sub}(\mathcal{L}, \mathcal{L}') \subseteq \mathcal{L}']$; *and*

(b) $\sigma(\mathcal{L}) = Sub_\infty(\mathcal{L}, \mathcal{L})$ *and* $\hat{\sigma}(\mathcal{L}) = \hat{Sub}_\infty(\mathcal{L}, \mathcal{L})$.

Proof: We shall give the argument for $\hat{\sigma}(\mathcal{L})$ only.

Let $\mathcal{L}_0$ be the smallest family $\mathcal{L}'$ containing $\mathcal{L}$ such that $\hat{\text{Sub}}(\mathcal{L}, \mathcal{L}') \subseteq \mathcal{L}'$. Since the family of all languages is such an $\mathcal{L}'$ and since the intersection of all such $\mathcal{L}'$ is also such an $\mathcal{L}'$, $\mathcal{L}_0$ exists.

We first show that $\mathcal{L}_0 = \hat{\text{Sub}}_\infty(\mathcal{L}, \mathcal{L})$. By definition, $\hat{\text{Sub}}_0(\mathcal{L}, \mathcal{L}) = \mathcal{L} \subseteq \mathcal{L}_0$. Continuing by induction, suppose $\hat{\text{Sub}}_i(\mathcal{L}, \mathcal{L}) \subseteq \mathcal{L}_0$ for all i, $0 \leqq i < k$, $k \geqq 1$. Then

$$\begin{aligned} \hat{\text{Sub}}_k(\mathcal{L}, \mathcal{L}) &= \hat{\text{Sub}}\left[\mathcal{L}, \bigcup_0^{k-1} \hat{\text{Sub}}_i(\mathcal{L}, \mathcal{L})\right] \\ &\subseteq \hat{\text{Sub}}\,[\mathcal{L}, \mathcal{L}_0], \quad \text{by induction,} \\ &\subseteq \mathcal{L}_0. \end{aligned}$$

Thus the induction is extended. Then $\hat{\text{Sub}}_\infty(\mathcal{L}, \mathcal{L}) = \bigcup_0^\infty \hat{\text{Sub}}_i(\mathcal{L}, \mathcal{L}) \subseteq \mathcal{L}_0$. To see the reverse inclusion, we have

$$\hat{\text{Sub}}\,[\mathcal{L}, \hat{\text{Sub}}_\infty(\mathcal{L}, \mathcal{L})] = \hat{\text{Sub}}\left[\mathcal{L}, \bigcup_0^\infty \hat{\text{Sub}}_k(\mathcal{L}, \mathcal{L})\right].$$

Let L be in $\mathcal{L}$ and τ a substitution on Σ_L^* by languages of $\bigcup_0^\infty \hat{\text{Sub}}_k(\mathcal{L}, \mathcal{L})$. Thus, for each a in Σ_L there exists $m_a \geqq 0$ such that $\tau(a)$ is in $\bigcup_0^{m_a} \hat{\text{Sub}}_k(\mathcal{L}, \mathcal{L})$. Let $m = \max\{m_a/a \text{ in } \Sigma_L\}$. Since Σ_L is finite, m exists. Then $\tau(a)$ is in $\bigcup_{k=0}^m \hat{\text{Sub}}_k(\mathcal{L}, \mathcal{L})$ for each a in Σ_L. Therefore $\tau(L)$ is in $\hat{\text{Sub}}\left[\mathcal{L}, \bigcup_0^m \hat{\text{Sub}}_k(\mathcal{L}, \mathcal{L})\right] = \hat{\text{Sub}}_{m+1}(\mathcal{L}, \mathcal{L}) \subseteq \hat{\text{Sub}}_\infty(\mathcal{L}, \mathcal{L})$. Thus

$$\hat{\text{Sub}}\,[\mathcal{L}, \hat{\text{Sub}}_\infty(\mathcal{L}, \mathcal{L})] \subseteq \hat{\text{Sub}}_\infty(\mathcal{L}, \mathcal{L}),$$

so that $\mathcal{L}_0 \subseteq \hat{\text{Sub}}_\infty(\mathcal{L}, \mathcal{L})$.

To complete the proof of the proposition it suffices to show that $\hat{\sigma}(\mathcal{L}) = \hat{\text{Sub}}_\infty(\mathcal{L}, \mathcal{L})$. Now

$$\begin{aligned} \hat{\text{Sub}}\,(\mathcal{L}, \hat{\sigma}(\mathcal{L})) &\subseteq \hat{\text{Sub}}\,(\hat{\sigma}(\mathcal{L}), \hat{\sigma}(\mathcal{L})) \\ &\subseteq \hat{\sigma}(\mathcal{L}), \quad \text{since } \hat{\sigma}(\mathcal{L}) \text{ is substitution closed.} \end{aligned}$$

Then $\hat{\text{Sub}}_\infty(\mathcal{L}, \mathcal{L}) \subseteq \hat{\sigma}(\mathcal{L})$ since, by the above paragraph, $\hat{\text{Sub}}_\infty(\mathcal{L}, \mathcal{L})$ is the smallest family $\mathcal{L}'$ containing $\mathcal{L}$ such that $\hat{\text{Sub}}(\mathcal{L}, \mathcal{L}') \subseteq \mathcal{L}'$. To see the reverse inclusion, it is enough to show that $\hat{\text{Sub}}_\infty(\mathcal{L}, \mathcal{L})$ is substitution closed. [For this will imply that $\hat{\sigma}(\mathcal{L}) \subseteq \hat{\text{Sub}}_\infty(\mathcal{L}, \mathcal{L})$.] By the above paragraph,

$$\hat{\text{Sub}}\,[\hat{\text{Sub}}_0(\mathcal{L}, \mathcal{L}), \hat{\text{Sub}}_\infty(\mathcal{L}, \mathcal{L})] = \hat{\text{Sub}}\,[\mathcal{L}, \hat{\text{Sub}}_\infty(\mathcal{L}, \mathcal{L})] \subseteq \hat{\text{Sub}}_\infty(\mathcal{L}, \mathcal{L}).$$

Continuing by induction, assume that $\hat{\text{Sub}}\,[\hat{\text{Sub}}_j(\mathcal{L}, \mathcal{L}), \hat{\text{Sub}}_\infty(\mathcal{L}, \mathcal{L})] \subseteq \hat{\text{Sub}}_\infty(\mathcal{L}, \mathcal{L})$ for all j, $0 \leqq j < k$, $k \geqq 1$. Then for $\mathcal{L}^{(k)} = \bigcup_{j=0}^{k-1} \hat{\text{Sub}}_j(\mathcal{L}, \mathcal{L})$,

$$(*)\ \hat{\text{Sub}}\,[\mathcal{L}^{(k)}, \hat{\text{Sub}}_\infty(\mathcal{L}, \mathcal{L})] = \bigcup_{j=0}^{k-1} \hat{\text{Sub}}\,[\hat{\text{Sub}}_j(\mathcal{L}, \mathcal{L}), \hat{\text{Sub}}_\infty(\mathcal{L}, \mathcal{L})] \subseteq \hat{\text{Sub}}_\infty(\mathcal{L}, \mathcal{L}).$$

Furthermore, by definition, $\hat{\text{Sub}}_k(\mathcal{L}, \mathcal{L}) = \hat{\text{Sub}}(\mathcal{L}, \mathcal{L}^{(k)})$. Thus

$$\begin{aligned}\hat{\text{Sub}}\,[\hat{\text{Sub}}_k(\mathcal{L}, \mathcal{L}), \hat{\text{Sub}}_\infty(\mathcal{L}, \mathcal{L})] &= \hat{\text{Sub}}\,[\hat{\text{Sub}}\,(\mathcal{L}, \mathcal{L}^{(k)}), \hat{\text{Sub}}_\infty(\mathcal{L}, \mathcal{L})]\\ &\subseteq \hat{\text{Sub}}\,(\mathcal{L}, \hat{\text{Sub}}\,[\mathcal{L}^{(k)}, \hat{\text{Sub}}_\infty(\mathcal{L}, \mathcal{L})]),\\ &\quad \text{by the remark after Lemma 6.1.1,}\\ &\subseteq \hat{\text{Sub}}\,[\mathcal{L}, \hat{\text{Sub}}_\infty(\mathcal{L}, \mathcal{L})], \quad \text{by } (*),\\ &\subseteq \hat{\text{Sub}}_\infty(\mathcal{L}, \mathcal{L}).\end{aligned}$$

Hence the induction is extended. Therefore

$$\begin{aligned}\hat{\text{Sub}}\,[\hat{\text{Sub}}_\infty(\mathcal{L}, \mathcal{L}), \hat{\text{Sub}}_\infty(\mathcal{L}, \mathcal{L})] &= \hat{\text{Sub}}\left[\bigcup_{k=0}^{\infty} \hat{\text{Sub}}_k(\mathcal{L}, \mathcal{L}), \hat{\text{Sub}}_\infty(\mathcal{L}, \mathcal{L})\right]\\ &= \bigcup_{k=0}^{\infty} \hat{\text{Sub}}\,[\hat{\text{Sub}}_k(\mathcal{L}, \mathcal{L}), \hat{\text{Sub}}_\infty(\mathcal{L}, \mathcal{L})]\\ &\subseteq \hat{\text{Sub}}_\infty(\mathcal{L}, \mathcal{L}),\end{aligned}$$

and the proof is complete.

Let $\mathcal{L} = \{U/U \subseteq a^+\}$ for some given symbol a. Then $\mathcal{L}$ is ϵ-free and substitution closed, but not an AFL. Since our main objects of concern are AFL we introduce the following concepts:

Notation: For each family $\mathcal{L}$ of languages, let

(a) $\mathcal{F}_\sigma(\mathcal{L})$ be the smallest AFL containing $\mathcal{L}$ and closed under ϵ-free substitution.

(b) $\mathcal{F}_{\hat{\sigma}}(\mathcal{L})$ be the smallest AFL containing $\mathcal{L}$ and closed under arbitrary substitution.

(c) $\hat{\mathcal{F}}_\sigma(\mathcal{L})$ be the smallest full AFL containing $\mathcal{L}$ and closed under ϵ-free substitution.

(d) $\hat{\mathcal{F}}_{\hat{\sigma}}(\mathcal{L})$ be the smallest full AFL containing $\mathcal{L}$ and closed under arbitrary substitution.

Clearly $\mathcal{F}_\sigma(\mathcal{L})$, $\mathcal{F}_{\hat{\sigma}}(\mathcal{L})$, $\hat{\mathcal{F}}_\sigma(\mathcal{L})$, and $\hat{\mathcal{F}}_{\hat{\sigma}}(\mathcal{L})$ exist.

Note that if $\mathcal{L}_1 \subseteq \mathcal{L}_2$, then $\mathcal{F}_\sigma(\mathcal{L}_1) \subseteq \mathcal{F}_\sigma(\mathcal{L}_2)$, $\hat{\mathcal{F}}_\sigma(\mathcal{L}_1) \subseteq \hat{\mathcal{F}}_\sigma(\mathcal{L}_2)$, $\mathcal{F}_{\hat{\sigma}}(\mathcal{L}_1) \subseteq \mathcal{F}_{\hat{\sigma}}(\mathcal{L}_2)$, and $\hat{\mathcal{F}}_{\hat{\sigma}}(\mathcal{L}_1) \subseteq \hat{\mathcal{F}}_{\hat{\sigma}}(\mathcal{L}_2)$. From this it immediately follows that $\mathcal{F}_\sigma(\mathcal{L}) = \mathcal{F}_\sigma(\mathcal{F}(\mathcal{L}))$, $\mathcal{F}_{\hat{\sigma}}(\mathcal{L}) = \mathcal{F}_{\hat{\sigma}}(\mathcal{F}(\mathcal{L}))$, $\hat{\mathcal{F}}_\sigma(\mathcal{L}) = \hat{\mathcal{F}}_\sigma(\hat{\mathcal{F}}(\mathcal{L}))$, and $\hat{\mathcal{F}}_{\hat{\sigma}}(\mathcal{L}) = \hat{\mathcal{F}}_{\hat{\sigma}}(\hat{\mathcal{F}}(\mathcal{L}))$ for each family $\mathcal{L}$. Thus we may always assume that $\mathcal{L}$ is an AFL when considering $\mathcal{F}_\sigma(\mathcal{L})$ and $\mathcal{F}_{\hat{\sigma}}(\mathcal{L})$, and that $\mathcal{L}$ is a full AFL when considering $\hat{\mathcal{F}}_\sigma(\mathcal{L})$ and $\hat{\mathcal{F}}_{\hat{\sigma}}(\mathcal{L})$.

By Proposition 3.3.3, each trio, thus each semi-AFL, closed under (ϵ-free) substitution is an AFL. Hence there is no need to introduce separate symbolism for the smallest trio or semi-AFL containing a given family and closed under (ϵ-free) substitution. Similarly, there is no need to consider separately the smallest full trio or semi-AFL containing a given family and closed under (ϵ-free) substitution.

We next examine some relations between the families $\mathcal{F}_\sigma(\mathcal{L})$, $\hat{\mathcal{F}}_\sigma(\mathcal{L})$, etc.

PROPOSITION 6.3.2: *For each family $\mathcal{L}$ of languages*:

(a) $\hat{\mathcal{F}}_{\hat{\sigma}}(\mathcal{L}) = \hat{\mathcal{F}}_\sigma(\mathcal{L})$.

(b) *If $\mathcal{L}$ contains a language with ϵ in it, then* $\mathcal{F}_{\hat{\sigma}}(\mathcal{L}) = \hat{\mathcal{F}}_\sigma(\mathcal{L})$. *If $\mathcal{L}$ is ϵ-free, then* $\mathcal{F}_{\hat{\sigma}}(\mathcal{L}) = \mathcal{F}_\sigma(\mathcal{L})$.

Proof: (a) We may assume that $\mathcal{L}$ is a full AFL. Clearly $\hat{\mathcal{F}}_\sigma(\mathcal{L}) \subseteq \hat{\mathcal{F}}_{\hat{\sigma}}(\mathcal{L})$.

Now $\hat{\mathcal{F}}_\sigma(\mathcal{L})$ is a full AFL containing $\mathcal{L}$ and

$$\hat{\mathrm{Sub}}(\hat{\mathcal{F}}_\sigma(\mathcal{L}), \hat{\mathcal{F}}_\sigma(\mathcal{L})) = \mathrm{Sub}(\hat{\mathcal{F}}_\sigma(\mathcal{L}), \hat{\mathcal{F}}_\sigma(\mathcal{L})), \quad \text{by Corollary 1 of Theorem 6.1.1,}$$

$$\subseteq \hat{\mathcal{F}}_\sigma(\mathcal{L}).$$

Then $\hat{\mathcal{F}}_{\hat{\sigma}}(\mathcal{L}) \subseteq \hat{\mathcal{F}}_\sigma(\mathcal{L})$, whence equality.

(b) We may assume that $\mathcal{L}$ is an AFL. Suppose $\mathcal{L}$ contains a language L with ϵ in it. Then $\mathcal{F}_{\hat{\sigma}}(\mathcal{L})$ is an AFL containing L, thus $\{\epsilon\}$, and is closed under arbitrary substitution. Hence $\mathcal{F}_{\hat{\sigma}}(\mathcal{L})$ is a full AFL, so that $\hat{\mathcal{F}}_\sigma(\mathcal{L}) \subseteq \mathcal{F}_{\hat{\sigma}}(\mathcal{L})$. To see the reverse containment, note that $\mathcal{F}_{\hat{\sigma}}(\mathcal{L}) \subseteq \hat{\mathcal{F}}_{\hat{\sigma}}(\mathcal{L}) = \hat{\mathcal{F}}_\sigma(\mathcal{L})$, the last equality by (a).

Suppose $\mathcal{L}$ is ϵ-free. Obviously $\mathcal{F}_\sigma(\mathcal{L}) \subseteq \mathcal{F}_{\hat{\sigma}}(\mathcal{L})$. Consider the reverse containment. Since $\mathcal{L}$ is ϵ-free, $\mathcal{F}_\sigma(\mathcal{L})$ is ϵ-free. [Otherwise, let $\mathcal{M}(\mathcal{L}) = \{L \text{ in } \mathcal{F}_\sigma(\mathcal{L})/L\ \epsilon\text{-free}\}$. Since $\mathcal{F}_\sigma(\mathcal{L})$ is an AFL, so is $\mathcal{M}(\mathcal{L})$. Since $\mathcal{L}$ is ϵ-free, $\mathcal{M}(\mathcal{L})$ contains $\mathcal{L}$. Clearly $\mathcal{M}(\mathcal{L}) \subsetneq \mathcal{F}_\sigma(\mathcal{L})$. Since $\mathrm{Sub}(\mathcal{M}(\mathcal{L}), \mathcal{M}(\mathcal{L})) \subseteq \mathrm{Sub}(\mathcal{F}_\sigma(\mathcal{L}), \mathcal{F}_\sigma(\mathcal{L})) \subseteq \mathcal{F}_\sigma(\mathcal{L})$ and $\mathrm{Sub}(\mathcal{M}(\mathcal{L}), \mathcal{M}(\mathcal{L}))$ is ϵ-free,

Sub $(\mathcal{M}(\mathcal{L}), \mathcal{M}(\mathcal{L})) \subseteq \mathcal{M}(\mathcal{L})$. Thus $\mathcal{M}(\mathcal{L})$ is an AFL containing $\mathcal{L}$, is closed under ϵ-free substitution, and is a proper subfamily of $\mathcal{F}_\sigma(\mathcal{L})$. This contradicts the definition of $\mathcal{F}_\sigma(\mathcal{L})$.] Therefore $\hat{\text{Sub}}(\mathcal{F}_\sigma(\mathcal{L}), \mathcal{F}_\sigma(\mathcal{L})) =$ Sub $(\mathcal{F}_\sigma(\mathcal{L}), \mathcal{F}_\sigma(\mathcal{L})) \subseteq \mathcal{F}_\sigma(\mathcal{L})$. Hence $\mathcal{F}_\sigma(\mathcal{L})$ is closed under arbitrary substitution. Thus $\mathcal{F}_{\hat{\sigma}}(\mathcal{L}) \subseteq \mathcal{F}_\sigma(\mathcal{L})$, whence equality.

In view of Proposition 6.3.2, instead of examining the four families $\mathcal{F}_\sigma(\mathcal{L})$, $\mathcal{F}_{\hat{\sigma}}(\mathcal{L})$, $\hat{\mathcal{F}}_\sigma(\mathcal{L})$, and $\hat{\mathcal{F}}_{\hat{\sigma}}(\mathcal{L})$, we need only study two, namely $\mathcal{F}_\sigma(\mathcal{L})$ and $\hat{\mathcal{F}}_\sigma(\mathcal{L})$ $[= \hat{\mathcal{F}}_{\hat{\sigma}}(\mathcal{L})]$.

We now establish some equalities for $\sigma(\mathcal{L})$ and $\hat{\sigma}(\mathcal{L})$ when $\mathcal{L}$ is an AFL or a full AFL.

LEMMA 6.3.2: (a) *For each* $k \geqq 0$ *and each trio* $\mathcal{L}$, $Sub_k(\mathcal{L}, \mathcal{L})$, $\hat{Sub}_k(\mathcal{L}, \mathcal{L})$, $Sub_\infty(\mathcal{L}, \mathcal{L})$, *and* $\hat{Sub}_\infty(\mathcal{L}, \mathcal{L})$ *are trios.*

(b) *For each* $k \geqq 0$ *and each full trio* $\mathcal{L}$, $Sub_k(\mathcal{L}, \mathcal{L}) = \hat{Sub}_k(\mathcal{L}, \mathcal{L})$, $Sub_\infty(\mathcal{L}, \mathcal{L}) = \hat{Sub}_\infty(\mathcal{L}, \mathcal{L})$, *and both are full trios.*

Proof: We shall just prove (b), an analogous, but simpler, argument holding for (a).

For $k = 0$, $\text{Sub}_0(\mathcal{L}, \mathcal{L}) = \mathcal{L} = \hat{\text{Sub}}_0(\mathcal{L}, \mathcal{L})$ and is a full trio. Continuing by induction, suppose $\text{Sub}_i(\mathcal{L}, \mathcal{L}) = \hat{\text{Sub}}_i(\mathcal{L}, \mathcal{L})$ and is a full trio for all i, $0 \leqq i < k$, $k \geqq 1$. Then

$$\bigcup_{i=0}^{k-1} \text{Sub}_i(\mathcal{L}, \mathcal{L}) = \bigcup_{i=0}^{k-1} \hat{\text{Sub}}_i(\mathcal{L}, \mathcal{L}), \quad \text{by induction,}$$
$$= \hat{\text{Sub}}_{k-1}(\mathcal{L}, \mathcal{L}), \quad \text{by Lemma 6.3.1(a),}$$

and thus is a full trio. Therefore

$$\begin{aligned}\text{Sub}_k(\mathcal{L}, \mathcal{L}) &= \text{Sub}\left[\mathcal{L}, \bigcup_{i=0}^{k-1} \text{Sub}_i(\mathcal{L}, \mathcal{L})\right] \\ &= \text{Sub}\left[\mathcal{L}, \bigcup_{i=0}^{k-1} \hat{\text{Sub}}_i(\mathcal{L}, \mathcal{L})\right] \\ &= \hat{\text{Sub}}\left[\mathcal{L}, \bigcup_{i=0}^{k-1} \hat{\text{Sub}}_i(\mathcal{L}, \mathcal{L})\right], \quad \text{by Theorem 6.1.1,} \\ &= \hat{\text{Sub}}_k(\mathcal{L}, \mathcal{L}).\end{aligned}$$

Since $\mathcal{L}$ and $\bigcup_{i=0}^{k-1} \hat{\text{Sub}}_i(\mathcal{L}, \mathcal{L})$ are full trios, $\hat{\text{Sub}}\left[\mathcal{L}, \bigcup_{i=0}^{k-1} \hat{\text{Sub}}_i(\mathcal{L}, \mathcal{L})\right] =$ $\hat{\text{Sub}}_k(\mathcal{L}, \mathcal{L})$ is a full trio and the induction is extended. Then $\text{Sub}_\infty(\mathcal{L}, \mathcal{L}) =$

$\bigcup_{0}^{\infty} \mathrm{Sub}_i(\mathscr{L}, \mathscr{L}) = \bigcup_{0}^{\infty} \mathrm{S\hat{u}b}_i(\mathscr{L}, \mathscr{L}) = \mathrm{S\hat{u}b}_\infty(\mathscr{L}, \mathscr{L})$. Since the arbitrary union of full trios is a full trio, $\mathrm{S\hat{u}b}_\infty(\mathscr{L}, \mathscr{L})$ is a full trio.

THEOREM 6.3.1: (a) *For each trio* $\mathscr{L}$, $\hat{\sigma}(\mathscr{L}) = \mathit{S\hat{u}b}_\infty(\mathscr{L}, \mathscr{L}) = \mathscr{F}_{\hat{\sigma}}(\mathscr{L})$, $\sigma(\mathscr{L}) = \mathit{Sub}_\infty(\mathscr{L}, \mathscr{L}) = \mathscr{F}_\sigma(\mathscr{L})$, *and both are AFL.*

(b) *For each full trio* $\mathscr{L}$, $\mathscr{F}_{\hat{\sigma}}(\mathscr{L}) = \hat{\mathscr{F}}_\sigma(\mathscr{L}) = \hat{\mathscr{F}}_{\hat{\sigma}}(\mathscr{L}) = \mathscr{F}_\sigma(\mathscr{L}) = \hat{\sigma}(\mathscr{L}) = \sigma(\mathscr{L}) = \mathit{S\hat{u}b}_\infty(\mathscr{L}, \mathscr{L}) = \mathit{Sub}_\infty(\mathscr{L}, \mathscr{L})$ *and is a full AFL.*

Proof: (a) We shall give the argument for $\hat{\sigma}(\mathscr{L})$, an analogous proof holding for $\sigma(\mathscr{L})$.

By Proposition 6.3.1, $\hat{\sigma}(\mathscr{L}) = \mathrm{S\hat{u}b}_\infty(\mathscr{L}, \mathscr{L})$. By Lemma 6.3.2, $\hat{\sigma}(\mathscr{L})$ is a trio. Since $\hat{\sigma}(\mathscr{L})$ is substitution closed, it is an AFL by Proposition 3.3.3. Since $\hat{\sigma}(\mathscr{L})$ also contains $\mathscr{L}$, $\mathscr{F}_{\hat{\sigma}}(\mathscr{L}) \subseteq \hat{\sigma}(\mathscr{L})$. On the other hand, $\hat{\sigma}(\mathscr{L})$ is the smallest family containing $\mathscr{L}$ and closed under substitution. Thus $\hat{\sigma}(\mathscr{L}) \subseteq \mathscr{F}_{\hat{\sigma}}(\mathscr{L})$. Therefore $\hat{\sigma}(\mathscr{L}) = \mathscr{F}_{\hat{\sigma}}(\mathscr{L})$.

(b) By (a), $\mathscr{F}_{\hat{\sigma}}(\mathscr{L}) = \hat{\sigma}(\mathscr{L}) = \mathrm{S\hat{u}b}_\infty(\mathscr{L}, \mathscr{L})$ and $\mathscr{F}_\sigma(\mathscr{L}) = \sigma(\mathscr{L}) = \mathrm{Sub}_\infty(\mathscr{L}, \mathscr{L})$. By Lemma 6.3.2(b), $\mathrm{S\hat{u}b}_\infty(\mathscr{L}, \mathscr{L}) = \mathrm{Sub}_\infty(\mathscr{L}, \mathscr{L})$. By (b) and (c) of Proposition 6.3.2, $\hat{\mathscr{F}}_{\hat{\sigma}}(\mathscr{L}) = \hat{\mathscr{F}}_\sigma(\mathscr{L}) = \mathscr{F}_{\hat{\sigma}}(\mathscr{L})$. Therefore the equalities hold. Since $\hat{\mathscr{F}}_\sigma(\mathscr{L})$ is a full AFL, the resulting family of languages is a full AFL.

Given a trio $\mathscr{L}$, there are certain commutative relations among the operations $\hat{\mathscr{H}}$, $\mathscr{F}_\sigma$, $\mathscr{F}_{\hat{\sigma}}$, etc. We now consider these.

LEMMA 6.3.3: *For each* $k \geqq 0$ *and each trio* $\mathscr{L}$,

$$\mathit{Sub}_k(\hat{\mathscr{H}}(\mathscr{L}), \hat{\mathscr{H}}(\mathscr{L})) = \hat{\mathscr{H}}(\mathit{Sub}_k(\mathscr{L}, \mathscr{L})) \quad \text{and}$$

$$\mathit{S\hat{u}b}_k(\hat{\mathscr{H}}(\mathscr{L}), \hat{\mathscr{H}}(\mathscr{L})) = \hat{\mathscr{H}}(\mathit{S\hat{u}b}_k(\mathscr{L}, \mathscr{L})).$$

Proof: We shall only prove the case involving $\hat{\mathscr{H}}(\mathrm{Sub}_k(\mathscr{L}, \mathscr{L}))$, an analogous argument holding for $\hat{\mathscr{H}}(\mathrm{S\hat{u}b}_k(\mathscr{L}, \mathscr{L}))$.

For $k = 0$, $\mathrm{Sub}_0(\hat{\mathscr{H}}(\mathscr{L}), \hat{\mathscr{H}}(\mathscr{L})) = \hat{\mathscr{H}}(\mathscr{L}) = \hat{\mathscr{H}}(\mathrm{Sub}_0(\mathscr{L}, \mathscr{L}))$. Continuing by induction, suppose that $\mathrm{Sub}_i(\hat{\mathscr{H}}(\mathscr{L}), \hat{\mathscr{H}}(\mathscr{L})) = \hat{\mathscr{H}}(\mathrm{Sub}_i(\mathscr{L}, \mathscr{L}))$ for all i,

$0 \leqq i < k$, $k \geqq 1$. Then

$$\begin{aligned}
\mathrm{Sub}_k(\hat{\mathscr{H}}(\mathscr{L}), \hat{\mathscr{H}}(\mathscr{L})) &= \mathrm{Sub}\left(\hat{\mathscr{H}}(\mathscr{L}), \bigcup_0^{k-1} \mathrm{Sub}_i(\hat{\mathscr{H}}(\mathscr{L}), \hat{\mathscr{H}}(\mathscr{L}))\right) \\
&= \mathrm{Sub}\left(\hat{\mathscr{H}}(\mathscr{L}), \mathrm{Sub}_{k-1}(\hat{\mathscr{H}}(\mathscr{L}), \hat{\mathscr{H}}(\mathscr{L}))\right), \\
&\qquad \text{by Lemma 6.3.1(a),} \\
&= \mathrm{Sub}\left(\hat{\mathscr{H}}(\mathscr{L}), \hat{\mathscr{H}}(\mathrm{Sub}_{k-1}(\mathscr{L}, \mathscr{L}))\right), \quad \text{by induction,} \\
&= \hat{\mathscr{H}}(\mathrm{Sub}\,(\mathscr{L}, \mathrm{Sub}_{k-1}(\mathscr{L}, \mathscr{L})), \\
&\qquad \text{by Corollary 2 of Theorem 6.1.1,} \\
&= \hat{\mathscr{H}}\left(\mathrm{Sub}\left(\mathscr{L}, \bigcup_{i=0}^{k-1} \mathrm{Sub}_i(\mathscr{L}, \mathscr{L})\right)\right), \quad \text{by Lemma 6.3.1 (a),} \\
&= \hat{\mathscr{H}}\,(\mathrm{Sub}_k(\mathscr{L}, \mathscr{L})).
\end{aligned}$$

Hence the induction is extended and the lemma is true.

THEOREM 6.3.2: *For each trio* $\mathscr{L}$,

$$\begin{aligned}
\mathscr{F}_\sigma(\hat{\mathscr{H}}(\mathscr{L})) &= \mathscr{F}_{\hat{\sigma}}(\hat{\mathscr{H}}(\mathscr{L})) = \hat{\mathscr{F}}_\sigma(\hat{\mathscr{H}}(\mathscr{L})) = \hat{\mathscr{F}}_{\hat{\sigma}}(\hat{\mathscr{H}}(\mathscr{L})) \\
&= \hat{\mathscr{H}}(\mathscr{F}_\sigma(\mathscr{L})) = \hat{\mathscr{H}}(\hat{\mathscr{F}}_\sigma(\mathscr{L})) = \hat{\mathscr{H}}(\mathscr{F}_{\hat{\sigma}}(\mathscr{L})) \\
&= \hat{\mathscr{H}}(\hat{\mathscr{F}}_{\hat{\sigma}}(\mathscr{L})) = \hat{\mathscr{F}}_\sigma(\mathscr{L}).
\end{aligned}$$

Proof: By Theorem 6.3.1(b),

(1) $\mathscr{F}_\sigma(\hat{\mathscr{H}}(\mathscr{L})) = \mathscr{F}_{\hat{\sigma}}(\hat{\mathscr{H}}(\mathscr{L})) = \hat{\mathscr{F}}_\sigma(\hat{\mathscr{H}}(\mathscr{L})) = \hat{\mathscr{F}}_{\hat{\sigma}}(\hat{\mathscr{H}}(\mathscr{L}))$.

Next,

$$\begin{aligned}
\hat{\mathscr{F}}_\sigma(\hat{\mathscr{H}}(\mathscr{L})) &= \mathrm{Sub}_\infty(\hat{\mathscr{H}}(\mathscr{L}), (\hat{\mathscr{H}}(\mathscr{L})), \quad \text{by Theorem 6.3.1 (b),} \\
&= \bigcup_0^\infty \mathrm{Sub}_k(\hat{\mathscr{H}}(\mathscr{L}), \hat{\mathscr{H}}(\mathscr{L})) \\
&= \hat{\mathscr{H}}\left(\bigcup_0^\infty \mathrm{Sub}_k(\mathscr{L}, \mathscr{L})\right), \quad \text{by Lemma 6.3.3,} \\
&= \hat{\mathscr{H}}(\mathrm{Sub}_\infty(\mathscr{L}, \mathscr{L})) \\
&= \hat{\mathscr{H}}(\mathscr{F}_\sigma(\mathscr{L})), \quad \text{by Theorem 6.3.1(a),} \\
&\subseteq \hat{\mathscr{H}}(\hat{\mathscr{F}}_\sigma(\mathscr{L})) \\
&= \hat{\mathscr{F}}_\sigma(\mathscr{L}), \quad \text{since } \hat{\mathscr{F}}_\sigma(\mathscr{L}) \text{ is full,} \\
&\subseteq \hat{\mathscr{F}}_\sigma(\hat{\mathscr{H}}(\mathscr{L})).
\end{aligned}$$

Thus

(2) $\hat{\mathcal{F}}_\sigma(\hat{\mathcal{H}}(\mathcal{L})) = \hat{\mathcal{H}}(\mathcal{F}_\sigma(\mathcal{L})) = \hat{\mathcal{H}}(\hat{\mathcal{F}}_\sigma(\mathcal{L})) = \hat{\mathcal{F}}_\sigma(\mathcal{L})$.

By (a) of Proposition 6.3.2,

(3) $\hat{\mathcal{H}}(\hat{\mathcal{F}}_\sigma(\mathcal{L})) = \hat{\mathcal{H}}(\hat{\mathcal{F}}_{\hat{\sigma}}(\mathcal{L}))$.

Combining (1), (2), and (3), we get

$$(4)\ \mathcal{F}_\sigma(\hat{\mathcal{H}}(\mathcal{L})) = \mathcal{F}_{\hat{\sigma}}(\hat{\mathcal{H}}(\mathcal{L})) = \hat{\mathcal{F}}_\sigma(\hat{\mathcal{H}}(\mathcal{L})) = \hat{\mathcal{F}}_{\hat{\sigma}}(\hat{\mathcal{H}}(\mathcal{L}))$$
$$= \hat{\mathcal{H}}(\mathcal{F}_\sigma(\mathcal{L})) = \hat{\mathcal{H}}(\hat{\mathcal{F}}_\sigma(\mathcal{L})) = \hat{\mathcal{H}}(\hat{\mathcal{F}}_{\hat{\sigma}}(\mathcal{L})) = \hat{\mathcal{F}}_\sigma(\mathcal{L}).$$

Also,

$$\begin{aligned}\hat{\mathcal{H}}(\mathcal{F}_\sigma(\mathcal{L})) &\subseteq \hat{\mathcal{H}}(\mathcal{F}_{\hat{\sigma}}(\mathcal{L}))\\ &\subseteq \hat{\mathcal{H}}(\hat{\mathcal{F}}_{\hat{\sigma}}(\mathcal{L}))\\ &= \hat{\mathcal{H}}(\mathcal{F}_\sigma(\mathcal{L})), \quad \text{by (4)},\end{aligned}$$

so that $\hat{\mathcal{H}}(\mathcal{F}_\sigma(\mathcal{L})) = \hat{\mathcal{H}}(\mathcal{F}_{\hat{\sigma}}(\mathcal{L}))$, completing the proof.

Finally, we give a representation for $\mathcal{F}_\sigma(\mathcal{L}^t(\mathcal{D}))$ and $\mathcal{F}_{\hat{\sigma}}(\mathcal{L}(\mathcal{D}))$ in terms of nested acceptors.

THEOREM 6.3.3: *For each AFA* $\mathcal{D}$,

$$\mathcal{L}^t((\wedge\mathcal{D})^{\mathrm{N}}) = \mathcal{F}_\sigma(\mathcal{L}^t(\mathcal{D})) \quad \textit{and} \quad \mathcal{L}((\wedge\mathcal{D})^{\mathrm{N}}) = \mathcal{F}_{\hat{\sigma}}(\mathcal{L}(\mathcal{D})).$$

Proof: For each $i \geqq 1$, let $\mathcal{D}_i = \mathcal{D}$. Then

$$\begin{aligned}\mathcal{L}^t((\wedge\mathcal{D})^{\mathrm{N}}) &= \bigcup_{n\geqq 1} \mathcal{L}^t((\mathcal{D}_1\wedge\ldots\wedge\mathcal{D}_n)^{\mathrm{N}})\\ &= \bigcup_{n\geqq 1} \mathrm{Sub}(\mathcal{L}^t(\mathcal{D}_1), \ldots, \mathcal{L}^t(\mathcal{D}_n)), \quad \text{by Theorem 6.2.2,}\\ &= \bigcup_{n\geqq 0} \mathrm{Sub}_n(\mathcal{L}^t(\mathcal{D}), \mathcal{L}^t(\mathcal{D})), \quad \text{by Lemma 6.3.1(b),}\\ &= \mathrm{Sub}_\infty(\mathcal{L}^t(\mathcal{D}), \mathcal{L}^t(\mathcal{D}))\\ &= \mathcal{F}_\sigma(\mathcal{L}^t(\mathcal{D})), \quad \text{by Theorem 6.3.1(b).}\end{aligned}$$

Similarly, $\mathcal{L}((\wedge\mathcal{D})^{\mathrm{N}}) = \mathcal{F}_{\hat{\sigma}}(\mathcal{L}(\mathcal{D}))$.

EXAMPLE 6.3.1: For each i let $\mathcal{D}_i = \mathcal{D}_{\mathrm{C}}$. For each $n \geqq 1$, let

$$\begin{aligned}\mathcal{L}_n &= \mathcal{L}((\mathcal{D}_1\wedge\ldots\wedge\mathcal{D}_n)^{\mathrm{N}})\\ &= \widehat{\mathrm{Sub}}(\overbrace{\mathcal{L}_{\mathrm{C}}, \ldots, \mathcal{L}_{\mathrm{C}}}^{n}).\end{aligned}$$

Then

$$\mathcal{F}_{\hat{\sigma}}(\mathcal{L}_C) = \mathcal{L}((\wedge \mathcal{D})^N), \quad \text{by Theorem 6.3.3,}$$
$$= \bigcup_1^\infty \mathcal{L}_n.$$

Clearly $\mathcal{L}_i \subseteq \mathcal{L}_{i+1}$ for each i. For each n, let

$$L_n = \{a_1^{i_1} \ldots a_n^{i_n} c a_n^{i_n} \ldots a_1^{i_1} / \text{each } i_j \geqq 1\},$$

where $a_1, \ldots, a_n, c$ are distinct symbols. It can be shown (see Exercise 6.3.17) that L_{n+1} is in $\mathcal{L}_{n+1} - \mathcal{L}_n$. Hence $\mathcal{L}_i \subsetneq \mathcal{L}_{i+1}$ for each i. Thus $\mathcal{F}_{\hat{\sigma}}(\mathcal{L}_C)$ is not (full) principal. This implies that $\mathcal{L}_C$ is not substitution closed and that $\mathcal{F}_{\hat{\sigma}}(\mathcal{L}_C) \subsetneq \mathcal{L}_{CF}$.

EXAMPLE 6.3.2: Let $\mathcal{L}_{DB} = \hat{\mathcal{F}}_{\hat{\sigma}}(\mathcal{L}_{lin})$. The family $\mathcal{L}_{DB}$ is called the "derivation-bounded languages" [GS4], the "standard matching choice languages" [Yn], and the "quasi-rational languages" [Ni]. Let $\mathcal{L}_0 = \hat{\mathcal{F}}(\{wcw^R/w \text{ in } \{a, b\}^*\})$ and let $\mathcal{D}$ be the 1-turn pda AFA given in Exercise 4.2.6. As noted in Exercise 4.3.7, $\mathcal{L}^t(\mathcal{D}) = \mathcal{L}(\mathcal{D}) = \mathcal{L}_0$. Then

$$\mathcal{L}((\wedge \mathcal{D})^N) = \mathcal{F}_{\hat{\sigma}}(\mathcal{L}(\mathcal{D})), \quad \text{by Theorem 6.3.3,}$$
$$= \mathcal{F}_{\sigma}(\mathcal{L}(\mathcal{D})), \quad \text{by Theorem 6.3.1,}$$
$$= \mathcal{F}_{\sigma}(\mathcal{L}^t(\mathcal{D}))$$
$$= \mathcal{L}^t((\wedge \mathcal{D})^N), \quad \text{by Theorem 6.3.3.}$$

EXERCISE 6.3.1: Prove that $\mathcal{F}_\sigma(\mathcal{L}_1) \subseteq \mathcal{F}_\sigma(\mathcal{L}_2)$ if $\mathcal{L}_1 \subseteq \mathcal{L}_2$, $\mathcal{L}_1$ and $\mathcal{L}_2$ arbitrary families of languages.

EXERCISE 6.3.2: Let $\mathcal{L}$ be a family of languages. Prove the following:

(a) If L is in $\sigma(\mathcal{L})$ $[\hat{\sigma}(\mathcal{L})]$ then there exists a finite, nonempty, sequence of languages $L_1, \ldots, L_n$ in $\mathcal{L}$ such that L is in $\sigma(\{L_1, \ldots, L_n\})$ $[\hat{\sigma}(\{L_1, \ldots, L_n\})]$.

(b) If L is in $\mathcal{F}_\sigma(\mathcal{L})$ $[\hat{\mathcal{F}}_{\hat{\sigma}}(\mathcal{L})]$ then there exists a finite, nonempty, sequence of languages $L_1, \ldots, L_n$ in $\mathcal{L}$ such that L is in $\mathcal{F}_\sigma(\{L_1, \ldots, L_n\})$ $[\hat{\mathcal{F}}_{\hat{\sigma}}(\{L_1, \ldots, L_n\})]$.

EXERCISE 6.3.3: Let $\mathcal{L}$ be a symmetric family of languages containing $\mathcal{R}_0$ such that $\hat{\text{Sub}}(\mathcal{R}_0, \mathcal{L}) \subseteq \mathcal{L}$. Prove that $\hat{\mathcal{F}}(\hat{\sigma}(\mathcal{L})) = \hat{\sigma}(\hat{\mathcal{F}}(\mathcal{L}))$ [GS5].

EXERCISE 6.3.4: Let $\mathcal{L}$ be a family of languages containing Σ_1^* for every Σ_1 and such that $\hat{\text{Sub}}(\mathcal{L}, \mathcal{F}_0) \subseteq \mathcal{L}$, where $\mathcal{F}_0$ is the family of all finite languages. Prove that $\hat{\sigma}(\mathcal{L})$ is a full AFL if and only if $\mathcal{H}(\mathcal{L} \wedge \mathcal{R}) \subseteq \hat{\sigma}(\mathcal{L})$ [GS5].

EXERCISE 6.3.5: Prove that $\hat{\mathscr{H}}(\mathscr{L})$ is substitution closed for each substitution-closed trio $\mathscr{L}$ [GS5].

The following notation is used in Exercises 6.3.6–6.3.11. For each family $\mathscr{L}$ of languages let $\mathrm{Sub}^0(\mathscr{L}, \mathscr{L}) = \hat{\mathrm{Sub}}^0(\mathscr{L}, \mathscr{L}) = \mathscr{L}$ and, by induction, let $\mathrm{Sub}^{k+1}(\mathscr{L}, \mathscr{L}) = \mathrm{Sub}\left[\bigcup_{i=0}^{k} \mathrm{Sub}^i(\mathscr{L}, \mathscr{L}), \mathscr{L}\right]$ and $\hat{\mathrm{Sub}}^{k+1}(\mathscr{L}, \mathscr{L}) = \hat{\mathrm{Sub}}\left[\bigcup_{i=0}^{k} \hat{\mathrm{Sub}}^i(\mathscr{L}, \mathscr{L}), \mathscr{L}\right]$ for each $k \geqq 0$. Let $\mathrm{Sub}^\infty(\mathscr{L}, \mathscr{L}) = \bigcup_{i=0}^{\infty} \mathrm{Sub}^i(\mathscr{L}, \mathscr{L})$ and $\hat{\mathrm{Sub}}^\infty(\mathscr{L}, \mathscr{L}) = \bigcup_{i=0}^{\infty} \hat{\mathrm{Sub}}^i(\mathscr{L}, \mathscr{L})$.

EXERCISE 6.3.6: Show that $\mathrm{Sub}^k(\mathscr{L}, \mathscr{L}) \subseteq \mathrm{Sub}^{k+1}(\mathscr{L}, \mathscr{L})$ and $\hat{\mathrm{Sub}}^k(\mathscr{L}, \mathscr{L}) \subseteq \hat{\mathrm{Sub}}^{k+1}(\mathscr{L}, \mathscr{L})$ for each $k \geqq 1$ [GS5].

EXERCISE 6.3.7: Show the following [GS5]:

(a) $\mathrm{Sub}^0(\mathscr{L}, \mathscr{L}) \subseteq \mathrm{Sub}^1(\mathscr{L}, \mathscr{L})$ and $\hat{\mathrm{Sub}}^0(\mathscr{L}, \mathscr{L}) \subseteq \hat{\mathrm{Sub}}^1(\mathscr{L}, \mathscr{L})$ both may be false.

(b) $\mathrm{Sub}^0(\mathscr{L}, \mathscr{L}) \subseteq \mathrm{Sub}^1(\mathscr{L}, \mathscr{L})$ and $\hat{\mathrm{Sub}}^0(\mathscr{L}, \mathscr{L}) \subseteq \hat{\mathrm{Sub}}^1(\mathscr{L}, \mathscr{L})$ if $\mathscr{L}$ contains $\{a\}$ for each a in Σ.

EXERCISE 6.3.8: Prove the following [GS5]:

(a) $\mathrm{Sub}^\infty(\mathscr{L}, \mathscr{L})$ is the smallest family $\mathscr{L}'$ containing $\mathscr{L}$ such that $\mathrm{Sub}(\mathscr{L}', \mathscr{L}) \subseteq \mathscr{L}'$.

(b) $\hat{\mathrm{Sub}}^\infty(\mathscr{L}, \mathscr{L})$ is the smallest family $\mathscr{L}'$ containing $\mathscr{L}$ such that $\hat{\mathrm{Sub}}(\mathscr{L}', \mathscr{L}) \subseteq \mathscr{L}'$.

EXERCISE 6.3.9: For all $k \geqq 0$ and each (full) trio, semi-AFL, or AFL, resp., prove that (a) $\mathrm{Sub}^k(\mathscr{L}, \mathscr{L})$, (b) $\hat{\mathrm{Sub}}^k(\mathscr{L}, \mathscr{L})$, (c) $\mathrm{Sub}^\infty(\mathscr{L}, \mathscr{L})$, and (d) $\hat{\mathrm{Sub}}^\infty(\mathscr{L}, \mathscr{L})$ are (full) trio, semi-AFL, or AFL, resp. [GS5].

EXERCISE 6.3.10: Prove that for each trio $\mathscr{L}$, (a) $\sigma(\mathscr{L}) = \mathrm{Sub}^\infty(\mathscr{L}, \mathscr{L})$ and (b) $\hat{\sigma}(\mathscr{L}) = \hat{\mathrm{Sub}}^\infty(\mathscr{L}, \mathscr{L})$ [GS5].

EXERCISE 6.3.11: Prove that for each full trio $\mathscr{L}$, $\mathrm{Sub}^\infty(\mathscr{L}, \mathscr{L}) = \hat{\mathrm{Sub}}^\infty(\mathscr{L}, \mathscr{L}) = \hat{\sigma}(\mathscr{L})$ [GS5].

EXERCISE 6.3.12: Prove that $\mathscr{L}(\mathscr{D}_{n,\omega}) = \mathscr{L}_n$ for each $n \geqq 1$, where $\mathscr{D}_{n,\omega}$ is as in Exercise 5.3.19 and $\mathscr{L}_n$ is as in Example 6.3.1 [GrG].

EXERCISE 6.3.13: Exhibit an AFL $\mathscr{L}$ containing $\{\epsilon\}$ such that $\mathscr{F}_\sigma(\mathscr{L}) \neq \mathscr{F}_{\hat{\sigma}}(\mathscr{L})$.

EXERCISE 6.3.14: Given an AFA $(\Omega, \mathcal{D})$, with $\Omega = (K, \Sigma, \Gamma, I, f, g)$, let ξ, PUSH, and POP be three new symbols. Consider the AFA $(\Omega', \mathcal{D}')$, $\Omega' = (K, \Sigma, \Gamma \cup \{\xi\}, I \cup \{\text{PUSH, POP}\}, f', g')$, where f' and g' are defined as follows (for each w in $(\Gamma \cup \{\xi\})^*$, x in Γ^*, z in Γ^+, and u in I): $f'(x, u) = f(x, u)$, $f'(w\xi x, u) = w\xi f(x, u)$, $f'(w, \text{PUSH}) = w\xi$, $f'(w\xi, \text{POP}) = w$, $g'(x) = g(x)$, $g'(w\xi z) = g(z)$, and $g'(w\xi) = \{\xi\}$. Prove the following [Gr4]:

(a) Let $\mathcal{E}_1(\mathcal{E}_2)$ be the set of all (quasi-realtime) acceptors $D = (K_1, \Sigma_1, \delta, p_0, F)$ in $\mathcal{D}'$ with the following property: There exists $k \geqq 1$ such that for all p in K_1 and w in Σ_1^*, if $(p_0, w, \epsilon) \overset{*}{\underset{D}{\vdash}} (p, \epsilon, \gamma)$ then γ has at most k occurrences of ξ. Then $\mathcal{L}(\mathcal{E}_1) = \hat{\mathcal{F}}_\sigma(\mathcal{L}(\mathcal{D}))$ and $\mathcal{L}(\mathcal{E}_2) = \mathcal{F}_\sigma(\mathcal{L}^t(\mathcal{D}))$.

(b) If $\mathcal{D}$ is nontrivial, then $\mathcal{L}(\mathcal{D}')$ is the smallest superAFL[1] containing $\mathcal{L}(\mathcal{D})$.

(c) If $\mathcal{D}$ is nontrivial and finitely encoded, then $\mathcal{L}(\mathcal{D}')$ is a full principal AFL. Thus infer that if $\mathcal{L}$ is a full principal AFL, then so is the smallest superAFL containing $\mathcal{L}$.

EXERCISE 6.3.15: Let $(\Omega, \mathcal{D}) = (\Omega_{\text{PDA}}, \mathcal{D}_{\text{PDA}})$, with $\Omega = (K, \Sigma, \Gamma, I, f, g)$, and let ξ, POP, and DUP be three new symbols. Let $\Omega' = (K, \Sigma, \Gamma \cup \{\xi\}, I \cup \{\text{POP, DUP}\}, f', g')$, where f' and g' are defined as follows (for each w in $(\Gamma \cup \{\xi\})^*$, x in Γ^*, z in Γ^+, and u in I): $f'(x, u) = f(x, u)$, $f'(w\xi x, u) = w\xi f(x, u)$, $f'(x, \text{DUP}) = x\xi x$, $f'(w\xi x, \text{DUP}) = w\xi x\xi x$, $f'(w\xi, \text{POP}) = w$, $g'(x) = \{x\}$, $g'(w\xi z) = \{z\}$, and $g'(w\xi) = \{\xi\}$. Prove that $\mathcal{L}^t(\mathcal{D}') = \mathcal{L}^t(\mathcal{D}_{\text{NSA}})$ and $\mathcal{L}(\mathcal{D}') = \mathcal{L}(\mathcal{D}_{\text{NSA}})$.

EXERCISE 6.3.16: Prove that each countable AFL is contained in a substitution-closed, full principal, countable AFL.

EXERCISE 6.3.17: Using the symbolism of Exercise 5.3.19 and Example 6.3.1, suppose that L_{n+1} is in $\mathcal{L}_n$ for some $n \geqq 1$. Prove the following [Gr1]:

(a) L_{n+1} is in $\mathcal{L}_{n+1}$.

(b) $L_{n+1} = L(D)$ for some $D = (K_1, \Sigma_1, \delta, p_0, F)$, in $\mathcal{D}_{n,\,\omega}$, with the following property: There exists a positive integer k such that for each word w in L_{n+1}, a sequence $(p_0, w_0, \gamma_0) \vdash \ldots \vdash (p_t, w_t, \gamma_t)$ can be found satisfying $w_0 = w$, $w_t = \gamma_0 = \gamma_t = \epsilon$, p_t is in F, and $|\gamma_i| \leqq k|w|$ for each i. [Hint: Use Exercise 6.3.12.]

[1] See Exercise 6.1.17.

(c) For each positive integer r, let $f(r) = \#\{y/y \text{ in } H_n, |y| \leqq r\}$. Then $f(r)$ is a polynomial (in r) of degree n.

(d) For each positive integer s, let $U(s) = \{a_1^{i_1} \ldots a_{n+1}^{i_{n+1}}/0 \leqq i_j \leqq s, 1 \leqq j \leqq n+1\}$. For each word w in $U(s)$ let (p_w, γ_w) be a specific pair, guaranteed by (b), such that $(p_0, wcw^R) \overset{*}{\vdash} (p_w, cw^R, \gamma_w) \overset{*}{\vdash} (p, \epsilon, \epsilon)$ for some p in F, with $|\gamma_w| \leqq k(2(n+1)s+1)$. Then there are at least s^{n+1} different pairs (p_w, γ_w).

(e) There are at most $\#(K_1) f\big(k(2(n+1)s+1)\big)$ pairs (p_w, γ_w).

(f) L_{n+1} is not in $\mathscr{L}_n$.

6.4 Substitution of Principal (Semi-)AFL

We now consider the questions of whether Sub $(\mathscr{L}_1, \mathscr{L}_2)$ is a principal (semi-)AFL if $\mathscr{L}_1$ and $\mathscr{L}_2$ are, and whether Sûb $(\mathscr{L}_1, \mathscr{L}_2)$ is a full principal (semi-)AFL if $\mathscr{L}_1$ and $\mathscr{L}_2$ are. We shall see that the answers to both questions are yes. In addition, we shall present (full) generators for Sub $(\mathscr{L}_1, \mathscr{L}_2)$ (Sûb $(\mathscr{L}_1, \mathscr{L}_2)$) which are explicitly expressed in terms of the (full) generators of $\mathscr{L}_1$ and $\mathscr{L}_2$.

We start with two technical lemmas. The first asserts that a certain type of a-transducer may be assumed to have no ϵ-input move from its start state. The second lemma asserts that Sub $(\mathscr{M}(L_1), \mathscr{M}(L_2))$ is a subset of $\mathscr{M}(L_3)$, where L_3 is a language related to L_1 and L_2 in a special way.

LEMMA 6.4.1: *Let L be an ϵ-free language and $M = (K_1, \Sigma_1, \Sigma_2, H, p_0, F)$ a 1-bounded, ϵ-output bounded a-transducer such that H contains no element (p_0, u, ϵ, p). Then there exists a 1-bounded, ϵ-output bounded a-transducer $M' = (K', \Sigma_1, \Sigma_2, H', q_0, F)$ such that $M'(L) = M(L)$, q_0 is not in F, and H' contains no element (q_0, ϵ, v, q) and no element (q_0, u, ϵ, q).*

Proof: First assume that there exists some element a in Σ_1 such that each word in L begins with a. For each p in K_1 let p' be a new symbol. Let q_0 be a new symbol. Let $K' = K_1 \cup \{q_0, p'/p \text{ in } K_1\}$ and let H' consist of the following 4-tuples:

(1) (p_1, u, v, p_2) for all (p_1, u, v, p_2) in H.
(2) (q_0, a, v, p) for all (p_0, a, v, p) in H.
(3) $(p_1', \epsilon, v, p_2')$ for all (p_1, ϵ, v, p_2) in H.
(4) (q_0, a, v, p') for all (p_0, ϵ, v, p) in H.
(5) (p_1', ϵ, v, p_2) for all (p_1, a, v, p_2) in H.

Let $M' = (K', \Sigma_1, \Sigma_2, H', q_0, F)$. Clearly M' satisfies the conclusion of the lemma. Furthermore, (q_1, u, v, q_2) in H' implies $q_2 \neq q_0$.

Now let L be any ϵ-free language. For each a in Σ_1, let $L_a = a\Sigma_1^* \cap L$. Clearly $M(L) = \bigcup_{L_a \neq \emptyset} M(L_a)$. By the previous paragraph, for each a, $L_a \neq \emptyset$, there exists an a-transducer $M'_a = (K'_a, \Sigma_1, \Sigma_2, H'_a, q_0, F)$, satisfying the conclusion of the lemma for L_a, such that

(6) (q_1, u, v, q_2) in H'_a implies $q_2 \neq q_0$.

Without loss of generality, we may therefore assume that $K'_a \cap K'_b = \{q_0\} \cup K_1$ for each a and b in Σ_1, $a \neq b$. Then $M' = \left(\bigcup_{a \text{ in } \Sigma_1} K'_a, \Sigma_1, \Sigma_2, \bigcup_{a \text{ in } \Sigma_1} H'_a, q_0, F\right)$ satisfies the conclusion of the lemma for L.

For the next lemma we need a particular kind of "uniformly marked substitution". This type of substitution will occur frequently in the sequel.

Notation: Given languages L_1 and L_2, with $\Sigma_{L_1} \cap \Sigma_{L_2} = \emptyset$, let τ_{L_2} be the substitution on $\Sigma_{L_1}^*$ defined by $\tau_{L_2}(a) = aL_2$ for each a in Σ_{L_1}.

LEMMA 6.4.2: *Let L_1 and L_2 be nonempty languages such that L_1 is ϵ-free and $\Sigma_{L_1} \cap \Sigma_{L_2} = \emptyset$. Let c be a new symbol. Then $Sub(\mathscr{M}(L_1), \mathscr{M}(L_2)) \subseteq \mathscr{M}(\tau_{(L_2c)^+}(L_1))$.*

Proof: Let L be in Sub $(\mathscr{M}(L_1), \mathscr{M}(L_2))$. Then $L = \tau(L_3)$, where L_3 is in $\mathscr{M}(L_1)$ and, for each b in Σ_{L_3}, $\tau(b)$ is an ϵ-free set in $\mathscr{M}(L_2)$. Since L_1 is ϵ-free, so is L_3. By Lemmas 3.2.5 and 6.4.1, we may assume that $L_3 = M_1(L_1)$, where $M_1 = (K_1, \Sigma_{L_1}, \Sigma_{L_3}, H_1, p_0, F_1)$ is a 1-bounded, ϵ-output bounded a-transducer such that p_0 is not in F_1, and H_1 contains no element (p_0, u, ϵ, p) and no element (p_0, ϵ, v, p). For each b in Σ_{L_3}, there exists an ϵ-free a-transducer $M_b = (K_b, \Sigma_{L_2}, \Sigma_b, H_b, q_b, F_b)$ such that q_b is not in F_b and $\tau(b) = M_b(L_2)$. Clearly we may assume that all sets of states are pairwise disjoint.

Let w be a specific element in L_2. Let $M = \left(K_M, \Sigma_{L_1} \cup \Sigma_{L_2} \cup \{c\}, \bigcup_{b \text{ in } \Sigma_{L_3}} \Sigma_b, H, (p_0, \epsilon), F\right)$ be the a-transducer where $K_M = (K_1 \times \{\epsilon\}) \cup \left(K_1 \times \bigcup_{b \text{ in } \Sigma_{L_3}} K_b\right)$, $F = F_1 \times \{\epsilon\}$, and H contains the following 4-tuples (for a in $\Sigma_{L_1} \cup \{\epsilon\}$):

(1) $((p, \epsilon), awc, \epsilon, (p', \epsilon))$ if (p, a, ϵ, p') is in H_1.

(2) $((p, \epsilon), a, \epsilon, (p', q_b))$ if (p, a, b, p') is in H_1, with b in Σ_{L_3}.

(3) $((p, q), u, v, (p, q'))$ for each p in K_1, if (q, u, v, q') is in H_b.

(4) $((p, q), c, \epsilon, (p, \epsilon))$ for all p in K_1, b in Σ_{L_3}, and q in F_b.

Intuitively, M simulates the operation of M_1 on the first coordinate and M_b on L_2 on the second coordinate. The idea of the simulation is as follows. While M_1 reads a_i, a_i in $\Sigma_{L_1} \cup \{\epsilon\}$, and outputs b_i, b_i in $\Sigma_{L_3} \cup \{\epsilon\}$, M reads a_iL_2c and outputs $\tau(b_i) = M_{b_i}(L_2)$. The start and end of this subroutine always occurs at states in $K_1 \times \{\epsilon\}$. [Initially, M_1 reads a symbol a_1 in Σ_{L_1} since H_1 contains no rule of the form (p_0, ϵ, v, p). Hence $a_1(L_2c)^+$ supplies an appropriate number of occurrences of L_2c.] If M_1 reads a_i in $\Sigma_{L_1} \cup \{\epsilon\}$ and outputs ϵ, then by (1), M reads exactly one word, a_iwc, in a_iL_2c, and outputs $\{\epsilon\} = \tau(\epsilon)$. If M_1 reads a_i in $\Sigma_{L_1} \cup \{\epsilon\}$ and outputs b_i in Σ_{L_3}, then by (2), (3), and (4), M reads a_iL_2c and outputs $M_{b_i}(L_2) = \tau(b_i)$. In particular, by (2), M reads a_i, outputs ϵ, and goes to the start state of M_b. By (3), M reads all words of L_2 and outputs all words of $M_b(L_2)$. By (4), M is in an accepting state of M_b and, under c, gets ready to simulate the processing of M_1 on a_{i+1}.

More formally, we now show that $M(\tau_{(L_2c)^+}(L_1)) = \tau(M_1(L_1))$. Suppose $(p_0, a_1, b_1, p_1), \ldots, (p_{k-1}, a_k, b_k, p_k)$ is a sequence of elements in H_1, with p_k in F_1 and $a_1 \ldots a_k$ in L_1. Let $m(1) < \ldots < m(t)$ be those indices i for which a_i is in Σ_{L_1}. Note that $m(1) = 1$ since H_1 has no elements of the form (p_0, ϵ, v, p). Let U be the set of all words $z_{m(1)} \ldots z_{m(t)}$, where for all i, $1 \leqq i < t$, $z_{m(i)} = a_{m(i)}w_{m(i)}c_{m(i)}w_{m(i)+1}c_{m(i)+1} \ldots w_{m(i+1)-1}c_{m(i+1)-1}$, $z_{m(t)} = a_{m(t)}w_{m(t)}c_{m(t)} \ldots w_kc_k$, and for all j, $1 \leqq j \leqq k$, $c_j = c$ and w_j is obtained as follows. If $b_j = \epsilon$ then $w_j = w$. If b_j is in Σ_{L_3} then w_j is in L_2. Obviously $U \subseteq a_{m(1)}(L_2c)^+ \ldots a_{m(t)}(L_2c)^+$. From (1), (2), (3), and (4), $\tau(b_1) \ldots \tau(b_k) \subseteq M(U)$. Therefore $\tau M_1(L_1) \subseteq M(\tau_{(L_2c)^+}(L_1))$.

To see the reverse inclusion, let v be in $M(\tau_{(L_2c)^+}(L_1))$. Then there exist u in $\tau_{(L_2c)^+}(L_1)$ and a sequence

(5) $(r_1, u_1, v_1, r_2), \ldots, (r_k, u_k, v_k, r_{k+1})$

of elements in H such that $r_1 = (p_0, \epsilon)$, r_{k+1} is in F, $u = u_1 \ldots u_k$, and $v = v_1 \ldots v_k$. Let $m(1) < \ldots < m(t)$ be those integers i such that r_i is in $K_1 \times \{\epsilon\}$. For each j, let $r_{m(j)} = (p'_j, \epsilon)$. Then $m(1) = 1$ and $m(t) = k+1$. For each j, $1 \leqq j < t$, consider

(6) $(r_{m(j)}, u_{m(j)} \ \ldots \ u_{m(j+1)-1}, \epsilon) \vdash \ldots \vdash (r_{m(j+1)}, \ \epsilon, v_{m(j)} \ldots v_{m(j+1)-1})$

as obtained from (5). Two possibilities arise.

(α) $m(j+1) - m(j) = 1$. By (2), (3), and (4), (6) is obtained by an application of a type 1 rule. Thus $v_{m(j)} = \epsilon$, $u_{m(j)}$ is of the form $a_{m(j)}wc$, and $(p'_j, a_{m(j)}, b_{m(j)}, p'_{j+1})$ is in H_1, with $b_{m(j)} = \epsilon$. Thus

(7) $v_{m(j)}$ is in $\tau(b_{m(j)})$.

(β) $m(j+1) - m(j) > 1$. Then a type 1 rule is not used. Thus $(r_{m(j)}, u_{m(j)}, v_{m(j)}, r_{m(j)+1})$ is type 2, $(r_{m(j+1)-1}, u_{m(j+1)-1}, v_{m(j+1)-1}, r_{m(j+1)})$ is type 4, and each $(r_{m(j)+l}, u_{m(j)+l}, v_{m(j)+l}, r_{m(j)+l+1})$, $1 \leq l < m(j+1)-1$, is type 3. Since a state of the form (p, ϵ) can be entered only after reading (in part) an occurrence of c (type 1 and 4 rules), $u_{m(j)} \ldots u_{m(j+1)-1}$ is in $u_{m(j)}L_2c$, with $u_{m(j)+1} \ldots u_{m(j+1)-1}$ in L_2c. Since $(r_{m(j)}, u_{m(j)}, v_{m(j)}, r_{m(j)+1})$ is type 2, $(p'_j, a_{m(j)}, b_{m(j)}, p'_{j+1})$ is in H_1 for some $b_{m(j)}$ in Σ_{L_3}, with $a_{m(j)} = u_{m(j)}$. From rules (2), (3), and (4), $v_{m(j)} = v_{m(j+1)-1} = \epsilon$ and

(8) $v_{m(j)} \ldots v_{m(j+1)-1}$ is in $M_{b_{m(j)}}(L_2) = \tau(b_{m(j)})$.

Since $u_1 \ldots u_k$ is in $\tau_{(L_2c)^+}(L_1)$, with u_i in $\Sigma_{L_2} \cup \{\epsilon\}$ if i is not of the form $m(j)$ for some $j < t$, and $u_{m(j)}$ is either $a_{m(j)}$ in $\Sigma_{L_1} \cup \{\epsilon\}$ or $u_{m(j)} = a_{m(j)}wc$, with $a_{m(j)}$ in $\Sigma_{L_1} \cup \{\epsilon\}$, it follows that $a_{m(1)} \ldots a_{m(t-1)}$ is in L_1. Then

$$(p'_1, a_{m(1)}, b_{m(1)}, p'_2) \ldots (p'_{t-1}, a_{m(t-1)}, b_{m(t-1)}, p'_t)$$

is a sequence of elements in H_1, with $p'_1 = p_0$, p'_t in F_1, and $a_{m(1)} \ldots a_{m(t-1}$ in L_1. Then $b_{m(1)} \ldots b_{m(t-1)}$ is in $M_1(a_{m(1)} \ldots a_{m(t-1)})$ and, by (7) and (8), $v_1 \ldots v_k$ is in $\tau(b_{m(1)} \ldots b_{m(t-1)})$. Thus v is in $\tau M_1(L_1)$. Therefore $M(\tau_{(L_2c)^+}(L_1)) \subseteq \tau M_1(L_1)$, whence equality.

To complete the proof we need to show that $M(\tau_{(L_2c)^+}(L_1))$ is in $\mathcal{M}(\tau_{(L_2c)^+}(L_1))$. This is not obvious since, by construction, M is not ϵ-free. Since H_1 contains no element (p_0, u, ϵ, p), it follows from (1), (2), (3), and (4) that H contains no element $((p_0, \epsilon), u, \epsilon, r)$, r in K_M. Hence $M(L_1) = M(L_1) - \{\epsilon\}$. By Theorem 3.2.2 it suffices to show M is ϵ-output bounded. Since M_1 is ϵ-output bounded, there exists k_1 such that M_1 has at most k_1 consecutive moves with ϵ as output. Each type 1 rule simulates an ϵ-rule in M_1. Types 2 and 4 rules add ϵ-output rules to H. Since each M_b is an ϵ-free a-transducer, no type 3 rule is an ϵ-output rule. Since no q_b is in F_b, only a type 3 rule can follow a type 2 rule. Thus M has at most k_1+2 consecutive ϵ-output rules, namely one of type 4, followed by k_1 of type 1, followed by one of type 2. Hence M is ϵ-output bounded.

We are finally ready for the theorem on the substitution of (full) principal [semi-]AFL into (full) principal [semi-]AFL.

THEOREM 6.4.1: *Let L_1 and L_2 be nonempty languages, with $\Sigma_{L_1} \cap \Sigma_{L_2} = \emptyset$. For new symbols c_1 and c_2*

(a) *Sub* $(\mathcal{F}(L_1), \mathcal{F}(L_2)) = \mathcal{F}\big(\tau_{(L_2c_2)^+}((L_1c_1)^+)\big)$ *if L_1 is ϵ-free,*

(b) *Sub* $(\mathcal{F}(L_1), \mathcal{F}(L_2)) = \mathcal{F}\big(\tau_{(L_2c_2)^+}((L_1c_1)^*)\big)$ *if L_1 contains ϵ,*

(c) *Sub* $(\hat{\mathcal{F}}(L_1), \hat{\mathcal{F}}(L_2)) =$ *Sûb* $(\hat{\mathcal{F}}(L_1), \hat{\mathcal{F}}(L_2)) = \hat{\mathcal{F}}\big(\tau_{(L_2c_2)^+}((L_1c_1)^+)\big)$,

(d) *Sub* $(\mathcal{S}(L_1), \mathcal{S}(L_2)) = \mathcal{S}(\tau_{(L_2c_2)^+}(L_1))$ *if $L_1 \neq \{\epsilon\}$, and*

(e) *Sub* $(\hat{\mathcal{S}}(L_1), \hat{\mathcal{S}}(L_2)) =$ *Sûb* $(\hat{\mathcal{S}}(L_1), \hat{\mathcal{S}}(L_2)) = \hat{\mathcal{S}}(\tau_{(L_2c_2)^+}(L_1))$ *if $L_1 \neq \{\epsilon\}$.*

Proof: (a) Suppose L_1 is ϵ-free. Clearly $\tau_{(L_2c_2)^+}((L_1c_1)^+)$ is in Sub $(\mathcal{F}(L_1), \mathcal{F}(L_2))$. By Theorem 6.1.1, Sub $(\mathcal{F}(L_1), \mathcal{F}(L_2))$ is an AFL. Thus $\mathcal{F}(\tau_{(L_2c_2)^+}((L_1c_1)^+)) \subseteq$ Sub $(\mathcal{F}(L_1), \mathcal{F}(L_2))$.

Consider the reverse containment. Note that

$$\begin{aligned}\text{Sub}(\mathcal{M}(L_1), \mathcal{M}(L_2)) &\subseteq \mathcal{M}(\tau_{(L_2c_2)^+}(L_1)), \quad \text{by Lemma 6.4.2,}\\ &\subseteq \mathcal{F}(\tau_{(L_2c_2)^+}(L_1)).\end{aligned}$$

Let w be a word in L_2. Let h_1 and h_2 be the homomorphisms on $(\Sigma_{L_1} \cup \Sigma_{L_2} \cup \{c_1, c_2\})^*$ defined by $h_1(c_1) = c_1wc_2$, $h_2(c_1) = \epsilon$, and $h_1(x) = h_2(x) = x$ for all x in $\Sigma_{L_1} \cup \Sigma_{L_2} \cup \{c_2\}$. Let

$$U_1 = \tau_{(L_2c_2)^+}((L_1c_1)^+) \cap ((\Sigma_{L_1} \cup \Sigma_{L_2} \cup \{c_2\})^+ c_1wc_2)$$

and $U_2 = h_1^{-1}(U_1)$. Then U_1 and U_2 are in $\mathcal{F}(\tau_{(L_2c_2)^+}((L_1c_1)^+))$, and $\tau_{(L_2c_2)^+}(L_1) = h_2(U_2)$. Since L_1 is ϵ-free, $\tau_{(L_2c_2)^+}(L_1)$ is ϵ-free. Thus $h_2(U_2) = h_2(U_2) - \{\epsilon\}$. Since h_2 is ϵ-limited on U_1, $\tau_{(L_2c_2)^+}(L_1) = h_2(U_2) - \{\epsilon\}$ is in $\mathcal{F}(\tau_{(L_2c_2)^+}((L_1c_1)^+))$ by Corollary 2 of Theorem 3.2.2. Thus $\mathcal{F}(\tau_{(L_2c_2)^+}(L_1)) \subseteq \mathcal{F}(\tau_{(L_2c_2)^+}((L_1c_1)^+))$. Hence

$$\begin{aligned}\text{Sub}(\mathcal{M}(L_1), \mathcal{M}(L_2)) &\subseteq \mathcal{F}(\tau_{(L_2c_2)^+}(L_1))\\ &\subseteq \mathcal{F}(\tau_{(L_2c_2)^+}((L_1c_1)^+)),\end{aligned}$$

so that

$$\text{Sub}(\mathcal{R}_0, \text{Sub}(\mathcal{M}(L_1), \mathcal{M}(L_2)) \subseteq \mathcal{F}(\tau_{(L_2c_2)^+}((L_1c_1)^+)).$$

Finally, note that

$$\begin{aligned}\text{Sub}(\mathcal{F}(L_1), \mathcal{F}(L_2)) &= \text{Sub}(\mathcal{F}(L_1), \{L \text{ in } \mathcal{F}(L_2)/L\ \epsilon\text{-free}\})\\ &= \text{Sub}(\mathcal{F}(L_1), \mathcal{F}(L_2 - \{\epsilon\})), \quad \text{by Proposition 3.4.1,}\\ &= \hat{\text{Sub}}(\mathcal{F}(L_1), \mathcal{F}(L_2 - \{\epsilon\})), \quad \text{since } \mathcal{F}(L_2 - \{\epsilon\}) \text{ is } \epsilon\text{-free,}\\ &= \hat{\text{Sub}}(\mathcal{F}(L_1), \hat{\text{Sub}}(\mathcal{R}_0, \mathcal{S}(L_2 - \{\epsilon\}))), \quad \text{by Theorem 3.4.1,}\\ &= \hat{\text{Sub}}(\hat{\text{Sub}}(\mathcal{F}(L_1), \mathcal{R}_0), \mathcal{S}(L_2 - \{\epsilon\})), \quad \text{by Lemma 6.1.1,}\\ &= \hat{\text{Sub}}(\mathcal{F}(L_1), \mathcal{S}(L_2 - \{\epsilon\}))\\ &= \hat{\text{Sub}}(\hat{\text{Sub}}(\mathcal{R}_0, \mathcal{S}(L_1)), \mathcal{S}(L_2 - \{\epsilon\})), \quad \text{by Theorem 3.4.1,}\\ &= \hat{\text{Sub}}(\mathcal{R}_0, \hat{\text{Sub}}(\mathcal{S}(L_1), \mathcal{S}(L_2 - \{\epsilon\}))), \quad \text{by Lemma 6.1.1,}\\ &= \text{Sub}(\mathcal{R}_0, \text{Sub}(\mathcal{S}(L_1), \mathcal{S}(L_2 - \{\epsilon\}))), \quad \text{since } \mathcal{S}(L_2 - \{\epsilon\})\\ &\qquad \text{and Sub}(\mathcal{S}(L_1), \mathcal{S}(L_2 - \{\epsilon\})) \text{ are } \epsilon\text{-free,}\\ &= \text{Sub}(\mathcal{R}_0, \text{Sub}(\mathcal{S}(L_1), \mathcal{S}(L_2))), \quad \text{by Proposition 3.4.1,}\\ &= \text{Sub}(\mathcal{R}_0, \text{Sub}(\mathcal{M}(L_1), \mathcal{M}(L_2))), \quad \text{by Proposition 5.1.1.}\end{aligned}$$

Hence

$$\begin{aligned}\operatorname{Sub}(\mathcal{F}(L_1), \mathcal{F}(L_2)) &= \operatorname{Sub}(\mathcal{R}_0, \operatorname{Sub}(\mathcal{M}(L_1), \mathcal{M}(L_2)))\\ &\subseteq \mathcal{F}\big(\tau_{(L_2c_2)^+}((L_1c_1)^+)\big).\end{aligned}$$

Therefore $\operatorname{Sub}(\mathcal{F}(L_1), \mathcal{F}(L_2)) = \mathcal{F}\big(\tau_{(L_2c_2)^+}((L_1c_1)^+)\big)$.

(b) Suppose L_1 contains ϵ. Assume $L_1 = \{\epsilon\}$. Then

$$\begin{aligned}\operatorname{Sub}(\mathcal{F}(L_1), \mathcal{F}(L_2)) &= \operatorname{Sub}(\mathcal{R}, \mathcal{F}(L_2))\\ &= \{L, L \cup \{\epsilon\}/L \text{ in } \mathcal{F}(L_2)\}\\ &= \mathcal{F}(L_2 \cup \{\epsilon\}), \quad \text{by Proposition 3.4.1.}\end{aligned}$$

Now $\{\epsilon\}$ and L_2 are in $\mathcal{F}(\tau_{(L_2c_2)^+}(c_1^*))$, so that $\mathcal{F}(L_2 \cup \{\epsilon\}) \subseteq \mathcal{F}(\tau_{(L_2c_2)^+}(c_1^*))$. On the other hand, $\tau_{(L_2c_2)^+}(c_1^*) = (c_1(L_2c_2)^+)^*$ is obviously in $\mathcal{F}(L_2 \cup \{\epsilon\})$. Therefore $\mathcal{F}(\tau_{(L_2c_2)^+}(c_1^*)) \subseteq \mathcal{F}(L_2 \cup \{\epsilon\})$, whence equality. Thus

$$\begin{aligned}\operatorname{Sub}(\mathcal{F}(L_1), \mathcal{F}(L_2)) &= \mathcal{F}(L_1 \cup \{\epsilon\})\\ &= \mathcal{F}\big(\tau_{(L_2c_2)^+}(c_1^*)\big)\\ &= \mathcal{F}\big(\tau_{(L_2c_2)^+}((L_1c_1)^*)\big).\end{aligned}$$

Now assume that $L_1 \neq \{\epsilon\}$, so that $L_1 - \{\epsilon\} \neq \emptyset$. Then

$$\begin{aligned}\operatorname{Sub}(\mathcal{F}(L_1), \mathcal{F}(L_2)) &= \operatorname{Sub}(\mathcal{F}(L_1 - \{\epsilon\}), \mathcal{F}(L_2))\\ &\quad \cup \{L \cup \{\epsilon\}/L \text{ in } \operatorname{Sub}(\mathcal{F}(L_1 - \{\epsilon\}), \mathcal{F}(L_2))\}\\ &= \mathcal{F}\big(\tau_{(L_2c_2)^+}(((L_1 - \{\epsilon\})c_1)^+)\big)\\ &\quad \cup \{L \cup \{\epsilon\}/L \text{ in } \mathcal{F}\big(\tau_{(L_2c_2)^+}(((L_1 - \{\epsilon\})\, c_1)^+)\big)\},\\ &\qquad \text{by (a) since } L_1 - \{\epsilon\} \neq \emptyset.\end{aligned}$$

Note that

$$\tau_{(L_2c_2)^+}\big(((L_1 - \{\epsilon\})c_1)^+\big) = \tau_{(L_2c_2)^+}((L_1c_1)^+) \cap \big((\Sigma_{L_1}(\Sigma_L^* c_2)^+)^+ c_1 (\Sigma_{L_2}^* c_2)^+\big)^+$$

and

$$\tau_{(L_2c_2)^+}((L_1c_1)^+) = \tau_{(L_2c_2)^+}\big(c_1^*[((L_1 - \{\epsilon\})c_1)^+ c_1^*]^+ \cup c_1^+\big),$$

so that

$$\mathcal{F}\big(\tau_{(L_2c_2)^+}(((L_1 - \{\epsilon\})c_1)^+)\big) = \mathcal{F}\big(\tau_{(L_2c_2)^+}((L_1c_1)^+)\big).$$

Thus

$$\begin{aligned}\operatorname{Sub}(\mathcal{F}(L_1), \mathcal{F}(L_2)) &= \mathcal{F}\big(\tau_{(L_2c_2)^+}((L_1c_1)^+)\big) \cup \big\{L \cup \{\epsilon\}/L \text{ in}\\ &\qquad \mathcal{F}\big(\tau_{(L_2c_2)^+}((L_1c_1)^+)\big)\big\}\\ &= \mathcal{F}\big(\tau_{(L_2c_2)^+}((L_1c_1)^*)\big), \quad \text{by Exercise 6.4.2.}\end{aligned}$$

(c) Suppose $L_1 = \{\epsilon\}$. Then $\operatorname{Sub}(\hat{\mathcal{F}}(L_1), \hat{\mathcal{F}}(L_2)) = \operatorname{Sub}(\mathcal{R}, \hat{\mathcal{F}}(L_2)) = \widehat{\operatorname{Sub}}(\mathcal{R}, \hat{\mathcal{F}}(L_2)) = \hat{\mathcal{F}}(L_2) = \hat{\mathcal{F}}\big(\tau_{(L_2c_2)^+}((L_1c_1)^+)\big)$. Suppose $L_1 \neq \{\epsilon\}$. Then

$$\begin{aligned}
\hat{\text{Sub}}(\hat{\mathcal{F}}(L_1), \hat{\mathcal{F}}(L_2)) &= \text{Sub}(\hat{\mathcal{F}}(L_1), \hat{\mathcal{F}}(L_2)), \\
&\qquad \text{by Corollary 1 of Theorem 6.1.1,} \\
&= \text{Sub}\big(\hat{\mathcal{H}}(\mathcal{F}(L_1 - \{\epsilon\})), \hat{\mathcal{H}}(\mathcal{F}(L_2))\big) \\
&= \hat{\mathcal{H}}\big(\text{Sub}(\mathcal{F}(L_1 - \{\epsilon\}), \mathcal{F}(L_2))\big), \\
&\qquad \text{by Corollary 2 of Theorem 6.1.1,} \\
&= \hat{\mathcal{H}}\big(\mathcal{F}\big(\tau_{(L_2c_2)^+}(((L_1 - \{\epsilon\})c_1)^+)\big)\big), \quad \text{by (a),} \\
&= \hat{\mathcal{F}}\big(\mathcal{F}\big(\tau_{(L_2c_2)^+}((L_1c_1)^+)\big)\big) \\
&= \hat{\mathcal{F}}\big(\tau_{(L_2c_2)^+}((L_1c_1)^+)\big).
\end{aligned}$$

(d) Suppose $L_1 \neq \{\epsilon\}$. Two cases arise.

(i) L_1 is ϵ-free. First note that

$$\begin{aligned}
\text{Sub}(\mathcal{S}(L_1), \mathcal{S}(L_2)) &= \text{Sub}\big(\text{Sub}(\mathcal{S}(L_1), \mathcal{R}_0), \mathcal{S}(L_2)\big), \quad \text{by Theorem 3.3.2,} \\
&= \text{Sub}(\mathcal{S}(L_1), \text{Sub}(\mathcal{R}_0, \mathcal{S}(L_2))), \quad \text{by Proposition 6.1.1,} \\
&= \text{Sub}\big(\mathcal{S}(L_1), \text{Sub}(\mathcal{R}_0, \mathcal{S}(L_2 - \{\epsilon\}))\big), \quad \text{by Proposition 3.4.1,} \\
&= \text{Sub}\big(\mathcal{S}(L_1), \hat{\text{Sub}}(\mathcal{R}_0, \mathcal{S}(L_2 - \{\epsilon\}))\big) \\
&= \text{Sub}(\mathcal{S}(L_1), \mathcal{F}(L_2 - \{\epsilon\})).
\end{aligned}$$

Now $\tau_{(L_2c_2)^+}(L_1)$ is in Sub $(\mathcal{S}(L_1), \mathcal{F}(L_2 - \{\epsilon\}))$. Since $\mathcal{S}(L_1)$ and $\mathcal{F}(L_2 - \{\epsilon\})$ are semi-AFL,

$$\mathcal{S}(\tau_{(L_2c_2)^+}(L_1)) \subseteq \text{Sub}(\mathcal{S}(L_1), \mathcal{F}(L_2 - \{\epsilon\})) = \text{Sub}(\mathcal{S}(L_1), \mathcal{S}(L_2)).$$

On the other hand,

$$\begin{aligned}
\text{Sub}(\mathcal{S}(L_1), \mathcal{S}(L_2)) &= \text{Sub}(\mathcal{M}(L_1), \mathcal{M}(L_2)) \\
&\subseteq \mathcal{M}(\tau_{(L_2c_2)^+}(L_1)), \quad \text{by Lemma 6.4.2,} \\
&= \mathcal{S}(\tau_{(L_2c_2)^+}(L_1)).
\end{aligned}$$

Therefore Sub $(\mathcal{S}(L_1), \mathcal{S}(L_2)) = \mathcal{S}(\tau_{(L_2c_2)^+}(L_1))$.

(ii) L_1 contains ϵ. Let $L_1' = L_1 - \{\epsilon\}$. Since $L_1 \neq \{\epsilon\}$, $L_1' \neq \emptyset$. Then

$$\begin{aligned}
\text{Sub}(\mathcal{S}(L_1), \mathcal{S}(L_2)) &= \text{Sub}(\mathcal{S}(L_1') \cup \{L \cup \{\epsilon\}/L \text{ in } \mathcal{S}(L_1')\}, \mathcal{S}(L_2)) \\
&= \text{Sub}(\mathcal{S}(L_1'), \mathcal{S}(L_2)) \cup \text{Sub}(\{L \cup \{\epsilon\}/L \text{ in } \mathcal{S}(L_1')\}, \mathcal{S}(L_2)) \\
&= \mathcal{S}(\tau_{(L_2c_2)^+}(L_1')) \cup \{L \cup \{\epsilon\}/L \text{ in } \mathcal{S}(\tau_{(L_2c_2)^+}(L_1'))\}, \\
&\qquad \text{by (i) since } L_1' \text{ is } \epsilon\text{-free,} \\
&= \mathcal{S}(\tau_{(L_2c_2)^+}(L_1' \cup \{\epsilon\})) \\
&= \mathcal{S}(\tau_{(L_2c_2)^+}(L_1)).
\end{aligned}$$

(e) Suppose $L_1 \neq \{\epsilon\}$. Then

$$\begin{aligned}
\mathrm{Sub}(\hat{\mathcal{S}}(L_1), \hat{\mathcal{S}}(L_2)) &= \mathrm{Sub}(\hat{\mathcal{S}}(L_1), \hat{\mathcal{S}}(L_2)), \quad \text{by Corollary 1 of Theorem 6.1.1,}\\
&= \mathrm{Sub}\big(\hat{\mathcal{H}}(\mathcal{S}(L_1)), \hat{\mathcal{H}}(\mathcal{S}(L_2))\big)\\
&= \hat{\mathcal{H}}\big(\mathrm{Sub}(\mathcal{S}(L_1), (\mathcal{S}(L_2))\big), \text{ by Corollary 2 of Theorem 6.1.1,}\\
&= \hat{\mathcal{H}}\big(\mathcal{S}(\tau_{(L_2c_2)^+}L_1)\big). \quad \text{by (d),}\\
&= \hat{\mathcal{S}}(\tau_{(L_2c_2)^+}(L_1)).
\end{aligned}$$

COROLLARY 1: *If $\mathcal{L}_1$ and $\mathcal{L}_2$ are (full) principal* [*semi-*]*AFL, then so is Sub* $(\mathcal{L}_1, \mathcal{L}_2)$ (*Sûb* $(\mathcal{L}_1, \mathcal{L}_2) =$ *Sub* $(\mathcal{L}_1, \mathcal{L}_2)$).

Proof: Let $\mathcal{L}_1$ and $\mathcal{L}_2$ be (full) principal AFL. Then there exist $\mathcal{L}_1$ and $\mathcal{L}_2$, with $\Sigma_{L_1} - \Sigma_{L_2} = \emptyset$, such that $\mathcal{L}_1 = \mathcal{F}(L_1)$ and $\mathcal{L}_2 = \mathcal{F}(L_2)$ ($\mathcal{L} = \hat{\mathcal{F}}(L_1)$ and $\mathcal{L}_2 = \hat{\mathcal{F}}(L_2)$). If $L_1 \neq \emptyset$ and $L_2 \neq \emptyset$, then the corollary follows immediately from Theorem 6.4.1. If $L_1 = \emptyset$, then $\mathcal{F}(L_1) = \mathcal{F}(\{a\})$ and $\hat{\mathcal{F}}(L_1) = \hat{\mathcal{F}}(\{a\})$ for a in $\Sigma - (\Sigma_{L_1} \cup \Sigma_{L_2})$. If $L_2 = \emptyset$, the $\mathcal{F}L_2) = \mathcal{F}(\{b\})$ and $\hat{\mathcal{F}}L_2) = \hat{\mathcal{F}}(\{b\})$ for b in $\Sigma - (\{a\}) \cup \Sigma_{L_1} \cup \Sigma_{L_2})$. Thus the corollary is also true if $L_1 = \emptyset$ or $L_2 = \emptyset$.

The proof for (full) principal semi-AFL is similar.

By induction, we get

COROLLARY 2: *If $\mathcal{L}_1, \ldots, \mathcal{L}_n$ are (full) principal* [*semi-*]*AFL, then so is Sub* $(\mathcal{L}_1, \ldots, \mathcal{L}_n)$ (*Sûb* $(\mathcal{L}_1, \ldots, \mathcal{L}_n) =$ *Sub* $(\mathcal{L}_1, \ldots, \mathcal{L}_n)$).

Consider Sûb $(\mathcal{F}(L_1), \mathcal{F}(L_2))$. If L_2 is ϵ-free, then Sûb $(\mathcal{F}(L_1), \mathcal{F}(L_2)) =$ Sub $(\mathcal{F}(L_1), \mathcal{F}(L_2))$ and so is principal. It need not be full principal. [For example, Sûb $(\mathcal{R}_0, \mathcal{R}_0) = \mathcal{R}_0$ is not full principal.] Let L_0 be a language such that $\hat{\mathcal{F}}(L_0)$ is not principal [Ui]. Then Sûb $(\mathcal{F}(L_0), \mathcal{R}) = \hat{\mathcal{F}}(L_0)$ and so is not principal. Hence no general statement about Sûb $(\mathcal{F}(L_1), \mathcal{F}(L_2))$ can be made without additional hypotheses.

The problem arises as to whether the converse to Corollary 1 above is true, i.e., if $\mathcal{L}_1$ and $\mathcal{L}_2$ are (full) [semi-]AFL and Sub $(\mathcal{L}_1, \mathcal{L}_2)$ (Sûb $(\mathcal{L}_1, \mathcal{L}_2) =$ Sub $(\mathcal{L}_1, \mathcal{L}_2)$) is (full) principal, does it follow that $\mathcal{L}_1$ and $\mathcal{L}_2$ are (full) principal. The answer turns out to be no. For let $\mathcal{L}_1 = \mathcal{L}_{\mathrm{CF}}$ and $\mathcal{L}_2 = \mathcal{L}_{\mathrm{DB}}$. Then Sûb $(\mathcal{L}_1, \mathcal{L}_2) =$ Sub $(\mathcal{L}_1, \mathcal{L}_2) = \mathcal{L}_1$ is (full) principal, but, as will be shown in Example 6.5.2, $\mathcal{L}_2$ is not (full) principal. There is a partial converse to Corollary 1, however, in the full principal case. In particular, we shall prove that for full (semi-)AFL $\mathcal{L}_1$ and $\mathcal{L}_2$, if Sub $(\mathcal{L}_1,$

$\mathscr{L}_2$) is full principal, then either $\mathscr{L}_1$ or $\mathscr{L}_2$ is full principal. To do this we establish two preliminary results, the first of which we use on a number of other occasions.

LEMMA 6.4.3: *Let L_1 and L_2 be ϵ-free, nonempty languages, with $\Sigma_{L_1} \cap \Sigma_{L_2} = \emptyset$. Let $\mathscr{L}_1$ be a full trio and $\mathscr{L}_2$ a full semi-AFL. If $\tau_{L_2}(L_1)$ is in $\hat{Sub}$ ($\mathscr{L}_1$, $\mathscr{L}_2$), then either L_1 is in $\mathscr{L}_1$ or L_2 is in $\mathscr{L}_2$.*

Proof: Let $L = \tau_{L_2}(L_1)$ be in $\hat{\text{Sub}}(\mathscr{L}_1, \mathscr{L}_2)$. By Theorem 6.1.1, $\hat{\text{Sub}}(\mathscr{L}_1, \mathscr{L}_2) = \text{Sub}(\mathscr{L}_1, \mathscr{L}_2)$. Hence there exist U in $\mathscr{L}_1$ and an ϵ-free substitution τ such that $L = \tau(U)$, with $\tau(b)$ in $\mathscr{L}_2$ for each b in Σ_U. We may assume that $\tau(b) \neq \emptyset$ for each b. [Otherwise, let $\Sigma_3 = \{b \text{ in } \Sigma_U / \tau(b) \neq \emptyset\}$. Then $L = \tau(U \cap \Sigma_3^*)$, $U \cap \Sigma_3^*$ is in $\mathscr{L}_1$, and $\tau(b) \neq \emptyset$ for each b in Σ_3^*.] Clearly U is nonempty and ϵ-free. Since $\mathscr{L}_1$ is closed under ϵ-free homomorphism, we may assume that $\Sigma_U \cap (\Sigma_{L_1} \cup \Sigma_{L_2}) = \emptyset$.

By a *factor marking* of a word y in L we shall mean an expression of the form $a_1y_1\ldots a_ny_n$, where $y = y_1\ldots y_n$, $a_1\ldots a_n$ is a Σ_U-word in U, and y_i is in $\tau(a_i)$ for each i. For each Σ_{L_1}-word $b_1\ldots b_m$ in L_1 and each word z in L_2 let $\tau_z(b_1\ldots b_m)$ be the word $b_1z\ldots b_mz$.[1] We shall say that a factor marking $a_1y_1\ldots a_ny_n$ of $\tau_z(b_1\ldots b_m)$ *splits* if each y_i contains at most one b_j, i.e., $\{y_1, \ldots, y_n\} \subseteq \Sigma_{L_2}^*(\Sigma_{L_1} \cup \{\epsilon\})\Sigma_{L_2}^*$.

Suppose that L_1 is not in $\mathscr{L}_1$. We shall show that L_2 is in $\mathscr{L}_2$. Let h_1 be the homomorphism on $(\Sigma_{L_1} \cup \Sigma_{L_2})^*$ defined by $h_1(x) = x$ for each x in Σ_{L_1} and $h_1(x) = \epsilon$ for x in Σ_{L_2}. Let $\bar{\tau}$ be the substitution on Σ_U^* defined by $\bar{\tau}(a) = h_1(\tau(a) \cap [\Sigma_{L_2}^*\Sigma_{L_1}\Sigma_{L_2}^* \cup \Sigma_{L_2}^*])$ for each a in Σ_U. Since h_1 is ϵ on Σ_{L_2}, $\bar{\tau}(a)$ is a finite subset of $\Sigma_{L_1} \cup \{\epsilon\}$, and thus regular, for each a in Σ_U. Let $U' = \bar{\tau}(U)$. Then U' is in $\mathscr{L}_1$ by Theorem 3.3.1. (This is the only place in the argument which requires $\mathscr{L}_1$ to be full.)

Suppose that $a_1y_1\ldots a_ny_n$ is a factor marking of $\tau_z(b_1\ldots b_m)$ which splits. For each i, y_i is in $\tau(a_i)$ and y_i is $\Sigma_{L_2}^*(\Sigma_{L_1} \cup \{\epsilon\})\Sigma_{L_2}^*$, so that $h_1(y_1)$ is in $\bar{\tau}(a_i)$. Since $b_1z\ldots b_mz = y_1\ldots y_n$,

$$(*)\ b_1\ldots b_m = h_1(b_1z\ldots b_mz) = h_1(y_1\ldots y_n) \text{ is in } \bar{\tau}(a_1\ldots a_n) \subseteq \bar{\tau}(U) = U'.$$

Also, $U' = \bar{\tau}(U) \subseteq h_1\tau(U) = h_1(L_1) = L_1$. Assume there exists a word z in L_2 such that for each $b_1\ldots b_m$ in L_1, $\tau_z(b_1\ldots b_m)$ has a factor marking which splits. From $(*)$, $L_1 \subseteq U'$. Since $U' \subseteq L_1$, it follows that $L_1 = U'$. Thus L_1 is in $\mathscr{L}_1$, a contradiction. Therefore,

[1] This is consistent with the symbolism for the substitution τ_L defined prior to Lemma 6.4.2.

($_{**}$) for each word z in L_2 there exists some $b_1 \ldots b_m$ in L_1 such that $\tau_z(b_1 \ldots b_m)$ has no factor marking which splits.

For each element b in $\Sigma_{L_1} \cup \Sigma_{L_2}$ let $\bar{b}$ be a new symbol and let $\Sigma_4 = \{\bar{b}/b$ in $\Sigma_{L_1} \cup \Sigma_{L_2}\}$. Let h_2 and h_3 be the homomorphisms on $(\Sigma_{L_1} \cup \Sigma_{L_2} \cup \Sigma_4)^*$ defined by $h_2(x) = x$ for each x in Σ_{L_2}, $h_2(x) = \epsilon$ for each x in $\Sigma_{L_1} \cup \Sigma_4$, and $h_3(\bar{b}) = h_3(b) = b$ for each b in $\Sigma_{L_1} \cup \Sigma_{L_2}$. Let

$$R = \bigcup_{b_1, b_2 \text{ in } \Sigma_{L_1}} \Sigma_4^* \bar{b}_1 \Sigma_{L_2}^* \bar{b}_2 \Sigma_4^* \quad \text{and}$$

$$L_2' = \bigcup_{a \text{ in } \Sigma_U} h_2(h_3^{-1}[\tau(a)] \cap R).$$

Since $\mathcal{L}_2$ is a full semi-AFL and $\tau(a)$ is in $\mathcal{L}_2$ for each a, it follows that L_2' is in $\mathcal{L}_2$. To complete the proof we shall show that $L_2 = L_2'$.

Suppose x is in L_2'. Then there exist a in Σ_U, y in $\tau(a)$, and v in $h_3^{-1}(y) \cap R$ such that $x = h_2(v)$. Since a is in Σ_U and U is nonempty and ϵ-free, there exist words u_1 and u_2 such that $u_1 a u_2$ is in U. Then $\tau(u_1) y \tau(u_2)$ is a nonempty subset of L, so that y is a subword of a word in L. Since v is in R, $v = v_1 \bar{b}_1 z \bar{b}_2 v_2$ for some (v_1, b_1, z, b_2, v_2) in $\Sigma_4^* \times \Sigma_{L_1} \times \Sigma_{L_2}^* \times \Sigma_{L_1} \times \Sigma_4^*$. Then $x = h_2(v) = z$. Since v is in $h_3^{-1}(y)$, $h_3(v) = h_3(v_1)\, b_1 x b_2 h_3(v_2) = y$ is a non-ϵ subword of a word in L. Since $L = \tau_{L_2}(L_1)$, x is in L_2. Therefore $L_2' \subseteq L_2$.

To see the reverse containment, let z be a word in L_2. By ($_{**}$) there exist symbols $b_1, \ldots, b_m$ such that $\tau_z(b_1 \ldots b_m)$ has a factor marking which does not split. Let $a_1 y_1 \ldots a_n y_n$ be such a factor marking. Thus for some i, there exist w_1 and w_2 in $(\Sigma_{L_1} \cup \Sigma_{L_2})^*$ and j, $1 \leqq j < m$, such that $y_i = w_1 b_j z b_{j+1} w_2$. Since y_i is in $\tau(a_i)$, $h_3^{-1}(y_i) \cap R \neq \emptyset$. Therefore z is in $h_2[h_3^{-1}(y_i) \cap R] \subseteq L_2'$. Hence $L_2 \subseteq L_2'$, whence $L_2 = L_2'$.

Open Question: Does Lemma 6.4.3 remain true if $\mathcal{L}_1$ and $\mathcal{L}_2$ are just closed under ϵ-free homomorphism instead of arbitrary homomorphism?

Open Question: Does Lemma 6.4.3 remain true if $\mathcal{L}_2$ is a full trio instead of a full semi-AFL?

A number of results in the sequel depend on Lemma 6.4.3. In view of the unresolvability of the above two open questions, some of the structures in the hypotheses of the results alluded to above are full semi-AFL instead of arbitrary semi-AFL or full trios.

LEMMA 6.4.4: *Let $\mathcal{L}_1$ be a trio and $\mathcal{L}_2$ a semi-AFL. If L is in Sub($\mathcal{L}_1$, $\mathcal{L}_2$), then there exist L_1 in $\mathcal{L}_1$ and ϵ-free L_2 in $\mathcal{L}_2$ such that L is in $\mathcal{S}(\tau_{L_2}(L_1))$. Furthermore, L_1 is ϵ-free if L is.*

Proof: Let $L = \tau(L_1')$ for some L_1' in $\mathscr{L}_1$ and some substitution τ on $\Sigma_{L_1'}^*$ such that $\tau(a)$ is an ϵ-free language in $\mathscr{L}_2$ for each a in $\Sigma_{L_1'}$. Let a' and a'' be new symbols for each a in $\Sigma_{L_1'}$. Let $\Sigma_1 = \{a'/a \text{ in } \Sigma_{L_1'}\}$ and $\Sigma_2 = \{a''/a \text{ in } \Sigma_{L_1'}\} \cup \bigcup_{a \text{ in } \Sigma_{L_1'}} \Sigma_{\tau(a)}$. Then $\Sigma_1 \cap \Sigma_2 = \emptyset$. Let h_1 be the homomorphism on $(\Sigma_1 \cup \Sigma_2)^*$ defined by $h_1(a') = h_1(a'') = \epsilon$ for each a in $\Sigma_{L_1'}$ and $h_1(b) = b$ for each b in $\bigcup_{a \text{ in } \Sigma_{L_1'}} \Sigma_{\tau(a)}$. Let h_2 be the homomorphism on $\Sigma_{L_1'}^*$ defined by $h_2(a) = a'$ for each a in $\Sigma_{L_1'}$. Let $L_2 = \bigcup_{a \text{ in } \Sigma_{L_1'}} a''\tau(a)$ and $L_1 = h_2(L_1')$. Then $L = h_1(\tau_{L_2}(L_1) \cap R)$, where $R = \left(\bigcup_a a'a''\Sigma_{\tau(a)}^+\right)^*$. Clearly R is regular and h_1 is ϵ-limited on R. Note that L_1 is in $\mathscr{L}_1$, and that L_2 is ϵ-free and in $\mathscr{L}_2$. Then $L - \{\epsilon\} = h_1(\tau_{L_2}(L_1) \cap R) - \{\epsilon\}$ is in $\mathscr{S}(\tau_{L_2}(L_1))$ by Corollary 2 of Theorem 3.2.2. Now L contains ϵ if and only if L_1', thus L_1, contains ϵ. If L_1 contains ϵ then $\{\epsilon\}$, thus $L = (L - \{\epsilon\}) \cup \{\epsilon\}$, is in $\mathscr{S}(\tau_{L_2}(L_1))$. If L_1 is ϵ-free, then $L = L - \{\epsilon\}$ is in $\mathscr{S}(\tau_{L_2}(L_1))$. In either case, L is in $\mathscr{S}(\tau_{L_2}(L_1))$.

We are now ready for the partial converse to Corollary 1 of Theorem 6.4.1.

THEOREM 6.4.2: *Let $\mathscr{L}_1$ and $\mathscr{L}_2$ be full (semi-) AFL. If Sub $(\mathscr{L}_1, \mathscr{L}_2)$ is full principal, then either $\mathscr{L}_1$ or $\mathscr{L}_2$ is full principal.*

Proof: First consider the semi-AFL case. Suppose Sub $(\mathscr{L}_1, \mathscr{L}_2)$ is full principal. Then Sub $(\mathscr{L}_1, \mathscr{L}_2) = \hat{\mathscr{S}}(L)$ for some nonempty language L. Since $\hat{\mathscr{S}}(L - \{\epsilon\}) = \hat{\mathscr{S}}(L)$, we may assume that L is ϵ-free. Since L is in Sub $(\mathscr{L}_1, \mathscr{L}_2)$, by Lemma 6.4.4 there exist (nonempty) languages L_1 in $\mathscr{L}_1$ and L_2 in $\mathscr{L}_2$ such that L is in $\mathscr{S}(\tau_{L_2}(L_1))$. Then $\hat{\mathscr{S}}(L_1) \subseteq \mathscr{L}_1$, $\hat{\mathscr{S}}(L_2) \subseteq \mathscr{L}_2$, and

$$\begin{aligned}
\text{Sub}(\mathscr{L}_1, \mathscr{L}_2) &= \hat{\mathscr{S}}(L)\\
&\subseteq \hat{\mathscr{S}}(\tau_{L_2}(L_1))\\
&\subseteq \text{Sub}\,(\hat{\mathscr{S}}(L_1), \hat{\mathscr{S}}(L_2)), \quad \text{since Sub}\,(\hat{\mathscr{S}}(L_1), \hat{\mathscr{S}}(L_2)) \text{ is a full semi-}\\
&\qquad \text{AFL containing } \tau_{L_2}(L_1) \text{ by Corollary 1 of Theorem 6.1.1,}\\
&\subseteq \text{Sub}\,(\mathscr{L}_1, \mathscr{L}_2).
\end{aligned}$$

Thus Sub $(\mathscr{L}_1, \mathscr{L}_2) =$ Sub $(\hat{\mathscr{S}}(L_1), \hat{\mathscr{S}}(L_2))$. We shall show that either $\mathscr{L}_1 = \hat{\mathscr{S}}(L_1)$ or $\mathscr{L}_2 = \hat{\mathscr{S}}(L_2)$, thereby completing the proof.

Suppose $\mathscr{L}_1 \neq \hat{\mathscr{S}}(L_1)$, so that $\hat{\mathscr{S}}(L_1) \subsetneq \mathscr{L}_1$. Then there exists a nonempty language L_3 in $\mathscr{L}_1 - \hat{\mathscr{S}}(L_1)$. Clearly, we may assume L_3 is ϵ-free. Let L_4 be any language in $\mathcal{L}_2$. If $L_4 = \{\epsilon\}$ or $L_4 = \emptyset$, then L_4 is in $\hat{\mathcal{S}}(L_2)$. Assume $L_4 \neq \{\epsilon\}$ and $L_4 \neq \emptyset$. For each a in Σ_{L_4} let $\bar{a}$ be a new symbol and let $\Sigma_5 = \{\bar{a}/a$ in $\Sigma_{L_4}\}$. Let h be the homomorphism from $\Sigma_{L_4}^*$ into Σ_5^* defined by $h(a) = \bar{a}$ for each a in Σ_{L_4} and let $L_5 = h(L_4) - \{\epsilon\}$. Then L_5 is nonempty and ϵ-free, and $\tau_{L_5}(L_3)$ is in Sub $(\mathcal{L}_1, \mathcal{L}_2) =$ Sub $(\hat{\mathcal{S}}(L_1), \hat{\mathcal{S}}(L_2))$. By assumption, L_3 is not in $\hat{\mathcal{S}}(L_1)$. Thus L_5 is in $\hat{\mathcal{S}}(L_2)$ by Lemma 6.4.3. Since $L_4 = h^{-1}(L_5) \cup (L_4 \cap \{\epsilon\})$, L_4 is in $\hat{\mathcal{S}}(L_2)$. Thus $\mathcal{L}_2 \subseteq \hat{\mathcal{S}}(L_2)$, whence $\mathcal{L}_2 = \hat{\mathcal{S}}(L_2)$.

Consider the AFL case. By the corollary to Theorem 5.4.1, a full principal AFL is a full principal semi-AFL. Thus Sub $(\mathcal{L}_1, \mathcal{L}_2)$ is a full principal semi-AFL. By the semi-AFL case, $\mathcal{L}_1$ or $\mathcal{L}_2$ is a full principal semi-AFL. Note that a full AFL which is a full principal semi-AFL is a full principal AFL. [For if $\mathcal{L}$ is a full AFL and $\mathcal{L} = \hat{\mathcal{S}}(L)$, then $\mathcal{L} = \hat{\mathcal{S}}(L) \subseteq \hat{\mathcal{F}}(L) \subseteq \mathcal{L}$.] Thus $\mathcal{L}_1$ or $\mathcal{L}_2$ is a full principal AFL.

REMARK: The proof of Theorem 6.4.2 actually shows the following slightly stronger result in the semi-AFL case: Let $\mathcal{L}_1$ be a full trio and $\mathcal{L}_2$ a full semi-AFL. If Sub $(\mathcal{L}_1, \mathcal{L}_2)$ is a full principal semi-AFL, then either $\mathcal{L}_1$ or $\mathcal{L}_2$ is a full principal semi-AFL.

From Corollary 1 of Theorem 6.4.1 and from Theorem 6.4.2, we immediately get:

THEOREM 6.4.3: *Let $\mathcal{L}$ be a full (semi-) AFL. Then Sub $(\mathcal{L}, \mathcal{L})$ is full principal if and only if $\mathcal{L}$ is full principal.*

Open Problem: Is Theorem 6.4.2 or Theorem 6.4.3 true if "full" is removed?

EXERCISE 6.4.1: For each full AFL $\mathcal{L}$ let IP($\mathcal{L}$) be the family of all languages U with the following property: For each language L in $\mathcal{L}$, if $\Sigma_L \cap \Sigma_U = \emptyset$ then $\tau_U(L)$ is in $\mathcal{L}$. Prove that IP($\mathcal{L}$) $\subseteq \mathcal{L}$ and is a substitution-closed full AFL [Le, b].

EXERCISE 6.4.2: Verify in the proof of (b) of Theorem 6.4.1 that

$$\mathcal{F}\big(\tau_{(L_2c_2)^+}((L_1c_1)^*)\big) = \mathcal{F}\big(\tau_{(L_2c_2)^+}((L_1c_1)^+)\big) \cup \big\{L \cup \{\epsilon\}/L \text{ in } \mathcal{F}\big(\tau_{(L_2c_2)^+}((L_1c_1)^+)\big)\big\}.$$

EXERCISE 6.4.3: Prove that an AFL $\mathcal{L}$ is closed under ϵ-free substitution if and only if $\mathcal{L}$ is closed under all substitutions of the form $\tau_{L_2}(L_1)$ for L_1 and L_2 in $\mathcal{L}$.

EXERCISE 6.4.4: Let L_1 and L_2 be languages, with $\Sigma_{L_1} \cap \Sigma_{L_2} = \emptyset$ and $L_2-\{\epsilon\} \neq \emptyset$. If L_3 is in $\mathscr{M}(L_2-\{\epsilon\})$, with $\Sigma_{L_1} \cap \Sigma_{L_3} = \emptyset$, prove that $\tau_{L_3}(L_1)$ is in $\mathscr{F}(\tau_{L_2-\{\epsilon\}}(L_1))$.

EXERCISE 6.4.5: Let L_1, L_2, and L_3 be languages, with $\Sigma_{L_1} \cap \Sigma_{L_2} = \Sigma_{L_2} \cap \Sigma_{L_3} = \emptyset$ and $L_1-\{\epsilon\} \neq \emptyset$. Let L_3 be in $\mathscr{M}(L_1-\{\epsilon\})$. Prove that there exists L_4 in $\mathscr{F}(L_2)$ such that $\Sigma_{L_1} \cap \Sigma_{L_4} = \emptyset$ and $\tau_{L_2}(L_3)$ is in $\mathscr{F}(\tau_{L_4}(L_1-\{\epsilon\}))$. Furthermore, L_4 is ϵ-free if L_2 is.

EXERCISE 6.4.6: Prove Corollary 1 of Theorem 6.4.1 for principal semi-AFL, i. e., prove that Sub $(\mathscr{L}_1, \mathscr{L}_2)$ is a principal semi-AFL if $\mathscr{L}_1$ and $\mathscr{L}_2$ are principal semi-AFL.

EXERCISE 6.4.7: Let L_1 and L_2 be languages such that $\Sigma_{L_1} \cap \Sigma_{L_2} = \emptyset$. Let c_1 and c_2 be new symbols. Prove the following:

(a) If $L_2 \neq \emptyset$, then $\mathscr{F}\big(\tau_{(L_2c_2)^+}((L_1c_1)^*)\big) = \mathscr{F}\big(\tau_{(L_2c_2)^*}((L_1c_1)^*)\big)$.

(b) If ϵ is in L_1 and $L_2 \neq \emptyset$, then Sub $(\mathscr{F}(L_1 \cup \{\epsilon\}), \mathscr{F}(L_2 \cup \{\epsilon\})) = \mathscr{F}\big(\tau_{(L_2c_2)^*}((L_1c_1)^*) \cup \{\epsilon\}\big)$.

(c) If ϵ is in L_1, $L_1 \neq \emptyset$, and $L_2 \neq \emptyset$, then Sub $(\mathscr{F}(L_1 \cup \{\epsilon\}), \mathscr{F}(L_2 \cup \{\epsilon\})) = \mathscr{F}\big(\tau_{(L_2c_2)^*}((L_1c_1)^*) \cup \{\epsilon\}\big)$.

(d) If $L_1 \neq \emptyset$, then Sub$\big(\mathscr{F}(L_1 \cup \{\epsilon\}), \mathscr{F}(L_2 \cup \{\epsilon\})\big) = \mathscr{F}\big(\tau_{(L_2c_2)^*}((L_1c_1)^*) \cup \{\epsilon\}\big)$ [GGG].

EXERCISE 6.4.8: Let L_1 and L_2 be ϵ-free, nonempty languages, with $\Sigma_{L_1} \cap \Sigma_{L_2} = \emptyset$. For full semi-AFL $\mathscr{L}_1$ and $\mathscr{L}_2$, prove that if $\tau_{L_2}(L_1)$ is in Sûb $(\mathscr{R}, \mathscr{L}_1 \cup \mathscr{L}_2)$ then either L_1 is in $\hat{\mathscr{F}}(\mathscr{L}_2)$ or L_2 is in $\mathscr{L}_1$ [Gr3].

EXERCISE 6.4.9: Let L_1 and L_2 be ϵ-free, nonempty languages, with $\Sigma_{L_1} \cap \Sigma_{L_2} = \emptyset$. Suppose $\mathscr{L}_1$ and $\mathscr{L}_2$ are full AFL and $\tau_{L_2}(L_1)$ is in Sûb $(\mathscr{R}, \mathscr{L}_1 \cup \mathscr{L}_2)$. Prove that either L_1 is in $\mathscr{L}_1 \cap \mathscr{L}_2$, L_2 is in $\mathscr{L}_1 \cap \mathscr{L}_2$, L_1 and L_2 are in $\mathscr{L}_1$, or L_1 and L_2 are in $\mathscr{L}_2$.

EXERCISE 6.4.10: Extend Lemma 6.4.3 to the following: Let L_1 and L_2 be ϵ-free, nonempty languages, with $\Sigma_{L_1} \cap \Sigma_{L_2} = \emptyset$. Let $\mathscr{L}_1$ and $\mathscr{L}_2$ be full trios. If $\tau_{L_2}(L_1)$ is in Sûb $(\mathscr{L}_1, \mathscr{L}_2)$, then either L_1 is in $\mathscr{L}_1$ or L_2 is in $\hat{\mathscr{S}}(\mathscr{L}_2)$.

EXERCISE 6.4.11: Let $\tau_{L_2}(L_1)$ be in Sub $(\mathscr{L}_1, \mathscr{L}_2)$, with $\mathscr{L}_1$ and $\mathscr{L}_2$ semi-AFL, and L_1 and L_2 ϵ-free. Prove the following:

(a) L_1 is in Sub $(\mathscr{L}_1, \mathscr{L}_2)$.

(b) L_2 is in Sub $(\mathscr{L}_1, \mathscr{L}_2)$.

EXERCISE 6.4.12: Let $\mathcal{L}_1$ and $\mathcal{L}_2$ be full semi-AFL, with $\mathcal{L}_2 \subsetneq \hat{\text{Sub}}(\mathcal{L}_1, \mathcal{L}_2)$. For OP($\mathcal{L}$) as in Exercise 6.1.12 prove the following [Le, a]:

(a) OP($\hat{\text{Sub}}(\mathcal{L}_1, \mathcal{L}_2)$) $\subseteq \mathcal{L}_1$. [Hint: Let L_4 be in $\hat{\text{Sub}}(\mathcal{L}_1, \mathcal{L}_2) - \mathcal{L}_2$ and L in OP($\hat{\text{Sub}}(\mathcal{L}_1, \mathcal{L}_2)$). Show that $\tau_{L_4}(L)$ is in $\hat{\text{Sub}}(\mathcal{L}_1, \mathcal{L}_2)$. Then use Lemma 6.4.3 to infer that L is in $\mathcal{L}_1$.]

(b) If $\mathcal{L}_1$ is substitution closed, then OP($\hat{\text{Sub}}(\mathcal{L}_1, \mathcal{L}_2)$) $= \mathcal{L}_1$.

6.5 Substitution Closure and Principal (Semi-) AFL

We now consider substitution closure and (full) principal AFL. We shall see that for a full principal AFL $\mathcal{L}$, $\hat{\mathcal{F}}_{\hat{\sigma}}(\mathcal{L})$ is not necessarily a full principal (semi-) AFL. We then present a condition which guarantees that $\hat{\mathcal{F}}_{\hat{\sigma}}(\mathcal{L})$ is not a full principal (semi-)AFL, and a condition on full (semi-)AFL $\mathcal{L}_1$ and $\mathcal{L}_2$ which guarantees that $\acute{\mathcal{F}}_{\hat{\sigma}}(\mathcal{L}_1 \cup \mathcal{L}_2)$ is not a full principal (semi-) AFL.

We first turn to a characterization of when a full semi-AFL is substitution closed. For this we need a preliminary result.

LEMMA 6.5.1: *Let $\mathcal{L}_1$, $\mathcal{L}_1'$, $\mathcal{L}_2$ be full trios, and $\mathcal{L}_2'$ a full semi-AFL such that $\mathcal{L}_1 - \mathcal{L}_1' \neq \emptyset$ and $\mathcal{L}_2 - \mathcal{L}_2' \neq \emptyset$. Then $\hat{\text{Sub}}(\mathcal{L}_1, \mathcal{L}_2) - \hat{\text{Sub}}(\mathcal{L}_1', \mathcal{L}_2') \neq \emptyset$.*

Proof: Let L_1 be in $\mathcal{L}_1 - \mathcal{L}_1'$ and L_2 in $\mathcal{L}_2 - \mathcal{L}_2'$. Since all structures are full, we may assume that $\Sigma_{L_1} \cap \Sigma_{L_2} = \emptyset$ and L_1 and L_2 are ϵ-free. Let $L = \tau_{L_2}(L_1)$. By definition, L is in $\hat{\text{Sub}}(\mathcal{L}_1, \mathcal{L}_2)$. Suppose L is in $\hat{\text{Sub}}(\mathcal{L}_1', \mathcal{L}_2')$. By Lemma 6.4.3 either L_1 is in $\mathcal{L}_1'$, a contradiction, or L_2 is in $\mathcal{L}_2'$, a contradiction. Thus L is not in $\hat{\text{Sub}}(\mathcal{L}_1', \mathcal{L}_2')$, so that L is in $\hat{\text{Sub}}(\mathcal{L}_1, \mathcal{L}_2) - \hat{\text{Sub}}(\mathcal{L}_1', \mathcal{L}_2')$.

COROLLARY 1: *If $\mathcal{L}_1$ and $\mathcal{L}_2$ are incomparable full semi-AFL, then $\hat{\text{Sub}}(\mathcal{L}_1, \mathcal{L}_2)$ and $\hat{\text{Sub}}(\mathcal{L}_2, \mathcal{L}_1)$ are incomparable.*

Suppose that $\mathcal{L}_1$ and $\mathcal{L}_2$ are semi-AFL. Then $\mathcal{L}_1 \subseteq \hat{\text{Sub}}(\mathcal{L}_1, \mathcal{L}_2)$ and $\mathcal{L}_2 \subseteq \hat{\text{Sub}}(\mathcal{L}_1, \mathcal{L}_2)$, so that

$$\hat{\text{Sub}}(\mathcal{L}_2, \mathcal{L}_1) \subseteq \hat{\text{Sub}}(\hat{\text{Sub}}(\mathcal{L}_1, \mathcal{L}_2), \hat{\text{Sub}}(\mathcal{L}_1, \mathcal{L}_2)).$$

Thus $\hat{\text{Sub}}(\mathcal{L}_1, \mathcal{L}_2)$ is not substitution closed if $\hat{\text{Sub}}(\mathcal{L}_2, \mathcal{L}_1) \subseteq \hat{\text{Sub}}(\mathcal{L}_1, \mathcal{L}_2)$ is false. From Corollary 1 we therefore get:

COROLLARY 2: *If $\mathcal{L}_1$ and $\mathcal{L}_2$ are incomparable full semi-AFL, then Sûb($\mathcal{L}_1$, $\mathcal{L}_2$) is not substitution closed.*

THEOREM 6.5.1: *A full semi-AFL $\mathcal{L}$ is substitution closed if and only if Sûb ($\mathcal{L}$, $\mathcal{L}$) is substitution closed.*

Proof: If $\mathcal{L}$ is substitution closed, then so is Sûb ($\mathcal{L}$, $\mathcal{L}$) $= \mathcal{L}$. Now suppose $\mathcal{L}$ is not substitution closed. Then Sûb ($\mathcal{L}$, $\mathcal{L}$)$-\mathcal{L} \neq \emptyset$. By Lemma 6.5.1,

$$\text{Sûb}\,(\text{Sûb}\,(\mathcal{L}, \mathcal{L}), \text{Sûb}\,(\mathcal{L}, \mathcal{L})) - \text{Sûb}\,(\mathcal{L}, \mathcal{L}) \neq \emptyset.$$

Hence Sûb ($\mathcal{L}$, $\mathcal{L}$) is not substitution closed.

COROLLARY 1: *A full semi-AFL $\mathcal{L}$ is substitution closed if and only if $\hat{\mathcal{F}}(\mathcal{L})$ is substitution closed, in which case*[1] $\mathcal{L} = \hat{\mathcal{F}}(\mathcal{L})$.

Proof: Suppose $\mathcal{L}$ is substitution closed. By Theorem 3.4.1, $\hat{\mathcal{F}}(\mathcal{L}) =$ Sûb ($\mathcal{R}$, $\mathcal{L}$). By Theorem 3.1.1, $\mathcal{R} \subseteq \mathcal{L}$. Then

$$\mathcal{L} \subseteq \hat{\mathcal{F}}(\mathcal{L}) = \text{Sûb}(\mathcal{R}, \mathcal{L}) \subseteq \text{Sûb}(\mathcal{L}, \mathcal{L}) \subseteq \mathcal{L},$$

so that $\mathcal{L} = \hat{\mathcal{F}}(\mathcal{L})$. Thus $\hat{\mathcal{F}}(\mathcal{L})$ is substitution closed.

Suppose $\mathcal{L}$ is not substitution closed. By Theorem 6.5.1, Sûb ($\mathcal{L}$, $\mathcal{L}$) is not substitution closed. Suppose $\hat{\mathcal{F}}(\mathcal{L})$ is substitution closed. Then

$$\text{Sûb}(\mathcal{L}, \mathcal{L}) \subseteq \text{Sûb}\,(\hat{\mathcal{F}}(\mathcal{L}), \hat{\mathcal{F}}(\mathcal{L})) \subseteq \hat{\mathcal{F}}(\mathcal{L})$$

and

$$\hat{\mathcal{F}}(\mathcal{L}) = \text{Sûb}\,(\mathcal{R}, \mathcal{L}) \subseteq \text{Sûb}\,(\mathcal{L}, \mathcal{L}).$$

Thus $\hat{\mathcal{F}}(\mathcal{L}) =$ Sûb ($\mathcal{L}$, $\mathcal{L}$), so that $\hat{\mathcal{F}}(\mathcal{L})$ is not substitution closed.

COROLLARY 2: *If $\mathcal{L}$ is a full semi-AFL which is not a full AFL, then $\hat{\mathcal{F}}(\mathcal{L})$ is not substitution closed.*

Proof: Let $\mathcal{L}$ be a full semi-AFL which is not a full AFL. Since $\mathcal{R} \subseteq \mathcal{L}$ and $\mathcal{L} \subsetneq \hat{\mathcal{F}}(\mathcal{L}) =$ Sûb ($\mathcal{R}$, $\mathcal{L}$), $\mathcal{L}$ is not substitution closed. By Corollary 1, $\hat{\mathcal{F}}(\mathcal{L})$ is not substitution closed.

EXAMPLE 6.5.1: Since $\mathcal{L}_{\text{lin}} \neq \hat{\mathcal{F}}(\mathcal{L}_{\text{lin}})$, $\hat{\mathcal{F}}(\mathcal{L}_{\text{lin}})$ is not substitution closed by Corollary 2.

[1] Compare with the corollary to Proposition 3.3.3.

We next consider the problem of when the substitution closure of a full semi-AFL is full principal. First though, we prove a lemma that asserts the existence of a sequence of properly increasing full semi-AFL.

LEMMA 6.5.2: *Let $\mathcal{L}$ be a full semi-AFL which is not substitution closed. Then $\{\hat{Sub}_k(\mathcal{L}, \mathcal{L})/k \geqq 0\}$ is an infinite chain of full semi-AFL, and $\hat{Sub}_k(\mathcal{L}, \mathcal{L}) \subsetneqq \hat{Sub}_{k+1}(\mathcal{L}, \mathcal{L})$ for each $k \geqq 0$.*

Proof: For each $n \geqq 0$ let $\mathcal{L}_n = \hat{\text{Sub}}_n(\mathcal{L}, \mathcal{L})$. By Lemma 6.3.1(b) and Corollary 1 of Theorem 6.1.1, each $\mathcal{L}_n$ is a full semi-AFL. Suppose $\mathcal{L}_k = \mathcal{L}_{k+1}$ for some $k \geqq 0$. Then $\mathcal{L}_{k+i} = \mathcal{L}_k$ for all $i \geqq 0$. [For assume $\mathcal{L}_{k+i} = \mathcal{L}_k$ for all i, $0 \leqq i < n$, $n \geqq 2$. Then $\mathcal{L}_{k+n} = \hat{\text{Sub}}\,(\mathcal{L}, \mathcal{L}_{n-1}) = \hat{\text{Sub}}\,(\mathcal{L}, \mathcal{L}_{n-2})$, by induction, $= \mathcal{L}_{n-1} = \mathcal{L}_k$. Hence the induction is extended.] Thus it suffices to exhibit an infinite sequence $k_0 < \ldots < k_r < \ldots$ such that $\mathcal{L}_{k_r} \subsetneqq \mathcal{L}_{k_{r+1}}$ for each r.

For each $r \geqq 0$, let $k_r = 2^r - 1$. Since $\mathcal{L}$ is not substitution closed, $\mathcal{L}_{k_0} = \mathcal{L} \subsetneqq \hat{\text{Sub}}\,(\mathcal{L}, \mathcal{L}) = \mathcal{L}_{k_1}$. By Theorem 6.5.1, $\mathcal{L}_{k_1}$ is not substitution closed. Continuing by induction, suppose $\mathcal{L}_{k_{r-1}} \subsetneqq \mathcal{L}_{k_r}$ and $\mathcal{L}_{k_r}$ is not substitution closed. Then

$$\begin{aligned}
\mathcal{L}_{k_r} &\subsetneqq \hat{\text{Sub}}\,(\mathcal{L}_{k_r}, \mathcal{L}_{k_r})\\
&= \hat{\text{Sub}}\,(\hat{\text{Sub}}(\overbrace{\mathcal{L}, \ldots, \mathcal{L}}^{2^r}), \hat{\text{Sub}}\,(\overbrace{\mathcal{L}, \ldots, \mathcal{L}}^{2^r})), \quad \text{by Lemma 6.3.1 (b)},\\
&= \hat{\text{Sub}}\,(\overbrace{\mathcal{L}, \ldots, \mathcal{L}}^{2^r+1})\\
&= \mathcal{L}_{k_{r+1}}.
\end{aligned}$$

By Theorem 6.5.1, $\mathcal{L}_{k_{r+1}}$ is not substitution closed. Hence the induction is extended.

THEOREM 6.5.2: *Let $\mathcal{L}$ be a full semi-AFL. Then the following statements are equivalent, and each implies $\mathcal{L} = \hat{\mathcal{F}}(\mathcal{L}) = \hat{\mathcal{F}}_{\hat{\sigma}}(\mathcal{L})$:*

(a) *$\hat{\mathcal{F}}_{\hat{\sigma}}(\mathcal{L})$ is a (full) principal semi-AFL.*

(b) *$\hat{\mathcal{F}}_{\hat{\sigma}}(\mathcal{L})$ is a (full) principal AFL.*

(c) *$\mathcal{L}$ is a (full) principal semi-AFL and substitution closed.*

(d) *$\mathcal{L}$ is a (full) principal AFL and substitution closed.*

Proof: By the corollary to Theorem 5.4.1, a full AFL is a (full) principal AFL if and only if it is a (full) principal semi-AFL. Thus (a) and (b) are equivalent. By the corollary to Proposition 3.3.3 and the corollary to Theorem 5.4.1, (c) and (d) are equivalent.

We now show that (a) implies (c) and (c) implies (a) for the case when $\mathscr{L}$ is a full AFL. Suppose (a) holds, i. e., $\hat{\mathscr{F}}_{\hat{\sigma}}(\mathscr{L})$ is a (full) principal semi-AFL. Assume $\mathscr{L}$ is not substitution closed. By Lemma 6.5.2, $\hat{\text{Sub}}_k(\mathscr{L}, \mathscr{L})$ is a full semi-AFL and $\hat{\text{Sub}}_k(\mathscr{L}, \mathscr{L}) \subset \hat{\text{Sub}}_{k+1}(\mathscr{L}, \mathscr{L})$ for each $k \geqq 0$. Since $\hat{\mathscr{F}}_{\hat{\sigma}}(\mathscr{L}) = \bigcup_k \hat{\text{Sub}}_k(\mathscr{L}, \mathscr{L})$, $\hat{\mathscr{F}}_{\hat{\sigma}}(\mathscr{L})$ is not a (full) principal semi-AFL by Lemma 5.1.2, a contradiction. Hence $\mathscr{L}$ is substitution closed. Therefore $\mathscr{L} = \hat{\mathscr{F}}_{\sigma}(\mathscr{L})$, and $\mathscr{L}$ is a (full) principal semi-AFL and substitution closed, i. e., (c) holds. Now suppose (c) holds. Then $\hat{\mathscr{F}}_{\hat{\sigma}}(\mathscr{L}) = \mathscr{L}$, and so is (full) principal, i. e., (a) holds.

Consider the general case, i.e., when $\mathscr{L}$ is just a full semi-AFL. Suppose (a) holds. Now $\hat{\mathscr{F}}_{\hat{\sigma}}(\mathscr{L}) = \hat{\mathscr{F}}_{\hat{\sigma}}(\hat{\mathscr{F}}(\mathscr{L}))$. By the case for full AFL, $\hat{\mathscr{F}}(\mathscr{L})$ is a (full) principal semi-AFL and substitution closed. By Corollary 1 of Theorem 6.5.1, $\mathscr{L} = \hat{\mathscr{F}}(\mathscr{L})$. Thus $\mathscr{L}$ is (full) principal and substitution closed, i.e., (c) holds. Now suppose (c) holds. By Corollary 1 of Theorem 6.5.1, $\mathscr{L} = \hat{\mathscr{F}}(\mathscr{L})$, i.e., $\mathscr{L}$ is a full AFL. By the case for full AFL, $\hat{\mathscr{F}}_{\hat{\sigma}}(\mathscr{L})$ is (full) principal, i.e., (a) holds.

Finally, suppose (a), (b), (c), or (d) holds. Then (a), (b), (c), and (d) hold. As noted above, $\mathscr{L} = \hat{\mathscr{F}}(\mathscr{L}) = \hat{\mathscr{F}}_{\hat{\sigma}}(\hat{\mathscr{F}}(\mathscr{L})) = \hat{\mathscr{F}}_{\hat{\sigma}}(\mathscr{L})$, completing the proof.

COROLLARY: *Let $\mathscr{L}$ be a semi-AFL for which $\hat{\mathscr{H}}(\mathscr{L})$ is not substitution closed. Then $\mathscr{L}$ is not closed under ϵ-free substitution. Furthermore, neither $\mathscr{F}_{\sigma}(\mathscr{L})$, $\mathscr{F}_{\hat{\sigma}}(\mathscr{L})$, $\hat{\mathscr{F}}_{\sigma}(\mathscr{L})$, nor $\hat{\mathscr{F}}_{\hat{\sigma}}(\mathscr{L})$ is a principal or full principal semi-AFL.*

Proof: Suppose $\mathscr{L}$ is closed under ϵ-free substitution. Then Sub $(\mathscr{L}, \mathscr{L}) = \mathscr{L}$. Thus

$$\begin{aligned} \hat{\mathscr{H}}(\mathscr{L}) &= \hat{\mathscr{H}}(\text{Sub}(\mathscr{L}, \mathscr{L})) \\ &= \text{Sub}\,(\hat{\mathscr{H}}(\mathscr{L}), \hat{\mathscr{H}}(\mathscr{L})), \quad \text{by Corollary 2 of Theorem 6.1.1,} \\ &= \hat{\text{Sub}}\,(\hat{\mathscr{H}}(\mathscr{L}), \hat{\mathscr{H}}(\mathscr{L})), \end{aligned}$$

a contradiction.

Suppose either $\mathscr{F}_{\sigma}(\mathscr{L}) = \mathscr{F}_{\sigma}(\mathscr{F}(\mathscr{L}))$, $\mathscr{F}_{\hat{\sigma}}(\mathscr{L}) = \mathscr{F}_{\hat{\sigma}}(\mathscr{F}(\mathscr{L}))$, $\hat{\mathscr{F}}_{\sigma}(\mathscr{L}) = \hat{\mathscr{F}}_{\sigma}(\mathscr{F}(\mathscr{L}))$, or $\hat{\mathscr{F}}_{\hat{\sigma}}(\mathscr{L}) = \hat{\mathscr{F}}_{\hat{\sigma}}(\mathscr{F}(\mathscr{L}))$ is a [full] principal semi-AFL. By Theorem 6.3.2, $\hat{\mathscr{F}}_{\hat{\sigma}}(\hat{\mathscr{F}}(\mathscr{F}(\mathscr{L}))) = \mathscr{F}_{\sigma}(\hat{\mathscr{F}}(\mathscr{F}(\mathscr{L}))) = \hat{\mathscr{F}}(\mathscr{F}_{\sigma}(\mathscr{F}(\mathscr{L}))) = \hat{\mathscr{F}}(\mathscr{F}_{\hat{\sigma}}(\mathscr{F}(\mathscr{L}))) - \hat{\mathscr{F}}(\hat{\mathscr{F}}_{\sigma}(\mathscr{F}(\mathscr{L}))) = \hat{\mathscr{F}}_{\sigma}(\mathscr{F}(\mathscr{L}))$. Thus $\hat{\mathscr{F}}_{\hat{\sigma}}(\hat{\mathscr{F}}(\mathscr{F}(\mathscr{L})))$ is a full principal semi-AFL. By Theorem 6.5.2, this implies that $\hat{\mathscr{F}}(\mathscr{F}(\mathscr{L})) =$

$\hat{\mathscr{F}}(\hat{\mathscr{H}}(\mathscr{L}))$ is substitution closed. By Corollary 1 of Theorem 6.5.1, $\hat{\mathscr{H}}(\mathscr{L})$ is substitution closed, a contradiction.

Open Problem: Does Theorem 6.5.2 remain valid if "full semi-AFL" is replaced by "semi-AFL"? In other words, let $\mathscr{L}$ be a semi-AFL (or AFL). Is it true that $\mathscr{F}_\sigma(\mathscr{L})$ is principal if and only if $\mathscr{L}$ is principal and substitution closed, in which case $\mathscr{L} = \mathscr{F}(\mathscr{L}) = \mathscr{F}_\sigma(\mathscr{L})$?

EXAMPLE 6.5.2: Let $\mathscr{L} = \hat{\mathscr{F}}(\mathscr{L}_{\text{lin}})$. As noted in Example 6.5.1, $\mathscr{L}$ is not substitution closed. By Theorem 6.5.2, $\hat{\mathscr{F}}_{\hat{\sigma}}(\mathscr{L}) = \mathscr{L}_{\text{DB}}$ is not a (full) principal AFL. Since $\mathscr{L} \subseteq \mathscr{L}_{\text{CF}}$, $\hat{\mathscr{F}}_{\hat{\sigma}}(\mathscr{L}) \subseteq \hat{\mathscr{F}}_{\hat{\sigma}}(\mathscr{L}_{\text{CF}}) = \mathscr{L}_{\text{CF}}$. Since $\mathscr{L}_{\text{CF}}$ is a full principal AFL, $\mathscr{L}_{\text{DB}} \subsetneq \mathscr{L}_{\text{CF}}$, so that $\mathscr{L} \subsetneq \mathscr{L}_{\text{CF}}$.

EXAMPLE 6.5.3: It can be shown [Gr2] that $\mathscr{L}_{\text{S}}$ is not closed under substitution. Now $\mathscr{L}_{\text{NSA}}$ is full principal and, by Exercise 5.2.13, is substitution closed. Furthermore, $\mathscr{L}_{\text{S}} \subseteq \mathscr{L}_{\text{NSA}}$. Hence $\hat{\mathscr{F}}_{\hat{\sigma}}(\mathscr{L}_{\text{S}}) \subsetneq \mathscr{L}_{\text{NSA}}$.

We conclude this section by proving that for all incomparable full semi-AFL $\mathscr{L}_1$ and $\mathscr{L}_2$, $\hat{\mathscr{F}}(\mathscr{L}_1 \cup \mathscr{L}_2)$ is not substitution closed and $\hat{\mathscr{F}}_{\hat{\sigma}}(\mathscr{L}_1 \cup \mathscr{L}_2)$ is not full principal. To do this we first introduce an auxiliary operation and establish a preliminary result.

Notation: For all families $\mathscr{L}_1$ and $\mathscr{L}_2$ of languages, let

$$\mathscr{L}_1 \vee \mathscr{L}_2 = \{L_1 \cup L_2 / L_1 \text{ in } \mathscr{L}_1,\ L_2 \text{ in } \mathscr{L}_2\}.$$

EXAMPLE 6.5.4: Let $\mathscr{L}_1 = \{a^*, \{bc\}\}$ and $\mathscr{L}_2 = \{\{a^nb^n/n \geqq 0\}\}$. Then $\mathscr{L}_1 \vee \mathscr{L}_2 = \{\{a^n, a^nb^n/n \geqq 0\}, \{bc, a^nb^n/n \geqq 0\}\}$.

Note that $\mathscr{L}_1 \vee \mathscr{L}_2$ is a (full) trio, resp. (full) semi-AFL if $\mathscr{L}_1$ and $\mathscr{L}_2$ are (full) trios, resp. (full) semi-AFL. (See Exercises 6.5.9 and 6.5.10.)

LEMMA 6.5.3: *Let $\mathscr{L}_1$ and $\mathscr{L}_2$ be incomparable full semi-AFL. Then $\mathscr{L}_1 \cup \mathscr{L}_2 \subsetneq \mathscr{L}_1 \vee \mathscr{L}_2 \subsetneq \hat{\mathscr{F}}(\mathscr{L}_1 \cup \mathscr{L}_2)$.*

Proof: Since $\mathscr{L}_1$ and $\mathscr{L}_2$ are incomparable, there exist L_1 in $\mathscr{L}_1 - \mathscr{L}_2$ and L_2 in $\mathscr{L}_2 - \mathscr{L}_1$. Since $\mathscr{L}_1$ and $\mathscr{L}_2$ are semi-AFL, we may assume that $\Sigma_{L_1} \cap \Sigma_{L_2} = \emptyset$.

Clearly $\mathscr{L}_1 \cup \mathscr{L}_2 \subseteq \mathscr{L}_1 \vee \mathscr{L}_2$. Now $L_1 \cup L_2$ is in $\mathscr{L}_1 \vee \mathscr{L}_2$. However, $L_1 \cup L_2$ is not in $\mathscr{L}_1$ since otherwise $(L_1 \cup L_2) \cap \Sigma_{L_2}^* = L_2$ would be in $\mathscr{L}_1$. Similarly, $L_1 \cup L_2$ is not in $\mathscr{L}_2$. Thus $\mathscr{L}_1 \cup \mathscr{L}_2 \subsetneq \mathscr{L}_1 \vee \mathscr{L}_2$.

Clearly $\mathcal{L}_1 \vee \mathcal{L}_2 \subseteq \hat{\mathcal{F}}(\mathcal{L}_1 \cup \mathcal{L}_2)$. Let c be a new symbol and consider L_1cL_2. Obviously L_1cL_2 is in $\hat{\mathcal{F}}(\mathcal{L}_1 \cup \mathcal{L}_2)$. Suppose L_1cL_2 is in $\mathcal{L}_1 \vee \mathcal{L}_2$. Then $L_1cL_2 = L_3 \cup L_4$ for some L_3 in $\mathcal{L}_1$ and L_4 in $\mathcal{L}_2$. Let h_1 and h_2 be the homomorphisms on $(\Sigma_{L_1} \cup \Sigma_{L_2} \cup \{c\})^*$ defined by $h_1(x) = x$, $h_1(y) = \epsilon$, $h_2(x) = \epsilon$, $h_2(y) = y$, and $h_1(c) = h_2(c) = \epsilon$ for all x in Σ_{L_1} and y in Σ_{L_2}. Two cases arise.

(α) There exists a word w in L_1 such that $wcL_2 \subseteq L_3$. Then $L_2 = h_2(L_3)$ is in $\mathcal{L}_1$, a contradiction.

(β) There is no word w in L_1 such that $wcL_2 \subseteq L_3$. Then for each word w in L_1 there exists a word z in L_2 such that wcz is in L_4. Hence $L_1 = h_1(L_4)$ and is in $\mathcal{L}_2$, a contradiction.

In either case, a contradiction arises. Therefore L_1cL_2 is not in $\mathcal{L}_1 \vee \mathcal{L}_2$, so that $\mathcal{L}_1 \vee \mathcal{L}_2 \subsetneq \hat{\mathcal{F}}(\mathcal{L}_1 \cup \mathcal{L}_2)$.

REMARK: The condition that the semi-AFL be full was only used in showing $\mathcal{L}_1 \vee \mathcal{L}_2 \subsetneq \hat{\mathcal{F}}(\mathcal{L}_1 \cup \mathcal{L}_2)$. Thus $\mathcal{L}_1 \cup \mathcal{L}_2 \subsetneq \mathcal{L}_1 \vee \mathcal{L}_2$ holds for arbitrary semi-AFL $\mathcal{L}_1$ and $\mathcal{L}_2$.

THEOREM 6.5.3: *Let $\mathcal{L}_1$ and $\mathcal{L}_2$ be incomparable full semi-AFL. Then*

(a) *$\hat{\mathcal{F}}(\mathcal{L}_1 \cup \mathcal{L}_2)$ is not substitution closed.*

(b) *$\hat{\mathcal{F}}_\sigma(\mathcal{L}_1 \cup \mathcal{L}_2)$ is neither a full principal AFL nor a full principal semi-AFL.*

Proof: Since $\mathcal{L}_1$ and $\mathcal{L}_2$ are incomparable, one of them is not $\mathcal{R}$. Thus $\mathcal{L}_1 \cup \mathcal{L}_2$ contains a nonregular set. Hence $\hat{\mathcal{F}}(\mathcal{L}_1 \cup \mathcal{L}_2) - \mathcal{R} \neq \emptyset$. By Lemma 6.5.3, $\hat{\mathcal{F}}(\mathcal{L}_1 \cup \mathcal{L}_2) - (\mathcal{L}_1 \vee \mathcal{L}_2) \neq \emptyset$. Now

$$\begin{aligned}\hat{\mathcal{F}}(\mathcal{L}_1 \cup \mathcal{L}_2) &= \hat{\mathcal{F}}(\mathcal{L}_1 \vee \mathcal{L}_2), && \text{by Exercise 6.5.12,}\\ &= \hat{\text{Sub}}(\mathcal{R}, \mathcal{L}_1 \vee \mathcal{L}_2), && \text{by Theorem 3.4.1 since } \mathcal{L}_1 \vee \mathcal{L}_2 \\ & && \text{is a full trio.}\end{aligned}$$

Thus

$$\begin{aligned}&\hat{\text{Sub}}(\hat{\mathcal{F}}(\mathcal{L}_1 \cup \mathcal{L}_2), \hat{\mathcal{F}}(\mathcal{L}_1 \cup \mathcal{L}_2)) - \hat{\mathcal{F}}(\mathcal{L}_1 \cup \mathcal{L}_2) = \\ &\qquad = \hat{\text{Sub}}(\hat{\mathcal{F}}(\mathcal{L}_1 \cup \mathcal{L}_2), \hat{\mathcal{F}}(\mathcal{L}_1 \cup \mathcal{L}_2)) - \hat{\text{Sub}}(\mathcal{R}, \mathcal{L}_1 \vee \mathcal{L}_2) \\ &\qquad \neq \emptyset, \qquad\qquad \text{by Lemma 6.5.1.}\end{aligned}$$

(b) Clearly $\hat{\mathcal{F}}_\sigma(\mathcal{L}_1 \cup \mathcal{L}_2) = \hat{\mathcal{F}}_\sigma(\hat{\mathcal{F}}(\mathcal{L}_1 \cup \mathcal{L}_2))$. By (a), $\hat{\mathcal{F}}(\mathcal{L}_1 \cup \mathcal{L}_2)$ is not substitution closed. By Theorem 6.5.2, $\hat{\mathcal{F}}_\sigma(\hat{\mathcal{F}}(\mathcal{L}_1 \cup \mathcal{L}_2))$ is neither a full principal AFL nor a full principal semi-AFL.

EXAMPLE 6.5.5: Let $\mathscr{L}_1 = \mathscr{L}_{\text{lin}}$ and $\mathscr{L}_2 = \mathscr{L}_C$. Now $\{wcw^R/w \text{ in } \{a, b\}^*\}$ is in $\mathscr{L}_1$, but, by Exercise 4.5.3, is not in $\mathscr{L}_2$. Let W_1 be the Dyck set over one letter. Then W_1 is in $\mathscr{L}_2$, but (see Exercise 6.5.14) is not in $\mathscr{L}_1$. Thus $\mathscr{L}_1$ and $\mathscr{L}_2$ are incomparable full semi-AFL. Since $\mathscr{L}_1 \cup \mathscr{L}_2 \subseteq \mathscr{L}_{\text{CF}}$, $\hat{\mathscr{F}}_{\hat{\sigma}}(\mathscr{L}_1 \cup \mathscr{L}_2) \subseteq \mathscr{L}_{\text{CF}}$. By Theorem 6.5.3, $\hat{\mathscr{F}}_{\hat{\sigma}}(\mathscr{L}_1 \cup \mathscr{L}_2)$ is not a full principal AFL. Since $\mathscr{L}_{\text{CF}}$ is a full principal AFL, $\hat{\mathscr{F}}_{\hat{\sigma}}(\mathscr{L}_1 \cup \mathscr{L}_2) \subsetneqq \mathscr{L}_{\text{CF}}$.

Open Question: If $\mathscr{L}_1$ and $\mathscr{L}_2$ are incomparable full semi-AFL, does it necessarily follow that $\hat{\mathscr{S}}(\mathscr{L}_1 \cup \mathscr{L}_2)$ is not substitution closed?

EXERCISE 6.5.1: Prove that each of the following pair of AFL are incomparable:

(a) $\mathscr{C}_i$ and $\mathscr{L}_{\text{CF}}$, for each $i \geqq 2$.

(b) $\bigcup_{i \geqq 1} \mathscr{C}_i$ and $\mathscr{L}_{\text{CF}}$.

(c) $\mathscr{S}_i$ and $\mathscr{L}_{\text{CF}}$, for each $i \geqq 1$, $\mathscr{S}_i$ as in Exercise 4.5.4 [BGi].

EXERCISE 6.5.2: A full AFL $\mathscr{L}$ is said to be *uniformly star closed* if, for each family $\mathscr{U}$, $\mathscr{L} = \hat{\mathscr{F}}(\mathscr{U})$ implies $\mathscr{L} = \hat{\mathscr{S}}(\mathscr{U})$. Prove that a substitution-closed full AFL is uniformly star closed [Gr6]. Thus $\mathscr{L}_{\text{CF}}$, $\mathscr{L}_{\text{RE}}$, $\mathscr{L}_{\text{DB}}$, and $\mathscr{L}_{\text{NSA}}$ are uniformly star closed.

EXERCISE 6.5.3: Let $\mathscr{L}_1$ and $\mathscr{L}_2$ be full AFL, neither of which is uniformly star closed. Prove that Sûb $(\mathscr{L}_1, \mathscr{L}_2)$ is not uniformly star closed [Le, b].

EXERCISE 6.5.4:Let OP($\mathscr{L}$) be as in Exercise 6.1.12. Let $\mathscr{L}_1$ be a substitution-closed full AFL and $\mathscr{L}_2$ a full AFL which is not uniformly star closed. Using Exercise 6.4.12, prove that OP(Sûb $(\mathscr{L}_1, \mathscr{L}_2)) = \mathscr{L}_1$ [Le, b].

EXERCISE 6.5.5: Let $\mathscr{L}$ be a full AFL such that $\bigcup_{n \geqq 1} a^n L b^n$ is in $\mathscr{L}$ for each L in $\mathscr{L}$ and distinct symbols a and b not in Σ_L. Prove the following [BN]:

(a) Let $\mathscr{U}$ be a family such that $\mathscr{L} = \hat{\mathscr{F}}(\mathscr{U})$. Let $L \neq \emptyset$ be in $\mathscr{L}$ and a and b distinct symbols not in Σ_L. Then there exist $R \neq \emptyset$ in $\mathscr{R}_0$ and a substitution τ on Σ_R^* with the following properties: (i) $\tau(R) = \bigcup_{n \geqq 1} a^n L b^n$. (ii) $\tau(c)$ is e-free, $\tau(c) \neq \emptyset$, and there exist U_c in $\mathscr{U}$ and an a-transducer M_c such that $M_c(U_c) = \tau(c)$ for each c in Σ_R.

(b) For each c in Σ_R, there exists an integer $n(c)$ such that $\#_a(x) - \#_b(x) = n(c)$ for all x in $\tau(c)$.

(c) A word x is in L if and only if there exist c in Σ_R and positive integers s, t such that $a^s x b^t$ is in $\tau(c)$.

(d) Let h be the homomorphism on $(\Sigma_L \cup \{a, b\})^*$ defined by $h(a) = h(b) = \epsilon$, and $h(d) = d$ for each element d in Σ_L. Then $L = \bigcup_{c \text{ in } \Sigma_R} hM_c(U_c)$.

(e) $\mathscr{L}$ is uniformly star closed. Thus $\mathscr{L}_S$ and $\mathscr{L}_{NES}$ are uniformly star closed.

EXERCISE 6.5.6: Let $\mathscr{U}$ be a countable family of infinite languages and L_0 a given countable language. Using a diagonalization argument, prove that there exists a language L containing no member of $\mathscr{U}$ as a subset such that L_0 is in $\hat{\mathscr{F}}(L)$.

(*) EXERCISE 6.5.7: Let Σ be countable and $\mathscr{L}_1$ the family of all languages. Prove that there is no full AFL $\mathscr{L}_2 \subsetneqq \mathscr{L}_1$ with the following property: If $\mathscr{L}$ is a full AFL such that $\mathscr{L}_2 \subseteq \mathscr{L} \subseteq \mathscr{L}_1$, then either $\mathscr{L} = \mathscr{L}_1$ or $\mathscr{L} = \mathscr{L}_2$. [Hint: Suppose such an AFL $\mathscr{L}_2$ exists. Let L_0 be some language in $\mathscr{L}_1 - \mathscr{L}_2$ and $\mathscr{U} = \{L \text{ in } \hat{\mathscr{F}}(L_0)/L \text{ infinite}\}$. Then show (i) there exists L containing no language in $\mathscr{U}$ such that L_0 is in $\hat{\mathscr{F}}(L)$, (ii) L is in $\mathscr{L}_1 = \hat{\mathscr{F}}(\mathscr{L}_2 \cup \{L_0\}) = \hat{\mathscr{S}}(\mathscr{L}_2 \cup \{L_0\})$, (iii) $L = L_1 \cup L_2$ for some L_1 in $\hat{\mathscr{M}}(L_0) \subseteq \hat{\mathscr{F}}(L_0)$ and L_2 in $\mathscr{L}_2$, (iv) L_1 is not in $\mathscr{U}$, so L_1 is finite, and (v) L, thus L_0, is in $\mathscr{L}_2$.]

EXERCISE 6.5.8: Let $\mathscr{L}$ be a full AFL which is not substitution closed. Prove that $\hat{\mathscr{F}}_{\hat{\sigma}}(\mathscr{L}) \subsetneqq \mathscr{L}'$, where $\mathscr{L}'$ is the smallest superAFL[1] containing $\mathscr{L}$ [Gr4].

EXERCISE 6.5.9: Let $\mathscr{L}_1$ and $\mathscr{L}_2$ be (full) semi-AFL. Prove that

(a) $\mathscr{L}_1 \vee \mathscr{L}_2$ is a (full) semi-AFL.

(b) $\mathscr{L}_1 \vee \mathscr{L}_2 = \mathscr{S}(\mathscr{L}_1 \cup \mathscr{L}_2)(\hat{\mathscr{S}}(\mathscr{L}_1 \cup \mathscr{L}_2))$.

EXERCISE 6.5.10: Let $\mathscr{L}_1$ and $\mathscr{L}_2$ be (full) trios. Prove that

(a) $\mathscr{L}_1 \vee \mathscr{L}_2$ is a (full) trio.

(b) $\mathscr{L}_1 \vee \mathscr{L}_2$ and $\mathscr{M}(\mathscr{L}_1 \cup \mathscr{L}_2)(\hat{\mathscr{M}}(\mathscr{L}_1 \cup \mathscr{L}_2))$ need not coincide.

EXERCISE 6.5.11: Exhibit two AFL $\mathscr{L}_1$ and $\mathscr{L}_2$ such that $\mathscr{L}_1 \vee \mathscr{L}_2$ is not an AFL.

EXERCISE 6.5.12: Verify that $\mathscr{F}(\mathscr{L}_1 \vee \mathscr{L}_2) = \mathscr{F}(\mathscr{L}_1 \cup \mathscr{L}_2)$ and $\hat{\mathscr{F}}(\mathscr{L}_1 \vee \mathscr{L}_2) = \hat{\mathscr{F}}(\mathscr{L}_1 \cup \mathscr{L}_2)$ if $\mathscr{L}_1$ and $\mathscr{L}_2$ are semi-AFL.

[1] See Exercise 6.1.17.

EXERCISE 6.5.13: Let $\mathcal{L}_1$ be a trio and $\mathcal{L}_2$ be a full trio. Suppose L is a nonempty ϵ-free language and a is a symbol not in Σ_L such that $(La)^+$ is in $\mathcal{L}_1 \vee \mathcal{L}_2$. Prove that $(La)^+$ is either in $\mathcal{L}_1$ or in $\mathcal{L}_2$ [Gr7].

EXERCISE 6.5.14: Let W_1 be the Dyck set over one letter. Prove that W_1 is not in $\mathcal{L}_{\text{lin}}$. More strongly, prove that W_1 is not in $\hat{\mathcal{F}}(\mathcal{L}_{\text{lin}})$ [Gr1].

EXERCISE 6.5.15: Let $\mathcal{L}_1$ and $\mathcal{L}_2$ be incomparable full AFL. Prove that $\hat{\mathcal{F}}(\mathcal{L}_1 \cup \mathcal{L}_2) \subset \hat{\text{Sub}}(\mathcal{L}_1, \mathcal{L}_2)$ [Gr3].

6.6 Substitution-Closed Full Principal AFL

We now consider substitution-closed full principal AFL. We first characterize when a substitution-closed full AFL is full principal. Then we prove that each such AFL $\mathcal{L} \neq \mathcal{R}$ contains a largest proper full AFL.

Def: Given a full AFL $\mathcal{L}$, a family $\mathcal{T}$ of languages is said to be a *full generating family* (*for* $\mathcal{L}$) if $\mathcal{L} = \hat{\mathcal{F}}(\mathcal{T})$. If, in addition, $\hat{\mathcal{F}}(\mathcal{T}) \neq \hat{\mathcal{F}}(\mathcal{T}-\{L\})$ for each L in $\mathcal{T}$, then $\mathcal{T}$ is said to be *independent*.

Note that $\mathcal{R}$ has no independent full generating family. For suppose $\mathcal{T}$ is any subfamily of $\mathcal{R}$ and L is in $\mathcal{T}$. Then $\hat{\mathcal{F}}(\mathcal{T}) = \hat{\mathcal{F}}(\mathcal{T}-\{L\}) = \mathcal{R}$, since $\hat{\mathcal{F}}(\{\emptyset\}) = \hat{\mathcal{F}}(\emptyset) = \mathcal{R}$.

Every finite full generating family for $\mathcal{L} \neq \mathcal{R}$ has a subset which is an independent full generating family. [For let $\mathcal{T}_1$ be a finite full generating family for $\mathcal{L} \neq \mathcal{R}$. Let $\mathcal{T}_2$ be a minimal subfamily of $\mathcal{T}_1$ which is a full generating family. By the minimality of $\mathcal{T}_2$ and the fact that $\mathcal{L} \neq \mathcal{R}$, $\hat{\mathcal{F}}(\mathcal{T}_2-\{L\}) \neq \mathcal{L}$ for each L in $\mathcal{T}_2$. Thus $\mathcal{T}_2$ is independent.]

EXAMPLE 6.6.1: It is shown in [Go1] that

(a) the family $\{Q_k/k \geqq 2\}$, where $Q_k = \{a^{n^k}/n \geqq 1\}$, is independent.

(b) the family $\{P_j/j \text{ in } A\}$, where $A \subseteq \{2, 3, \ldots\}$ and $P_j = \{a^{j^n}/n \geqq 1\}$, is independent if and only if no two integers in A are powers of the same integer.

LEMMA 6.6.1: *Let* $\mathcal{L} = \hat{\mathcal{F}}(\mathcal{T})$ *be a substitution-closed full AFL. If* $\mathcal{T} = \mathcal{T}_1 \cup \mathcal{T}_2$, *then either* $\mathcal{L} = \hat{\mathcal{F}}(\mathcal{T}_1)$ *or* $\mathcal{L} = \hat{\mathcal{F}}(\mathcal{T}_2)$.

Proof: Let $\mathcal{T} = \mathcal{T}_1 \cup \mathcal{T}_2$. If either $\mathcal{T}_1 = \emptyset$ or $\mathcal{T}_2 = \emptyset$, then the lemma is clearly true. Suppose $\mathcal{T}_1 \neq \emptyset$ and $\mathcal{T}_2 \neq \emptyset$. Then $\mathcal{L} = \hat{\mathcal{F}}(\mathcal{T}_1 \cup \mathcal{T}_2) =$

$\hat{\mathcal{F}}(\hat{\mathcal{F}}(\mathcal{T}_1) \cup \hat{\mathcal{F}}(\mathcal{T}_2))$. Since $\mathcal{L}$ is substitution closed, it follows from Theorem 6.5.3 that $\hat{\mathcal{F}}(\mathcal{T}_1)$ and $\hat{\mathcal{F}}(\mathcal{T}_2)$ are not incomparable. Thus $\hat{\mathcal{F}}(\mathcal{T}_1) \subseteq \hat{\mathcal{F}}(\mathcal{T}_2) \subseteq \mathcal{L}$ or $\hat{\mathcal{F}}(\mathcal{T}_2) \subseteq \hat{\mathcal{F}}(\mathcal{T}_1) \subseteq \mathcal{L}$. Hence $\mathcal{L} = \hat{\mathcal{F}}(\hat{\mathcal{F}}(\mathcal{T}_1) \cup \hat{\mathcal{F}}(\mathcal{T}_2)) = \hat{\mathcal{F}}(\hat{\mathcal{F}}(\mathcal{T}_2)) = \hat{\mathcal{F}}(\mathcal{T}_2)$ or $\mathcal{L} = \hat{\mathcal{F}}(\hat{\mathcal{F}}(\mathcal{T}_1) \cup \hat{\mathcal{F}}(\mathcal{T}_2)) = \hat{\mathcal{F}}(\hat{\mathcal{F}}(\mathcal{T}_1)) = \hat{\mathcal{F}}(\mathcal{T}_1)$.

We are now ready for the characterization result.

THEOREM 6.6.1: *Let $\mathcal{L}$ be a substitution-closed full AFL. Then*

(a) *$\mathcal{L}$ is full principal if and only if every full generating family contains a full generator.*

(b) *$\mathcal{L} \neq \mathcal{R}$ is not full principal if and only if $\mathcal{L}$ has no independent full generating family.*

Proof: (a) It suffices to show the "only if". Thus let $\mathcal{L}$ be a full principal AFL, i.e., $\mathcal{L} = \hat{\mathcal{F}}(L)$ for some L. If $\mathcal{L} = \mathcal{R}$, then the conclusion is obviously true. Suppose $\mathcal{L} \neq \mathcal{R}$, so that L is nonregular. Let $\mathcal{T}$ be any full generating family for $\mathcal{L}$. Then there exists a finite subset $\mathcal{T}_1$ of $\mathcal{T}$ such that L is in $\hat{\mathcal{F}}(\mathcal{T}_1)$. Since L is nonregular, $\mathcal{T}_1$ contains a nonempty language and so is a family of languages. Now $\mathcal{L} = \hat{\mathcal{F}}(L) \subseteq \hat{\mathcal{F}}(\mathcal{T}_1) \subseteq \hat{\mathcal{F}}(\mathcal{T}) = \mathcal{L}$, so that $\mathcal{L} = \hat{\mathcal{F}}(\mathcal{T}_1)$. As noted earlier, $\mathcal{T}_1$ contains a subfamily $\mathcal{T}_2$ which is an independent full generating family. Let L_1 be a language in $\mathcal{T}_2$. By Lemma 6.6.1, either $\mathcal{L} = \hat{\mathcal{F}}(L_1)$ or $\mathcal{L} = \hat{\mathcal{F}}(\mathcal{T}_2 - \{L_1\})$. If $\mathcal{L} = \hat{\mathcal{F}}(L_1)$, there is nothing to prove. Suppose $\mathcal{L} = \hat{\mathcal{F}}(\mathcal{T}_2 - \{L_1\})$. Since $\mathcal{T}_2$ is independent, $\mathcal{T}_2 - \{L_1\}$ is not a family of languages. Therefore $\mathcal{T}_2 - \{L_1\} = \{\emptyset\}$ or $\mathcal{T}_2 - \{L_1\} = \emptyset$. If $\mathcal{T}_2 - \{L_1\} = \{\emptyset\}$, then $\hat{\mathcal{F}}(\mathcal{T}_2 - \{\emptyset\}) = \hat{\mathcal{F}}(\mathcal{T}_2) = \mathcal{L}$, contradicting $\mathcal{T}_2$ being independent. If $\mathcal{T}_2 - \{L_1\} = \emptyset$, then $\mathcal{T}_2 = \{L_1\}$, so that $\mathcal{L} = \hat{\mathcal{F}}(\mathcal{T}_2) = \hat{\mathcal{F}}(L_1)$.

(b) Suppose $\mathcal{L} \neq \mathcal{R}$ has no independent full generating family. Assume $\mathcal{L} = \hat{\mathcal{F}}(L)$ for some language L. Since $\mathcal{L} \neq \mathcal{R}$, $L \neq \emptyset$. Then $\{L\}$ is an independent full generating family, a contradiction. Thus $\mathcal{L}$ is not full principal. On the other hand, suppose $\mathcal{L}$ is not full principal. Let $\mathcal{T}$ be a full generating family for $\mathcal{L}$ and let L be in $\mathcal{T}$. By Lemma 6.6.1, either $\mathcal{L} = \hat{\mathcal{F}}(L)$ or $\mathcal{L} = \hat{\mathcal{F}}(\mathcal{T} - \{L\})$. Since $\mathcal{L}$ is not full principal, $\mathcal{L} = \hat{\mathcal{F}}(\mathcal{T} - \{L\})$. Thus $\mathcal{T}$ is not independent.

EXAMPLE 6.6.2: The full AFL $\mathcal{L}_{\mathrm{DB}} = \hat{\mathcal{F}}_{\hat{\sigma}}(\mathcal{L}_{\mathrm{lin}})$ is substitution closed, but not full principal. Hence $\mathcal{L}_{\mathrm{DB}}$ has no independent full generating family.

EXAMPLE 6.6.3: Let $\mathscr{L}$ be either $\mathscr{L}_{CF}$, $\mathscr{L}_{NSA}$, or $\mathscr{L}_{RE}$. Then $\mathscr{L}$ is a full principal AFL and substitution closed. Thus each full generating family contains a full generator.

We now establish the second result mentioned at the beginning of the section.

THEOREM 6.6.2: *Let $\mathscr{L} \neq \mathscr{R}$ be a substitution-closed full principal AFL. Then $\{L$ in $\mathscr{L}/\hat{\mathscr{F}}(L) \neq \mathscr{L}\}$ is a substitution-closed full AFL and is the* (*unique*) *largest full AFL properly contained in $\mathscr{L}$.*

Proof: Let $\mathscr{L}_1 = \{L \text{ in } \mathscr{L}/\hat{\mathscr{F}}(L) \neq \mathscr{L}\}$. Suppose $\mathscr{L}_2$ is a full AFL properly contained in $\mathscr{L}$. Then no element of $\mathscr{L}_2$ can be a full generator for $\mathscr{L}$. Hence $\mathscr{L}_2 \subseteq \mathscr{L}_1$. Since $\mathscr{L}$ is full principal, $\mathscr{L} = \hat{\mathscr{F}}(L_0)$ for some L_0 in $\mathscr{L}$. Then L_0 is not in $\mathscr{L}_1$. Thus $\mathscr{L}_1 \subsetneq \mathscr{L}$.

To see that $\mathscr{L}_1$ is a full AFL, suppose $\mathscr{L}_1 \neq \hat{\mathscr{F}}(\mathscr{L}_1)$. Since $\mathscr{L} \neq \mathscr{R}$, $\mathscr{R} \subseteq \mathscr{L}_1$. Therefore $\mathscr{L}_1 \neq \emptyset$. Since $\mathscr{L}_1 \subseteq \hat{\mathscr{F}}(\mathscr{L}_1)$ and $\mathscr{L}_1 \neq \hat{\mathscr{F}}(\mathscr{L}_1)$, $\hat{\mathscr{F}}(\mathscr{L}_1) - \mathscr{L}_1 \neq \emptyset$. Hence $\hat{\mathscr{F}}(\mathscr{L}_1)$ contains a full generator for $\mathscr{L}$, so that $\mathscr{L} = \hat{\mathscr{F}}(\mathscr{L}_1)$. By (a) of Theorem 6.6.1, $\mathscr{L}_1$ contains a full generator for $\mathscr{L}$, a contradiction. Hence $\hat{\mathscr{F}}(\mathscr{L}_1) = \mathscr{L}_1$, i. e., $\mathscr{L}_1$ is a full AFL.

Suppose $\mathscr{L}_1$ is not substitution closed. By Lemma 6.5.2,

$$\mathscr{L}_1 \subsetneq \hat{\text{Sub}}(\mathscr{L}_1, \mathscr{L}_1) \subsetneq \hat{\text{Sub}}(\mathscr{L}_1, \hat{\text{Sub}}(\mathscr{L}_1, \mathscr{L}_1)) \subseteq \mathscr{L}.$$

Then $\hat{\text{Sub}}(\mathscr{L}_1, \mathscr{L}_1)$ is a full AFL properly contained in $\mathscr{L}$. Therefore $\hat{\text{Sub}}(\mathscr{L}_1, \mathscr{L}_1) \subseteq \mathscr{L}_1$, a contradiction. Hence $\mathscr{L}_1$ is substitution closed.

EXAMPLE 6.6.4: Each of the AFL $\mathscr{L}_{CF}$, $\mathscr{L}_{NSA}$, and $\mathscr{L}_{RE}$ properly contains a largest full AFL.

Theorem 6.6.2 raises a host of problems pertaining to the nature of the largest proper full subAFL. Two are stated below. (The reader should easily be able to imagine others.) A generalization of Theorem 6.6.2, as well as some results in Section 6.5, will be found in [Gr6].

Open Problem: Identify the unique maximal full AFL in the conclusion of Theorem 6.6.2 for well-known AFL satisfying the hypotheses, such as $\mathscr{L}_{CF}$, $\mathscr{L}_{NSA}$, and $\mathscr{L}_{RE}$.

Open Question: What additional conditions must be placed on $\mathscr{L}$ in Theorem 6.6.2 to guarantee that the largest full AFL properly contained in $\mathscr{L}$ is full principal?

EXERCISE 6.6.1: Let $\mathscr{L}_1$ be a substitution-closed, principal or full principal AFL and let $\mathscr{L}_2$ be a full AFL incomparable with $\mathscr{L}_1$. Prove that $\hat{\mathscr{F}}_{\hat{\sigma}}(\mathscr{L}_2)$ is also incomparable with $\mathscr{L}_1$ [GS7].

EXERCISE 6.6.2: A language L is said to be *fully prime* if for all full AFL $\mathscr{L}_1$ and $\mathscr{L}_2$ such that L is in $\hat{\mathscr{F}}(\mathscr{L}_1 \cup \mathscr{L}_2)$, either L is in $\mathscr{L}_1$ or L is in $\mathscr{L}_2$. Prove that a language L for which $\hat{\mathscr{F}}(L)$ is substitution closed is fully prime [GS7]. [Hint: Use Lemma 6.4.3.]

EXERCISE 6.6.3: A full AFL $\mathscr{L}$ is said to *fully split* if there are incomparable full AFL $\mathscr{L}_1$ and $\mathscr{L}_2$ such that $\mathscr{L} = \hat{\mathscr{F}}(\mathscr{L}_1 \cup \mathscr{L}_2)$. Prove that if L is fully prime then $\hat{\mathscr{F}}(L)$ does not fully split [GS7]. [It is shown in [Gr6] that $\hat{\mathscr{F}}(\{a^n cb^n/n \geqq 1\}) = \hat{\mathscr{F}}(\{a^n b^n/n \geqq 1\})$ does not fully split, and in [GS7] that $\{a^n b^n/n \geqq 1\}$ is not fully prime. Thus the converse to Exercise 6.6.3 is false.]

EXERCISE 6.6.4: For each full principal AFL $\mathscr{L} \neq \mathscr{R}$ let $\hat{N}_g(\mathscr{L}) = \{L \text{ in } \mathscr{L}/\hat{\mathscr{F}}(L) \neq \mathscr{L}\}$. Prove that the following are equivalent [Gr6]:

(a) $\hat{N}_g(\mathscr{L})$ is a full AFL.

(b) $\hat{N}_g(\mathscr{L})$ is closed under union.

(c) $\mathscr{L}$ does not fully split.

(d) There are no two incomparable full principal AFL $\mathscr{L}_1$ and $\mathscr{L}_2$ such that $\mathscr{L} = \hat{\mathscr{F}}(\mathscr{L}_1 \cup \mathscr{L}_2)$.

(e) $\mathscr{L}$ has no independent full generating family with more than one element.

(f) $\hat{N}_g(\mathscr{L})$ is the largest full AFL properly contained in $\mathscr{L}$.

[From Theorem 6.6.2 and (c) above, no substitution-closed full AFL $\mathscr{L} \neq \mathscr{R}$ fully splits. The same result follows from Exercises 6.6.2 and 6.6.3.]

EXERCISE 6.6.5: Let $\mathscr{L}$ be a full AFL which is not full principal and does not fully split. Prove that $\mathscr{L}$ has no independent full generating family [Gr6].

6.7 Historical References

The initial paper on substitution of AFL was [GS5]. Lemma 6.1.1 and Theorem 6.1.1, with the exception of the second sentence in (b), were proved there. The remaining part of (b) of Theorem 6.1.1 is in [GrG] as is the notion of a nested multitape AFA. Theorems 6.2.1 and 6.2.2 are also in [GrG]. The concepts of $\hat{\sigma}$ and $\hat{\text{Sub}}_\infty$ are in [GS5], while that of $\hat{\mathcal{F}}_{\hat{\sigma}}$ and $\mathcal{F}_\sigma$ are in [GrG]. The statements and proofs of Theorems 6.3.1 and 6.3.2 are split between [GS5] and [GrG]. Theorem 6.3.3 appears in [GrG]. Theorem 6.4.1 was demonstrated in [GGr2]. The special substitution τ_L originated in [Gr2]. Lemma 6.4.3 and Theorem 6.4.3, in addition to the subject matter of Sections 6.5 and 6.6, were published in [Gr3]. Theorem 6.4.2 was established in an early version of [Gr3].

(+)CHAPTER 7

GENERATION BY FAMILIES OF BOUNDED LANGUAGES

One of the concepts which plays an important subsidiary role in the study of context-free languages is that of a "bounded" language. There is growing evidence that bounded languages will play an analogous role in the study of (semi-)AFL theory. In this chapter we consider trios, semi-AFL, and AFL [fully] generated by families of bounded languages. We shall see that no (semi-)AFL generated by a family of bounded languages can contain a (semi-)AFL, with at least one nonregular set, which is closed under ϵ-free substitution. We also derive some necessary conditions on certain kinds of bounded languages U and V in order that V be in $\mathcal{O}(U)$ $[\hat{\mathcal{O}}(U)]$, $\mathcal{O} = \mathcal{M}$, $\mathcal{S}$, or $\mathcal{F}$. As a consequence, we are able to show that various [full] principal (semi-)AFL, [fully] generated by bounded languages, are different. In particular, we shall find that $\hat{\mathcal{F}}(\{a^{n^2}b^{n^2}/n \geqq 0\}) \neq \hat{\mathcal{F}}(\{a^{n^2}b^{(n+1)^2}/n \geqq 0\})$.

7.1 (*m*-)Bounded Languages

In this section we first define the notion of an (*m*-) bounded language. Then we show that each of our three structures, i. e., trio, semi-AFL, and AFL, "fully generated" by a family of (*m*-) bounded languages is "generated" by some family of (*m*-) bounded languages. In other words, the bounded languages can be chosen so that all homomorphisms used are ϵ-free. This result generalizes, but in a weakened form, the corollary to Theorem 3.5.1 from 1-bounded to *m*-bounded.

Def: A language L is said to be *m-bounded*, $m \geqq 1$, if there exist words $w_1, \ldots, w_m$ such that $L \subseteq w_1^* \ldots w_m^*$. A language L is said to be *bounded* if it is *m*-bounded for some *m*. A trio, semi-AFL, AFL $\mathcal{L}$ is said to be (*full*) *generating-family-bounded* if there exists a family $\mathcal{U}$ of bounded languages such that $\mathcal{L} = \mathcal{M}(\mathcal{U})(\hat{\mathcal{M}}(\mathcal{U}))$, $\mathcal{S}(\mathcal{U})(\hat{\mathcal{S}}(\mathcal{U}))$, $\mathcal{F}(\mathcal{U})(\hat{\mathcal{F}}(\mathcal{U}))$, resp.

Since $w_1^* \ldots w_m^* \subseteq w_1^* \ldots w_m^* w_{m+1}^* \ldots w_n^*$, each *m*-bounded language is *n*-bounded for all $n \geqq m$.

EXAMPLE 7.1.1: For a in Σ, $\mathcal{R}_0 = \mathcal{M}(\{a\}) = \mathcal{S}(\{a\}), = \mathcal{F}(\{a\})$, $\mathcal{R} = \mathcal{M}(\{a, \epsilon\}) = \mathcal{S}(\{a, \epsilon\}) = \mathcal{F}(\{a, \epsilon\})$, and $\mathcal{R} = \hat{\mathcal{M}}(\{a\}) = \hat{\mathcal{S}}(\{a\}) = \hat{\mathcal{F}}(\{a\})$. Thus $\mathcal{R}_0$ and $\mathcal{R}$ are generating-family-bounded trios, semi-AFL, and AFL; and $\mathcal{R}$ is a full generating-family-bounded trio, semi-AFL, and AFL.

It is known [Gi] that for each a and b in Σ, $a \neq b$, the language $\{a, b\}^+$ is not bounded. Hence every trio contains some language which is not bounded.

Agreement: The symbols $a_1, \ldots, a_k$, $k \geqq 1$, will always denote k distinct elements in Σ.

In anticipation of Theorem 7.1.1 below, we now present a lemma which asserts that each (full) semi-AFL (fully) generated by a finite family of m-bounded languages, for some m, is (fully) generated by a single language $L \subseteq a_1^* \ldots a_m^*$. In other words, a finite family of m-bounded languages may be replaced by one m-bounded language, and this language is a subset of $a_1^* \ldots a_m^*$. Formally, we have:

LEMMA 7.1.1: *For each finite family $\mathcal{L}$ of m-bounded languages, there exists a language $L \subseteq a_1^* \ldots a_m^*$ such that $\mathcal{M}(L) = \mathcal{S}(\mathcal{L})$ and $\hat{\mathcal{M}}(L) = \hat{\mathcal{S}}(\mathcal{L})$.*

Proof: We shall just establish the $\mathcal{S}$ case, the $\hat{\mathcal{S}}$ case being similar.

Let $\mathcal{L} = \{L_1, \ldots, L_n\}$. Without loss of generality we may assume that

$$(*) \qquad L_i \subseteq a_1^* \ldots a_m^* \quad \text{for each } i.$$

For suppose that $L_i \subseteq w_{i1}^* \ldots w_{im}^*$ for each i, every w_{ij} a word. Clearly we may assume that each w_{ij} is a non-ϵ word. For each i, let h_i be the ϵ-free homomorphism on $\{a_1, \ldots, a_m\}^*$ defined by $h_i(a_j) = w_{ij}$ for each a_j, and let $\bar{L}_i = a_1^* \ldots a_m^* \cap h_i^{-1}(L_i)$. Then $L_i = h_i(\bar{L}_i)$ for each i. Thus $\{\bar{L}_1, \ldots, \bar{L}_n\} \subseteq \mathcal{S}(\{L_1, \ldots, L_n\})$ and $\{L_1, \ldots, L_n\} \subseteq \mathcal{S}(\{\bar{L}_1, \ldots, \bar{L}_n\})$. Hence $\mathcal{S}(\{\bar{L}_1, \ldots, \bar{L}_n\}) \subseteq \mathcal{S}(\{L_1, \ldots, L_n\})$ and $\mathcal{S}(\{L_1, \ldots, L_n\}) \subseteq \mathcal{S}(\{\bar{L}_1, \ldots, \bar{L}_n\})$, so that $\mathcal{S}(\{\bar{L}_1, \ldots, \bar{L}_n\}) = \mathcal{S}(\{L_1, \ldots, L_n\}) = \mathcal{S}(\mathcal{L})$. Also, for each i, $\bar{L}_i \subseteq a_1^* \ldots a_m^*$, and if $L_i \neq \emptyset$ then $\bar{L}_i \neq \emptyset$. Thus we may consider that $\mathcal{L} = \{\bar{L}_1, \ldots, \bar{L}_n\}$, i. e., $(*)$ holds.

Two cases arise.

(α) Suppose each L_i is ϵ-free. For each i, let

$$L_i' \subseteq \{a_1^{i+nr_1} a_2^{r_2} \ldots a_m^{r_m} / a_1^{r_1} \ldots a_m^{r_m} \text{ in } L_i\}.$$

Let $L = \bigcup_1^n L_i'$ and let c be a new symbol. Since $L_i \neq \emptyset$ for some i, $L \neq \emptyset$.

Let f and h be the homomorphisms on $\{a_1, \ldots, a_m, c\}^*$ defined by $f(c) = \epsilon$, $h(c) = a_1$, $f(a_j) = a_j$, $h(a_1) = a_1^n$, and $h(a_k) = a_k$ for all j and k, $1 \leqq j \leqq m$, $1 < k \leqq m$. For each i, let $R_i = c^i a_1^* \ldots a_m^*$. Then R_i is regular and $L_i' = h(c^i L_i) = h(f^{-1}(L_i) \cap R_i)$ is in $\mathcal{S}(\mathcal{L})$ for each i. Thus L is in $\mathcal{S}\mathcal{S}(\mathcal{L}) = \mathcal{S}(\mathcal{L})$, so that $\mathcal{M}(L) \subseteq \mathcal{M}(\mathcal{S}(\mathcal{L})) = \mathcal{S}(\mathcal{L})$.

To see the reverse containment, it suffices to show that each L_i is in $\mathcal{M}(L)$. [For this implies that $\mathcal{L} \subseteq \mathcal{M}(L)$. Then $\mathcal{S}(\mathcal{L}) \subseteq \mathcal{S}\mathcal{M}(L) = \mathcal{M}(L)$ by Proposition 5.1.1.] Thus let i be an integer, $1 \leqq i \leqq n$. Let $R_i' = a_1^i(a_1^n)^* a_2^* \ldots a_m^*$ and let f_i be the homomorphism on $\{c, a_1, \ldots, a_m\}^*$ defined by $f_i(c) = a_1^i$, $f_i(a_1) = a_1^n$, and $f_i(a_j) = a_j$ for each j, $1 < j \leqq m$. Let $R' = ca_1^* \ldots a_m^*$. Then R' and each R_i' are regular sets, $L_i' = L \cap R_i'$, and $cL_i = f_i^{-1}(L_i') \cap R' = f_i^{-1}(L \cap R_i') \cap R'$. Hence cL_i is in $\mathcal{M}(L)$. Let g be the homomorphism on $\{c, a_1, \ldots, a_m\}^*$ defined by $g(c) = \epsilon$ and $g(a_j) = a_j$ for all j, $1 \leqq j \leqq m$. Obviously g is ϵ-limited on cL_i and $L_i = g(cL_i)$. Since each L_j is ϵ-free, L and $\mathcal{M}(L)$ are ϵ-free. By Corollary 2 of Theorem 3.2.2, $L_i = g(cL_i)$ is in $\mathcal{M}(L)$.

(β) Suppose some of the L_i contain ϵ. Let $\mathcal{L}' = \{L_1 - \{\epsilon\}, \ldots, L_n - \{\epsilon\}\}$. By (b) of the corollary to Proposition 3.4.1, $\mathcal{S}(\mathcal{L}) = \{U, U \cup \{\epsilon\} / U \text{ in } \mathcal{S}(\mathcal{L}')\}$. Suppose $L_i - \{\epsilon\} = \emptyset$ for each i. Then $\mathcal{S}(\mathcal{L}') = \mathcal{R}_0$ and $\mathcal{S}(\mathcal{L}) = \mathcal{R}$. Hence $\mathcal{S}(\mathcal{L}) = \mathcal{M}(L)$, where $L = \{\epsilon\}$. Thus suppose some of the $L_i - \{\epsilon\}$ are nonempty. Therefore $\mathcal{L}'$ is a family of languages. By (α), there exists a language $L' \subseteq a_1^* \ldots a_m^*$ such that $\mathcal{M}(L') = \mathcal{S}(L')$. Then

$$\begin{aligned} \mathcal{M}(L' \cup \{\epsilon\}) &= \{U, U \cup \{\epsilon\} / U \text{ in } \mathcal{M}(L')\}, \quad \text{by (b) of Proposition 3.2.1,} \\ &= \{U, U \cup \{\epsilon\} / U \text{ in } \mathcal{S}(\mathcal{L}')\} \\ &= \mathcal{S}(\mathcal{L}). \end{aligned}$$

In studying trios, semi-AFL, and AFL generated by bounded languages we shall frequently be examining a-transducers very carefully with respect to inputs, moves, and outputs. The notation on a-transducers already introduced is not precise enough for our purposes. Hence we present some specialized symbolism, to be used in the remainder of the chapter.

Def: Let $M = (K_1, \Sigma_1, \Sigma_2, H, p_0, F)$ be an a-transducer. A *computation* (*of* M) is any word of the form $(p_0, u_0, v_0, p_1) \ldots (p_{n-1}, u_{n-1}, v_{n-1}, p_n)$, where $n \geqq 1$, each (p_i, u_i, v_i, p_{i+1}) is in H, and p_n is in F, together with ϵ if p_0 is in F.

Notation: Let Π_M be the set of all computations of M.

Thus Π_M is the set of all sequences of moves from the start state to an accepting state.

It follows from Lemma 3.2.1 that Π_M is a regular set.

Notation: For $M = (K_1, \Sigma_1, \Sigma_2, H, p_0, F)$ let h_1 and h_2 be the homomorphisms on H^* defined by $h_1((p, u, v, q)) = u$ and $h_2((p, u, v, q)) = v$ for each (p, u, v, q) in H.

Thus h_1 selects the inputs of the sequences of moves and h_2 the outputs.

By the method of proof of Lemma 3.2.2, $M(L) = h_2[h_1^{-1}(L) \cap \Pi_M]$ for each language L.

Def: A *loop* of M, $M = (K_1, \Sigma_1, \Sigma_2, H, p_0, F)$, is a word of the form

$$(p_1, u_1, v_1, p_2) \ldots (p_n, u_n, v_n, p_{n+1}),$$

where $n \geqq 1$, each (p_i, u_i, v_i, p_{i+1}) is in H, and $p_1 = p_{n+1}$.

Hence a loop is a sequence of moves in which the first state coincides with the last, regardless of the intermediate states. For example, $(p_1, a_1^2 a_2, a_2^2, p_2)$ $(p_2, a_1^3, a_2 a_1, p_2)(p_2, a_2 a_1, a_1^2, p_1)$ is a loop.

We are now ready for the main result of the section.

THEOREM 7.1.1: *Let $\mathcal{L}$ be a family of* (m-) *bounded languages* (*for some* $m \geqq 1$). *Then there exists a family $\mathcal{L}'$ of* (m-) *bounded languages such that* $O(\mathcal{L}') = \hat{O}(\mathcal{L})$ *for* $O = \mathcal{M}$, $\mathcal{S}$, *and* $\mathcal{F}$.

Proof: It suffices to establish the theorem for $\hat{\mathcal{M}}(\mathcal{L})$. For suppose there exists $\mathcal{L}'$ such that $\hat{\mathcal{M}}(\mathcal{L}) = \mathcal{M}(\mathcal{L}')$. Then

$$\hat{\mathcal{S}}(\mathcal{L}) = \left\{\bigcup_1^n M_i(L_i)/n \geqq 1, L_i \text{ in } \mathcal{L}, M_i \text{ an a-transducer}\right\}, \quad \text{by Theorem 3.4.2,}$$

$$= \left\{\bigcup_1^n M_i(L_i)/n \geqq 1, L_i \text{ in } \mathcal{L}', M_i \text{ an } \epsilon\text{-free a-transducer}\right\}, \quad \text{since } \hat{\mathcal{M}}(\mathcal{L}) = \mathcal{M}(\mathcal{L}'),$$

$$= \mathcal{S}(\mathcal{L}'), \quad \text{by Theorem 3.4.2;}$$

and

$$\hat{\mathcal{F}}(\mathcal{L}) = \text{Sûb}(\mathcal{R}_0, \hat{\mathcal{M}}(\mathcal{L})), \quad \text{by Theorem 3.4.1,}$$

$$= \text{Sûb}(\mathcal{R}_0, \mathcal{M}(\mathcal{L}')), \quad \text{since } \hat{\mathcal{M}}(\mathcal{L}) = \mathcal{M}(\mathcal{L}'),$$

$$= \mathcal{F}(\mathcal{L}'), \quad \text{by Theorem 3.4.1.}$$

Thus consider the $\hat{\mathcal{M}}(\mathcal{L})$ case. Let $\mathcal{L}' = \hat{\mathcal{M}}(\mathcal{L}) \cap \{L \subseteq a_1^* \ldots a_m^*/ m \geqq 1\}$ ($\mathcal{L}' = \hat{\mathcal{M}}(\mathcal{L}) \cap \{L/L \subseteq a_1^* \ldots a_m^*\}$). Then $\mathcal{M}(\mathcal{L}') \subseteq \mathcal{M}(\hat{\mathcal{M}}(\mathcal{L})) \subseteq \hat{\mathcal{M}}(\mathcal{L})$. Also, $\mathcal{L}'$, thus $\mathcal{M}(\mathcal{L}')$, is closed under union with $\{\epsilon\}$. To complete the argument we shall show that $\hat{\mathcal{M}}(\mathcal{L}) \subseteq \mathcal{M}(\mathcal{L}')$. Let $\mathcal{L}_0 = \{L-\{\epsilon\}/L$

in $\hat{\mathcal{M}}(\mathcal{L})\}$. Clearly $\mathcal{L}_0 = \{L$ in $\hat{\mathcal{M}}(\mathcal{L})/L$ ϵ-free$\}$ and $\hat{\mathcal{M}}(\mathcal{L}) = \mathcal{L}_0 \cup \{L \cup \{\epsilon\}/L$ in $\mathcal{L}_0\}$. Thus it suffices to prove that $\mathcal{L}_0 \subseteq \mathcal{M}(\mathcal{L}')$. [For then $\{L \cup \{\epsilon\}/L$ in $\mathcal{L}_0\} \subseteq \{L \cup \{\epsilon\}/L$ in $\mathcal{M}(\mathcal{L}')\} \subseteq \mathcal{M}(\mathcal{L}')$, since $\mathcal{M}(\mathcal{L}')$ is closed under union with $\{\epsilon\}$.]

Let L_0 be an arbitrary nonempty language in $\mathcal{L}_0$. Then there exist a nonempty language U in $\mathcal{L}$ and an a-transducer M_0 such that $L_0 = M_0(U)$. By hypothesis, U is m-bounded for some $m \geqq 1$ (or for the given m which bounds $\mathcal{L}$). It thus suffices to prove that:

(1) There exist nonempty languages $L_1, \ldots, L_n$, $n \geqq 1$, such that $L_i \subseteq a_1^* \ldots a_m^*$ for each i, $M_0(U)$ is in $\mathcal{S}(\{L_1, \ldots, L_n\})$, and $\mathcal{S}(\{L_1, \ldots, L_n\}) \subseteq \hat{\mathcal{M}}(U)$.

For suppose (1) is true. By Lemma 7.1.1, there exists a nonempty language $L' \subseteq a_1^* \ldots a_m^*$ such that $\mathcal{M}(L') = \mathcal{S}(\{L_1, \ldots, L_n\})$. Thus $M_0(U)$ is in $\mathcal{M}(L')$ and L' is in $\mathcal{M}(L') \subseteq \hat{\mathcal{M}}(U) \subseteq \hat{\mathcal{M}}(\mathcal{L})$. Hence L' is in $\hat{\mathcal{M}}(\mathcal{L}) \cap \{L/L \subseteq a_1^* \ldots a_m^*\} = \mathcal{L}'$. Therefore $M_0(U)$ is in $\mathcal{M}(L') \subseteq \mathcal{M}(\mathcal{L}')$.

By Lemma 7.1.1, there exists a nonempty language $L \subseteq a_1^* \ldots a_m^*$ such that $\hat{\mathcal{M}}(U) = \hat{\mathcal{S}}(U) = \hat{\mathcal{M}}(L)$. Then $\hat{\mathcal{M}}_0(U) = M(L)$ for some a-transducer M. Thus (1) becomes:

(2) There exist nonempty languages $L_1, \ldots, L_n$, $n \geqq 1$, such that $L_i \subseteq a_1^* \ldots a_m^*$ for each i and $M(L)$ is in $\mathcal{S}(\{L_1, \ldots, L_n\}) \subseteq \hat{\mathcal{M}}(L)$.

Consider (2). Informally, we shall group the computations of M into classes according to which states of M are encountered during the computations. Within each class C_J, almost all the loops with ϵ-output in each computation will be deleted without altering the output of the computation, providing the input language L is changed. This will result in 1-bounded ϵ-output bounded a-transducers M_J and languages $L_J' \subseteq a_1^* \ldots a_m^*$, with $M(L) = \bigcup_J M_J(L_J')$, such that the computations of each M_J will contain very few loops with ϵ-output.

Formally, let $M = (K_1, \Sigma_1, \Sigma_2, H, p_0, F)$. By Lemma 3.2.3, we may assume that M is 1-bounded. Let σ be the function from H^* into 2^{K_1} defined by $\sigma(\epsilon) = \emptyset$, $\sigma(\theta) = \{p, q\}$ for each $\theta = (p, u, v, q)$ in H, and $\sigma(\theta_1 \ldots \theta_t) = \bigcup_{i=1}^{t} \sigma(\theta_i)$, for each $t \geqq 1$ and each θ_i in H. Thus σ applied to a computation is the set of states the computation passes through. Let $\mathcal{J}$ be the set of all m-tuples $(J_1, \ldots, J_m)$, each $J_i \subseteq K_1$. Clearly $\mathcal{J}$ is finite. For each $J = (J_1, \ldots, J_m)$ in $\mathcal{J}$, let

$$C_J = \{\alpha_1 \ldots \alpha_m \text{ in } \Pi_M/\text{each } \alpha_i \text{ in } H^*, h_1(\alpha_i) \text{ in } a_i^*, \sigma(\alpha_i) = J_i\}.$$

Now $L \subseteq a_1^* \ldots a_m^*$ and, since M is 1-bounded, h_1 is length decreasing. Hence each word α in $h_1^{-1}(L) \cap \Pi_M$ may be written as $\alpha_1 \ldots \alpha_m$, each α_i in H^* and $h_1(\alpha_i)$ in a_i^*, and is in C_J, where $J = (\sigma(\alpha_1), \ldots, \sigma(\alpha_m))$. Consequently,

$$h_1^{-1}(L) \cap \Pi_M \subseteq \bigcup_{J \text{ in } \mathcal{J}} (h_1^{-1}(L) \cap C_J).$$

Since $C_J \subseteq \Pi_M$ for each J, J in $\mathcal{J}$, the reverse containment holds. Therefore

$$h_1^{-1}(L) \cap \Pi_M = \bigcup_{J \text{ in } \mathcal{J}} (h_1^{-1}(L) \cap C_J).$$

Thus

$$\begin{aligned} M(L) &= h_2(h_1^{-1}(L) \cap \Pi_M) \\ &= h_2\Big(\bigcup_{J \text{ in } \mathcal{J}} (h_1^{-1}(L) \cap C_J)\Big) \\ &= \bigcup_{J \text{ in } \mathcal{J}} h_2(h_1^{-1}(L) \cap C_J). \end{aligned}$$

For each J in $\mathcal{J}$ let $L_J = h_2(h_1^{-1}(L) \cap C_J)$. Then $M(L) = \bigcup_{J \text{ in } \mathcal{J}} L_J$. To complete the proof, it suffices to show that:

(3) For each J in $\mathcal{J}$ there exists $L_J' \subseteq a_1^* \ldots a_m^*$ such that L_J is in $\mathcal{M}(L_J')$ and L_J' is in $\hat{\mathcal{M}}(L)$.

For let $\mathcal{J} = \{J^{(1)}, \ldots, J^{(n)}\}$. Then $M(L) = \bigcup_{i=1}^{n} L_{J^{(i)}}$ is in $\mathcal{S}(\{L'_{J^{(1)}}, \ldots, L'_{J^{(n)}}\}) = \mathcal{S}(\{L'_{J^{(i)}} \neq \emptyset / 1 \leqq i \leqq n\}) \subseteq \hat{\mathcal{S}}(L) = \hat{\mathcal{M}}(L)$, by Proposition 5.1.1. Thus (2) holds.

To see (3), let $J = (J_1, \ldots, J_m)$ be an element of $\mathcal{J}$. Let

$$\Gamma = \{\gamma \text{ a loop of } M / |\gamma| \leqq \#(K_1), h_2(\gamma) = \varepsilon\}.$$

Clearly Γ is finite. For each i, $1 \leqq i \leqq m$, let

$$\begin{aligned} \Gamma_i &= \{\gamma \text{ in } \Gamma / h_1(\gamma) \text{ in } a_i^*, \sigma(\gamma) \subseteq J_i\}, \\ S_i &= \{s / a_i^s = h_1(\gamma) \text{ for some } \gamma \text{ in } \Gamma_i\}, \\ T_i &= \{s_1 + \ldots + s_k / k \geqq 0, \text{ each}^1\ s_j \text{ in } S_i\}, \quad \text{and} \\ L_J' &= \{a_1^{r_1 - t_1} \ldots a_m^{r_m - t_m} / a_1^{r_1} \ldots a_m^{r_m} \text{ in } L, \text{ each } t_j \text{ in } T_j\}. \end{aligned}$$

[Note that Γ_i, S_i, and T_i depend on J.] Since 0 is in each T_j, $L \subseteq L_J'$. For each i, $1 \leqq i \leqq m$, and each s in S_i, let c_{is} be a new symbol in Σ. Let f and h

[1] For $k = 0$, $s_1 + \ldots + s_k$ is defined to be 0.

be the homomorphisms on $(\{a_1, \ldots, a_m\} \cup \{c_{is}/\text{all } i, s\})^*$ defined by $f(c_{is}) = a_i^s$, $f(a_i) = a_i$, $h(c_{is}) = \epsilon$, and $h(a_i) = a_i$ for each i, $1 \leqq i \leqq m$, and each s in S_i. Obviously $L'_J = h(f^{-1}(L))$. Therefore L'_J is in $\hat{\mathscr{M}}(L)$. It remains to show that L_J is in $\mathscr{M}(L'_J)$.

For each i, $1 \leqq i \leqq m$, let

$$A_i = \{\alpha \text{ in } H^*/h_1(\alpha) \text{ is in } a_i^*,\ \sigma(\alpha) = J_i\}.$$

Note that $C_J = \Pi_M \cap A_1 \ldots A_m$ and each A_i depends on J. Since

$$A_i = h_1^{-1}(a_i^*) \cap \{\theta \text{ in } H/\sigma(\theta) \subseteq J_i\}^* \cap \bigcap_{p \text{ in } J_i} H^*\{\theta \text{ in } H/p \text{ in } \sigma(\theta)\}\ H^*,[1]$$

A_i is regular. For all i, $1 \leqq i \leqq m$, let

$$B_i = A_i - \bigcup_{\gamma \text{ in } \Gamma} H^*\gamma H^*\gamma H^*.$$

Since Γ is finite and A_i is regular, B_i is regular. Let

$$C'_J = \Pi_M \cap B_1 \ldots B_m.$$

Since Π_M and every B_i are regular, C'_J is regular. Clearly $C'_J \subseteq C_J = \Pi_M \cap A_1 \ldots A_m$, and each word in C'_J has at most $2m-1$ nonoverlapping occurrences of each loop of Γ. Observe that h_2 is ϵ-limited on C'_J. [This follows from the fact that a "long" subword w, of a word in B_i, such that $h_2(w) = \epsilon$, would contain two occurrences of some γ in Γ, contradicting the definition of B_i.] To show that $L_J = h_2(h_1^{-1}(L) \cap C_J)$ is in $\mathscr{M}(L'_J)$ it suffices to prove that

(4) $h_2(h_1^{-1}(L) \cap C_J) = h_2(h_1^{-1}(L'_J) \cap C'_J)$.

[For since $L_J \subseteq M(L)$ and $M(L)$ is ϵ-free, L_J is ϵ-free. Thus $h_2(h_1^{-1}(L'_J) \cap C'_J) = h_2(h_1^{-1}(L'_J) \cap C'_J) - \{\epsilon\}$. Then $h_2(h_1^{-1}(L'_J) \cap C'_J) - \{\epsilon\} = h_2(h_1^{-1}(L'_J) \cap C'_J)$ is in $\mathscr{M}(L'_J)$ by Corollary 2 of Theorem 3.2.2, since h_2 is ϵ-limited on C'_J.]

We first establish that

(5) $h_2(h_1^{-1}(L) \cap C_J) \subseteq h_2(h_1^{-1}(L'_J) \cap C'_J)$.

Since $L \subseteq L'_J$, $h_2(h_1^{-1}(L) \cap C_J) \subseteq h_2(h_1^{-1}(L'_J) \cap C_J)$. It thus suffices to show that

(6) $h_2(h_1^{-1}(L'_J) \cap C_J) \subseteq h_2(h_1^{-1}(L'_J) \cap C'_J)$.

Suppose (6) is false. Then there is a word, hence one of minimal length, α in $h_1^{-1}(L'_J) \cap C_J$ such that $h_2(\alpha)$ is not in $h_2(h_1^{-1}(L'_J) \cap C'_J)$. Since α is in C_J

[1] If $J_i = \emptyset$, then $\bigcap_{p \text{ in } J_i} H^*\{\theta \text{ in } H/p \text{ in } \sigma(\theta)\}\ H^*$ is to be interpreted as $\{\epsilon\}$.

$= \Pi_M \cap A_1 \ldots A_m$, $\alpha = \alpha_1 \ldots \alpha_m$ for some $\alpha_1, \ldots, \alpha_m$, each α_i in A_i. Now α is not in $C'_J = \Pi_M \cap B_1 \ldots B_m$. [Otherwise, α is in $h_1^{-1}(L'_J) \cap C'_J$, so that $h_2(\alpha)$ is in $h_2(h_1^{-1}(L'_J) \cap C'_J)$, a contradiction.] Thus there exists k such that α_k is not in $B_k = A_k - \bigcup_{\gamma \text{ in } \Gamma} H^*\gamma H^*\gamma H^*$. Therefore α_k is in $H^*\gamma H^*\gamma H^*$ for some γ in Γ. Then $\alpha_k = \pi_1\gamma\pi_2\gamma\pi_3$ for some π_1, π_2, π_3 in H^*. Let $\alpha'_k = \pi_1\gamma\pi_2\pi_3$ and $\alpha' = \alpha_1 \ldots \alpha_{k-1}\alpha'_k\alpha_{k+1} \ldots \alpha_m$. Since γ is a loop, α' is in Π_M. Then α'_k is in A_k, since $\sigma(\alpha'_k) = \sigma(\pi_1) \cup \sigma(\pi_2) \cup \sigma(\pi_3) \cup \sigma(\gamma) = \sigma(\alpha_k)$ and α_k is in A_k. Hence α' is in C_J. Furthermore, $\sigma(\gamma) \subseteq \sigma(\alpha_k) = J_k$. Since $h_1(\alpha_k)$ is in a_k^*, $h_1(\gamma)$ is in a_k^*. Thus γ is in Γ_k. Therefore $h_1(\gamma) = a_k^s$ for some s in S_k. Let $h_1(\alpha) = a_1^{n_1} \ldots a_m^{n_m}$. Then $h_1(\alpha') = a_1^{n_1} \ldots a_k^{n_k - s} \ldots a_m^{n_m}$. Since α is in $h_1^{-1}(L'_J)$, $h_1(\alpha)$ is in L'_J. From the fact that s is in S_k, $h_1(\alpha')$ is in L'_J, i. e., α' is in $h_1^{-1}(L'_J)$. Thus α' is in $h_1^{-1}(L'_J) \cap C_J$. Also, $|\alpha'| < |\alpha|$ implies that $h_2(\alpha')$ is in $h_2(h_1^{-1}(L'_J) \cap C'_J)$ by the minimality of α. Since γ is in Γ, $h_2(\gamma) = \epsilon$. Thus $h_2(\alpha') = h_2(\alpha)$. Hence $h_2(\alpha)$ is in $h_2(h_1^{-1}(L'_J) \cap C'_J)$, a contradiction. Therefore (6) holds.

Finally, we verify that

(7) $h_2(h_1^{-1}(L'_J) \cap C'_J) \subseteq h_2(h_1^{-1}(L) \cap C_J)$.

Since $C'_J \subseteq C_J$, $h_2(h_1^{-1}(L'_J) \cap C'_J) \subseteq h_2(h_1^{-1}(L'_J) \cap C_J)$. Suppose (7) is false. Then there exists a word α in $h_1^{-1}(L'_J) \cap C_J$ such that $h_2(\alpha)$ is not in $h_2(h_1^{-1}(L) \cap C_J)$. Since $C_J = \Pi_M \cap A_1 \ldots A_m$, $\alpha = \alpha_1 \ldots \alpha_m$ for some $\alpha_1, \ldots, \alpha_m$, each α_i in A_i. Then for each i, $h_1(\alpha_i) = a_i^{r_i}$ for some $r_i \geqq 0$. Since $h_1(\alpha)$ is in L'_J, there exist $t_1, \ldots, t_m$, each t_i in T_i, such that $a_1^{r_1+t_1} \ldots a_m^{r_m+t_m}$ is in L. We may assume that α has been selected to minimize $t_1 + \ldots + t_m$. If $t_i = 0$ for each i, then α is in $h_1^{-1}(L) \cap C_J$, a contradiction. Hence $t_k > 0$ for some k. Then $t_k = s_1 + \ldots + s_n$ for some $n \geqq 1$ and $s_1, \ldots, s_n$, each s_j in S_k, $s_1 > 0$. Thus $a_k^{s_1} = h_1(\gamma)$ for some loop γ in Γ_k. Let p be the first and last states of γ. Thus p is in $\sigma(\gamma) \subseteq J_k = \sigma(\alpha_k)$. Hence $\alpha_k = \beta\beta'$, where (i) p is the last state of β and the first of β' if β and β' are in H^+, or (ii) $\beta' = \epsilon$, and p is the first and last states of $\alpha_k = \beta$. Let $\alpha'_k = \beta\gamma\beta'$ and $\alpha' = \alpha_1 \ldots \alpha_{k-1}\alpha'_k\alpha_{k+1} \ldots \alpha_m$. Then α' is in Π_M. Since γ is in Γ_k, $\sigma(\gamma) \subseteq J_k$ and $h_1(\gamma)$ is in a_k^*. Thus α'_k is in A_k. Therefore α' is in $C_J = \Pi_M \cap A_1 \ldots A_m$. Let $r'_k = r_k + s_1$. Then $h_1(\alpha') = a_1^{r_1} \ldots a_k^{r'_k} \ldots a_m^{r_m}$. Let $t'_k = t_k - s_1$. Then $t'_k = s_2 + \ldots + s_n$ is in T_k and $r'_k + t'_k = r_k + t_k$. Thus $a_1^{r_1+t_1} \ldots a_k^{r'_k+t'_k} \ldots a_m^{r_m+t_m}$ is in L. Consequently $a_1^{r_1} \ldots a_k^{r'_k} \ldots a_m^{r_m}$ is in L'_J. Hence $h_1(\alpha')$ is in L'_J and α' is in $h_1^{-1}(L'_J) \cap C_J$. Since γ is in Γ, $h_2(\gamma) = \epsilon$. Thus $h_2(\alpha') = h_2(\alpha)$ and $h_2(\alpha')$ is not in $h_2(h_1^{-1}(L) \cap C_J)$. But $t_1 + \ldots + t'_k + \ldots + t_m < t_1 + \ldots + t_k + \ldots + t_m$, a contradiction of the minimality of $t_1 + \ldots + t_m$. Hence (7) holds and the proof of Theorem 7.1.1 is complete.

COROLLARY: *For each family* $\mathcal{L}$ *of* (m-) *bounded languages, there is a family* $\mathcal{L}'$ *of* (m-) *bounded languages such that* $\mathcal{F}_\sigma(\mathcal{L}') = \hat{\mathcal{F}}_{\hat{\sigma}}(\mathcal{L})$.

Proof: By Theorem 7.1.1, there exists a family $\mathcal{L}'$ of (m-) bounded languages such that $\mathcal{F}(\mathcal{L}') = \hat{\mathcal{F}}(\mathcal{L})$. By (b) of Theorem 6.3.1, $\mathcal{F}_\sigma(\hat{\mathcal{F}}(\mathcal{L})) = \hat{\mathcal{F}}_{\hat{\sigma}}(\hat{\mathcal{F}}(\mathcal{L}))$. Therefore, $\mathcal{F}_\sigma(\mathcal{L}') = \mathcal{F}_\sigma(\mathcal{F}(\mathcal{L}')) = \mathcal{F}_\sigma(\hat{\mathcal{F}}(\mathcal{L})) = \hat{\mathcal{F}}_{\hat{\sigma}}(\mathcal{L})$.

EXERCISE 7.1.1: Let $\mathcal{L} = \mathcal{O}(\mathcal{U})$, where $\mathcal{U}$ is a family of m-bounded languages and $\mathcal{O} = \mathcal{S}$ or $\mathcal{F}$. If $\mathcal{L}$ is principal, prove that $\mathcal{L}$ has some m-bounded generator [Go1].

EXERCISE 7.1.2: Show that $\mathcal{L}'$ as constructed in the proof of Theorem 7.1.1 is always an infinite family.

EXERCISE 7.1.3: For each of the following m and families $\mathcal{L}$ of m-bounded languages find an m-bounded family $\mathcal{L}'$ such that $\mathcal{F}(\mathcal{L}') = \hat{\mathcal{F}}(\mathcal{L})$.

(a) $m = 2$ and $\mathcal{L} = \{\{a^n b^n / n \geqq 1\}\}$.
(b) $m = 1$ and $\mathcal{L} = \{\{a^{n^2+3n} / n \geqq 1\}\}$.
(c) $m = 2$ and $\mathcal{L} = \{\{a^{n^2} / n \geqq 1\}, \{a^n b^n / n \geqq 1\}\}$.
(d) $m = 3$ and $\mathcal{L} = \{\{a^n b^n c^n / n \geqq 1\}, \{a^{n^3} / n \geqq 1\}\}$.

7.2 Pumping Languages

We now consider languages L for which there exist positive integers m and p having the following property:

($*$) For each word w in L, $|w| > p$, there exist words $x_0, y_1, x_1, \ldots, y_m, x_m$ such that $w = x_0 y_1 x_1 \ldots y_m x_m$, $y_1 \ldots y_m \neq \epsilon$, $|y_i| \leqq p$ for all i, and for each positive integer k, $x_0 y_1^{k_1} x_1 \ldots y_m^{k_m} x_m$ is in L for some integers $k_1 \geqq k$, $\ldots, k_m \geqq k$.

Roughly speaking, such a language has the property that each sufficiently large word w may be "pumped up" in certain ways to produce other words in the language. [Such languages are sometimes used to show the distinctness of families $\mathcal{L}_1$ and $\mathcal{L}_2$. In particular, one proves that each language in $\mathcal{L}_1$ has property ($*$) and then exhibits a language in $\mathcal{L}_2$ not having that property.] The two main results in the section are that (i) given m, the family of all such languages for some p is closed under ϵ-free substitution, and (ii) each language in $\hat{\mathcal{F}}_{\hat{\sigma}}(\mathcal{L})$, where $\mathcal{L}$ is a family of m-bounded languages, satisfies $(_*)$ for some p.

We start with a more tractable statement of $(*)$.

Def: Let L be a language and m, p positive integers. Given a word w in L, $(x_0, y_1, x_1, \ldots, y_m, x_m)$ is said to be an *(L, m, p)-factorization of* w if the following conditions hold: (i) $w = x_0y_1x_1 \ldots y_mx_m$, (ii) $|y_i| \leqq p$ for each i, (iii) $y_1 \ldots y_m \neq \epsilon$, and (iv) for each k in N there exist $k_1, \ldots, k_m$ in N, each $k_i \geqq k$, so that $x_0y_1^{k_1+1}x_1 \ldots y_m^{k_m+1}x_m$ is in L.

Notation: For each $m \geqq 1$ let $\mathcal{E}_m$ be the family of all languages L with the following property: There exists an integer $p = p_m(L)$ such that each word w, $|w| > p$, in L has an (L, m, p)-factorization. Let $\mathcal{E} = \bigcup_{m \geqq 1} \mathcal{E}_m$.

If $(x_0, y_1, \ldots, y_m, x_m)$ is an (L, m, p)-factorization of w, then $(x_0, y_1, \ldots, y_m, x_m, \epsilon, \epsilon)$ is an $(L, m+1, p)$-factorization of w. Therefore $\mathcal{E}_1 \subseteq \ldots \subseteq \mathcal{E}_m \subseteq \ldots \subseteq \mathcal{E}$.

Suppose L_1 and L_2 are in $\mathcal{E}_m$. Then $L_1 \cup L_2$ is in $\mathcal{E}_m$ since each word in $L_1 \cup L_2$ has an (L, m, p)-factorization, where $p = \max\{p_m(L_1), p_m(L_2)\}$. Thus $\mathcal{E}_m$ is closed under union.

EXAMPLE 7.2.1: Each regular set is in $\mathcal{E}_1$.[1] Thus $\mathcal{R} \subseteq \mathcal{E}_m$ for every m.

EXAMPLE 7.2.2: Each context-free language is in $\mathcal{E}_2$.[2]

EXAMPLE 7.2.3: Let ϱ be a function from $\{1, \ldots, q\}$ into $\{1, R\}$ and let $\mathcal{L} = \mathcal{L}_{CF}$. As noted in Exercise 5.6.17, $\hat{\mathcal{F}}(\mathcal{L}_\varrho)$ is in $\mathcal{E}_{2q}$.

We turn to the first of the results mentioned earlier.

THEOREM 7.2.1: *For each m, $\mathcal{E}_m$ is closed under ϵ-free substitution.*

Proof: Suppose L is in $\mathcal{E}_m$ and τ is an ϵ-free substitution such that $\tau(a)$ is in $\mathcal{E}_m$ for each a in Σ_L. Let $p' = \max\{p_m(\tau(a))/a \text{ in } \Sigma_L\}$ and $p = p_m(L)p'$. Let w, $|w| > p$, be an arbitrary word in $\tau(L)$. We shall show that w has a $(\tau(L), m, p)$-factorization.

Since w is a non-ϵ word in $\tau(L)$, there exist $n \geqq 1$, $z_1, \ldots, z_n$ in Σ_L, and words $w_1, \ldots, w_n$ such that $z_1 \ldots z_n$ is in L, each w_i is in $\tau(z_i)$, and $w = w_1 \ldots w_n$. Two cases arise.

[1] See Section 2.2.
[2] See Section 2.3.

(α) Suppose $|w_i| > p'$ for some i. Then $|w_i| > p_m(\tau(z_i))$ and $\tau(z_i)$ is in $\mathcal{E}_m$. Thus w_i has a $(\tau(z_i), m, p_m(\tau(z_i)))$-factorization $(x_0, y_1, \ldots, y_m, x_m)$. Then

$$(w_1 \ldots w_{i-1}x_0, y_1, x_1, \ldots, y_m, x_mw_{i+1} \ldots w_n)$$

is a $(\tau(L), m, p)$-factorization of w.

(β) Suppose $|w_i| \leqq p'$ for each i. Then $p_m(L)\, p' = p < |w| \leqq np'$, since $w = w_1 \ldots w_n$. Thus $n > p_m(L)$. Hence $z_1 \ldots z_n$ has an $(L, m, p_m(L))$-factorization

$$(*) \qquad (z_{t_0} \ldots z_{t_1}, z_{t_1+1} \ldots z_{t_2}, \ldots, z_{t_{2m}+1} \ldots z_{t_{2m+1}}),$$

with $t_0 = 1$, $t_{2m+1} = n$, and $t_{i+1}-t_i = |z_{t_i+1} \ldots z_{t_{i+1}}| \leqq p_m(L)$ for $i = 1, 3, \ldots, 2m-1$. For each j, $|w_j| \leqq p'$. Therefore

$$|w_{t_i+1} \ldots w_{t_{i+1}}| \leqq (t_{i+1}-t_i)\, p' \leqq p_m(L)\, p' = p$$

for $i = 1, 3, \ldots, 2m-1$. Since τ is an ϵ-free substitution, $w_j \neq \epsilon$ for each j, $1 \leqq j \leqq n$. Hence $w_{t_i+1} \ldots w_{t_{i+1}} \neq \epsilon$ if $z_{t_i+1} \ldots z_{t_{i+1}} \neq \epsilon$. Thus

$$(w_{t_0} \ldots w_{t_1}, w_{t_1+1} \ldots w_{t_2}, \ldots, w_{t_{2m}+1} \ldots w_{t_{2m+1}})$$

is a $(\tau(L), m, p)$-factorization of w.

COROLLARY 1: *For each m, $\mathcal{E}_m$ is closed under union, concatenation, $+$, and $*$.*

Proof: This follows from Theorem 7.2.1 and the fact that $\mathcal{R} \subseteq \mathcal{E}_m$.

COROLLARY 2: *$\mathcal{E}$ is closed under ϵ-free substitution.*

Proof: Let L be in $\mathcal{E}$ and τ an ϵ-free substitution such that $\tau(a)$ is in $\mathcal{E}$ for each a in Σ_L. Then L is in $\mathcal{E}_{m_L}$ and $\tau(a)$ is in $\mathcal{E}_{m_{\tau(a)}}$ for some integers m_L and $m_{\tau(a)}$, a in Σ_L. Let $m = \max\{m_L, m_{\tau(a)}/a \text{ in } \Sigma_L\}$. Since Σ_L is finite, m exists. Clearly L and each $\tau(a)$ is in $\mathcal{E}_m$. By Theorem 7.2.1, $\mathcal{E}_m$ is closed under ϵ-free substitution. Hence $\tau(L)$ is in $\mathcal{E}_m \subseteq \mathcal{E}$.

Using Theorem 7.2.1, we now demonstrate the second main result.

THEOREM 7.2.2: *$\hat{\mathcal{F}}_{\hat{\sigma}}(\mathcal{L}) \subseteq \mathcal{E}_m$ for each family $\mathcal{L}$ of m-bounded languages.*

Proof: The proof is by induction on m. (The argument for $m = 1$ will be given simultaneously.)

Suppose either $m=1$, or $m>1$ and the theorem is true for each family of $(m-1)$-bounded languages. Let $\mathcal{L}$ be a family of m-bounded languages. By the corollary to Theorem 7.1.1, there exists a family $\mathcal{L}'$ of m-bounded languages such that $\hat{\mathcal{F}}_{\hat{\sigma}}(\mathcal{L}) = \mathcal{F}_\sigma(\mathcal{L}')$. Note that $\mathcal{L}'$ has a language with ϵ in it, since $\mathcal{F}_\sigma(\mathcal{L}')$ is a full AFL. To prove the theorem, it suffices to show that

(1) $\mathcal{M}(\mathcal{L}') \subseteq \mathcal{E}_m$.

For suppose (1) holds. Then

$$\begin{aligned}
\mathcal{F}(\mathcal{L}') &= \hat{\text{Sub}}\,(\mathcal{R}_0, \mathcal{M}(\mathcal{L}')), \quad \text{by Theorem 3.4.1,}\\
&= \text{Sub}\,(\mathcal{R}, \mathcal{M}(\mathcal{L}')), \quad \text{by Lemma 3.4.1,}\\
&\subseteq \text{Sub}\,(\mathcal{E}_m, \mathcal{M}(\mathcal{L}')), \quad \text{since } \mathcal{R} \subseteq \mathcal{E}_m,\\
&\subseteq \text{Sub}\,(\mathcal{E}_m, \mathcal{E}_m), \quad \text{by (1),}\\
&\subseteq \mathcal{E}_m, \quad \text{since } \mathcal{E}_m \text{ is closed under } \epsilon\text{-free substitution.}
\end{aligned}$$

By (a) of Theorem 6.3.1, $\mathcal{F}_\sigma(\mathcal{L}') = \mathcal{F}_\sigma(\mathcal{F}(\mathcal{L}'))$ is the ϵ-free substitution closure of $\mathcal{F}(\mathcal{L}')$. Hence $\hat{\mathcal{F}}_{\hat{\sigma}}(\mathcal{L}) = \mathcal{F}_\sigma(\mathcal{L}') \subseteq \mathcal{E}_m$, since $\mathcal{E}_m$ is closed under ϵ-free substitution.

Consider (1). It suffices to show that $\mathcal{M}(L) \subseteq \mathcal{E}_m$ for each m-bounded language $L \neq \emptyset$. By Lemma 7.1.1, we may assume that $L \subseteq a_1^* \ldots a_m^*$. Let $M = (K_1, \Sigma_1, \Sigma_2, H, p_0, F)$ be an ϵ-free a-transducer. By the construction in Lemma 3.2.3, we may assume that M is 1-bounded and that h_2 is ϵ-limited on Π_M. Thus there exists a positive integer r such that for each α in Π_M, if $\alpha = \alpha_1\alpha_2\alpha_3$ and $h_2(\alpha_2) = \epsilon$, then $|\alpha_2| < r$. Let $n = (r\#(K_1))!$ and let ν be the function from N^m into $a_1^* \ldots a_m^*$ defined by $\nu(r_1, \ldots, r_m) = a_1^{r_1} \ldots a_m^{r_m}$ for each $r_1, \ldots, r_m$ in N. For each word $w = \nu(s_1, \ldots, s_m)$ let

$$L_w = \{\nu(s_1+k_1n, \ldots, s_m+k_mn) \text{ in } L/\text{each } k_i \geqq 0\}.$$

Then L is the union of all L_w for which $w = \nu(s_1, \ldots, s_m)$, $0 \leqq s_i < n$ for each i. Note that there are only a finite number of such L_w. Thus $M(L)$ is the union of a finite number of sets, each of the form $M(L_w)$. Since $\mathcal{E}_m$ is closed under union, it suffices to show that each $M(L_w)$ is in $\mathcal{E}_m$.

Let $s_1, \ldots, s_m$ be arbitrary nonnegative integers and let $w = \nu(s_1, \ldots, s_m)$. For each i, $1 \leqq i \leqq m$, and $j \geqq 0$ let

$$L_{ij} = \{\nu(t_1, \ldots, t_m) \text{ in } L_w/t_i = j\}.$$

Then for each i and j,

(2) $M(L_{ij})$ is in $\mathcal{E}_m$.

For suppose $m = 1$. Then L_{ij} is finite and thus regular. Therefore $M(L_{ij})$ is in $\mathcal{R} \subseteq \mathcal{E}_m$. Suppose $m > 1$. Let

$$L'_{ij} = \{\nu(t_1, \ldots, t_{i-1}, t_{i+1}, \ldots, t_m)/\nu(t_1, \ldots, t_{i-1}, j, t_{i+1}, \ldots, t_m) \text{ in } L_{ij}\}.$$

Clearly L_{ij} is in $\hat{\mathscr{M}}(L'_{ij})$. Since L'_{ij} is $(m-1)$-bounded, $\hat{\mathscr{M}}(L'_{ij}) \subseteq \mathscr{E}_{m-1}$ by induction. Thus $M(L_{ij})$ is in $\hat{\mathscr{M}}(L'_{ij}) \subseteq \mathscr{E}_{m-1} \subseteq \mathscr{E}_m$. Hence (2) holds.

Suppose there exists some $k \geqq 0$ with the property that for each $v(t_1, \ldots, t_m)$ in L_w, $t_i \leqq k$ for some i. Then $L_w = \bigcup_{\substack{1 \leqq i \leqq m \\ 0 \leqq j \leqq k}} L_{ij}$, so that $M(L_w)$ is in $\mathscr{E}_m$. On the other hand, suppose

(3) for each $k \geqq 0$ there exists a word $v(t_1, \ldots, t_m)$ in L_w such that $t_i > k$ for all i, $1 \leqq i \leqq m$.

Let $L'' = \bigcup_{\substack{1 \leqq i \leqq m \\ 0 \leqq j < r\#(K_1)}} L_{ij}$ and $L' = L_w - L''$. By (2) and Corollary 1 of Theorem 7.2.1, $M(L'')$ is in $\mathscr{E}_m$. Since $L'' \subseteq L_w$, $M(L_w) = M(L') \cup M(L'')$. It thus suffices to prove that $M(L')$ is in $\mathscr{E}_m$.

To this end let u be a word in $M(L') = h_2(h_1^{-1}(L') \cap \Pi_M)$. Then there exist α in Π_M and $r_1, \ldots, r_m$ in N such that $u = h_2(\alpha)$ and $h_1(\alpha) = v(r_1, \ldots, r_m)$ is in L'. Since M is 1-bounded, h_1 is length decreasing. Hence there exist $\alpha_1, \ldots, \alpha_m$ such that $\alpha = \alpha_1 \ldots \alpha_m$ and $h_1(\alpha_i) = a_i^{r_i}$ for each i. Now $v(r_1, \ldots, r_m)$ is in $L' = L_w - L''$. Thus $v(r_1, \ldots, r_m)$ is not in L''. Therefore $r_i \geqq r\#(K_1)$ for each i. Let i be an arbitrary integer, $1 \leqq i \leqq m$. Since h_1 is length decreasing, $|\alpha_i| \geqq |h_1(\alpha_i)| = r_i \geqq r\#(K_1)$. Thus there exist $\beta_0, \ldots, \beta_{\#(K_1)}$, where $|\beta_j| = r$ for each j, $1 \leqq j \leqq \#(K_1)$, such that $\alpha_i = \beta_0 \ldots \beta_{\#(K_1)}$. Since there are only $\#(K_1)$ states and there are $\#(K_1)$ words β_j, $1 \leqq j \leqq \#(K_1)$, α_i contains a loop of the form $\gamma_i = \beta_p\beta_{p+1} \ldots \beta_q$ for some p and q, $1 \leqq p \leqq q \leqq \#(K_1)$. Also, there exist α'_i and α''_i such that $\alpha_i = \alpha'_i\gamma_i\alpha''_i$. Since h_2 is length decreasing, $|h_2(\gamma_i)| \leqq |\gamma_i| \leqq r\#(K_1)$. Since $|\gamma_i| \geqq |\beta_p| = r$, $h_2(\gamma_i) \neq \epsilon$ from the definition of r. Thus

(4) $h_2(\gamma_i) \neq \epsilon$ for each i, $1 \leqq i \leqq m$.

Two cases arise.

(α) Suppose $h_1(\gamma_i) = \epsilon$ for some i. Since $\alpha_i = \alpha'_i\gamma_i\alpha''_i$,

$$\alpha = \alpha_1 \ldots \alpha_{i-1}\alpha'_i\gamma_i\alpha''_i\alpha_{i+1} \ldots \alpha_m.$$

Now $|h_2(\gamma_i)| \leqq r\#(K_1)$ and, by (4), $h_2(\gamma_i) \neq \epsilon$. For each $k \geqq 0$ let

$$\pi_k = \alpha_1 \ldots \alpha'_i\gamma_i^{k+1}\alpha''_i \ldots \alpha_m.$$

Since γ_i is a loop and α is in Π_M, π_k is in Π_M. Since $h_1(\gamma_i) = \epsilon$, $h_1(\pi_k) = h_1(\alpha)$. Thus $h_1(\pi_k)$ is in L', so that π_k is in $h_1^{-1}(L') \cap \Pi_M$. Hence $h_2(\pi_k)$ is in $M(L')$. Therefore

$$(h_2(\alpha_1 \ldots \alpha'_i), h_2(\gamma_i), h_2(\alpha''_i\alpha_{i+1} \ldots \alpha_m), \epsilon, \ldots, \epsilon)$$

is an $(M(L'), m, r\#(K_1))$-factorization of $h_2(\alpha)$.

(β) Suppose $h_1(\gamma_i) \neq \epsilon$ for each i. Let $n_i = |h_1(\gamma_i)|$, so that $n_i \geqq 1$ for each i. Observe that

$$\alpha = \alpha_1 \ldots \alpha_m = \alpha_1'\gamma_1\alpha_1'' \ldots \alpha_m'\gamma_m\alpha_m''.$$

Let k be an arbitrary integer in N, and let $k' = \max \{kn_i+r_i/1 \leqq i \leqq m\}$. By (3), there exists a word $\nu(t_1, \ldots, t_m)$ in L_w such that $t_i > k'$ for each i. Since $t_i > k' \geqq r_i \geqq r\#(K_1)$, $\nu(t_1, \ldots, t_m)$ is in L'. Thus $\nu(t_1, \ldots, t_m)$ and $\nu(r_1, \ldots, r_m)$ are both in $L' \subseteq L_w$. Hence $t_i - r_i$ is a positive multiple of n. But $n = (r\#(K_1))!$ and $n_i = |h_1(\gamma_i)| \leqq |\gamma_i| \leqq r\#(K_1)$. Therefore $t_i - r_i$ is a positive multiple of n_i. Thus $t_i = r_i + k_i n_i$ for some integer $k_i > 0$. Then $k_i n_i = t_i - r_i > k' - r_i \geqq kn_i$, so that $k_i > k$. Let

$$\alpha' = \alpha_1'\gamma_1^{k_1+1}\alpha_1'' \ldots \alpha_m'\gamma_m^{k_m+1}\alpha_m''.$$

Then α' is in Π_M. Since $h_1(\alpha_i)$ is in a_i^*, $h_1(\gamma_i)$ is in a_i^*. Therefore $h_1(\gamma_i) = a_i^{n_i}$. Then $h_1(\alpha_i'\gamma_i^{k_i+1}\alpha_i'') = h_1(\alpha_i)h_1(\gamma_i)^{k_i} = a^{r_i+k_in_i}$. Hence

$$\begin{aligned} h_1(\alpha') &= \nu(r_1+k_1n_1, \ldots, r_m+k_mn_m) \\ &= \nu(t_1, \ldots, t_m), \end{aligned}$$

and is in L'. Thus α' is in $h_1^{-1}(L') \cap \Pi_M$. Consequently $h_2(\alpha')$ is in $M(L')$. Since $k_i \geqq k$,

$$(h_2(\alpha_1'), h_2(\gamma_1), h_2(\alpha_1''\alpha_2'), h_2(\gamma_2), \ldots, h_2(\alpha_m''))$$

is an $(M(L'), m, r\#(K_1))$-factorization of $h_2(\alpha)$.

It thus follows that $h_2(\alpha)$ has an $(M(L'), m, r\#(K_1))$-factorization in both cases. Hence $M(L')$ is in $\mathscr{E}_m$.

COROLLARY: *$\hat{\mathscr{F}}_{\hat{\sigma}}(\mathscr{L}) \subseteq \mathscr{E}$ for each family $\mathscr{L}$ of bounded languages.*

Proof: Let L be in $\hat{\mathscr{F}}_{\hat{\sigma}}(\mathscr{L})$. Then there exists a finite, nonempty sequence of languages $L_1, \ldots, L_n$ in $\mathscr{L}$ such that L is in $\hat{\mathscr{F}}_{\hat{\sigma}}(\{L_1, \ldots, L_n\})$. [See Exercise 6.3.2.] Since $\mathscr{L}$ is a family of bounded languages, each L_i is m_i-bounded for some m_i. Then $\{L_1, \ldots, L_n\}$ is a family of m-bounded languages, where $m = \max \{m_i/1 \leqq i \leqq n\}$. Therefore

$$\begin{aligned} L &\subseteq \hat{\mathscr{F}}_{\hat{\sigma}}(\{L_1, \ldots, L_n\}) \\ &\subseteq \mathscr{E}_m, \quad \text{by Theorem 7.2.2,} \\ &\subseteq \mathscr{E}. \end{aligned}$$

The question arises as to whether or not there exists some m such that $\mathcal{E}_m = \mathcal{E}_{m+1}$. This is resolved negatively by the corollary to the next result.

PROPOSITION 7.2.1: *Let $m \geqq 2$ and let L be an infinite subset of $a_1^* \ldots a_m^*$ with the following property*:

(∗) *For all words $u = a_1^{r_1} \ldots a_m^{r_m}$ and $v = a_1^{s_1} \ldots a_m^{s_m}$ in L, $u = v$ if $r_i = s_i$ for some i.*

Then L is not in $\mathcal{E}_{m-1}$.

Proof: Suppose L is in $\mathcal{E}_{m-1}$. Then there exists an integer p such that each word w, $|w| > p$, in L has an $(L, m-1, p)$-factorization. Since L is infinite, there is a word $u = a_1^{r_1} \ldots a_m^{r_m}$ in L with $|u| > p$. Hence there exist words $x_0, y_1, x_1, \ldots, y_{m-1}, x_{m-1}$ such that $u = x_0 y_1 x_1 \ldots y_{m-1} x_{m-1}$, $y_j \neq \epsilon$ for some j, and $v = x_0 y_1^{k_1} x_1 \ldots y_{m-1}^{k_{m-1}} x_{m-1}$ is in L for some integers $k_1, \ldots, k_{m-1}$, each $k_i > 1$. Since v is in L, $v = a_1^{s_1} \ldots a_m^{s_m}$ for some non-negative integers $s_1, \ldots, s_m$. For each i, y_i^2 is a subword of v. Since v is in $a_1^* \ldots a_m^*$ and $a_1, \ldots, a_m$ are distinct symbols, no y_i can contain occurrences of two different symbols. Since each y_i, $1 \leqq i \leqq m-1$, contains occurrences of at most one symbol, there is some k, $1 \leqq k \leqq m$ such that a_k does not occur in the word $y_1 \ldots y_{m-1}$. Then $s_k = r_k$. By (∗), $u = v$. But $y_j \neq \epsilon$, so that $|u| < |v|$, a contradiction. Hence L is not in $\mathcal{E}_{m-1}$.

For each $m \geqq 1$, $\{a_1^i \ldots a_{m+1}^i / i \geqq 1\}$ is in $\mathcal{E}_{m+1}$ by Theorem 7.2.2 but is not in $\mathcal{E}_m$ by Proposition 7.2.1. Hence we have:

COROLLARY: *For all $m \geqq 1$, $\mathcal{E}_m \subsetneq \mathcal{E}_{m+1}$.*

EXERCISE 7.2.1: Prove that $\{(a^i b^i)^k / i \geqq 1, k \geqq 1\}$ is not in $\mathcal{E}$ [Go1].

EXERCISE 7.2.2: Prove that each $\mathcal{E}_m(\mathcal{E})$ is closed under ϵ-free homomorphism.

EXERCISE 7.2.3: Prove that Lc^+ is in $\mathcal{E}_1$ for each $L \subseteq \{a, b\}^*$.

EXERCISE 7.2.4: Using Exercises 7.2.1 and 7.2.3, show that for each m, $\mathcal{E}_m(\mathcal{E})$ is:

(a) not closed under arbitrary homomorphism.
(b) not closed under intersection with regular sets.

EXERCISE 7.2.5: Using Proposition 7.2.1, give another proof of Theorem 5.6.3.

7.3 Substitution

We now consider substitution of semi-AFL generated by families of bounded languages. Specifically, we shall show that if $\mathscr{L}_1$ and $\mathscr{L}_2$ are semi-AFL, each containing at least one nonregular set, then Sub $(\mathscr{L}_1, \mathscr{L}_2)$ cannot be a subfamily of any (semi-)AFL generated by a family of bounded languages. It follows as a corollary that no such semi-AFL, excluding $\mathscr{R}_0$ and $\mathscr{R}$, can be closed under ϵ-free substitution.

We shall need five lemmas to obtain our results on substitution. The first lemma asserts that if L_1cL_2 is in $\hat{\mathscr{M}}(L)$, where L is m-bounded and c is a new symbol, then either L_1 or L_2 is in $\hat{\mathscr{S}}(\mathscr{U}) \subseteq \hat{\mathscr{M}}(L)$, where $\mathscr{U}$ is a family of either 1-bounded or $(m-1)$-bounded languages. The others will be described as encountered.

Lemma 7.3.1: *Let L_1 and L_2 be subsets of Σ_1^* and let c be a new symbol. Let L be a nonempty subset of $a_1^* \ldots a_m^*$, $m \geqq 2$, and let L_1cL_2 be in $\hat{\mathscr{M}}(L)$. Then either L_1 is in $\hat{\mathscr{S}}(\mathscr{U}) \subseteq \hat{\mathscr{M}}(L)$ for some family $\mathscr{U}$ of $(m-1)$-bounded languages, or L_2 is in $\hat{\mathscr{S}}(\mathscr{U}') \subseteq \hat{\mathscr{M}}(L)$ for some family $\mathscr{U}'$ of* 1*-bounded languages.*

Proof: If $L_1 = \emptyset$ or $L_2 = \emptyset$ then the lemma is obviously true. Suppose that $L_1 \neq \emptyset$ and $L_2 \neq \emptyset$. Let $L_1cL_2 = M(L)$, where M is the a-transducer $(K_1, \Sigma_2, \Sigma_1 \cup \{c\}, H, p_0, F)$. Without loss of generality, we may assume that

(1) each element in H involving c is of the form (p, ϵ, c, p').

[For let $\bar{p}$ be a new symbol for each p in K_1. Let $M' = (K_1', \Sigma_2, \Sigma_1 \cup \{c\}, H', p_0, F)$, where $K_1' = K_1 \cup \{\bar{p}/p \text{ in } K_1\}$ and $H' = (H-(K_1 \times \Sigma_1 \times \{c\} \times K_1)) \cup \{(p, a, \epsilon, \bar{p}), (\bar{p}, \epsilon, c, q)/(p, a, c, q) \text{ in } H \text{ for some } a \text{ in } \Sigma_2\}$. Then $M'(L) = M(L)$ and each element in H' involving c is of the form (p, ϵ, c, p').] Let $K_2 = \{(p, p')/(p, \epsilon, c, p') \text{ in } H\}$. For each p_1, p_2 in K_1 let M_{p_1, p_2} be the a-transducer $(K_1, \Sigma_2, \Sigma_1 \cup \{c\}, H, p_1, \{p_2\})$ and $\tilde{M}_{p_1, p_2}$ be the a-transducer $(K_1, \Sigma_1 \cup \{c\}, \Sigma_2, \tilde{H}, p_1, \{p_2\})$, where $\tilde{H} = \{(p, v, u, p')/(p, u, v, p') \text{ in } H\}$. For each p in K_1, let

$$R(p) = \{w/M_{p_0, p}(w) \neq \emptyset\}$$

and

$$S(p) = \{w/M_{p, p'}(w) \neq \emptyset \text{ for some } p' \text{ in } F\}.$$

Note that $R(p)$ is regular for each p. This follows from the fact that $R(p) = \tilde{M}_{p_0, p}((\Sigma_1 \cup \{c\})^*)$ and $(\Sigma_1 \cup \{c\})^*$ is regular. Similarly, $S(p)$ is regular for each p.

For each (p, p') in K_2 and i, $1 \leqq i \leqq m$, let

(2) $L(i, p, p') = M_{p_0, p}\big((L/S(p')) \cap a_1^* \ldots a_i^*\big)$ and
(3) $L'(i, p, p') = \bigcup_{p'' \text{ in } F} M_{p', p''}\big((R(p)\backslash L) \cap a_i^* \ldots a_m^*\big)$.

We now show that for each i, p, and p', with (p, p') in K_2,

(4) $L(i, p, p') \subseteq L_1$ and
(5) $L'(i, p, p') \subseteq L_2$.

To see (4), suppose x is in $M_{p_0, p}\big((L/S(p')) \cap a_1^* \ldots a_i^*\big)$ for some i, p, and p'. Then there exist u_1 in $L/S(p')$ and u_2 in $S(p')$ such that x is in $M_{p_0, p}(u_1)$ and $u_1 u_2$ is in L. From the definition of $S(p')$, there exist p'' in F and y in $M_{p', p''}(u_2)$. Then xcy is in $M(u_1 u_2)$, so that x is in L_1. The argument for (5) is similar.

We next define three languages, A, B, and D. Let

$$A = \bigcup_{1 \leqq i \leqq m-1} \; \bigcup_{(p, p') \text{ in } K_2} L(i, p, p'),$$

$$B = \bigcup_{(p, p') \text{ in } K_2} L(m, p, p'),$$

and

$$D = \bigcup_{(p, p') \text{ in } K_2} L'(m, p, p').$$

Suppose that x is in L_1. Let y be some element in L_2. Since xcy is in $L_1 c L_2$, there exist (p, p') in K_2, p'' in F, i in $\{1, \ldots, m\}$, u_1 in $a_1^* \ldots a_i^*$, and u_2 in $a_i^* \ldots a_m^*$ such that $u_1 u_2$ is in L, x is in $M_{p_0, p}(u_1)$, and y is in $M_{p', p''}(u_2)$. Since u_2 is in $S(p')$, x is in $L(i, p, p')$. Since x is an arbitrary element of L_1, $L_1 \subseteq A \cup B$. From (4), $A \cup B \subseteq L_1$. Thus $L_1 = A \cup B$. Two alternatives arise.

(α) Suppose $L_1 = A$. Consider an arbitrary $L(i, p, p')$. By (2), $L(i, p, p') = M_{p_0, p}\big((L/S(p')) \cap a_1^* \ldots a_i^*\big)$. Since $S(p')$ and $a_1^* \ldots a_i^*$ are regular, $(L/S(p')) \cap a_1^* \ldots a_i^*$ is in $\hat{\mathscr{M}}(L)$ by Theorem 3.2.1 and Corollary 4 of Theorem 3.2.2. Thus $L(i, p, p')$ is in $\hat{\mathscr{M}}(L)$. Hence $L_1 = A$ is in $\hat{\mathscr{S}}(\mathscr{U}) \subseteq \hat{\mathscr{M}}(L)$, where $\mathscr{U}$ is the finite family of $(m-1)$-bounded languages $(L/S(p')) \cap a_1^* \ldots a_i^*$, with $1 \leqq i \leqq m-1$ and (p, p') in K_2.

(β) Suppose $L_1 \neq A$. Then $L_1 - A \neq \emptyset$. Let x be some element in $L_1 - A$ and y an arbitrary element in L_2. Then there exist (p, p') in K_2, p'' in F, and words u_1 and u_2 such that $u_1 u_2$ is in L, x is in $M_{p_0, p}(u_1)$, and y is in $M_{p', p''}(u_2)$. Thus u_2 is in $S(p')$ and u_1 is in $L/S(p')$. Since x is not in A, it follows that u_1 is not in $a_1^* \ldots a_{m-1}^*$. Thus u_1 is in $a_1^* \ldots a_{m-1}^* a_m^+$, and u_2 is in a_m^*. Therefore u_2 is in $a_m^* \cap (R(p)\backslash L)$. Hence y is in $L'(m, p, p') \subseteq D$. Since y is an arbitrary element in L_2, $L_2 \subseteq D$. By (5), $D \subseteq L_2$. Thus $L_2 = D$. Then L_2 is in $\hat{\mathscr{S}}(\mathscr{U}')$, where $\mathscr{U}'$ is the finite family of 1-bounded languages $a_m^* \cap (R(p)\backslash L)$, with (p, p') in K_2.

The second lemma, which is needed for the third lemma, asserts that the quotient of a language $L \subseteq a^*$ by a certain type of regular subset of a^* is regular.

LEMMA 7.3.2: *Let a be a symbol in Σ, $L \subseteq a^*$, and r a positive integer. Then $L/(a^r)^* a^k$ is regular for each nonnegative integer k.*

Proof: Let $L' = L/(a^r)^* a^k$. For each i, $0 \leqq i \leqq r-1$, let $U_i = L \cap (a^r)^* a^{i+k}$, $R_i = U_i/(a^r)^* a^k$ if U_i is finite, and $R_i = (a^r)^* a^i$ if U_i is infinite. Then

(∗) R_i is a regular subset of L' for each i.

For let i be an arbitrary integer, $0 \leqq i \leqq r-1$. Clearly R_i is regular. If U_i is finite, then $R_i = U_i/(a^r)^* a^k \subseteq L/(a^r)^* a^k = L'$. Suppose U_i is infinite. Let w be in R_i. Then $w = a^{tr+i}$ for some $t \geqq 0$. Since U_i is infinite, L contains a word $a^{sr+i+k} = a^{tr+i} a^{(s-t)r+k}$ for some $s \geqq t$. Since $a^{(s-t)r+k}$ is in $(a^r)^* a^k$, $w = a^{tr+i}$ is in L'. Therefore $R_i \subseteq L'$ and (∗) holds.

Consider L'. Then

$$\begin{aligned} L' &= L/(a^r)^* a^k \\ &= \left(L \cap \left(\bigcup_{i=0}^{r-1} (a^r)^* a^{i+k}\right)\right)\Big/(a^r)^* a^k \\ &= \left(\bigcup_{i=0}^{r-1} (L \cap (a^r)^* a^{i+k})\right)\Big/(a^r)^* a^k \\ &= \bigcup_{i=0}^{r-1} \left((L \cap (a^r)^* a^{i+k})/(a^r)^* a^k\right), \quad \text{since } \left(\bigcup_{\alpha} L_\alpha\right)/\bar{L} = \bigcup_{\alpha} (L_\alpha/\bar{L}), \\ &\subseteq \bigcup_{i=0}^{r-1} R_i \\ &\subseteq L'. \end{aligned}$$

Thus $L' = \bigcup_{0}^{r-1} R_i$, so that L' is regular.

The third lemma states that when $L \subseteq a^*$ and $M(L) = L_1 c L_2$, then either L_1 or L_2 is regular. More precisely, we have

LEMMA 7.3.3: *Let L_1 and L_2 be subsets of Σ_1^* and c a new symbol. Let a be in Σ, $L \subseteq a^*$, and M an a-transducer such that $M(L) = L_1 c L_2$. Then either L_1 or L_2 is regular.*

Proof: Let $M = (K_1, \{a\}, \Sigma_1, H, p_0, F)$, K_2, M_{p_1, p_2}, $R(p)$, and $S(p)$ be as in Lemma 7.3.1. For each p in K_1, $\{i/a^i \text{ in } S(p)\}$ is ultimately periodic since $S(p) \subseteq a^*$ and is regular. Thus, for each p in K_1, there exists a finite (possibly empty) set A_p of nonnegative integers, a finite (possibly empty) set B_p of positive integers, and a positive integer $s(p)$ such that

$$S(p) = A'_p \cup \bigcup_{t \text{ in } B_p} (a^{s(p)})^* a^t,$$

where A'_p is the finite set $\{a^k/k \text{ in } A_p\}$.

We next show that

(1) $L_1 = \bigcup_{(p, p') \text{ in } K_2} M_{p_0, p}(L/S(p'))$ and

(2) $L_2 = \bigcup_{(p, p') \text{ in } K_2} \bigcup_{p'' \text{ in } F} M_{p', p''}(R(p)\backslash L)$.

To see (1), observe that $L_1 \subseteq \bigcup_{(p, p') \text{ in } K_2} M_{p_0, p}(L/S(p'))$. To obtain the reverse containment, suppose that x is in $M_{p_0, p}(L/S(p'))$ for some (p, p') in K_2. Then there exist u_1 in $L/S(p')$ and u_2 in $S(p')$ such that x is in $M_{p_0, p}(u_1)$ and u_1u_2 is in L. From the definition of $S(p')$, there exist p'' in F and y in $M_{p', p''}(u_2)$. Then xcy is in $M(u_1u_2)$, so that x is in L_1. Thus (1) holds. A similar argument occurs for (2).

Now consider the languages

$$V_1 = \bigcup_{(p, p') \text{ in } K_2} \bigcup_{t \text{ in } B_{p'}} M_{p_0, p}(L/(a^{s(p)})^* a^t)$$

and

$$V_2 = \bigcup_{(p, p') \text{ in } K_2} M_{p_0, p}(L/A'_{p'}).$$

Since $L/\bigcup_{\alpha \text{ in } A} L_\alpha = \bigcup_{\alpha \text{ in } A} L/L_\alpha$,

$$\begin{aligned} L_1 &= \bigcup_{(p, p') \text{ in } K_2} M_{p_0, p}(L/S(p')), \quad \text{by (1)}, \\ &= \bigcup_{(p, p') \text{ in } K_2} M_{p_0, p}\Big(L/\Big(A'_{p'} \cup \bigcup_{t \text{ in } B_{p'}} (a^{s(p')})^* a^t\Big)\Big) \\ &= V_1 \cup V_2. \end{aligned}$$

By Lemma 7.3.2, each set $L/(a^{s(p')})^*a^t$ is regular. Thus V_1 is regular. Suppose $V_1 = L_1$. Then L_1 is regular. Suppose $V_1 \subsetneq L_1$. Then there exists a word x in $L_1 - V_1$. Hence x is in V_2. Let y be an arbitrary element in L_2. Since $M(L) = L_1cL_2$, xcy is in $M(L)$. Hence there exist some (p, p') in K_2, p'' in F, u_1 in $L/A'_{p'}$, and u_2 in $A'_{p'}$ such that x is in $M_{p_0, p}(u_1)$, y is in $M_{p', p''}(u_2)$, and u_1u_2 is in L. [Otherwise, x would be in V_1.] Then u_2 is also in $R(p)\backslash L$.

Therefore u_2 is in $A'_{p'} \cap (R(p)\backslash L)$ and y is in $M_{p',p''}\big(A'_{p'} \cap (R(p)\backslash L)\big)$. Since y is an arbitrary element of L_2,

$$\begin{aligned} L_2 &\subseteq \bigcup_{(p,p')\text{ in }K_2}\ \bigcup_{p''\text{ in }F} M_{p',p''}\big(A'_{p'} \cap (R(p)\backslash L)\big) \\ &\subseteq L_2, \quad \text{by (2).} \end{aligned}$$

Thus

$$L_2 = \bigcup_{(p,p')\text{ in }K_2}\ \bigcup_{p''\text{ in }F} M_{p',p''}\big(A'_{p'} \cap (R(p)\backslash L)\big).$$

Now each set $A'_{p'}$ is finite and thus regular. Hence each set $M_{p',p''}\big(A'_{p'} \cap (R(p)\backslash L)\big)$ is regular. Since K_2 and F are both finite, L_2 is regular.

The next lemma, a technical result, is needed for the fifth lemma.

LEMMA 7.3.4: *Let $\mathcal{U}$ be a family of m-bounded languages, L a language, and c a new symbol. If $(Lc)^{2m}$ is in $\hat{\mathcal{S}}(\mathcal{U})$, then L is regular.*

Proof: Suppose $m = 1$ and $LcLc$ is in $\hat{\mathcal{S}}(\mathcal{U})$. Then Lc_1Lc is in $\hat{\mathcal{S}}(\mathcal{U})$, where c_1 is a new symbol. Thus Lc_1Lc is in $\hat{\mathcal{S}}(\mathcal{U}')$ for some finite family $\mathcal{U}' \subseteq \mathcal{U}$. By Lemma 7.1.1, $Lc_1Lc = M(L_1)$ for some a-transducer M and some $L_1 \subseteq a_1^*$, where a_1 is a symbol. By Lemma 7.3.3, either L or Lc is regular. The result then follows from the fact that Lc regular implies L is regular.

Continuing by induction, suppose the lemma is true for all $\mathcal{U}$ and all $m = j$, $j < n$, where $n \geqq 2$. Consider $m = n$. Suppose $(Lc)^{2n}$ is in $\hat{\mathcal{S}}(\mathcal{U})$., Then $(Lc)^{2(n-1)}c_1(Lc)^2$ is in $\hat{\mathcal{S}}(\mathcal{U})$, where c_1 is a new symbol. As above there exists an a-transducer M and a language $L_1 \subseteq a_1^* \ldots a_n^*$ such that $M(L_1) = (Lc)^{2(n-1)}c_1(Lc)^2$. By Lemma 7.3.1, either $(Lc)^{2(n-1)}$ is in $\hat{\mathcal{S}}(\mathcal{U}'')$ for some family $\mathcal{U}''$ of $(n-1)$-bounded languages or $(Lc)^2$ is in $\hat{\mathcal{S}}(\mathcal{U}''')$ for some family $\mathcal{U}'''$ of 1-bounded languages. In either case, L is regular by induction.

The final lemma asserts that for each family $\mathcal{U}$ of bounded languages, $\hat{\mathcal{S}}(\mathcal{U})$ can contain no AFL other than $\mathcal{R}_0$ or $\mathcal{R}$.

LEMMA 7.3.5: *Let $\mathcal{U}$ be a family of bounded languages. If $\mathcal{L} \subseteq \hat{\mathcal{S}}(\mathcal{U})$ and $\mathcal{L}$ is an AFL, then either $\mathcal{L} = \mathcal{R}_0$ or $\mathcal{L} = \mathcal{R}$.*

Proof: Suppose that $\mathcal{L} \subseteq \hat{\mathcal{S}}(\mathcal{U})$ and $\mathcal{L}$ is an AFL. Let L be in $\mathcal{L}$ and c be a symbol not in Σ_L. If $L = \emptyset$, then L is regular. Suppose $L \neq \emptyset$. Then

$(Lc)^+$ is in $\mathcal{L} \subseteq \hat{\mathcal{S}}(\mathcal{U})$. Hence $(Lc)^+$ is in $\hat{\mathcal{S}}(\mathcal{U}')$ for some finite family $\mathcal{U}' \subseteq \mathcal{U}$. Thus $\mathcal{U}'$ is a family of m-bounded languages for some $m \geqq 1$. Since $(Lc)^+$ is in $\hat{\mathcal{S}}(\mathcal{U}')$, $(LcLc)^m = (Lc)^+ \cap (\Sigma_L^* c)^{2m}$ is in $\hat{\mathcal{S}}(\mathcal{U}')$. By Lemma 7.3.4, L is regular. Since each language in $\mathcal{L}$ is regular, $\mathcal{L} = \mathcal{R}_0$ or $\mathcal{L} = \mathcal{R}$.

We are now ready for the main result of the section.

THEOREM 7.3.1: *Let $\mathcal{L}_1$ and $\mathcal{L}_2$ be (full) semi-AFL, each with a nonregular set, and let $\mathcal{L}$ be a (full) AFL or semi-AFL such that Sub $(\mathcal{L}_1, \mathcal{L}_2) \subseteq \mathcal{L}$. Then $\mathcal{L}$ is not a (full) generating-family-bounded AFL or semi-AFL resp.*

Proof: First consider the case when $\mathcal{L}_1$, $\mathcal{L}_2$ are full and $\mathcal{L}$ is a full AFL. Suppose that $\mathcal{L}$ is a full generating-family-bounded AFL. Then $\mathcal{L} = \hat{\mathcal{F}}(\mathcal{U})$ for some family $\mathcal{U}$ of bounded languages. By Theorem 3.4.1 and Proposition 3.3.2, $\mathcal{L} = \hat{\mathcal{F}}(\mathcal{U}) = \widehat{\text{Sub}}(\mathcal{R}, \hat{\mathcal{M}}(\mathcal{U})) \subseteq \widehat{\text{Sub}}(\mathcal{R}, \hat{\mathcal{S}}(\mathcal{U}))$. Let L_1 and L_2 be nonregular sets in $\mathcal{L}_1$ and $\mathcal{L}_2$ respectively. By hypothesis, L_1 and L_2 exist. We may assume that L_1 and L_2 are ϵ-free. [Otherwise, consider $L_1 - \{\epsilon\}$ and $L_2 - \{\epsilon\}$.] Also, we may assume that $\Sigma_{L_1} \cap \Sigma_{L_2} = \emptyset$. Since L_1 and L_2 are nonregular, $L_1 \neq \emptyset$ and $L_2 \neq \emptyset$. Let c be a new symbol. Then $(L_2 c)^+$ is in $\hat{\mathcal{F}}(\mathcal{L}_2)$ and is ϵ-free. Clearly $(L_2 c)^+$ is not a regular set. [For otherwise, let S be a gsm which is the identity on $\Sigma_{L_2}^*$ until the first occurrence of c and is ϵ on $(\Sigma_{L_2} \cup \{c\})^*$ thereafter. Then $S((L_2 c)^+) = L_2$, so that L_2 is regular, a contradiction.] Now

$$
\begin{aligned}
\text{Sub}(\mathcal{L}_1, \mathcal{L}_2) &= \widehat{\text{Sub}}\,(\mathcal{L}_1, \mathcal{L}_2), \quad \text{since } \mathcal{L}_1 \text{ and } \mathcal{L}_2 \text{ are full,}\\
&= \widehat{\text{Sub}}\,(\widehat{\text{Sub}}\,(\mathcal{L}_1, \mathcal{R}), \mathcal{L}_2), \quad \text{by Theorem 3.3.2,}\\
&= \widehat{\text{Sub}}\,(\mathcal{L}_1, \widehat{\text{Sub}}\,(\mathcal{R}, \mathcal{L}_2)), \quad \text{by Lemma 6.1.1,}\\
&= \widehat{\text{Sub}}\,(\mathcal{L}_1, \hat{\mathcal{F}}(\mathcal{L}_2)), \quad \text{by Theorem 3.4.1,}\\
&= \text{Sub}\,(\mathcal{L}_1, \hat{\mathcal{F}}(\mathcal{L}_2)).
\end{aligned}
$$

Hence $\tau_{(L_2 c)^+}(L_1)$ is in $\text{Sub}(\mathcal{L}_1, \hat{\mathcal{F}}(\mathcal{L}_2)) = \text{Sub}\,(\mathcal{L}_1, \mathcal{L}_2) \subseteq \mathcal{L} \subseteq \widehat{\text{Sub}}\,(\mathcal{R}, \hat{\mathcal{S}}(\mathcal{U}))$. By Lemma 6.4.3, either L_1 is in $\mathcal{R}$ or $(L_2 c)^+$ is in $\hat{\mathcal{S}}(\mathcal{U})$. Since L_1 is not regular, $(L_2 c)^+$ is in $\hat{\mathcal{S}}(\mathcal{U})$. Then $\hat{\mathcal{M}}((L_2 c)^+) \subseteq \hat{\mathcal{S}}(\mathcal{U})$. By Theorem 5.4.1, $\mathcal{M}((L_2 c)^+) = \mathcal{F}(L_2 - \{\epsilon\}) = \mathcal{F}(L_2)$. Then $\hat{\mathcal{M}}((L_2 c)^+) = \hat{\mathcal{F}}(L_2)$. Therefore $\hat{\mathcal{F}}(L_2) \subseteq \hat{\mathcal{S}}(\mathcal{U})$, which contradicts Lemma 7.3.5.

Next consider the case where $\mathcal{L}_1$, $\mathcal{L}_2$ are just semi-AFL and $\mathcal{L}$ is an AFL. Suppose that $\mathcal{L}$ is a generating-family-bounded AFL. Then

$$
\begin{aligned}
\text{Sub}\,(\hat{\mathcal{H}}(\mathcal{L}_1), \hat{\mathcal{H}}(\mathcal{L}_2)) &= \hat{\mathcal{H}}(\text{Sub}\,(\mathcal{L}_1, \mathcal{L}_2)), \quad \text{by Corollary 2 of Theorem 6.1.1,}\\
&\subseteq \hat{\mathcal{F}}(\mathcal{L}).
\end{aligned}
$$

Since $\mathscr{L}$ is a generating-family-bounded AFL, $\mathscr{L} = \mathscr{F}(\mathscr{U})$ for some family $\mathscr{U}$ of bounded languages. Then $\hat{\mathscr{F}}(\mathscr{L})$ is a full generating-family-bounded AFL. Since $\mathscr{L}_1 \subseteq \hat{\mathscr{H}}(\mathscr{L}_1)$ and $\mathscr{L}_2 \subseteq \hat{\mathscr{H}}(\mathscr{L}_2)$, $\hat{\mathscr{H}}(\mathscr{L}_1)$ and $\hat{\mathscr{H}}(\mathscr{L}_2)$ both contain nonregular sets. However, it was shown in the previous case that $\hat{\mathscr{F}}(\mathscr{L})$ is not a full generating-family-bounded AFL, a contradiction.

Finally, suppose that $\mathscr{L}$ is a (full) generating-family-bounded semi-AFL. Then $\mathscr{F}(\mathscr{L})$ ($\hat{\mathscr{F}}(\mathscr{L})$) is a (full) generating-family-bounded AFL and $\mathrm{Sub}(\mathscr{L}_1, \mathscr{L}_2) \subseteq \mathscr{L} \subseteq \mathscr{F}(\mathscr{L})$ ($\hat{\mathscr{F}}(\mathscr{L})$), a contradiction of the previous cases. Thus $\mathscr{L}$ is not a (full) generating-family-bounded semi-AFL.

Corollary 1: *Let $\mathscr{L}_1$ be a (full) generating-family-bounded AFL or semi-AFL. If $\mathscr{L}_2 \subseteq \mathscr{L}_1$ is a (full) semi-AFL with a nonregular set, then $\mathscr{L}_2$ is not closed under ϵ-free (arbitrary) substitution.*

Proof: Suppose $\mathscr{L}_2 \subseteq \mathscr{L}_1$ is a (full) semi-AFL with a nonregular set and is closed under ϵ-free (arbitrary) substitution. Then $\mathrm{Sub}(\mathscr{L}_2, \mathscr{L}_2)$ ($= \hat{\mathrm{Sub}}(\mathscr{L}_2, \mathscr{L}_2)$) $\subseteq \mathscr{L}_2 \subseteq \mathscr{L}_1$, a contradiction of Theorem 7.3.1.

By the corollary to Theorem 3.6.2, an AFL closed under intersection is closed under ϵ-free substitution. Thus we have

Corollary 2: *Let $\mathscr{L}$ be an AFL containing a nonregular language. If $\mathscr{L} \subseteq \mathscr{L}'$ for some generating-family-bounded AFL $\mathscr{L}'$, then $\mathscr{L}$ is not closed under intersection.*

Corollary 3: *Let $\mathscr{L}$ be a full semi-AFL containing a nonregular set. If $\mathscr{L} \subseteq \mathscr{L}'$ for some (full) generating-family-bounded AFL or semi-AFL $\mathscr{L}'$, then $\hat{\mathscr{F}}_{\hat{\sigma}}(\mathscr{L})$ is neither principal nor full principal.*

Proof: Suppose $\mathscr{L} \subseteq \mathscr{L}'$ for some (full) generating-family-bounded AFL or semi-AFL $\mathscr{L}'$. By Corollary 1, $\mathrm{Sub}(\mathscr{L}, \mathscr{L}) = \hat{\mathrm{Sub}}(\mathscr{L}, \mathscr{L}) \subseteq \mathscr{L}$ is false. By Theorem 6.5.2, $\hat{\mathscr{F}}_{\hat{\sigma}}(\mathscr{L})$ is neither principal nor full principal.

Example 7.3.1: Let $\mathscr{L} = \mathscr{F}(L)$, where $L = \{a^n b^n / n \geqq 1\}$. Then $\mathscr{L}$ is not closed under ϵ-free substitution by Corollary 1 above.

Example 7.3.2: The AFL $\mathscr{L}_{\mathrm{CF}}$ is closed under ϵ-free substitution and contains a nonregular set. Therefore $\mathscr{L}_{\mathrm{CF}}$ is not a subfamily of any generating-family-bounded AFL.

EXAMPLE 7.3.3: Let $\mathscr{L} \subseteq \mathscr{L}_{CF}$ be a generating-family-bounded AFL containing a nonregular set. Then $\mathscr{L}' = \hat{\mathscr{F}}(\mathscr{L}) \subseteq \mathscr{L}_{CF}$ is a full generating-family-bounded AFL containing a nonregular set. Since $\mathscr{L}_{CF}$ is closed under substitution, $\hat{\mathscr{F}}_{\hat{\sigma}}(\mathscr{L}') \subseteq \mathscr{L}_{CF}$. By Corollary 3, $\hat{\mathscr{F}}_{\hat{\sigma}}(\mathscr{L}')$ is not full principal. As noted earlier, $\mathscr{L}_{CF}$ is full principal. Thus $\hat{\mathscr{F}}_{\hat{\sigma}}(\mathscr{L}) \subseteq \hat{\mathscr{F}}_{\hat{\sigma}}(\mathscr{L}') \subsetneq \mathscr{L}_{CF}$.

EXERCISE 7.3.1: Show that $\{a^{2^n}/n \geqq 1\}/(a^4)^* = (a^4)^*$ for each element a in Σ.

EXERCISE 7.3.2: Prove that $\{a^{2^n}/n \geqq 1\}/((a^4)^* \cup \{a\})$ is not regular, for each element a in Σ. Thus infer that Lemma 7.3.2 cannot be generalized to the case where $(a^r)^*a^k$ is replaced by an arbitrary infinite regular set.

EXERCISE 7.3.3: Let $\mathscr{L}_1$ and $\mathscr{L}_2$ be AFL, each containing a nonregular set. Prove that $\mathscr{L}_1 \wedge \mathscr{L}_2$ is contained in no generating-family-bounded AFL [Go1].

EXERCISE 7.3.4: Prove that if $\mathscr{D}$ is an AFA such that $\mathscr{L}^t(\mathscr{D})$ contains a nonregular set, then $\mathscr{L}^t(\mathscr{D} \wedge \mathscr{D})$ is contained in no generating-family-bounded AFL.

EXERCISE 7.3.5: Let $L \subseteq a_1^* \ldots a_n^*$ and let M be an a-transducer such that $M(L) = L_1c \ldots cL_{2n+2}$ for languages $L_1, \ldots, L_{2n+2}$ and a symbol c not in $\bigcup_i \Sigma_{L_i}$. Prove that at least one of the L_i is regular [Le, b].

EXERCISE 7.3.6: Let $\mathscr{U}$ be a family of m-bounded languages and $\mathscr{L} \subseteq \hat{\mathscr{S}}(\mathscr{U})$ a semi-AFL closed under concatenation. Prove that either $\mathscr{L} = \mathscr{R}_0$ or $\mathscr{L} = \mathscr{R}$ [Gr6].

EXERCISE 7.3.7: Let $\mathscr{U}$ be a family of bounded languages. Prove that $\hat{\mathscr{F}}(\mathscr{U}) - \hat{\mathscr{S}}(\mathscr{U}) = \emptyset$ if and only if $\mathscr{U} \subseteq \mathscr{R}$ [Gr6; Le, b].

In Exercises 7.3.8, 7.3.9, and 7.3.10, let OP($\mathscr{L}$) be as in Exercise 6.1.12.

EXERCISE 7.3.8: Let $\mathscr{L}_1$ be a family of bounded languages and $\mathscr{L}_2 = \hat{\mathscr{F}}(\mathscr{L}_1)$. Prove each of the following [Le, a]:

(a) OP($\mathscr{L}_2$) $= \mathscr{R}$.
(b) OP(Sûb ($\mathscr{L}_3$, $\mathscr{L}_2$)) $= \mathscr{L}_3$ for each substitution-closed full AFL $\mathscr{L}_3$.

EXERCISE 7.3.9: Let $\mathscr{L}_1$ and $\mathscr{L}_2$ be incomparable full semi-AFL. Prove each of the following for $\mathscr{L} = \hat{\mathscr{F}}(\mathscr{L}_1 \cup \mathscr{L}_2)$ [Le, a]:

(a) $\mathrm{OP}(\mathscr{L}) = \mathscr{R}$.
(b) $\mathrm{OP}(\hat{\mathrm{Sub}}\,(\mathscr{L}_3, \mathscr{L})) = \mathscr{L}_3$ for each substitution-closed full AFL $\mathscr{L}_3$.

EXERCISE 7.3.10: Let $\mathscr{L}_1$ be a substitution-closed full AFL not containing every language. Prove that there exists a full AFL $\mathscr{L}_2 \neq \mathscr{L}_1$ such that $\mathrm{OP}(\mathscr{L}_2) = \mathscr{L}_1$ and $\mathscr{L}_2$ is not substitution closed [Le, b].

EXERCISE 7.3.11: Let a and b be two symbols. Prove that if L is a non-regular subset of a^*b^* then $\hat{\mathrm{Sub}}(\mathscr{R}, L)$ and $\hat{\mathscr{M}}(L)$ are incomparable families of languages [Le, a]. [Hint: Use Lemma 7.3.4.]

EXERCISE 7.3.12: Let a, b, and c be three elements of Σ. Show that:
(a) $\mathscr{L}_{\mathrm{CF}}$ and $\hat{\mathscr{F}}(\{a^n b^n c^n / n \geqq 1\})$ are incomparable.
(b) $\mathscr{L}_{\mathrm{lin}}$ and $\hat{\mathscr{F}}(\{a^n b^n c^n / n \geqq 1\})$ are incomparable.

EXERCISE 7.3.13: Let $\mathscr{L}$ be the largest full AFL properly contained in $\mathscr{L}_{\mathrm{RE}}$. [See Example 6.6.4.] Prove that there is no bounded language in $\mathscr{L}_{\mathrm{RE}} - \mathscr{L}$.

7.4 Symbol Loops

For $\mathcal{O} = \mathscr{M}$ or $\mathscr{F}$ and for nonempty languages U and V, consider the problem of determining if $\mathcal{O}(V) \subseteq \mathcal{O}(U)[\hat{\mathcal{O}}(V) \subseteq \hat{\mathcal{O}}(U)]$. As a rule, it is usually much easier to show, when so, that $\mathcal{O}(V) \subseteq \mathcal{O}(U)[\hat{\mathcal{O}}(V) \subseteq \hat{\mathcal{O}}(U)]$ than to establish, when so, its denial.[1] One standard approach to the latter problem consists in (i) deriving some necessary conditions for $\mathcal{O}(V) \subseteq \mathcal{O}(U)\,[\hat{\mathcal{O}}(V) \subseteq \hat{\mathcal{O}}(U)]$ to hold and then (ii) verifying that at least one of the conditions is violated for the pair (U, V). The case when U and V are bounded will now be treated. The situation is quite complicated and, as yet, not fully understood. In the present section, two types of loops, the "symbol loops" and "a-symbol loops" are examined. The main result (Lemma 7.4.7) is that under certain conditions, each computation may be replaced by an equivalent one, i. e., by one with the same input and the same output, which has certain restrictions on the nature and number of occurrences of its symbol loops. Using this result and two lesser ones (Lemma 7.4.3 and 7.4.4), some progress is made in Section 7.5 on (i) and (ii) for bounded

[1] Since the generators involved are nonempty, the trio and semi-AFL cases coincide. Thus $\mathcal{O} = \mathscr{S}$ is not specifically mentioned.

languages U and V, in particular, when $U \subseteq a_1^* \ldots a_m^*$ and $V \subseteq b_1^* \ldots b_n^*$, where $b_1, \ldots, b_n$ are distinct symbols.

The two types of loops of interest to us are the following:

Def: Let $M = (K_1, \Sigma_1, \Sigma_2, H, p_0, F)$ be an a-transducer. A word

$$(*) \qquad (p_1, u_1, v_1, p_2) \ldots (p_t, u_t, v_t, p_{t+1})$$

is said to be a *symbol loop* (*of* M) if $t \geqq 1$, each (p_i, u_i, v_i, p_{i+1}) is in H, $p_1 = p_{t+1}$, $p_i \neq p_j$ for $i \neq j$, $1 \leqq i, j \leqq t$, $u_1 \ldots u_t$ is in a^* for some a in Σ_1, and $v_1 \ldots v_t$ is in b^* for some b in Σ_2. If, in addition, $u_1 \ldots u_t$ is in a^+, then $(*)$ is called an *a-symbol loop*.

Clearly each symbol loop is a loop. The converse is not true. For example, $(p_1, a^2, b^3, p_2)(p_2, a, \epsilon, p_2)(p_2, a^2, b, p_1)$ and (p_1, ab, b^2, p_1) are loops, but not symbol loops.

No proper subword of a symbol loop can be a loop. Hence there are only a finite number of symbol loops in each a-transducer.

For each symbol loop γ in M and each integer $k > 1$ there are $|\gamma|-1$ other symbol loops, each a subword of γ^k, occurring exactly $k-1$ times in γ^k, and consisting of the same elements of H as γ. For example, if $\gamma = \alpha_1\alpha_2\alpha_3$ is a symbol loop, α_1, α_2, and α_3 in H, then $\alpha_2\alpha_3\alpha_1$ and $\alpha_3\alpha_1\alpha_2$ are symbol loops, each occurring exactly four times in γ^5. For our purposes, these $|\gamma|$ symbol loops are "essentially the same". This idea of "essentially the same" is abstracted under the technical term "associated with" next given.

Def: A symbol loop γ_1 is said to be *associated with* a symbol loop γ_2 if there exist words α_1 and α_2 in H^* such that $\gamma_1 = \alpha_1\alpha_2$ and $\gamma_2 = \alpha_2\alpha_1$. Otherwise, γ_1 is said to be *nonassociated with* γ_2.

Clearly the concept of "associated with" is symmetric (and transitive). Thus "γ_1 associated with γ_2" can be read as "γ_1 and γ_2 are associated", and "γ_1 nonassociated with γ_2" as "γ_1 and γ_2 are nonassociated".

Note that if γ_1 and γ_2 are associated, then $h_1(\gamma_1) = h_1(\gamma_2)$ and $h_2(\gamma_1) = h_2(\gamma_2)$.

In studying $M(U)$, where M is an a-transducer, $U \subseteq a_1^* \ldots a_m^*$, and $M(U) \subseteq b_1^* \ldots b_n^*$, we shall be examining certain computations of M. Those computations which can be factored into a form displaying powers of nonassociated symbol loops, with the subwords between these symbol loops containing no symbol loops, play a particularly important role. Hence the following:

Def: A computation α is said to be in *standard form* if

$$\alpha = w_1\gamma_1^{k_1}w_2 \ldots w_r\gamma_r^{k_r}w_{r+1},$$

where $\gamma_1, \ldots, \gamma_r$, $r \geqq 0$, are pairwise nonassociated symbol loops, no w_i contains a symbol loop, and $k_j \geqq 1$ for each j.

When speaking of a computation $\alpha = w_1\gamma_1^{k_1} \ldots w_r\gamma_r^{k_r}w_{r+1}$ in standard form, it will be assumed that $\gamma_1, \ldots, \gamma_r$ are nonassociated symbol loops, no w_i contains a symbol loop, and $k_j \geqq 1$ for each j.

It turns out, as proved in Lemma 7.4.1, that a computation in $h_1^{-1}(U) \cap \Pi_M$ may always be assumed in standard form.

Notation: In the sequel, $n \geqq 1$ and $b_1, \ldots, b_n$ are distinct symbols in Σ.

LEMMA 7.4.1: *Let M be an a-transducer, $U \subseteq a_1^* \ldots a_m^*$, and $M(U) \subseteq b_1^* \ldots b_n^*$. Then for every computation α in $h_1^{-1}(U) \cap \Pi_M$ there exists a computation α' in standard form such that $h_1(\alpha') = h_1(\alpha)$ and $h_2(\alpha') = h_2(\alpha)$.*

Proof: If α contains no symbol loop, then $\alpha' = \alpha$ satisfies the conclusion of the lemma. Suppose α contains a symbol loop. Then $\alpha = w_1\gamma_1u_1$, where γ_1 is a symbol loop and w_1 contains no symbol loop.

Using induction, suppose that for $j = 1, \ldots, r$, α_j is defined and of the form $w_{j1}\gamma_{j1}^{l_{j1}} \ldots w_{js(j)}\gamma_{js(j)}^{l_{js(j)}}u_{j+1}$, where the γ_{ji} are pairwise nonassociated, each l_{ji} is a positive integer, no w_{ji} contains a symbol loop, $|\alpha_j| = |\alpha|$, $h_1(\alpha_j) = h_1(\alpha)$, $h_2(\alpha_j) = h_2(\alpha)$, $|u_{j+1}| < |u_j|$, and u_j contains a symbol loop. If u_{r+1} contains no symbol loop, let $\alpha' = \alpha_r$. Clearly α' satisfies the conclusion of the lemma. Suppose u_{r+1} contains a symbol loop. To simplify the notation let $w_{r1} = w_1$, $\gamma_{r1} = \gamma_1$, $l_{r1} = l_1, \ldots, w_{rs(r)} = w_s$, $\gamma_{rs(r)} = \gamma_s$, and $l_{rs(r)} = l_s$. Two cases arise.

(α) u_{r+1} contains some symbol loop associated with some γ_i. Let t be the smallest integer such that u_{r+1} contains a symbol loop γ associated with γ_t. Hence there exist words v_1 and v_2 in H^* such that $\gamma_t = v_1v_2$ and $\gamma = v_2v_1$. Then $\alpha_r = \beta_rv_1v_2\beta_r'u_{r+1}'v_2v_1u_{r+1}''$ for some β_r, β_r', u_{r+1}', and u_{r+1}'' in H^* such that $\beta_r = w_1\gamma_1^{l_1}w_2 \ldots \gamma_t^{l_t-1}$, $\beta_r' = \epsilon$ if $s = t$ and $\beta_r' = w_{t+1} \ldots \gamma_s^{l_s}$ if $t < s$, and $u_{r+1} = u_{r+1}'v_2v_1u_{r+1}''$. Obviously $h_1(\gamma_t\beta_r'u_{r+1}'\gamma) = h_1(\gamma_t\gamma_t\beta_r'u_{r+1}')$ if $h_1(\gamma_t) = \epsilon$. Suppose $h_1(\gamma_t) \neq \epsilon$. Then $h_1(\gamma_t) = h_1(\gamma)$ is in a_i^+ for some i. From this and the fact that $U \subseteq a_1^* \ldots a_m^*$, it follows that $h_1(\beta_r'u_{r+1}')$ is in a_i^*. Then $h_1(\gamma_t\beta_r'u_{r+1}'\gamma) = h_1(v_1v_2\beta_r'u_{r+1}'\gamma) = h_1(v_1\gamma v_2\beta_r'u_{r+1}') = h_1(v_1v_2v_1v_2\beta_r'u_{r+1}') = h_1(\gamma_t^2\beta_r'u_{r+1}')$. Similarly, $h_2(\gamma_t\beta_r'u_{r+1}'\gamma) = h_2(\gamma_t^2\beta_r'w_{r+1}')$. Let $\alpha_{r+1} = w_1\gamma_1^{l_1} \ldots w_t\gamma_t^{l_t+1} \ldots \gamma_s^{l_s}u_{r+2}$, where $u_{r+2} = u_{r+1}'u_{r+1}''$.

(β) u_{r+1} contains no symbol loop associated with some γ_i. Let $\alpha_{r+1} = w_1\gamma_1^{l_1}w_2\gamma_2^{l_2} \ldots w_s\gamma_s^{l_s}w_{s+1}\gamma_{s+1}u_{r+2}$, where γ_{s+1} is a symbol loop, $u_{r+1} = w_{s+1}\gamma_{s+1}u_{r+2}$, and w_{s+1} contains no symbol loop.

In each case, the γ_i are pairwise nonassociated, the exponents on the γ_i are positive integers, no w_i contains a symbol loop, $|\alpha_{r+1}| = |\alpha|$, $h_1(\alpha_{r+1}) = h_1(\alpha_r) = h_1(\alpha)$, $h_2(\alpha_{r+1}) = h_2(\alpha_r) = h_2(\alpha)$, $|u_{r+2}| < |u_{r+1}|$, and u_{r+1} contains a symbol loop. Thus the induction is extended. Since $|u_{j+1}| < |u_j|$ for each j, the process terminates for some integer r_0. This can only occur if u_{r_0+1} contains no symbol loop. Then $\alpha' = \alpha_{r_0}$ satisfies the conclusion of the lemma.

In the previous lemma, "moving a symbol loop γ" meant deleting γ at one place and inserting it at another, without changing either the total input or output. The next lemma asserts that it is possible to make "exchanges" in a computation so that most of the occurrences of a symbol loop at one place are replaced by some occurrences of a second symbol loop at another place, while still preserving the total input (although the output may be changed). In this way, a computation is obtained in which, for each i, "most" of the a_i-symbol loops are associated.

LEMMA 7.4.2: *Let M be an a-transducer, $U \subseteq a_1^* \ldots a_m^*$, and $M(U) \subseteq b_1^* \ldots b_n^*$. Let $k = \max\{|h_1(\gamma)|+1, 2/\gamma$ a symbol loop$\}$. Then for every computation $\alpha = w_1\gamma_1^{k_1}w_2\gamma_2^{k_2}w_3$ in $h_1^{-1}(U) \cap \Pi_M$, where γ_1 and γ_2 are nonassociated a_i-symbol loops for some i and k_1, k_2 are positive integers; there exist computations α' and α'' such that*

(a) $\alpha' = w_1\gamma_1^{l_1}w_2\gamma_2^{l_2}w_3$, $0 < l_1 < k$, *and*
$\alpha'' = w_1\gamma_1^{p_1}w_2\gamma_2^{p_2}w_3$, $0 < p_2 < k$,
(b) $h_1(\alpha') = h_1(\alpha'') = h_1(\alpha)$, *and*
(c) $l_2 > k_2 (p_1 > k_1)$ *if* $k_1 \geqq k$ $(k_2 \geqq k)$.

Proof: Since there are only finitely many symbol loops in M, k exists. Clearly $k \geqq 2$. Consider α', an analogous argument holding for α''. If $k_1 < k$, then $\alpha' = \alpha$ satisfies the conclusion of the lemma. Suppose $k_1 \geqq k$. Let t be the smallest nonnegative integer such that $0 < k_1 - t\,|h_1(\gamma_2)| < k$. Since γ_2 is an a_i-symbol loop, $h_1(\gamma_2) \neq \epsilon$. Furthermore, $|h_1(\gamma_2)| < k$. Thus t exists. Let $\alpha' = w_1\gamma_1^{l_1}w_2\gamma_2^{l_2}w_3$, where $l_1 = k_1 - t\,|h_1(\gamma_2)|$ and $l_2 = k_2 + t|\,h_1(\gamma_1)|$. Clearly α' satisfies (a). Since $U \subseteq a_1^* \ldots a_m^*$, with the $a_1, \ldots, a_m$ distinct symbols, and since both γ_1 and γ_2 are a_i-symbol loops, $h_1(w_2)$ is in a_i^*. Obviously $|h_1(\gamma_1^{l_1}w_2\gamma_2^{l_2})| = |h_1(\gamma_1^{k_1}w_2\gamma_2^{k_2})|$. Thus $h_1(\gamma_1^{l_1}w_2\gamma_2^{l_2}) = h_1(\gamma_1^{k_1}w_2\gamma_2^{k_2})$. Hence $h_1(\alpha') = h_1(\alpha)$, so that (b) is satisfied. Since γ_1 is an a_i-symbol loop, $|h_1(\gamma_1)| \geqq 1$. Then $t \geqq 1$ and $t|\,h_1(\gamma_1)| \geqq 1$. Thus $l_2 > k_2$, and (c) holds.

In Lemma 7.4.2 we were able to show that $h_1(\alpha) = h_1(\alpha')$. In general, $h_2(\alpha) = h_2(\alpha')$ is false. [See Exercise 7.4.5.] In order to guarantee that

$h_2(\alpha) = h_2(\alpha')$, as is done in Lemma 7.4.7, we have to restrict both the type of output language and the type of a-transducer. The type of output language used in Lemma 7.4.7 is the following:

Notation: Let $\langle b_1^{g_1(x)} \dots b_n^{g_n(x)} \rangle$ denote the set $\{b_1^{g_1(x)} \dots b_n^{g_n(x)}/x \geqq 0\}$, where $n \geqq 2$ and $g_1, \dots, g_n$ are strictly increasing functions from N into N.

EXAMPLE 7.4.1: The set $\{b_1^{x^3} b_2^{x^2+3x+7}/x \geqq 0\}$ can be written as $\langle b_1^{x^3} b_2^{x^2+3x+7} \rangle$. The set $\{b_1^{x^3} b_2^{x^2-4x+9}/x \geqq 0\}$ cannot be written as $\langle b_1^{x^3} b_2^{x^2-4x+9} \rangle$ since x^2-4x+9 is not a strictly increasing function.

The type of a-transducer used in Lemma 7.4.7 is:

Def: An a-transducer M is said to be ϵ-*loop-free* if $h_1(\gamma) \neq \epsilon$ or $h_2(\gamma) \neq \epsilon$ for each symbol loop of M.

Thus an a-transducer is ϵ-loop-free if there is no symbol loop γ such that $h_1(\gamma) = h_2(\gamma) = \epsilon$.

There is no real loss, as is now shown, in restricting the a-transducer to be ϵ-loop-free.

LEMMA 7.4.3: *For each* (ϵ-*free*) *a-transducer M there exists an* (ϵ-*free*) ϵ-*loop-free a-transducer M' such that $M'(L) = M(L)$ for each language L.*

Proof: If M is ϵ-free, there is nothing to prove since each ϵ-free a-transducer is, perforce, ϵ-loop-free. Suppose M is an arbitrary a-transducer. Let $M = (K_1, \Sigma_1, \Sigma_2, H, p_0, F)$ and let

$$A(p) = \{q \text{ in } K_1/(p, \epsilon, \epsilon) \overset{*}{\vdash} (q, \epsilon, \epsilon)\}$$

for each p in K_1. Let $H' = A_1 \cup A_2$, where

$$A_1 = \{p, u, v, q)/uv \neq \epsilon, (p, u, v, p') \text{ in } H \text{ and } q \text{ in } A(p')\}$$

and

$$A_2 = \{(p_0, \epsilon, \epsilon, p)/p \text{ in } A(p_0) - \{p_0\}\}.$$

Let $M' = (K_1, \Sigma_1, \Sigma_2, H', p_0, F)$. By construction, if $(p, \epsilon, \epsilon, q)$ is in H' then $p = p_0$ and $q \neq p_0$. This implies that M' is ϵ-loop-free. Clearly $M'(L) = M(L)$ for each language L.

The next lemma asserts that, in an ϵ-loop-free a-transducer whose output is of the form $\langle b_1^{g_1(x)} \dots b_n^{g_n(x)} \rangle$, each symbol loop in a computation is an a_i-symbol loop for some i. This result is used both in Lemma 7.4.7 and in Section 7.5.

LEMMA 7.4.4: *Let M be an ϵ-loop-free a-transducer, $U \subseteq a_1^* \ldots a_m^*$, and $M(U) = \langle b_1^{g_1(x)} \ldots b_n^{g_n(x)} \rangle$. Then $h_1(\gamma) \neq \epsilon$ for each symbol loop γ in a computation in $h_1^{-1}(U) \cap \Pi_M$.*

Proof: Suppose the contrary. Then there exist α in $h_1^{-1}(U) \cap \Pi_M$ and a symbol loop γ such that $\alpha = v_1\gamma v_2$, with v_1v_2 in H^* and $h_1(\gamma) = \epsilon$. Since M is ϵ-loop-free, $h_2(\gamma) \neq \epsilon$. Let $\alpha' = v_1\gamma\gamma v_2$. Clearly α' is in $h_1^{-1}(U) \cap \Pi_M$ and $h_1(\alpha') = h_1(\alpha)$. Since γ is a symbol loop and $h_2(\gamma) \neq \epsilon$, $h_2(\gamma) = b_j^l$ for some j, $1 \leqq j \leqq n$, and some $l \geqq 1$. Let $h_2(\alpha) = b_1^{k_1} \ldots b_n^{k_n}$. Then $h_2(\alpha') = b_1^{k_1} \ldots b_j^{k_j+l} \ldots b_n^{k_n}$. Since each function g_i is strictly increasing, $n \geqq 2$, and $k_j + l > k_j$, $h_2(\alpha')$ is in $M(U)$ but not in $\langle b_1^{g_1(x)} \ldots b_n^{g_n(x)} \rangle$. This is a contradiction.

We need two more lemmas to establish Lemma 7.4.7. The first asserts that for each a_i, all the displayed a_i-symbol loops occurring a large number of times in a given computation in standard form have the same ratio of output length to input length. The second lemma provides a characterization of when two symbol loops are associated.

LEMMA 7.4.5: *Let M be an ϵ-loop-free a-transducer, $U \subseteq a_1^* \ldots a_m^*$, and $M(U) = \langle b_1^{g_1(x)} \ldots b_n^{g_n(x)} \rangle$. Let $k = \max \{|h_1(\gamma)| + 1, 2 / \gamma \text{ a symbol loop}\}$ and let $\alpha = v_1\gamma_1^{k_1} \ldots v_r\gamma_r^{k_r}v_{r+1}$ in $h_1^{-1}(U) \cap \Pi_M$ be a computation in standard form. Then for each i, $1 \leqq i \leqq m$, a_i-symbol loops γ_s and γ_t, $1 \leqq s, t \leqq r$, and $k_s \geqq k$, the following hold*:

(a) *$h_2(\gamma_s)$ and $h_2(\gamma_t)$ are both in b_j^* for some j, $1 \leqq j \leqq n$, and*

(b) $\dfrac{|h_2(\gamma_s)|}{|h_1(\gamma_s)|} = \dfrac{|h_2(\gamma_t)|}{|h_1(\gamma_t)|}$.

Proof: By definition of symbol loop there exist integers j and l, $1 \leqq j, l \leqq n$, such that $h_2(\gamma_s)$ is in b_j^* and $h_2(\gamma_t)$ is in b_l^*. If $s = t$ then the lemma holds trivially. Suppose $s \neq t$, say $s < t$. (An analogous argument holds for $s > t$.) Then $\alpha = w_1\gamma_s^{k_s}w_2\gamma_t^{k_t}w_3$ for appropriate w_1, w_2, and w_3, with $k_s \geqq k$ and $k_t \geqq 1$. Since $h_2(\alpha)$ is in $M(U)$, $h_2(\alpha) = b_1^{z_1} \ldots b_n^{z_n}$ for some $z_1, \ldots, z_n$. By Lemma 7.4.2, there exists a computation α' such that (i) $\alpha' = w_1\gamma_s^{l_s}w_2\gamma_t^{l_t}w_3$, $0 < l_s < k$, (ii) $h_1'(\alpha') = h_1(\alpha)$, and (iii) $l_t > k_t$. Note that $h_2(\alpha')$ is in $M(U)$. Four cases arise:

(α) $h_2(\gamma_s) = \epsilon$ and $h_2(\gamma_t) = \epsilon$. Then (a) and (b) are satisfied, since $|h_1(\gamma_s)| \neq 0$ and $|h_1(\gamma_t)| \neq 0$.

(β) $h_2(\gamma_s) = \epsilon$ and $h_2(\gamma_t) \neq \epsilon$. Then $h_2(\gamma_t) = b_u^e$ for some u, $1 \leqq u \leqq n$, and $e \geqq 1$. Since $h_2(\gamma_s) = \epsilon$,

$$\begin{aligned} h_2(\alpha') &= h_2(w_1\gamma_s^{l_s}w_2\gamma_t^{l_t}w_3) \\ &= h_2(w_1w_2\gamma_t^{l_s}w_3). \end{aligned}$$

Since $h_2(\gamma_t) = b_u^e$ and $l_t > k_t$,

$$\begin{aligned} h_2(\alpha') &= h_2(w_1 w_2 \gamma_t^{k_t} \gamma_t^{l_t - k_t} w_3) \\ &= h_2(w_1 w_2 \gamma_t^{k_t})\, h_2(\gamma_t^{l_t - k_t})\, h_2(w_3) \\ &= b_1^{z_1} \dots b_u^{z_u} b_u^{e(l_t - k_t)} b_{u+1}^{z_{u+1}} \dots b_n^{z_n}. \end{aligned}$$

Then $b_1^{z_1} \dots b_n^{z_n}$ and $b_1^{z_1} \dots b_u^{z_u + e(l_t - k_t)} \dots b_n^{z_n}$ are both in $M(U)$. Since $l_t - k_t > 0$ and $e \geqq 1$, this contradicts the fact that $g_1, \dots, g_n$ are strictly increasing functions. Thus (β) does not occur.

(γ) $h_2(\gamma_s) \neq \epsilon$ and $h_2(\gamma_t) = \epsilon$. This case produces a contradiction similar to (β).

(δ) $h_2(\gamma_s) \neq \epsilon$ and $h_2(\gamma_t) \neq \epsilon$. Then $h_2(\gamma_s) = b_j^d$ and $h_2(\gamma_t) = b_u^e$ for some j and u, $1 \leqq j, u \leqq n$, and $d, e \geqq 1$.

Consider (a). Suppose $j \neq u$. Then $j < u$, since $s < t$. Thus

$$\begin{aligned} h_2(\alpha') &= h_2(w_1 \gamma_s^{l_s} w_2 \gamma_t^{l_t} w_3) \\ &= h_2(w_1 \gamma_s^{k_s - (k_s - l_s)} w_2 \gamma_t^{k_t + (l_t - k_t)} w_3) \\ &= b_1^{z_1} \dots b_j^{z_j - (k_s - l_s) d} \dots b_u^{z_u + (l_t - k_t) e} \dots b_n^{z_n}. \end{aligned}$$

This is a contradiction, since $g_1, \dots, g_n$ are strictly increasing functions, $h_2(\alpha)$ and $h_2(\alpha')$ are in $M(U)$, $l_t - k_t > 0$, $k_s - l_s > 0$, $e > 0$, and $d > 0$. Hence $j = u$, and (a) holds.

Consider (b). Let $\bar{\alpha} = w_1 \gamma_s^{k_s - |h_1(\gamma_t)|} w_2 \gamma_t^{k_t + |h_1(\gamma_s)|} w_3$. (Note that $k_s - |h_1(\gamma_t)| > 0$, since $k_s \geqq k$.) Since (a) holds, $h_2(w_2)$ is in b_j^*. Then $h_2(\bar{\alpha}) = b_1^{z_1} \dots b_j^{z_j + k'} \dots b_n^{z_n}$, where

$$k' = |h_1(\gamma_s)|\,|h_2(\gamma_t)| - |h_1(\gamma_t)|\,|h_2(\gamma_s)|.$$

Since γ_s and γ_t are a_i-symbol loops and $U \subseteq a_1^* \dots a_m^*$, $h_1(w_2)$ is in a_i^*. Clearly $h_1(\alpha) = h_1(\bar{\alpha})$. Hence $h_2(\bar{\alpha})$ is in $M(U)$. Now $g_1, \dots, g_n$ are strictly increasing functions. Thus $h_2(\bar{\alpha})$ is not in $\langle b_1^{g_1(x)} \dots b_n^{g_n(x)} \rangle$ if $k' \neq 0$, a contradiction. Therefore $k' = 0$. Since γ_s and γ_t are a_i-symbol loops, $|h_1(\gamma_s)| \neq 0$ and $|h_1(\gamma_t)| \neq 0$. Thus (b) holds.

LEMMA 7.4.6: *The following statements are equivalent for symbol loops* γ_1 *and* γ_2:

(1) γ_1 *is associated with* γ_2.

(2) γ_1 *is a subword of* γ_2^2.

(3) γ_1 *is a subword of* γ_2^k *for some integer* k.

Proof: Suppose (1) holds. Hence $\gamma_1 = \alpha_1\alpha_2$ and $\gamma_2 = \alpha_2\alpha_1$ for some α_1, α_2 in H^*. Then $\gamma_2\gamma_2 = \alpha_2\alpha_1\alpha_2\alpha_1 = \alpha_2\gamma_1\alpha_1$, so that (2) holds.

Consider (2) implies (1). Suppose γ_1 is a subword of $\gamma_2\gamma_2$. Let $\gamma_1 = \theta_1 \ldots \theta_m$ and $\gamma_2 = \theta'_1 \ldots \theta'_n$, where $m, n \geqq 1$, and each θ_i, θ'_j is in H. Let $\theta'_i = (p_i, u_i, v_i, p_{i+1})$ for each i, with $p_1 = p_{n+1}$. Since γ_1 is a subword of $\gamma_2\gamma_2$, there exist words α_1 and α_2 such that $\gamma_2 = \alpha_2\alpha_1$ and γ_1 is an initial subword of $\alpha_1\alpha_2\alpha_1$. Since $\theta_i \neq \theta_j$ for all $i \neq j$, γ_1 is an initial subword of $\alpha_1\alpha_2$. Let $\alpha_2 = \theta'_1 \ldots \theta'_s$ and $\alpha_1 = \theta'_{s+1} \ldots \theta'_n$ for some s, $0 \leqq s \leqq n$. Suppose $s = n$. Then $\alpha_1 = \epsilon$ and γ_1 is an initial subword of $\alpha_2 = \gamma_2$, whence $\gamma_1 = \gamma_2 = \alpha_1\alpha_2$. Suppose $s = 0$. Then $\alpha_2 = \epsilon$ and γ_1 is an initial subword of $\alpha_1 = \gamma_2$, whence $\gamma_1 = \gamma_2 = \alpha_1\alpha_2$. Suppose $1 \leqq s < n$. If γ_1 is a proper initial subword of $\alpha_1\alpha_2 = \theta'_{s+1} \ldots \theta'_n\theta'_1 \ldots \theta'_s$, then $p'_{s+1} = p'_{t+1}$ for some $t \neq s$, $1 \leqq t < n$, contradicting the fact that $\alpha_2\alpha_1$ is a symbol loop. Thus $\gamma_1 = \alpha_1\alpha_2$. Hence (1) holds.

Obviously (2) implies (3). To complete the proof it thus suffices to show that (3) implies (2). Suppose (3) holds. Assume γ_1 is not a subword of γ_2^2. Then $k \geqq 3$, so that γ_2 is a proper subword of γ_1 since γ_1 is a subword of γ_2^k. But no symbol loop can be a proper subword of another symbol loop. Hence γ_1 is a subword of γ_2^2, i.e., (2) holds.

We are now ready for the main result of the section, Lemma 7.4.7. This asserts that each computation may be assumed to be of the form $v_1\gamma_1^{k_1} \ldots v_m\gamma_m^{k_m}v_{m+1}$, where each $k_i \geqq 0$, each γ_i is an a_i-symbol loop, and $v_1 \ldots v_{m+1}$ has a bounded number (depending only on M) of symbol loops.

LEMMA 7.4.7: *Let M be an ϵ-loop-free a-transducer, $U \subseteq a_1^* \ldots a_m^*$, and $M(U) = \langle b_1^{g_1(x)} \ldots b_n^{g_n(x)} \rangle$. Then there exists an integer $\bar{k}$, depending only on M, with the following property*: *For each computation α in $h_1^{-1}(U) \cap \Pi_M$ there exists $\alpha' = v_1\gamma_1^{k_1} \ldots v_m\gamma_m^{k_m}v_{m+1}$ in $h_1^{-1}(U) \cap \Pi_M$, each $k_i \geqq 0$, such that*

(a) $h_1(\alpha') = h_1(\alpha)$ *and* $h_2(\alpha') = h_2(\alpha)$;

(b) *each γ_i is an a_i-symbol loop*; *and*

(c) *for each symbol loop γ in M and each i, $1 \leqq i \leqq m+1$, v_i has at most $\bar{k}-1$ occurrences of γ.*

Proof: By the addition of new states p_i and rules (p_i, a_i, b_1, p_i), we may assume that M has an a_i-symbol loop for each i. By Lemma 7.4.1, we may assume that $\alpha = w_1\gamma_1'^{l_1} \ldots w_r\gamma_r'^{l_r}w_{r+1}$ is in standard form. By Lemma 7.4.5, $h_1(\gamma'_i) \neq \epsilon$ for each i. Let R_α be the set of all i such that γ'_j is an a_i-symbol loop for some j, and let $R'_\alpha = \{1, \ldots, m\} - R_\alpha$. For each i in R_α let $j(i)$ be the smallest integer such that $\gamma'_{j(i)}$ is an a_i-symbol loop. Let $Q_\alpha = \{j(i)/i \text{ in } R_\alpha\}$. Let $k = \max\{|h_1(\gamma)|+1, 2/\gamma$ a symbol loop in $M\}$ and $Q'_\alpha = \{j$ not in $Q_\alpha/l_j \geqq k\}$. Let $s_\alpha = \#(Q'_\alpha)$. Let $\gamma_i = \gamma'_{j(i)}$ for i in R_α and γ_i be an arbitrary a_i-symbol loop in M for each i in R'_α. Clearly γ_i is defined for each i. Let $\bar{k} = k+2k'$, where k' is the number of symbol loops in M. Note that $\bar{k}$ depends only on M. The proof will be by induction on s_α.

Suppose $s_\alpha = 0$. Let $k_i = l_{j(i)}$ for i in R_α and $k_i = 0$ for i in R'_α. For each i, $1 \leqq i \leqq m+1$, let $t(i) = j(i-1)+1$ and $t'(i) = j(i)-t(i)$, with $j(m+1) = r+1$. Clearly $\alpha = v_1\gamma_1^{k_1}\ldots v_m\gamma_m^{k_m}v_{m+1}$, where $v_1 = w_1$, and for each i, $1 < i \leqq m+1$,

$$v_i = w_{t(i)}\gamma_{t(i)}^{\prime l_{t(i)}} w_{t(i)+1}\ldots\gamma_{t(i)+t'(i)-1}^{\prime l_{t(i)+t'(i)-1}} w_{t(i)+t'(i)}$$

if $t'(i) > 0$ and $v_i = w_{t(i)}$ if $t'(i) = 0$. Then $\alpha' = \alpha$ satisfies (a) and (b). Consider (c). Since $v_1 = w_1$, v_1 contains no symbol loop. Let γ be a symbol loop in M. Suppose γ occurs in v_i for some i. Since $\alpha = w_1\gamma_1'^{l_1}\ldots w_r\gamma_r'^{l_r}w_{r+1}$ is in standard form, no w_j contains a symbol loop. Hence there are only the three possibilities: (α) γ occurs in $\gamma_j'^{l_j}$ for some j, $t(i) \leqq j \leqq t(i)+t'(i)-1$; ($\beta$) γ consists of a non-ϵ terminal subword of some w_j followed by an initial subword of γ'_j; or (γ) γ consists of a non-ϵ terminal subword of some γ'_j followed by an initial subword of w_{j+1}. Since $s_\alpha = 0$, $l_j < k$ for each j, $t(i) \leqq j \leqq t(i)+t'(i)-1$. Since α is in standard form, γ cannot occur as a subword of both $\gamma_j'^{l_j}$ and $\gamma_u'^{l_u}$ for $j \neq u$ by Lemma 7.4.6. Thus γ occurs at most $k-1$ times in some γ'^{l_j}. There are at most $t'(i)$ occurrences of γ in case (β) and $t'(i)$ in case (γ). Hence there are at most $z = k-1+2t'(i)$ occurrences of γ in v_i. Since $t'(i) \leqq r \leqq k'$, $z < k+2k' = \bar{k}$ and (c) holds.

Continuing by induction suppose the lemma holds for all computations α in $h_1^{-1}(U) \cap \Pi_M$ with $s_\alpha \leqq s$. Let α be in $h_1^{-1}(U) \cap \Pi_M$, with $s_\alpha = s+1$. Select j in Q'_α and let γ'_j be an a_i-symbol loop. Then $\alpha = u_1\gamma_iu_2\gamma_j'^{l_j}u_3$ for some u_1, u_2, and u_3. By Lemma 7.4.2, there exists $\bar{\alpha}$ in $h_1^{-1}(U) \cap \Pi_M$ such that (i) $\bar{\alpha} = u_1\gamma_i^{r_1}u_2\gamma_j'^{r_2}u_3$, where $r_1 = 1+t\,|h_1(\gamma'_j)|$, $r_2 = l_j - t\,|h_1(\gamma_i)|$, and t is the smallest integer such that $0 < l_j - t\,|h_1(\gamma_i)| < k$; and (ii) $h_1(\bar{\alpha}) = h_1(\alpha)$. Clearly $s_{\bar{\alpha}} = s_\alpha - 1 = s$. It thus suffices to prove that $h_2(\bar{\alpha}) = h_2(\alpha)$ since, by induction, there will then exist α' satisfying (b), (c), and $h_1(\alpha') = h_1(\bar{\alpha}) = h_1(\alpha)$ and $h_2(\alpha') = h_2(\bar{\alpha}) = h_2(\alpha)$.

Suppose $h_2(\gamma_i) = h_2(\gamma'_j) = \epsilon$. Then $h_2(\bar{\alpha}) = h_2(u_1\gamma_i^{r_1}u_2\gamma_j'^{r_2}u_3) = h_2(u_1u_2u_3) = h_2(u_1\gamma_iu_2\gamma_j'^{l_j}u_3) = h_2(\alpha)$. Suppose either $h_2(\gamma_i) \neq \epsilon$ or $h_2(\gamma'_j) \neq \epsilon$. By (b) of Lemma 7.4.5, $h_2(\gamma_i) \neq \epsilon$ and $h_2(\gamma'_j) \neq \epsilon$. By (a) of Lemma 7.4.5, $h_2(\gamma_i)$

$= b_e^{z_1}$ and $h_2(\gamma_j') = b_e^{z_2}$ for some e, $1 \leqq e \leqq n$, $z_1 \geqq 1$, and $z_2 \geqq 1$. Thus $h_2(u_2) = b_e^{z_3}$ for some $z_3 \geqq 0$. Then

$$\begin{aligned} h_2(\bar{\alpha}) &= h_2(u_1)\, h_2(\gamma_i^{r_1})\, h_2(u_2)\, h_2(\gamma_j'^{r_2})\, h_2(u_3) \\ &= h_2(u_1)\, b_e^{z_1 r_1 + z_2 r_2 + z_3} h_2(u_3). \end{aligned}$$

Similarly, $h_2(\alpha) = h_2(u_1)\, b_e^{z_1 + z_2 l_j + z_3} h_2(u_3)$. Let $y_1 = |h_1(\gamma_i)|$ and $y_2 = |h_1(\gamma_j')|$. By (b) of Lemma 7.4.5, $z_1/y_1 = z_2/y_2$. Then

$$\begin{aligned} r_1 z_1 + r_2 z_2 &= (1 + t y_2)\, z_1 + (l_j - t y_1)\, z_2 \\ &= z_1 + l_j z_2 + t(y_2 z_1 - y_1 z_2) \\ &= z_1 + l_j z_2. \end{aligned}$$

Hence $h_2(\bar{\alpha}) = h_2(\alpha)$ and the induction is extended.

EXERCISE 7.4.1: For each of the following $M = (K_1, \Sigma_1, \Sigma_2, H, p_0, F)$ and $\Sigma_1 = \Sigma_2 = \{a, b, c\}$, list all symbol loops.

(a) $H = \{(p_0, \epsilon, \epsilon, p_1), (p_0, a^2, b, p_1), (p_1, ab, b^2, p_2),$
$(p_1, a^2, b, p_0), (p_1, a^3, ba, p_0), (p_1, b, c^2, p_2), (p_2, b, \epsilon, p_1)\}$.

(b) $H = \{(p_0, a, b^2, p_1), (p_0, \epsilon, c^2, p_1), (p_1, a^2, b^3, p_0),$
$(p_1, \epsilon, \epsilon, p_2), (p_2, a^2, b, p_0), (p_2, a, \epsilon, p_0), (p_2, b, c, p_1)\}$.

EXERCISE 7.4.2: Give an example of a computation having at least two different standard forms.

EXERCISE 7.4.3: Let $M = (K_1, \Sigma_1, \Sigma_2, H, p_0, F)$ be an a-transducer, $m_1 = \max\{|h_1(\theta)| / \theta \text{ in } H\}$, $m_2 = \#(H)$, and $m_3 = \max\{\#(S)/S$ a set of pairwise nonassociated symbol loops in $M\}$. Let $U \subseteq a_1^* \ldots a_m^*$ and $M(U) \subseteq b_1^* \ldots b_n^*$. Let $\alpha = w_1 \gamma_1^{k_1} w_2 \ldots w_r \gamma_r^{k_r} w_{r+1}$ be a computation in standard form in $h_1^{-1}(U) \cap \Pi_M$ and $k \geqq 1$ an arbitrary integer. Prove the following for each j, $1 \leqq j \leqq n$: If $\#_{b_j}(h_2(\alpha)) > 3km_1m_2m_3$, then there exists an integer i, $1 \leqq i \leqq r$, such that $h_2(\gamma_i)$ is in b_j^+ and $k_i > k$ [Rv].

EXERCISE 7.4.4: Let M be an a-transducer, $U \subseteq a_1^* \ldots a_m^*$, and $M(U) \subseteq b_1^* \ldots b_n^*$. Prove that there exists an integer k with the following property: Let $\alpha = v_1 \gamma_1^{l_1} \ldots v_s \gamma_s^{l_s} v_{s+1}$ be a computation in standard form in $h_1^{-1}(U) \cap \Pi_M$ and let $B(\alpha) = \{j/\gamma_i$ is an a_j-symbol loop for some i, $1 \leqq i \leqq s\}$. Let $r = \#(B(\alpha))$ and let $B'(\alpha) = \{i_1, \ldots, i_r\} \subseteq \{1, \ldots, s\}$ be any set of indices such that $\{\gamma_j / j \text{ in } B'(\alpha)\}$ is a set of a_i-symbol loops over r distinct symbols. Then there exists a computation $\alpha' = w_1 v_1^{k_1} w_2 \ldots v_m^{k_m} w_{m+1}$ in $h_1^{-1}(U) \cap \Pi_M$, each $k_i \geqq 0$, such that (i) $h_1(\alpha') = h_1(\alpha)$; (ii) v_i is an a_i-symbol loop for all i, $1 \leqq i \leqq m$; (iii) for each i in $B(\alpha)$, $v_i = \gamma_j$ for some j in $B'(\alpha)$; and (iv) for each symbol loop γ in M and each i, $1 \leqq i \leqq m+1$, w_i contains at most $k-1$ occurrences of γ [Rv].

EXERCISE 7.4.5: Show that Lemma 7.4.2 cannot be strengthened to require $h_2(\alpha) = h_2(\alpha')$. [Hint: Consider the case when $U = a^+$ and $M = (\{p_0\}, \{a\}, \{b\}, H, p_0, \{p_0\})$, where $H = \{(p_0, a, b, p_0), (p_0, a, b^2, p_0)\}$.]

EXERCISE 7.4.6: Let U be an infinite subset of $\langle a_1^{f_1(x)} \ldots a_m^{f_m(x)} \rangle$. Prove that $U = \langle a_1^{g_1(x)} \ldots a_m^{g_m(x)} \rangle$ for appropriate functions $g_1, \ldots, g_m$.

EXERCISE 7.4.7: Prove that an a-transducer is ϵ-loop-free if and only if it has no loop γ such that $h_1(\gamma) = h_2(\gamma) = \epsilon$.

EXERCISE 7.4.8: Let M be an ϵ-loop-free a-transducer, $U \subseteq a_1^* \ldots a_m^*$, and $M(U) \subseteq b_1^* \ldots b_n^*$, where $m \geqq 1$ and $n \geqq 2$. Suppose that for each j in N and each i, $1 \leqq i \leqq n$, there are only a finite number of words in $M(U)$ having exactly j occurrences of b_i. Prove that

(a) $h_1(\gamma) \neq \epsilon$ for each symbol loop γ occurring in a computation in $h_1^{-1}(U) \cap \Pi_M$. [This is an extension of Lemma 7.4.4.]

(b) $M(w)$ is finite for each word w in U.

EXERCISE 7.4.9: Let M be an ϵ-loop-free a-transducer, $U \subseteq a_1^* \ldots a_m^*$, and $M(U) \subseteq b_1^* \ldots b_n^*$, where $m \geqq 1$ and $n \geqq 3$. Suppose there exists an integer l such that for each j in N and each i, $1 \leqq i \leqq n$, there are at most l words in $M(U)$ having exactly j occurrences of b_i. Prove that there exists an integer k with the following property: Let $\alpha = v_1\gamma_1^{k_1} \ldots v_r\gamma_r^{k_r}v_{r+1}$ in $h_1^{-1}(U) \cap \Pi_M$ be a computation in standard form. Then (a) and (b) of Lemma 7.4.5 hold for every i, $1 \leqq i \leqq m$, a_i-symbol loops γ_s and γ_t, $1 \leqq s, t \leqq r$, and $k_s \geqq k$.

EXERCISE 7.4.10: Let $V = \{a^nb^n/n \geqq 1\}$. Suppose U is a subset of V such that $M(U) = V$ for some a-transducer M. Using Lemma 7.4.7 prove [GS7] that there exists a real number

(a) $k_1 > 0$ such that $|w'| \geqq k_1|w|$, where w is in $M(w')$ and w' is in U, for all but a finite number of w in V;

(b) $k_2 > 0$ such that $|w'| \leqq k_2|w|$, where w is in $M(w')$ and w' is in U, for all but a finite number of w in V.

EXERCISE 7.4.11: Let $V = \{a^nb^n/n \geqq 1\}$ and $U = \{a^nb^n/(2m)! \leqq n < (2m+1)!$ for some $m \geqq 1\}$. Using Exercise 7.4.10 prove that V is not in $\hat{\mathscr{M}}(U)$ [GS7].

7.5 [Full] Principal (Semi-)AFL with $\langle a_1^{f_1(x)} \ldots a_m^{f_m(x)} \rangle$ Generators

We are now ready to derive necessary conditions on bounded languages U and V in order that $\mathcal{O}(V) \subseteq \mathcal{O}(U)(\hat{\mathcal{O}}(V) \subseteq \hat{\mathcal{O}}(U))$ hold, equivalently, that V be in $\mathcal{O}(U)(\hat{\mathcal{O}}(U))$, for $\mathcal{O} = \mathcal{M}$ or $\mathcal{F}$. We shall always restrict V to be of the form $\langle b_1^{g_1(x)} \ldots b_n^{g_n(x)} \rangle$, and in most cases, place the same restriction on U.[1]

We start by establishing a necessary and sufficient condition for $V = \langle b_1^{g_1(x)} \ldots b_n^{g_n(x)} \rangle$ to be in $\mathcal{M}(U)$ ($\hat{\mathcal{M}}(U)$), where U is a given subset of $a_1^* \ldots a_m^*$. The condition is that V be a finite union of languages of a fairly complicated form. This condition is also shown to be necessary and sufficient for V to be in $\mathcal{F}(U)$ ($\hat{\mathcal{F}}(U)$).

Notation: For each $c = (c_1, \ldots, c_m)$ and $l = (l_1, \ldots, l_m)$ in N^m and each $L \subseteq a_1^* \ldots a_m^*$ let

$$\mathcal{K}(L, c, l) = \{(k_1, \ldots, k_m) \text{ in } N^m / a_1^{c_1+k_1 l_1} \ldots a_m^{c_m+k_m l_m} \text{ in } L\}.$$

THEOREM 7.5.1: *Let $U \subseteq a_1^* \ldots a_m^*$ and $V = \langle b_1^{g_1(x)} \ldots b_n^{g_n(x)} \rangle$ (with ϵ in U if ϵ is in*[2] *V). Then V is in $\hat{\mathcal{M}}(U)$ ($\mathcal{M}(U)$) if and only if the following holds:*

$$(*)\ V = \bigcup_{i=1}^{q} V_i \text{ for some } q \geqq 1, \text{ each } V_i \text{ of the form } \psi^{-1}_{\langle b_1, \ldots, b_n \rangle}$$

$$\left[\left\{\left(d_{i1} + \sum_{j=z_{i1}}^{z_{i2}-1} k_j p_{ij}, \ldots, d_{in} + \sum_{j=z_{in}}^{z_{i(n+1)}-1} k_j p_{ij}\right) \Big/ (k_1, \ldots, k_m) \text{ in } \mathcal{K}(U, c_i, l_i)\right\}\right],$$

where $c_i, l_i = (l_{i1}, \ldots, l_{im}), (p_{i1}, \ldots, p_{im})$ are in N^m, all $l_{ij} > 0$, (all $p_{ij} > 0$), $(d_{i1}, \ldots, d_{in})$ is in N^n, and $(z_{i1}, \ldots, z_{i(n+1)})$ is in N^{n+1}, with $1 = z_{i1} < \ldots < z_{i(n+1)} = m+1$.

Proof: We shall only give the argument for $\mathcal{M}(U)$, the $\hat{\mathcal{M}}(U)$ case being similar. Suppose $(*)$ holds. By Theorem 3.2.2 and by Corollary 1 of Theorem 3.2.2, it suffices to show that $V = M(U)$ for some ϵ-output bounded a-transducer M.

[1] The reader is referred to [Rv] for a relaxation of this restriction.

[2] This condition is needed just for the "if". For the "only if", i. e., if V is in $\mathcal{M}(U)$, then clearly ϵ is in U when ϵ is in V.

For each i, $1 \leq i \leq q$, let $c_i = (c_{i1}, \ldots, c_{im})$, and

$$U_i = \{a_1^{c_{i1}+k_1 l_{i1}} \ldots a_m^{c_{im}+k_m l_{im}} \text{ in } U/(k_1, \ldots, k_m) \text{ in } N^m\}.$$

For each i and j, $1 \leq i \leq q$ and $1 \leq j \leq m$, let s_i and s_{ij} be distinct states. Let $F = \{s_{im}/1 \leq i \leq q\}$. Construct $M = (K_1, \Sigma_1, \Sigma_2, H, p_0, F)$ as follows. (We omit some of the formal details.) Starting at p_0, M nondeterministically goes to one of the s_i via the 4-tuple $(p_0, \epsilon, \epsilon, s_i)$ in H. At s_i, M checks to see if the input word is of the form $a_1^{c_{i1}+k_1 l_{i1}} \ldots a_m^{c_{im}+k_m l_{im}}$, and simultaneously maps the input into $b_1^* \ldots b_n^*$ by the following 4-tuples of H:

(a) $(s_i, a_1^{c_{i1}}, b_1^{d_{i1}}, s_{i1})$;

(b) $(s_{ij}, a_{j+1}^{c_{i(j+1)}}, b_r^t, s_{i(j+1)})$ for $1 \leq j < m$, where r is the unique integer such that $z_{ir} \leq j+1 < z_{i(r+1)}$, $t = d_{ir}$ if $j+1 = z_{ir}$ and $t = 0$ otherwise; and

(c) $(s_{ij}, a_j^{l_{ij}}, b_r^{p_{ij}}, s_{ij})$ for $1 \leq j \leq m$, where r is the unique integer such that $z_{ir} \leq j < z_{i(r+1)}$.

Clearly M is ϵ-output bounded on U if each $p_{ij} > 0$. Note that once in state s_i, M blocks on each word in U which is not in U_i. Then $M(U_i) = V_i$ and $M(U) = V$.

Consider the "only if". Thus let $V = M(U)$ for some ϵ-free a-transducer M. By Lemma 7.4.3, we may assume that M is ϵ-loop-free. As in Lemma 7.4.7, we may assume that M has at least one a_i-symbol loop for each i. By Lemma 7.4.4, $h_1(\gamma) \neq \epsilon$ for each symbol loop γ occurring in a computation in $h_1^{-1}(U) \cap \Pi_M$. For each i, $1 \leq i \leq m$, let Q_i be the set of all a_i-symbol loops in M. Obviously each Q_i is finite. Let $\bar{k}$ be an integer satisfying the conclusion of Lemma 7.4.7. Let W be the set of all subwords w of words in Π_M such that

(1) w contains at most $\bar{k}-1$ occurrences of each symbol loop in M,
(2) $h_1(w)$ is in $a_1^* \ldots a_m^*$, and
(3) $h_2(w)$ is in $b_1^* \ldots b_n^*$.

Clearly W is finite. Let e be a new symbol and let

$$Q = WeQ_1eWeQ_2 \ldots WeQ_meW.$$

Since the Q_i and W are finite, Q is finite. For each word $\alpha = w_{\alpha 1}e\gamma_{\alpha 1}e \ldots w_{\alpha m}e\gamma_{\alpha m}w_{\alpha(m+1)}$ in Q, let

$$Z_\alpha = \{w_{\alpha 1}\gamma_{\alpha 1}^{k_1} \ldots w_{\alpha m}\gamma_{\alpha m}^{k_m} w_{\alpha(m+1)}/(k_1, \ldots, k_m) \text{ in } N^m\} \cap h_1^{-1}(U) \cap \Pi_M.$$

By Lemma 7.4.7,[1] for each computation β in $h_1^{-1}(U) \cap \Pi_M$ there exists a

[1] This is the only place where Lemma 7.4.7 is used in Section 7.5.

computation β' such that β' is in Z_α for some α in Q, $h_1(\beta) = h_1(\beta')$, and $h_2(\beta) = h_2(\beta')$. Therefore $V = \bigcup_{\alpha \text{ in } Q} h_2(Z_\alpha)$.

Now V is infinite. Thus there exist α_0 in Q such that $h_2(Z_{\alpha_0})$ is infinite. Then $\{\#_{b_{i_0}}(w)/w \text{ in } h_2(Z_{\alpha_0})\}$ is infinite for some i_0. Since $h_2(Z_{\alpha_0}) \subseteq V$ and $V = \langle b_1^{g_1(x)} \ldots b_n^{g_n(x)} \rangle$, the set $\{\#_{b_i}(w)/w \text{ in } h_2(Z_{\alpha_0})\}$ is infinite for each i, $1 \leqq i \leqq n$. Hence for each i, $1 \leqq i \leqq n$, there exists j, $1 \leqq j \leqq m$, such that $h_2(\gamma_{\alpha_0 j})$ is in b_i^+. Therefore $n \leqq m$.

Let α be an arbitrary element in Q. Two cases arise.

(α) $\#(h_2(Z_\alpha)) < 2$. Let $(z_{\alpha 1}, \ldots, z_{\alpha(n+1)})$ be any $(n+1)$-tuple of integers satisfying $1 = z_{\alpha 1} < \ldots < z_{\alpha(n+1)} = m+1$. Since $n \leqq m$, $(z_{\alpha 1}, \ldots, z_{\alpha(n+1)})$ exists.

(β) $h_2(Z_\alpha)$ has at least two elements. Since $g_1, \ldots, g_n$ are strictly increasing, for each i, $1 \leqq i \leqq n$, b_i occurs in $h_2(\gamma_{\alpha j})$ for some symbol loop $\gamma_{\alpha j}$. From the definition of symbol loop, $h_2(\gamma_{\alpha j})$ is in b_i^+. Let $z_{\alpha 1} = 1$, $z_{\alpha(n+1)} = m+1$, and for each i, $1 < i \leqq n$, let $z_{\alpha i}$ be the smallest j such that $h_2(\gamma_{\alpha j})$ is in b_i^+. Clearly $1 = z_{\alpha 1} < \ldots < z_{\alpha(n+1)} = m+1$.

For either case, (α) or (β),

$$h_2(Z_\alpha) = \psi^{-1}_{\langle b_1, \ldots, b_n \rangle}\left[\left\{\left(d_{\alpha 1} + \sum_{j = z_{\alpha 1}}^{z_{\alpha 2}-1} k_j |h_2(\gamma_{\alpha j})|, \ldots, d_{\alpha n} + \sum_{j = z_{\alpha n}}^{z_{\alpha(n+1)}-1} k_j |h_2(\gamma_{\alpha j})|\right)\middle/ (k_1, \ldots, k_m) \text{ in } \mathcal{K}(U, c_\alpha, t_\alpha)\right\}\right],$$

where $t_\alpha = (|h_1(\gamma_{\alpha 1})|, \ldots, |h_1(\gamma_{\alpha m})|)$ and $c_\alpha = (c_{\alpha 1}, \ldots, c_{\alpha m})$, with $c_{\alpha i} = \#_{a_i}(h_1(w))$ and $d_{\alpha j} = \#_{b_j}(h_2(w))$ if $Z_\alpha = \{w\}$, and $c_{\alpha i} = \#_{a_i}(h_1(w_{\alpha 1} \ldots w_{\alpha(m+1)}))$ and $d_{\alpha j} = \#_{b_j}(h_2(w_{\alpha 1} \ldots w_{\alpha(m+1)}))$ otherwise.

Let $q = \#(Q)$. Let μ be a one-to-one function from Q onto $\{1, \ldots, q\}$. Let $V_{\mu(\alpha)} = h_2(Z_\alpha)$, $l_{\mu(\alpha)j} = |h_1(\gamma_{\alpha j})|$, and $p_{\mu(\alpha)j} = |h_2(\gamma_{\alpha j})|$. Since each $\gamma_{\alpha j}$ is an a_j-symbol loop, $l_{\mu(\alpha)j} > 0$. Since M is e-free, $p_{\mu(\alpha)j} > 0$. Thus (*) holds and the proof is complete.

The above result provides a necessary and sufficient condition in order that V be in $\hat{\mathcal{M}}(U)$ ($\mathcal{M}(U)$). We shall extend it to the AFL case. To do this we need a technical lemma which indicates how a language L in $\hat{\mathcal{F}}(\mathcal{L})$ ($\mathcal{F}(\mathcal{L})$), of the form $\langle b_1^{g_1(x)} \ldots b_n^{g_n(x)} \rangle$, can be obtained from languages in $\mathcal{M}(\mathcal{L})$ ($\hat{\mathcal{M}}(\mathcal{L})$).

LEMMA 7.5.1: *Let L be of the form* $\langle b_1^{g_1(x)} \ldots b_n^{g_n(x)} \rangle$ *and let* $\mathcal{L}$ *be a family of languages. Suppose there exists a sequence* $U_1, \ldots, U_k$ *of languages such that* $L = U_k$ *and for each* l, $1 \leqq l \leqq k$, *either*

(i) U_l *is in* $\hat{\mathcal{M}}(\mathcal{L})$ ($\mathcal{M}(\mathcal{L})$); (ii) $U_l = U_i \cup U_j$ *for some* $i, j < l$; (iii) $U_l = U_j^+$ *for some* $j < l$; *or* (iv) $U_l = U_i U_j$ *for some* $i, j < l$. *Then there exists a sequence* $V_1, \ldots, V_r$, *with* $L = V_r$, *of languages for which only* (i) *and* (ii) *occur.*

Proof: We shall give the argument for $\mathcal{M}(\mathcal{L})$, an analogous demonstration holding for $\hat{\mathcal{M}}(\mathcal{L})$. The proof is by induction on the length k of a shortest sequence $U_1, \ldots, U_k = L$ satisfying (i)–(iv). The lemma is obviously true for $k = 1$. Suppose the lemma holds for all languages with a shortest sequence of length $k \leqq r, r \geqq 1$. Let $L = \langle b_1^{g_1(x)} \ldots b_n^{g_n(x)} \rangle$ be a language for which a shortest sequence is $U_1, \ldots, U_{r+1} = L$ of length $r+1$. Then L is not in $\mathcal{M}(\mathcal{L})$, since otherwise the sequence $U_1 = L$ of length 1 exists, contradicting the minimality of $U_1, \ldots, U_{r+1}$.

Suppose $L = U_l^+$ for some $l < r+1$. Since $n \geqq 2$ and each g_i is strictly increasing, L contains a word with an occurrence of at least two distinct letters. Thus U_l cannot be over a one-letter alphabet. Hence $L = U_l^+$ is not in $b_1^* \ldots b_n^*$, a contradiction. Therefore U_{r+1} is not of type (iii).

Suppose $L = U_i U_j$ for some $i, j < r+1$. We may assume $U_i \neq \{\epsilon\}$ and $U_j \neq \{\epsilon\}$. [For otherwise $U_1, \ldots, U_j = L$, resp. $U_1, \ldots, U_i = L$, gives a shorter sequence for L, contradicting the minimality of $U_1, \ldots, U_{r+1}$.] Four cases arise.

(α) U_i and U_j both contain at least two distinct words, say v_1, v_2 and w_1, w_2 resp. Suppose one of the words v_1, v_2, w_1, or w_2 contains at least two distinct letters, say $v_1 = a^s bw$, a and b distinct symbols. Then $v_1 w_1 = a^s bww_1$ and $v_1 w_2 = a^s bww_2$ are both in L. This contradicts the fact that all the g_i are strictly increasing. Thus neither v_1, v_2, w_1, nor w_2 contains two distinct letters. Then v_1 is in a^*, v_2 is in b^*, w_1 is in c^*, and w_2 is in d^* for some symbols a, b, c, and d. Assume $a \neq c$ and $a \neq d$. Then $v_1 w_1$ and $v_1 w_2$ are both in L, contradicting the fact that all the g_i are strictly increasing. Assume $a = c$ and $a = d$. Then $v_1 w_1$ and $v_1 w_2$ are both in L, contradicting the fact that $n \geqq 2$ and all the g_i are strictly increasing. Thus $c \neq d$ and a is one of the symbols c or d. Similarly, b is one of the symbols c or d, $a \neq b$, c is one of the symbols a or b, and d is one of the symbols a or b. Hence $a \neq b$, $c \neq d$, and either $a = c$ and $b = d$, or $a = d$ and $b = c$. Then $v_1 w_1$ and $v_2 w_2$, or $v_1 w_2$ and $v_2 w_1$, are in L. One of these pairs contradicts the fact that $n \geqq 2$ and all the g_i are strictly increasing. Hence case (α) does not occur.

(β) $U_i = \{w\}$ for some word w. By assumption, $w \neq \epsilon$. Since $\mathcal{M}(\mathcal{L})$ contains every ϵ-free finite set and $L = U_i U_j$ is not in $\mathcal{M}(\mathcal{L})$, L, thus U_j, is infinite. Suppose $w = a^p b\bar{w}$ for some $p \geqq 1$ and distinct letters a and b.

Then $a^p b\bar{w}w_1$ and $a^p b\bar{w}w_2$ are both in L for distinct words w_1 and w_2 in U_j. This contradicts the fact that all the g_i are strictly increasing. Thus $w = a^s$ for some $s > 0$. Clearly $a = b_1$. Then $U_j = \langle b_1^{g_1(x)-s} b_2^{g_2(x)} \ldots b_n^{g_n(x)} \rangle$. Let $U_1', \ldots, U_t' = U_j$ be a shortest sequence for U_j. Obviously $t \leqq j \leqq r$. By induction, there exists a sequence $V_1, \ldots, V_h = U_j$ in which only (i) and (ii) occur. Let $V_1', \ldots, V_h'$ be the sequence defined inductively by $V_g' = b_1^s V_g$ if V_g is in $\mathscr{M}(\mathscr{L})$ and $V_g' = V_k' \cup V_l'$ if $V_g = V_k \cup V_l$. Clearly V_g' is in $\mathscr{M}(\mathscr{L})$ if V_g is in $\mathscr{M}(\mathscr{L})$. It is easily seen that $V_g' = b_1^s V_g$ for each g. Thus $V_h' = b_1^s V_h = b_1^s U_j = L$, and $V_1', \ldots, V_h'$ is a sequence for L in which only (i) and (ii) occur.

(γ) Suppose $U_j = \{w\}$ for some word w. An argument analogous to (β) holds.

(δ) Suppose U_i or U_j is empty. Then L is empty and thus is in $\mathscr{M}(\mathscr{L})$, a contradiction.

Therefore the induction is extended if $L = U_i U_j$.

Now suppose $L = U_i \cup U_j$ for some $i, j < r+1$. Since $L = \langle b_1^{g_1(x)} \ldots b_n^{g_n(x)} \rangle$, L is infinite. Thus either U_i or U_j is infinite. By a relabeling if necessary, we may assume that U_i is infinite. Since U_i is an infinite subset of L, $U_i = \langle b_1^{f_1(x)} \ldots b_n^{f_n(x)} \rangle$ for some functions $f_1, \ldots, f_n$. [See Exercise 7.4.6.] Since the length of a shortest sequence for U_i is less than $r+1$, by the induction hypothesis there exists a sequence $V_1, \ldots, V_t = U_i$ in which only (i) and (ii) occur. If U_j is finite, then U_j is in $\mathscr{M}(\mathscr{L})$ and $V_1, \ldots, V_t, U_j, V_t \cup U_j = L$ is a sequence for L in which only (i) and (ii) occur. Suppose U_j is infinite. Then by induction, there exists a sequence $V_1', \ldots, V_s' = U_j$ in which only (i) and (ii) occur. Then $V_1, \ldots, V_t, V_1', \ldots, V_s', V_t \cup V_s' = L$ is a sequence for L in which only (i) and (ii) occur. Thus the induction is extended if $L = U_i \cup U_j$, and the proof is complete.

THEOREM 7.5.2: *Let $U \subseteq a_1^* \ldots a_m^*$ be nonempty and $V = \langle b_1^{g_1(x)} \ldots b_n^{g_n(x)} \rangle$. Then V is in $\hat{\mathscr{F}}(U)(\mathscr{F}(U))$ if and only if V is in $\hat{\mathscr{M}}(U)(\mathscr{M}(U))$, thus (when ϵ is in U if ϵ is in V) if and only if ($*$) of Theorem 7.5.1 holds.*

Proof: It suffices to show that

($*$) for $V = \langle b_1^{g_1(x)} \ldots b_n^{g_n(x)} \rangle$ and U a nonempty language, V is in $\hat{\mathscr{F}}(U)$ ($\mathscr{F}(U)$) if and only if V is in $\hat{\mathscr{M}}(U)(\mathscr{M}(U))$.

We shall give the proof of ($*$) for $\mathscr{F}(U)$, an analogous argument holding for $\hat{\mathscr{F}}(U)$.

Since the "if" is trivially true, we shall establish the "only if". By Theorem 3.4.1, each language in $\mathscr{F}(U)$ is obtained from languages in $\mathscr{M}(U)$ by a finite number of applications of union, concatenation, and $+$. Suppose V is in $\mathcal{F}(U)$. Then there exists a sequence of languages $U_1, \ldots, U_k$ such that $U_k = V$ and for each l, $1 \leqq l \leqq k$, either (i) U_l is in $\mathcal{M}(U)$; (ii) $U_l = U_i \cup U_j$ for some $i, j < l$; (iii) $U_l = U_j^+$ for some $j < l$; or (iv) $U_l = U_iU_j$ for some $i, j < l$. By Lemma 7.5.1, we may assume that only cases (i) and (ii) occur. Since $\mathcal{M}(U)$ is a semi-AFL, it is closed under union. Hence each U_i is in $\mathcal{M}(U)$. Therefore V is in $\mathcal{M}(U)$.

Theorems 7.5.1 and 7.5.2, while presenting necessary and sufficient conditions, do not lend themselves easily to specific examples. In order to derive necessary conditions which are more readily violated, we restrict the form of the U-language and trivially generalize the form of the V-language.

Notation: Let $m \geqq 2$, θ be in N, and f_i be a function from N into N, strictly increasing on the set $\{x \text{ in } N/x \geqq \theta\}$, for each i, $1 \leqq i \leqq m$. Then $\langle a_1^{f_1(x)} \ldots a_m^{f_m(x)} \rangle_\theta$ denotes the set $\{a_1^{f_1(x)} \ldots a_m^{f_m(x)}/x \geqq \theta\}$.

Thus $\langle a_1^{f_1(x)} \ldots a_m^{f_m(x)} \rangle = \langle a_1^{f_1(x)} \ldots a_m^{f_m(x)} \rangle_0$.

COROLLARY: *Let $U \subseteq a_1^* \ldots a_m^*$ be nonempty and $V = \langle b_1^{g_1(x)} \ldots b_n^{g_n(x)} \rangle_\theta$. Then V is in $\hat{\mathcal{F}}(U)(\mathcal{F}(U))$ if and only if V is in $\hat{\mathcal{M}}(U)(\mathcal{M}(U))$.*

Proof: We give the argument for $\mathcal{F}(U)$, the one for $\hat{\mathcal{F}}(U)$ being similar.

If V is in $\mathcal{M}(U)$, then V is obviously in $\mathcal{F}(U)$. Suppose V is in $\mathcal{F}(U)$. For each i, $1 \leqq i \leqq n$, let g_i' be the function on N defined by $g_i'(x) = g_i(x+\theta)$ for each x in N. Note that each g_i' is strictly increasing on N. Let $F = \{b_1^{g_1(x)} \ldots b_n^{g_n(x)}/0 \leqq x < \theta\}$ if $\theta > 0$ and $F = \emptyset$ if $\theta = 0$. Then F is a finite subset of V and $V - F = \langle b_1^{g_1'(x)} \ldots b_n^{g_n'(x)} \rangle$. Clearly $V - F$ is in $\mathcal{F}(U)$. By Theorem 7.5.2, $V - F$ is in $\mathcal{M}(U)$. If F is ϵ-free, then $V = (V-F) \cup F$ is in $\mathcal{M}(U) = \mathcal{S}(U)$. Suppose F contains ϵ. Then V, and hence U, contains ϵ. Again $V = (V-F) \cup F$ is in $\mathcal{M}(U) = \mathcal{S}(U)$.

In view of the above corollary, any necessary conditions for V to be in $\hat{\mathcal{M}}(U)(\mathcal{M}(U))$, $U \subseteq a_1^* \ldots a_m^*$ nonempty and $V = \langle b_1^{g_1(x)} \ldots b_n^{g_n(x)} \rangle_\theta$, serve as necessary conditions for V to be in $\hat{\mathcal{F}}(U)(\mathcal{F}(U))$, and conversely. The more practical necessary conditions involve languages U and V, each of the form $\langle a_1^{f_1(x)} \ldots a_m^{f_m(x)} \rangle_\theta$. Before presenting some of them, we first prove a necessary condition of theoretical import. For this we need the following lemma.

LEMMA 7.5.2: *Let* $U = \langle a_1^{f_1(x)} \ldots a_m^{f_m(x)} \rangle_{\theta_1}$ *and* $V = \langle b_1^{g_1(x)} \ldots b_n^{g_n(x)} \rangle_{\theta_2}$, *with* V *in* $\hat{\mathcal{O}}(U)(\mathcal{O}(U))$, $\mathcal{O} = \mathcal{M}$ *or* $\mathcal{F}$. *Let* $\theta = \max\{\theta_1, \theta_2\}$. *Then there exist* θ', $\theta \leqq \theta' \leqq \theta+1$, $l_i > 0$, $\bar{c}_i$, $\bar{d}_j$, $\bar{z}_j$, *and* $\bar{p}_i\,(>0)$ *in* N, $1 \leqq i \leqq m$, $1 \leqq j \leqq n$, $1 \leqq \bar{z}_1 < \ldots < \bar{z}_{n+1} = m+1$, *with the following properties: Given the system of equations*

(1) $\bar{c}_i + k_i \bar{l}_i = f_i(x)$, $1 \leqq i \leqq m$, *and*

(2) $\bar{d}_j + \sum_{s=\bar{z}_j}^{\bar{z}_{j+1}-1} k_s \bar{p}_s = g_j(y)$, $1 \leqq j \leqq n$,

(a) *The set of all* $x \geqq \theta'$ *in* N *such that* $(k_1, \ldots, k_m, x, y)$ *in* N^{n+2} *is a solution of* (1) *and* (2) *for some* $k_1, \ldots, k_m, y$, *with* $y \geqq \theta'$, *is infinite.*

(b) *For each* $x \geqq \theta'$ *in* N *there is at most one* $(m+2)$*-tuple* $(k_1, \ldots, k_m, x, y)$ *in* N^{m+2}, *with* $y \geqq \theta'$, *which is a solution of* (1) *and* (2).

(c) *The set of all* $y \geqq \theta'$ *such that* $(k_1, \ldots, k_m, x, y)$ *in* N^{m+2} *is a solution of* (1) *and* (2), *for some* $k_1, \ldots, k_m, x$, *with* $x \geqq \theta'$, *is infinite.*

Proof: In view of Theorem 7.5.2, it suffices to give the argument for $\mathcal{O} = \mathcal{M}$. The proof for $\mathcal{M}(U)$ is presented, the $\hat{\mathcal{M}}(U)$ case being similar.

Two alternatives arise.

(α) $\theta_1 = \theta_2 = 0$. Then $\theta = 0$. Let $\theta' = 0$. By Theorem 7.5.1, there exist $q \geqq 1$, $c_i = (c_{i1}, \ldots, c_{im})$, $l_i = (l_{i1}, \ldots, l_{im})$, and $(p_{i1}, \ldots, p_{im})$ in N^m, with all the d_{ij} and p_{ij} positive; $(d_{i1}, \ldots, d_{in})$ in N^n; and $(z_{i1}, \ldots, z_{i(n+1)})$ in N^{n+1} such that $V = \bigcup_{i=1}^{q} V_i$, each V_i being as in Theorem 7.5.1. For each i, $1 \leqq i \leqq q$, let

$$U_i = \{a_1^{c_{i1}+k_1 l_{i1}} \ldots a_m^{c_{im}+k_m l_{im}} \text{ in } U/(k_1, \ldots, k_m) \text{ in } N^m\}.$$

Note that for each i,

$$(*) \qquad V_i = \psi^{-1}_{\langle b_1, \ldots, b_n\rangle}\left[\left\{\left(d_{i1} + \sum_{j=z_{i1}}^{z_{i2}-1} k_j p_{ij}, \ldots, d_{in} + \sum_{j=z_{in}}^{z_{i(n+1)}-1} k_j p_{ij}\right) \Big/ (k_1, \ldots, k_m) \text{ in } \mathcal{K}(U_i, c_i, l_i)\right\}\right].$$

Since V is infinite, at least one of the V_i, say V_t, is infinite. Therefore $\mathcal{K}(U_t, c_t, l_t)$ is infinite. Since each $l_{ij} > 0$, U_t is infinite. Let $\bar{c}_i = c_{ti}$, $\bar{l}_i = l_{ti}$, $\bar{p}_i = p_{ti}$, $\bar{d}_j = d_{tj}$, and $\bar{z}_k = z_{tk}$ for all i, j, k. By ($*$), each solution $(k_1, \ldots, k_m, x)$ of (1) gives rise to a word in V_t, thus an integer y such that $(k_1, \ldots, k_m, x, y)$ is a solution to both (1) and (2). Hence (a) holds.

Consider (b). Suppose for some x, $(k_1, \ldots, k_m)$ and $(k_1', \ldots, k_m')$ in N^m are solutions of (1). Then $\bar{c}_i k_i \bar{l}_i = \bar{c}_i k_i' \bar{l}_i$, $1 \leqq i \leqq m$, whence $(k_1', \ldots, k_m') = (k_1, \ldots, k_m)$. Thus for each x in N there is at most one m-tuple $(k_1, \ldots, k_m)$ in N^m such that $(k_1, \ldots, k_m, x)$ is a solution of (1). Since the functions g_i are strictly increasing, and therefore one to one, there is at most one y satisfying (2). Hence for each x in N there is at most one $(m+2)$-tuple $(k_1, \ldots, k_m, x, y)$ in N^{m+2} which is a solution of both (1) and (2), i. e., (b) holds.

Finally, (c) follows from $(*)$ and the fact that V_t is infinite.

(β) θ_1 or θ_2 is nonzero. Let $\theta' = 1+\max\{\theta_1, \theta_2\}$. Let $f_i'(x) = f_i(x+\theta')$ and $g_j'(x) = g_j(x+\theta')$ for all i and j, $1 \leqq i \leqq m$ and $1 \leqq j \leqq n$. Since $\theta' > \max\{\theta_1, \theta_2\}$, all the functions f_i' and g_j' are strictly increasing on N. Let $U' = \langle a_1^{f_1'(x)} \ldots a_m^{f_m'(x)} \rangle$ and $V' = \langle b_1^{g_1'(x)} \ldots b_n^{g_n'(x)} \rangle$. Then $U' = U - U''$ and $V' = V - V''$ for certain finite sets U'' and V''. Clearly ϵ is not in $U' \cup V'$. Then V' is in $\mathscr{M}(U')(\hat{\mathscr{M}}(U'))$.[1] By ($\alpha$), there exist nonnegative integers $\bar{c}_i$, positive integers $\bar{l}_i$, positive (nonnegative) integers $\bar{p}_i$, $1 \leqq i \leqq m$, and nonnegative integers $\bar{d}_j$ and $\bar{z}_j$, $1 \leqq j \leqq n$, $1 \leqq \bar{z}_1 < \ldots < \bar{z}_{n+1} = m+1$, such that the system of equations

$$(1') \quad \bar{c}_i + k_i \bar{l}_i = f_i'(x), \quad 1 \leqq i \leqq m, \text{ and}$$

$$(2') \quad \bar{d}_j + \sum_{s=\bar{z}_j}^{\bar{z}_{j+1}-1} k_s \bar{p}_s = g_j'(x), \quad 1 \leqq j \leqq n,$$

satisfies (a), (b), and (c) for $\theta' = 0$. Now for each solution $(k_1, \ldots, k_m, x', y')$ of (1′) and (2′), with $x' \geqq 0$ and $y' \geqq 0$, there corresponds a solution $(k_1, \ldots, k_m, x, y)$ of (1) and (2), with $x = x'+\theta'$ and $y = y'+\theta'$; and conversely, to each solution $(k_1, \ldots, k_m, x, y)$ of (1) and (2), with $x = x'+\theta'$ and $y = y'+\theta'$, $x' \geqq 0$ and $y' \geqq 0$, $(k_1, \ldots, k_m, x', y')$ is a solution of (1′) and (2′). Clearly (a), (b), and (c) are satisfied with respect to (1) and (2).

Using Lemma 7.5.2 we now establish a major result for V to be in $\hat{\mathscr{M}}(U)$ ($\mathscr{M}(U)$), U and V each of the form $\langle a_1^{f_1(x)} \ldots a_m^{f_m(x)} \rangle_\theta$. It involves the notion of an arbitrary "r-ary real-valued function".

Def: Let r be a positive integer. An *r-ary real-valued function* is a function which maps r-tuples of real numbers into real numbers. An r-ary real-valued function $F(x_1, \ldots, x_r)$ is frequently abbreviated $F(\ldots, x_u, \ldots)$.

THEOREM 7.5.3: *Let $U = \langle a_1^{f_1(x)} \ldots a_m^{f_m(x)} \rangle_{\theta_1}$ and $V = \langle b_1^{g_1(x)} \ldots b_n^{g_n(x)} \rangle_{\theta_2}$, with V in $\hat{\mathscr{O}}(U)(\mathscr{O}(U))$, $\mathscr{O} = \mathscr{M}$ or $\mathscr{F}$. Then there exist a set $Q \subseteq \{1, \ldots, m\}$ ($Q =$*

[1] See Exercise 3.4.1.

$\emptyset$) and integers $z_1, \ldots, z_{n+1}$, $1 = z_1 < \ldots < z_{n+1} = m+1$, with the following two properties:

(i) *$Q_i = \{s/z_i \leqq s < z_{i+1}$, s not in $Q\} \neq \emptyset$ for all i, $1 \leqq i \leqq n$.*

(ii) *There exist real numbers t_j and positive real numbers t_{js} for all j and s, $1 \leqq j \leqq n$ and s in Q_j, such that for every n-ary real-valued function $F(x_1, \ldots, x_n)$,*

$$\lim_{x\to\infty} F(\ldots, g_u(x), \ldots) = \lim_{x\to\infty} F\Big(\ldots, t_u + \sum_{Q_u} t_{us} f_s(x), \ldots\Big)$$

if[1] *both limits exist.*

Proof: Let $\bar{c}_i, \bar{l}_i, \bar{p}_i, \bar{d}_j, \bar{z}_1, \ldots, \bar{z}_{n+1}, \theta$, and θ' be as given in the conclusion of Lemma 7.5.2. For simplicity of notation, let $c_i = \bar{c}_i$, $l_i = \bar{l}_i$, $p_i = \bar{p}_i$, $d_j = \bar{d}_j$, $z_1 = \bar{z}_1, \ldots$, and $z_{n+1} = \bar{z}_{n+1}$. Consider the system of equations

(1) $c_i + k_i l_i = f_i(x)$, $1 \leqq i \leqq m$, and

(2) $d_j + \sum_{s=z_j}^{z_{j+1}-1} k_s p_s = g_j(y)$, $1 \leqq j \leqq n$.

By (b) of Lemma 7.5.2, for each $x \geqq \theta'$ in N there is at most one $(m+2)$-tuple $(k_1(x), \ldots, k_m(x), x, y(x))$ in N^{m+2}, $y(x) \geqq \theta'$, which is a solution of (1) and (2). Let A be the set of all $x \geqq \theta'$ in N for which there is such a solution. By (a) of Lemma 7.5.2, A is infinite. It follows from (c) of Lemma 7.5.2 that for each j there exists s_j, $z_j \leqq s_j < z_{j+1}$, such that $p_{s_j} > 0$. Let $Q = \{i/p_i = 0\}$. Clearly (i) holds.

Consider (ii). Let $t_j = d_j - \sum_{Q_j} (c_s p_s / l_s)$ and $t_{js} = (p_s/l_s)$ for all j and s, $1 \leqq j \leqq n$ and s in Q_j. Let $F(x_1, \ldots, x_n)$ be an arbitrary n-ary real-valued function such that $\lim_{x\to\infty} F(\ldots, g_u(x), \ldots)$ and $\lim_{x\to\infty} F(\ldots, t_u + \sum_{Q_u} t_{us} f_s(x), \ldots)$ both exist. Since $l_i > 0$ and f_i is strictly increasing on A, $\lim_{\substack{x\to\infty \\ x \text{ in } A}} k_i(x) = \lim_{\substack{x\to\infty \\ x \text{ in } A}} ((f_i(x) - c_i)/l_i) = \infty$ for all i. This and the fact that $Q_j \neq \emptyset$ imply that $\lim_{\substack{x\to\infty \\ x \text{ in } A}} g_j(y(x)) = \infty$ for all j. Since each g_j is strictly increasing on $\{y/y \geqq \theta\}$, $\lim_{\substack{x\to\infty \\ x \text{ in } A}} y(x) = \infty$. Then

$$\begin{aligned} \lim_{y\to\infty} F(\ldots, g_u(y), \ldots) &= \lim_{\substack{x\to\infty \\ x \text{ in } A}} F\big(\ldots, g_u(y(x)), \ldots\big) \\ &= \lim_{\substack{x\to\infty \\ x \text{ in } A}} F\Big(\ldots, d_u + \sum_{Q_u} k_s(x)\, p_s, \ldots\Big) \end{aligned}$$

[1] $+\infty$ and $-\infty$ are permitted to be values of the limit.

$$= \lim_{\substack{x\to\infty \\ x \text{ in } A}} F\Big(\ldots, d_u+\sum_{Q_u}((f_s(x)-c_s)/l_s)p_s, \ldots\Big)$$

$$= \lim_{\substack{x\to\infty \\ x \text{ in } A}} F\Big(\ldots, d_u-\sum_{Q_u}(c_sp_s/l_s)+\sum_{Q_u}(p_s/l_s)f_s(x), \ldots\Big)$$

$$= \lim_{\substack{x\to\infty \\ x \text{ in } A}} F\Big(\ldots, t_u+\sum_{Q_u} t_{us}f_s(x), \ldots\Big)$$

$$= \lim_{x\to\infty} F\Big(\ldots, t_u+\sum_{Q_u} t_{us}f_s(x), \ldots\Big).$$

When $m = n$ in Theorem 7.5.3, we get:

COROLLARY: *Let* $U = \langle a_1^{f_1(x)} \ldots a_n^{f_n(x)}\rangle_{\theta_1}$ *and* $V = \langle b_1^{g_1(x)} \ldots b_n^{g_n(x)}\rangle_{\theta_2}$, *with* V *in* $\hat{\mathcal{O}}(U)$ $(\mathcal{O}(U))$, $\mathcal{O} = \mathcal{M}$ *or* $\mathcal{F}$. *Then there exist real numbers* t_j *and positive real numbers* t'_j, $1 \leqq j \leqq n$, *such that for every n-ary real-valued function* $F(x_1, \ldots, x_n)$,

$$\lim_{x\to\infty} F(\ldots, g_u(x), \ldots) = \lim_{x\to\infty} F(\ldots, t_u+t'_uf_u(x), \ldots)$$

if both limits exist.

EXAMPLE 7.5.1: Let $U = \langle a^{2^{2^x}}b^{x^2}\rangle$ and $V = \langle a^{2^{2^x}}b^x\rangle$. Suppose that V is in $\hat{\mathcal{F}}(U)$. Let $F(x, y)$ be the function defined by $F(x, 0) = F(0, y) = 0$ for all x, y and[1] $F(x, y) = (\log_2 \log_2 x)/y$ for $xy \neq 0$. For all real numbers t_1, t_2 and all positive real numbers t'_1, t'_2,

$$\lim_{x\to\infty} F(g_1(x), g_2(x)) = \lim_{x\to\infty} \frac{\log_2 \log_2 2^{2^x}}{x} = 1$$

and

$$\lim_{x\to\infty} F(t_1+t'_1f_1(x), t_2+t'_2f_2(x)) = \lim_{x\to\infty} \frac{\log_2 \log_2 (t_1+t'_1 2^{2^x})}{t_2+t'_2x^2} = 0.$$

Since this contradicts the corollary to Theorem 7.5.3, V is not in $\hat{\mathcal{F}}(U)$.

Theorem 7.5.3 is quite general in that the conclusion holds for every n-ary real-valued function $F(x_1, \ldots, x_n)$. By imposing special forms on $F(x_1, \ldots, x_n)$, as is done in the next three theorems, different necessary conditions are obtained.

[1] By definition, $\log_2 x = 0$ for $x \leqq 0$.

Def: Let $f_1, \ldots, f_m$ be functions from N into N. Then f_i, $1 \leqq i \leqq m$, is a *dominating* element of $\{f_1, \ldots, f_m\}$ if, for each j, $\lim_{x \to \infty} (f_i(x)/f_j(x))$ exists and is nonzero.

THEOREM 7.5.4: *Let* $U = \langle a_1^{f_1(x)} \ldots a_m^{f_m(x)} \rangle_{\theta_1}$ *and* $V = \langle b_1^{g_1(x)} \ldots b_n^{g_n(x)} \rangle_{\theta_2}$, *with* V *in* $\hat{\mathcal{O}}(U)$ $(\mathcal{O}(U))$, $\mathcal{O} = \mathcal{M}$ *or* $\mathcal{F}$. *Then there exist a set* $Q \subseteq \{1, \ldots, m\}$ $(Q = \emptyset)$ *and integers* $z_1, \ldots, z_{n+1}$, $1 = z_1 < \ldots < z_{n+1} = m+1$, *with the following two properties*:

(i) $Q_i = \{s/z_i \leqq s < z_{i+1}, s \text{ not in } Q\} \neq \emptyset$ *for all* i, $1 \leqq i \leqq n$.

(ii) *For all integers* i *and* j, $1 \leqq i, j \leqq n$, *and for all positive real numbers* k *and* l *the following holds: Suppose there exist a dominating element* f_i' *of* $\{f_s/s \text{ in } Q_i\}$ *and a dominating element* f_j' *of* $\{f_s/s \text{ in } Q_j\}$. *Then*

$$(*) \qquad \lim_{x\to\infty} \frac{(g_i(x))^k}{(g_j(x))^l} > 0 \text{ if and only if } \lim_{x\to\infty} \frac{(f_i'(x))^k}{(f_j'(x))^l} > 0,$$

if both limits exist.

Proof: Let $Q \subseteq \{1, \ldots, m\}$, $z_1, \ldots, z_{n+1}$, $t_1, \ldots, t_n$, and t_{js}, $1 \leqq j \leqq n$ and s in Q_j, be as guaranteed by Theorem 7.5.3. Let i and j be in $\{1, \ldots, n\}$ and let k and l be positive real numbers. Let $F(x_1, \ldots, x_n) = (x_i^k/x_j^l)$ if $x_j > 0$ and $F(x_1, \ldots, x_n) = 0$ if $x_j \leqq 0$. Suppose

$$f_i'(x), f_j'(x), \lim_{x\to\infty} \frac{(g_i(x))^k}{(g_j(x))^l}, \quad \text{and} \quad \lim_{x\to\infty} \frac{(f_i'(x))^k}{(f_j'(x))^l} \quad \text{exist.}$$

Then

$$\begin{aligned}
&\lim_{x\to\infty} F\Big(t_1 + \sum_{Q_1} t_{1s} f_s(x), \ldots, t_n + \sum_{Q_n} t_{ns} f_s(x)\Big) \\
&= \lim_{x\to\infty} \frac{\Big(t_i + \sum_{Q_i} t_{is} f_s(x)\Big)^k}{\Big(t_j + \sum_{Q_j} t_{js} f_s(x)\Big)^l} \\
&= \lim_{x\to\infty} \frac{(f_i'(x))^k}{(f_j'(x))^l} \frac{\left[\lim_{x\to\infty} \left(\dfrac{t_i}{f_i'(x)} + \sum_{Q_i} t_{is} \dfrac{f_s(x)}{f_i'(x)}\right)\right]^k}{\left[\lim_{x\to\infty} \left(\dfrac{t_j}{f_j'(x)} + \sum_{Q_j} t_{js} \dfrac{f_s(x)}{f_j'(x)}\right)\right]^l} \\
&= \frac{p}{q} \lim_{x\to\infty} \frac{(f_i'(x))^k}{(f_j'(x))^l},
\end{aligned}$$

for some positive real numbers p and q, the last equality occurring since

$\lim_{x\to\infty} f_i'(x) = \lim_{x\to\infty} f_j'(x) = \infty$, all appropriate t_{is} and t_{js} are positive real numbers, and $\lim_{x\to\infty} (f_s(x)/f_i'(x))$ and $\lim_{x\to\infty} (f_s'(x)/f_j'(x))$ are nonnegative real numbers for all appropriate s and s'. Hence $\lim_{x\to\infty} F\left(t_1+\sum_{Q_1} t_{1s} f_s(x), \ldots, t_n+\sum_{Q_n} t_{ns} f_s(x)\right)$ exists. By Theorem 7.5.3,

$$\lim_{x\to\infty} \frac{(g_i(x))^k}{(g_j(x))^l} = \frac{p}{q} \lim_{x\to\infty} \frac{(f_i'(x))^k}{(f_j'(x))^l}.$$

Thus (∗) holds.

COROLLARY: *Let* $U = \langle a_1^{f_1(x)} \ldots a_n^{f_n(x)} \rangle_{\theta_1}$ *and* $V = \langle b_1^{g_1(x)} \ldots b_n^{g_n(x)} \rangle_{\theta_2}$, *with* V *in* $\hat{\mathcal{O}}(U)$ ($\mathcal{O}(U)$), $\mathcal{O} = \mathcal{M}$ *or* $\mathcal{F}$. *Then for every pair of integers* i, j, $1 \leqq i, \leqq n$, *and for all positive real numbers* k *and* l,

$$\lim_{x\to\infty} \frac{(g_i(x))^k}{(g_j(x))^l} > 0 \quad \textit{if and only if} \quad \lim_{x\to\infty} \frac{(f_i(x))^k}{(f_j(x))^l} > 0,$$

if both limits exist.

Proof: Since $z_i = i$, $1 \leqq i \leqq n$, $Q = \emptyset$ in (i) of Theorem 7.5.4. Then $f_i'(x) = f_i(x)$ and the result follows from (ii) of Theorem 7.5.4.

EXAMPLE 7.5.2: Let $U = \langle a_1^{2^{3x}} a_2^{2^{2x}} a_3^{2^x} \rangle$ and $V = \langle b_1^{2^{4x}} b_2^{2^{3x}} \rangle$. Suppose V is in $\mathcal{F}(U)$. Using Theorem 7.5.4, $Q = \emptyset$ and there are only two possible choices for z_1, z_2, and z_3.

(a) $z_1 = 1$, $z_2 = 2$, and $z_3 = 4$. Then $f_1'(x) = 2^{3x}$ and $f_2'(x) = 2^{2x}$. For $k = 4$, $l = 3$, $i = 2$, and $j = 1$ we have

$$\lim_{x\to\infty} \frac{(g_i(x))^k}{(g_j(x))^l} = \lim_{x\to\infty} \frac{(2^{3x})^4}{(2^{4x})^3} = 1$$

and

$$\lim_{x\to\infty} \frac{(f_i'(x))^4}{(f_j'(x))^3} = \lim_{x\to\infty} \frac{(2^{2x})^4}{(2^{3x})^3} = 0.$$

Thus (∗) of Theorem 7.5.4 does not hold.

(b) $z_1 = 1$, $z_2 = 3$, and $z_3 = 4$. Then $f_1'(x) = 2^{3x}$ and $f_2'(x) = 2^x$. For $k = 4$, $l = 3$, $i = 2$, and $j = 1$ we get

$$\lim_{x\to\infty} \frac{(g_i(x))^k}{(g_j(x))^l} = \lim_{x\to\infty} \frac{(2^{3x})^4}{(2^{4x})^3} = 1$$

and

$$\lim_{x\to\infty} \frac{(f_i'(x))^k}{(f_j'(x))^l} = \lim_{x\to\infty} \frac{(2^x)^4}{(2^{3x})^3} = 0.$$

Thus (*) of Theorem 7.5.4 does not hold.

Hence V is not in $\mathcal{F}(U)$.

EXAMPLE 7.5.3: Let $U = \langle a^{x^2} b^x \rangle$ and $V = \langle a^x b^{x^2} \rangle$. Suppose V is in $\hat{\mathcal{F}}(U)$. By the corollary to Theorem 7.5.4, $\lim_{x\to\infty} (x/x^2) > 0$ if and only if $\lim_{x\to\infty} (x^2/x) > 0$, a contradiction. Thus V is not in $\hat{\mathcal{F}}(U)$. From Exercise 3.4.1, it follows that $\{a^n b^{n^2} / n \geqq 1\}$ is not in $\hat{\mathcal{F}}(\{a^{n^2} b^n / n \geqq 1\})$. This result was already noted in Exercise 4.8.3.

We now derive a necessary condition for a large class of languages $U = \langle a_1^{f_1(x)} \ldots a_n^{f_n(x)} \rangle_{\theta_1}$ and $V = \langle b_1^{g_1(x)} \ldots b_n^{g_n(x)} \rangle_{\theta_2}$, with f_i and g_i polynomials.

THEOREM 7.5.5: *Let* $U = \langle a_1^{f_1(x)} \ldots a_n^{f_n(x)} \rangle_{\theta_1}$ *and* $V = \langle b_1^{g_1(x)} \ldots b_n^{g_n(x)} \rangle_{\theta_2}$, *with* V *in* $\hat{\mathcal{O}}(U)(\mathcal{O}(U))$, $\mathcal{O} = \mathcal{M}$ *or* $\mathcal{F}$, *and all* $f_i(x)$ *and* $g_i(x)$ *polynomials. For each polynomial* $h(x)$ *let deg* (h) *be the degree of* $h(x)$.

(a) *If deg* $(f_i) =$ *deg* (g_i) *for some* i, $1 \leqq i \leqq n$, *then deg* $(f_j) =$ *deg* (g_j) *for all* j, $1 \leqq j \leqq n$.

(b) *Let* $f_i(x) = cx$ *and* $g_i(x) = dx$ *for some* i, $1 \leqq i \leqq n$, $c \neq 0$, *and* $d \neq 0$. *Then there exist real numbers* $p, r, q_1, \ldots, q_n, q_1', \ldots, q_n'$, *with* p *and each* q_j *positive, such that* $g_j(px+r) = q_j f_j(x) + q_j'$ *for each* j, $1 \leqq j \leqq n$.

Proof: Consider (a). Suppose the contrary. Then there exist i and j, $1 \leqq i$, $j \leqq n$, satisfying deg $(f_i) =$ deg (g_i) and deg $(f_j) \neq$ deg (g_j). Suppose deg $(f_j) <$ deg (g_j), an analogous argument holding if deg $(f_j) >$ deg (g_j). Since f_i is strictly increasing for $x \geqq \theta_1$, deg $(f_i) \geqq 1$. For

$$k = \frac{\deg (f_j)}{\deg (f_i)} \quad \text{and} \quad l = 1,$$

$$\lim_{x\to\infty} \frac{(f_i(x))^k}{(f_j(x))^l} = s \quad \text{and} \quad \lim_{x\to\infty} \frac{(g_i(x))^k}{(g_j(x))^l} = 0$$

for some appropriate positive real number s. This contradicts the corollary to Theorem 7.5.4. Hence (a) holds.

Consider (b). By (a), deg $(g_j) =$ deg (f_j) for each j. Let $g_j(x) = d_h x^h + \ldots + d_1 x + d_0$ and $f_j(x) = c_h x^h + \ldots + c_1 x + c_0$, with $d_h > 0$ and $c_h > 0$.

Let t_u and t'_u, $1 \leqq u \leqq n$, be real numbers, with $t_u > 0$, guaranteed by the corollary to Theorem 7.5.3. Let $F(x_1, \ldots, x_n) = (1/x_i)(x_j - g_j(x_i/d))$ if $x_i > 0$ and $F(x_1, \ldots, x_n) = 0$ otherwise. Clearly $\lim_{x \to \infty} F(g_1(x), \ldots, g_n(x)) = 0$ and

$$\lim_{x \to \infty} F(t_1 + t'_1 f_1(x), \ldots, t_n + t'_n f_n(x)) =$$

$$= \lim_{x \to \infty} \frac{1}{t_i + t'_i cx}\left(t_j + t'_j f_j(x) - g_j\left(\frac{t_i + t'_i cx}{d}\right)\right)$$

$$= \lim_{x \to \infty} \frac{1}{t_i + t'_i cx}(t'_j f_j(x) - g_j(px + r))$$

exists, with $p = (t'_i c)/d > 0$ and $r = t_i/d$. By the corollary to Theorem 7.5.3,

$$\lim_{x \to \infty} F(\ldots, t_u + t'_u f_u(x), \ldots) = \lim_{x \to \infty} F(\ldots, g_u(x), \ldots) = 0.$$

This implies that $\deg(t'_j f_j(x) - g_j(px + r)) < 1$. Thus $g_j(px + r) = t'_j f_j(x) + q'_j$ for some real number q'_j. The theorem then holds with $q_j = t'_j$.

EXAMPLE 7.5.4: Let $U = \langle a_1^x a_2^{x^3+x} a_3^{x^3+x^2} \rangle$ and $V = \langle b_1^x b_2^{x^3+x^2+x} b_3^{x^3+5x^2+x} \rangle$. Suppose V is in $\hat{\mathscr{F}}(U)$. By (b) of Theorem 7.5.5, there exist real numbers p and r, $p > 0$, such that

(1) $(px+r)^3 + (px+r)^2 + (px+r) = q_2(x^3+x) + q'_2$ and

(2) $(px+r)^3 + 5(px+r)^2 + (px+r) = q_3(x^3+x^2) + q'_3$

for some real numbers q_2, q'_2, q_3, and q'_3, with q_2 and q_3 positive. Comparing coefficients of x^2 in (1) yields $r = -\frac{1}{3}$. Comparing coefficients of x in (2) (with $r = -\frac{1}{3}$) yields $p = 0$, a contradiction. Thus V is not in $\hat{\mathscr{F}}(U)$.

For our final result we have:

THEOREM 7.5.6: *Let* $U = \langle a_1^{f_1(x)} \ldots a_m^{f_m(x)} \rangle$ *and* $V = \langle b_1^{g_1(x)} \ldots b_n^{g_n(x)} \rangle$, *with* V *in* $\hat{\mathcal{O}}(U)(\mathcal{O}(U))$, $\mathcal{O} = \mathscr{M}$ *or* $\mathscr{F}$. *Then there exist a set* $Q \subseteq \{1, \ldots, m\}$ $(Q = \emptyset)$ *and integers* $z_1, \ldots, z_{n+1}$, $1 = z_1 < \ldots < z_{n+1} = m+1$, *with the following two properties*:

(i) $Q_i = \{s/z_i \leqq s < z_{i+1}, s$ *not in* $Q\} \neq \emptyset$ *for all* i, $1 \leqq i \leqq n$.

(ii) *Let* i *in* $\{1, \ldots, n\}$ *and real numbers* $q_1, \ldots, q_n$, l, $l > 0$, *be such that*

(a) *there exists a dominating element* f'_i *of* $\{f_s/s$ *in* $Q_i\}$,

(b) $\lim_{x \to \infty} \dfrac{\sum_{j=1}^{n} q_j g_j(x)}{(g_i(x))^l}$ *exists, and*

(c) $\lim\limits_{x\to\infty} \dfrac{\sum_{s=1}^{m} r_s f_s(x)}{(f_i'(x))^l}$ *exists for all real numbers* r_s

which satisfy sgn $(r_s) =$ sgn (q_j) *for all s in* Q_j, $1 \leqq j \leqq n$, *and* $r_s = 0$ *for all s in Q, where for each real number y*, sgn (y) *is* $-1, 0$ *or* 1 *according as* $y < 0$, $y = 0$, *or* $y > 0$ *resp.*

Then there exist real numbers $v_1, \ldots, v_m$, *with* sgn $(v_s)=$sgn (q_j) *for all s in* Q_j, $1 \leqq j \leqq n$, *and* $v_s = 0$ *for s in Q, such that*

$$\lim_{x\to 0} \frac{\sum_{j=1}^{n} q_j g_j(x)}{(g_i(x))^l} = \lim_{x\to\infty} \frac{\sum_{s=1}^{m} v_s f_s(x)}{(f_i'(x))^l}.$$

Proof: Let $Q \subseteq \{1, \ldots, m\}$, $z_1, \ldots, z_{n+1}$, $t_1, \ldots, t_n$, and t_{js}, $1 \leqq j \leqq n$ and s in Q_j, be as guaranteed by Theorem 7.5.3. Let $F(x_1, \ldots, x_n) = (1/x_i^l) \sum_{j=1}^{n} q_j x_j$ if $x_i > 0$ and $F(x_1, \ldots, x_n) = 0$ otherwise. Then

$$\lim_{x\to\infty} F\Big(t_1 + \sum_{Q_1} t_{1s} f_s(x), \ldots, t_n + \sum_{Q_n} t_{ns} f_s(x)\Big) =$$

$$= \lim_{x\to\infty} \frac{\sum_{j=1}^{n} q_j \Big(t_j + \sum_{Q_j} t_{js} f_s(x)\Big)}{\Big(t_i + \sum_{Q_i} t_{is} f_s(x)\Big)^l}$$

$$= \lim_{x\to\infty} \frac{\sum_{j=1}^{n} q_j t_j + \sum_{j=1}^{n} \sum_{Q_j} q_j t_{js} f_s(x)}{(f_i'(x))^l \left(\dfrac{t_i}{f_i'(x)} + \sum_{Q_i} \dfrac{t_{is} f_s(x)}{f_i'(x)}\right)^l}$$

$$= \lim_{x\to\infty} \frac{\sum_{j=1}^{n} q_j t_j}{k(f_i'(x))^l} + \lim_{x\to\infty} \frac{\sum_{j=1}^{n} \sum_{Q_j} q_j t_{js} f_s(x)}{k(f_i'(x))^l}$$

$$= \lim_{x\to\infty} \frac{\sum_{s=1}^{m} v_s f_s(x)}{(f_i'(x))^l},$$

where $k>0$ is an appropriate real number, $v_s=0$ for s in Q, and $v_s=(q_j t_{js})/k$ for s in Q_j, $1 \leqq j \leqq n$. Then for each s in Q_j, sgn $(v_s) =$ sgn (q_j) since each

$t_{js} > 0$. By (c), the last limit above exists. Now $\lim_{x\to\infty} F(g_1(x), \ldots, g_n(x)) = \lim_{x\to\infty} (1/(g_i(x))^l) \sum_{j=1}^{n} q_j g_j(x)$. By (b) and by Theorem 7.5.3, it follows that

$$\lim_{x\to\infty} \sum_{j=1}^{n} \frac{q_j g_j(x)}{(g_i(x))^l} = \lim_{x\to\infty} \frac{\sum_{s=1}^{m} v_s f_s(x)}{(f_i'(x))^l}.$$

Hence the theorem holds.

EXAMPLE 7.5.5: Let $U = \langle a^{(x+1)^2} b^{x^2} \rangle$ and $V = \langle a^{x^2} b^{x^2} \rangle$. Suppose V is in $\hat{\mathscr{F}}(U)$. Using Theorem 7.5.6, $Q = \emptyset$, $z_1 = 1$, $z_2 = 2$, and $z_3 = 3$. Let $q_1 = 1$, $q_2 = -1$, $i = 2$, and $l = 1/2$. Clearly (a), (b), and (c) of (ii) of Theorem 7.5.6 hold. However,

$$\lim_{x\to\infty} \frac{g_1(x) - g_2(x)}{(g_2(x))^{1/2}} = \lim_{x\to\infty} \frac{x^2 - x^2}{(x^2)^{1/2}} = 0$$

and

$$\lim_{x\to\infty} \frac{v_1 f_1(x) + v_2 f_2(x)}{(f_2'(x))^{1/2}} = \lim_{x\to\infty} \frac{v_1 (x+1)^2 + v_2 x^2}{(x^2)^{1/2}} \neq 0$$

for every choice of nonzero real numbers v_1 and v_2. This is a contradiction. Hence V is not in $\hat{\mathscr{F}}(U)$.

EXERCISE 7.5.1: Let $\mathscr{L}$ be a family of languages and $L = \langle b_1^{g_1(x)} \ldots b_n^{g_n(x)} \rangle$. Prove that if L is in $\hat{\mathscr{F}}(\mathscr{L})(\mathscr{F}(\mathscr{L}))$, then $L = \bigcup_{i=1}^{r} M_i(L_i)$ for some $r \geq 1$, $L_1, \ldots, L_r$ in $\mathscr{L}$, and (ϵ-free) a-transducers $M_1, \ldots, M_r$ [Rv].

EXERCISE 7.5.2: Using Exercise 7.4.11, prove that L_0 is not in $\hat{\mathscr{F}}(L_1)$, where $L_0 = \{a^n b^n / n \geq 1\}$ and $L_1 = \{a^n b^n / (2m)! \leq n < (2m+1)!$ for some $m \geq 1\}$ [GS7].

EXERCISE 7.5.3: Prove that V is not in $\hat{\mathscr{F}}(U)$, where $U = \langle a^{2^x} b^{x^2} \rangle$ and $V = \langle a^{2^x} b^x \rangle$. [Hint: In the corollary to Theorem 7.5.3, let $F(x, y)$ be the function defined by $F(0, y) = F(x, 0) = 0$ for all x, y and $F(x, y) = (\log_2 x)/y$ for all $xy \neq 0$.]

EXERCISE 7.5.4: Prove that V is not in $\hat{\mathscr{F}}(U)$, where[1] $U = \langle a^{(x \log_2 x) \log_2 \log_2 x} b^{x^2 (\log_2 x)^2} c^{2^x} \rangle_{1000}$ and $V = \langle a^{x \log_2 x} b^{x^2} c^{2^x} \rangle_{1000}$. [Hint: In the corollary to

[1] Given an expression $\langle a_1^{f_1(x)} \ldots a_m^{f_m(x)} \rangle_\theta$, with each f_i a function from N into the nonnegative real numbers, every function f_i is to be interpreted as $\bar{f}_i$, where $\bar{f}_i(x)$ is the largest integer not greater than $f_i(x)$.

Theorem 7.5.3, let $F(x, y, z)$ be the function defined by $F(x, y, z) = (1/\log_2 \log_2 z)(x/\sqrt{y})$ for all $y > 0$, $z > 2$, and $F(x, y, z) = 0$ otherwise.]

EXERCISE 7.5.5: Let $U = \langle a_1^{x^2} a_2^{x^2 \log_2 x} a_3^x \rangle_{1000}$ and $V = \langle b_1^{x \log_2 x} b_2^x \rangle_{1000}$. Prove that V is not in $\hat{\mathcal{F}}(U)$.

EXERCISE 7.5.6: Prove that $\langle b_1^x b_2^{2^{2^x}} b_3^x \rangle$ is not in $\mathcal{F}(\langle a_1^x a_2^{2^{2^x}} a_3^x a_4^{2^{2^x}} \rangle)$.

EXERCISE 7.5.7: Prove that $\{a^{x^2} b^7 c^{x^3} / x \geqq 1\}$ is not in $\hat{\mathcal{F}}(\langle a^{x^3} b^{x^2} c^{x^4} \rangle)$.

EXERCISE 7.5.8: Prove that V is not in $\hat{\mathcal{F}}(U)$, where $U = \{a^x b a^{x^2} b a^{x^4} / x \geqq 1\}$ and $V = \{a^{x^3} b a^{x^5} / x \geqq 1\}$.

EXERCISE 7.5.9: Prove that $\langle a^{2x^2+1} b^{3x^2-2x+1} c^{5x} \rangle$ is not in $\hat{\mathcal{F}}(\langle a^{7x^2+3} b^{2x^2+7} c^{3x} \rangle)$.

EXERCISE 7.5.10: Prove that $\langle a^{x^2+7} b^{3x^2+5} c^{5x+3} \rangle$ is not in $\hat{\mathcal{F}}(\langle a^{2x^2+1} b^{x^2+7x+1} c^x \rangle)$.

EXERCISE 7.5.11: Let $\mathcal{L}$ be a family of languages and let $L = \langle b_1^{g_1(x)} \ldots b_n^{g_n(x)} \rangle$ be in the smallest [full] AFL generated by $\mathcal{L}$. Prove that L is in $\mathcal{S}(\mathcal{L})$ [$\hat{\mathcal{S}}(\mathcal{L})$] [Rv].

EXERCISE 7.5.12: Let $\mathcal{L}$ be a family of languages, each of the form $\langle a_1^{f_1'(x)} \ldots a_m^{f_m'(x)} \rangle_\theta$. Thus m, $f_1'(x)$, $\ldots$, $f_m'(x)$, and θ vary from language to language in $\mathcal{L}$. Let $V = \langle b_1^{g_1(x)} \ldots b_n^{g_n(x)} \rangle_{\theta_2}$ be in $\hat{\mathcal{O}}(\mathcal{L})$ ($\mathcal{O}(\mathcal{L})$), $\mathcal{O} = \mathcal{M}$ or $\mathcal{F}$. Prove each of the following [Rv]:

(a) There exist a language $U = \langle a_1^{f_1(x)} \ldots a_m^{f_m(x)} \rangle_{\theta_1}$ in $\mathcal{L}$, $Q \subseteq \{1, \ldots, m\}$ ($Q = \emptyset$) and integers $z_1, \ldots, z_{n+1}$, $1 = z_1 < \ldots < z_{n+1} = m+1$, satisfying Theorem 7.5.4.

(b) There exist a language $U = \langle a_1^{f_1(x)} \ldots a_m^{f_m(x)} \rangle_{\theta_1}$ in $\mathcal{L}$, $Q \subseteq \{1, \ldots, m\}$ ($Q \neq \emptyset$) and integers $z_1, \ldots, z_{n+1}$, $1 = z_1 < \ldots < z_{n+1} = m+1$, satisfying Theorem 7.5.6.

EXERCISE 7.5.13: Let $\mathcal{L} = \{\langle a^x b^{x^2} \rangle, \langle a^{x^2} b^x c^{x^3} \rangle, \langle a^{x^3} b^x c^{x^2} \rangle\}$. Using (a) of Exercise 7.5.12, show that $\mathcal{F}(\mathcal{L})$ is not closed under reversal [Rv]. [Hint: Prove that $\langle a^{x^2} b^x \rangle$ is not in $\mathcal{F}(\mathcal{L})$.]

EXERCISE 7.5.14: Let n be a positive integer. Let $\mathcal{L}$ be a family of languages, each of the form $\langle a_1^{f_1'(x)} \ldots a_n^{f_n'(x)} \rangle_\theta$, with every $f_j'(x)$ a polynomial. Let $V = \langle b_1^{g_1(x)} \ldots b_n^{g_n(x)} \rangle_{\theta_2}$ be in $\hat{\mathcal{O}}(\mathcal{L})$, $\mathcal{O} = \mathcal{M}$ or $\mathcal{F}$, with every $g_j(x)$ a polynomial. For each polynomial $h(x)$ let deg (h) be the degree of $h(x)$.

(a) If, for each $\langle a_1^{f_1'(x)} \ldots a_n^{f_n'(x)} \rangle_\theta$ in $\mathscr{L}$, there exists some i, $1 \leqq i \leqq n$, such that $\deg (f_i') = \deg (g_i)$, prove that there exists some $U = \langle a_1^{f_1(x)} \ldots a_n^{f_n(x)} \rangle_{\theta_1}$ in $\mathscr{L}$ such that $\deg (f_j) = \deg (g_j)$ for all j, $1 \leqq j \leqq n$.

(b) If, for each $\langle a_1^{f_1(x)} \ldots a_n^{f_n(x)} \rangle_\theta$ in $\mathscr{L}$, there exist some i, c, and d, $1 \leqq i \leqq n$, such that $f_i'(x) = cx$ and $g_i(x) = dx$, prove that there exist $U = \langle a_1^{f_1(x)} \ldots a_n^{f_n(x)} \rangle_{\theta_1}$ in $\mathscr{L}$ and real numbers $p, r, q, q_1, \ldots, q_n, q_1', \ldots, q_n'$, p and each q_j positive, such that $g_j(px+r) = q_j f_j(x) + q_j'$ for each j, $1 \leqq j \leqq n$.

7.6 Historical References

Historically, the first paper on (full) generating-family-bounded AFL was [Ui], and the first massive study [Go1]. Theorem 7.3.1 and Sections 7.1 and 7.2 are in [Go1]. Sections 7.4 and 7.5 appear in [Rv].

REFERENCES AND RELATED PAPERS

[Ah1] Aho, A. V., "Indexed Grammars – An Extension of Context-Free Grammars," *Journal of the Association for Computing Machinery*, vol. 15, 1968, pp. 647–671.

[Ah2] Aho, A. V., "Nested Stack Automata," *Journal of the Association for Computing Machinery*, vol. 16, 1969, pp. 383–406.

[AU] Aho, A. V., and Ullman J. D., "A Characterization of Two-Way Deterministic Classes of Languages," *Journal of Computer and System Sciences*, vol. 4, 1970, pp. 523–538.

[BB] Baker, B., and Book, R. V., "Reversal-Bounded Multi-Pushdown Machines," *Journal of Computer and System Sciences*, vol. 8, 1974, pp. 315–332.

[Be1] Berstel, J., "Contribution à l'Etude des Propriétés Arithmétiques des Langages Formels," Doctor of Science Thesis, University of Paris VII, January 1972.

[Be2] Berstel, J., "Une Hiérarchie des Parties Rationnelles de N^2," *Mathematical Systems Theory*, vol. 7, 1973, pp. 114–137.

[Bo1] Boasson, L., "Cônes Rationnels et Familles Agréables de Langages – Application au Langages à Compteur," University of Paris VII Thesis, 1971.

[Bo2] Boasson, L., "An Iteration Theorem for One-Counter Languages," *Proceedings of the 3rd Annual ACM Symposium on Theory of Computing*, 1971, pp. 116–120.

[Bo3] Boasson, L., "Two Iteration Theorems for Some Families of Languages," *Journal of Computer and System Sciences*, vol. 7, 1973, pp. 583–596.

[BCN] Boasson, L., Crestin, J. P. and Nivat, M., "Familles de Langages Translatables et Fermees par Crochet," *Acta Informatica*, vol. 2, 1973, pp. 383–393.

[BN] Boasson, L., and Nivat, M., "Sur Diverses Familles de Langages Fermées par Transduction Rationelle," *Acta Informatica*, vol. 2, 1973, pp. 180–188.

[Bk1] Book, R. V., "Time-Bounded Grammars and Their Languages," *Journal of Computer and System Sciences*, vol. 5, 1971, pp. 397–429.

[Bk2] Book, R. V., "On Languages Accepted in Polynomial Time," *SIAM Journal on Computing*, vol. 1, 1972, pp. 281–287.

[BGi] Book, R. V., and Ginsburg, S., "Multi-Stack-Counter Languages," *Mathematical Systems Theory*, vol. 6, 1972, pp. 37–48.

[BGr] Book, R. V., and Greibach, S. A., "Quasi-Realtime Languages," *Mathematical Systems Theory*, vol. 4, 1970, pp. 97–111.

[BGIW] Book, R. V., Greibach, S. A., Ibarra, O. H., and Wegbreit, B., "Tape-Bounded Turing Acceptors and Principal AFLs," *Journal of Computer and System Sciences*, vol. 4, 1970, pp. 622–625.

[BGW] Book, R. V., Greibach, S. A., and Wegbreit, G., "Time and Tape-Bounded Turing Acceptors and AFL," *Journal of Computer and System Sciences*, vol. 4, 1970, pp. 606–621.

[BW] Book, R. V., and Wegbreit, B., "A Note on AFLs and Bounded Erasing," *Information and Control*, vol. 19, 1971, pp. 18–29.

[Ch] Chandler, W. J., "Abstract Families of Deterministic Languages," *Proceedings of the First ACM Symposium on Theory of Computing*, 1969, pp. 21–30.

[Co] Cook, S. A., "Characterizations of Pushdown Machines in Terms of Time-Bounded Computers," *Journal of the Association for Computing Machinery*, vol. 18, 1971, pp. 4–18.

[Cu1] Culik, K., II, "Abstract Families of Relations," *Journal of Computer and System Sciences*, vol. 5, 1971, pp. 596–606.

[Cu2] Culik, K., II, "On Some Families of Languages Related to Developmental Systems," University of Waterloo Report, C7–73–12, 1973.

[CO] Culik, K., II, and Opatrny, J., "Macro 0L-Systems," University of Waterloo Report, CS-73-06, 1973.

[EM] Elgot, C. C., and Mezei, J. E., "On Relations Defined by Generalized Finite Automata," *IBM Journal of Research and Development*, vol. 9, 1965, pp. 47–68.

[FMR] Fischer, P. C., Meyer, A. K., and Rosenberg, A. L., "Counter Machines and Counter Languages," *Mathematical Systems Theory*, vol. 2, 1968, pp. 265–283.

[GaG] Gabrielian, A., and Ginsburg, S., "Structured Storage AFA," *IEEE Transactions on Electronic Computers*, vol. C-22, 1973, pp. 534–537.

[Gi] Ginsburg, S., *The Mathematical Theory of Context-Free Languages*, McGraw-Hill Book Company, New York, 1966.

[GGo1] Ginsburg, S., and Goldstine, J., "On the Largest Full SubAFL of an AFL," *Mathematical Systems Theory*, vol. 6, 1972, pp. 241–242.

[GGo2] Ginsburg, S., and Goldstine, J., "Intersection-Closed Full AFL and the Recursively Enumerable Languages," *Information and Control*, vol. 22, 1973, pp. 201–231.

[GGr1] Ginsburg, S., and Greibach, S. A., "Abstract Families of Languages," in *Studies in Abstract Families of Languages*, Memoirs of the American Mathematical Society, no. 87, 1969, pp. 1–32.

[GGr2] Ginsburg, S., and Greibach, S. A., "Principal AFL," *Journal of Computer and System Sciences*, vol. 4, 1970, pp. 308–338.

[GGr3] Ginsburg, S., and Greibach, S. A., "On AFL Generators for Finitely Encoded AFA, "*Journal of Computer and System Sciences*, vol. 7, 1973, pp. 1–27.

[GGG] Ginsburg, S., Goldstine, J., and Greibach, S. A., "Uniformly Erasable AFL," *Proceedings of the Fourth Annual ACM Symposium on Theory of Computing*, May 1972, pp. 207–213.

[GGHa1] Ginsburg, S., Greibach, S. A., and Harrison, M. A., "Stack Automata and Compiling," *Journal of the Association for Computing Machinery*, vol. 14, 1967, pp. 172–201.

[GGHa2] Ginsburg, S., Greibach, S. A., and Harrison, M. A., "One-Way Stack Automata," *Journal of the Association for Computing Machinery*, vol. 14, 1967, pp. 389–418.

[GGHo] Ginsburg, S., Greibach, S. A., and Hopcroft, J. E., "Pre-AFL," in *Studies in Abstract Families of Languages*, Memoirs of the American Mathematical Society, no. 87, 1969, pp. 41–51.

[GHa1] Ginsburg, S., and Harrison, M. A., "One-Way Nondeterministic Real-Time

List-Storage Languages," *Journal of the Association for Computing Machinery*, vol. 15, 1968, pp. 428–446.

[GHa2] Ginsburg, S., and Harrison, M. A., "On the Closure of AFL Under Reversal," *Information and Control*, vol. 17, 1970, pp. 395–409.

[GHo1] Ginsburg, S., and Hopcroft, J. E., "Two-Way Balloon Automata and AFL," *Journal of the Association for Computing Machinery*, vol. 17, 1970, pp. 3–13.

[GHo2] Ginsburg, S., and Hopcroft, J. E., "Images of AFL under Certain Families of Homomorphisms," *Mathematical Systems Theory*, vol. 5, 1971, pp. 216–227.

[GR1] Ginsburg, S., and Rose, G. F., "On the Existence of Generators for Certain AFL," *Information Sciences*, vol. 2, 1970, pp. 431–446.

[GR2] Ginsburg, S., and Rose, G. F., "The Equivalence of Stack-Counter Acceptors and Quasi-Realtime Stack-Counter Acceptors," *Journal of Computer and System Sciences*, vol. 8, 1974, pp. 243–269.

[GS1] Ginsburg, S., and Spanier, E. H., "Quotients of Context-Free Languages," *Journal of the Association for Computing Machinery*, vol. 10, 1963, pp. 487–492.

[GS2] Ginsburg, S., and Spanier, E. H., "Bounded Regular Sets," *Proceedings of the American Mathematical Society*, vol. 17, 1966, pp. 1043–1049.

[GS3] Ginsburg, S., and Spanier, E. H., "Control Sets on Grammars," *Mathematical Systems Theory*, vol. 2, 1968, pp. 159–177.

[GS4] Ginsburg, S., and Spanier, E. H., "Derivation-Bounded Languages," *Journal of Computer and System Sciences*, vol. 2, 1968, pp. 228–250.

[GS5] Ginsburg, S., and Spanier, E. H., "Substitutions in Families of Languages," *Information Sciences*, vol. 2, 1970, pp. 83–110.

[GS6] Ginsburg, S., and Spanier, E. H., "AFL with the Semilinear Property," *Journal of Computer and System Sciences*, vol. 5, 1971, pp. 365–396.

[GS7] Ginsburg, S., and Spanier, E. H., "On Incomparable AFL," to appear in the *Journal of Computer and System Sciences*.

[Go1] Goldstine, J., "Abstract Families of Languages Generated by Bounded Languages," Ph.D. Thesis, University of California at Berkeley, 1970.

[Go2] Goldstine, J., "Substitution and Bounded Languages," *Journal of Computer and System Sciences*, vol. 6, 1972, pp. 9–29.

[Gr1] Greibach, S. A., "An Infinite Hierarchy of Context-Free Languages," *Journal of the Association for Computing Machinery*, vol. 16, 1969, pp. 91–106.

[Gr2] Greibach, S. A., "Checking Automata and One-Way Stack Languages," *Journal of Computer and System Sciences*, vol. 3, 1969, pp. 196–217.

[Gr3] Greibach, S. A., "Chains of Full AFL's," *Mathematical Systems Theory*, vol. 4, 1970, pp. 231–242.

[Gr4] Greibach, S. A., "Full AFLs and Nested Iterated Substitution," *Information and Control*, vol. 16, 1970, pp. 7–35.

[Gr5] Greibach, S. A., "Characteristic and Ultrarealtime Languages," *Information and Control*, vol. 18, 1971, pp. 65–98.

[Gr6] Greibach, S. A., "Simple Syntactic Operators on Full Semi-AFLs," *Journal of Computer and System Sciences*, vol. 6, 1972, pp. 30–76.

[Gr7] Greibach, S. A., "Erasing in Context-Free AFLs," *Information and Control*, vol. 21, 1972, pp. 436–465.

[Gr8] Greibach, S. A., "A Generalization of Parikh's Semilinear Theorem," *Discrete Mathematics*, vol. 2, 1972, pp. 347–355.

[GrG] Greibach, S. A., and Ginsburg, S., "Multitape AFA," *Journal of the Association for Computing Machinery*, vol. 19, 1972, pp. 193–221.

[GrH1] Greibach, S. A., and Hopcroft, J. E., "Independence of AFL Operations," in *Studies in Abstract Families of Languages*, Memoirs of the American Mathematical Society, no. 87, 1969, pp. 33–40.

[GrH2] Greibach, S. A., and Hopcroft, J. E., "Scattered Context Grammars," *Journal of Computer and System Sciences*, vol. 3, 1969, pp. 233–247.

[HH] Hartmanis, J., and Hopcroft, J. E., "What Makes Some Language Theory Problems Undecidable," *Journal of Computer and System Sciences*, vol. 4, 1970, pp. 368–376.

[He] Herman, G. T., "Closure Properties of Some Families of Languages Associated with Biological Systems," *Information and Control*, vol. 24, 1974, pp. 101–121.

[HU1] Hopcroft, J. E., and Ullman, J. D., *Formal Languages and their Relation to Automata*, Addison-Wesley Publishing Company, Reading, Massachusetts, 1969.

[HU2] Hopcroft, J. E., and Ullman, J. D., "An Approach to a Unified Theory of Automata," *The Bell System Technical Journal*, vol. XLVI, 1967, pp. 1793–1829.

[Ib1] Ibarra, O. H., "Simple Matrix Languages," *Information and Control*, vol. 17, 1970, pp. 359–394.

[Ib2] Ibarra, O. H., "Characterizations of Transductions Defined by Abstract Families of Transducers," *Mathematical Systems Theory*, vol. 5, 1971, pp. 271–281.

[Ib3] Ibarra, O. H., "Controlled Pushdown Automata," *Information Sciences*, vol. 6, 1973, pp. 327–342.

[Kn] Kain, R. Y., *Automata Theory: Machines and Languages*, McGraw-Hill Book Company, New York, 1972.

[Ka] Kasai, T., "An Hierarchy Between Context-Free and Context-Sensitive Languages," *Journal of Computer and System Sciences*, vol. 4, 1970, pp. 492–508.

[Ki] Kiel, D. I., "Two-Way a-Transducers and AFL," Ph.D. Thesis, University of Southern California, 1973.

[Ko] Kobayashi, K., "Classification of Formal Languages by their Structural Complexity," Report of the Research Institute of Science and Technology, Nihon University, Report No. 12, March 1971.

[Kr] Kral, J., "A Modification of a Substitution Theorem and Some Necessary and Sufficient Conditions for Sets to be Context-Free," *Mathematical Systems Theory*, vol. 4, 1970, pp. 129–139.

[Le, a] Lewis, D. J., "Closure of Families of Languages under Substitution Operators," *Proceedings of the 2nd Annual ACM Symposium on Theory of Computing*, 1970, pp. 100–108.

[Le, b] Lewis, D. J., "Closure of Families of Languages under Substitution Operators," Ph.D. Thesis, Cornell University, 1971.

[MB] MacLane, S., and Birkhoff, G., *Algebra*, The MacMillan Company, New York, 1967.

[Mc] McCloskey, T., "Abstract Families of Length-Preserving Processors," Ph.D. Thesis, Case Western Reserve University, January 1972.

[Mi] Minsky, M. L., "Recursive Unsolvability of Post's Problem of 'Tag' and other Topics in the Theory of Turing Machines," *Annals of Mathematics*, vol. 74, 1961, pp. 437–455.

[Ni] Nivat, M., "Transductions des Languages de Chomsky," Ph.D. Thesis, Paris, 1967.

[Og, a] Ogden, W. F., "Intercalation Theorems for Pushdown Store and Stack Languages," Ph.D. Thesis, Stanford University, 1968.

[Og, b] Ogden, W. F., "Intercalation Theorems for Pushdown Store and Stack Languages," *Proceedings of the First ACM Symposium on Theory of Computing*, 1969, pp. 31–42.

[Ra] Rajlich, V., "Absolutely Parallel Grammars and Two-Way Finite State Transducers," *Journal of Computer and System Sciences*, vol. 6, 1972, pp. 324–342.

[Ro] Rose, G. F., "Abstract Families of Processors," *Journal of Computer and System Sciences*, vol. 4, 1970, pp. 193–204.

[Rv] Rovan, B., "Necessary Conditions for Containment of Principal (Semi-)AFL with Bounded Generators," to appear in the *Journal of Computer and System Sciences*.

[Sm] Salomaa, A., *Formal Languages*, Academic Press, Inc., New York, 1973.

[Sa] Savitch, W. J., "Relationships Between Nondeterministic and Deterministic Tape Complexities," *Journal of Computer and System Sciences*, vol. 4, 1970, pp. 177–192.

[SHL] Stearns, R. E., Hartmanis, J., and Lewis, P. M., II, "Hierarchies of Memory Limited Computations," *1965 IEEE Conference Record on Switching Circuit Theory and Logical Design*, pp. 191–202.

[Ui] Ullian, J. S., "Three Theorems Concerning Principal AFL," *Journal of Computer and System Sciences*, vol. 5, 1971, pp. 304–314.

[Um] Ullman, J. D., "Halting Stack Automata," *Journal of the Association for Computing Machinery*, vol. 16, 1969, pp. 550–563.

[Va] Van Der Walt, A. P. J., "Random Context Languages," *Proceedings of the IFIP Congress 71*, vol. 1, North-Holland Publishing Company, Amsterdam, pp. 66–69.

[Wa] Walljasper, S. J., "Left-Derivation Bounded Languages," *Journal of Computer and System Sciences*, vol. 8, 1974, pp. 1–7.

[We] Wegbreit, B., "A Generator of Context-Sensitive Languages," *Journal of Computer and System Sciences*, vol. 3, 1969, pp. 456–461.

[Yn] Yntema, M. K., "Inclusion Relations Among Families of Context-Free Languages," *Information and Control*, vol. 10, 1967, pp. 572–597.

SYMBOL INDEX

AUTHOR INDEX

SUBJECT INDEX

[illegible]